Byzantium

Byzantium

Church, Society, and Civilization
Seen through Contemporary Eyes

UNIVERSITY OF CHICAGO PRESS · CHICAGO AND LONDON

DENO JOHN GEANAKOPLOS

FRONTISPIECE. Detail from *Christ Raising Adam and Eve from Hell* (Anatatis), by an anonymous painter of the Palaeologan Renaissance. From a fresco in the Kariye Djami, Constantinople. Courtesy of Dumbarton Oaks, Center for Byzantine Studies, Washington, D.C.

Publication of this book was supported in part by the Greek Orthodox Archdiocese of North and South America.

The University of Chicago Press, Chicago 60637
The University of Chicago Press, Ltd., London

17 16 15 14 13 12 11 10   8 9 10 11

ISBN-13: 978-0-226-28461-3 (paper)
ISBN-10: 0-226-28461-1 (paper)

Library of Congress Cataloging-in-Publication Data
Main entry under title:
Byzantium: church, society, and civilization
   seen through contemporary eyes.
   Includes index.
   1. Byzantine Empire—History—Sources.
I. Geanakoplos, Deno John.
DF503.B983   1984   949.5   83-4806
ISBN 0-226-28460-3 (cloth)
ISBN 0-226-28461-1 (paper)

To the memory of the greatest of modern Greek Orthodox patriarchs, His All-holiness Patriarch Athenagoras of Constantinople (1962–72), and to his exarch in the Western Hemisphere, Archbishop Iakovos, who almost single-handedly has achieved recognition of Orthodoxy as the fourth major faith in America.

CONTENTS

• • • • • • • • • • • • • • • • • ◆

PROLOGUE

◆ ◆ ◆ ◆ ◆ ◆ ◆ ◆ ◆ ◆ ◆ ◆ ◆ ◆ ◆ ◆ ◆ ◆ ◆

        The study of Byzantine history has finally come into its own. This is due not only to its importance as one of the world's great civilizations, but also to an increasing awareness of its role in the formation of the Western, Slavic, and, to a lesser extent, Islamic cultures. Byzantium served as a kind of buffer for the West against repeated waves of invaders from the East, thus providing backward Latin Europe with the time to revive from the low state of civilization to which it had sunk after the German, Viking, and Magyar invasions. More than that, it preserved ancient Greek learning, the fountainhead of Western philosophy, literature, and science, which otherwise would be almost lost to us today. And, finally, as is only now being fully realized, Byzantium made original cultural contributions of its own. It is these contributions—passed on in varying degrees to its neighboring civilizations—in art and architecture, in forms of Christian worship and theology, in law and statecraft, in industry and refinements of living, together with its work as preserver of ancient Greek culture, that makes this civilization worth studying.

        This book constitutes the first systematic attempt to treat as comprehensively as possible all of the main themes in the history of the Byzantine church, society, and civilization through the use of primary sources, a great many translated here for the first time into English. The selections are drawn not only from Byzantine writers but also from more obscure documents and chronicles written in Latin, Arabic, Slavic, Italian, French, Armenian, and other languages. The matters they treat include the traditional areas of political, ecclesiastical, socioeconomic, administrative, and military life of the Byzantines. More unusually, the selections also concern the empire's relations with the Latin West, the Slavs, Arabs, Turks, and other neighboring peoples, and, notably, include a considerable number devoted to Byzantine culture—in particular to education, philosophy, literature, hymnography, and science.

        This work is not a source book in the usual sense. Rather it is an up-to-date, scholarly account of the development of Byzantine history in which contemporary sources are systematically and chronologically inserted to illustrate the development of the particular theme, institution, or aspect of culture under discussion. In order to provide a sense of continuity and to place each source accurately in historical context, the book contains a running commentary. This commentary reflects the most recent scholarly research in Byzantine studies and enables the reader to examine the translated source materials with the help of the most authoritative interpretations offered by specialists in the field. This dy namic interaction between primary and secondary materials is, to my knowledge, a feature found in no other book on Byzantium. The interweaving of contemporary sources and commentary will, I hope, provide the effect of a "living" history and lend vividness to the various phenomena that pass in review.

It has been my aim to select those source materials that give the clearest possible illustrations for each topic under consideration—for example, the development of the Senate; treatment of women and Jews; types of imperial succession; ways to achieve mystical union with God; amusements; clothing; law; sexual crimes; the navy; religious poetry and drama; education; astronomy; and so on. I have drawn on sources from each successive period of Byzantine history: first, the period of Constantine and his successors, then the periods of Justinian, Heraclius, the Iconoclast and Amorian emperors, the Macedonian and Comnenan rulers, the Latin Empire, and, finally, the Palaeologan era.

Each major theme in Byzantium's history and civilization is treated in a separate section: the universal empire; defense of the empire; the church; social and economic life; relations with the outside world; and culture. Within each of these broad sections the selections are arranged, insofar as possible, in chronological order. For those readers, however, who wish to study the selections under the rubric of major historical *periods*—for example, the age of Justinian or the Iconoclastic epoch—the Chronological Table of Contents (appendix B) lists all selections in the book by historical eras.

It is my hope that the particular features of this work, while fostering a clearer understanding of the broader, sometimes conflicting dimensions of Byzantium's history, will provide a detailed depiction of the inner workings of Byzantine society, church, and civilization—in other words, a more nuanced portrait of contemporary life "in action" in sophisticated Constantinople and among the peasants in the countryside.

In general I have retained the Greek form of names and terms except where they are better known in English in their Latin spelling.

Unless specifically noted, all translations are my own.

ACKNOWLEDGMENTS

♦ ♦ ♦ ♦ ♦ ♦ ♦ ♦ ♦ ♦ ♦ ♦ ♦ ♦ ♦ ♦ ♦ ♦ ♦

It would be difficult to list all those persons who, during the fifteen-year gestation period of this volume, contributed in one way or another to what became the final version. My thanks go first to John Erickson, now professor at St. Vladimir's Orthodox Theological Seminary, who, as one of my first assistants at Yale, helped in the initial stage of organizing the voluminous material. Other assistants during successive years to whom I express my thanks are Christopher Bender and Peter Kochenberger. Most of all I am deeply grateful to Andrew Cappel, my graduate assistant during the last several years, for his dedicated aid in all manner of problems, whether organizational or involving suggestions for translating not infrequently convoluted passages in the Byzantine texts. Two of my secretaries at Yale, Ruth Kurzbauer and Katrin van der Vaart, have been indefatigable in typing successive drafts of the text. I am grateful to Emmy Varouxakis of Athens, who helped translate several selections. Nor can I refrain from expressing warm gratitude to two colleagues in Byzantine studies, Constantine Trypanis of Oxford University and the University of Chicago, and Charles Brand of Bryn Mawr. Professor Trypanis read through the completed manuscript and made valuable suggestions especially in his field of primary expertise, Byzantine literature. In an earlier stage Professor Brand generously offered perceptive comments on the organization of the work as a whole, particularly on the sequence of selections, and suggested inclusion of certain additional materials. To my dear friend Alexander Turyn, whose death Byzantine scholarship mourns, I am indebted for unstinting support and unfailing willingness to answer any and all questions. Finally, I express my appreciation to my wife and children for their forbearance in my seemingly endless labors on this tome.

Grateful acknowledgment for permission to reprint the selections, maps, and illustrations that have already been published is made to the following:

American Historical Association: Selection 144 ("The Relics of Constantinople"), from E. Joranson, trans., "The Problem of the Spurious Letter of Emperor Alexius to the Count of Flanders," *American Historical Review* 55, no. 4 (1950): 815.

Bowes & Bowes at The Bodley Head: Selections 50A ("From the Preface to the *Ecloga*"), 50B ("The *Ecloga* on Sexual Crimes"), 216 ("The Contract of Marriage"), reprinted with permission of Bowes & Bowes at The Bodley Head, from E. Freshfield, trans., *A Manual of Roman Law: The "Ecloga"* (Cambridge, 1926), pp. 67–68; pp. 108–12; pp. 72–74.

Cambridge University Press: Selections 212A ("Government Regulation of the Silk Industry"), 212B ("Bankers and Money Lenders"), from E. Freshfield, *Roman Law in the Later Roman Empire: Byzantine Guilds, Professional and Commercial Ordinances of Leo VI c. 895, from the "Book of the Eparch"* (Cambridge, 1938), pp. 16–17 and 20–23; pp. 25–27. Diagram on p. 464 ("Constantinople"), from *Cambridge Medieval History*, vol. 4, *The Eastern Roman Empire*, ed. J. B. Bury (Cambridge, 1927).

Catholic University of America Press: Selection 121 ("An Example of St. Basil's 'Longer Rules'"), from M. M. Wagner, *Saint Basil: Ascetical Works*, in series *Fathers of the Church* (Washington, D.C., 1950), vol. 9, pp. 247–50 and 289–91.

Central Trust Company: Selections 48 ("Plan of the *Digest*"), 49A ("The Principles of Law from the *Institutes*"), 49B ("Concerning Natural Law, the Law of Nations, and the Civil Law"), 57B ("Senatorial Rank Is Hereditary"), 191 ("Jews Shall Live in Accordance with the Rites of Christianity"), 219 ("Women Shall Not Act as Witnesses in the Execution of Contracts"), 221B ("Disposition of Property of Imperial Slaves"), from S. P. Scott, *The Civil Law* (Cincinnati, 1932), vol. 2, pp. 179–82; vol. 2, pp. 3–4; vol. 2, pp. 5–7; vol. 15, p. 24; vol. 17, p. 255; vol. 17, p. 249; vol. 17, p. 241.

Dumbarton Oaks: Selections 89A ("On the Importance of the Pechenegs"), 89B ("On Byzantine Relations with Barbarian Peoples"), 90 ("Imperial Marriages with Foreigners"), 205 ("The Varangian Route to Constantinople"), 328B ("An Astrological Prediction on the Arabs"), from R. Jenkins, trans., Constantine Porphyrogenitus, *De administrando imperio*, ed. G. Moravcsik (Washington, D.C., 1967), pp. 49–55; pp. 67–71; pp. 73–75; pp. 57–63; p. 81.

Dumbarton Oaks, Center for Byzantine Studies, Washington, D.C.: Frontispiece (detail from *Christ Raising Adam and Eve from Hell*), p. 446 (detail of the head of Adam from *Christ Raising Adam and Eve from Hell*).

E. P. Dutton: Selections 137 ("The *Russian Primary Chronicle* on Byzantine Liturgy"), 262 ("Princess Olga Becomes a Christian"), 263 ("Vladimir's Road to Conversion"), from Serge A. Zenkovsky, ed., *Medieval Russia's Epics, Chronicles, and Tales* (New York, 1963), pp. 67–68; pp. 61–62; pp. 66–67 and 70. Copyright © 1963 by Serge A. Zenkovsky. Reprinted with permission of the publisher, E. P. Dutton, Inc.

Editions du Centre National de la Recherche Scientifique: Selections 6 ("Warm and Cool Receptions"), 33 ("Official Ranks in the Fourteenth Century"), 66 ("The Senate Participates at Ceremonial Banquets"), 78 ("The Grand Domestic"), 80 ("Commanders of the Byzantine Navy"), from Pseudo-Codinus, *Traité des offices*, ed. J. Verpeaux (Paris, 1966), p. 235; pp. 133–37; p. 272; p. 248; p. 167.

Editions E. de Boccard: Selection 257 ("On Emperor Nicephorus, Who Left His Bones in Bulgaria"), from I. Dujcev, "La chronique byzantine de l'an 811," *Travaux et mémoires* (Paris, 1965), vol. 1, pp. 210–12.

Wm. Eerdmans: Selections 92A ("Eusebius Lauds Constantine"), 106 ("Socrates on the Council of Nicaea"), 107 ("Socrates's Account of the Second Ecumenical Council"), 112 ("The Council of 754 Condemns Icons"), 113 ("The Seventh Ecumenical Council Condemns Iconoclasm"), 120 ("From Athanasius, *Life of Saint Anthony*"), 241 ("Ulfila Converts the Goths"), from P. Schaff and H. Wace, eds., *A Select Library of Nicene and Post-Nicene Fathers of the Christian Church*, 2d ser. (reprint, Grand Rapids, Mich., 1955 and 1976), vol. 1, p. 606; vol. 2, pp. 10–12; vol. 2, p. 121; vol. 14, pp. 543–44; vol. 14, p. 550; vol. 4, pp. 196, 200, 210; vol. 2, p. 373. Used by permission of the publisher, Wm. B. Eerdmans Publishing Co.

Fordham University Press: Selections 149 ("Theodore of Studius on the Ecclesiastical Pentarchy"), 153 ("A Byzantine Moderate's View of Papal Primacy"), from F. Dvornik, *Byzantium and the Roman Primacy*, trans. Edwin A. Quain, S.J. (New York, 1966/1979), p. 101; pp. 145–46. Selection 167 ("The Anonymous Fiscal Treatise on Villages"), from C. Brand, "Two Byzantine Treatises on Taxation," *Traditio* 25 (1969): 49–50.

Fribourg University Press: Selection 139 ("The Akathistos Hymn"), from G. Meersseman, *The Acathistos Hymn* (Fribourg, 1958), pp. 25–37.

Harper & Row, Publishers: map on p. 469 ("The Byzantine Empire in 1265 Shortly after Michael VIII's Recovery of Constantinople from the Latins") and map on p. 470 ("The Byzantine Empire and the Ottoman Turks in 1355") based on Maps I and II (p. 89), from *Shepherd's Historical Atlas*, 9th ed., by William R. Shepherd. Copyright © 1964 by Barnes & Noble, Inc. (A Division of Harper & Row, Publishers). Reprinted by permission of Harper & Row, Publishers, Inc.

Harvard University Press: Selection 93 ("Julian's Decree on Christian Teachers"), from W. Wright, *The Works of Emperor Julian* (Cambridge, Mass., 1932), vol. 3, pp. 117–23. Selection 261 ("Homily of Photius on the First Attacks of the Rus"), from C. Mango, *The Homilies of Photius* (Cambridge, Mass., 1958), pp. 95–110. Selection 296A ("St. Basil on the Study of Classical Greek Literature"), from R. J. Deferrari and M. R. McGuire, trans., *St. Basil: The Letters*, Loeb Classical Library (Cambridge, Mass., 1934), vol. 4, pp. 387–93 and 431. Reprinted by permission of Harvard University Press.

Hutchinson Publishing Group Ltd.: map on p. 468 ("The Aegean World, c. 1214–54"), from Joan Hussey, *The Byzantine World* (New York: Harper Torchbooks, 1961; first published by Hutchinson & Co., London, 1957).

Institut Français d'Etudes Byzantines: Selection 24 ("An Ecclesiastical Oath of Fidelity to the Emperor"), from N. Oikonomides, "Cinq actes inédits du Patriarch Michiel Autoreianos," *Revue des études byzantines* 25 (1967): 122–24. Selection 104 ("Imperial Privileges over the Church"), from V. Laurent, "Les droits de l'empereur en matière ecclésiastique: L'accord de 1380–82," *Revue des études byzantines* 13 (1955): 5–20. Selection 126 ("A Patriarchal Indictment of the Practice of Granting Charistikia"), from P. Gautier, "Réquisitoire du Patriarche Jean d'Antioche contre le charisticiat," *Revue des études byzantines* 33 (1975): 115–19.

Medieval Academy of America: Selections 84 ("The *Russian Primary Chronicle* on the Same Episode"), 206 ("Byzantine-Russian Treaties"), from S. Cross and O. Sherbowitz, trans., *Russian Primary Chronicle* (Cambridge, Mass., 1953), p. 72; pp. 65–68.

Ohio University Press: Selection 9 ("The Ideal of the Imperial Image in

Digenes Akritas"), from D. B. Hull, *Digenes Akritas: The Two-blooded Border Lord* (Athens, Ohio, 1972), pp. 60–61.

Orientalia Christiana Edizioni: Selections 131 ("The Vision of St. Symeon"), 134 ("Methods of Holy Prayer and Attention"), from "Vie de Symeon le nouveau theologien," ed. I. Hausherr, in *Orientalia Christiana* 12 (1918): 8–11, 9 (1927): 150–59.

Oxford University Press: Selections 169 ("Opening Verses of *Digenes Akritas, Border Warlord*"), 315 ("Epic: Border Fights and Beauties, from *Digenes Akritas*"), from J. Mavrogordato, ed., *Digenes Akritas* (Oxford, 1956), pp. 3–4; pp. 83 and 89. Selections 110A ("Decree of the Fifth Ecumenical Council"), 110B ("Decisions of the Sixth Ecumenical Council against Monotheletism"), from H. Bettenson, *Documents of the Christian Church* (Oxford, 1947), pp. 128–29; pp. 130–31. Selection 243 ("Synesius Cautions against the Gothic Threat"), from A. Fitzgerald, *The Letters of Synesius of Cyrene* (London, 1926), pp. 13–24. Map on p. 465 ("The Byzantine Empire in 565 A.D. under Emperor Justinian"), from N. Baynes and H. Moss, eds., *Byzantium: An Introduction to East Roman Civilization* (Oxford: Clarendon Press, 1961).

Prentice-Hall: Selections 288A ("Byzantine Views of Western Icons"), 288B ("Latin Religious Art Unappreciated by Byzantines"), from C. Mango, *The Art of the Byzantine Empire, 312–1453* (Englewood Cliffs, N.J., 1972), pp. 253–54; p. 254.

Rutgers University Press: map on p. 466 ("The Organization of the Themes in Asia Minor in the Seventh to Ninth Centuries"), from G. Ostrogorsky, *History of the Byzantine State* (New Brunswick, N.J., 1969). Copyright © 1969 by Rutgers, The State University.

St. Vladimir's Orthodox Theological Seminary and A. R. Mowbray & Co., Ltd.: Selections 119 ("The Bishop Takes Care of His People"), 128 ("The Charisma of Monks"), 213 ("Tradesmen and Craftsmen in Early Byzantine Asia Minor"), 227 ("The Philanthropy of John 'the Almsgiver'"), 234 ("Fun at the Baths"), 317 ("Hagiography: St. Theodore of Sykeon Performs an Exorcism"), from E. Dawes and N. Baynes, trans., *Three Byzantine Saints* (Crestwood, N.Y.: St. Vladimir's Seminary Press, and Oxford: A. R. Mowbray, 1977; originally published by Blackwell, Oxford, 1948), pp. 202, 221, 223; pp. 106–7; pp. 185–86; pp. 229–31; p. 178; pp. 146–47.

P. Schreiner and A. Hohlweg, Institut für Byzantinistik, Neugriechische Philologie und Byzantinische Kunstgeschichte der Universität München: Selection 10 ("The Coronation of Emperor Manuel II and Helena Dragaš"), from P. Schreiner, ed., "Hochzeit und Krönung Kaiser Manuels II. im Jahre 1392," *Byzantinische Zeitschrift* 60 (1967): 76–79.

Société d'Edition Les Belles Lettres: Selection 4 ("Preface to *On Ceremonies*"), from Constantine VII Porphyrogenitus, *De ceremoniis*, in A. Vogt, ed., *Le livre de cérémonie* (Paris, 1935), vol. 1, pp. 1–2. Selections 63 ("The Sapping of Senatorial Authority"), 178 ("Abrogation of Laws on Duties of Curiales"), 186 ("Space Regulations for Constantinople's Residential Buildings with Balconies"), 188A ("Edict of Leo VI regarding Eunuchs"), 217 ("Inheritances and Guardians for the Young"), from *Les novelles de Léon VI le Sage*, ed. P. Noailles and A. Dain (Paris, 1944), p. 271; pp. 183–85; no. 113, p. 373; no. 60, p. 223; no. 28, pp.

111–13. Selections 21 ("On the Macedonian 'Dynasty'"), 22 ("Succession through Marriage"), 103A ("The Boldness of Michael Cerularius"), 187 ("Michael Psellus: Self-Portrait"), 188B ("The Eunuch John the Orphanotrophos"), from Michael Psellus, *Chronographie*, ed. E. Rénauld (Paris, 1926 and 1928), vol. 1, p. 117; vol. 1, pp. 53–54; vol. 2, p. 123; vol. 1, pp. 138–40; vol. 1, pp. 59–60. Selections 30 ("Alexius Comnenus 'Invents' New Titles"), 116A ("The Trial of Basil the Bogomil"), 198 ("Forced Resettlement of the Paulicians"), 218 ("A Matriarch of the Early Twelfth Century"), 223 ("Imperial Vestments"), 228 ("A Philanthropic Emperor"), 270 ("Anna Comnena on the Crusaders"), 304 ("Suppressing the Teachings of Italus"), 305 ("Alexius Comnenus and the State of Education"), 309 ("Anna Comnena on Writing History"), 328A ("Anna Comnena on Astrology"), from Anna Comnena, *Alexiade*, ed. B. Leib (Paris, 1945), vol. 1, pp. 113–15; vol. 3, pp. 218–19 and 226–27; vol. 3, pp. 178–81; vol. 1, pp. 123–25; vol. 1, pp. 115–16; vol. 3, p. 217; vol. 2, pp. 206–9; vol. 2, pp. 38–40; vol. 3, p. 218; vol. 3, pp. 173–75; vol. 2, pp. 57–79.

University of Oklahoma Press: Selections 138 ("The Byzantine Liturgy"), 297 ("Appreciation for Literary Excellence"), from G. Downey, *Constantinople in the Age of Justinian* (Norman, Okla., 1960), pp. 124–35; p. 155. Copyright © 1960 by the University of Oklahoma Press, Publishing Division of the University.

Vatican Library: Selection 286 ("Cydones's Apologia for His Interest in the Teachings of Aquinas"), from G. Mercati, *Studi e testi*, no. 56, *Notizie di Procoro e Demetrio Cidone . . .* (Vatican, 1931), pp. 362–63.

Viking Penguin: Selection 330 ("Bessarion Pleads for Western Aid against the Turks"), from J. B. Ross and M. M. McLaughlin, eds., *The Portable Renaissance Reader* (New York, 1953), pp. 70–73; copyright © 1953 by The Viking Press, Inc.; copyright renewed 1981 by Viking Penguin Inc.; reprinted by permission of Viking Penguin Inc.

Wayne State University Press: Selection 319 ("'Devotional' Poetry: Monastic Love for the Divine"), reprinted from H. Magoulias, *Byzantine Christianity: Emperor, Church and the West* (Detroit, 1970), pp. 77–78, by permission of the Wayne State University Press. Copyright © 1970 by Rand McNally & Company. All rights reserved.

Weidenfeld & Nicolson Ltd.: map on p. 467 ("The Byzantine Empire in the Middle of the Eleventh Century A.D."), from R. Jenkins, *Byzantium: The Imperial Centuries, A.D. 610–1071* (London; originally published by Random House, New York, 1966).

Yale University Press: Selections 260 ("Byzantines and Rus at a Western Court"), 264 ("Russian Reaction to the Council of Florence and Metropolitan Isidore"), 265 ("The Russians Elect Their Own Metropolitan"), 333A ("A Muscovite Response to the Fall of Constantinople"), from G. Vernadsky, *A Source Book for Russian History* (New Haven, Conn., and London, 1972), vol. 1, p. 11; pp. 126–27; p. 127; p. 160.

INTRODUCTION:
Byzantium's History in Outline

◆ ◆ ◆ ◆ ◆ ◆ ◆ ◆ ◆ ◆ ◆ ◆ ◆ ◆ ◆ ◆ ◆ ◆

THE NEW ROME: CONSTANTINE AND HIS SUCCESSORS

In 330 A.D. Constantine the Great dedicated Constantinople (formerly the Greek city Byzantium) as the new capital of the Roman Empire. During his reign Emperor Constantine completed many of the reforms instituted by his predecessor, Diocletian, and the blueprint, administratively speaking, for the Later Roman ("Byzantine") Empire was laid down.

One of Constantine's first cares was the reform of the civil organization of the empire. Since the empire was too large to be governed effectively by one person, it was split (although not definitively until 395) into two large segments, the East, with its capital at Constantinople, and the West, with Rome as its capital. Both areas (excluding the capital cities) were in turn divided into four praetorian prefectures, themselves composed of smaller divisions called dioceses. The smallest imperial administrative unit was the province, under the jurisdiction of a governor. This entire system of provincial administration was firmly based on the principle of separation of powers between civil and military authorities so as to avert concentration of power in the hands of a few provincial officials—something that had contributed in large part to a series of ruinous rebellions earlier in the third century.

Complementing the administrative system was the complex bureaucratic machinery of the capital cities. This bureaucracy serviced the needs of the imperial court, including the massive imperial correspondence: edicts, responses to questions from provincial governors, petitions from provincials—in short, everything involved in managing a far-flung empire. The entire administrative system was theoretically under the absolute control of the emperor, although in practice local authorities often enjoyed a surprisingly large degree of authority. Taxation was now more regularly imposed than before. All persons, whether lower or upper class, were liable to contribute to the revenues of the state, and some, like the *curiales* (local senators of the provincial cities), were required to make up out of their own resources the taxes owed by delinquent taxpayers. At the same time, the economic chaos caused by debasement of the coinage was alleviated and then definitively rectified by the reforms of the Emperor Anastasius at the end of the fifth century. When Constantine transferred the capital from Rome to Constantinople, he also transferred many senators to the new center to create a new Senate. His sons and their successors continued his policies, especially his administrative and fiscal reforms.

Like his predecessors, Constantine had to face the severe problem of the German invasions. In time the entire West was stripped from the empire by the Germanic invaders (Visigoths, Anglo-Saxons, Ostrogoths, Franks, and several other groups). Owing in part to its greater prosperity and administrative cohesiveness, the eastern half of the empire did not succumb to the invaders. Yet Byzantium experienced its own German problem, especially during the fifth century, when the Goths threatened to take over from within by controlling the chief offices and the army in Constantinople itself. An even more serious threat to the East was posed by the neighboring and frequently hostile Sassanid Persian state.

The "translation" of the capital from Rome to Constantinople, a city henceforth always to be associated with Christianity, marked the transformation of the pagan Roman Empire into the *Christian* Roman Empire. But Constantine's adoption of Christianity as a state religion brought a host of new problems. The question of paganism was not definitively resolved until the reign of Theodosius I, who completely prohibited sacrifices to the old gods. Also important was the problem of the emerging relations between church and state and the reconciliation of pagan Greek culture with Christian beliefs. Perhaps most significant, however, were the acute difficulties connected with formulating an orthodox Christian dogma that could be accepted by all groups in the empire. With respect to Christian doctrine, the most dangerous heresy was Arianism, which threatened the integrity of the Trinity and was defeated only by the intercession of Emperor Constantine and the imperial government.

The heresy that posed the greatest threat to the survival of the Byzantine state itself, however, was Monophysitism. Unable to accept the dogmas formulated at the Fourth Ecumenical Council (one of seven such ecclesiastical assemblies all held in the Byzantine East primarily to resolve doctrinal differences within the church), the adherents of Monophysitism formed a majority of the population in Syria and Palestine and, especially, in what was then the empire's richest and most important province, Egypt. This doctrinal dispute concerned the relation between the divine and human natures in Christ. The Monophysites generally maintained (contrary to the conciliar pronouncements) that after the Incarnation Christ had only one nature—the divine. But this heresy may also have had another significance, for it seems to have served as a focus for the disaffection of the local inhabitants of these largely Semitic eastern areas against the Hellenized ruling class in the large cities and, especially, against imperial domination from Constantinople.

The Age of Justinian

At the accession of Justinian in 527, the empire consisted of the Balkan Peninsula, Asia Minor, Egypt, Syria, and Armenia. Egypt and Syria were still rich provinces, with the Greek-speaking cities of Alexandria and Antioch as their capital cities. Asia Minor had increasingly come to constitute the heartland of the empire, dotted as it was with Greek cities celebrated from patristic times.

Justinian, in a persistent attempt to reconquer the western areas of the empire lost to the German peoples, engaged in several wars, during which he recovered most of Africa from the Vandals, southern Spain from the Visigoths, and, most important, Italy from the Ostrogoths. The Ostrogothic War lasted for twenty years and was costly and destructive both for Italy and for Byzantium. Eventually Rome (the pope still recognized the emperor in Constantinople as his political superior), Naples, and Ravenna were all retaken, and Ravenna became the Byzantine capital in Italy, the seat of the imperial governor. But Justinian's conquests in the West were accomplished at the price of Persian advances in the East, where the centuries-long Byzantine-Persian rivalry (based on political and economic factors) continued in full force. Ultimately Justinian's costly military successes in the West proved ephemeral, and, by bringing the empire to the brink of economic collapse, they seriously weakened the defense of the eastern borders.

The significance of Justinian's work in certain cultural spheres, especially legislation, is noteworthy. By this time the emperor was considered to be the sole source of law. But since the imperial enactments of his predecessors had fallen into almost complete disorder, Justinian appointed a special commission to codify and systematize Roman law. Four great works were published, constituting the famous Civil Law: the *Codex Justinianus*, a codification of the imperial edicts; the *Digest*, a collection of the opinions of jurisconsults on the law; the *Institutes*, a handbook for students; and the *Novellae*, the new laws issued under Justinian.

Meantime, there broke out, with greater intensity than before, a new phase of religious conflict over Monophysitism. Several of the Byzantine emperors, notably Justinian (and later Heraclius), aware of the dangers inherent in the disaffection of the empire's eastern provinces, made determined attempts to placate the Monophysites. They tried to effect a compromise on the question of the natures of Christ and thereby find a solution acceptable to both sides, Orthodox and Monophysite. But these efforts were consistently thwarted by the intransigent opposition of the papacy, which, far removed in the West, cared little for eastern political and military exigencies, preferring to pursue a more or less independent policy.

In the field of imperial administration, the Roman civil service was retained from the earlier period and was in some ways improved. Consisting of a group of highly educated officials trained primarily at the university or, rather, "higher school" of Constantinople, the civil service was organized into a hierarchical system of considerable complexity even by today's standards. Taxes were collected regularly, justice was administered, armies were raised and put into the field, and the functions of the state in general were very adequately carried out. It may be said that in its period of greatest power (330–c. 1050) the Byzantine government, despite all its faults (excessive love of pomp and protocol, bureaucratic tendencies, and frequent venality), functioned more effectively, and for a longer period, than virtually any other political organism in history.

Byzantine commerce was based on the Byzantine gold coin, the *nomisma* (called "bezant" in the West). By the sixth century it had become the standard gold coin in a large part of the world and was used to some extent even in the Far East. Constantinople's extensive commercial activity made the city one of the world's great trade emporia, supporting much of the empire's economy and providing a rich source of revenue to the government, which taxed all trade coming to and from Constantinople. State customhouses dotted the Bosporus and Black Sea regions.

The Persian and Arab Invasions: Heraclius and His Successors

After Justinian's death in 565, the empire, exhausted by his military endeavors, lay open to the advance of the Persians. Approaching through Asia Minor, they besieged Constantinople. But in 610 Heraclius came to the throne, and he was able to marshal Byzantine strength and mount a counter-offensive. Heraclius recaptured all the eastern provinces that had been lost to the Persians and completely eliminated Persia as a military threat. Before he died, however, a new and greater danger erupted from Arabia. In a short time, all the eastern provinces—whose Monophysite population welcomed the Arabs as liberators from Orthodox persecution—as well as North Africa, Crete, Cyprus, and Rhodes, were taken by the Arabs. Only in the early eighth century was the extraordinary Muslim advance checked in the East by Emperor Leo III, founder of the new Isaurian dynasty.

It was during this time of Persian and Arab incursions that the empire was completely reorganized. Martial law was established in the provinces, and military commanders were now given joint military and civil authority over what came to be called the "themes." The thematic system first began to take form under Emperor Maurice, certainly under Heraclius, and it seems roughly to have reached its completed form in Asia Minor in the late seventh century. To increase revenues, the taxation system was also overhauled, and heavy, sometimes crushing, taxes were levied on the peaant villages. If a villager could not pay his tax, it was decreed that his neighbors had to contribute for him.

The Iconoclastic Period

In the year 726 a celebrated struggle broke out over the question of the icons, the sacred images of Christ, the Virgin, and the saints. The conflict resulted from an order of Emperor Leo III that all icons should be destroyed. (Precisely why he issued this order is still uncertain.) A storm of opposition immediately arose, especially in Italy on the part of the pope, and in what is today Greece. Monks, the special guardians of the faith, were severely persecuted by the Iconoclastic emperors. Finally, in 787, after the dispute had convulsed the empire, the images were restored by decree of the Seventh Ecumenical Council. Iconoclasm underwent a brief revival in 813, but the movement had lost its early vitality and was definitively crushed at the ceremony of the Feast of Orthodoxy in 843. But the conflict left its scars, for in the course of it the pope excommunicated the Byzantine emperor, who, in retaliation, removed Greece, southern Italy, and much of the Balkans from papal ecclesiastical control and transferred them to the patriarch of Constantinople.

These events constituted the prelude to a long process of political and ecclesiastical alienation between East and West. Even when organically united in the ancient Roman Empire, East and West had in the main spoken different languages and employed different liturgical practices. The West, for example, used Latin in its liturgy in contrast to the Greek of the East. The Byzantine clergy, unlike the Western, were allowed to marry (before ordination), and the East used leavened instead of the Western unleavened bread in the Eucharist. To these ecclesiastical differences was added, in the early ninth century, an even more serious political schism. In 800 the pope crowned Charlemagne "Roman" emperor in direct contradiction to Byzantine claims to the imperial title. This event marked the beginning of a bitter rivalry over the imperial title, which served to exacerbate East-West relations virtually until 1453.

A new threat to Byzantium emerged with the rise of the Bulgar state. The Bulgars, originally a Turkic people, dominated, and were eventually assimilated into, the large Slavic population of present-day Bulgaria. Virtually from the time of their arrival in the Balkans the Bulgars had close, though very often hostile, relations with the empire. Several times, notably in 813, Bulgar armies crushed their Byzantine counterparts and were thwarted in their ambition to conquer Constantinople itself only by their inability to breach the city's massive walls.

The turning point in Byzantine-Bulgar relations came with the Bulgars' conversion to Christianity in the latter half of the ninth century. Bulgaria was brought into the Byzantine cultural orbit, but only at the cost of a serious Byzantine rift with the papacy. The Bulgarian conversion in fact forms the background to the so-called Photian schism. The papacy, anxious to extend its ecclesiastical authority over the Bulgars, tried to force the emperors to restore Roman ecclesiastical jurisdiction over southern Italy and Illyricum (the Balkans), earlier taken away by the Iconoclast emperors. Photius, the great patriarch of Constantinople, countered Roman demands with accusations of Western doctrinal deviation in connection with the Latin addition of the term *filioque* to the Nicene-Constantinopolitan creed, an addition that in the eyes of the Byzantines was forbidden by the ecumenical councils. The charges and countercharges between Rome and Constantinople led in 867 to the first really serious break in the ecclesiastical unity of Christendom.

The Macedonian Dynasty: Apogee of Empire

In the midst of the Photian crisis the Byzantine world was shaken by the murder of Emperor Michael III and the accession of Basil I (867), a Macedonian stable boy who had risen to the throne and founded what was to become the most glorious dynasty in Byzantine history. Basil quickly ended the ecclesiastical breach with Rome. But in doing so he did not surrender Constantinople's jurisdictional claims over the Balkans, and the conversion of the Bulgars proceeded speedily under Byzantine auspices.

The Macedonian dynasty was most noted for its military achievements. From 867 to 1025 Byzantium was able to recover its strength and take the offensive against the Arabs. Crete was retaken, as was Syria, and Byzantine armies penetrated almost as far as Jerusalem, with the empire making Palestine a virtual protectorate. In southern Italy the Byzantines not only consolidated their control but instituted administrative reforms, organizing Calabria and Apulia into the theme of Langobardia. At the same time, the Bulgar threat was neutralized and ultimately eliminated during the reign of Basil II (d. 1025), who completely crushed the Bulgar state and incorporated its territories into the empire.

These conquests were made possible by the Byzantine army and navy, armed forces without peer in the medieval world. Although drawing in large part on the military tradition of the later Roman Empire, the Byzantines developed new tactics, new formations, and even a new secret weapon, "Greek" fire, which made their navy nearly invincible in battle. In the field, Byzantine armies under the command of the *strategoi* (commanders of themes) were carefully organized; the chief military arm was the Byzantine heavy cavalry (the cataphracts), horsemen fully clad in armor and/or leather. An attack by this cavalry, meticulously organized into a wedge-shaped formation, was virtually irresistible.

In addition to Byzantium's military triumphs, political and ecclesiastical diplomacy brought about a notable expansion in the empire's sphere of influence. After years of commercial and military contact with Byzantium, the Viking rulers of Kiev, together with their Slavic subjects, converted to Orthodoxy in 989. Constantinople controlled this newly established church, and Byzantine influence soon became paramount in the development of Orthodox Russian culture. In addition, other foreign rulers sought to emulate imperial ceremonial and especially to gain a place for themselves in the honorific Byzantine political hierarchy as members of the "family of princes" under the paternal aegis of the emperor. Even the Western Empire, restored to vigor under a line of capable German rulers, came under Byzantine cultural influence with the marriage of the Greek princess Theophano to Otto II and the semi-Byzantinization, however ephemeral, of the German court under her son Otto III.

The Macedonian emperors Basil I and, notably, his son Leo VI were the greatest legislators in Byzantine history after Justinian. Their achievement was the promulgation of the *Basilica*, a massive compilation and updating of the *Corpus Juris Civilis* of Justinian. The new code was written in Greek, the spoken language of the empire, rather than Latin, as was most of the Justinianic corpus. In addition, the *Basilica* presented in unified form the body of law that Justinian had divided into several parts, thus making it more useful for jurists than the cumbersome older work. It quickly supplanted the *Corpus* as the fundamental Byzantine law code and remained so until the fall of the empire.

The political and legislative efflorescence of the Macedonian period was matched by the vitality of Byzantine trade. Constantinople was indisputably the commercial capital of the Christian world, and through it flowed eastern goods to the West, following both the sea route through the Mediterranean and the famous "Varangian" route of the Rus traders through Russia and the Baltic Sea. Internal commerce flourished under the direction of native Greek traders, and the Byzantine merchant marine formed a potent commercial force. Industry also prospered, and several Byzantine exports, especially luxurious silk fabrics, were prized through much of the world.

Yet some portents of danger began to reveal themselves in this period. In 992 Basil II granted the Venetians a set of trade privileges in Constantinople. Although these concessions were not in themselves detrimental to the economic health of the empire, they foreshadowed the rapid expansion of the Italian maritime cities into the markets of Asia Minor and Syria. By the end of the eleventh century Venice had been granted a quarter in Constantinople for her merchants, significant tariff reductions, and other privileges; her rivals, principally Pisa and Genoa, were later to obtain similar concessions. Control of trade thus began to slip from native Byzantine merchants into the hands of privileged foreign competitors.

Perhaps the most dramatic internal phenomenon of the period was the bitter struggle between the emperors and the landed aristocracy concerning control of peasant lands. As we have noted, the free peasantry—especially that of Asia Minor—formed the backbone of the Byzantine state, providing both a major source of tax revenue and the primary recruiting ground for the army. By the tenth century the large lay and ecclesiastical estates, which had never completely disappeared since the early years of the empire, began to expand tremendously, absorbing peasant lands and putting the peasants themselves into a semiservile state of dependence on their landlords. This process was facilitated by the crushing taxes levied on the peasants, many of whom were driven into bankruptcy or into debt to their more powerful neighbors, and also by a series of severe famines in the mid-tenth century, which forced many small farmers to turn over their land in return for subsistence. Several Macedonian emperors, notably Romanus I Lecapenus and Basil II, realizing the danger to the state inherent in this situation, enacted stringent laws to curb the growing power of the magnate landlords. Indeed, Basil tried to curb the power of the magnates decisively, and during his lifetime he succeeded to a certain extent. But with his death this imperial policy was discarded, and the growth of the large estates continued unabated. Nevertheless, despite its growing internal problems, the empire continued under the Macedonian dynasty to maintain its position as the leading power of Europe and the Middle East.

The Partial Collapse of the Empire in the Eleventh Century

After the century and a half of Macedonian glory, the empire began to experience a decline that rapidly accelerated in the course of the mid-eleventh century. The malaise that gripped the empire—the result primarily of its unsolved internal problems—became glaringly apparent in 1071, when Byzantine armies suffered two almost fatal disasters. In the West, Norman adventurers captured Bari, the Byzantine capital of southern Italy, forever ending Byzantine political control there. In the East, the Byzantines were defeated at Manzikert (near Armenia) by the advancing armies of a new invader, the Seljuk Turks. It was this latter defeat that in the long run proved catastrophic for Byzantium, for henceforth the Byzantine heartland of Asia Minor suffered constantly from Turkish incursions and much of it was absorbed by the Seljuks into their state, an independent sultanate with its capital at Iconium.

The Norman and Turkish threats were indeed severe, but Byzantium had survived even greater external dangers in the past. It is therefore clear that the empire's partial collapse must be attributed primarily to internal factors. There were two main causes of internal decay in the years between 1025 and 1071. We have already noted that after Basil II's death no attempt was made to stop the growth of the large estates. In time the magnates not only eliminated most of the free peasantry but also came to enjoy a partial or (much later) even complete immunity from taxation and some forms of state control. While this process was by no means complete by 1071, the vaunted central authority of the empire had begun to disintegrate, to be replaced ultimately by quasi-feudal landlords holding independent jurisdiction over a servile peasantry. An equally important cause of decline was the struggle between the court bureaucracy in Constantinople, from whose ranks were drawn most of the emperors in this era, and the rural magnates, who composed the army's high command. The bureaucratic class, fearing domination by the military, allowed the army to fall into decay in order to destroy the power base of the rural nobility. They succeeded so well in this objective that the armed forces were unable to protect the state from the sudden appearance of the Seljuk Turks and the Normans, despite the best efforts of the two soldier-emperors, Isaac I Comnenus and Romanus IV Diogenes, whose attempts to repair the damage were too little and too late.

Meantime, the Norman conquest of southern Italy precipitated the most serious—and what in later centuries came to be viewed as the definitive—split between East and West in the ecclesiastical sphere. While Byzantium and the papacy were involved in political negotiations in response to the Norman invasion of southern Italy, the patriarch of Constantinople, Michael Cerularius, condemned the papacy's attempts to introduce Latin liturgical practices among the Greek communities of that area. This led to a serious clash between pope and patriarch, with the result that, on 15 July 1054, papal legates entered the cathedral of Hagia Sophia and excommunicated the patriarch. In retaliation, a synod of bishops residing in Constantinople anathematized the papal legates. Although neither the emperor nor the pope was excommunicated, this famous event has traditionally been taken to mark the beginning of the schism that today still divides the Greek and Latin churches.

By 1081 the empire, attacked by the ever-advancing Seljuk Turks, isolated from the West by ecclesiastical schism, and increasingly unable effectively to enforce the authority of the state over all segments of its population, seemed on the verge of extinction. In its hour of extreme crisis Byzantium was saved by a brilliant soldier and diplomat, the Emperor Alexius I Comnenus.

The Comnenan and Angelid Period: The Early Crusades

At his accession in 1081 Alexius Comnenus found himself in a desperate situation. Constantinople faced determined attacks from two sides by Turkish forces. To save his capital, Alexius melted down and sold many church treasures, the proceeds of which he used to buy the military services of a third Turkic people, the Cumans, with whose aid he temporarily turned back the dual threat. During this crisis Alexius was also compelled to turn to the West for assistance against the Seljuk Turks advancing in Asia Minor. It was perhaps in part as a response to this appeal that Pope Urban II called forth the First Crusade. At the Council of Clermont, in southern France, in 1095, Urban delivered an impassioned address that set in motion the crusading movement. Thousands of Westerners of all classes took up the Cross to recover the Holy Sepulcher from the Turks and, presumably, to aid Alexius. The main forces of the crusading knights soon converged on the Byzantine capital, the meeting point on the way to Jerusalem. But Alexius was amazed at the vast army massed before the gates of his capital. Instead of the mercenary troops he had sought to protect his empire againt the Turks, he was confronted by powerful and dangerous armies of haughty Western knights, whose primary aim was not to defend Byzantium but to conquer Jerusalem. Alexius agreed to aid the Western leaders in their campaign in the Holy Land, but in return he insisted that all former Byzantine territory reconquered in Asia Minor be handed over to him. The leaders of the Crusade were, in the Western manner, obliged to swear an oath of allegiance to him as their feudal overlord. But the Crusaders and Alexius had very different ideas about the meaning of the oath.

After several minor altercations between Latins and Greeks, the crusading host advanced toward the Holy Land. Soon a more severe dispute broke out over possession of the recaptured city of Antioch, and the Norman leader, Bohemund, in violation of his agreement with Alexius, seized the old Byzantine city for himself. The remaining Latin leaders moved southward against Jerusalem. After a long siege, the Holy City fell to the crusading host, and in June 1099 a Latin kingdom of Jerusalem was established by the Western conquerors.

In 1147 the Second Crusade, composed of Germans and Franks, was organized in the West to recover the Christian city of Edessa in the Holy Land, recently lost to the Muslims. Again Western armies converged on Constantinople. After the same sort of misunderstandings as before, the Byzantine Emperor Manuel I Comnenus transported the Crusaders across the Bosporus to Asia Minor, where, at Damascus in Syria they eventually met a disastrous end, both the French and German rulers and their forces being routed by the Muslims.

Three decades later the Byzantines made their own last great effort to recapture important regions of Asia Minor, the empire's key area, from the Seljuk Turks. But the battle of Myriocephalon (1176) was a disastrous defeat for Byzantine arms and sealed the fate of Asia Minor, closing most of it forever to Byzantine authority.

When, in 1187, Jerusalem fell to the Muslim ruler Saladin, the West for the third time launched a crusade. Several Western rulers participated in this expedition: Emperor Frederick Barbarossa and kings Philip Augustus of France and Richard I of England. But, just as in the Second Crusade, the Westerners failed in their objectives. More significant for Byzantium, however, was the ever-widening mistrust between itself and the West, a distrust that had greatly increased since 1054.

The shattering climax of Byzantine-Latin hostility came during the Fourth Crusade. This time the Latin Crusaders, instead of proceeding to the Holy Land to recover Jerusalem, diverted their course in order to attack and seize Christian

Constantinople. The main protagonists among the Western Crusaders in this predatory expedition were the Venetians, who probably saw an unprecedented opportunity to gain a monopoly over the lucrative trade of Constantinople. In June 1203 the Crusader fleet arrived before Constantinople. After a brief siege the city fell and the Crusaders handed the city over to a Byzantine pretender whose claims to the throne they were supporting. But when a popular revolution broke out in Constantinople and its citizenry selected a new emperor hostile to the Crusaders, the latter decided to take the city for themselves. After drawing up a treaty partitioning the Byzantine Empire among their leaders, the Crusaders stormed the city walls while the Venetian fleet attacked from the sea. Constantinople succumbed on 13 April 1204.

The Crusader army was granted a three-day period of sack, which resulted in an unparalleled looting of the city and the destruction of many churches, monasteries, and works of art, and the transfer of countless relics of ancient Christianity to the West. The Byzantine Empire was now reorganized along Western feudal lines. A Latin emperor was chosen as suzerain and received much of the city of Constantinople. Other Western nobles secured lands on the mainland of Greece as fiefs of the new Latin emperor. (Some of these principalities were to remain in Latin hands long after Constantinople's reconquest by the Greeks in 1261.) To the Venetians fell the greatest share. They secured the remaining part of Constantinople and numerous strategically situated islands in the Aegean Sea. To complement Latin political control in the East, a "Latinization" of the Greek church and population was attempted.

But not all areas of the Byzantine Empire were conquered by the Crusaders. The two most important "successor" Greek states, the Despotate of Epirus and the "empire" established by Theodore Lascaris at Nicaea (in Asia Minor), vied vigorously to retake the capital and establish the legitimacy of their ruling houses. In 1261 a Byzantine noble from Nicaea, Michael Palaeologus, retook Constantinople and thus restored the heart of the empire to the Byzantines. Byzantium, however, was never to regain its former prestige. After the reign of Michael VIII, the empire became essentially a small Balkan power, though it still retained enough strength and diplomatic skill to resist the pressure of the advancing Ottoman Turks until 1453.

The Last Centuries of the Empire

Constantinople's recapture by Michael VIII Palaeologus in 1261 did not end the Western threat to Byzantium's existence. Indeed, in the face of the grave dangers confronting him on all sides, it is a tribute to Michael's remarkable diplomatic skill that he was able to thwart the last and greatest Latin attempt to reconquer Byzantium, that of Charles of Anjou, the ambitious king of Sicily and inheritor of the old Norman designs against Constantinople. In the course of his conflict with Charles, Michael saved his empire from the threat of a second Latin invasion, but at the same time, through buying off his enemies and other diplomatic endeavors, he drained Byzantium of its financial resources. Moreover, his policy of trying to gain papal support through negotiations for religious union of the churches created a fundamental religious dissension in Byzantium that lasted to the very end of the empire. Worst of all, while preoccupied with the West, he largely neglected the defense of his eastern borders against the now rapidly advancing Ottoman Turks.

First appearing in eastern Asia Minor at the end of Michael's reign (1261–82), the Ottomans gradually took over much of the territory of the Seljuk sultanate, which itself had been shattered by the Mongol invasions earlier in the thirteenth century. By 1301 the Ottoman Turks, rising increasingly to power as the Seljuks declined, had penetrated the vital Byzantine province of Bithynia as far as Nicaea.

In his first act as emperor, Michael's son, Andronicus II Palaeologus, denounced the religious union with Rome signed by his father and punished all the prounionists who had been active under his father. Yet these measures did not avert a bitterly divisive religious conflict between a radical group of antiunionist churchmen and a more moderate (and much smaller) group of ecclesiastics who favored a pro-Western orientation in political and religious affairs. This rivalry was further inflamed in the second half of the fourteenth century by the outbreak of the Hesychast controversy. The Hesychasts, a group of monks from the great monastic center of Mount Athos, believed that through contemplation and a particular method of prayer a type of mystical union with God (*theosis*) could be achieved already in this life. Their views often (though not always) came to be associated with the Byzantine nationalist party, just as their opponents' views were not infrequently equated with the pro-Latin faction.

Byzantine long-range commerce, control of which had for long been gradually passing to the Italian cities, now fell almost entirely into Venetian and Genoese hands as the native Byzantine mercantile class tended largely to disappear, though a large group of Greek tradesmen and artisans controlled the retail trade. The dominance of these two cities in the commercial life of the empire constituted a threat to Byzantium's very existence. Their powerful navies, stationed in Byzantine waters, enabled them to intervene almost at will in the internal affairs of the empire. In addition, rivalry between the Venetian and Genoese inhabitants of Constantinople frequently erupted into open warfare, creating a continual source of disorder in the streets of the city. Significantly, by this time the merchants of Venice and Genoa enjoyed total exemption from Byzantine customs duties. Vital revenues were lost to the imperial treasury. Since a large number of great Byzantine lay and ecclesiastical landholders also enjoyed immunity from taxation, the treasury, at a time when vast amounts were required to defend the empire against its enemies, found itself perpetually short of funds. Andronicus raised the rates of the remaining taxes, but this action did not provide nearly enough revenue and, at the same time, by further impoverishing the lower classes, it helped foment the urban social unrest that occurred in the period. In another desperate financial expedient, Andronicus scrapped the Byzantine navy, which had been laboriously rebuilt by his father. Henceforth Byzantium was almost completely dependent on its often untrustworthy and independent-minded Genoese ally for naval forces.

A common fiscal device of the Palaeologan emperors, however, was coinage depreciation. By the mid-fourteenth century the *nomisma* (now called *hyperpyron*) had fallen to only half its original value and was displaced as the international currency of the mercantile world by the newly minted Italian gold coins. The resulting monetary chaos, when combined with the collapse of the Byzantine merchant marine and the loss, by 1350, of virtually all of the best agricultural lands in Asia Minor, left the empire, in the last century and a half of its existence, economically prostrate.

To these severe crises were added the disaster of the Black Death and two major civil wars, which raged through most of the early decades of the fourteenth century: first a rebellion in which Andronicus III overthrew his grandfather Andronicus II; then the confused struggle against John V Palaeologus and his mother, Anna of Savoy, led by John Cantacuzene, a major provincial magnate and former supporter of Andronicus III. Thus, throughout the Palaeologan period, Byzantium, which needed to marshal all of its now limited resources against the advancing Ottomans, found itself bitterly divided by both political and ecclesiastical conflicts.

The political, social, and economic situation of Byzantium seemed almost hopeless. It appeared as if the capital would fall to anyone who wished to seize it. Yet the empire showed an amazing tenacity for life until the very end. Paradoxically, in this period of ruin Byzantium experienced a remarkable cultural revival (the so-called Palaeologan Renaissance) in art, literature, philosophy, and learning in general—a fact that shows that, though the state was bankrupt, its civilization was in many ways still vigorous.

The West, at last recognizing that the Turkish successes in the Balkans posed a threat to its own existence, began to take an interest in the fate of Byzantium. But it was the Slavs of the Balkans who now confronted the Turkish advance. In 1389, at Kossovo, the Serb army was destroyed by the Turks. With the Bulgars already subjugated, almost the entire Balkan area, except for parts of Greece, had fallen to the Ottomans. The Byzantine Empire was now reduced to the environs of Constantinople, the Peloponnesus, Thessalonika, and one or two islands. A similar debacle occurred in 1396 when the last great Western crusading army was destroyed by the Ottomans at Nicopolis. Byzantium, now in deadly peril, was granted a reprieve of several decades, however, by the defeat of Sultan Bayazid at the hands of another Turkish leader, the Tatar Timur the Lame. At the battle of Ankara, in 1402, the vaunted Turkish troops were cut to pieces by the Tatar host.

Emperor Manuel II Palaeologus made every effort to prepare his tiny empire to resist the Turkish onslaught that he knew was coming. A formidable antagonist came to the fore in the person of Sultan Murad II, who was able to restore the unity and power of the Ottoman Empire. When Murad, in 1422, laid siege to Constantinople, the new emperor, John VIII Palaeologus, realized that he must make a supreme effort to bring the West to his aid.

After considerable negotiations with the pope and other Western rulers, John decided to go personally to the West to attend a great council, to be summoned to discuss the problem of ecclesiastical union between the two churches. In return for bringing about religious union, John expected to receive effective Western military aid against the Ottoman Turks.

On 16 July 1439, after about a year and a half of protracted theological wrangling, the ceremony of ecclesiastical union took place at the famous Council of

Florence. Despite signatures of acceptance on the part of almost all of the Greek delegates, they repudiated the union on their return to Constantinople, and so did the great majority of the Byzantine populace. Popular opposition was based not only on the belief that the union was obtained under duress but on the Byzantines' deep-rooted mistrust and, by now, nearly fanatical hatred of the Latins. The memory of the atrocities committed in 1204 and of their own enforced conversion to "Roman Catholicism" still rankled.

As for the Latins, their antagonism toward the Byzantines was further inflamed by the Greek repudiation of the union signed at Florence. Byzantium, as a result, secured no effective aid from the West. A final (but vain) attempt to help Constantinople was made only by two eastern European powers—the Poles and the Hungarians—at the Battle of Varna in 1444.

After very intensive planning, the new Ottoman sultan, Mehmed II, began his attack on Constantinople in April 1453, after amassing a huge army against the few thousand military defenders of the city. Mehmed's bombardment of Constantinople lasted fifty days and exhausted the defenders, who each night rushed to repair the damaged walls. Mehmed, exasperated, ordered a final assault, which began on Tuesday, 29 May, at one o'clock in the morning. After the Greeks repulsed several attacks, Mehmed stormed the weakened gate where Emperor Constantine XI Palaeologus was fighting. Making a breach, the Turks poured in through the walls.

The fall of Constantinople marked the end of a millennium. Not only was it the end of medieval Europe's most durable political organism; it was technically the end of the venerable Roman Empire, which harked back in an unbroken line to the reign of Augustus, though of course many of its institutions were in reality no longer operative. But the Eastern concept of the "Roman" Empire did not perish; for the idea of a "third Rome," to replace the fallen Byzantium, was taken up by distant Moscow, which now proclaimed itself the heir of Byzantium and the protector of all the Orthodox peoples.

PART I
The Universal Empire

◆ ◆ ◆ ◆ ◆ ◆ ◆ ◆ ◆ ◆ ◆ ◆ ◆ ◆ ◆ ◆ ◆ ◆ ◆ ◆

A.
THE IMPERIAL IMAGE

1.

Introduction. The key to an understanding of Byzantine polity and civilization is the figure of the emperor. While Constantine the Great (306–37) and his Christian successors rejected the titles of divinity adopted by their pagan predecessors in the Hellenistic and Roman periods, they retained the substance of the belief in their cosmic function. Their predecessors had been proclaimed gods; the Byzantine emperors were content with the only slightly less distinguished role of "imitation" (*mimesis*) of God, the heavenly king. Like their predecessors, the emperors of Byzantium were described as possessing, among other attributes, the qualities of *philanthropeia* (love of mankind), *eusebeia* (piety), *phronesis* (wisdom), and *sophrosyne* (temperance).

The emperor's role in the cosmic order is well described by Eusebius of Caesarea, the noted church historian and adviser to Constantine, in a discourse that he composed for the thirtieth year of Constantine's reign. Eusebius expresses the belief that the emperor, like God, is an absolute monarch, the vicar of God on earth. As the Christian God is one, so there can be but one Christian emperor and one earthly empire. (Throughout Byzantine history there may be junior emperors, or coemperors, but never more than one senior emperor at a time. By the seventh century the title of the senior emperor became "Basileus and Autokrator"; see selection 248.)

The following excerpt is taken from Eusebius's "Tridecennial Oration," delivered in 336 to celebrate three decades of rule by the Emperor Constantine.

THE EMPEROR'S QUALITIES

(From Eusebius Pamphyli, *Oratio de laudibus Constantini*, ed. I. Heikel [Leipzig, 1902], pp. 198–202.)

And it is from and through This Very One—who is the Lord of the entire universe, who is over all, through all, and in all both visible and invisible, who is the all-pervasive Logos of God [i.e., Christ, the Word]—that the emperor, the bearer of the image of the heavenly kingdom and one dear to God, directs, in imitation of the Higher Power, the helm of the earth and guides all its affairs.

Just as the light of the sun shines upon settlers in very distant lands through its rays reflected far into the distance, so too does he [Constantine] assign this son here to us who live in the East, an offspring worthy of himself. Also, a second of his progeny he appoints to another segment of the world, and still another elsewhere,* to be beacons and reflectors of the brilliance emanating from himself. Accordingly, after yoking the four most noble caesars [junior emperors] like spirited colts, under the single yoke of his own imperial chariot, he directs their course by the reins of sacred harmony and concord. Standing on high above them and grasping the reins, he traverses all the lands of the earth on which the sun shines, while still being present everywhere and watching over all things.

Thus invested with the image of the kingship of heaven, he pilots affairs on earth while looking upward in order to steer according to the pattern of his archetype. Indeed, he waxes strong as he follows this model of monarchic authority, which the Ruler over all has given to man alone of all beings on earth. For He [God] only is the author of sovereign power, the law that decrees a single authority over all men. Monarchy transcends every other kind of constitution and form of government. Indeed, polyarchy [i.e. democracy], which is the alternative, because it embodies equality of status gives rise to anarchy and conflict. Hence there is one God, not two or three or even more. Polytheism is actually atheism; there is one Supreme Ruler, and his Logos [Word] and imperial law are one, not expressed in letters and syllables or in writings or tablets that perish with time, but in the living, self-subsisting Word, who is himself God, and who governs the kingdom of his Father in behalf of all those who are under and after him. . . .

He [God] has modeled the kingdom on earth into an image of that in heaven, and he urges all men to strive toward it, holding out to them this radiant hope. And in this heavenly kingdom, the one dear to God [i.e., the emperor] shall henceforth participate, for he has been endowed by God with natural virtues and has received in his soul the outpouring of God's favor. He has become rational from the Universal Logos [reason], he has become wise from his communion with Wisdom, become good through association with the Good, and become just from his connection with Justice. And he is prudent in the ideal of Prudence, and from his sharing in the Supreme Authority he acquires courage. And in truth he should merit the imperial title who has shaped his soul to royal virtues, according to the model of that celestial kingdom.

*Constantine's sons were Constantine, Constantius, and Constans, all given the title of caesar. On these "junior emperors" see selection 19.

2.

Introduction. Eusebius's formulation of the emperor's central role in the world order was to remain normative throughout Byzantine history, all subsequent statements on the subject expressing much the same point of view. For example, the famous treatise by the sixth-century deacon of St. Sophia, Agapetus, reiterates the substance of Eusebius's message while, at the same time, drawing on the writings of the ancient Athenian orator

Isocrates and the Greek Fathers of the Church. Agapetus's work, consisting of seventy-two brief chapters, is an early example of the "mirror of princes" literature later much in vogue in Byzantium and the West. In literary works of this type, advice and counsel were given on the proper conduct of Christian heads of state.

AGAPETUS'S POINTS OF ADVICE TO THE EMPEROR JUSTINIAN

(From Agapetus, *Expositio capitum amonitoriorum . . . imperatori Justiniano,* MPG [Migne Patrologie Graeca], vol. 86, cols. 1164–74.)

Possessing a dignity, O Emperor, surpassing all others in honor, you should, above all, render honor to God, who has bestowed that rank upon you. For he has given you the scepter over terrestrial power in imitation of the celestial kingdom in order that you may teach men to cultivate justice, and you should punish the howling of those who rage against it—you who are yourself subject to the laws of justice and who lawfully govern those subject to you.

Like the pilot of a vessel, the many-eyed mind of the emperor is constantly vigilant, firmly holding the rudder of equity and strongly repelling the waves of lawlessness so that the ship of this commonwealth of the world may not be overwhelmed by the waves of injustice.

Nothing renders a man more esteemed than to be able to accomplish the things he wishes while always willing and doing these things humanely (*philanthropa*). Since, then, there comes to you from God the power that your goodwill toward us desired for our benefit, may you both wish and do all things in a manner pleasing to Him who granted this authority to you.

Just as, on a voyage, an error committed by a sailor does little damage to the passengers, but if the pilot himself makes an error catastrophe results for the entire vessel, so in states, when one of the subjects does wrong, he does not injure society so much as he damages himself, but when the ruler himself commits injustice, he gravely injures the entire state. Since, then, he will have to account for great responsibilities if he neglects to do what he should do, may he speak as well as act with great carefulness.

I consider you as truly emperor, since you have the authority of an emperor and are master of your passions, and also since you are adorned with the crown of temperance and are clothed in the purple of justice. Other kinds of authority have death as their heir, but such imperial authority lasts forever. And other powers find their end in this world, but this power is saved from eternal punishment.

If you want to reap the benefits of being honored by all men, become the common benefactor to all. For there is nothing that moves men to feel goodwill [to their ruler] more than his grace bestowed upon those who need it. Service which results from fear is merely false flattery: it cheats those who give heed to it in the guise of false honor.

The emperor is equal to all men in the nature of his body, but in the authority of his rank he is similar to God, who rules all. For there is no one on earth higher than he. Thus, like God, he should not give way to anger, and as a mortal he should not be arrogant. If he is honored as the image of the divine, he is at the same time connected with the earthly image. And through this he is reminded of his equality with other men.

Impose upon yourself the necessity of obeying the laws, since no one on earth can force you to do so. For in this way you will show respect to the laws by reverencing them above everything else. Thus also your subjects will clearly comprehend that any infraction of the laws will not be without peril.

3.

Introduction. Another example of the continuity of Eusebian political theory regarding the emperor is found in a selection from the treatise *Logos nouthetetikos* (*Words of Counsel*) formerly attributed (erroneously) to the twelfth-century writer Nikulitzas, but probably the work of an anonymous author of the eleventh century. Although Eusebius and Agapetus represent the emperor as law incarnate (in effect, above the law), the author of this treatise qualifies this authority to a certain degree. Revealing a new emphasis in the doctrine of kingship, he advises the emperor to show himself in various areas of his dominions in order to encourage continued loyalty—a suggestion absent in Eusebius or Agapetus, who advocate the emperor's inaccessibility to his subjects in order to encourage an aura of mystery around the imperial office.

COUNSELS FOR THE EMPEROR

(From *Cecaumeni strategicon et incerti scriptoris de officiis regiis Libellus,* ed. B. Wassiliewsky and V. Jernstedt [St. Petersburg, 1896], pp. 93, 99, 103–4.)

Some affirm that the emperor is not subject to the law but is the law. And I say the same. However, whenever he acts and legislates, he does well and we obey him. But if he should say, "Drink poison," you will of course not do so. And if he should affirm, "Go to the sea and cross it like a diver," neither can you do this. From this, know that the emperor, being a man, is subject to the laws of piety. For this reason we write this treatise for the pious and Christian emperors who will follow.

Holy Lord, God has elevated you to the imperial authority and has made you by his grace, as you are called, a god on earth, to do and to act as you will. Let then your acts and your deeds be full of understanding and truth, and may justice dwell in your heart. Look, therefore, and act toward all—toward those who are in a position of authority and toward all others—with an equal eye. And do not evilly coerce some while bestowing benefits on others against just reason. But let there be equality for all. . . .

The emperor is the model and example for all, and all men look up to him and imitate his conduct. And if his ways are good, men are eager to follow them quickly; but if they are bad and worthy of blame, men will do the same. Therefore, I beg you, take hold of and adopt the four virtues: courage (I mean that of the soul), justice, temperance, and wisdom. . . .

I know, Your Majesty, that by nature man is desirous of relaxation. But there has come into fashion a custom not helpful but rather damaging: that the emperor not go abroad into the countries under his rule, both in the East and in the West, but that he spend his time in Constantinople, as if in prison there. If someone had indeed restricted you to a single city, in that case you would have to make an effort to leave that area. But the fact is that you have done this to yourself. What, then, is to be said? Go out into the countries under your rule and into your provinces and see for yourself what injustices the poor suffer and what the tax collectors, whom you dispatch, are doing. Ascertain whether the poor have been wronged, and correct all wrong things. Thus both the provinces of the Byzantines and the lands of the peoples under your rule will know that they have an emperor and lord who rules them. Then you yourself will know the strength of each province and fortress and land, how each is situated, and what damage it suffers and what benefits accrue to it. Then there will arise no rebellion or revolt against your agents, but all the areas under your rule will be at peace.

I realize that your ministers, in order to save you from trouble, will admonish you that this advice is not sound; they will tell you that, as you advance through your countries and provinces with your army and imperial entourage, you will oppress them. They may even say that, if you leave Byzantium, another will seize the imperial throne in your place. When I have thought of this, I have laughed. For the one left by you in the palace, charged with the direction of affairs that come there to your notice from the [foreign] nations and from the Byzantines, will, if he is energetic and adequate, be entirely effective, and he will be ever vigilant and will do whatever should be done.

4.

Introduction. The extensive rituals surrounding the activities of the emperor did much to impress the imperial image upon the minds of the people. Countless ceremonies filled everyday life at court, and these were so complex that lengthy manuals were drawn up for the guidance of the masters of protocol and the courtiers. The most important of these manuals were *On Ceremonies*, by the Emperor Constantine VII Porphyrogenitus in the tenth century, and the late fourteenth-century treatise by Pseudo-Codinus entitled *On the Offices* [of Constantinople].

In the introduction to *On Ceremonies*, Constantine VII clearly states why the ritualistic aspects of court life were significant: they were symbolic actions, projecting qualities of order, awe, and dignity, which helped to reinforce respect for government.

PREFACE TO *ON CEREMONIES*

(From Constantine VII Porphyrogenitus, *De ceremoniis*, in A. Vogt, ed., *Le livre de cérémonie* [Paris: Les Belles Lettres, 1935], vol. 1, pp. 1–2.)

Some, who do not much care for necessary matters, would perhaps view this present enterprise [the composition of this manual] as superfluous; for us, however, this work is very dear, for it appears worthy of all our care and more fitting, in fact, than all other cares, since, thanks to a praiseworthy ritual, the imperial power appears more majestic, grows in prestige, and at the same time evokes the admiration both of strangers and of our own subjects.

Many things, in fact, by nature tend to disappear with the passing of time, which has created and exhausted them. Of this number is the great and precious matter that is the expression and codification of imperial ceremonial. Because it was neglected and, so to speak, perishing, the empire was viewed truly as without adornment and without beauty. Moreover, just as one would call disorderly a body badly constituted, one in which the limbs are joined together pell-mell and without unity, so it is with the imperial government when it is not conducted and governed with order. When this is the case, the state differs in nothing from the conduct of an uneducated individual.

In order to escape that condition, [i.e., being swept along in disorder], and so that we do not appear to insult the imperial majesty, we have believed it would be appropriate to gather together carefully, from the right and the left, whatever was established by the ancients and transmitted by their contemporaries or seen by ourselves and established for us and introduced in our time, to set it forth in the present work in a synthesis easily understood, and to pass on to our successors the tradition of ancestral customs [which had] fallen into disuse. They will be like flowers we gather from the meadows to embellish incomparably the imperial splendor. They will be like a mirror, radiant and of a perfect clarity. And we will place them in the center of the palace [and] will see there what is appropriate to the imperial power and what befits the senatorial organization.

And, in order that our text be clear and of easy understanding, we have employed a common and simple style, and we have used the current language for words and expressions applied a long time ago to each matter. Therefore, may the imperial power, being employed with measure and good order, reproduce the harmonious movement that the Creator gives to this entire universe, and may [the empire] appear to our subjects more majestic and, at the same time, more pleasing and admirable. We must therefore speak of each ceremony in order to say how and according to what rules it is necessary to carry it out and complete it.

5.

Introduction. Famous throughout the entire medieval world were the mechanical devices (*automata*) used in the Byzantine imperial court to impress foreign ambassadors at official receptions. These contrivances—and their dazzling effects—are perhaps best described by the tenth-century bishop of Cremona, Liudprand, envoy to Constantinople of Berengar (c. 950), king of Italy, and later of the Holy Roman Emperor Otto I.

Dazzling Effects

(From Liudprand, *Antapodosis*, MPL [Migne Patrologie Latina], vol. 136, col. 895.)

A certain tree, bronze but covered over with gold, stood in front of the emperor's throne, and birds of various types, likewise made of gilded bronze, filled its branches and uttered the cries of [real] birds, each according to its species. The emperor's throne was constructed in such a way that at one moment it appeared to be very low, then higher, and at another moment it seemed very lofty. The throne was of immense size, made either of bronze or of wood. Lions covered with gold stood as if guarding it, and, beating the ground with their tails, they produced a roar with mouths open and tongues moving. Then, leaning on the shoulders of two eunuchs, I was led into the presence of the emperor. When, at my approach, the lions roared and the birds called in the manner of their species, I was moved by neither terror nor admiration, since I had learned much about all these things from men who knew them well.

Then prostrating myself [performing *proskynesis*] three times before the emperor, I raised my head, and him whom I had just seen sitting elevated only a little above the ground I now saw with his clothing changed and seated just below the level of the ceiling. In what manner this was effected I was unable to imagine, unless perhaps he was elevated through the sort of device by which the timbers of a winepress are raised up. The emperor at this time said nothing directly to me, since, even if he had so desired, the great distance would have rendered it indecorous. Instead, he asked through the logothete about Berengar's activities and health. After I had properly responded to him, the interpreter nodded. I then departed and soon returned to the lodging assigned to me.

6.

Introduction. The selection from the treatise of the Byzantine writer known as Pseudo-Codinus (fourteenth century) describes the reception of Venetian and Genoese envoys by Emperor Michael VIII Palaeologus (1259–82). The selection's importance lies not only in the way it reveals the use of court ceremonial to exalt the imperial image in the eyes of foreigners but, even more, in the way it shows how the reaction of foreigners to the imperial image could accurately reflect the political realities of the time.

WARM AND COOL RECEPTIONS

(From Pseudo-Codinus, *Traité des offices*, ed. J. Verpeaux [Paris: Editions du Centre national de la recherche scientifique, 1966], p. 235.)

Emperor Michael VIII Palaeologus concluded with the Genoese a perpetual peace, in which were specified the honors that had to be rendered to the emperor. When the *podestà* [leader of the Genoese] arrived from Genoa, for the first and only time, upon entering for the prostration [*proskynesis*] he flexed his knee twice, after which he entered the door of the *triklinium* [a special ceremonial room] and stood in the middle. Then he advanced and kissed the foot and hand of the emperor, who was seated on the throne. At the same time, other Genoese nobles, coming from other places [in the room], prostrated themselves and kissed the foot and hand of the emperor. Each day when they came for the prostration, they removed their hats and bent their knees twice. When their ships arrived, whether many or few or only one, they acclaimed the emperor. And that is how it is with the Genoese.

As for the Venetians, since the emperor, soon after, wanted to make war on them, he did not conclude a definitive peace but rather a short truce. Also, he did not establish with precision the ceremonies regarding them, as he had with the Genoese. When the [Venetian] *baiulus* arrived, the first day, when he was supposed to prostrate himself, he and the men of his suite only bent the knee; they did not kiss the foot of the emperor. And in the future they only removed their hats and did not bend the knee. In the same way, they did not participate in the *polychronia* ceremony ["Many happy years to you"]. . . . Nor do their ships acclaim him [the emperor]. And so, too, for the Franks [from Western Europe].

7.

Introduction. Another aspect of the imperial image had to do with the emperor's role as commander-in-chief of the military forces. Victorious emperors often enjoyed magnificent triumphal processions in the manner of the victorious generals and emperors of ancient Rome. These processions served not only to glorify the emperors but also to instill confidence in the population (and in visitors) in the strength of the Byzantine Empire. The following selection is a contemporary description of the solemn entry in 1159 of Emperor Manuel I into Antioch (taken by the Crusaders in 1098). Adorned with the imperial insignia, Manuel Comnenus rode on horseback, while the Crusader (Latin) king of Jerusalem followed behind at a considerable distance. Walking beside Manuel was the prince of Antioch, holding the stirrup of Manuel's horse.

PROTOCOL OF A TRIUMPH IN ANTIOCH
(From John Kinnamos, *Epitome rerum ab Ioanne et Alexio Comnenis gestarum*, ed. A. Meineke [Bonn, 1836], pp. 187–88.)

When he [Emperor Manuel] was about to enter the city, he put on a double breastplate, moved to do so by the indefatigable strength of his body. Above this he placed a garment decorated with precious stones, which weighed hardly less than that underneath, and a crown and the other customary imperial insignia. I marvel very much at this, that the emperor, after he had celebrated a triumph in the manner customarily observed at Byzantium [Constantinople] and had arrived at the Church of the Apostle Peter, dismounted nimbly from his horse and, when he was going to remount, jumped again upon it as if he were unarmed and not wearing armor.

Then the bishop of the city, wearing priestly robes, came to the emperor, accompanied by the entire order of priests. They held crosses in their hands and carried before them the Holy Scriptures. All of the foreigners and visitors present were amazed when they saw, in addition to these things, Reginald [of Chatillon, Latin prince of Antioch] and the Antiochene nobles running on foot alongside the emperor's horse. Baldwin, a man who himself had been crowned [Latin king of Jerusalem], rode much further back on horseback but without insignia. In such manner the triumph was celebrated. The emperor remained eight days in the city and then departed. But the Antiochenes held the emperor in such veneration that, as long as Manuel stayed in Reginald's palace, no one involved in a legal dispute had his case judged by those of his own nation but rather by Romans [Byzantines].

8.

Introduction. Although "dazzling effects" and the emperor's habit of making his appearance only on magnificent state occasions had an impressive effect on foreign ambassadors and natives alike, this quality of aloofness tended to make the emperor appear remote from most of his subjects, who only very occasionally were able to catch a glimpse of him (and even then from a distance, as in the Hippodrome). In the following selection (c. 950) we have a rare example of a story—reported to us in Latin by the Western envoy Liudprand of Cremona—that circulated among the people of the capital. The story points up the sharp contrast between the impact on the Byzantine populace of the all-pervasive "presence" of the imperial image and the actuality of the man himself, who was virtually unknown to his people.

A COMMON MAN'S VIEW OF THE EMPEROR

(From Liudprand, *Antapodosis*, MPL, vol. 136, col. 795.)

And so Leo the august emperor, desiring to test the faithfulness and constancy of the guards, went out alone from his palace after nightfall and came to the first guard station. When the guards saw him, he feigned flight, turning away as if with fear. After he had been caught, the guards inquired of him who he was and where he was going. He said that he was nobody in particular and that he was searching for a brothel. They then replied, "We are going to beat you thoroughly, manacle your legs, and hold you until tomorrow." To which Leo responded, "*Me, adelphoi, me*," (which means, "No, brothers, no.") "Take what I have on me, and let me go where I wish." After they had received twenty gold coins, they let him go. Leaving there, Leo came to the second guard station, where he was detained in the same manner and released after the guards there had received twenty gold coins. When he came to the third guard station, however, he was again seized, but here, unlike the two earlier instances, he was not released. Instead, since all his money had been taken from him, he was bound with heavy manacles, beaten for a while with fists and whips and placed in prison to appear before the judge on the following morning.

When the soldiers had gone away, the emperor called out to his jailer, "Phile mou [My friend], do you know the emperor Leo?" "How could I know him," the man responded, "a man I do not remember having seen? Certainly, on public occasions when he passes by, I have seen him from a distance (for I was unable to get close), but I felt I was looking at a marvel and not a man."

9.

Introduction. A view of the imperial image as held by members of the aristocratic group of Anatolian border lords is exemplified in the Byzantine "epic" poem *Digenes Akritas*, written in the tenth or eleventh century. This celebrated work describes the life and exploits of a Byzantine hero, the half-Byzantine, half-Arab Digenes (two-blooded) Akritas, in the Byzantine-Arab border region near the northern Euphrates. In the section of the poem quoted here, the young Digenes meets his overlord, the emperor of Byzantium. In the epithets used by the soldier to address his ruler we may derive an idea of his views of the traits of an ideal emperor.

THE IDEAL OF THE IMPERIAL IMAGE IN DIGENES AKRITAS

(Translated by D. B. Hull, *Digenes Akritas: The Two-blooded Border Lord* [Athens, Ohio: Ohio University Press, 1972], pp. 60–61.)

Since he [the emperor] wished strongly to behold
    the youth,
He took along with him a hundred soldiers,
Some spearmen too, and went to the Euphrates,
Ordering all on no account to utter
A word offensive to the Border Lord.
Those posted to keep watch on his account
Shortly announced the Emperor's arrival
To the marvelous Two-Blood Border Lord.
The Two-Blood came out all alone to meet him,
And bowed his head down to the ground, and said,
"Hail, you who take imperial power from God,
And rule us all because of the heathen's sins.
Why has it happened that the whole world's master
Comes before me, who am of no account?"
The Emperor, astonished when he saw him,
Forgot the burden of his majesty,
Advanced a little from his throne, embraced him,
Joyfully kissed him, and admired his stature,
And the great promise of his well-formed beauty.
"My son," he said, "you've proof of all your deeds;
The way you're put together shows your courage.
Would that Romania [Land of the Romans—i.e.
    Byzantium] had four such men!
So speak, my son, freely and openly,
And then take anything you wish from us."
"Keep everything, my lord," the boy replied,
"Because your love alone is enough for me.
It's not more blessed to receive than give.
You have immense expenses in your army.
So I beseech your glorious majesty:
Love him who is obedient, pity the poor,
Deliver the oppressed from malefactors,
Forgive those who unwittingly make blunders,
And heed no slanders, nor accept injustice,
Sweep heretics out, confirm the orthodox.

These, master, are the arms of righteousness
With which you can prevail over all foes.
To rule and reign are not part of that power
Which God and His right hand alone can give.

10.

Introduction. In order to be accepted as legitimate, the emperor had to be crowned by the patriarch—the chief religious hierarch and the citizen of the empire next in importance to the emperor—in the great church of St. Sophia in Constantinople. The very elaborate ceremonial also included the coronation of the empress and sometimes, in order to ensure the royal succession, the emperor's son (who was crowned by his father).

The following detailed account, probably written by an eyewitness, describes the coronation of Emperor Manuel II Palaeologus in 1392. The ceremony was typical of coronations throughout Byzantine history except for the anointment of the emperor by the patriarch, mentioned here, which may well have resulted from the influence of the Latin Empire, established in Byzantine territory for fifty-seven years (1204–61). In the earlier periods of the empire, anointment was not part of the consecration of the emperor.

THE CORONATION OF EMPEROR MANUEL II AND HELENA DRAGAŠ (1392)

(From P. Schreiner, ed., "Hochzeit und Krönung Kaiser Manuels II. im Jahre 1392," *Byzantinische Zeitschrift* 60 [1967]: 76–79.)

After the censing of the emperor as he approached the holy altar, one of the bishops took the crown from his head [doubtless an inferior type of crown worn *before* the imperial coronation itself] and gave it to the *prokathemenos tou vestiariou* [the one in charge of the wardrobe]. The patriarch took the censer from the hands of the emperor and himself censed the latter. Then they left the altar and ascended to the ambo [pulpit], and there, as the emperor was bending his head, the patriarch by himself privately said a prayer, which the prelates and deacons heard. . . .

Immediately within the hearing of the bishops and deacons [gathered] in the ambo, the patriarch said, "Holy, holy, holy," and the archdeacon, in the hearing of all the people, proclaimed "holy" three times, and the entire assembly in the same way [uttered] "holy" thrice; and again the patriarch [said] "holy" three times; then the archdeacon and in turn the people, three times; then again the patriarch three times said "holy," and then the archdeacon and people; that is, the patriarch [said] the triple "holy" three times, just as [did] the archdeacon and the people. And the patriarch anointed him with the unguent of nard and placed upon him a hood, after which the patriarch put the crown upon his head. But if the emperor is a son whose father is also an emperor, or there is already an emperor in office,* the patriarch anoints him, but the father-emperor places the crown on his [son's] head and all the people hail him [literally, wish him "many years"]. The patriarch placed the cross in his right hand, and, descending, they stood before the throne.

Then the *augusta* [empress], having approached, lowered her head, and her husband, [just] crowned emperor, placed the crown that is customary for *augustae* upon her head and put in her right hand a gold scepter ornamented with precious stones and pearls.

After they had worshiped at the altar and ascended the platform, they sat down on their thrones. And the patriarch, after entering the sanctuary, sat on his throne, and one of the deacons who was standing by the doors of the sanctuary voiced the acclamation of the emperors and the patriarch. And all the people, as is the custom, hailed them with song. Behind the ambo were two platforms constructed of wood, one on the right, the other on the left. Upon them stood the *maïstores* [important court officials] guiding the ceremonies, along with the choir, wearing above their clothing outer garments of gold material issued by the imperial wardrobe. For such is their function. The chief chanter and the *domestikos* [at this time probably a leading household official] stood motionless before the throne while the torchbearer with a double lamp [stood] before the emperor below the imperial platform, and the chief regulator of the service stood at the center of the pulpit, toward the back part, and in a loud voice directed [the singing of] the verses. The *maïstores* during each verse chanted in many voices, "Indeed holy," and then [chanted] the verse. And the verses are as follows:

> Many years to you, emperors of the Romans.
> Many your years, Manuel, emperor of the Romans.
> Many your years, Helen, empress of the Romans.
> For the glory and prosperity of the Romans, this
>   indeed is the Lord's great day.
>
> Glory, glory, glory in the highest to God and peace
>   on earth and goodwill toward men.
> Glory to God, who has crowned you rulers of the
>   Romans.

And again they began, "Many your years, emperors of the Romans" and in turn the other verses just mentioned. And they chanted them so that the beginning extended from the [opening of] the holy liturgy to its conclusion. But at the time of the coronation, the reading from the Apostle and the Holy Gospels, the Great Entrance [when the Holy Eucharist was taken to the altar], the Holy Symbol [Eucharist], the [prayer] "Our Father," and the Elevation of the Eucharist, they remained quiet. And again they began (to chant):

> Many, many years up to many,
> Many years to many,
> Many years to many,
> Many years to many.

The [reading] of the Apostle is: "Brothers, receive the kingdom of God." And that of the Gospel according to John: "Whoever does not enter through the door into the sheepfold."

When they came to the Great Entrance, the archdeacon, coming forth from the sanctuary, called the emperor. And the *deputatoi* [a group of honored laymen] dressed the emperor in a gold garment [in the manner of a bishop] and placed in his right hand a staff, and he approached the priests and with him his bodyguard. They came up to the throne, and the emperor, turning back and ascending, again sat down on his throne while the priests entered the sanctuary. After the elevation of the holy objects [the eucharist], they summoned the emperor again into the sanctuary, and, having entered, he took holy communion with his own hand and once more went up to the platform [where his throne was].

After the end of the service the emperor, riding on horseback, made his way from the church to the palace. And the highest officials, that is, the despots, sebastokrators, and caesars, led the horses of the emperor and empress by the bridle from the church to the palace.

*This refers to the typical Byzantine practice of naming coemperors. See selection 20.

11.

Introduction. Many emperors were in reality neither strikingly virtuous nor extraordinarily capable. In fact, a succession of mediocre emperors in the mid-eleventh century brought the empire to the verge of collapse. Michael Psellus, imperial private secretary and man of letters, gives us a vivid picture of one of these emperors, Constantine IX Monomachus (1042–55), and details with psychological insight and perhaps some exaggeration the corruption and gracious life at his court.

PORTRAIT OF EMPEROR CONSTANTINE IX

(Translated by E. Sewter from Michael Psellus, *Chronographia* [New Haven, Conn.: Yale University Press, 1953], pp. 124–25, 127, 131–32.)

Naturally I would have wished that my favourite emperor had been perfect, even if such a compliment was impossible for all the others, but the events of history do not accommodate themselves to our desires. . . . At the start of his reign Constantine ruled neither with vigour nor with discretion. Apparently, before his accession, he had imagined that being an emperor was to confer on him undreamed-of happiness, something he had never experienced in his life. He had visions, quite unreasonably, of a sudden and complete reversal of his fortunes, and no sooner had he ascended the throne than he attempted to realize these ambitions. Now two things in particular contribute to the hegemony of the Romans, namely, our system of honours and our wealth, to which one might add a third: the wise control of the other two, and prudence in their distribution. Unfortunately Constantine's idea was to exhaust the treasury of its money, so that not a single *obol* was to be left there, and as for the honours, they were conferred indiscriminately on a multitude of persons who had no right to them, especially on the more vulgar sort who pestered the man, and on those who amused him by their witticisms. It is well known, of course, that there is in the political world a proper scale of honours, with an invariable rule governing promotion to a higher office, but Constantine reduced this *cursus honorum* to mere confusion and abolished all rules of advancement. The doors of the Senate* were thrown open to nearly all the rascally vagabonds of the market, and the honour was bestowed not on two or three, nor on a mere handful, but the whole gang was elevated to the highest offices of state by a single decree, immediately after he became emperor. Inevitably this provided occasion for rites and solemn ceremonies, with all the city overjoyed at the thought that their new sovereign was a person of such generosity. The new state of affairs seemed incomparably better than that to which they had been accustomed, for the truth is, folk who live in the luxury of a city have little conception of government, and those who do understand such matters neglect their duties, so long as their desires are satisfied.

Gradually the error of this policy became apparent when privileges, much coveted in the old days, were now distributed with a generous abandon that knew no limits, with the consequence that the recipients lost distinction. At the time, though, most people had not yet recognized the implications of all this profusion, and so the squandering and waste went on, all to no purpose. . . .

Although he could scarcely be called an advanced student of literature, or in any sense of the word an orator, yet he admired men who were, and the finest speakers were invited to the imperial court from all parts of the Empire, most of them very old men.

. . . Constantine had no very clear conception of the nature of monarchy. He failed to realize that it entailed responsibility for the well-being of his subjects, and that an emperor must always watch over the administration of his realm and ensure its development on sound lines. To him the exercise of power meant rest from his labours, fulfilment of desire, relaxation from strife. He had entered the harbour of the palace, so to speak, to enjoy the advantages of a calm retreat and to avoid the duties of helmsman in the future. As for the administration of public affairs, and the privilege of dispensing justice, and the superintendence of the armed forces, they were delegated to others. Only a fraction of these duties was reserved for himself. Instead, he chose a life of pleasure and luxury, as if it were his natural right (not without some justification, for he had inherited an innate predilection for such things). Now, having acquired supreme power, he had greater opportunity for pleasure, and he indulged himself more than ever.

*On the Senate, see selections 57–66.)

12.

Introduction. In keeping with the Eusebian political ideal of the imperial image, Byzantine emperors up to 1453 regarded themselves as rulers of the continuation of the unified Roman Empire of the fourth and fifth centuries. Thus Justinian in the sixth century attempted to wrest from "barbarian" German hands the former western provinces of the Roman Empire. Although, according to most scholars, Justinian's efforts in the end proved disastrous for the economy and finances of Byzantium, his venture is understandable in the light of this Byzantine ideal of the universality of the empire and the inalienability of its territory. Moreover, as vicar of God, Justinian felt it his duty to impose, in the restored provinces of the empire, the one Orthodox Christian faith among the western "heretical" Arians and pagans.

JUSTINIAN'S SACRED OBLIGATION TO RECOVER LOST IMPERIAL TERRITORY

(Translated by H. Dewing from Procopius, *De bello Gothico*, Loeb Classical Library [Cambridge, Mass.: Harvard, 1961], vol. 2, pp. 96–99.)

[John the Cappadocian, the praetorian prefect, said to Justinian:] "Thou art purposing to make an expedition against Carthage, to which, if one goes by land, the journey is one of a hundred and forty days, and if one goes by water, he is forced to cross the whole open sea and go to its very end. So that he who brings thee news of what will happen in the camp must needs reach thee a year after the event. And one might add that if thou art victorious over thy enemy, thou couldst not take possession of Libya while Sicily and Italy lie in the hands of others; and at the same time, if any reverse befall thee, O Emperor, the treaty having already been broken by thee, thou wilt bring the danger upon our own land. In fact, putting all in a word, it will not be possible for thee to reap the fruits of victory, and at the same time any reversal of fortune will bring harm to what is well established. It is before an enterprise that wise planning is useful. For when men have failed, repentance is of no avail, but before disaster comes there is no danger in altering plans. Therefore it will be of advantage above all else to make fitting use of the decisive moment."

Thus spoke John; and the Emperor Justinian, hearkening to his words, checked his eager desire for the war. But one of the priests, with the title of Bishop, came from the East, and after having asked to speak to Justinian, told him that God had commanded him in a dream to come and find him [Justinian] and to rebuke him, that after having resolved to go and deliver the Christians in Libya [the Roman provinces located in North Africa] from tyranny, Justinian had for no good reason become afraid. "And yet," [God] said, "I Myself will join with him to wage the war and will make him the Lord of Libya." When the emperor heard these things, he could no longer contain his impatience, but he amassed an army and ships and he prepared supplies of weapons and food and he ordered Belisarius to make himself ready to go and take command of the expedition into Libya.

Meanwhile Prudentius, one of the natives of Tripolis in Libya, caused this district to revolt from the Vandals, and sending to the emperor he begged that he should despatch an army to him; for, he said, he would with no trouble win the land for the emperor. And Justinian sent him Tattimuth and an army of no very great size. This force Prudentius joined with his own troops and, the Vandals being absent, he gained possession of the land and made it subject to the emperor.

13.

Introduction. The Byzantines, who viewed their emperor as the lord of the world, the vicar of God on earth, saw all other rulers as deriving their legitimacy and authority from him. Hence the theory of a "family of princes" headed by the Byzantine emperor, a hierarchical arrangement that gave theoretical justification to a reality of multiple rulers while still affirming the universality of the empire under one "father" emperor. In the document that follows, the duke of Istria urges his ally, the Merovingian king of Austrasia Childebert II, to adhere with filial devotion to the pact recently signed with the Byzantine emperor against the Lombards in Italy.

THE BYZANTINE "FAMILY OF PRINCES": CHILDEBERT OF THE FRANKS AND THE DUKE OF ISTRIA, FAITHFUL "SONS" OF THE BYZANTINE EMPEROR (C. 581)

(From *Epistolae Austrasicae*, MGH, vol. 3, no. 48, pp. 152–53.)

And so, after all things are carried out, do as you see fit. And let us try to avenge equally God's injuries and the blood of our Roman relatives, with Christ as leader, in such a way that these matters may end in the security of a perpetual peace or, with regard to the remaining matters and with appropriate parties on both sides cooperating, there may finally be an end to things. Moreover, we demand that, if the vigor of a priest is lacking in you, you may either financially carry out all these things or make an end to them as rational order demands. Let legates proceed from the side of the most pious emperor when they are strengthened in these purposes by certain specified goals. As long as the winter weather prevents the sailing of ships, it would be easy through you (if there be a direct connection) that these troops be brought over into our borders. Here, in expectation of them, as is proper, worthy preparations are being made, so that there should be no delay in coming and that favorable opportunities in these areas should be very quickly taken advantage of. . . .

Lest it be said that we [Childebert and the duke of Istria] on our part show some delay, [may] you [Childebert] proceed without delay, and let us see you advance with perfect deliberation and security from the regions of your state. We are ready to attack our adversaries with you in vengeance, and we seek an opportunity and desire to show by our actions how the most pious [Byzantine] emperor may consider it worthy to accept us into the number of his sons.

14.

Introduction. In addition to being accepted into the imperial "family," foreign kings were often given high, although not the highest, Byzantine official titles: the king of the Franks, Clovis, accepted the title of consul (see selection 246), while the king of the Armenians received that of *Kouropalates* (keeper of the palace). In the following excerpt, taken from the *Kleitorologion* of Philotheus—a ninth-century manual of ranks and court ceremonials—we see how Byzantine protocol carefully ranked foreign ambassadors (here Bulgars, Saracens, and Franks), in effect incorporating them into the Byzantine hierarchy of official dignitaries.

Hierarchy of Envoys to Constantinople

(From Philotheus, *Kleitorologion*, in J. Bury, *The Imperial Administrative System in the Ninth Century* [London: H. Frowde, 1911], pp. 155–57.)

Saracen Friends. Our friends from the Agarenes [Arabs] rank behind the class of [Byzantine] *patrikioi* and *strategoi* [generals] with respect to their seats, those from the East ranking before those from the West. They are seated in an honored place, either as the fourth friends or the fifth, as happens in the second sitting at the table.

Bulgar Friends. Those from the Ounnon,* that is, the Bulgars, friends who came at the summons to the *kletorion* [imperial banquet], are chosen as fourth or fifth in honorable place, that is, ranking below the [Byzantine] patricians and generals and all the patrician archons in their seating. They, too, partake of the second mess at the imperial table. In the hall of the 19 *akoubitoi* for feast days, they are ranked eighth and ninth, that is, coming after those in the previous group.

Envoys of the Franks. The envoys of the Frangoi [Franks], if they are prelates, are ranked thus: If they are not so, they rank below the group of *offikialioi*. And if others come as friends from other peoples, they all rank below the *spatharokandidatoi.*

*Doubtless Huns, according to N. Oikonomides, *Les listes de préséance byzantines* (Paris, 1972), p. 163.

15.

Introduction. The exalted, increasingly anachronistic Eusebian image of the universality of the Byzantine emperor's authority and the inalienability of Roman territory was not, of course, always shared by the West. In Western documents (especially after the church schism of the mid-eleventh century) Byzantines were often slightingly called *Rhomaioi* (the Greek form of "Romans") or more often *Graeci* (Greeks) rather than *Romani* ("Romans," a classical Latin term employed by medieval Westerners, who saw themselves as the rightful heirs of ancient, imperial Rome). The Byzantines, for their part, called the Westerners not "Romans" but "Franks," emphasizing the latter's "barbarian" Germanic origins. The following passage, taken from the writings of Bishop Liudprand, the proud envoy of the Western Roman Emperor Otto I to the Byzantine Emperor Nicephorus II Phocas (963–69), reveals the acrimonious claims and counterclaims made by East and West to the mantle of imperial Rome.

Sibling Rivalry

(From Liudprand, *Relatio de legatione Constantinopolitana*, MPL, vol. 136, col. 928.)

To increase my misfortunes, on the day of the Assumption of the Holy Mother of God, the Virgin Mary, the envoys—for me ill-omened—of the apostolic lord and universal Pope John, came [to Constantinople] with a letter entreating Nicephorus, emperor of the Greeks [*imperator Graecorum*], to create a "parental" and firm friendship with his beloved and spiritual "son" Otto, august emperor of the Romans [*Romanorum imperator*]. As to why this manner of address and these titles, which to the Greeks are sinful and audacious, did not produce an overwhelming reaction and even result in death for the letter-bearer before the letter was read, I (who am in other matters usually talkative and loquacious) am as silent as a fish. The Greeks scolded the sea and rebuked it; they marveled exceedingly at how the sea could have conveyed this transgression, why it had not opened up into an abyss and swallowed the ship. They cried, "It is disgusting to address the universal emperor of the Romans, the great Augustus, only as Nicephorus, 'emperor of the Greeks,' while calling the wretched barbarian pauper 'emperor of the Romans.' O heaven! O earth! O sea! What will we do with such wicked and criminal men? They are paupers, and if we kill them, we will pollute our hands with worthless blood. They are ragged, they are slaves, they are bumpkins. If we flog them, we disgrace ourselves and not them; they are worthy neither of the gilded Roman lash nor of any other tortures of this kind. Oh, if only one were a bishop, the other a marquess so that we could sew them up into leather bags and, after soundly beating them with rods and plucking out their beards and hairs, we could throw them into the sea. But instead let their lives be spared, and until Nicephorus, the most holy emperor of the Romans, hears about these insults, let them be held under heavy guard."*

* For more on the rivalry of the Eastern and Western empires, see the section "Byzantium and the West," selections 266–88.

16.

Introduction. Constantinople was at once the physical capital and the central symbol of the empire. The occupation of their great city in 1204 by Latin Crusaders forced the Byzantines, at least in part, to face reality and to limit their theoretical claims to political hegemony. Whereas during the height of the empire in the early eleventh century the Byzantines frequently propounded their legal claims over all former territory of the (Roman) empire, the years after 1204 saw the emphasis shift to more modest assertions of territorial integrity centering on Constantinople, Asia Minor, and "Greece." This is demonstrated in the document from which we quote below, a vehement letter from the "Nicene" Emperor John Vatatzes to Pope Gregory IX in 1237. Note that, although on the surface Vatatzes concerns himself with the lofty question of whether he or the (new) Latin emperor of Constantinople is the true heir to the mantle of Constantine the Great, the thrust of his argument focuses on his right as Roman emperor to control Constantinople. The former far-reaching Byzantine claims of jurisdiction over the *ecumene* are now nowhere to be found.

CONSTANTINOPLE, THE INALIENABLE CAPITAL

(From John Vatatzes's letter to Pope Gregory IX, in J. Sakellion, ed., *Athenaion* [Athens, 1889], vol. 1, p. 469.)

The envoys from Your Holiness, bearers of this letter, maintain that it comes from Your Holiness, but our imperial majesty, having read the writing, did not wish to believe that it was from you but from a man experiencing the final stages of madness and with his soul full of vanity and audacity. . . .

We have no need of wisdom to understand what your throne is and how it was established. But how is it that you overlook or do not understand with what wisdom the imperial throne was allotted to our race by Constantine the Great? Who is unaware that the lot of his succession fell to our people and that we are his successors and inheritors [and not the Latins occupying Constantinople]?

You ask me not to overlook your throne and its privileges, but we too have our claims, as you should see and recognize, our rights of government and of authority over Constantinople which go back over a thousand years to Constantine the Great. The ancestors of our majesty, of the families of Ducas and Comneni— let me not mention the others—came from the "Greek" race and for many centuries held sway over Constantinople; and even the Roman church and its bishops called them "emperors of the Romans." How is it, then, that we appear to you not entitled to rule and govern, but rather [you say] that John of Brienne [the Latin emperor] was consecrated [emperor] by you? By what right did he rule? How can you piously praise this unjust and wicked view, and regard as lawful the rapacious and shameful occupation of Constantinople by the Latins?

We had forcibly to leave the place [Constantinople], but we do not relinquish our lawful rights to the government and to authority over Constantinople. Anyone who rules has authority and hegemony over a nation, its people, and its inhabitants, not over stones and wood, which are only the walls and fortifications.

Your letter also notes that Your Holiness has proclaimed a crusade throughout the whole world and that a multitude of fighting men have hastened to volunteer for the recovery of the Holy Land. When we heard this, we were very pleased and full of hope that these Crusaders wished to begin the recovery from that [area] of our homeland [Constantinople] and that they wished to punish the conquerors of Constantinople as desecrators of holy places, as defilers of the holy vessels [in the churches], and for all the impieties they have committed against Christians. . . . Since Your Holiness in your letter asks that we do not disturb your friend and son, John of Brienne, we make known to Your Holiness that we do not know where on land or sea this John has his authority. If it is a question of Constantinople, we should note to Your Holiness and to all Christians that we have never ceased to fight and make war against those holding Constantinople. For we would do an injustice to the laws of nature, to the principles of our people, to the graves of our fathers, and to the holy and sacred places if we did not with all our strength seek to recover Constantinople.*

But if anyone doubts this at all and prepares to take up arms against us, we have every means of arming ourselves against him, first with the aid of God, then with the arms and forces and masses of armed men and soldiers we have now, who often fought the [earlier] crusaders. And you, as imitator of Christ [*mimetes Christou*]† and as successor of the first of the Apostles, with your knowledge of the divine and canonical laws and of the laws of men, should praise us who defend our homeland and fight in behalf of our priceless liberty.

These things, then, will happen in accordance with God's will. Our majesty is indeed willing and eager to offer the proper respect to the holy church of Rome and to honor the throne of Peter, chief of the Apostles, and to have relations with Your Holiness and respect you as a son, and to do all with respect and reverence. But Your Holiness must not overlook the legal rights of our majesty and should not write to me in this insensitive and improper manner. As we are inclined toward peace with Your Holiness, we have accepted your lack of understanding of [the contents of] our letters without distress, and we have conducted ourselves with kindness toward its bearers.

*The authenticity of this letter had been questioned because of its vehement tone and style, but it has been shown to be genuine by V. Grumel, *Echos d'Orient* 29 (1930): 452–54.
†This title was also applied by the Byzantines to their emperor.

17.

Introduction. After the long-awaited Byzantine recovery of Constantinople by Michael VIII Palaeologus in 1261, that emperor in an address to his people linked the loss of the empire to the Latins and its subsequent recovery to God's punishment of Byzantine sins and his bestowal once again of his grace upon the Byzantines. Note Michael's comparison of the Byzantine return to Constantinople with the Jews' return to the Promised Land after their captivity in Egypt.

GOD'S GRACE: THE BYZANTINES RECOVER CONSTANTINOPLE (1261)

(From Pachymeres, *De Michaele et Andronico Palaeologis*, ed. I. Bekker [Bonn, 1835], vol. 1, pp. 153–55.)

You know, subjects of the empire of the Romans, both notables and men of the people, how sometime ago when God was angered he made use of the Italians as an impetuous wind to punish the Greeks, and our fathers were driven from their country and their rule was limited to a narrow area [Nicaea]. I will not refer to the olden period when the empire was bordered on the east by the Euphrates and Tigris rivers, on the west by Sicily and Apulia, on the south by Ethiopia, and on the north by peoples near the Pole. I shall omit this, but you who hear know that once we possessed a vast extent of sea that cannot be crossed in two or three days and a stretch of land more than ten days in extent not counting all the islands, very great ones too. But at God's will, or at least by his permission for the chastisement of the sins we had committed, when the heart of the empire [Constantinople] suffered, all became lifeless and the Italians, Persians, Bulgars, Slavs, and all the others divided up our lands. Even rebellious subjects of the empire stripped us of lands. And there remained to us only Nicaea, Brusa, and Philadelphia and the lands around them. Is it necessary to recall how we have recovered a part of the empire [and how] it has pleased God to regard us in a more favorable light? But then we held nothing of this remaining patrimony securely while we were still deprived of the imperial City. . . . When we demanded what had been usurped from us they [the Latins] responded with taunts and railleries, and ridiculed us for trying to reenter towns and lands where we no longer possessed anything. . . .

But if we have just retaken Constantinople in spite of the resistance of those who defended it, and if we are going to maintain ourselves there despite the efforts of the Franks . . . to strip our conquest from our hands, it is the result of the Divine Power, who renders impregnable (when it pleases him) the towns which appear most feeble and renders feeble those which appear impregnable. If we have undergone so much fatigue trying to take Constantinople without securing any result (although we were greater in number than those who defended it), it is because God wished us to recognize that the possession of the City is a grace that depends only on his bounty. He has reserved this to our reign through his grace—which obliges us to an eternal appreciation—and, in according it to us, he makes us hope that with Constantinople we may retake the provinces that were lost with it.* He will revenge our injuries; he will crush the pride of our enemies. He has seen fit to show us this great compassion that he refused to our fathers, and he has bestowed it upon us through his inscrutable divine will, according to which, rather than distributing his grace and his favor to those who have merited them, he grants these only to their descendants. Formerly, he promised the Israelites an abundant land and all kinds of possessions. Yet, when they left Egypt, they died in the desert and were interred in a foreign land. The promise he had made to the nation in the person of Abraham was fulfilled only after a long period. That is how [God] dispenses his favors, with a weightiness and a full measure of justice. The happy time has arrived when we no longer live under the branches of trees [i.e. we are not homeless].

*This clearly refers to the diminished extent of the empire just before the Latin conquest.

18.

Introduction. Though theoretically the majestic and powerful image of the ideal emperor ruling a mighty, unified empire persisted to the very end of the Byzantine Empire, by the last centuries, with the extreme diminution of imperial territory, this image had become almost completely detached from reality. This may be seen in the following passage, which describes the impression made by Byzantine Emperor Manuel II Palaeologus on the early fifteenth-century English chronicler Adam Usk. Manuel had gone to London in 1400 to beg financial assistance from the English for the defense of Constantinople against the Ottoman Turks.

LAMENT FOR A BELEAGUERED EMPEROR

(Translated by E. M. Thompson, from Adam Usk, *Chronicon*, A.D. 1377–1421 [London: H. Frowde, 1904], pp. 219–20, 246.)

The emperor of the Greeks, seeking to get aid against the Saracens, visited the king of England in London, on the day of Saint Thomas the Apostle [21st December], being well received by him, and abiding with him, at very great cost, for two months, being also comforted at his departure with very great gifts. This emperor always walked with his men, dressed alike and in one colour, namely white, in long robes cut like tabards; he finding fault with the many fashions and distinctions in dress of the English, wherein he said that fickleness and changeable temper was betokened. No razor touched head or beard of his chaplains. These Greeks were most devout in their church services, which were joined in as well by soldiers as by priests, for they chanted them without distinction in their native tongue. I thought within myself, what a grievous thing it was that this great Christian prince from the farther east should perforce be driven by unbelievers to visit the distant islands of the west, to seek aid against them. My God! What dost thou, ancient glory of Rome? Shorn is the greatness of thine empire this day; and truly may the words of Jeremiah be spoken unto thee: "Princess among the provinces, how is she become tributary?" Who would ever believe that thou shouldst sink to such depth of misery, that, although once seated on the throne of majesty thou didst lord it over all the world, now thou hast no power to bring succour to the Christian faith.

B.
SUCCESSION TO THE THRONE

19.

Introduction. One inescapable weakness afflicted even those emperors who most closely approximated the Eusebian ideal: mortality. The Byzantine Empire developed no simple, clearly defined law or method of succession to the throne. To be sure, in the earliest period, beginning with Diocletian (284–305) and continuing intermittently under Constantine and several of his successors, an attempt was made to ensure orderly succession by explicitly naming heirs to the throne. This system of two senior emperors (*augusti*) ruling in East and West, together with two junior emperors (called caesars), was termed the Tetrarchy. The following selection from the fourth-century Latin Father Lactantius quotes the argument used by the caesar under Diocletian, supporting his own accession to the rank of *augustus* in accord with the Diocletianic system.

THE TETRARCHY
(From Lactantius, *De mortibus persecutorum*, ed. J. Moreau [Paris, 1954], pp. 97–99.)

But the caesar [Galerius], who already in his hopes saw himself as master of the world, . . . said that it was necessary to conserve in perpetuity the arrangements of this man [Diocletian] that there be two greater [rulers] in the state to hold the highest authority over affairs [and] likewise two lesser ones to be of assistance to them, since harmony can be preserved easily among two but by no means among four equals. And in the case where Diocletian would fail to give up his rule, he [the caesar] would then look after his own interest, since he was unable any longer to remain in an inferior rank [that is, as caesar].

20.

Introduction. The tetrarchic system of orderly succession of two *augusti* and two caesars proved unworkable. Yet the idea of seeking to ensure a stable, orderly succession by means of the appointment of an heir to the throne during the lifetime of the reigning emperor continued to remain a very important feature of imperial policy. Indeed, the most common method of succession came to be for a strong emperor to coopt and crown his own son as "coemperor" during his lifetime. In the following selection, drawn from Theophanes, we see the steps Emperor Leo III took to ensure the coronation of his infant son, Constantine. Note especially that in this instance Leo's wife was even crowned *Augusta after* the child was born. This was, at least in part, an effort to further legitimize young Constantine's claim to the throne.

SUCCESSION BY COOPTATION

(From Theophanes, *Chronographia*, ed. C. de Boor, vol. 1 [Leipzig, 1883], pp. 399–401.)

In the same year [718] there was born to the impious emperor Leo, an even more impious son, Constantine, the precursor of Antichrist.* On December 25 his wife, Maria, was crowned in the *triklinium* [a special chamber] of the Augusteum and she went with a solemn retinue, but without her husband, into the Great Church [Hagia Sophia] and, passing before the entrance to the altar, she went into the great baptistery, her husband preceding her with a few courtiers, where the patriarch Germanos baptized Constantine, their successor to the empire and to evil. . . . In this year [719], in the third indiction, on Easter Sunday, Constantine was crowned by Emperor Leo, his father, in the chamber of the nineteen *Akoubitoi* [in the palace], by the blessed patriarch Germanos who, according to custom, pronounced the benediction.

*Because of Leo and Constantine's Iconoclastic policy Theophanes was prejudiced against them (see selections 111–15).

21.

Introduction. With the accession of several strong emperors from the same family, a "dynasty" might be on the way to being established. Indeed, in time some of these dynasties, especially the Macedonian (867–1056), came to be looked upon by the people as the legitimate ruling house, and in consequence the Macedonian emperors evoked general support against would-be usurpers. In the following brief selection Michael Psellus writes about this greatest imperial house, the Macedonian. Note especially the tone of admiration employed by the author.

ON THE MACEDONIAN "DYNASTY"

(From Michael Psellus, *Chronographie*, ed. E. Rénauld [Paris, 1926], vol. 1, p. 117.)

I do not know if any other family has been so beloved by God as this one [the Macedonian house], and I marvel at this when I think that the house was not established and planted legitimately, but rather in murder and bloodshed . But so implanted it took root and grew, and it put forth so many shoots, each bearing imperial fruit, that it is not possible for any other [house] to be compared to it, either in beauty or grandeur.

22.

Introduction. Besides cooptation, another way to legitimize accession to the imperial throne was through marriage. This was the case in the mid-eleventh century when Zoë, last of the famous Macedonian dynasty, brought to the throne a succession of three husbands, one of whom, Michael IV, had been an official prominent in the Senate. Michael Psellus describes the quick change from old to new emperor.

SUCCESSION THROUGH MARRIAGE

(From Michael Psellus, *Chronographie*, ed. E. Rénauld [Paris, 1926], vol. 1, pp. 53–54.)

Thus died Romanus after reigning five and one-half years. But Empress Zoë, when she found out that he had died (for she was not present at his death), immediately took control of affairs just as if she were, by divine will, the next inheritor of the throne. But actually she was more concerned to take over power briefly so that she might turn over authority to Michael (concerning whom I have just spoken). Those in the palace, however, who occupied high ranks, the larger part of whom happened to have been servants from the time of her father, and those who had been the retainers of her husband [Romanus]—who had served his family since his father's time—sought to prevent her from taking any hasty action. They advised her for her own good to consider and ponder the best course before making any decision. They insisted that she select as emperor one among them who excelled over the rest and who would agree to treat her not as a consort but as an actual ruler.

The latter group pressed her, seeking to persuade her in short order to agree with their views. But in all her judgments and thoughts she persisted in supporting Michael, not regarding him rationally but emotionally. Since it was necessary to designate a day on which Michael would be crowned and assume the other insignia of authority, John the eunuch, Michael's elder brother, a man most resourceful in thought and vigorous in action, went secretly to the empress and said to her: "We shall die if there is any delay in Michael's assumption of power." He won her over entirely to his way of thinking.

Immediately she summoned Michael and dressed him in robes interwoven with gold thread. Then, placing the imperial crown on his head, she sat him down on the sumptuous throne with herself dressed in similar garb seated next to him. She ordered everyone who was living in the palace at this time to perform *proskynesis* and to acclaim them both together. And they did so. This development soon became known to those outside the palace, and the entire city wished to join the celebration prescribed by imperial order. Many feigned rejoicing and flattered the emperor, and, professing to be disencumbered of the dead emperor [Romanus III] (as if putting aside a heavy burden), they accepted Michael lightly and easily with joy and pleasure.

After this proclamation had been carried out in the evening by those at court, a double edict was received by the eparch [roughly, governor] of Constantinople that all members of the Senate come to the palace in the morning in order to perform *proskynesis* before the new emperor as well as to observe the customary funeral rites for the dead man. They came in compliance with the order. Approaching the seated monarchs, each one touched his head to the ground. For the empress they performed only this act, but they also kissed the right hand of the emperor. In the presence of these men [the senators], Michael was proclaimed emperor and immediately had to consider what would be beneficial for the empire. The ceremony for the dead emperor, Romanus, who had been laid out on a magnificent bier, was already prepared, and everyone withdrew in order to pay the customary respects to him.

23.

Introduction. A change of dynasty might often involve a judicious murder or mutilation. The case of Empress Irene, who in 797 had her son, the rightful heir Constantine VI, blinded, may be rather extraordinary, but it is really only a more extreme example of a type of succession not uncommon in Byzantium. The chronicler of this period, Theophanes, tells in his *Chronographia* about the blinding of Constantine by order of his mother:

> And the sun was darkened during seventeen days, and gave no light, so that ships ran off their course and drifted, and all men said and confessed that it was because the emperor was blinded that the sun had set aside its rays. And thus it was that power came into the hands of Irene, his mother.*

Usurpers of course always tried to lend an air of legitimacy to their accession. Thus Michael VIII Palaeologus, the thirteenth-century emperor, after usurping the throne at Nicaea elaborately and ostentatiously assumed the names of Angelus, Comnenus, and Ducas, to all of which imperial families he was in fact related. Earlier, before his accession, Michael had tried by every possible means, especially flattery, to ingratiate himself with the Patriarch Arsenius and other important elements of Byzantine society.

Nicephorus Gregoras describes Michael's role in the events before 1258–59 in the following selection taken from his *History.*

USURPATION: MICHAEL VIII'S RISE TO POWER

(From Nicephorus Gregoras, *Byzantina historia*, ed. I. Bekker and
L. Schopen [Bonn, 1829], vol. 1, p. 68.)

Michael Palaeologus . . . was among the highest offi-
cials, superior to the rest, with a cheerful countenance, smooth in speech, urbane
in manner, and also generous. All of these qualities brought him affection in the
hearts of all. He attracted all easily, including leaders of the army, both the commanders and the officers, also the plebs and the senators. Preoccupation with
matters of the empire influenced them to pay heed to him and to feel great loyalty to him. . . . But there were certain reasons, far greater than others, pushing
the throne toward him from the start. And he and his friends, seizing upon
them, justified his claim to the throne with such reasons as these:

His grandmother Irene was the first of the daughters of Alexius [III] the emperor, who, lacking male offspring, ordered [imperial] red boots to be put on her
so that she and the one who married her would then be the cosuccessors to the
empire. Whereupon, marrying her to Alexius Palaeologus, the emperor at once
created him despot, and had the latter not died he would have become emperor
after his father-in-law, Alexius.

But when he [Alexius Palaeologus] died, he left only a daughter [Theodora],
and after a short time the emperor married her to Andronicus Palaeologus,
whom later Emperor Theodore honored with the title of grand domestic. Of
them was born Michael Palaeologus Comnenus, who was therefore doubly a Palaeologus, on both his father's and his mother's side. Therefore, given these considerations, he [Michael] had not a few reasons to claim the throne. To put it
simply, he was a man remarkable in all respects and admired by all, and his fame
spread quickly, beguiling the ears of all. . . .

Then the patriarch [Arsenius] took counsel with him in ecclesiastical matters,
and, even more, he entrusted to him alone the keys of the imperial fisc in order
to provide funds whenever military exigency and public affairs required such
expenditure. Michael was thus provided with what was most effectual for secret
councils. . . . After he had received the power to handle so much money, which
he had desired but never dared to hope for, he then poured it forth into the
hands of the nobles and the appointed leaders of the army, and thus they were
able to influence the people by persuasion through the art of demagoguery.
Among these were included many ecclesiastics. Many opinions were voiced by all
these, urging the patriarch not to be hesitant but to take a stand and to be properly diligent . . . and so he [Michael] proceeded to take care of the affairs [of the
empire] as the times required . . . in the present situation of imminent ruin, like
a ship in the middle of the sea laden with infinite goods or like a great house
whose foundations have been shaken.

Most people had the name of Michael on their lips as capable of assuming the
burden of imperial authority because of his serious manner and experience in
public affairs—that is, [they wanted him] to assume this power until the emperor's son reached the proper age. The patriarch now agreed with these and
proceeded to carry out what was decided. So Michael was put in charge of state
affairs, assuming the whole authority [becoming regent] but without the imperial

insignia. . . . A few days went by, and Michael's supporters held a second meeting, affirming that it was not proper that the one who governs imperial and public affairs, receiving embassies from many nations, should not have the insignia of one closest to the imperial rank and also the rank of honor. . . . So the rank of despot was granted to him by the patriarch and by the son of the emperor. [In subsequent passages Gregoras relates how Michael capitalized on the turmoil in church and state to blind his young charge, the boy-emperor, John, and finally to have himself crowned emperor.]

*Translated by R. Jenkins, *Byzantium: The Imperial Centuries* (London, 1966), p. 101.

24.

Introduction. During the difficult times of the early thirteenth century (and later), Byzantine emperors, in an effort to ensure the preservation of their thrones, often insisted that their subjects, both laymen and clergy, take an oath of allegiance to them. Thus, in the critical years 1208–10, when parts of the former empire were being seized by the Latins, the Nicene Emperor Theodore I Lascaris issued an order demanding that his subjects swear fidelity to his rule and to the imperial family. The following is the text of the oath taken by the Patriarch Michael Autoreianos and his prelates.

AN ECCLESIASTICAL OATH OF FIDELITY TO THE EMPEROR

(From N. Oikonomides, "Cinq actes inédits du Patriarch Michiel Autoreianos," *Revue des études byzantines* 25 [1967]: 122–24.)

It is worthy of an appreciative soul to recognize its benefactors and demonstrate kindness to them with the greatest straightforwardness. If the obligation of the appreciation aims at the benefit and preservation of the secular situation in this world, all the more reason that this good should be pursued with the assiduous efforts it merits. That is why we, the clergy—having noted that first the blood relations of our powerful and holy emperor, then the nobles and other magistrates, and finally the citizens [of Nicaea], soldiers, and inhabitants of the towns and countryside of the state of the Byzantines, have affirmed by oath their sincere loyalty and their favorable disposition toward our powerful and holy emperor and his son, the well-loved Kyr [Lord] Nicholas—have judged it necessary to give written assurance of the goodwill and submission that we have in regard to our powerful and holy emperor, our holy empress, and their well-loved son Emperor Nicholas, inheritor and successor to their throne. [We have done this], on the one hand, to show that we are sincere in our support of you and, on the other, to encourage still more our very powerful and holy *autokrator* in his numerous battles against arrogant enemies who now, in a more oppressive manner than ever, have invaded our lands on account of our sins.

We, then, the prelates who are found in this city guarded by God, Nicaea, following the imperial order addressed to us for this purpose and in accordance with the jurisdiction given us by our Lord God and his grace, compose the present *tomos* to affirm and to declare that we pledge ourselves by our signatures that we will preserve toward you, our lord, the powerful and hóly emperor of the Byzantines, the Comnenan Kyr Theodore Lascaris, a pure faith and a very favorable disposition. We will never foster ideas or plans which will go against you, your body, or your throne. We will not be partisans of any other, of an enemy of your majesty whoever it may be, Byzantine or barbarian, crowned or not, not even of the grandson of Kyr Andronikos. On the contrary, we agree to do everything possible so that the thoughts and acts of those in our provinces, whatever their family, wealth, or rank, may conduce to the honor and the maintenance of your majesty. If it happens that you die, we promise to keep all these promises without modification toward the heir and successor of your throne, our very dear son, Emperor Kyr Nicholas. Toward our powerful and holy empress we will show the proper respect and submission which our office demands of us. . . .

It has been decided that the absent metropolitans and archbishops, wherever they may be, shall have to sign the present *tomos*, as well as the patriarchal archons. The participants at this great synod will take care that the bishops who are under them act according to our decision.

C.
THE COURT AND ITS OFFICES:
THE CIVIL BUREAUCRACY IN CONSTANTINOPLE

25.

Introduction. One basic reason for the remarkable longevity of the Byzantine Empire was the efficiency of its governmental bureaucracy. The governmental administration was probably more centralized than that of any other state in the medieval world, including the caliphates of the Arabs and certainly the Western empire. This well-developed and tightly organized administrative system was in large part inherited from the late Roman Empire of the time of the emperors Diocletian and Constantine. To be sure, in time the system was substantially altered to maintain its efficiency under changing circumstances, in particular during wars with the Persians and, above all, the Arabs. But in all periods authority was concentrated in the hands of the emperor, who held the power to appoint or remove all officials of state.

The officials of the provincial administration (for example, the praetorian prefects), although often high dignitaries residing in Constantinople, will be treated in a later section of this book focusing on the provincial administration. Here we will concentrate on the imperial court and the administrative machinery connected with the central government in Constantinople. In the earliest period, from Constantine through Justinian, the central bureaucracy consisted of a number of central bureaus (or departments), each under a chief. The head of the entire civil service was the *magister officiorum* (minister of offices), whose control of the imperial bureaucracy (as well as the secret service) often made him, in this period, a kind of prime minister. Under his control were the principal secretarial bureaus of the imperial palace, which handled record keeping and correspondence. The chief legal minister of the empire was the quaestor of the sacred palace, who drafted the laws for the emperor's approval. The head of all palace officials and servants was the *praepositus sacri cubiculae* (the grand chamberlain), almost invariably a eunuch and a dignitary of the highest class.

While the administration of the provinces, as already noted, was controlled by four praetorian prefects, the capital cities of Rome and Constantinople (in this early period) were separately administered by two officials, called urban prefects, who were part of the civil bureaucracy of the capital(s). The following selection, drawn from the writer-bureaucrat John the Lydian of the sixth century, describes the duties of the *magister officiorum* (master of offices) during this period and notes something of the development of that office from the time of Emperor Constantine.

THE MAGISTER OFFICIORUM

(From John the Lydian, *De magistratibus populi Romani*, ed. R. Wuensch, Teubner [Stuttgart, 1967], pp. 80–81.)

For the name *magister officiorum* means simply the head of the court catalog [of titles], as we have said. Among these the combined horse and foot forces of the empire are considered to number in the thousands, and the master of the horse (*hipparchos*) used to hold this responsibility as his only one. But the *magister officiorum* holds an even greater responsibility, since the empire has been so greatly extended [under Justinian]. In the past the [ancient] Romans controlled only Italy, but, with God leading, they now hold the entire earth and sea.

And whoever in the past was named to the office of *magister* [*officiorum*] I cannot tell, since history remains silent. For before Martinian, who was *magister* under Licinius, the record provides the name of no other. After Martinian had served under Licinius, Constantine, when he had taken sole control of the entire empire, chose Palladius as magister of the court, an intelligent man who had become a friend of the Persians earlier through a Roman embassy he had gone on for Maximian Galerius. . . .

Therefore the authority of a *magister* extends even beyond the magistracy, for the *magister* is entrusted not only with receiving the embassies of foreign peoples, with the public post, and—in the past—with the heavy responsibility of the corn provisions, but now with all the magistrates and with the preparation and control of arms, as well as with political matters. And this Peter [the contemporary *magister*], who is great and second to none in skills, guards the court and keeps it safe, and does not besmirch Byzantine glory, which was almost lost by the stupidity of the ones before him. Wise and well read in everything, he restores all these things.

26.

Introduction. Advancement in the complex Byzantine bureaucracy could be achieved through merit, through patronage, or perhaps through judicious flattery of superiors, including even the emperor. But to hold office in the civil bureaucracy of Constantinople, one also needed a good education in the ancient classics.

The following selection, drawn from the treatise *De magistratibus* (*On Magistracies*), written by John the Lydian during the reign of Justinian (c. 554), describes the training and talents, the blend of scholarship and administrative work, necessary for advancement in the Byzantine administrative system—characteristics that continued to be important to bureaucrats up to the very end of the empire.

THE TRAINING OF A BUREAUCRAT

(Translated by P. Ure, *Justinian and His Age* [Harmondsworth: Penguin, 1951], pp. 114–15, as revised by D. Geanakoplos, from Ioannes Lydus, *De magistratibus populi Romani*, ed. R. Wuensch [Stuttgart, 1967], pp. 113–15.)

When I was in my twenty-first year : . . . I came from my native Philadelphia, which lies at the foot of Mount Tmolus in Lydia, to this blessed city [Constantinople]; and after much consideration I decided to join the *memoriales* of the court and take a post among them.* To avoid seeming to waste the intervening time, I resolved to attend the classes of a philosopher. Agapius was flourishing at that time, about whom Christodorus the poet, in his volume about the pupils of the great Proclus, speaks thus: "Agapius [was] last but foremost of them all." Under him it was my fortune to study the first part of the Aristotelian doctrine and to attend some lectures on the philosophy of Plato. But fortune, having it in view rather to thrust me aside into this service, advanced Zoticus, a fellow citizen of mine who took an extreme delight in me, to the prefecture of the praetorians under the mildest of all monarchs, Emperor Anastasius; and having it in his power not only to persuade but also to compel me, he enrolled me among the clerks [*tachygraphoi*] of his office. . . .

To prevent any chance of my growing slack, the prefect pointed out to me every road to [monetary] gain, so that all through his period of office—it was not long, just over a year—I gained no less than a thousand pieces of gold through my prudent behavior. So naturally, being grateful—how could I have been otherwise?—I composed a brief encomium on him. He was delighted and told me to take from the "table" a gold piece for each line. And those who are summoned to serve as aides by the official called *ab actis* [head of a branch of the quaestor's office] invited and accepted me—a thing that had never happened before—to be first *chartularius* [chief clerk]. There were only two others, both old men who had been appointed only after first agreeing to make a present of money; and not only this, but they further appointed me a yearly stipend of twenty-four gold pieces.

Similarly . . . I was appointed to be one of the *souggestiones*, about whom it might be said that all, without exception . . . shone by their excellent education, and they especially took care to become more learned in the Latin language, for it was necessary to them in their work. When a case of appeal happened to come up and was referred to the Senate for review, the most important of the officials arranged that the so-called *souggestio* (in Greek, termed *didaskalia*, that is, interpretation) should be conducted in such a manner, in the presence of the council, so as to amaze the quaestor of the council and those formerly called [in Latin] *antecensores* but according to us *antigrapheis* [clerk-copyists]. With God's help and my own zeal—fostered by the encouragement surrounding me—which rendered the work easy, I not only fulfilled the aforementioned duties of the *scrinium* but also acted as chief among the secretaries [speed writers], in addition to giving help to other clerks in the chamber of justice that is called the *secretum*. Not small was my reputation on account of my actions, and the encouragement accorded me in these actions was infinite. Thence, as if I had become winged, I was propelled forward amidst those who are called *a secretis* [the secretariat] of the court [*aule*].

*The *memoriales* were secretaries in the branch of the imperial bureaucracy that handled records.

27.

Introduction. It is difficult to know the exact function of any given Byzantine official at a specific time, since extant sources for many periods are relatively scanty. In fact almost all the sources we now have on the bureaucracy (such as John the Lydian, *On Magistracies*, Constantine VII, *On Ceremonies*, Philotheos, *Kleitorologion*, and Pseudo-Codinus, *On the Offices*) describe the position or role of officials in the court ceremonials but often do not specify exactly what duties were attached to the positions named. Moreover, as time went on, certain officials would be granted honorary positions in the ceremonies that sometimes did not correspond to their actual duties in the government.

And yet, despite these developments, a certain continuity in some titles may be observed, extending from the time of Constantine or Justinian almost to the end of the empire (though, of course, many new titles were adopted in later centuries and some older titles fell out of use).

Our next selection is drawn from the famous *Kleitorologion* of Philotheus, written in 899. Philotheus, whose title was *protospatharios* and *atriklines*, was in effect the master of ceremonies for the emperor and in this capacity drew up a manual of protocol and list of ranks according to which officials would be formally received and seated at imperial functions, especially banquets. Philotheus lists first the "grades of dignity," along with the particular insignia conferred on each rank by the emperor. Note that some of the titles are in Latin (e.g. *mandator*), indicating continuity back to the time of Constantine or Justinian.

PHILOTHEUS'S LIST OF RANKS AT IMPERIAL CEREMONIES (IN ASCENDING ORDER)

(From Philotheus, *Kleitorologion*, in J. Bury, *The Imperial Administrative System in the Ninth Century* [London: H. Frowde, 1911], pp. 20–22.)

Title	Insignia
*1. (a) *Stratelates*	
(b) *Apo eparchon*	diploma
*2. *Silentiarios*	
(chief duty: marshal at imperial ceremonies)	gold staff
*3. *Vestetor*	
(officer of the wardrobe)	*fiblatorion*
4. *Mandator*	
(officer in imperial communications)	red wand
5. *Kandidatos*	special gold chain
6. *Strator*	jeweled gold whip

Title	Insignia
*7. Hypatos (belonging to the consular order of the Senate, an honorary title)	diploma
' 8. Spatharios	sword with gold hilt
9. Spatharokandidatos	special gold chain
*10. Disypatos (a senatorial rank given to only a few)	diploma
11. Protospatharios (chief of taxeis, rank of the Spatharioi)	jeweled gold collar
12. Patrikios	inscribed ivory tablets
13. (Patrikios and) Anthypatos	inscribed purple tablets
14. Magistros (in the eighth century he was titled magister officiorum [master of offices], though he was already shorn of most of the functions attached to this rank in late Roman times)	gold-embroidered white tunic
15. Zoste patrikia (a woman, mistress of the robes)	ivory tablets
16. Couropalates (an honorary title [held by Philotheus] usually bestowed on relatives of the emperor; in the tenth century the king of Iberia held this title)	red tunic, mantle, and belt
17. Nobilissimus	purple tunic, mantle, and belt
18. Caesar (the highest rank in this period, sometimes given to the successor to the throne)	crown without a cross

* Those ranks marked with an asterisk were senatorial in their very origin.
' In the seventh century the titles spatharios and hypatos were often combined.

28.

Introduction. Even more important than the list of ranks and insignia is the list of classes of government officials, arranged according to actual duties performed, provided by Philotheus, again in his *Kleitorologion.* Most important officials possessed both a functional and a ceremonial rank, and indeed with the passing of time there came to be a great multiplicity of gradations and differentiations involved. This circumstance, plus the fact that the information we have from the extant sources is scant, does not permit us to make an exact structural analysis of the system.

PHILOTHEUS'S LIST OF MAJOR OFFICES ACCORDING TO FUNCTION (IN DESCENDING ORDER)

(From Philotheus, *Kleitorologion,* in J. Bury, *The Imperial Administrative System in the Ninth Century* [London: H. Frowde, 1911], pp. 39–121 passim.)

1. *Strategoi*
   [Generals (governors) of the themes (provinces), commanding civil as well as military employees.]

2. *Domestikoi*

[Chiefs of the *tagmatic* (household) troops. One of these, the domestic of the *scholae*, was often the commander-in-chief of the field army.]

3. *Kritai*

[Judges, including the prefect of the city (*eparchos*), with wide judicial powers, and judges to examine petitions.]

4. *Sekretikoi*

[Treasurers, including the *sakellarios* (comptroller general) and the logothete; the *chartularios* (a high-ranking chancery clerk) and the *protoasecretes* (imperial secretary); two curators, one supervising the naval and military arsenal and workshop of the Mangana; the *orphanotrophos*, who headed the Great Orphanage of Constantinople.]

5. *Democratai*

[The two demarchs, supervisors of the Green and Blue Demes (see below, selection 181).]

6. *Stratarchai*

[Chiefs of the imperial guard, made up of foreign mercenaries; the Lord High Admiral; the official supervising cavalry remounts; the *basilikoi*, who headed the office of special emissaries; and the count of the stables.]

7. Various Offices

[Including the rector, who at this time was chief of the imperial household; the *synkellos*, an ecclesiastical liaison official between emperor and patriarch; the master of ceremonies; the palace eunuchs.]

[Each one of the above officials reported directly to the throne.]

29.

Introduction. An excellent example of the rigid protocol, according to rank, followed by officials at the imperial court is provided by the following passage, drawn from the tenth-century Emperor Constantine VII's *On Ceremonies*, concerning the activities involved in the imperial reception of foreign ambassadors.

COURT PROTOCOL AT THE RECEPTION FOR FOREIGN ENVOYS

(From Constantine VII Porphyrogenitus, *De ceremoniis*, ed. J. Reiske [Bonn, 1829], pp. 567–70.)

And when everything has been made ready by the master of ceremonies and the *praepositi* [chamberlains] and the logothete of the *dromos* [foreign minister], the *praepositi* approach and inform the emperor and empress. They withdraw immediately, and official garments and garlands are brought to them. These they put on under the direction of the *praepositi*; then they reenter and sit on their thrones, and the people standing around the two drawn curtains at the west end of the hall loudly shout acclamations to them. Then, leaving the hall, the *praepositus* leads in the household officials in two groups, one from the right side and one from the left, as custom dictates. The *praepositus* directs the usher with the golden staff that these men stand, and [the usher] exits and leads in the *magistri* in the first group. Then, by order of the *praepositus*, another usher goes out and, according to the same procedure, leads in the second group, the patricians. Then, by order of the *praepositus*, another usher goes out and leads in the third group, the senators, and [this continues for] as many groups as custom and the arrangement of the ceremony dictate. The *katepanos* [a military official] enters behind the domestic and the men in gold clothing, and they stand to the right and left of the two drawn curtains at the west end.

After they are standing, the *praepositus* orders the usher with the golden staff to bring in the foreigner, conducted by the *katepanos* of the empire or by the count of the stables [the *protostrator*] with an interpreter also [to be] near them. The logothete of the *dromos* leads all of these men forward. This man [the foreign ambassador], after approaching, prostrates himself before the emperor and empress, and immediately organs start to play. Then he approaches and stands at a distance from the emperor, and suddenly the organs cease. . . . Then lions begin to roar and the birds on the throne begin to sing, just like those in the trees. All the animals on the throne stand upright. After this has taken place, the gifts [for the emperor] are brought in by the *protonotarios*, and after a short time the organ ceases [*sic*], and the lions become quiet, the birds stop singing, and the beasts return to their original positions. After the presentation of the gifts which have been brought forward by the logothete, the foreigner prostrates himself and leaves while the organ plays, each animal makes its particular noises, and all the beasts stand upright. After the visitor has left the curtain, the organ stops playing and the animals sit down again. If there is another honored guest and the emperor orders him to enter, [that guest] comes in and departs according to the same protocol and procedure, in the manner thus described. Regardless of how many visitors seek to enter, the protocol is followed for each that has just been recounted. It should be noted that when the foreigners are leaving, the *praepositus* loudly exclaims, "At your service," and the *magistri*, patricians, and senators say, "[May you, O Emperor] live many years." . . . When everyone has departed, the rulers descend from the throne and remove the golden vestments, garlands, and cloaks. And they secretly return to their God-protected palace.

Commentary. Beginning with the end of the eleventh century, certain new titles or variations of older titles came to the fore. Most notable was that of grand logothete, earlier a financial (and postal) official—equivalent perhaps to our secretary of the treasury—then becoming a sort of comptroller general and evolving at times in the fourteenth century into a kind of prime minister of the empire.

30.

Introduction. One administrative consequence of the deteriorating political and military conditions in the empire at the end of the eleventh century was what may be called an "inflation" of titles. Indeed, though the empire's territory became increasingly constricted, with the passing of time the number of titles actually increased. For example, the title *sebastos* (*augustus*), common in the earlier period and referring originally only to the emperor, came later to be outranked by the newly created title *pansebastos*, then even by *hyperpansebastos* ("all most august one"). Court politics encouraged this hyperbole, as revealed in the following passage taken from the history of the Byzantine Princess Anna, daughter of Emperor Alexius Comnenus (1081–1118)—a passage in which Anna also shows her insight into the philosophy ("science") of government. Note the addition of the prefixes "pan" and "hyper" to several of the titles listed in Philotheus's *Kleitorologion*. (See also, on the great increase in honors awarded senators, selection 64, by Michael Attaleiates.)

ALEXIUS COMNENUS "INVENTS" NEW TITLES

(From Anna Comnena, *Alexiade*, ed. B. Leib [Paris, 1945], vol. 1, pp. 113–15.)

Since Alexius had promised to grant the title of caesar to Nicephorus Melissenus [his brother-in-law], it was necessary that Isaac, the eldest of his brothers, be honored with some higher dignity. But because there existed no other rank [between emperor and caesar], Emperor Alexius created a new title, a combination of *sebastos* and *autokrator*, and he bestowed upon his brother this rank of *sebastokrator*, making him virtually a second emperor. He subordinated the caesar to him and made the caesar third in the rank of acclamations after the emperor. Further, he ordered that in the public festivals both the *sebastokrator* and the caesar wear crowns, though greatly inferior in splendor to the one he himself wore.

At the same time, Taronites, who was the husband of the sister of the emperor, was also honored with the dignities of *protosebastos* and *protovestiarios*, and shortly thereafter he was raised to the rank of *panhypersebastos* with the right to sit with the caesar. In addition, Adrian, his [Alexius's] brother, was given the rank of most illustrious *protosebastos*. And Nicephorus, the last of his brothers, who had been elevated to grand *drungarios* [commander] of the fleet, also was raised to the rank of the *sebastoi*. My father himself invented these new ranks, some being compounds [of older titles] just as has been described above, and others being put to a new use. For on the one hand he "composed" *panhypersebastos* and *sebastokrator* and other such names, while on the other he gave a new meaning to the rank of *sebastos*. In earlier times the emperors were termed *sebastoi* and the name *sebastos* was properly applied only to the emperor. But Alexius was the first to bring it into wider usage. One who considers the art of ruling a science and a highest form of philosophy, the art of arts and the science of sciences, would admire my father as both a kind of scientist and an architect since he invented in the empire these functions and titles. The difference is that the masters of the logical sciences invented names for the sake of clarity, while Alexius, master of the science of government, instituted all this in the best interest of the empire, and often made innovations with respect to both the division of duties and the designation of titles.

31.

Introduction. Though the court offices operated with considerable efficiency for some years after Alexius's reign, venality became an increasingly severe problem in the bureaucracy. Certain offices, in fact, from the mid-eleventh century on, came to be awarded by the emperor to grasping relatives or, worse, sold by the emperor (who at times was in dire need of money) to those unsuited to perform whatever duties of state may have been required. Such conditions were rampant by the time of the Angeloi emperors in the late twelfth century when the empire had lost a good deal of its wealth, as bitterly described by the contemporary historian Nicetas Choniates in the following selection.

SALE OF IMPERIAL OFFICES

(From Nicetas Choniates, *Historia*, ed. I. Van Dieten [Berlin, 1975], vol. 1, p. 444.)

Also after adulterating the silver coinage, he [Emperor Isaac II] rendered the *nomisma* spurious. Nor did he collect the taxes in a just manner and without reproach, but he increased the exactions with respect to the public imposts in order to maintain his extravagances. And he put up offices for sale just as men of the marketplace hawk their fruits for sale. At times he sent officials into the provinces without money or wallet, in the manner of the Apostles, but he knew that they would carry out justice with severity and that they would bring back faithfully to his treasury what they exacted from the people.

32.

Introduction. In the period between the fall of Constantinople to the Latins (1204) and the restoration of the empire in 1261, four of the problems besetting the Byzantine central administration to which we have paid particular attention—purchase of offices, inflation of titles, bloated size of the bureaucracy, and noncorrespondence of office and duties—became even more glaringly apparent.

In the following selection Bishop Demetrius Chomatianos of Epirus, an expert in canon law, provides a list of officials appointed at the Byzantine court at Epirus during the interregnum between 1204 and 1261. This list, which was obviously modeled after the old Byzantine court protocol of Constantinople, carried the inflation of titles to an extreme, almost ridiculous, degree.

INFLATION OF TITLES AT THE COURT OF EPIRUS

(From Demetrius Chomatianos, *Synoptikon*, in J. Pitra, ed., *Analecta sacra et classica* [Paris, 1891], vol. 6, col. 785ff.)

Dukes

Nicephorus Mazaris
Alexis Pegonetes

Pansebastos sebastos [All-august, august one]	Constantine Aspietes
Megalodoxotatos [Great, most glorious one]	Andronikos Skutariotes
Protopansebastohypertatos First, all-august, most high one]	Eudaimonoiannis
Paneutechestatos [The all most fortunate one]	John Chamaretos and others
Paneugenestatos [All most noble one]	Andronikos Comnenos
Megalepifanestatos [The great, most high-appearing one]	Gregory Gavras

33.

Introduction. The last comprehensive listing of Byzantine administrative officials that survives is the *Treatise on Offices* (*De officiis*) of the fourteenth-century court official known as Pseudo-Codinus, from which we take the following list of ranks. A comparison of this list of officials with the somewhat analogous list of Philotheus provided earlier reveals the degree of continuity and, even more, of change in titles, and also the fact that the most important titles were reserved for members of the imperial family (doubtless in large part for security reasons).

OFFICIAL RANKS IN THE FOURTEENTH CENTURY

(From Pseudo-Codinus, *Traité des offices*, ed. J. Verpeaux [Paris: Editions du Centre national de la recherche scientifique, 1966], pp. 133–37.)

The sons of the emperor, the despots, take precedence over the brothers and the close relatives of the emperor who are also despots [the ranks following despot are:]

Sebastokrator

Caesar

Protovestiarios

Emperor Michael VIII Palaeologus, having taken away from the *protosebastos* the green vestments, conferred them on his nephew Michael Tarchaneiotes, after having honored him with the title of *protovestiarios*: [then follow]

Grand duke

Grand domestic

Emperor Andronicus II Palaeologus, having stripped the eparch of the yellow ornaments that he wore from the beginning, conferred them, after creating him *protohypersebastos*, on his nephew John Palaeologus, the son of the Porphyrogenitus, giving him precedence over all his nephews and also over the *protovestiarios*, the grand duke, the grand domestic, and others. Emperor Andronicus III and his grandfather [Emperor Andronicus II] made John Cantacuzene grand domestic [he later became emperor], a rank equal to *panhypersebastos*. Then Emperor Andronicus III, after the death of his grandfather, placed Grand Domestic Cantacuzene above all others in order to honor him—over the nephews of his grandfather, the emperor, over his own uncles, as well as over all others including the *protovestiarios*. The latter, the grand domestic, was then the first after the caesar, with the rest following:

Panhypersebastos
Protovestiarios
Grand duke
Protostrator
Grand stratopedarch
Grand primicerius
Grand constable
Grand logothete
Protosebastos
Pincernes
Kouropalates
Parakoimomenos of the Seal
Parakoimomenos of the Chamber
Logothete of the Genikon . . .

34.

Introduction. An excellent example of the lack of correspondence between title of office and duty performed during the last century of the empire is provided in the account of the Byzantine chronicler Ducas, who describes the fall of Constantinople to the Turks in 1453. In the following selection Ducas describes the actions of the *megas dukas* (grand duke, a title referring to the fleet admiral), Lucas Notaras, although by now the navy as a military force was almost nonexistent.

THE MEGAS DUKAS AT THE FALL OF CONSTANTINOPLE

(From Ducas, *Ducae historia Turcobyzantina, 1341–1462*, ed. V. Grecu [Bucharest, 1958], p. 355.)

The troops within the city were deployed in the following manner: the emperor and John Giustiniani [Genoese lord of Chios] [were] at the collapsed walls beyond the [improvised] earthworks, having with them about three thousand Latins and Romans [Byzantines]. The grand duke [*megas dukas*] was stationed at the Imperial Gate with about five hundred men. More than five hundred crossbowmen and archers defended the sea walls and ramparts from the Xyloporta Gate to the Horaia [Beautiful] Gate. Completing the circuit, a single archer, crossbowman, or gunner was posted in each bastion, extending from the Horaia Gate to the Golden Gate. They passed the entire night on guard and did not go to sleep at all.

D.
TAXATION

35.

Introduction. The most important section of the imperial administration in all periods was that entrusted with the vital responsibility of collecting the tax revenues. In the early period of the empire dating from Diocletian and Constantine's time, by far the most significant tax was the land tax. This tax was levied according to the amount and arability of the land, expressed in a unit called the *iugum*, and the amount of labor, measured by the *caput*, or "head." The populace of the cities did not pay the land tax. Rather, they paid the "urban tribute," an analogous tax on urban sites. Other sources of governmental revenue were the toll on receipts (a form of income tax), death duties, judicial fines, and, above all, duties levied on imported goods. Following is the text of the decree of Emperor Theodosius I increasing the number of individuals included in one *caput*.

THE CAPITATION TAX (386)

(Translated by C. Pharr, *The Theodosian Code* [Princeton, 1952], 13-11-2, p. 402.)

From Emperor Theodosius I to his praetorian prefect:
Although formerly the norm of the capitation tax unit was assessed on the basis of one man but two women for each such unit,* now the burden of the payment of one capitation tax unit is assigned to two or three men, or to four women. Wherefore, your Sublime Authority shall order, throughout the cities of the Comanians and of the Ariarathians of Second Armenia, of the Amasians of Helenopontus, and of the Diocaesarians of Second Cappadocia, that the measure of this salutary and temperate equalization shall be annexed to the public records for such tax lists.

* In the tax system established by Diocletian.

36.

Introduction. During the period of Constantine and his successors the responsibility for collecting the taxes in the cities lay with the *curiales* (decurions). Indeed, if they were unable to collect the prescribed amount of taxes, they were required by law to make up the deficit with their own funds. This increasingly became a severe hardship on the curiales, and by the fourth and fifth centuries, many curiales even preferred to flee from their homes in order to escape their onerous duties. The following decree shows how the decurions, though themselves here receiving a remission in their tax obligations, tried to prevent the taxpayers of their cities from enjoying the same benefit.

THE CURIALES (DECURIONS) AND TAXES (415)

(Translated by C. Pharr, *The Theodosian Code*, [Princeton, 1952], 11-28-10, pp. 319–20.)

Some men appear to have converted to their own gain and booty the remission of taxes which We distributed as of general effect throughout all the provinces and peoples, from the eleventh year of the indiction of Valens up to the fifth year of the indiction just completed, so that what had been public debts became private debts. Therefore, in order that the provincials may enjoy Our bounty in fact and not merely in name, nothing further shall be exacted from them by any member of a municipal senate under the pretext of a tax payment anticipated by him, since the members of the municipal senates must find sufficient as a remedy whatever they personally obtained from the aforesaid remission of taxes, which they have attempted to violate with their sacrilegious intent.

37.

Introduction. The reign of Emperor Anastasius I (491–518) was especially significant from the fiscal point of view. His important currency reform in 498 prescribed a new copper coin to replace the older ones. He also established a new ratio between the gold *nomisma*, the silver *denarius*, and the copper *follis*, a ratio which remained stable until the mid-eleventh century, a result of the remarkable fact that the coinage remained undepreciated during these centuries.

Moreover, Anastasius regularized the taxes, especially abolishing the payment of the hated *chrysargyron* (498), a tax paid in gold and silver and applied to all handicrafts and professions in the empire (even to servants, beggars, and prostitutes). This tax dated from the time of the reforms by Diocletian and Constantine. Levied perhaps even on the tools and livestock of farmers, the *chrysargyron* weighed heavily on the poor. Moreover, it was often arbitrarily collected. The *Chronicle* of the monk Joshua the Stylite of this period relates the effect of the abolition of the *chrysargyron* on the jubilant population of the city of Edessa in Syria.

ANASTASIUS ABOLISHES THE TAX OF THE CHRYSARGYRON

(Translated by W. Wright, *The Chronicle of Joshua the Stylite Composed in Syria in 507* [Cambridge University Press, 1882], p. 22.)

In this same year was issued an edict of the emperor Anastasius that the money should be remitted which the artisans used to pay once in four years [the *chrysargyron*], and that they should be freed from the impost. This edict was issued not only in Edessa but in all the cities of the Greek [Byzantine] empire. The Edessenes used to pay once in four years one hundred and forty pounds of gold. The whole city rejoiced, and they all put on white garments, both small and great, and carried lighted tapers and censers full of burning incense, and went forth with psalms and hymns, giving thanks to God and praising the emperor, to the church of St. Sergius and St. Simeon, where they celebrated the eucharist. They then reentered the city, and kept a glad and merry festival during the whole week, and enacted that they should celebrate this festival every year. All the artisans were reclining and enjoying themselves, bathing, and feasting in the court of the [great] Church and in all the porticoes of the city.

38.

Introduction. By the middle period (after Heraclius, that is) the minister of imperial finances was called the general logothete (*logothetes tou genikou*). Under him was the *sakellarios*, the chief of the imperial treasury, who was the chief financial officer in charge of the actual receipts and disbursement of tax revenues. Apart from this, the emperor had his own revenues from his own private estates administered by the grand curator. (The army and imperial palace, at least at times, had their own separate officials in charge of income and expenditures.) Beneath these main officials was a large group of lesser administrators who made up the bulk of the Byzantine financial administration.

Although in the earliest Byzantine period, the late Roman fiscal system was in the main continued, the financial administration underwent numerous changes and revisions throughout the empire's history. One of the most basic and far-reaching financial reforms was that undertaken by Emperor Nicephorus I, who himself had been general logothete before his accession in 802. The following selection, drawn from the monk-chronicler Theophanes, gives a detailed but hostile, account of Nicephorus's wide-ranging fiscal reforms (810), which (besides providing for the first census taken in seventy-five years) above all rescinded the immunity from taxation granted to certain groups (especially the church and the monks) by his predecessors, in particular the pious Empress Irene.

THEOPHANES ON NICEPHORUS I'S TAX AND
FINANCIAL REFORMS

(From Theophanes, *Chronographia*, ed. C. de Boor [Leipzig,
1883] vol. 1, pp. 486–87.)

In this year, after ignominious vacillations, Nicepho-
rus . . . ordered Christians from every theme, under pain of compulsion, to sell
their property and to go and settle in the Sclavinian areas.* But it was a question
of nothing less than slavery, and some blasphemed from lack of understanding
. . . while others wailed at their ancestors' graves and blessed the dead. . . . Second, along with this harassment, the emperor ordered poor [farmers] to be con-
scripted into the army and to be armed by fellow farmers who were jointly [*allelengyos*] to provide eighteen and one-half *nomismata* to the public treasury as
taxes for the poor farmers.

Nicephorus's third evil idea was to order that the property of each person be
re-examined and that the taxes be increased so that each had to pay two additional *keratia* [one-twelfth *nomisma*] as an administrative fee. In the fourth place
he ordered that all remissions from taxation be revoked. Fifth, from the *paroikoi*
[tenants] of charitable foundations, the *orphanotropheion* [the great orphanage],
hostleries and old people's homes, churches, and imperial monasteries [many in
great part exempt from taxation], he demanded that the hearth tax be paid, extending from the first year of his tyranny [reign] onward . . .

Sixth [he ordered] that military governors seek out those persons who had
suddenly risen from penury [without paying taxes, that is] and that they be taxed
as if they were finders of treasure trove. Seventh [he ordered], regarding those
who during the last twenty years had found a jar or vase of any kind, that they be
taxed. Eighth, he ordered that during the same period those poor who had
shared in a legacy from grandparents or parents, pay a tax to the treasury. Also
that those who had profited from the importation of household slaves without
their passing through [the main customs-station of] Abydos be ordered to pay
two *nomismata* in tax; this applied especially to those in the Dodecanese.

Ninth [he ordered] that those living along the shores, especially of Asia Minor,
shipowners who had never lived off agriculture, be forced, against their will, to
purchase the property that he had seized so that it could be taxed.† Tenth, he
brought together the chief shipowners of Constantinople and gave a loan to
them of twelve pounds of gold, [to be repaid] at an interest rate of four *keratia*
per *nomisma*,‡ while also demanding payment of the customary *commerkia* [port
and market duties.]

Of the many things [he did], these few I have compiled as in a chapter, so that
they might reveal his [the emperor's] shrewdness in every kind of machina-
tion. . . He also induced wicked servants to inform against their masters and,
although at the beginning he hypocritically pretended to doubt their testimony,
later, after making certain of the servants' lies, he pitted insignificant people
against important ones and rewarded those who made successful accusations. . .
As something worthy of notice and piquant, I mention also this example: a certain candlemaker in the forum had become rich through his own efforts, so the
voracious one [the emperor], sending for him, said: "Put your hand on my head

and swear to me how much gold you have." The poor man hesitated a bit as being unworthy, but he was compelled to do this. And he confessed he had nine *litras* [100 pounds] of gold. The emperor ordered the money to be brought before him within the hour, telling him: "What need have you for distraction? Dine with me and take one hundred *nomismata* and go, satisfied."

Commentary. Nicephorus's reforms were harsh only in the sense that they now applied the taxes equally to all groups. Since the church, the rich, and government officials had hitherto often been guilty of tax evasion (or exemption from taxation), the result was to increase the taxes on these groups in particular. Nicephorus's reforms, which were basically sound, were continued under his successors and, once established, do not seem to have been considered oppressive.

* Presumably to bring back into cultivation land that had been deserted during the Slavic invasions.
† Another possible intention was to make them, legally, sailors of the naval theme.
‡ This amounted to roughly 16% interest.

39.

Introduction. In the later centuries these taxes were augmented by other kinds of taxes. At the same time the practice began, evidently in the eleventh century, of the emperor's granting to the most powerful monasteries and lay landholders immunities from all taxation, in the case of the monasteries often to further the welfare of the monastery, and in the case of the powerful laylords to curry favor with them. In the following selection, drawn from a chrysobull dated 1235 (during the period of the Latin Empire of Constantinople), Emperor John III Vatatzes of Nicaea grants immunity to the monastery of Lembos (in Asia Minor). This is a good example not only of the granting of exemption from taxation (*exkusseia*) but of the many different types of taxes which existed in that later period.

A MONASTERY SECURES (TOTAL) IMMUNITY FROM TAXATION (1235)

(Translated by A. Cappel and D. Geanakoplos, from F. Miklosich and J. Müller, eds., *Acta et diplomata Graeca medii aevi* [Vienna, 1890], vol. 4, p. 21.)

My Majesty protects the monks, and the present chrysobull for the holy monastery of Lembos provides means through which it is ordered permanently and unalterably that the monastery possesses through imperial permission all the things enumerated above, and obtains free access to them, and that all of the *paroikoi* [dependent peasants] and persons unknown to the fisc which it has, are released from taxation [*exkouseuein*] and from all obligations [*epereia*], that is, from feudal dues [*angareia*], payments [*zemia*], bread-tax [*psomozemia*], construction levy [*kastroktisia*], naval levy [*katergoktisia*], the compulsory cutting down of wood, flax, hemp, pitch, or charcoal, the obligations of hospitality to imperial officials [*katathesis mitatou kai aplektou*], obligations to the duke [i.e., *strategos*] or *katepan* [another provincial official], the compulsory furnishing of ships for the fleet or armaments, forcible alienation of bequests, the surrendering of sheep, removal of oxen teams [zeugoamaxia], the handing over of judicial fines [aer], pasturage area, or private livestock of the monastery or of its paroikoi, and from any other obligation [epereia] whatsoever, even if not stated explicitly in this chrysobull. For according to the principle of exemption [exkousseia], My Majesty sees fit to exempt all things belonging to the monastery, and also the fishing area from the fishing tax [bibaropakton], tribute [proskynetikion], navigation taxes [zetesis ploïmon], and any other annual and customary things demanded of fishing areas.

E.
THE PROVINCIAL
ADMINISTRATION:
PROVINCES,
THEMES, AND PRONOIA

40.

Introduction. Along with the centralization of power in Constantinople, Emperor Constantine introduced a new type of provincial administration. This was actually not really new, rather, it was the culmination of a process originally begun in the time of Diocletian. The entire empire of East and West (excluding Rome and Constantinople) was now divided into four vast prefectures, each under a praetorian prefect, the most important officials of the time after the emperor. The prefectures were in turn broken down into dioceses, each under a vicar. The dioceses finally were divided into provinces, the fundamental governmental unit, each headed by a governor. Our main source for the provincial structure of Constantine and his successors' imperial organization is the early fifth-century *Notitia dignitatum,* an official list of court, civil, and military offices which also contains a list of 120 provinces. At this time the governors had strictly administrative and judicial functions, not military. The following is a list of the dioceses and their provinces in the eastern part of the empire as listed in the *Notitia dignitatum.*

A. TITLES AND PROVINCES IN THE *NOTITIA DIGNITATUM*

(From *Notitia dignitatum,* ed. O. Seeck [Berlin, 1876], pp. 5–7.)

[Under the praetorian prefect of the East are the following five dioceses, each under a vicar:]

Oriens, Egypt, Asia, Pontus, Thrace

[The following fifteen provinces are included under the diocese Oriens:]

Palestine, Phoenicia, Syria, Cilicia, Cyprus, Arabia, Isauria, Palestine Salutaris, Palestine Secunda, Lebanese Phoenicia, Euphrates, Syria Salutaris, Osrhoëne, Mesopotamia, Cilicia Secunda.

[The following five provinces are listed under the diocese of Egypt:]

Libya Superior, Libya Inferior, Thebes, Egypt, Arcadia

[The following ten provinces are listed under the diocese of Asia:]

Pamphylia, Hellespont, Lydia, Pisidia, Lycaonia, Phrygia Pacatiana, Phrygia Salutaris, Lycia, Caria, Insulae.

[The following ten provinces are listed under the diocese of Pontus:]

Galatia, Bithynia, Honorias, Cappadocia Prima, Cappadocia Secunda, Pontus Polemoniacus, Helenopontus, Armenia Prima, Armenia Secunda, Galatia Salutaris

[The following six provinces, under the diocese of Thrace:]

Europe, Thrace, Haeminmontus, Rhodopa, Moesia Secunda, Scythia

Introduction. The following selection is a decree from the Theodosian Code (353) delineating the duties of the vicar in this provincial bureaucracy.

B. DUTIES OF THE VICAR

(Translated by C. Pharr, *The Theodosian Code* [Princeton, 1952], 1-15-3, p. 25.)

When the governors of the provinces wish to refer any matter to Us [the Emperor], this matter shall be referred first to the Vicar to whom written instructions have been given that he shall receive the reports and references of the official messengers, which are to be transmitted to My imperial court, and that he shall perform that which he sees ought to be done. Indeed, in this way, in addition to other advantages, the public post will be strengthened by great relief.

41.

Introduction. The seventh century was one of grave crisis for the empire. Hardly had Byzantium thrown back the Sassanid Persian invaders when a new enemy appeared on the scene—the Arabs—who overran most of the empire's eastern provinces and succeeded even in blockading Constantinople, at one time for seven years. In this critical period, the organization of the old Roman Empire, based on the old provincial organization of the era of Diocletian and Constantine, foundered, and a new form of organization based on the need for constant military preparedness gradually emerged: the themes.

The themes (provinces), which took their name from the military units permanently stationed there (from the verb *tithemi*, to place) were military districts under the command of military generals, the *strategoi*. In the hands of the *strategoi* were combined both civil and military functions. The origins of the thematic system, arising as it did during a time of permanent martial law, are still rather obscure. But the system probably began to take shape during the reigns of Emperors Maurice and Heraclius with the Exarchates of Ravenna (Italy) and Carthage (Africa), as a response to their particular military needs against the Lombards and Persians at a time when Constantinople could ill afford to send aid.

The question of when the "true" thematic system was established in Asia Minor is clouded by controversy. The earliest references to thematic "provincial" organization seem to come from Theophanes, writing about Heraclius's campaigns against the Persians in the early seventh century. Thus for the year 622 Theophanes writes:

VERY EARLY REFERENCES TO THEMES

(From Theophanes, *Chronographia*, ed. C. de Boor [Leipzig, 1883] pp. 303 and 325.)

Then he [Heraclius], having set out through the territories of the themes [*choras ton thematon*], assembled the footsoldiers and added to them a new army . . .

Later, writing for the year 627, Theophanes states:

The emperor [Heraclius] ordered George the Turmarch [subordinate to the *strategos*] of the Armeniakon to approach the river and investigate if [the river] Narbas had a ford suitable for crossing.

42.

Introduction. Another of the earliest surviving documents which seems to point to the formation of this new thematic organization (note that the term *thema* is here nowhere *explicitly* stated) is the letter written by Emperor Justinian II (c. 685) to Pope John, confirming the decisions of the Sixth Ecumenical Council (680) which had taken place (in the presence of a papal legate) in Constantinople.

JUSTINIAN II'S LETTER TO POPE JOHN ON THE SIXTH ECUMENICAL COUNCIL

(From J. Mansi, *Sacrorum conciliorum nova et amplissima collectio* [Venice, 1770], vol. 11, cols. 753–54.)

But then we brought in our most holy fathers and most blessed patriarchs along with the representative [*apocrisiarius*] of Your Holiness, and the most holy Senate, and also the metropolitans and bishops, beloved of God, who were residing here in the imperial city, and then the soldiers who are stationed in the sacred palace and also some members of the popular guilds and *excubitors* [palace guards] and even certain members from the armies beloved by God—from the East from the Thracian [theme?] and similarly from the Armenian, also from the army of Italy, then from among the Cabarisiani [Carabisiani], and Septensiani [sp.?], that is from Sardinia [?] and from the African army—who had come to Our Piety.

We ordered that the aforementioned records of the Synodal Acts be brought into our midst and that they be read before all. And with everyone listening diligently, we made all sign these. And all the listeners put written agreements in our hands [affirming] that we ought to defend these [decisions of the Sixth Ecumenical Council] as inviolate, so that there might not arise opportunity at any other time for those who have no fear of God to subvert or corrupt them in any way.

43.

Introduction. The later thematic organization, on the other hand, is relatively well known. This above all due to the informative work, *On the Themes*, written by the tenth-century Emperor Constantine VII Porphyrogenitus (913–59). In the selection which follows (and which begins his book), Constantine, after a few words of explanation, plunges at once into a historical and geographical description of the most important theme, the Anatolikon, located in Asia Minor. The complexity and diffuseness of the explanation is typical of the style of Constantine's book.

THE ANATOLIKON THEME

(From Constantine VII Porphyrogenitus, *De thematibus*, ed. A. Pertusi [Vatican: Biblioteca Apostolica Vaticana, 1952], pp. 59–61.)

This is the work of the Emperor Constantine, son of Leo, on the themes of the empire of the Romans, whence they derive their names and what they mean and their nomenclature, of which the first group of names is from ancient times but the second received their names more recently.

The first theme is called Anatolikon. It seems to me that the titles of the themes did not originate in the manner commonly believed. For not one is ancient nor has any historian mentioned such names as the themes possess today. But formerly and at the beginning there were battalions and legions enrolled according to nation [people from the same place of origin], as for instance the legion of the forty martyrs which was called Thunderbolt, and another, Marmariton, and another, Pisidian, still another, Thessalian; and still others otherwise named. These were often under the authority of a duke and lord or a *praepositus*. And when was this? When the emperors with their army went on a campaign and attacked the enemies of Roman rule, they besieged almost the entire *ecumene* [world], which was in disorder and revolt; these were such men as Julius Caesar, the remarkable Augustus, and the famous Trajan, and among the emperors the great Constantine and Theodosius and their successors who accepted Christianity and showed piety toward God. For it was not proper, it seems, when the emperor was along, for a general to give orders. For the officers were under the command of lords and [civil] commanders, and everything concerning matters of warfare depended on the will of the emperor. The entire army looked to the command only of the emperor. And when the emperors ceased to go on expeditions, they then established *strategoi* and themes. The authority of the Romans extends until today.

But now the Roman Empire is no longer united in East and West, and, having been dismembered during the reign of Heraclius of Libya (since those who ruled after him did not know how best to exercise their authority), they [the Byzantine emperors] divided their own authority and their battalions into smaller segments, and they [the emperors] were Hellenized and discarded the language of their fathers, the Roman [Latin] tongue. The *chiliarchoi* [commanders of 1,000 men], they used to call *longinoi*, and those [with units of] over 100 men, centurions, and what we now call *strategoi*, counts. The name of this theme [to be discussed below] is Greek, and not Roman, and received its name from its geographical location.

On the First Theme, Called Anatolikon. This theme is called Anatolikon, not because it is above and in the direction of the east whence the sun rises, but because it lies east of us who are the inhabitants of Byzantium and Europe. But by the people of Mesopotamia, Syria, and greater Asia, in which live Indians, Ethiopians, and Egyptians, it is called "western" and it is within Asia Minor. . . . In order not to babble and mislead [anyone] about the names of the themes, we shall say only that the truth is as follows: the Anatolikon theme, as we now call it, consists of five peoples. Beginning with the town of Merou [Myra], it is called Phrygia Salutaria, up to Contum. The regions close to Isauria, which extend up to the Taurus, are called Lycaonia. [Constantine then gives the boundaries of the areas of Phrygia, Caria, Pisidia, Lycia.] . . . All the areas which are in the middle and close to, and extending up to, the Taurus Mountains are called the theme of Anatolikon.

44.

Introduction. In the early eleventh century—at the apogee of the Byzantine Empire—there were over thirty themes: twelve in Asia Minor (especially the important Armeniakon and Anatolikon themes), twelve in Europe, two naval themes (based around the Aegean) established for the recruiting of sailors for the imperial navy, and others. The European themes included several which would today constitute parts of modern Greece and the Balkans—Hellas, Dyrrachium (Durazzo), and the Peloponnesus. And with the reconquest of southern Italy by the Emperor Basil I at the end of the ninth century, a new theme, Longobardia (from "Lombard"), was added to the older Calabrian theme. Note in Constantine's account of Longobardia the reference to past events affecting the area, especially the alliance between Emperor Basil I, the Carolingian ruler Louis II, and the pope.

THE THEME LONGOBARDIA

(From Constantine VII Porphyrogenitus, *De thematibus*, ed. A. Pertusi [Vatican: Biblioteca Apostolica Vaticana, 1952], pp. 96–97.)

The theme Longobardia is called in two different ways. By some it is called Longibardia, that is, long-bearded; by others, Longobardia, that is [lacuna]. The land which they inhabit—that is, the Sorrento [area], the metropolis of Naples, the Vesvian mountain [Vesuvius?], and Pyrchanos which is in it—these are colonies of the Greeks. And from the days of Justinian, or rather of Zeno, the Goths took Naples and other nearby cities. . . .

The Franks then were subdued, being co-mingled with the Lombards. And thenceforth until today the name Longobardia is listed as a theme. During the reign of Michael, son of Theophilus, there came from Africa a [Muslim] fleet of 36 galleys under the leadership of Soldan, Saba, and Kalfous. They plundered many cities of Dalmatia and Boutoba and Rosa and lower Dekatera. [These areas asked for and received aid from Constantinople against the raiders. When the Africans heard about the aid sent], they passed, "fleeing" as it were, into Longobardia and besieged the fortress at Bari. Capturing it, they seized the fortified places and all of Longobardia and the remaining forts of Calabria up to Rome, numbering 150. Then Basil, the immortal emperor, coming to the throne by the aid of God, as noted, dispatched an army of cavalry and 100 ships when he learned of all this. He wrote to Louis [Lodouchon], king of the Franks, and to the pope at Rome to join with the [Byzantine] forces. And both of them, responding to the imperial request and uniting with the mounted cavalry and the navy sent by the emperor, joined in battle against the Saracens from Africa and besieged the fortress of Bari, and took even Emir Soldan prisoner. And after he [Louis] had taken him [Soldan] with his Saracens, Louis, king of the Franks [Frangia], departed for home. Then the [Byzantine] emperor took all of Longobardia, and even today it is still ruled by the Byzantines.

45.

Introduction. The more important themes, in particular the Anatolikon and the Armeniakon, lay in Asia Minor, the heartland of the empire. There most of the resources of the state—troops, revenues, and means of communication—were concentrated.

Though this thematic structure concentrated great authority in the hands of a select number of military leaders, the *strategoi* (who sometimes fostered revolts against the emperor), the overall result was more effective control of the empire by the emperors. Administrative lines of communication between the central government and the local administration were tightly maintained. A number of excellent highways across Asia Minor facilitated the rapid movement of troops. All this made for a more smoothly functioning political and military organization under the authority of the emperor, one that could react quickly and decisively to repel invasion from any side.

Because of the grave dangers constantly threatening the empire and the central government's increasing need for troops (which by the late ninth and tenth centuries it could no longer secure through the existing administrative system), the emperors of that period were driven more and more to adopt the practice of assigning imperial or other lands to great magnates in return for military service to be provided by the magnate and his dependents, perhaps including the peasants on the land. The grant of these lands, called *pronoia* (roughly "care of") in Greek, often carried with it immunity from imperial taxation and sometimes also the right to exercise certain administrative privileges performed normally by the imperial government (for example, the right to administer justice among the peasants). This grant of *pronoia* was assigned at first only for the lifetime of the grantee (*pronoiar*). Evidence for what may have been the first recorded case of *pronoia* is found in a passage from the continuation, by John Curopalates, of Cedrenus's redaction of the *Synopsis historion* of John Scylitzes, as well as in a reference by John Zonaras, mentioning that Emperor Constantine IX (mid-eleventh century) assigned estates of the Mangana as *pronoia* to Constantine Leichoudes, the *protovestiarios* and later patriarch of Constantinople.*

A Very Early Grant of Pronoia

(From *Georgius Cedrenus Ioannis Scylitzae ope*, ed. I. Bekker [Bonn, 1839], vol. 2, pp. 644–45.)

Constantine Leichoudes, chief officer and *protovestiarios*, was appointed patriarch in his [Michael Cerularius's] place after a vote was taken on this matter by the metropolitans and prelates and all the people [1059]. He had been a man greatly excelling in imperial and political activities from the time of [Constantine] Monomachus up to the present. And he had acquired a great reputation in his administration of all affairs [of the government] and in the *pronoia* of the Mangana. He had been appointed custodian of the privileges by the aforesaid emperor. And though he had been elected [patriarch] he was not accepted without dissent from the archbishops and patriarchs.

(From John Zonaras, *Epitome historion*, ed. L. Dindorf [Leipzig, 1871], vol. 4, p. 194.)

[Emperor Constantine IX] also granted as *pronoia* the [lands attached to the] Mangana, and regarding matters concerning their immunity [from taxation and other governmental interference], he handed over [written] documents.

*P. Lemerle, *Cinq études sur 11ᵉ siècle byzantine* (Paris, 1977), pp. 273–83, believes rather that the form of this particular grant was not equivalent to later grants of *pronoia* but was related to a grant of *charistikion*. See below on *charistikion*, selections 126 and 127.

46.

Introduction. The penetration of the Seljuk Turks into Asia Minor following the fatal battle of Manzikert (1071) and the weakness of the Byzantine central government (due to a series of incompetent emperors and the lack of effective domestic and foreign policies) brought about the almost total collapse of the thematic structure in Asia Minor. In Europe, too, though the situation was somewhat less serious, the themes which remained ceased to function with their previous effectiveness. In order to remedy the situation, the dynasty of the Comnenoi, beginning with Alexius I (from 1081 onward), restructured the provincial organization along different lines.

The further development of the system of *pronoia* of course played havoc with the thematic organization of the empire. For lands held in *pronoia* were in the later period considered to be immune from the payment of taxes, the operation of imperial administration, and, ultimately, even from the duty of supplying soldiers for the imperial army. This system, which in effect rendered some areas of the empire (especially in Asia Minor and the Peloponnesus) virtually independent of the central government, may be termed "incipient" feudalism, when contrasted to the more developed medieval Western feudalism.

But *pronoia* differed fundamentally from Western feudalism in that it lacked both a hierarchy of feudal lords and the practice of subinfeudation. Lands granted in *pronoia* by the emperor could not, as in the West, in turn be sub-divided by the grantee and then regranted to others. Unlike Western feudal lords, each Byzantine grantee of a *pronoia* (roughly equivalent to a Western fief) owed allegiance directly to the emperor, there being no intermediary ranks of nobles between himself and the highest authority in the land. Thus Western-style feudalism, with its subinfeudation and complex system of vas-salage, was really foreign to the Byzantine world. Yet the very fact that the Byzantine Empire was gradually becoming less centralized, and especially the fact that its political and military systems now rested on what was a "semi-feudal" base, are precisely what facilitated the imposition of a complete Latin feudal system on Byzantine territories after the Latin conquest of 1204. It is notable that the initial opposition of Byzantine pronoiars to the Latin occupa-tion, especially in the Morea, lasted usually only until the new Latin rulers agreed to confirm the Greek magnates in the possession of their *pronoia* (now called fiefs). Evidence of the assimilation of Greek-held lands to the Western feudal system is found in the following legal document drawn up in Venetian-occupied Crete in 1222.

Byzantine Pronoia into Latin Fief

(From F. Cornelius, *Creta sacra* [Modena, reprint, 1971], vol. 2, pp. 265–66.)

In the name of the Father and the Son and the Holy Spirit, Amen. I, Nicholas Sevastos of Monianis and I, Sevastos Omollesinos Mi-chael [both evidently Greeks], and all the others who are inhabitants from the river Petrea up to the place which is called Actus, acknowledge that from you, our highest and noble Lord Bartholomew Gradonigo by order of our most high doge of Venice [and of] the duke of Crete, and from the smaller and larger councils [the Venetian Senate and Grand Council], we have received the area from the river Petrea up to the place called Actus as a fief [*feudum*] through the beneficence of the doge of Venice. We swear, and those who have not now sworn obedience to our lord the duke must swear, that we will be faithful and loyal to the honor of the doge and of his successors, and likewise to the duke of Crete.

We will keep all Venetians, both going and coming, safe and secure without any taxation [*datio*], and we will consider the friends of the Venetians as our friends, and their enemies as our enemies. We will keep true obedience and as much as we are able we will make the Anatolians [Byzantines] flee and place them outside this area, unless they will remain by your order. If they themselves wish to come over to your will and obedience they will hold lands from Petrea up to the head of the Selmon [river]. We will make war on them as much as we are able until they turn to the obedience of Your Highness and we will give praise and pounds of *denarii*, and as much wax as we ought to supply we will supply by the month of September. Concerning those serfs [*villani*, i.e. Greek peasants] who have been found belonging to the area of Rethimno, we will return them to those who hold fiefs there and similarly we will return all serfs of the commune.

47.

Introduction. By the final Palaeologan period of the empire (1261–1453), the Byzantine state, though still clinging theoretically to the old ideal of imperial unity—the one Roman Empire—in reality became a collection of semi-independent principalities under the virtually nominal authority of the emperor. In the following passage from the *Historia* of Nicephorus Gregoras, the conflict between the lingering Byzantine ideal of imperial unity and the strong centrifugal tendency inherent in the development of the *pronoia* system is clearly seen. In the fourteenth century, the tendency toward fragmentation was further exacerbated by the Latin-born empress of Byzantium, Eirene (Yolande of Montferrat), who went so far as to propose to her husband, Emperor Andronicus II (1282–1328), the adoption of what seemed to be the Latin system of royal inheritance, the *appanage*, as it was called in France.

A. A "LATIN" HERITAGE

(From Nicephorus Gregoras, *Byzantina historia*, ed. I. Bekker and L. Schopen [Bonn, 1835], vol. 1, pp. 233–34.)

Eirene, the wife of Emperor Andronicus, a woman ambitious by nature, desired that her sons and her descendants inherit in perpetuity, as successors, the imperial rule of the Romans, and that the imperial authority preserve her memory as immortal through the names of her descendants. Even more unusual, she desired, not according to the fashion of monarchy as is the custom prevailing among the Romans since antiquity, but in conformity with Latin practice, that [all of Andronicus's] sons divide the cities and provinces of the Romans among themselves, and that each son rule a portion, as if they were dividing a private inheritance and personal possession, and as if the empire were something passed down to them from their fathers in accordance with the laws concerning the property and possessions of vulgar people, and in the same manner transmitted in turn to their children and descendants. She proposed this because she was by birth a Latin and, having learned of this innovation from them, she wished to introduce it among the Roman people.

Introduction. The next two selections reveal the plans of two Byzantine emperors of the Palaeologan period to bring about—for personal reasons—a division of imperial territory among members of the imperial family.

B. MICHAEL VIII'S PLAN FOR HIS SONS

(From Nicephorus Gregoras, *Byzantina historia*, vol. 1, p. 187.)

For Emperor Michael VIII desired, and had for a long time cherished in his heart, the aim of cutting off the area around Thessalonika and Macedonia from the Roman Empire as a whole and giving it as a personal domain and private "empire" to his [younger] son [Constantine Porphyrogenitus]. And had not death anticipated him and removed him from the midst of men, his plans would possibly have emerged into the light as accomplished fact. But since God, so it seems, did not approve, the ill-starred project came to an end.

C. Cantacuzene's Plan for Division

(From John VI Cantacuzene, *Historia* [Bonn, 1832], vol. 3, pp. 280–81.)

For these reasons the Emperor Cantacuzene [the writer himself] was constrained, as it were, to appoint his son Matthew as emperor. But he had a notion, even after the public proclamation of his son, to cut off a portion of the Roman Empire and turn it over to him—a portion which the son might rule only for the duration of his life. When he died, however, he would not be permitted to leave a successor. Rather he was to return it again to the control of the Roman Emperor, his [Cantacuzene's] son-in-law John [V Palaeologus], if he was still alive, or to Andronicus, the latter's son. Cantacuzene wished, when the war against him would be over, to recall his son-in-law and to leave to him the entire Roman Empire, putting aside political affairs and seeking to acquire divine grace through the pursuit of wisdom for the rest of his life. But he wished to do these things later.

F.
CIVIL LAW

48.

Introduction. As the continuation of the Roman Empire, Byzantium prided itself on being ruled by law. Indeed, the foremost monument of Roman law, the codification of Justinian, is at the same time the first and primary source of Byzantine law. It consists of (1) the *Codex*, a collection of the imperial edicts of Justinian's predecessors; (2) the *Digest* (or *Pandects*), a compendium of interpretations of the law by leading Roman jurists; and (3) the *Institutes*, a brief handbook of law for judges and students of the law. Finally, the *Codex* was later supplemented by (4) the *Novellae* ("new edicts") issued by Justinian and his successors. This multi-volume corpus of law (later called the *Corpus juris civilis*) formed the basis for all subsequent Byzantine legislation and jurisprudence.

The following lengthy selection, drawn from Justinian's edict promulgating the first edition of the *Digest* (530) and addressed to its principal architect, the quaestor [chief legal official] Tribonian, indicates something of Justinian's attitude toward law (one shared by his successors): a belief in law as the regulator of society, and a concern that the empire be ruled by stable and just laws. In this passage Justinian also gives instructions for the selection and editing of the opinions of famous Roman jurists on the law.

PLAN OF THE *DIGEST*

(Translated by S. P. Scott, *The Civil Law* [Cincinnati: Central Trust Company, 1932], vol. 2, pp. 179–82.)

Therefore, since there is nothing to be found in all things so worthy of attention as the authority of the law, which properly regulates all affairs both divine and human and expels all injustice: We have found the entire arrangement of the law which has come down to us from the foundation of the City of Rome and the times of Romulus, to be so confused that it is extended to an infinite length and is not within the grasp of human capacity; and hence We were first induced to begin by examining what had been enacted by former most venerated princes, to correct their constitutions, and make them more easily understood; to the end that being included in a single Code, and having had removed all that is superfluous in resemblance and all iniquitous discord, they may afford to all men the ready assistance of their true meaning.

After having concluded this work and collected it all in a single volume under Our illustrious name, raising Ourself above small and comparatively insignificant matters, We have hastened to attempt the most complete and thorough amendment of the entire law, to collect and revise the whole body of Roman jurisprudence, and to assemble in one book the scattered treatises of so many authors; which no one else has heretofore ventured to hope for or to expect. . . .

Therefore We order you [Tribonian] to read and revise the books relating to the Roman law drawn up by the jurists of antiquity, upon whom the most venerated princes conferred authority to write and interpret the same; so that from these all the substance may be collected, and, as far as may be possible, there shall remain no laws either similar to or inconsistent with one another, but that there may be compiled from them a summary which will take the place of all. . . .

You shall divide the entire law into fifty books, and into a certain number of titles following, as far as may be convenient for you, the arrangement of Our Code, as well as that of the Perpetual Edict, so that nothing may be omitted from the above mentioned collection; and that all the ancient law which has been in a confused condition for almost fourteen hundred years shall be embraced in the said fifty books, and this ancient law, purified by Us, shall be, so to speak, surrounded by a wall, and shall have nothing beyond it. All legal authors shall possess equal authority, and no preference shall be given to any, because all of them are neither superior nor inferior to one another in every respect, but some are of greater or less weight as far as certain subjects are concerned.

But you must neither base your judgment as to what is best and most equitable upon the number of authors, as perhaps on some points the opinion of one who is inferior may be preferable to that of many and greater ones; and therefore you must not entirely reject what was formerly included in the notes to [the jurist] Aemilius Papinianus, taken from Ulpianus, Paulus, and Marcianus, although the said notes have hitherto had but little force, on account of the distinction of the most renowned Papinianus; but if you perceive that anything from them is required to supplement the labors of Papinianus, that man of eminent genius, or necessary for their interpretation, you must not hesitate, after having selected it, to give it the force of law. . . .

We desire you to be careful with regard to the following: if you find in the old books anything that is not suitably arranged, superfluous, or incomplete, you must remove all superfluities, supply what is lacking, and present the entire work in regular form, and with as excellent an appearance as possible. You must also observe the following, namely: if you find anything which the ancients have inserted in their old laws or constitutions that is incorrectly worded, you must correct this, and place it in its proper order, so that it may appear to be true, expressed in the best language, and written in this way in the first place; so that by comparing it with the orignal text, no one can venture to call in question as defective what you have selected and arranged. Since by an ancient law, which is styled the *Lex Regia*, all the rights and power of the Roman people were transferred to the Emperor, We do not derive Our authority from that of other different compilations, but wish that it shall all be entirely Ours, for how can antiquity abrogate our laws? . . .

Therefore, in no part of the aforesaid treatise, shall there be any place for *antinomia*, . . . but there must be such conformity and consistency therein that there will be no opportunity for contradiction.

We desire, as has already been stated, that all repetition shall also be banished from this compilation, and whatever has been provided by the most Sacred Constitutions which We have included in our Code We do not permit again to be considered as a part of the ancient law, since the sanction of the Imperial Constitutions is sufficient to confer authority upon them, unless perhaps this should take place either for the purpose of division, or supplement, or in order to secure greater exactness; and even this must be done very rarely, lest where this repetition occurs, something thorny may grow up in this meadow.

However, by no means do We allow you to insert into your treatise laws that appearing in ancient works have now fallen into desuetude, since We only desire that legal procedure to prevail which has been most frequently employed, or which long custom has established in this benign City. . . .

Therefore We order that everything shall be governed by these two works, one that of the Imperial Constitutions, the other, that of the law to be interpreted and compiled in a future Code; so that if anything else should be promulgated by Us in the form of an elementary treatise, the uninstructed mind of the student, being nourished by simple matters, may the more readily be conducted to a knowledge of the higher principles of jurisprudence.

We desire Our compilation which, God willing, is to be drawn up by you, to bear the name of the Digest or Pandects, and no person learned in the law shall dare hereafter to add any commentaries thereto, and to confuse by his own prolixity the abridgement of the aforesaid work, as was done in former times, for almost all law was thrown into confusion by the opposite opinions of those interpreting it; but it is sufficient merely by indexes, and a skilful use of titles which are called *paratitla*, to give such warning that no change may take place in the interpretation of the same.

49.

Introduction. The following two selections are drawn from Justinian's *Institutes*, or handbook of law (533). The first, taken from the preamble, provides the reasons for its compilation; the second, drawn from the body of the *Institutes*, explains the various types of law.

A. THE PRINCIPLES OF LAW FROM THE INSTITUTES

(Translated by S. P. Scott, The Civil Law [Cincinnati: Central Trust Company, 1932], vol. 2, pp. 3–4.)

This [compilation of *Codex* and *Digest*] having been concluded through the Grace of God, We summoned the illustrious Tribonian, Master and former Quaestor of Our Sacred Palace, along with Theophilus and

Dorotheus, eminent men and professors, whose skill, familiarity with the laws, and fidelity in obeying Our orders We have proved on many occasions, and especially directed them to draw up Institutes by Our authority, and with Our advice, that you [youth desirous of learning the laws] may be able to learn the first principles of the law, not from ancient fables, but acquire them from the Imperial Splendor; so that your ears as well as your minds may absorb nothing that is useless or incorrect, but whatever is in accordance with reason in all things.

Therefore, after the completion of the fifty books of the Digest or Pandects, in which all the ancient law has been collected, and which We have caused to be compiled by the said distinguished personage Tribonian and other eminent and most illustrious men, We have ordered these Institutes to be divided into the following four books, that they may constitute the first elements of the entire science of jurisprudence.

These Institutes collected from all those of the ancients and especially from the Commentaries of Our Gaius, embracing not only what is contained in his Institutes but also those of his work relating to daily transactions and compiled from those of many others, the three learned men aforesaid submitted to Us, and, after having read and examined them, We have accorded to them the full authority of Our Constitution.

B. Concerning Natural Law, the Law of Nations, and the Civil Law

(From *The Civil Law*, vol. 2, pp. 5–7.)

Natural Law is that which nature has taught to all animals, for this law is not peculiar to the human race, but applies to all creatures which originate in the air, on the earth, and in the sea. Hence arises the union of the male and the female which we designate marriage; and hence are derived the procreation and the education of children: for we see that other animals also act as though endowed with knowledge of this law.

The Civil Law and the Law of Nations are divided as follows. All peoples that are governed by laws and customs make use of the law which is partly peculiar to themselves and partly pertaining to all men; for what each people has established for itself is peculiar to that State, and is styled the Civil Law, being, as it were, the especial law of that individual commonwealth. But the law which natural reason has established among all mankind and which is equally observed among all peoples, is called the Law of Nations, as being that which all nations make use of. The Roman people also employ a law which is in part peculiar to them and in part common to all men. We propose to set forth their distinctions in their proper places. . . .

Our Law, which We make use of, is either written or unwritten, just as among the Greeks written and unwritten laws exist. The written law consists of the Statutes, the *Plebiscita*, the Decrees of the Senate, the Decisions of the Emperors, the Orders of the Magistrates and the Answers of Jurisconsults.

A Statute is what the Roman people have established as the result of an interrogatory of a senatorial magistrate, for example, a consul. The *Plebiscitum* is what the plebeians have established upon the interrogatory of a plebeian magistrate, for instance, a tribune. Plebeians differ from the people as a species does from a genus; for all citizens, including even patricians, and senators, are understood by the word people, and by the term plebeians all other citizens, exclusive of patricians and senators, are designated. *Plebiscita* have had the same force as statutes since the passage of the *Lex Hortensia*.

A Decree of the Senate is what the Senate orders and establishes, for since the Roman people have increased in numbers to such an extent that it is difficult for them to be convoked in an assembly for the purpose of adopting a law, it has seemed advisable for the Senate to be consulted instead of the people.

Whatever is approved by the sovereign has also the force of law, because by the *Lex Regia*, from whence his power is derived, the people have delegated to him all their jurisdiction and authority. Therefore, whatever the Emperor establishes by means of a Rescript or decrees as a magistrate, or commands by an Edict, stands as law, and these are called Constitutions. Some of these are personal and are not considered as precedents, because the sovereign does not wish them to be such; for any favor he grants on account of merit, or where he inflicts punishment upon anyone or affords him unusual assistance, this affects only the individual concerned; the others, however, as they are of general application unquestionably are binding upon all. . . .

The unwritten law is that which usage has confirmed, for customs long observed and sanctioned by the consent of those who employ them, resemble law.

50.

Introduction. Justinian's great codification remained the fundamental law of the empire, but later emperors occasionally attempted to revise and recodify the body of law to reflect changing social needs—as well as for reasons of dynastic pride. The first revision, the *Ecloga*, a condensed practical handbook of law, was issued during the Isaurian dynasty, probably to make the law more readily available to provincial judges far from the capital and its more sophisticated legal traditions. In the words of the new code's sponsor, Emperor Leo III, the *Ecloga* was "a selection of laws, made in an abridgement by Leo and Constantine [Leo's son], our wise and pious emperors, from the *Institutes, Digest, Code,* and *Novellae* of the great Justinian . . . and issued with a view to greater humanity."

A. FROM THE PREFACE TO THE *ECLOGA*

(Reprinted with permission of Bowes & Bowes at The Bodley Head, from E. Freshfield, trans., *A Manual of Roman Law: The "Ecloga"* [Cambridge, 1926], pp. 67–68.)

Whence, busied with such cares and watching with sleepless mind the discovery of those things which please God, and are conducive to the public interests, preferring Justice to all things terrestrial as the promise of things celestial, and as being, by the power of Him who is worshipped in her, sharper than any sword against foes; knowing moreover that the laws enacted by previous Emperors have been written in many books and being aware that the sense thereof is to some difficult to understand, to others absolutely unintelligible, and especially to those who do not reside in this our imperial God-protected city, we have called the most illustrious Patrician, our Quaestor, and our most illustrious patricians, and our most illustrious consulars and comptrollers, and others who have the fear of God, and we have ordered that all these books should be collected in our Palace; and having examined all with careful attention, going through both the contents of those books, and our own enactments, we considered it right that the decisions in many cases and the laws of contract and several penalties of crimes should be repeated more lucidly and minutely to ensure a eusynoptic [good, overall] knowledge of the force of such pious laws, and to facilitate the decision of such causes clearly, and to ensure a just prosecution of the guilty and to restrain and correct those who have a natural propensity to evil doing.

Commentary. Although the *Ecloga* was primarily intended as an abridgment of Justinian's law, nevertheless, there are several modifications to be noted in it. These have led some scholars to term the *Ecloga* the first law code to be influenced by Christian principles. This influence is apparent in the following list of criminal punishments, taken from the *Ecloga*. Although the frequently mentioned punishment of mutilation might offend modern sensibilities, it is important to note that such measures often replaced capital punishment and were considered to provide a time for penance, thus presumably allowing the wrongdoer to secure the forgiveness of God.

B. The *Ecloga* on Sexual Crimes

(Reprinted with permission of Bowes & Bowes at The Bodley Head, from E. Freshfield, trans., *A Manual of Roman Law: The "Ecloga"* [Cambridge, 1926], pp. 108–12.)

1. A married man who commits adultery shall by way of correction be flogged with twelve lashes; and whether rich or poor he shall pay a fine.

2. An unmarried man who commits fornication shall be flogged with six lashes.

3. A person who has carnal knowledge of a nun shall, upon the footing that he is debauching the Church of God, have his nose slit, because he committed wicked adultery with her who belonged to the Church; and she on her side must take heed lest similar punishment be reserved to her.

4. Anyone who, intending to take in marriage a woman who is his goddaughter in Salvation-bringing baptism, has carnal knowledge of her without marrying her, and being found guilty of the offence shall, after being exiled, be condemned to the same punishment meted out for other adultery, that is to say, both the man and the woman shall have their noses slit.

5. The husband who is cognizant of, and condones, his wife's adultery shall be flogged and exiled, and the adulterer and the adulteress shall have their noses slit.

6. Persons committing incest, parents and children, children and parents, brothers and sisters, shall be punished capitally with the sword. Those in other relationships who corrupt one another carnally, that is father and daughter-in-law, son and stepmother, father-in-law and daughter-in-law, brother and his brother's wife, uncle and niece, nephew and aunt, shall have their noses slit. And likewise he who has carnal knowledge with two sisters and even cousins.

7. If a woman is carnally known and, becoming pregnant, tries to produce miscarriage [abortion], she shall be whipped and exiled.

8. Those who are guilty whether actively or passively of committing unnatural offences shall be capitally punished with the sword. If he who commits the offence passively, is found to be under twelve years old, he shall be pardoned on the ground of youthful ignorance of the offence committed.

9. Those guilty of "abominable crime" [homosexuality] shall be emasculated.

51.

Introduction. The *Ecloga* was rejected by the succeeding Macedonian dynasty (ninth to early eleventh century), who considered the Isaurian emperors, as supporters of Iconoclasm (on Iconoclasm, see selections 111–15), to be heretics. The Macedonian emperors therefore began promulgation of a new code of law. The beginnings of this new codification are to be found in the compilation of two small manuals of law, intended to be the basis for the complete new corpus. These two were the *Epanagoge* (which was never officially promulgated but nonetheless remained influential) and the *Procheiron*. (On the *Epanagoge*, see selections 99b and 118 below.)

PROEMIUM FROM THE *PROCHEIRON* (870–79)

(From *Imperatorum Basilii, Constantini et Leonis Prochiron*, ed. Zacharia von Lingenthal [Heidelberg, 1837], pp. 6–8.)

We therefore . . . have ordered that work be studiously undertaken concerning the law(s) (since many had sought to appeal to this law), so that none of the things that come to us might be judged irrationally; for, on account of the infinite multitude of cases as well as changes of human condition, the vicissitudes of customs, and the variety of means, the passage of laws has grown to immense size. As a result, the loving zeal [of lawmakers] has brought irritation for men; because among those who have devoted effort to jurisprudence, several have made things larger and broader, others have subjected certain matters to emendation and have even omitted things, condemning them to perpetual silence.

Since this teaching of law is necessary for all, what were we able to devise in order to carry out the desire of men and render the teaching of the law easier? Nothing else than that, after the multitude of existing laws were scrutinized, we selected out of the individual books [of Justinian] the things that are necessary and useful and frequently referred to, and we wrote them under definite headings in this manual of law, permitting nothing to be excluded from among them which ought to be known to everyone. And so we have collected the body of law into this *Procheiron Nomon*, we have translated the collection of Roman [legal] pronouncements into Greek, we have restored the laws which have been adulterated, we have changed that which was necessary to correct for the better, and especially, concerning those things about which laws had not been promulgated, we have striven to provide new laws. . . . And having collected all these we have separated the entire law into forty titles.

52.

Introduction. The ultimate result of the legal reform of the Macedonian emperors was the sixty-volume work known as the *Basilica*, promulgated by Leo VI (886–912). In this code the emperors pointedly said that their purpose was "to return to the principles of Justinianic law." Indeed, although some scholars recently have shown that there are some innovations in the *Basilica* as compared with Justinian's work, yet most of the compilation is remarkably faithful to its predecessor.

The *Basilica* is composed of sixty titles, dealing with all major aspects of civil law; but in contrast to the Justinianic code, there is no formal division into *Codex, Digest,* and *Novellae.* All now is coherently integrated by subject into sixty titles, and commentary from several post-Justinianic legal scholars is also included. It is hardly surprising that the *Basilica* rapidly almost completely supplanted the Justinianic corpus. Although the fact that the work is in Greek seems to differentiate it from the Latin work of Justinian, most of the *Basilica* seems in fact to be derived from Greek translations of the Justinianic corpus— translations in common usage as early as the early seventh century.

The following selection, including much material from one of the titles of the *Basilica*, gives a clear overview of the organization and usefulness of the code. The first two sections are drawn verbatim from the *Digest,* while the remaining sections are faithfully paraphrased from book 4 of the *Codex.* Finally, we have included one of the numerous scholia by the noted sixth-century Byzantine commentator Theodore—scholia we know were cited as authoritative shortly after publication of the *Basilica.*

SELECTION FROM THE *BASILICA* (CONCERNING EXCHANGES)

(Translated by A. Cappel and D. Geanakoplos from the *Basilica,* ed. G. Heimbach [Leipzig, 1836], vol. 2, pp. 377–79, from bk. 20, title 3.)

I. (The jurisconsult Paul) Exchange differs from sale in that in a sale the purchaser is constrained to give the owner a sum of money, but for the seller it suffices to turn over the thing, to agree on [the terms of] its surrender, and to be without deceit. And if the object is not claimed [by the purchaser], he [the seller] owes nothing. But in an exchange it is necessary that each party receive ownership. And if one of the things given is claimed in the exchange, the action takes place in fact. On the one hand, sale without consideration stands by itself, and the other [types of property transfer] have their own names, such as lease or mandate. But if something is given which does not belong [to the one giving it up] there is no exchange. . . .

II. (The same jurisconsult) In an exchange, just as in a sale, a slave ought to be given in good health, and not under obligation for theft or punishment.

III. If someone receives something* and gives something else in return for it, for example, one who has received clothing gives a slave, this is not in itself an exchange. It is befitting that we inquire whether the one who had the clothing wished to sell it, and the one who had the slave wished to buy clothing, and whether—when they reached agreement concerning the price—it seemed more pleasing to give an object [i.e., the slave] in place of the price, or whether from the beginning they had no idea of making a sale, but wanted to exchange possessions. If we should find that he who gave the object [clothing] had wished to sell it and in place of the price took something else, a contract of this type is a sale and purchase. Whence, when eviction follows, if it is a sale, it is necessary to file suit under [the laws concerning] sales, since a thing which has been sold has been evicted [taken away]. But if there should be an exchange, [the injured party] is able to demand the restitution of the thing [which he gave to the other party] in an action *praescriptis verbis*.[†]

*[Scholium of Theodore on this phrase:] "When someone gives an object, not money, for something else, if he gave it in place of the price and it has been evicted, a legal action concerning the contract of purchase is fitting for the one who received it concerning that which is subject to dispute. But if the things are given not in the place of the price but for reason of exchange, [the injured party] is bound [to use] an action *praescriptis verbis*."

IV. An exchange, when it is in good faith, is similar to purchase and sale.

VI. If I will have given something to someone by reason of exchange and he will not give that which had been agreed to be given to me, and will sell that which had been given him by me, I have no legal recourse against the purchaser. But against him [who sold the property], I have action *praescriptis verbis*, demanding that he either present to me what had been agreed upon, or restore what I had given him.

IX. Purchases and sales are not concluded in terms of objects, but ought to be constituted [in terms of] a set amount of money. Wherefore if someone will give corn for the sake of receiving oil and the oil has not been received . . . he is able to sue for recovering the corn which was given.

† 1. *Praescriptis verbis* refers to a special type of litigation concerning "uncertain" contracts, i.e., implied or of an unusual form.

53.

Introduction. The *Basilica* theoretically remained in force until the end of the empire as the official collection of civil law. Nevertheless, in practice, earlier codifications did not lose all their authority, as judges in the more remote provinces would tend to use whatever law books they had at hand. (The *Basilica* with their scholia filled many volumes of text and would not be easily available everywhere.) Also, there was a whole body of law, the imperial chrysobulls *after* Justinian, which remained virtually unincorporated into the *Basilica*. Thus the more recent imperial edicts were sometimes incorporated into other manuals designed for provincial judges. Such manuals included simplified explanatory versions of the *Basilica* such as the anonymous treatise *Peri pekoulion* (*On Property*) and the manual the *Peira* (*Experience*), the last based on the interpretations of the noted judge Eustathius Romanus of the mid-eleventh century.

THE *PEIRA* ON THIEVES

(From the *Peira*, in J. and P. Zepos, eds., *Jus graecoromanum* [Athens, 1931], vol. 4, p. 227.)

If someone steals private property from a church, he is considered a thief and is not to be punished as one who has committed a sacrilege.

Whatever a thief, on the one hand, will steal openly, that is, if he is caught in the act, he shall be subject to a fourfold action and he shall make such restitution. But if he steals clandestinely, that is, at night, not being caught in the act but being convicted, he shall make twofold restitution.

[Eustathius's quotation from a law:] "Those who steal other people's deeds cannot use them as proof of ownership. For the possession of these does not give legitimacy to the one who has possession but to him to whom the content of the document pertains."

54.

Introduction. In the last Byzantine period (as in earlier centuries) there appeared synopses and handbooks to aid judges, but these were compiled by private individuals, without official sanction. Some of these collections, such as the *Hexabiblos* put out by Constantine Harmenopoulos in the fourteenth century, virtually supplanted the bulkier and more unwieldy *Basilica* collection (to judge from a comparison of the number of surviving manuscripts). Many of the legal complexities in the *Basilica* were removed or simplified even more in the *Hexabiblos*. We quote below from the interesting section on witnesses in the *Hexabiblos*. Note the repetitions and sometimes convoluted turns of phrase typical of Byzantine legal expression.

THE *HEXABIBLOS* OF HARMENOPOULOS ON WITNESSES (1345)

(Translated by M. Varouxakis and D. Geanakoplos from Constantine Harmenopoulos, *Manuale legum sive hexibiblos*, ed. G. Heimbach [Leipzig, 1851], pp. 98 and 100.)

1. Let witnesses be worthy of belief, provided they are not common people, or of the poor class, or utterly obscure. It is necessary that they be of good reputation with respect to honor[s] or military service, or [that they be persons] employed or [possessing] a skill. Witnesses who have no education can, if necessary, be tortured.

2. Let the witnesses testify concerning documents relating to debts; let them say whether they were present when the debt was paid or when it was legally deposited in the account of the man to whom the debt was owed. And there must be no less than five witnesses called [to testify] in such a case.

3. In the case that witnesses contradict each other or other witnesses, then let the judge accept the [testimony of the] more worthy of them, and cast blame on the suspect persons if they [the latter] appear to have committed a crime.

4. Let the judge send the testimony from city to city for the purpose of summoning witnesses. And this should be legally done in the provinces, before the presiding judge, and in Constantinople, before the holy judges.

5. In criminal cases it is absolutely necessary that witnesses be present personally, not only their voices [i.e., their testimony]. . . . Dignity and faith are required and [good] habits and gravity, so that there may be no contradictions [in testimony].

6. Regarding witnesses, their worth and good faith should be examined along with their moral habits and uprightness [of character] so that their opponents may not speak out against them when they testify.

7. Regarding every witness, it is necessary to seek out whether he is honorable and free of blame, or dishonest and vituperative, wealthy or destitute, so that he may not overlook something in order to profit, whether [he be] a friend to the one involved in the case or an enemy of the one against whom he is testifying. For if we have no suspicion of him he may [then] act as a witness. Regarding these matters, let the judge rule whether they shall simply testify or may present a prepared speech; and if they [the witnesses] respond to the question with probability, let the judge then decide which evidence should be accepted.

8. In a case of selling and buying and of other contracts, what is required for a good case is good faith and reliability on the part of witnesses. If a witness is proved to be unacceptable, the document is invalid. In the case of witnesses testifying regarding violence or insults, or in similar cases, it is not required [that] the conduct [or] the character of the witness or his way of life be examined by the magistrate, as the magistrate said [*hos ho Magistros elegen*].

9. Actors, fighters in public spectacles, dancers, and those who are accustomed to be on the stage, as well as those who have been condemned as calumniators, adulterers, flatterers, or thieves, or who have committed some other crime, and also the very poor [and] women and children not of legal age are forbidden to testify [as witnesses]. Yet women may act as witnesses, but only when the appearance of men is forbidden. There are also other persons who may testify if they so wish, but who may not be compelled to do so, such as the *protospatharios* and his superiors and the priests and those who are involved in [matters of] the holy liturgy. Priests neither willingly nor unwillingly may serve as witnesses, but only at their place of residence and if the case concerns holy [ecclesiastical] matters.

10. A heretic or a Jew cannot testify against an Orthodox but [they] can testify against one another.

11. An employee cannot testify in behalf of his employer, and the judge has ruled that this testimony must be free of suspicion [i.e., of personal interest], and a friend is not clear of suspicion. An employee with any interests involved is therefore unacceptable.

12. Regarding all those called to be witnesses in a case involving high treason, when the situation demands it, let them be tortured, both those under fourteen and those over fourteen years of age.

13. We accept [as valid] the testimony of witnesses in a hearing regarding questions of boundaries [of property already built] and of new buildings.

14. Let witnesses be preferred to documentary evidence because they can be

questioned by the judges personally regarding crimes; and he who is not able to demonstrate [prove] what he claims, let him be exiled.

(15. Scholium [a note added later to the manuscript]: The [ancient] Roman people preferred documentary evidence over witnesses, whereas now [the testimony of] witnesses is preferred over documents.

16. Different is the authority of the witness who is present, and different the authority of one whose testimony is read from a document. If anyone wishes to make use of witnesses, let him pay them.

17. Witnesses are required to remain only fifteen days in court in trials of a financial nature.

18. Father and son and two brothers may act as witnesses in the same case since there is no harm if several witnesses appear from one household in a case.

19. If it happens that a witness from the arena or similar persons be admitted, they are to be believed only when tortured.

20. If all the witnesses are of the same integrity and reputation but are not in agreement among themselves, the stronger party is not always to be believed. When any suspicion of friendship or enmity is lacking, the case is [to be] decided by the conscience of the judge and [on the basis of] the evidence.

55.

Introduction. A very important judge in the Byzantine legal system of the Palaeologan period was the so-called "general" or "universal" judge, usually an ecclesiastic. As part of the judicial reforms undertaken by Emperor Andronicus III in the early fourteenth century to remove corruption, the oath of the "general" judge was established.

THE OATH OF THE "GENERAL" JUDGE (1329)

(Translated by M. Varouxakis and D. Geanakoplos from P. Lemerle, "Le juge général des Grecs et la réforme judiciaire d'Andronic III," in *Mémorial L. Petit: Mélanges d'histoire et d'archéologie byzantine* [Bucharest, 1948], pp. 297–98.)

Since I was requested by our Mighty and Holy Lord and Emperor that as soon as I would be elected "general judge of the Romans," I would at the same time personally affirm and take an oath—which is befitting and proper to me as an ecclesiastic by God's grace in the same way as the Most Holy Metropolitan of Apro, the highly honored general judge of the Romans, gave assurance, and also as my other colleagues, the general judges, were required [to do], very willingly providing written affirmation in accordance with their status and condition—so now do I swear and bind myself as a religious [ecclesiastic], so to say, in the responsibility and execution [of my duties], that the aforesaid Most Holy Bishop of Apro, the All-praised and Universal Judge of the Romans, my colleague, according to the oath [affirmation] that is provided on the holy and divine canons by all the ecclesiastics for these purposes—that I maintain and observe at all times all the provisions of this written oath and affirmation [taken] by him and by my other colleagues, the general judges of the Romans, not because of any genuine fear of the high rank of any persons, nor on account of humility or friendship or enmity or sorrow or sympathy for any person under judgment, nor on account of any carelessness or laziness on my part, nor for any other possible reason that might arise or [that will] infringe on the authority that is dependent on judgments [legal rulings] and the laws.

I will try with all my power to remain free of all corruption and I will take care that all people around me stay aloof from any case, and if anybody around me should be found [trying to influence me], I will take care to correct the situation and I will get rid of him as if such a thing had never happened in any respect, whether it involved a servant or friend or relative. I will take responsibility for this before the Lord—I take this pledge before our Most Holy Ecumenical Patriarch and the Holy Circle [the Standing Synod] of the holy bishops: that I will take care to observe the holy canons, with all straightforwardness [and] truth will I execute [my duties]. [I will] struggle and be vigilant in behalf of all the people, whether archons or common men, rich or poor, enemies or friends. I will judge fairly and without corruption and with no personal interest, seeking only the vindication of a wronged party in accordance with the authority that is granted to me by the holy imperial edicts [*prostagmata*]. If I do not keep these promises, or if I neglect [to observe] any of the written laws, I will be guilty in my soul before the Holy Gospels and the honor that has been bestowed upon me by my colleague in [rendering] judgment, the Holy Bishop of Apro. And if ever I see that the vindication of any wronged party is not taken seriously and remains without authority and validity, I shall, as is the wish of our Mighty and Holy Lord the Emperor, speak out in accordance with the holy and imperial edict once issued on that matter, until I see that the vindication of the unjustly judged is observed and carried out. And if I do not succeed in carrying out the will of our Mighty and Holy Emperor and Ruler, I will at once resign from [the position of] general judge of the Romans, and thus absolve myself of any guilt.

56.

Introduction. Although Roman law prevailed throughout the entire history of the empire, there are a few indications that certain Western medieval ("barbarian") ways of proving guilt or innocence were resorted to in Byzantium, though on very rare occasions. In the following passage, taken from the *History* of the Byzantine scholar Acropolites, the young Michael Palaeologus (future emperor and restorer of Constantinople), accused of treason by Emperor John Vatatzes of Nicaea, is asked to clear himself not through the Roman legal process, but, surprisingly, by recourse to the Western-style judicial ordeal: first, the ordeal by fire, then the ordeal by combat. (The reason for proceeding in this fashion was that evidently no official charge of treason had been raised against Michael; the accusation against him was based on rumor.)

TRIAL BY ORDEAL (1253)

(From George Acropolites, *Historia*, ed. A. Heisenberg [Leipzig, 1903], pp. 95–98.)

Now the entire inquiry reverted to Michael Palaeologus himself. Then some, as if to judge him, said: "Since certain questionable words have been spoken against you, you must rid yourself of suspicion by some 'wonder-working act,' that is, through the ordeal by hot iron." But Michael—and he had truth on his side—said: "If there were anyone who would accuse me [directly], I would fight him and show he is lying. But since there is no accuser, what am I being judged for? I am really not a person who can perform miracles. If a red-hot iron touches the hand of a living man, I do not see but that it would burn him, unless he be sculpted from stone by Phidias or Praxiteles,* or fashioned from bronze."

Then the emperor took Michael aside alone, and I [Acropolites] heard him say: "You were born a nobleman from noble parents. Therefore, you should understand and do whatever is necessary for your reputation and faith; and since there is no counterproof from the witnesses in your behalf, you must demonstrate the truth by the ordeal of hot iron." Michael, very bravely and courageously (like a hero in a painting of a battle), said: "O Lord, I do not know why this ordeal is called holy. I am a sinful man, and I cannot perform such miracles; but if the metropolitan [who was present], a man of God, would advise me to perform this, let him then first put on his entire prelate's robes, as if he were about to enter the holy sanctuary [of a church] in order to meet with God. Then with his own hands let him take up the iron, by which you lay hold of the sacrifice of God, the body of our Lord Jesus Christ, which is offered for the world and is always done by you and the priests and prelates. And with these own hands of yours, put into my hand the iron. I have faith in Christ the Lord that this will remove every sin of mine and that the miracle will reveal the truth."

After Michael had spoken thus, the metropolitan replied: "O noble young man, this is not a part of our Roman institutions or even of our ecclesiastical traditions or our laws, nor was it received earlier from our divine and holy canons. The practice is barbaric and unknown to us, and it is done only by imperial command." Michael replied: "You are a prelate of God. If I myself were born of a barbarian race and reared in barbarian practices or were educated in such laws, I would pay the penalty in a barbaric manner. But I am a Roman born of Romans, and according to Roman laws and written tradition may my trial take place."

*Byzantine superstition considered these two sculptors miracle workers or sorcerers.

G.
THE SENATE

57.

Introduction. Constantine the Great (324–37), when he founded the Christian Roman Empire, maintained the new institutions established by his predecessor, Diocletian. Constantine's foundation of Constantinople led to the formation of a second Senate, modeled on that of Rome. In fact, however, his Senate more closely resembled the local senates of large cities like Antioch. The following short passage from the near contemporary *Anonymus Valesianus* records Constantine's action in creating a new Senate, of less important status, and calling to Constantinople many of the senators of Rome.

A. CONSTANTINE CREATES A NEW SENATE IN CONSTANTINOPLE

(From *Anonymus Valesianus*, in J. Rolfe, ed., *Ammianus Marcellinus* [Cambridge: Harvard University Press, 1964], pt. 1, 6.30, p. 527.)

Constantine called Byzantium Constantinople after his own name; and as if it were his native city, he adorned it with great magnificence and wished to make it equal to Rome. Then he sought out new citizens for it from every quarter, and lavished such wealth on the city that he all but exhausted the imperial fortunes. There he also established a Senate of the second rank, the members of which had the title of *clari* [a category of the senatorial class].

Introduction. In the following selection Constantine decrees that the rank of a senator shall pass, hereditarily, to his children.

B. SENATORIAL RANK IS HEREDITARY

(Translated by S. P. Scott, *The Civil Law* [Cincinnati; Central Trust Company, 1932], vol. 15, p. 24.)

If a senator, or any other man of illustrious rank, has children born to him before he was raised to the above-mentioned dignity (which rule applies to sons as well as daughters), they will follow the condition of their fathers. As children should not be excluded from the honors enjoyed by their fathers, a child born to a senator or other person of illustrious rank must be considered to be invested with that rank and dignity.

58.

Introduction. It was Constantine's son Constantius (337–61) who raised the Senate of Constantinople from the position of a municipal body to that of an imperial institution having legal equality with that of Rome. The following selection from the pagan orator Libanius documents an actual case of the transfer of a senator from Rome to Constantinople and reflects the still inferior status of the latter Senate in the popular mind.

TRANSFER OF A SENATOR FROM ROME TO CONSTANTINOPLE

(From Libanius, *Epistolae*, ed. R. Forster [Leipzig, 1920], epp. 70 and 251, pp. 70 and 237.)

[To Themistius, a high Roman dignitary in the East:]

This man [Olympius] has been transferred to your Senate [of Constantinople] from the greater one. For you will agree if I call the Senate of the Romans [in Rome] greater than the one of which you are a member. Treat him [Olympius] the same way among your people [in Constantinople] as he was treated in Rome. . . .

[To Honoratus, the administrator of the province of Asia:]

This Olympius whom you have done well by twice—for twice you were in charge of our area [Antioch]—you will also be favorably disposed to for a third time. For earlier he was a member of the Senate of the Romans [in Rome], but yesterday, so to speak, he became yours [a Senate member in Constantinople]. But thereupon he was disturbed by longstanding taxes, not because he owed them—for how could he yet owe anything to you?—but because his name is the same as that of another Olympius. . . . So, first of all, then, O benign one, it is fitting for you to clear up the confusion.

59.

Introduction. The rank of senator remained a hereditary one, and the normal way of becoming a senator was by holding a magistracy. By the time of Constantine and his immediate successors, the sons of senators were obliged to hold the office of praetor. (In the East there were eight praetors; their sole duty was to spend money on the exhibition of games and on public works). Men not born to the senatorial order could be admitted to the Senate by the emperor or by decree of the Senate itself. By the end of the fourth century the Senate numbered about two thousand members, not all of whom, of course, were active in Constantinople.

In time the power of the Senate began to crumble in the face of growing imperial absolutism, but it did not surrender all its constitutional functions all at once. Indeed, for several centuries the Senate (*synkletos*) of Constantinople played a genuine role in the life of the Byzantine state, acting primarily as an advisory body to the emperor.

The following passage, from the sixth-century historian Procopius, reveals the impotence of the Senate in Constantinople under the thinly veiled absolutism of Justinian (527–65).

JUSTINIAN DEMOTES THE SENATE

(From Procopius, *Anecdota*, ed. H. Dewing, Loeb Classical Library [Cambridge, Mass.: Harvard, 1960], p. 170.)

Many times matters which had been sanctioned by the Senate and the emperor came to another and final judgment. For the Senate sat as if in a picture, possessing no control over its vote, nor over the public welfare, and was convened only for the sake of appearance and of conformity with ancient law. It was absolutely not allowed for anyone of those assembled there to discuss anything [seriously]. Rather the *basileus* and his consort usually pretended to be of divided opinion concerning the matters which were in dispute, but, in these cases, that opinion prevailed which had been agreed upon by both of them in advance.

60.

Introduction. Although Justinian stripped the Senate of most of its authority, its prestige could still be an important influence on the common people, as is revealed by the next selection, from Theophanes.

THE SENATE ACTS TO DISPEL DANGEROUS RUMORS

(From Theophanes, *Chronographia*, ed. C. de Boor [Leipzig, 1883], vol. 1, pp. 234–35.)

At this time, on the fifth day of the ninth month of September, the ninth indiction [560], it was reported in Constantinople that the emperor [Justinian] had died. For he had come from Thrace and seen no one. And then the demes suddenly seized bread from the bakers and street vendors, and by the third hour there was no bread to be found in the entire city. And it rained heavily on the same day. Even the workshops were closed and it was rumored throughout the palace that no person of the Senate had seen the emperor because he had a headache. For this reason it was believed that he had died. Around the ninth hour, the Senate was convoked and the eparch was dispatched to have lights lit in the entire city [signifying] that the emperor was well. In this manner disorder in the city was averted.

61.

Introduction. Although the Senate's authority had been diminished by Emperor Justinian, that body experienced a genuine revival of authority in the seventh century. According to the chronicler Theophanes, the Senate played a major part in 610 in persuading the exarch of Africa, Heraclius, to attempt to overthrow the tyrant Phocas. Heraclius sent his son, also named Heraclius, with a navy against the capital. The coup succeeded and Heraclius ascended the imperial throne, thus founding a new dynasty.

HERACLIUS, BACKED BY THE SENATE, DETHRONES PHOCAS (610)

(From Theophanes, *Chronographia*, ed. C. de Boor [Leipzig, 1883], vol. 1, pp. 296–97.)

Phocas entrusted authority to Kosmas, the eparch of the city, and many persons were mutilated and they hanged their limbs in the *Sphendone* [the southern part of the Hippodrome]. But others he [Phocas] beheaded and still others he threw into the sea in sacks and drowned. When the Greens had gathered together they set fire to the *Praetorium* and burned the *Secreton* and the *Scrinia* [offices of the imperial secretaries] and the prisons. And when the prisoners came out of their cells they fled, and Phocas, furious, ordered the Greens no longer to meddle in the government. Then Heraclius, the strategos of Africa, impelled by the Senate, armed his son Heraclius and sent him [by sea] against Phocas the tyrant. Likewise, his lieutenant-general [*hypostrategos*] Gregory, sent his son, Nicetas, marching by land, so that whoever might reach there first and conquer the tyrant, would rule.

62.

Introduction. The restored power of the Senate was shown again in the seventh century when the Senate, by its order, deposed Empress Martina and Emperor Heraclonas, sealing its decision by mutilating both as a sign they were no longer capable of holding office. Thereupon, the Senate conferred the office of [senior] emperor upon a young boy, Constantine [Constans II], the son of Emperor Constantine III.

A. THE SENATE DEPOSES ONE EMPEROR AND NAMES ANOTHER (641)

(From Theophanes, *Chronographia*, ed. C. de Boor [Leipzig, 1883], vol. 1, p. 341.)

In that year the Senate deposed Heraclonas along with his mother Martina and [general] Valentine, and they [by order of the Senate] cut off the tongue of Martina and the nose of Heraclonas, and, expelling them, they [the Senators] raised to the throne Constans [II], the son of Constantine [and] grandson of Heraclius.

Introduction. Constans himself, in a formal speech before the assembled Senate, stressed the authority of the senators and requested the senators in the future to be his advisers and upholders of the common good for all the subjects of the empire.

B. CONSTANS REAFFIRMS SENATORIAL AUTHORITY

(From Theophanes, *Chronographia*, vol. 1, p. 342.)

In this year Emperor Constans said before the Senate: "I am the son of my father Constantine, who was son of his father, my grandfather Heraclius, who [Constantine] ruled with Heraclius a long time and after Heraclius, he also ruled for a very brief time. The jealousy of Martina, his stepmother, when it was aroused, took his life, and this for the sake of Heraclonas, born of her and Heraclius's lawlessness [incest]. Your decree [of the Senate] with the help of God justly deprived her and her child of the empire, because the senators, who were well known for their outstanding piety, could not endure lawlessness in the empire of the Romans. Therefore, I call on you to act as the advisers and judges for the common good of the subjects [of the empire.]" After saying this he gave the senators abundant gifts and dismissed the Senate.

63.

Introduction. It was in the reign of the Macedonian Emperor Leo VI (886–912) that the Senate's authority was revoked and that it lost, even in theory, virtually all of its authority. From Leo's time onward the Senate was less often convoked, and its only constitutional duty was the formal ratification of the selection of a new emperor. In the following selection Leo VI explicitly revokes and annuls the ancient legislative authority of the Senate.

THE SAPPING OF SENATORIAL AUTHORITY

(From *Les novelles de Léon VI le Sage*, ed. P. Noailles and A. Dain [Paris, 1944], p. 271.)

That which we have already done with respect to other laws not required by the condition of affairs—that is, the removal of superfluous material from our system of laws—we do now in the following respect: We ordain that the law which assigns to the Senate the authority of legislation shall be excised from the body of the laws. For the condition of affairs attests to that law's uselessness, ever since the imperial power took the [entire] government into his hands. It is therefore inopportune and inappropriate that a law which is no longer useful should retain its place by the side of laws which serve a purpose. . . .

64.

Introduction. Despite Leo's edict, the Senate continued to act as an advisory body to the emperor. In the eleventh century the emperors of the Ducas family, adherents of the party of the civil bureaucracy in Constantinople, sought to strengthen their position by extending among the citizens of the capital (meaning the middle and lower classes) the privilege of admission to the senatorial class and by granting to the new (and old) senators lavish gifts. Even somewhat earlier, as shown in the following passage from the historian Michael Attaleiates, emperors looking to the Senate for support, bestowed rich gifts on members of that body.

LIMITLESS HONORS FOR SENATORS

(From Michael Attaleiates, *Historia*, ed. I. Bekker [Bonn, 1853], p. 175.)

For no one among all the people made any request which was not at once granted, and this was true especially of the holy churches and the sacred places and all the monasteries and places of penance. And the result of this generosity and the constancy of this beneficence was extended to everything. This caused wonder and boundless amazement to all, since—in contrast to the previous emperor, Michael [V], who had always bewailed his need and terrible indigence and would say, in addition, that it was impossible for him to give a helping hand to the least benefaction because of the sudden (as he alleged) misfortune of the empire—from such sources of revenue his successor [Constantine IX], who had acceded to the scepter of the Romans [Byzantines], granted so many extraordinary benefactions, and gifts, and rich largesse and honors, more [even] than the sands of the sea and the company of the heavenly lights [stars]. On other days he distributed honors quietly on account of their great number and infinite quantity.

But what happened on Palm Sunday completely astonished everyone. For the entire Senate (*synkletos*), numbering more than thousands of persons, individually and according to rank, was considered worthy of great honors, which exceeded four and five times over [their previous ranks and honors], so that not even the *protovestiarios* [chief chamberlain] was able to receive from the emperor [all] those who were being honored, nor publicly even to call out their dignities, so overwhelmed was he by the vast number of honors. And he had to wheel around to the rostrum and turn back again and again. Even when standing constantly in the same place, he would hurry up the proclamation of the honors which were constantly being augmented and he did so much work that he lost his voice.

65.

Introduction. In Byzantium's later period it was, in time of crisis, possible to dispense with senatorial sanction even in the case of an imperial election. Thus in 1204, just before the Latin armies of the Fourth

Crusade captured and looted Constantinople, a Byzantine assembly was hastily convened at Hagia Sophia to vote on two candidates presented for the throne, Ducas and Lascaris. The Byzantine historian Nicetas Choniates writes succinctly as follows:

A Crisis Form of Imperial Election

(From Nicetas Choniates, *Historia*, ed. I. Van Dieten [Berlin, 1975], vol. 1, pp. 571–72.)

After the emperor [Alexius V] had fled, a split occurred over the rule [of the empire]—just as over control of a ship beset by a storm—between two sober-minded young men who were very able in battle, Dukas and Lascaris. Both had the same name as the imperial founder of the faith [i.e. Constantine the Great]. Since they viewed the highest and greatest good, that is, the empire of the Romans, as a reward of fate and the supreme "roll of the dice" of illogical chance, both entered into the Great Church. And vying with each other and being compared to each other by those present, neither seemed in any way greater or lesser than the other. But both were considered to be of the same caliber. Lascaris then won the draw of the lots which were cast. But he did not assume the insignia of empire. Going with the patriarch to the Milion,* he did not cease exhorting and cajoling those present to resist [the Latins who were about to storm the city].

Commentary. Lascaris, however, failed in his efforts to stir up resistance to the besieging Latins (especially on the part of the Varangian mercenaries), and he fled from the city to Asia Minor the following morning. This Lascaris is not generally listed by the historians as an emperor.

*Roughly the patriarchal area including Hagia Sophia and Hagia Irene. From the Milion, at this time a square building on pillars with a platform on top, distances were measured. Hagia Sophia and Hagia Irene were together termed "the Great Church," although the term often referred only to Hagia Sophia.

66.

Introduction. In the last, Palaeologan period of the empire, the Senate, now virtually powerless, continued to act in an advisory capacity and, as Pseudo-Codinus of the mid-fourteenth century shows in the following selection, also retained a role in important imperial ceremonies.

The Senate Participates at Ceremonial Banquets

(From Pseudo-Codinus, *Traité des offices*, ed. J. Verpeaux [Paris: Editions du Centre national de la recherche scientifique, 1966], p. 272.)

Therefore there were instituted, in those days that we have been speaking about, sumptuous banquets and feasts. And all the members of the Senate were [present], seated, joyfully dining before the emperors who themselves too were dining at their own tables. Then the domestic and the *epi tes trapezes* [the one in charge of ceremonial banquets] ministered to them. But if he did not, someone (who was without headdress* and of the family of the emperor) did so at the imperial bidding. The grand domestic, also reclining at the table, participates in the dinners in his proper place along with the other members of the Senate. Such an order [prevails] without any variation also at the marriages of the emperors.

*That is, *distinctive* headdress revealing rank.

PART II
The Defense of The Empire
◆ ◆ ◆ ◆ ◆ ◆ ◆ ◆ ◆ ◆ ◆ ◆ ◆ ◆ ◆ ◆ ◆ ◆ ◆

A.
THE ARMY

67.

Introduction. The Byzantine army, like many others of Byzantium's institutions, was a continuation of the Roman tradition. Its military organization, recruitment, tactics, armaments, and pay—all were set forth in the most minute detail in manuals often drawn up by the emperors themselves. In the following passages, drawn from the Theodosian and Justinianic codes, Theodosius I (379–95) and Valens (364–78) make provision for the hereditary recruitment of soldiers, a provision already established under Constantine the Great.

A. MILITARY RECRUITMENT OF SONS OF SOLDIERS

(From *Codex Justinianus*, bk. 12, title 47.3.)

If a soldier dies in any manner in battle, his son, if there is only one, or the eldest if there are many, straightway shall assume the place of his father and receive the same *annona* [support], if the father was of rank up to commisary general. But if the father was of higher rank than commisary general, then the son shall be only a commisary general. For it is assumed that when the older brother fulfills this obligation he fulfills also that of his brothers.

B. EDICT OF EMPEROR VALENS

(Translated by C. Pharr, *The Theodosian Code* [Princeton, 1952], 7-1-8, p. 156.)

Your Authority shall announce to all veterans whatsoever that if any of them should not, of his own free will, offer his son who is entirely worthy of the honor of bearing arms [i.e., capable of bearing arms] to the imperial service for which the veteran himself has toiled, he shall be involved in the toils of Our law.

68.

Introduction. In the earliest period, from the fourth century onward, the army, besides its regular troops, consisted also of foreign troops, for example, German *foederati* (tribes allied to Rome) or, a little later, Isaurians (from southwest Asia Minor) who, in exchange for military service, were given grants of land. This type of army organization and recruitment remained in force until a few decades after Justinian's death in 565. Then, because of the perils threatening the empire, a reform of the system of military recruitment took place.

This reorganization is well illustrated by passages from the *Strategikon*, ascribed to the Emperor Maurice and written ca. 579 to serve as the official handbook for the army. The barbarians, especially German mercenaries, were no longer used. All subjects of the empire under forty had an obligation to serve in the army, though we cannot really say that a system of universal military service was ever adopted in Byzantium. Nevertheless, Maurice apparently wished to remove the de facto exemption of the rich from military service (he emphasized, for example, the practice of archery for boys and men of all classes especially in the provinces) and also to recruit the army from entirely within Byzantine territories. Foreign auxiliaries loyal to the empire were becoming more difficult to find.

A. EMPEROR MAURICE'S MILITARY DIRECTIVE (579)

(Translated by C. Oman, from Emperor Maurice, *Strategikon*, in *The Art of War in the Middle Ages*, rev. ed. [New York, 1924], vol. 1, pp. 178–79.)

We wish that every young Roman of free condition should learn the use of the bow, and be constantly provided with that weapon and with two javelins.

Introduction. Several centuries later, in the late ninth century, Emperor Leo VI in his treatise *Tactica* stressed, as had Emperor Maurice, universal military preparedness, urging all men and boys to learn the use of the bow.

B. TRAINING FOR ALL IN THE USE OF THE BOW

(Translated by C. Oman, from Leo VI, *Tactica*, in *Art of War in the Middle Ages*, p. 179.)

The bow is the easiest of weapons to make, and one of the most effective. We therefore wish that those who dwell in castle, countryside, or town, in short, every one of our subjects, should have a bow of his own. Or if this be impossible, let every household keep a bow and forty arrows, and let practice be made with them in shooting both in the open and in broken ground and in defiles and woods. For if there come a sudden incursion of enemies into the bowels of the land, men using archery from rocky ground or in defiles or in forest paths can do the invader much harm; for the enemy dislikes having to keep sending out detachments to drive them off, and will dread to scatter far abroad after plunder, so that much territory can thus be kept unharmed, since the enemy will not desire to be engaging in a perpetual archery skirmish.

69.

Introduction. In the sixth century under Justinian the simple regiment (*tagma*) was enlarged and became the basis of military organization (similar to our brigade or division). But the size of each unit was not exactly specified, so that the enemy would not be able to ascertain the exact strength of the force opposing him. (These and other changes were connected with and led to the emergence of the theme system in the seventh century: see selections 41–44.)

The following passage from Emperor Leo VI's *Tactica* refers in general terms to the recruitment of troops and their officers. Note, from the careful provisions made for their lands, that most recruits at this time seem to have been landholders.

ON THE RECRUITMENT AND PRIVILEGES OF SOLDIER-FARMERS

(From Leo VI, *Tactica*, in R. Vari, ed., *Leonis Imperatoris Tactica* [Budapest, 1917], vol. 1, pp. 48–50.)

Therefore we [Emperor Leo VI] decree that you, the Most Glorious *Strategos*, in conformity with longstanding custom, select the soldiers and their officers, men whom you consider sufficient for the needs of the war. Choose soldiers from throughout your entire theme, neither boys nor old men, but those who are vigorous, strong, brave, and financially sound, so that they may leave others at home who will care for their *strateia* [military lands], while they are on campaign or garrison duty. And so that these [latter] farmers might be able to defray the costs for the soldiers who take up arms and complete the campaign, [let them] preserve their homes free from all other obligations to the fisc. For we do not wish that our fellow soldiers (for thus we call a man who is about to do his best in combat for the sake of our empire and the polity of the Romans which is beloved of Christ) be subject to any other obligation to the fisc except the land tax. . . . [According to Leo VI, the rank and file of the army were recruited in part from settlers in possession of military holdings, the *stratiotika ktemata* or *strateiai*, and from the ranks of other small free landowners. Their officers, especially of the higher ranks, were drawn from the best families of the Byzantine aristocracy.] Nothing forbids that [the officers] be rich, of noble birth, and also of the highest character. Their nobility insures that the [common soldiers] will be ready to do whatever the officers order during the height of battle, while the officers' [personal] wealth enables them, if it becomes necessary, to help defray the expenses of their troops. Perhaps even a small grant on the part of the commanders to their soldiers, if it is well-intentioned and fully appreciated by the latter, will induce the common soldiers to take part even unto death in the customary dangers [of war].

70.

Introduction. Under the impact of the great Persian and Arab invasions (seventh and eighth centuries), a drastic change in army organization took place. With the whole eastern civil administration in disarray, the administrative burden fell on the generals—and the military hierarchy served as the basis for the civil administration. The term *thema* (referring originally to an army battalion) came to be applied to the province in which such a military unit was permanently stationed [see selections 41–44]. The military forces under the *strategos* (chief commander) of a frontier theme usually consisted of eight to twelve thousand men (at times less). Subordinate to the *strategos* were two or three *turmarchs*, each commanding three to five thousand men. All frontier military forces included, as their main striking arm, about five thousand picked cavalry, while the garrisons of the towns were composed primarily of infantry. The make-up of the military forces of the themes is described in passages from the *Tactica*. (Note in this passage the mixture, still, of Latin and Greek terms.)

THE ORGANIZATION OF THE ARMY

(From Leo VI, *Tactica*, in A. Dain, ed., *Le "Extrait Tactique" tiré de Léon VI le Sage* [Paris, 1942], pp. 91–93.)

At the head of the [military] hierarchy comes the *strategos*. After him come the *merarchs* [= *turmarchs*], then the *drungarii*, then the *komites* (that is, those who have command over what are called *banda*), then the *centarchs*; following these come the *decarchs*, the first of which is called *akiai*, then the *pentarchs*, and finally the *tetrarchs*, who are called *ouragii* from the fact that, in the battle line, they are placed last in depth. In fact, the last of all the column or of the *akia* is placed there at the end of the formation.

Such are the names of those who hold commands. There are still other ranks, separate in each *tagma* or band, such as the horn players, the buglers or *buccinatores*, the ambulance men or doctors, the *deputati*, the *mandatores* [message carriers], the exhorters (those who by their words excite the army to combat); others, in addition, are detached for special service, such as the *scribones*, and the like. These are the names presently employed; the ancient names are passed over here.

Strategos, then, is the name given to the one who is in first place over the whole army, the chief of it. The *hypostrategos* is the one who, following him, occupies the second rank. I believe that our predecessors gave the name of *hypostrategos* to the *strategoi*; indeed, by law the emperor is the supreme *strategos* and in each theme the *strategos* functions only as his representative. For this reason the *strategos* is called *hypostrategos*, while one calls properly *strategos* the one who, representing the emperor, is put at the head of the whole army, having under his orders as *hypostrategos* the *strategoi* of the themes, a manner of organization that seems excellent.

From our days onward, one no longer uses the term *hypostrategos* except as the officer called *merarch*, he who is in charge of a *meros*.

A *drungarios* is the one who commands the *moira*, a lower section of the *meros* commanded by the *turmarch*. The *meros* is in fact the *tourma*, a unit composed of three *moirai* or *drungi*. As for the *moira* or *drungus*, it is the element consisting of *tagmata* [*numeri* or *banda*], commanded by those that are called *kometes*.

71.

Introduction. Although composition of the Byzantine army always contained a mixture of infantry and cavalry, the elite cavalry (*cataphractai*) provided the shock power that usually decided the outcome of close battles. A good example of this may be found in the campaign of Emperor John Tzimisces against the Rus in 971. Considered by some scholars to mark the zenith of the Byzantine military accomplishment, this campaign resulted in several defeats of the vaunted Rus infantry, heavily armed with double-headed axes. The final, crushing Byzantine cavalry charge in these various engagements is vividly depicted in the following selection taken from the Byzantine historian Leo Diaconus.

BYZANTINE CATAPHRACTS IN ACTION

(Translated by R. Jenkins, from Leo Diaconus, *Historia*, ed. K. Hase [Bonn, 1828], pp. 128ff., in P. Whiting, *Byzantium: An Introduction* [New York, 1971], p. 76.)

In the earlier clashes, neither side prevailed. The Russians felt it to be unendurable that they, who held among their neighbours a record of unbroken victory, should now lose it shamefully to the Byzantines, and they fought with desperate courage. But the Byzantines, for their part, thought it a foul disgrace if, hitherto successful against all opposition, they should now be worsted in a struggle against a foot-soldiering nation who couldn't even ride. The Russians, with their native savagery and spirit, leapt roaring on the Byzantines like men possessed. But the Byzantines fought back with military skill and technical knowledge. Losses on both sides were heavy. By the late afternoon, the issue was still in doubt. The evening star was already sinking when the Emperor John launched his final cavalry-charge on the Russians with devastating effect: "You are *Romans!*" he cried; "Now show your valour in your deeds!" Thus heartened, the cavalry burst out with irresistible ardour. The bugles sounded the charge. The Byzantine battle-cry rang out. The Russians wavered and fled. Their losses were enormous.

72.

Introduction. In general the cataphracts fought in a wedge formation, that is, in the shape of a blunt triangle. This allowed them to employ the shock force of a cavalry charge as a battering ram against the lines of their enemy. The following selection, drawn from a military manual probably written by Nicephorus Ouranos, the great general of the late Macedonian period, provides information on the organization and tactics of a squadron of the Byzantine cataphracts and indicates why they were the most powerful military force in medieval history.

CONCERNING THE BYZANTINE HEAVY CAVALRY (CATAPHRACTS)

(From *Strategika Imperatora Nikifora*, ed. I. Kulakovskii, *Mémoires de l'Académie Impériale des Sciences de St. Pétersbourg*, 8th ser., no. 9, *Classe historico-philologique* [St. Petersburg, 1908], pp. 10–12.)

It is necessary to understand that the triangular arrangement of the cataphracts, if there are a great many men, should amount in number to 504 and the depth of the formation should be twelve. That is to say, the first rank of the line should contain 20 men, the second 24, the third 28, the fourth 32, the fifth 36, the sixth 40, the seventh 44, the eighth 48, the ninth 52, the tenth 56, the eleventh 60, the twelfth 64, so as to amount to 504 men in the whole phalanx [regiment].

But if there are not so many men, such an arrangement has to be more modest, so as to have in the first line 10 men, in the second 14, the third 18, the fourth 22, the fifth 26, the sixth 30, the seventh 34, the eighth 38, the ninth 42, the tenth 46, the eleventh 50, the twelfth 54. The number of men in the entire regiment should be 384.

But if the army is greater or smaller, the commander must constitute the face of the formation, that is, the front line, of such a quantity of men as he may see at a glance and as pleases him. And let there be added, in each line from the second line proceeding backwards, two men to the right and left sides so as to render the regiment evenly triangular. . . .

It should be understood that there should be archers in the midst of the cataphracts, so that the archers can be protected by them. The ranks in front of them [the archers], that is, the first, second, third, and fourth ranks, shall not include archers. But from the fifth rank on to the rear they shall. If the number of the regiment of the cataphracts is 504, it shall include 150 archers. But if there are 300, it shall include 80 archers.

These are the [offensive] weapons of the cataphracts: [first are] iron maces with heads, and these heads shall be jagged so as to be three or four or five-sided, or even made of iron spikes. The others shall be daggers. All of these [cataphracts] shall have swords, and they shall hold iron maces and daggers in their hands and other iron rods either in their belts or in their saddles. The first rank, that is, the face of the regiment, and the second, third, and fourth shall be equipped in the same way, as well as the cataphracts on the flanks from the fifth rank onward, in order that these may be included among the lancers and iron mace-bearers or even among those holding daggers. And they shall be arranged thus up to the rear guard. But the archers should wear corselets and helmets only and, if possible, their horses shall be *cataphract* [fully armored].

73.

Introduction. Up to almost the middle of the eleventh century, at which point the Byzantine army was at its zenith, it constituted the strongest military force in Europe and western Asia. Its supply lines, so vital to any military action, especially an advance, were carefully prescribed, each man in the front lines having at least two or three men in the rear acting as quartermaster troops. Besides fighting men and supply troops, there were also special military units such as an ambulance corps (with surgeons) and an engineering corps (stationed with the vanguard). The corps of engineers at each stop would at once, according to instructions, mark out with stakes and ropes the best position for encampment in the most favorable and defensible area. Meantime, the infantry would dig a ditch along a line of ropes surrounding the encampment. All these preparations served to make a surprise attack against the Byzantine camp very difficult.

The tactics adopted depended usually on the strength of the Byzantine heavy cavalry (cataphracts), who were positioned surrounding the infantry. The cavalry itself was arranged in different ways in order to provide the greatest mobility and protection for the rest of the troops and also to preclude a surprise attack from any direction. An interesting feature was the provision for the mounting of at least five cavalry shock attacks in succession before the impetus would be gone, each line providing for the orderly absorption of whichever preceding line might have given way.

It is characteristic of Byzantine military manuals to specify the type of tactics to combat most effectively the enemy of the moment. Against the Cumans, Pechenegs, early Seljuks and Avars—all nomadic or near-nomadic peoples who liked to ambush the enemy—as well as the highly mobile Arab armies, Byzantine tactics were geared to avoid hit-and-run attacks. It was therefore prescribed that these swift enemies be suddenly assaulted from close quarters and especially by foot soldiers covered by cataphracts on their flanks, an attack which the enemy feared. On the other hand, when facing an enemy such as the "Franks" (a term used by Byzantines for all Western peoples), it was advisable for the Byzantines to avoid a pitched battle. Instead, the Byzantines were instructed to attack from the side and rear, wearing the Latins down by luring them away from their supply lines and splitting off various Latin troops from each other. The following passage from the military manual ascribed to Emperor Maurice (582–602) vividly prescribes the various types of tactics to be used against one specific enemy, the Germanic warriors.

Techniques and Tactics: Know Your Enemy

(From Emperor Maurice, *Strategikon*, in H. Mihǎescu, ed., *Mauricius Arta Militara* [Bucharest, 1970], pp. 274, 276.)

The yellow-haired nations are rash and dauntless in battle when it is a question of liberty. Being daring and reckless, they look disdainfully on even a short retreat as a sign of cowardice, and they calmly despise death, fighting violent hand-to-hand combat either on horse or on foot. When they are in a tight situation during a cavalry battle, they will dismount and arrange themselves in a single mass on foot; even if they are few, they do not decline battle against a greater number of cavalry. They are armed with shields and pikes and with broad swords which are carried on their shoulders. They take pleasure in infantry battles and in making raiding incursions. In these battles they arrange themselves—whether on foot or on horseback—into no formal divisions or order, neither into *moiras* or *mere* [smaller units in the Byzantine army], but only according to tribal affiliation, with bonds of kinship and friendship among their fellow soldiers. (For this reason in times of crisis, when [close] friends or relatives have been left behind [i.e., dead], they often plunge into the battle in order to avenge them.) In battle they make the face [front] of their battle formations equal and densely packed; their attacks, whether on horseback or on foot, are vehement and uncontrollable, as they alone of all peoples shun every form of timidity. Since they are disobedient to their officers and without [a sense of] responsibility, since they lack cunning, [concern for] safety, and any conception of their own best interest, they despise ordered tactics [i.e., discipline], especially when fighting on horseback.

They are easily corrupted by bribes, since they are lovers of gain. Ill-fate and [military] reverses trouble them grievously. For while they are of brave and bold spirit, their bodies are well taken care of, and soft and unable to bear hardship easily. Heat, cold, rain, a lack of provisions and especially wine—the excesses of war—bother them. In time of cavalry combat, bad terrain and forests are unfavorable to their fighting. But they calmly endure ambushes against the flanks or rear of their formation, and they do not even bother with guards and other security. Their ranks are broken easily through the tactics of feigned withdrawal and sudden counterattacks. Nocturnal raids by archers are also often effective against them, causing them to flee in disorder. Therefore, in battle one must, above all, not advance against them in clear formation, especially in the opening stage, but rather lie in wait in good order and utilize especially stealth and cunning, protracting the length of battle and not drawing up [our troops] opposite them in a disadvantageous manner, so that through lack of provisions or the extremities of heat or cold, their bravery and passion may be diminished.

Such conditions occur best when the [Byzantine] army is encamped in a fortified place or in rugged terrain, so that the enemy spears cannot be utilized easily against the defenders' position. If an opportunity arises, however, for formal battle array, the troops should be drawn up as we have elucidated in our [previous] discussion of battle formations.

74.

Introduction. The composition and organization of the Byzantine armies remained relatively constant from the seventh to the mid-eleventh century. But by the latter period, the bureaucratic class in Constantinople, through its policy of neglect of the military, had brought about a serious decline in the efficiency and morale of the army. It was during this time that the Byzantines suffered the most serious defeat in their history, at Manzikert in Armenia in 1071, where a large Byzantine army was completely shattered by the invading Seljuk Turks. Though the army's decay actually began earlier,

Manzikert marks the real turning point in the decline of Byzantine might, for it opened the way to conquest of Byzantium's most important area, its heartland Asia Minor.

At the battle of Manzikert, the Byzantine commander, Emperor Romanus Diogenes, seemed to violate many of Leo VI's principles of strategy and tactics. In addition there were serious defections from the Byzantine army by Turkish mercenaries, who deserted to their fellow (Seljuk) Turks, as well as the disobedience of a leading Greek general.

In the thirty-year chaos following Manzikert, the Byzantine army virtually disappeared as an effective force. And with the principal Asian themes now largely lost, recruitment of troops henceforth depended more and more on the use of foreign mercenaries. Under the Comneni and especially following the Fourth Crusade and the recovery of Constantinople in 1261 by the Greek Palaeologi, the army was often only a haphazardly organized, heterogeneous body. The old thematic system was, in effect, no longer operative.

In the following selection an unknown author of probably the eleventh century warns against certain aspects of the increasing role of mercenaries in place of native Byzantine troops. (Cf. views of Synesius, selection 243, and of Theodore Lascaris, selection 75.)

A WARNING CONCERNING THE USE OF FOREIGN MERCENARIES

(From *Cecaumeni strategicon et incerti scriptoris de officiis regius Libellus*, ed. B. Wassiliewsky and V. Jernstedt [St. Petersburg, 1896; reprint, Amsterdam, 1965], p. 95.)

If foreigners are not of royal descent in their own country, do not invest them with great honors nor entrust to them high offices. For in doing so you will not help yourself in any way, nor will you please your own officers who are of Byzantine origin. When you honor a man who has come from England by naming him to the rank of *primicerius* [colonel] or of general, of what value is it for a Byzantine to become a general? You will instead make him an enemy. But even in his own country when they hear he has achieved such honor and authority, they will all laugh and say, "Here we consider him to be nobody and only when he went to Romania did he gain such honor. It seems that in Romania no one is worthy and for that reason our compatriot was exalted. If the Byzantines were discerning, they would not have raised him to such rank." But perhaps your imperial highness will respond, "I conferred this honor upon him in order that others, observing it, will also come to serve me." That is not good policy. For, if you wish, I can bring you as many foreigners as you want for bread and water [alone]. It is in Romania's best interest, O Lord, not to bestow high ranks on foreigners. For if they later work only for clothing and subsistence, you should know that they will serve you faithfully and wholeheartedly, expecting to receive from you only a small measure of money and provisions.

75.

Introduction. A few emperors tried to return to reliance on a native, "Greek" army; one of these was Theodore II Lascaris of Nicaea. The following letter, written by him c. 1255, describes his determination to form an army henceforth primarily of "Greek nationals."

FORMATION OF A "NATIONAL" GREEK ARMY

(From *Theodori Ducae Lascaris epistulae*, ed. N. Festa. [Florence, 1898], letter 44, pp. 58–59.)

When the mob incites to enmity, and other nations war against us, who will come to our aid? How can a Persian help a Greek? Even more, the Italian is furious with us; and most of all, the Bulgarian and the Serb abandon us because they are moved only by force. And he who pretends to be our friend is not in truth our friend. Only the Greek [element] can help itself, finding its energy from within itself. Should we limit the size of the army or the funds through which the army is established? If we do the first, then we help our enemies; if the second, again I say we help our enemies. And this is no sophistry but is much clearer than any other truth. For the truth is one for me. One is my purpose and one thing I have established as my goal: namely, always to gather together the flock of God and to preserve it from the attacking wolves. . . . I am [therefore] amassing the country's gold to build an army not of Turkish, Italian, Bulgar, or Serb soldiers, but a Greek ["Hellenic"] one, which alone can truly be depended upon.

76.

Introduction. Although the centuries after Manzikert saw a tremendous change in the organization and especially composition of the army, the use of trickery, cleverness, and psychological pressure remained important weapons in the Byzantine defense arsenal until the very end of the empire. It was prescribed, for example, that, if negotiations with the enemy were going on, "soft words" should be employed by the *strategos* up to the next to the last day of the talks, after which a sudden attack should be launched. Precise instructions were given on how to confuse the enemy camp by falsifying messages and spreading rumors. As the Byzantine historian Gregoras, writing of the last centuries of Byzantium, records, Emperor Michael Palaeologus used such devious means along with force of arms when he faced a coalition of Franks and Epirot Byzantines at the battle of Pelagonia (1259). It was the victory at Pelagonia which opened the road to the recovery of Constantinople from the Latins.

BYZANTINE SABOTAGE AGAINST THE ENEMY (1259)

(From Nicephorus Gregoras, *Byzantina historia,* ed. L. Schopen and I. Bekker [Bonn, 1829], vol. 1, pp. 74–75.)

Since the Byzantines had pitched camp near the enemy [Franks], they sent a man very suitable for planting discord and sowing confusion in the ranks of the enemy. This was not impossible since the prince of Achaia and the king of Sicily [Manfred] were of different peoples and not of the same race as Michael Angelus [Greek despot of Epirus, siding with the Latins]. Leaving his camp, then, as if he were a deserter, the man went at night to the enemy, and coming secretly before the ruler of Aetolia, Michael Angelus [the Greek collaborator], he said: "Know that today great danger threatens you and all your men, for both your son-in-law and allies, the prince of the Peloponnesus and Achaia and the king of Sicily, have secretly sent envoys to the Romans [Byzantines] to make a deal for a certain sum of money. If you value your life, take heed at once, before their negotiations for peace and collusion are concluded." And Michael [Angelus] was persuaded; after quietly informing as many of his men as he could, he departed and fled before the sun rose. After the news of Michael's flight spread in whispers from man to man, his soldiers took off in disorderly fashion, each trying to escape before the other.

When the allies arose at dawn and heard of Michael's flight, they were unable to understand the cause and became confused. And so they forbade attacking the Romans [Byzantines] both because they were ignorant of what was happening and because they were now much reduced in number. Whereupon they too fled, believing themselves betrayed by Michael [Angelus]. The Byzantines then attacked and captured the rest, except for a few, and among the captured was Prince William of the Peloponnesus and Achaia. But the king of Sicily escaped with a very few of his men.

77.

Introduction. After 1261 the Byzantine armies sometimes still managed to present a semblance of their old military skill and organization. But the extensive use of expensive foreign mercenaries, the lack of a genuine esprit and cohesive organization, and territorial losses which meant losses in military manpower rendered the Byzantine armies increasingly incapable of stopping the attacks of the new and most dangerous of all enemies of Byzantium—the Ottoman Turks, who were inexorably advancing on Constantinople. At the final siege of Constantinople, when only some five thousand Greek soldiers fought to defend the capital city against a Turkish army of at least one hundred fifty thousand men, a principal group of defenders consisted of the Latin troops of the Genoese lord of Chios, Giustiniani. The Greek historian Ducas describes the final struggle for Constantinople.

OPPOSING ARMIES AT THE FINAL SIEGE OF
CONSTANTINOPLE (1453)

(From Ducas, *Historia Turko-byzantina*, ed. I. Bekker [Bonn, 1834],
pp. 221–23.)

The tyrant [Mehmed, sultan of the Turks] began to
wage all-out war on Sunday 27 May, the festival of All Saints. When evening
came, he gave no rest to the Romans, and when the morning light emerged, he
waged war only until the ninth hour. And after the ninth hour, he rearranged
the army, extending it from the palace up to the Golden [Gate], and the eighty
ships from the Xyloporta [Wooden Gate] up to the Platea [Gate]. And the rest [of
the ships] he stationed at the Double Columns; they surrounded the Acropolis,
extending from the Beautiful Gate and beyond St. Demetrius, and [they also
surrounded] the small gate at the monastery of Hodegetria. . . . He [Mehmed]
himself fought then immediately before the walls . . . along with his faithful and
very valiant young servants. And they, struggling like lions, numbered more
than ten thousand men. Behind them and on their flanks was the aggressive cavalry of more than 100,000. In the lower areas [of the city] up to the harbor of the
Golden [Horn] there were still another 100,000 men and more, and from the
place where the commander stood, extending up to the edges of the palace, another 50,000; and in the ships more men than can be counted.

[The Byzantines] inside the walls were also drawn up in battle array. The emperor, with John Giustiniani, defended the walls already breached outside the
fortress in the surrounding area, having with him Latins and Romans [Byzan-
tines] in the number of about 3,000, while the grand duke had with him about
500 men at the Imperial Gate. The walls on the seaward side and the fortifications extending from the Xyloporta Gate up to the *Horaia* [Beautiful] Gate were
defended by more than 500 *tzangras* [siege engines] and archers. In the area
from the Beautiful Gate, forming an entire circle up to the Golden Gate, in each
tower there was an armed man who was either an archer, a *tzangras* operator, or a
rock thrower.

And [the Byzantines] spent the whole night in vigil, unable to sleep at all.
Then the Turks with their leader rushed toward the walls, bringing with them
innumerable ladders which they had previously prepared. The tyrant, running
behind his men, steel sword in hand, urged his archers on, at times with flatter-
ing words, sometimes with threats. Meantime, the defenders of the city fought
back as valiantly as they could. John [Giustiniani] stood his ground bravely, with
his own men, having with him the emperor who too was armed and was fighting
alongside his men. But the brave deeds of these men were destined to result to
the advantage of the Turks, for God removed from the midst of the Roman army
the general Giustiniani, that valiant and powerful fighting man. He was wounded
in the arm by a lead shot while it was still dark, and it passed through his corselet
which was forged like the armor of Achilles. And he was in pain from his
wounds; thus he said to the emperor, "Stand your ground courageously, but I
will go to my ship, and I shall return quickly after my wound is bandaged."

78.

Introduction. In the very early period of the empire under Constantine and his successors the commanders-in-chief of the imperial armies were the *magistri militum* of East and West. From about the time of Heraclius, the *strategoi*, of course, commanded the forces in their themes, often under the general direction of the emperor or his representatives. But from the period of John Comnenus (twelfth century) onward, and especially during the Palaeologan period, the commander of the armies of the reduced empire was termed the grand domestic. Pseudo-Codinus of the mid-fourteenth century describes the duties of the grand domestic thus.

THE GRAND DOMESTIC

(From Pseudo-Codinus, *Traité des offices*, ed. J. Verpeaux [Paris: Editions du Centre national de la recherche scientifique, 1966], p. 248.)

The entire army [*fossaton*] is under the orders of the grand domestic. Therefore when the emperor is with the army, it is from the tent of the grand domestic that the trumpets sound the signal for the advance. When the army is deployed before the emperor, the maneuver is directed by the grand domestic himself, who decides which units ought to be placed ahead and also in the rear, and which should, on the other hand, be arranged laterally. And the emperor approves such a position.

79.

Introduction. Finally, in connection with defense on land, mention should be made of the famous walls of Constantinople, which for almost a millennium kept attacking land armies at bay. These walls were originally constructed during the reign of Theodosius II but as a single wall. The following edict of Theodosius (413) directs the praetorian prefect of the East, Anthemius, as to the use and repairs of the newly constructed wall.

A. THE WALLS OF THEODOSIUS II

(Translated by C. Pharr, *The Theodosian Code* [Princeton, 1952], 15-1-51, p. 429.)

We command that the towers of the New Wall, which has been constructed for the fortification of this most splendid City, shall after the completion of the work, be assigned to the use of those persons through whose lands this wall was duly erected by the zeal and foresight of Your Magnitude, pursuant to the decision of Our Serenity. This regulation and condition shall be observed in perpetuity, so that said landholders and those persons to whom the title to these lands may pass shall know that each year they must provide for the repair of the towers at their own expense, that they shall acquire the use of these towers as a special favor from the public, and that they shall not doubt that the care of repair and the responsibility therefore belong to them. . . .

Introduction. But the wall built by Anthemius was destroyed by an earthquake and it was later (447) expanded into a double wall with a moat and flanked by 192 towers in order to repel the threat of invaders such as the Huns. The following text of an inscription found on the walls attests to the swiftness with which the Theodosian walls were built.

B. Inscription on the Theodosian Walls

(From A. Van Millingen, *Byzantine Constantinople: The Walls of the City and Adjoining Historical Sites* [London, 1899], p. 47.)

By the commands of Theodosius, in less than two months, Constantine (praetorian prefect) triumphantly erected these strong walls.

B.
THE NAVY

80.

Introduction. At the apogee of the Byzantine empire, in the later tenth and early eleventh centuries, the Byzantine navy was unrivalled in the world. Of course, its organization, spirit of discipline, and certain of its skills were carried over from ancient Roman days. But the Byzantines modified or improved certain of these naval practices, as we shall see below. Like the Byzantine army, the navy was carefully structured and had its hierarchy of officers. The following selection from Pseudo-Codinus (fourteenth century) lists explicitly the titles of the ranking commanders of the navy, some the same as they had been at the height of empire in the later tenth century.

COMMANDERS OF THE BYZANTINE NAVY

(From Pseudo-Codinus, *Traité des offices*, ed. J. Verpeaux [Paris, 1966], p. 167.)

The grand duke is the head of the entire navy, as is the grand domestic over the entire land army. The chiefs who are at the head of the other galleys hoist the usual imperial standard, that is, the cross with flame-throwers, while the grand duke hoists the standard of the emperor on horseback. He [the Grand Duke] has under his orders the grand *drungarios* of the fleet, the admiral, the *protokomes*, the *drungarios*, and the *kometes* [Counts].

81.

Introduction. The Byzantine warship was the *dromon*, a long ship driven by oars. The term could also refer to a huge vessel with a crew of three hundred or more men. But the typical *dromon* was usually smaller, designed for speed, maneuverability, and, after the seventh century, for delivery of the deadly Greek fire against enemy vessels.

THE BYZANTINE DROMON

(From the *Taktikon* of Nicephorus Ouranos, in *Naumachika*, ed. A. Dain [Paris, 1943] pp. 71–72, sections 3–5, 8.)

The construction of the *dromon* should be neither too massive (for it will not respond easily) nor too light, or it will be too fragile to resist the force of the waves or an enemy collision. . . . Let the equipment of the *dromon* be absolutely complete in all respects, and everything should be in double supply: tillers, oars, pins [to which oars were fastened], blocks and tackle, masts, armature, and everything necessary for the vessel to function well. Let it also have extra wood, planking, ropes and pitch, solid as well as liquid. The ship should carry a carpenter with all his tools for woodworking: auger, saw, and other things. A nozzle mounted on the forward part of the prow should, as customarily, eject against the enemy the material that will burn. And above this, platforms should be constructed of planks and strengthened with the same materials for holding the sailors who are to repel the attacks from the enemy forecastle or attack their opponents with any kind of weapons at their disposal.

82.

Introduction. The following passage from the manual of Nicephorus Ouranos (probably of the early eleventh century) describes tactics to be used for a specific situation.

NAVAL TACTICS

(From the *Taktikon* of Nicephorus Ouranos, in *Naumachika*, ed. A. Dain [Paris, 1943], pp. 84–85, section 62.)

But it is also possible that an entire [enemy] ship can be capsized with its crew if the ship is grappled alongside a *dromon* and if the combatants on both sides, as is the custom, engage each other in hand-to-hand combat and the enemy ship bumps against the *dromon*. Meantime, another [Byzantine] *dromon*, moving toward the side of the stern [of the enemy ship], should strongly ram the enemy's ship while the first *dromon*, having freed itself of the grappling, should move away a little so that it in turn will not be struck by the enemy ship. The second [Byzantine] *dromon* should then with all its vigor collide with, and completely overturn, the enemy ship with all its men. The grappling [chain], however, should meanwhile be adjusted lest both ships be overturned, and an area should be left on the sides of the stern of the enemy ship so that, after the [second Byzantine] *dromon* has attacked, it may force the ship to be overturned along with its crew.

83.

Introduction. From the seventh century onward the Byzantine *dromones* were provided with the great advantage of a special secret weapon, the famed Greek fire (which worked even when it came into contact with water). This new incendiary weapon was invented by Callinicos, a Byzantine of Syria, in the last quarter of the seventh century. Its use was especially decisive during the years 674–78, when Constantinople was almost constantly under siege by an Arab fleet blockading the capital. But the use of Greek fire on a grand scale came in 941 when a huge number of Rus ships advanced from Kiev down the Dnieper River and across the Black Sea. Liudprand, the tenth-century German bishop and envoy to Byzantium, describes the steps taken by Emperor Romanus I to combat the threat of the Rus fleet under Prince Igor.

LIUDPRAND ON THE USE OF GREEK FIRE AGAINST THE RUS

(From Liudprand, *Antapodosis*, MPL, vol. 136, cols. 833–34.)

After [Emperor] Romanus had spent some sleepless nights lost in thought while Igor was ravaging all the coastal regions, Romanus was informed that he possessed some dilapidated galleys which the government had left out of commission on account of their age. When he heard this, he ordered the *kalaphatai*—that is, the shipwrights—to come to him, and he said to them, "Hurry without delay, and prepare these remaining galleys for service. Place the devices which shoot out fire, not only in the prow but also in the stern and on both sides of each ship." When the galleys had been outfitted according to his orders, he manned them with his most competent sailors and ordered them to proceed against King [Prince] Igor.

They set out, and when King Igor saw them out on the sea, he ordered his troops not to kill the sailors but to take them alive. But then God, merciful and compassionate, wished not only to protect but to honor with victory those who served and worshiped him and sought his aid [i.e., the Byzantines]. Therefore, he quieted the winds and calmed the sea. For otherwise it would have been difficult for the Greeks to shoot their fire. Then, having become surrounded by the Rus, the Greeks hurled their fire all around them. When the Rus saw this, they at once threw themselves from their ships into the sea, choosing to be drowned by the waves rather than cremated by the fire. Some, weighted down by their breastplates and helmets (which they would never see again) sank to the bottom of the sea. Others were burned as they swam on the waves. No one escaped that day unless he was able to flee to the shore [in his vessel]. For the ships of the Rus, on account of their small size, can sail in very little water whereas the galleys of the Greeks, because of their greater draught [*profunditas*], cannot do so.

84.

Introduction. The *Russian Primary Chronicle*, first compiled in the eleventh century and revised in the early twelfth century, also describes the Rus naval attack on Constantinople in 941. The "lightning from heaven" mentioned in the *Chronicle* is, of course, the famed Greek fire.

THE *RUSSIAN PRIMARY CHRONICLE* ON THE SAME
EPISODE (941)

(Translated by S. Cross and O. Sherbowitz, *Russian Primary Chronicle* [Cambridge, Mass.: Medieval Academy of America, 1953], p. 72.)

Theophanes [the Byzantine commander] pursued them in boats with Greek fire, and dropped it through pipes upon the Russian ships, so that a strange miracle was offered to view. Upon seeing the flames, the Rus cast themselves into the sea water, being anxious to escape, but the survivors returned home. When they came once more to their native land, where each recounted to his kinsfolk the course of events and described the fire launched from the ships, they related that the Greeks had in their possession the "lightning from heaven," and had set them on fire by pouring it forth, so that the Rus could not conquer them.

Commentary. It might be noted that Greek fire was still in use by the Byzantines at the final siege of Constantinople in 1453. But long before that the weapon had lost its shock value and was ultimately replaced by gunpowder and cannon.

85.

Introduction. For centuries the Byzantine navy had been manned primarily by recruits from the provinces, in particular from the Cibyrrhaeot (or Caravisianorum) theme, which consisted of the islands near and the extreme southwest coast of Asia Minor. By the early thirteenth century the Byzantine navy had declined from its formerly proud and effective state. But Emperor Michael Palaeologus, the restorer of Constantinople to Byzantium, set out to rebuild the navy (1261–82). In contrast to Byzantine recruitment of sailors in earlier days, Michael drew his sailors from new groups: from the Gasmules (the half-breed sons of Greco-Latin unions) and from the port towns of southern Greece. Pachymeres, in the passage below, tells us something about Michael's newly organized navy. (On the Gasmules, see selection 220.)

A. RECRUITMENT OF SAILORS: THE GASMULES AND THE BYZANTINE NAVY

(From George Pachymeres, *De Michaele et Andronico Palaeologis*, ed. I. Bekker [Bonn, 1835], vol. 1, p. 309.)

A brave man, [Alexis] Philanthropenos, commanded the navy, holding the rank of *protostrator*,* and he was placed over all. Those under him who were many and very important he divided into captains, majors, counts, and admirals. The navy consisted of many ships. . . . But while young men filled these ships, they were rather lacking in force and impetuosity. [The ships were manned by] the Gasmules, who were from "the City." (These the Byzantines called two-raced, that is, born of Greek women to Latin men.) But most [sailors] were from Laconia and they are wrongly called Tzakones. And these, coming from the Morea and the western areas, since they were numerous and warlike, the ruler at once transferred to Constantinople to live, together with their women and children.

Introduction. The historian Gregoras (d. 1360) has this to say about Michael and his navy:

B. The Gasmule and Laconian Sailors

(From Nicephorus Gregoras, *Byzantina historia*, ed. L. Schopen and I. Bekker [Bonn, 1829], vol. 1, p. 98.)

The emperor prepared a very great fleet, filling more than 60 triremes [a long ship powered by three banks of oars] from others and from the people of the Gasmules. These were brought up in both Greek and Latin customs. . . . And there was with these [Gasmules] also an armed naval army, Laconians who had come from the Peloponnesus. . . . And the imperial fleet, thus splendidly organized, sailed at Michael's order.

* Usually an army rank.

C.
DIPLOMACY

86.

Introduction. Perhaps more than any state in history, Byzantium was constantly being attacked by enemies from more than one side. But the empire preferred to avoid war, if at all possible, through the exercise of subtle diplomacy. Besides of course the exchange of envoys, such measures included the payment of bribes in the form of rich gifts to foreign rulers, the creation of suitable marriage alliances, and, not least, the conversion of other peoples, especially the barbarians, to the Orthodox faith.

DIPLOMACY THROUGH PRESENTATION OF GIFTS TO BARBARIANS

(From Theophylact Simocattes, *Ekumenike historia*, ed. C. de Boor [Leipzig, 1887], p. 226.)

When the armies of the Avars were ravaging the areas of Thrace, the Senate recommended to [Emperor] Maurice that he send an embassy to the *khagan*. And the emperor, having summoned Armaton, appointed him ambassador and sent him to the *khagan*. And Armaton at Drizipera was loaded down with gifts [to take with him]. But the *khagan* was at this moment bewailing his fate, lamenting inconsolably the loss of his son and the ruin of his forces. Ten days the envoy remained with the *khagan*, which was not according to plan. For the mourning was deep and the damage irreparable. Then on the twelfth day the envoy was brought to the tent of the barbarian and the envoy flattered the barbarian with soothing words, but the ruler could barely bring himself to accept the imperial gifts, all but consumed as he was by the events of the tragedy. Giftless gifts of the enemy!

Then the envoy, employing a great many words, prevailed upon the barbarian to be honored by [accepting] the gifts. On the next day the barbarian, having now negotiated peace, prepared to break camp. Thereupon, the *khagan* made the following speech: "O God, judge between [Emperor] Maurice and the *khagan*, between Avars and Romans [Byzantines]. Keep the emperor from wrecking the peace. . . . For if the Romans be falsifiers of the peace and creators of war, may terrible misfortunes befall them." . . . The Istros [river] is agreed upon by Romans and Avars as their border, but against the Slavs, [Byzantine] authority shall extend across the river. And then another 20,000 gold pieces were added to [the terms of] the treaty. Through these circumstances the war between Avars and Romans came to an end.

87.

Introduction. The following selection, taken from the sixth-century chronicle of John Malalas of Antioch, relates how a barbarian ruler during the reign of Justin used conversion to Orthodoxy in order to break away from Persia and presumably to secure Byzantine support.

CONVERSION OF THE LAZI TO ORTHODOXY

(Translated by M. Spinka and G. Downey and revised by D. Geanakoplos, from the *Chronicle of John Malalas* [Chicago: University of Chicago Press, 1940], pp. 121–23.)

During his [Justin's] reign there was a certain Tzath, [ruler] of the Lazi who came from Persia where [king] Kavad reigned and whose subject Tzath was. Tzath, ruler of the Lazi of Persia, was a pagan. Tzath ran away from Persia and came to Emperor Justin in Constantinople to beseech him to appoint a ruler over the Lazi, and he would then become a Christian. Accepted by the emperor, he was instructed and became Christian and took as wife a Byzantine woman, the granddaughter of Nomos, the *patricius*, by name of Valeriane. He took her with him back to his own land, after being crowned by Justin, the emperor of the Romans. He [Tzath] wore a small imperial Byzantine crown and a white chlamys all of silk, and under it, instead of a purple garment, there was a broad gold vestment in the middle of which there was a small medallion ornamented with a portrait of himself. And he wore a white tunic covered with even more gold and with a similar portrait of the emperor. The boots he wore were from his own land, decorated with pearls in a Persian design. He also had a belt with pearls on it. Both he and his wife Valeriane received many other gifts from Emperor Justin.

88.

Introduction. The use of spies was, of course, a common feature of diplomatic (as well as military) practice throughout the Byzantine period. The following is from the *Anecdota* of the contemporary historian Procopius on Justinian's reign.

BYZANTIUM SPIES ON FOREIGN NATIONS

(From Procopius of Caesarea, *Anecdota or Secret History*, Loeb Classical Library [Cambridge, 1960], pp. 350, 352).

And this about the activities of spies: Many men from the beginning were supported by the state, that is, those going to the wars which occurred under the Persian rule, or those who were involved under the guise of trading or in some other manner. They scrutinized everything [in foreign areas] very closely, then returned to the land of the Byzantines to relate to its rulers all they could about the secrets of their enemies. And these [Byzantine rulers] made provision to safeguard themselves, and thus nothing untoward happened to them. This practice had also been useful to the Medes of old. Chosroës [the Persian ruler] on his part [employed] many such, they say, and utilized the evidence gathered up by his spies from this area [the Byzantine empire]. Thus events occurring among the Byzantines did not deceive him.

89.

Introduction. Though priding themselves on the efficiency of their army and navy, the Byzantines, as noted, tried first in almost every case to avoid war and gain their ends through craft or devious diplomacy. (They were so celebrated for this that "byzantine" is today still used as an adjective implying political intrigue and manipulation.) The best evidence of this finely tempered diplomacy is provided in the secret instructions left by Emperor Constantine VII Porphyrogenitus to his son (c. 950) on diverse ways to handle threats from foreign peoples: whom to play up to and whom to utilize as allies in order to stave off impending dangers without the use of military force.

When Constantine VII wrote his confidential instructions, he emphasized that the key people, the linchpin of Byzantine diplomacy, were the Pechenegs (*Patzinaks*, in Greek). These people adjoined other tribes of Turks, Rus, and the Greek population in the Byzantine province of Cherson (located in present-day southern Russia). Constantine explains that it is the Pechenegs who hold other, more dangerous nomadic peoples in check, and that alliance with the Pechenegs would provide the key to Byzantine domination of the region north and east of the Black Sea. He then relates how to diplomatically resist giving up the secret of Greek fire.

A. ON THE IMPORTANCE OF THE PECHENEGS

(Translated by R. Jenkins, from Constantine Porphyrogenitus, *De administrando imperio,* ed. G. Moravcsik [Washington, D.C.: Dumbarton Oaks, 1967], pp. 49–55.)

I conceive, then, that it is always greatly to the advantage of the emperor of the Romans to be minded to keep the peace with the nation of the Pechenegs and to conclude conventions and treaties of friendship with them and to send every year to them from our side a diplomatic agent with presents befitting and suitable to that nation, and to take from their side sureties, that is, hostages and a diplomatic agent, who shall be collected together under charge of the competent minister in this city protected of God, and shall enjoy all imperial benefits and gifts suitable for the emperor to bestow.

This nation of the Pechenegs is neighbour to the district of Cherson, and if they are not friendly disposed towards us, they may make excursions and plundering raids against Cherson, and may ravage Cherson itself and the so-called Regions. . . .

The Pechenegs are neighbours to and march with the Russians also, and often, when the two are not at peace with one another, raid Russia, and do her considerable harm and outrage.

The Russians also are much concerned to keep the peace with the Pechenegs. For they buy of them horned cattle and horses and sheep, whereby they live more easily and comfortably, since none of the aforesaid animals is found in Russia. Moreover, the Russians are quite unable to set out for wars beyond their borders unless they are at peace with the Pechenegs, because while they are away from their homes, these may come upon them and destroy and outrage their property.

Nor can the Russians come at this imperial city of the Romans, either for war or for trade, unless they are at peace with the Pechenegs, because when the Russians come with their ships to the barrages of the river and cannot pass through unless they lift their ships off the river and carry them past by portaging them on their shoulders, then the men of this nation of the Pechenegs set upon them, and, as they cannot do two things at once, they are easily routed and cut to pieces. . . .

The tribe of the Turks, too, trembles greatly at and fears the said Pechenegs, because they have often been defeated by them and brought to the verge of complete annihilation. Therefore the Turks always look on the Pechenegs with dread, and are held in check by them. . . .

So long as the emperor of the Romans is at peace with the Pechenegs, neither Russians nor Turks can come upon the Roman dominions by force of arms, nor can they exact from the Romans large and inflated sums in money and goods as the price of peace, for they fear the strength of this nation which the emperor can turn against them while they are campaigning against the Romans. *For* the Pechenegs, if they are leagued in friendship with the emperor and won over by him through letters and gifts, can easily come upon the country both of the Russians and of the Turks, and enslave their women and children and ravage their country. . . .

To the Bulgarians also the emperor of the Romans will appear more formidable, and can impose on them the need for tranquillity, if he is at peace with the Pechenegs, because the said Pechenegs are neighbours to these Bulgarians also, and when they wish, either for private gain or to do a favour to the emperor of the Romans, they can easily march against Bulgaria, and with their preponderating multitude and their strength overwhelm and defeat them. And so the Bulgarians also continually struggle and strive to maintain peace and harmony with the Pechenegs. For from having frequently been crushingly defeated and plundered by them, they have learned by experience the value and advantage of being always at peace with them.

Yet another folk of these Pechenegs lies over against the district of Cherson; they trade with the Chersonites, and perform services for them and for the emperor in Russia and Chazaria and Zichia and all the parts beyond: that is to say, they receive from the Chersonites a prearranged remuneration in respect of this service proportionate to their labour and trouble, in the form of pieces of purple cloth, ribbons, loosely woven cloths, gold brocade, pepper, scarlet *or* "Parthian" leather, and other commodities which they require, according to a contract which each Chersonite may make or agree to with an individual Pecheneg.

For these Pechenegs are free men and, so to say, independent, and never perform any service without remuneration.

When an imperial agent goes over to Cherson on this service, he must at once send to Patzinacia and demand of them hostages and an escort, and on their arrival he must leave the hostages under guard in the city of Cherson, and himself go off with the escort to Patzinacia and carry out his instructions. Now these Pechenegs, who are ravenous and keenly covetous of articles rare among them, are shameless in their demands for generous gifts, the hostages demanding this for themselves and that for their wives, and the escort something for their own trouble and some more for the wear and tear of their cattle. Then, when the imperial agent enters their country, they first ask for the emperor's gifts, and then again, when these have glutted the menfolk, they ask for the presents for their wives and parents. Also, all who come with him to escort him on his way back to Cherson demand payment from him for their trouble and the wear and tear of their cattle.

B. On Byzantine Relations with Barbarian Peoples

(From Constantine Porphyrogenitus, *De administrando imperio*, pp. 67–71.)

Fix, my son, your minds's eye upon my words, and learn those things which I command you, and you will be able in due season as from ancestral treasures to bring forth the wealth of wisdom, and to display the abundance of wit. Know therefore that all the tribes of the north have, as it were implanted in them by nature, a ravening greed of money, never satiated, and so they demand everything and hanker after everything and have desires that know no limit or circumscription, but are always eager for more, and desirous to acquire great profits in exchange for a small service. And so these importunate demands and brazenly submitted claims must be turned back and rebutted by plausible speeches and prudent and clever excuses, which, in so far as our experience has enabled us to arrive at them, will, to speak summarily, run more or less as follows:

Should they ever require and demand, whether they be Chazars, or Turks, or again Russians, or any other nation of the northerners and Scythians, as frequently happens, that some of the imperial vesture or diadems or state robes should be sent to them in return for some service or office performed by them, then thus you shall excuse yourself: "These robes of state and the diadems, which you call 'kamelaukia', were not fashioned by men, nor by human arts devised or elaborated, but, as we find it written in secret stories of old history, when God made emperor the former Constantine the great, who was the first Christian emperor, He sent him these robes of state by the hand of His angel, and the diadems which you call 'kamelaukia', and charged him to lay them in the great and holy church of God, which, after the name of that very wisdom which is the property of God, is called St. Sophia; and not to clothe himself in them every day, but *only* when it is a great public festival of the Lord. And so by God's command he laid them up, and they hang above the holy table in the sanctuary of this same church, and are for the ornament of the church. And the rest of the imperial vestments and cloaks lie spread out upon this holy table. And when a festival of our Lord and God Jesus Christ comes round, the patriarch takes up such of these robes of state and diadems as are suitable and appropriated to that occasion, and sends them to the emperor, and he wears them in the procession, and only in it, as the servant and minister of God, and after use returns them again to the church, and they are laid up in it. Moreover, there is a curse of the holy and great emperor Constantine engraved upon this holy table of the church of God, according as he was charged by God through the angel, that if an emperor for any use or occasion or unseasonable desire be minded to take of them and either himself misuse them or give them to others, he shall be anathematized as the foe and enemy of the commands of God, and shall be excommunicated from the church; moreover, if he himself be minded to make others like them, these too the church of God must take, with the freely expressed approval of all the archbishops and of the senate; and it shall not be in the authority either of the emperor, or of the patriarch, or of any other, to take these robes of state or the diadems from the holy church of God. And mighty dread hangs over them who are minded to transgress any of these divine ordinances. For one of the emperors, Leo by name, who also married a wife from Chazaria, out of his folly and rashness took up one of these diadems when no festival of the Lord was toward, and without the approval of the patriarch put it about his head. And straightway a carbuncle came forth upon his forehead so that in torment at the pains of it he evilly departed his evil life, and ran upon death untimely. And, this rash act being summarily avenged, thereafter a rule was made, that when he is about to be crowned the emperor must first swear and give surety that he will neither do nor conceive anything against what has been ordained and kept from ancient times, and then may he be crowned by the patriarch and perform and execute the rites appropriate to the established festival."

Similar care and thought you must take in the matter of the liquid fire which is discharged through tubes, so that if any shall ever venture to demand this too, as they have often made demands of us also, you may rebut and dismiss them in words like these: "This too was revealed and taught by *God* through an angel to the great and holy Constantine, the first Christian emperor, and concerning this too he received great charges from the same angel, as we are assured by the faithful witness of our fathers and grandfathers, that it should be manufactured among the Christians only and in the city ruled by them, and nowhere else at all, nor should it be sent nor taught to any other nation whatsoever. And so, for the confirmation of this among those who should come after him, this great emperor caused curses to be inscribed on the holy table of the church of God, that he who should dare to give of this fire to another nation should neither be called a Christian, not be held worthy of any rank or office; and if he should be the holder of any such, he should be expelled therefrom and be anathematized and made an example for ever and ever, whether he were emperor, or patriarch, or any other man whatever, either ruler or subject, who should seek to transgress this commandment. And he adjured all who had the zeal and fear of God to be prompt to make away with him who attempted to do this, as a common enemy and a transgressor of this great commandment, and to dismiss him to a death most hateful and cruel.

90.

Introduction. For members of the Byzantine impe-
rial family, dynastic marriages to foreigners were not uncommon. Nevertheless,
there was always some suspicion on the part of the Byzantines that such marriages might legitimate claims of the "barbarian" rulers to the imperial dignity.
One example of Byzantine hesitation over marriage alliances of this kind may
be found in the reaction to Ambassador Liudprand's mission to Constantinople
in 968 to gain a Byzantine *porphyrogenita* (born in the purple chamber of the
palace) wife for his master's son, the German Emperor Otto II (see below, selection 267). In the next selection (c. 950), Emperor Constantine VII expresses
his displeasure at a marriage arranged shortly before by his father-in-law, the
usurper Romanus Lecapenus, between Romanus's daughter Maria and the barbarian Bulgar prince Peter (who was in fact now an Orthodox Christian). In
the last two or three centuries of the empire, however, marriage alliances of
Byzantine princes with Latin princesses became very common. All the former
Byzantine prejudices and condescension had finally given way to the realities
of the situation. (Cf. also selection 47 on Yolande of Montferrat and Emperor
Andronicus II.)

IMPERIAL MARRIAGES WITH FOREIGNERS

(Translated by R. Jenkins, from Constantine Porphyrogenitus, *De
administrando imperio*, ed. G. Moravcsik [Washington, D.C.: Dumbarton Oaks, 1967], pp. 73–75.)

"For how can it be admissible that Christians should
form marriage associations and ally themselves by marriage with infidels, when
the canon forbids it and the whole church regards it as alien to and outside the
Christian order? Or which of the illustrious or noble or wise emperors of the
Romans has admitted it?" But if they reply: "How then did the lord Romanus,
the emperor, ally himself in marriage with the Bulgarians, and give his granddaughter to the lord Peter the Bulgarian?", this must be the defence: "The lord
Romanus, the emperor, was a common, illiterate fellow, and not from among
those who have been bred up in the palace, and have followed the Roman national customs from the beginning; nor was he of imperial and noble stock, and
for this reason in most of his actions he was too arrogant and despotic, and in
this instance he neither heeded the prohibition of the church, nor followed the
commandment and ordinance of the great Constantine, but out of a temper arrogant and self-willed and untaught in virtue and refusing to follow what was
right and good, or to submit to the ordinances handed down by our forefathers,
he dared to do this thing; offering, that is, this alone by way of specious excuse,
that by this action so many Christian prisoners were ransomed, and that the Bulgarians too are Christians *and* of like faith with us, and that in any case she who
was given in marriage was not daughter of the chief and lawful emperor, but of
the third and most junior, who was still subordinate and had no share of authority in matters of government; but this was no different from *giving* any other
of the ladies of the imperial family, whether more distantly or closely related to
the imperial nobility, nor did it make any difference that she was given for some

service to the commonweal, or was daughter of the most junior, who had no authority to speak of. And because he did this thing contrary to the canon and to ecclesiastical tradition and the ordinance and commandment of the great and holy emperor Constantine, the aforesaid lord Romanus was in his lifetime much abused, and was slandered and hated by the senatorial council and all the commons and the church herself, so that their hatred became abundantly clear in the end to which he came; and after his death he is in the same way vilified and slandered and condemned inasmuch as he too introduced an unworthy and unseemly innovation into the noble polity of the Romans."

91.

Introduction. Finally, here is another, more unusual type of diplomacy to avoid war: as the Byzantine historian Pachymeres relates, Emperor Michael VIII Palaeologus of the late thirteenth century, after conquering the Latin Prince William of Achaia at the famous battle of Pelagonia (1259),* entered into an alliance with him, strengthening the bonds between them by making William godfather to one of his own children. The ties between the two rulers were further tightened by the invocation, as part of their formal oaths, of horrible curses should this bond (in effect relationship with the emperor in the Byzantine "family of princes") be broken. Note here the conflation of Western with Byzantine custom.

*See above, selection 76.

SOLEMN OATHS OF MICHAEL VIII AND WILLIAM OF ACHAIA

(From George Pachymeres, *De Michaele et Andronico Palaeologis,* ed. I. Bekker [Bonn, 1835], vol. 1, pp. 86–88.)

The Prince of Achaia was thrown into prison. . . . [This took place in 1261 after the city of Constantinople had been retaken by the Byzantines.] William humbled himself, offering to prostrate himself at the feet of the emperor, and to render the honors due him. He pledged to submit to him in obedience and to negotiate his liberty. The Emperor Michael Palaeologus, having examined his proposals and realizing that the towns the prince offered for his ransom [especially Mistra] constituted a considerable part of the Morea, accepted. Then he released him with all those of his entourage and rendered him great honors. Moreover, Michael contracted with him such a close bond that he had him hold one of his children at the baptismal font [act as godfather]. After that, they bound each other reciprocally by execrable oaths, each holding a lighted candle in his hand. They pronounced against each other (in case the oaths were broken) the most horrible curses and then at once extinguished their candles according to the custom of the Italians in their excommunications. . . . Then the emperor gave him his freedom and honored him with the office of grand domestic. . . . So the prince returned the lands and received the title of grand domestic.

PART III
The Church
◆ ◆ ◆ ◆ ◆ ◆ ◆ ◆ ◆ ◆ ◆ ◆ ◆ ◆ ◆ ◆ ◆ ◆

A.
THE TRIUMPH OF
CHRISTIANITY

92.

Introduction. The acceptance of Christianity on the part of Constantine as the new religion of the Roman Empire was one of the most momentous events in all of European history. To glorify the triumph of Christianity Eusebius, the emperor's adviser, in the thirtieth year of Constantine's reign wrote his panegyric of Constantine.

A. EUSEBIUS LAUDS CONSTANTINE (335)

(Translated by E. Richardson, from *De laudibus Constantini*, in P. Schaff and H. Wace, eds., *A Select Library of Nicene and Post-Nicene Fathers of the Christian Church*, 2d ser. [reprint, Grand Rapids, Mich.: Wm. Eerdmans, 1976], vol. 1, p. 606.)

One god was proclaimed to all mankind. At the same time one universal power, the Roman Empire, arose and flourished. . . . At the selfsame period . . . by the express appointment of the same God, two roots of blessing, the Roman Empire and the doctrine of Christian piety, sprang up together for the benefit of men. . . . Two mighty powers starting from the same point, the Roman Empire which henceforth was swayed by a single sovereign, and the Christian religion, subdued and reconciled all the contending elements.

Introduction. Although Constantine's Constantinople had become the new capital of the Christian Roman Empire, paganism was not at once proscribed. Not until 341 did Constantine's son, Emperor Constantius, decree that pagan sacrifices were forbidden.

B. CONSTANTIUS PROSCRIBES PAGAN SACRIFICES (341)

(Translated by C. Pharr, *The Theodosian Code* [Princeton, 1952], 16-10-2, p. 472.)

Superstition shall cease; the madness of sacrifices shall be abolished. For if any man in violation of the law of the sainted Emperor, our Father, and in violation of this command of Our Clemency, should dare to perform sacrifices, he shall suffer the infliction of a suitable punishment and the effect of an immediate sentence. . . .

[And in 346 Constantius decreed the following (16-10-4)]:

It is our pleasure that the temples shall be immediately closed in all places and in all cities, and access to them forbidden, so as to deny to all abandoned men the opportunity to commit sin. It is also our will that all men shall abstain from sacrifices. But if perchance any man should perpetrate any such criminality, he shall be struck down with the avenging sword. We also decree that the property of a man thus executed shall be vindicated to the fisc. The governors of the provinces shall be similarly punished if they should neglect to avenge such crimes.

93.

Introduction. When in 361 young Emperor Julian, nephew of Constantius, came to the throne, he sought to turn the clock back by restoring a Greek philosophic type of paganism and outlawing Christianity. But realizing the firm hold Christianity had achieved among many groups and individuals of Roman society, he went at his purpose slowly and systematically. His most damaging measure to Christianity was the issue of an edict on teaching in the schools.

JULIAN'S DECREE ON CHRISTIAN TEACHERS (362)*

(Translated by W. Wright, *The Works of Emperor Julian* [Cambridge, Mass.: Harvard University Press, 1932], vol. 3, pp. 117–23.)

I hold that a proper education results, not in laboriously acquired symmetry of phrases and language, but in a healthy condition of mind, I mean a mind that has understanding and true opinions about things good and evil, honorable and base. Therefore, when a man believes one thing [Christianity] and teaches his pupils another [pagan literature], in my opinion he fails to educate exactly in proportion as he fails to be an honest man. And if the divergence between a man's convictions and his utterances is merely in trivial matters, that can be tolerated somehow, though it is wrong. But if in matters of the greatest importance a man has certain opinions and teaches the contrary, what is that but the conduct of hucksters, and not honest but thoroughly dissolute men in that they praise most highly the things that they believe to be most worthless, thus cheating and enticing by their praises those to whom they desire to transfer their worthless wares. Now all who profess to teach anything whatever ought to be men of upright character, and ought not to harbour in their souls opinions irreconcilable with what they publicly profess and above all, I believe it is necessary that those who associate with the young and teach them rhetoric should be of that upright character, for they expound the writings of the ancients, whether they be rhetoricians or grammarians, and still more if they are sophists. For these claim to teach, in addition to other things, not only the use of words, but morals also, and they assert that political philosophy is their peculiar field. Let us leave aside, for the moment, the question whether this is true or not. But while I applaud them for aspiring to such high pretensions, I should applaud them still more if they did not utter falsehoods and convict themselves of thinking one thing and teaching their pupils another.

I think it is absurd that men who expound the works of these writers should dishonor the gods whom they used to honor. Yet, though I think this absurd, I do not say that they ought to change their opinions and then instruct the young. But I give them this choice: either not to teach what they do not think admirable, or, if they wish to teach, let them first really persuade their pupils that neither Homer nor Hesiod nor any of these writers whom they expound and have declared to be guilty of impiety, folly, and error in regard to the gods, is such as they declare. For since they make a livelihood and receive pay from the works of those writers, they thereby confess that they are most shamefully greedy of gain, and that, for the sake of a few drachmae, they would put up with anything. . . . But since the gods have granted us liberty, it seems to me absurd that men should teach what they do not believe to be sound. But if they believe that those whose interpreters they are and for whom they sit, so to speak, in the seat of the prophets, were wise men, let them be the first to emulate their piety towards the gods. If, however, they think that those writers were in error with respect to the most honored gods, then let them betake themselves to the churches of the Galileans to expound Matthew and Luke, since you Galileans are obeying them when you ordain that men shall refrain from temple worship. For my part, I wish that your ears and your tongues might be "born anew," as you would say, as regards these things in which may I ever have part, and all who think and act as is pleasing to me.

For religious and secular teachers let there be a general ordinance to this effect: Any youth who wishes to attend the schools is not excluded; nor indeed would it be reasonable to shut out from the best way boys who are still too ignorant to know which way to turn, and to overawe them into being led against their will to the beliefs of their ancestors. Though indeed it might be proper to cure these, even against their will, as one cures the insane, except that we concede indulgence to all for this sort of disease. For we ought, I think, to teach, but not punish, the demented.[†]

*The contemporary historian Ammianus Marcellinus (*Historiae*, ed. J. Fontaine [Paris, 1977], bk. 25, ch. 4, section 20) remarks on this edict: "Julian forbade without pity Christian masters of rhetoric and grammar to teach unless they passed to the cult of the gods."

†Not surprisingly, not a few Christians were pleased and believed that Christianity should have nothing at all to do with pagan Greek learning. For a different view, see below, selection 296, the famous discourse of St. Basil in this same period, which played a great role in making pagan learning acceptable and even useful to Christianity.

94.

Introduction. One of Theodosius I's edicts decreed the death penalty for pagan sacrifices. Although previous emperors had also issued edicts against paganism, they were not always strictly carried out. It was Theodosius's decided preference for Christianity that left no room whatever for toleration of paganism and marked Christianity's genuine triumph. Other decrees prohibited the offering of sacrifices, divination by animal entrails, and visiting the temples. The last decree of Theodosius against the pagans was issued in 392, specifying the most severe penalties for the offering of pagan sacrifices.

THE DEFINITIVE TRIUMPH OF CHRISTIANITY

(Translated by C. Pharr, *The Theodosian Code* [Princeton, 1952], 16-10-12, pp. 473–74.)

No person at all, of any class or order whatsoever of men or of dignitaries . . . shall sacrifice an innocent victim to senseless images in any place at all or in any city. . . . But if any man should dare to immolate a victim for purpose of sacrifice, or to consult the quivering entrails, according to the example of a person guilty of high treason, he shall be reported by an accusation which is permitted to all persons, and he shall receive the appropriate sentence, even though he has inquired nothing contrary to, or with reference to, the welfare of the emperors.

B.
RELATIONSHIP OF CHURCH
AND STATE

95.

Introduction. To speak of a relationship between "church and state" in Byzantium is perhaps misleading. For unlike modern Western society and to a degree even more than in the medieval West, Byzantium knew no such clear separation. Rather than two distinct, and sometimes even competing authorities within society, there was but one "Christian commonwealth" (*Basileia*), in which affairs we ordinarily ascribe to church or state were intermingled, and over which one emperor (*basileus*) ruled as vice regent of the one God. To be sure, according to the theory of imperial authority the emperor seemed to be in a position of firm control over all aspects of church life. But the question of the relationship of church and state, or, more precisely, the degree of the authority of the emperor over the church, its administration, spiritual life, and its ecclesiastical properties, is still debated by scholars. Pertinent here is the famous Byzantine theory of *mimesis*, that is, of the position of the Roman emperor and of his empire on earth as "imitating" or representing on earth God and his universal heavenly kingdom. This theory had been first formulated by the early fourth-century bishop of Caesarea, Eusebius, and seems to have been molded by views he expressed in his *Preparatio evangelica* ("Preparation for the New Testament"). This work emphasizes, above all, that the polytheism and polyarchy of the ancient world were ended with the coming of Christ—to Eusebius clear proof of the power of the Christian God. Since there is one God, he states, it follows that there can be but one emperor, one empire, and one church.

THE UNIVERSAL EMPIRE AND THE CHURCH UNIVERSAL

(From Eusebius, *La préparation evangélique*, in J. Sirinelli and E. des Places, eds., *Sources chrétiennes* [Paris, 1974], pp. 118–20.)

It was the result of divine and ineffable power that, together with his word and along with his teaching of the monarchy of the one God of the universe, he [God] delivered the human race at one and the same time both from the much-erring, deceitful influence of demons and from the polyarchy of various nations. Indeed, in the past there existed among the nations thousands of kings and local rulers who ruled in different cities and countries. Some were governed democratically, others tyranically, and in still others authority was shared by several. Naturally, as a result of this situation, all kinds of wars erupted, as peoples fought with other peoples and continually attacked their neighbors. Nations pillaged and were pillaged, and they besieged each other's cities to the point that all the inhabitants of the cities, the peasants in the fields, were all trained in war from infancy on. Only when they were armed did they circulate on the great roads and in their villages and fields.

But when Christ-God appeared, concerning whom the prophets had long ago prophesied: "In his days justice and a profound peace shall prevail" and "They shall beat their swords into ploughshares, and a nation shall no longer take up the sword against another and they shall no longer learn to make war," events followed what had been prophesied. All the polyarchy in the Roman world came to an end, since Augustus had established a monarchy at the same moment that our Savior appeared on earth. Henceforth and until the present, there were no longer seen, as before, cities waging war on other cities, or peoples combatting other peoples, or even life exhausting itself in the earlier confusion.

96.

Introduction. Early in the reign of Constantine (324–37), when so many precedents were established, especially for the relations between church and empire, the custom was confirmed of exempting a church and its ecclesiastics from performance of the so-called "political liturgies," that is, work for the benefit of state and society, to which, hitherto, all subjects of the empire had been liable on demand of the government. This point is well demonstrated in the following letter of the Emperor Constantine the Great to the governor of the province of Africa.

IMMUNITY OF THE CLERGY

(Translated by H. Lawlor and J. Oulton from Eusebius, *The Ecclesiastical History* and *Martyrs of Palestine* [London: Society for Promoting Christian Knowledge, 1927], vol. 1, p. 320.)

Since from many facts it appears that the setting at naught of divine worship, by which the highest reverence for the most holy and heavenly [Power] is preserved, has brought great dangers upon public affairs, and that its lawful restoration and preservation have bestowed the greatest good fortune on the Roman name and singular prosperity on all the affairs of mankind (for it is the Divine Providence which bestows these blessings): it has seemed good that those men who, with due holiness and constant observance of this law, bestow their services on the performance of divine worship, should receive the rewards of their own labours, most honoured Anulinus. Wherefore it is my wish that those persons who, within the province committed to you, in the Catholic Church over which Caecilian presides, bestow their service on this holy worship—those whom they are accustomed to call clerics—should once for all be kept absolutely free from all the public offices, that they be not drawn away by any error or sacrilegious fault from the worship which they owe to the Divinity, but rather without any hindrance serve to the utmost their own law. For when they render supreme service to the Deity, it seems that they confer incalculable benefit on the affairs of the State.

97.

Introduction. In addition to exemptions from certain of these "political liturgies" and of course from imperial taxation, in the early years of the reign of Constantine the Great the church needed help from the resources of the state. Accordingly, Constantine and many emperors following him gave grants of money to, or constructed at their own expense, churches, basilicas, and cathedrals. The following quotation indicating the grant of money to the church by the state is taken from a letter of Constantine the Great (early fourth century) addressed to the bishop of Carthage in North Africa.

GRANTS OF MONEY TO CHURCHES BY THE STATE

(Translated by H. Lawlor and J. Oulton from Eusebius, *The Ecclesiastical History* and *Martyrs of Palestine* [London: Society for Promoting Christian Knowledge, 1927], vol. 1, p. 319.)

Forasmuch as it has been our pleasure in all provinces, namely the African, the Numidian and the Mauretanian, that somewhat be contributed for expenses to certain specified ministers of the lawful and most holy Catholic religion, I have despatched a letter to Ursus, the most distinguished finance minister of Africa, and have notified him that he be careful to pay over to thy Firmness three thousand *folleis* [copper coins]. Do thou therefore, when thou shall secure delivery of the aforesaid sum of money, give orders that this money be distributed among all the above-mentioned persons in accordance with the schedule sent to you by Hosius. But if, after all, thou shalt find that there is aught lacking for the fulfilment of this my purpose in respect of them all, thou should ask without doubting whatsoever you find to be necessary from Heraclides our procurator fiscal. For indeed when he was here I gave him orders that if thy Firmness should ask any money from him, he should be careful to pay it over without any scruple.

98.

Introduction. In contrast to this official government support of the church, some emperors, in attempting especially to help the state ward off the threat of foreign enemies, had recourse to a peculiarly Byzantine ecclesiastical concept, that of *economia.* In essence this meant a certain elasticity in administrative and disciplinary matters of the church (dogma was normally excepted), especially when the safety and well-being of the state (*Basileia*) seemed to require it. We provide below three examples of the use of *economia.* The first, from the early seventh century (c. 622–23), describes how, despite the rigorous inalienability (canonically) of ecclesiastical property, Emperor Heraclius obtained the church's (reluctant) consent to melt down ecclesiastical treasures of gold and silver and he converted them into money in order to raise funds to push back the critical Persian onslaught in Asia Minor.

A. Heraclius Melts Down Church Treasures

(From Theophanes, *Chronographia*, ed. C. de Boor [Leipzig, 1883] vol. 1, pp. 302–3.)

In this year, on April 4, in the tenth indiction, immediately after Emperor Heraclius had celebrated the festival of Easter, on Monday evening, he moved against the Persian power. He seized the possessions of the blessed houses [churches] in loan, and, impelled by his lack of resources, he even took the many candles [gold and silver candle sticks] and other serviceable implements of the Great Church [Hagia Sophia] itself, and struck gold coins and very many *miliaresia* [silver coins.]

Introduction. In the later eleventh century (1081), when the Norman Robert Guiscard dangerously invaded the Balkans, aiming at Constantinople, Alexius I Comnenus, lacking funds to raise an army, had recourse to the same sort of *economia*, though many churchmen seemed extremely reluctant to comply. As Alexius's daughter (and apologist) Anna Comnena recounts:

B. Alexius Invokes Economia to Raise an Army

(Translated by E. Sewter, *The Alexiad of Anna Comnena* (Baltimore, 1969) p. 158.)

Then they examined the ancient laws and canons on the alienation of sacred objects. Among other things they discovered that it is lawful to expropriate sacred objects from churches for the ransoming of prisoners-of-war (and it was clear that all those Christians living in Asia under barbarian rule and all those who had escaped massacre were thus defiled because of their intercourse with infidels). In order to pay the soldiers and allies, therefore, they decided to convert into money a small quantity of such objects, which had long been idle and set aside as serving no purpose.

Introduction. The third example of *economia* we cite here (a rather different type) occurred in the later thirteenth century when Emperor Michael Palaeologus, seeking through religious union with Rome to block the aim of the king of Sicily, Charles of Anjou (the vassal of the pope), to seize Constantinople, declared to his clergy who were opposed to his policy:

C. Emperor Michael VIII Justifies Union with Rome

(From Pachymeres, *De Michaele et Andronico Palaeologis* [Bonn, 1835], vol. 1, pp. 387 and 457–59; translated by D. Geanakoplos, in *Emperor Michael Palaeologus and the West* [Cambridge, Mass.: Harvard University Press, 1959], pp. 265, 319.)

Far from being blamed for skillfully averting the danger threatening us . . . we shall instead be praised by all wise and prudent men. Only one thing impels me to seek union, and that is the absolute necessity of averting the peril that threatens us. Except for that I would never have begun this affair [ecclesiastical negotiations with Rome]. . . . My unionist efforts are due only to my desire to spare the Greeks the terrible wars and effusion of blood threatening the Empire. . . . For when would the Pope appear in Constantinople to take precedence over the Greek bishops and when would anyone traverse so vast a sea to carry an appeal to Rome? What is there contrary to the purity of the faith in the patriarchal commemoration of the Pope in liturgical matters [the diptychs]?*

Commentary. In another, even franker speech Michael cast aside any remaining pretense of moral justification for union and exposed completely his policy of pure expediency, or, as he clearly implied, of *economia*. Note, however, that Michael's arguments, involving, in the clergy's eyes, matters of dogma, failed to convince the vast majority of the churchmen.

You know very well with how much difficulty the present accord [of union pronounced in 1274 at Lyons] was achieved. . . . I realize that I have used force against many of you and have given offense to many friends, even grieving my own family. . . . I thought that the affair would now be ended and that the Latins would demand nothing more, as I promised you in my golden bulls in the church. But some of us, who, I am convinced, are attempting to create differences (I do not know why unless they spoke thus in order to test us and stir up trouble) when conversing with [Latin-minded] friars in Pera, called the union a farce and a fraud. They declared that further proof of union should be demanded. This then is the purpose of the present embassy. I wished to speak to you first and to inform you of this so that upon hearing them [the papal envoys] you will not suddenly become disturbed and accuse me of bad faith when you observe my conduct towards them. God is my witness that I will not alter one accent or one iota of the faith. I promise to hold aloft as a standard this divine symbol of our fathers and to combat not only the Latins but any people that would dispute this matter.

---

*A diptych was a two-leaved book the clergy read from during the liturgy, commemorating the names of the patriarchs and other dignitaries. The main question at issue was the Latin addition of the *filioque* to the creed. See selection 156.

99.

Introduction. By the time of Justinian the Eusebian ideal had been somewhat modified into a *theoretical* "dyarchy" of emperor and patriarch. This development finds its most famous expression in the preface to Justinian's *Novella* (edict) 6 (after 534) addressed to the patriarch of Constantinople. Here an ideal concord (*symphonia*) between *imperium* and *sacerdotium* is described—a harmony made possible because both spheres are instituted by the authority of God and both are contained within his Kingdom on earth (*Basileia*).

Nevertheless, as "vicar of God," Justinian in actuality exercised authority over all phases of church administration, appointing the patriarch, summoning ecumenical councils, establishing qualifications for the office of bishop and also for ordination, even—though there was no explicit legal basis for this—deposing recalcitrant patriarchs. Indeed, the emperor enjoyed certain "liturgical privileges" similar to those of the clergy, such as preaching to and censing the congregation and even with his own hands administering to himself the bread and wine of the Holy Eucharist (which, however, first had to be consecrated by an ecclesiastic). Imperial control of what we might call ecclesiastical "polity" was to characterize the Byzantine church throughout its entire history and, along with the emperor's liturgical privileges, is probably a major reason why in Western eyes the imperial authority was considered to be "Caesaropapistic."

A. JUSTINIAN'S *NOVELLA* VI: IMPERIAL AUTHORITY OVER THE CHURCH

(Justinian, *Novella* VI, in R. Schoell, ed., *Corpus Iuris Civilis*, vol. 3, *Novellae* [Berlin, 1912], pp. 35–36.)

The greatest blessings of mankind are the gifts of God which have been granted us by the mercy on high: the priesthood and the imperial authority. The priesthood ministers to things divine; the imperial authority is set over, and shows diligence in, things human; but both proceed from one and the same source, and both adorn the life of man. Nothing, therefore, will be a greater matter of concern to the emperor than the dignity and honor of the clergy; the more as they offer prayers to God without ceasing on his behalf. For if the priesthood be in all respects without blame, and full of faith before God, and if the imperial authority rightly and duly adorn the commonwealth committed to its charge, there will ensue a happy concord which will bring forth all good things for mankind. We therefore have the greatest concern for true doctrines of the Godhead and the dignity and honor of the clergy; and we believe that if they maintain that dignity and honor we shall gain thereby the greatest of gifts, holding fast what we already have and laying hold of what is yet to come. "All things," it is said, "are done well and truly if they start from a beginning that is worthy and pleasing in the sight of God." We believe that this will come to pass if observance be paid to the holy rules which have been handed down by the Apostles—those righteous guardians and ministers of the Word of God, who are ever to be praised and adored—and have since been preserved and interpreted by the holy Fathers.

Introduction. But the theory of a dyarchy attributes at once too much and too little power to both the emperor and patriarch. For their powers seemed in certain respects to overlap, if not in theory certainly in practice. For example, several emperors attempted to redefine dogma, most notably the Iconoclastic emperors of the eighth century and the later Palaeologan rulers of the last two centuries. Even Justinian, though acknowledging the two complementary spheres, was nevertheless closely involved in determining the final formulation of an important question of dogma, the relation of the human and the divine in Christ. (On the failure, however, of imperial attempts to alter dogma, see selections 100 and 106–13.)

On the other hand, the patriarch, under certain circumstances, also held a certain authority in the imperial administration. As the second leading personage in the empire, the patriarch, on the death of an emperor, would be provisionally in charge of administration. Moreover, should the heir to the throne be a minor, the patriarch often served as regent.

One view of the division of powers between emperor and patriarch is revealed in the document which follows, the introduction to one version of the *Epanagoge* (c. 880), probably drafted by the great ninth-century patriarch, statesman, and scholar, Photius. The *Epanagoge*, a revised lawcode commissioned by Emperor Basil I of the same period, seems never to have been officially promulgated. But these individual provisions dealing with the church were at least theoretically accepted, owing in large part to Photius's enormous personal prestige.

B. PHOTIUS DEFINES THE POWERS OF THE PATRIARCH

(From the *Epanagoge Aucta,** in J. and P. Zepos, eds., *Jus graecoromanum* [Athens, 1930–31], vol. 6, pp. 59–60.)

The attributes of the patriarch are to be a teacher, to behave with equality and indifference toward all men, high as well as low; to be merciful in [administering] justice but reproving of the unbelievers, while speaking forcefully in behalf of truth and the vindication of [orthodox] doctrines before kings, and not to be ashamed.

The patriarch alone should interpret the canons adopted by those men of old and the decrees instituted by the holy synods.

The patriarch should take care of and decide whatever problems arise from what was done and arranged, in particular and in general, by the ancient Fathers in ecumenical synods and in provincial synods. . . .

Since the constitution, analogous to man, consists of parts and members, the highest and most necessary parts are the emperor and the patriarch. For this reason the peace and happiness of the subjects in soul and body lie in the agreement and harmony of kingship and priesthood in all respects.

The [episcopal] throne of Constantinople, honored with dominion [over others], was declared by synodical votes to rank as the first [by the Second Ecumenical Council in 381]. Thus, those divine laws which followed decreed that matters brought before the other thrones should be referred to that [of Constantinople] for adjudication and decision.

*****Epanagoge Aucta* is an expanded version of the *Epanagoge.*

100.

Introduction. Almost from the time of Constantine's conversion to Christianity, however, there emerged within ecclesiastical circles a strong tradition of opposition to the exercise of imperial power over what the bishops considered to be the core of Christian belief: the formulation of dogma. This opposition became especially strong as a result of the attempts by certain emperors of the sixth and seventh centuries to placate the bitterly dissident Monophysites of Egypt, Syria, and Palestine (and later the Monotheletes), who refused to accept the orthodox doctrine of the dual natures in Christ. One of the best-known representatives of this ecclesiastical opposition was the famous seventh-century monk and theologian, Maximos the Confessor, whom (aside from Gregory Palamas) some scholars today consider the last truly creative thinker of the Eastern church.

A contemporary of the emperors Heraclius and Constans II, Maximos played an important part in the development of Byzantine mysticism through his theological exegesis of the mystical works of Pseudo-Dionysius "the Areopagite," which served to place Christ at the center of Dionysian mystical theology. In the following selection from a report of a formal interrogation, Maximos expresses what for him seems to have lain at the heart of clerical opposition to imperial "encroachments" of authority over the church: the fact that the emperor, despite his so-called "liturgical" privileges, was not truly a priest.

MAXIMOS THE CONFESSOR ON THE LIMITS OF IMPERIAL POWER OVER THE CHURCH

(From Maximos the Confessor, *Acta*, in MPG, vol. 90, col. 117.)

None of the emperors was able, through compromising measures, to induce the Fathers, who were theologians, to conform to the heretical teachings of their time. But in strong and compelling voices appropriate to the dogma in question, they declared quite clearly that it is the function of the clergy to discuss and define the "saving" dogmas of the universal church. And you said: "What then? Is not every emperor a Christian and a priest?" To which I responded: "He is not [a priest], for he does not participate in the sanctuary, nor, after the consecration of the bread, does he elevate it and say, 'The holy things [belong] to the holy.' He does not baptize nor perform the ceremony of chrismation; nor does he lay on hands and ordain bishops, priests, and deacons; nor does he consecrate churches; nor does he bear the symbols of the priesthood, the *omoforion* [cloak] and the Gospel, as he does bear the symbols of his rule, the crown and the purple robe."

101.

Introduction. Church councils and patriarchs repeatedly stressed that ecclesiastical personnel were to be tried and judged only in ecclesiastical courts. The state's attitude was often similar in principle, but more fluid in practice. Some emperors worked to protect the church's demand, notably Emperor Heraclius; but at other times the church complained of officials forcing clerics to answer charges in secular courts. (Nor was the later practice—reaffirmed by an edict of Alexius I—of trying a case in the court having jurisdiction over the defendant agreeable to the church, for a cleric would have to leave ecclesiastical domain to prosecute a layman.) The problem of secular versus ecclesiastical jurisdiction still vibrated in the ninth century, as evidenced by the provisions on courts of law found in the *Epanagoge*.

To Caesar What Is Caesar's; To God What Is God's

(From the *Epanagoge Aucta*, in J. and P. Zepos, eds., *Jus graeco-romanum* [Athens, 1930–31], vol. 6, pp. 75–76.)

There are two kinds of courts. The one acts in accord with [civil] laws, the other with [church] canons. But there is also a third kind, which combines and administers what is taken from both [civil] laws and canons.

The tribunal of the *autokrator* and *basileus* is not subject to appeal, nor can its findings be reversed by another court, but it is constantly reviewed by itself. In the same way also Moses who saw God remitted to the law the authority to review judgments.

The tribunal of the patriarch is not subject to appeal nor can its decrees be reviewed by another court; it is in itself the basis and source of ecclesiastical courts. All the ecclesiastical tribunals derive from it, and they all return to and end in it. Yet it is not derived from any other, and it does not return to and end in any other. . . . It is reviewed only spiritually and that by itself.

. . . We do not allow anyone of the ranks of the clergy, either bishop, priest, deacon, or anyone registered among the clergy, to appear before a lay court, be it voluntarily or against his will. If anyone should do this [bring an ecclesiastic before a lay court against his will], he shall be reprimanded properly by Our Serenity. If an ecclesiastic should appear voluntarily before a lay court, or at his initiative prefer the judgment of that court to that of an ecclesiastical court, he is condemned by the holy canons, although he may believe he has received [fair] judgment from that court.

None of the officials has the authority to force the God-loving bishops to appear at court and give testimony. But let the judge send to the bishops some of those serving him, so that the bishops may testify what they know before God, as is proper.

102.

Introduction. To encourage and protect the moral position of the clergy, the church sought by law to bar its officials from engaging in certain activities. For example, clergy could not serve in the civil bureaucracy, work in banking, or own private estates, though manual labor was permitted. (Many of the lower clergy, in fact, earned their living as tenant farmers.) Title IX of the *Epanagoge* sets forth some of these restrictions, not always maintained in practice.

THE CLERGY MAY NOT . . .

(From the *Epanagoge Aucta*, in J. and P. Zepos, eds., *Jus graeco-romanum* [Athens, 1931], vol. 2, pp. 257–59.)

We do not allow the holy bishops or monks to act, as a result of any legal regulation, as guardians or curators of any person whatever.

We do permit priests and deacons and subdeacons who may be named to the office of guardian or curator on the basis of kinship (but solely on that basis) to assume the duty of such office.

We do not permit a bishop or an *oikonomos* [steward], or any other cleric of any rank, or a monk, to act as a receiver or a "demander" or a farmer of taxes, or a curator of the possessions and house of another person, or as a summoner in a court case, or as a surety.

Hellenes [pagans], Jews, and heretics do not serve in the army or in the government but are completely disfranchised.

Those who have entered the ranks of the clergy or have taken monastic vows, and who then abandon their own status to assume the status of laymen, do not serve in the armed forces or in the government but, likewise, are disfranchised.

The monasteries and churches and, more specifically, the metropolitans and bishops, are not subject to any *angareia* [corvée] or any kind of service, either of a private or public nature. Their exemption from all of these services is owing to their service to God—just as the tribe of Levi, according to Mosaic law, was exempt from any obligations. If, however, some unavoidable crisis should arise in which the common good is at stake, and which calls upon them, too, to perform certain services in behalf of their own safety, they shall carry out such work but entirely at the direction of the bishops of their area and not of the laymen.

103.

Introduction. In general the emperor showed a certain discretion in selecting (and especially deposing) patriarchs, although if politics or personal interest demanded it, he would proceed with little restraint. In periods of imperial weakness the balance of power between emperor and patriarch might be occasionally reversed. Such was the case above all in the mid-eleventh century at the time of Patriarch Michael Cerularius. The scion of a powerful noble (even imperial) house who was forced initially into a clerical career against his will, he seemed determined, as patriarch, to elevate himself even above the emperor. Thus, against the policies of Emperor Constantine IX, Cerularius was, at least in part, responsible in 1054 for bringing about what is usually termed the "final schism" between the Eastern and Western churches (on this complex episode, see selection 151).

The following short paragraph from the history written by the imperial secretary Michael Psellus, who was a contemporary to these events, indicates the pretentions of this powerful Byzantine prelate who has been termed (exaggeratedly) by some modern scholars a "Byzantine Hildebrand."

A. The Boldness of Michael Cerularius

(From Michael Psellus, *Chronographie*, ed. E. Rénauld [Paris, 1928], vol. 2, p. 123.)

Michael had once spoken boldly to him [the emperor] in an audacious tone of voice. At that time the emperor, restraining his anger, let the incident pass, but he retained an unspoken resentment against him in his heart. . . .

Introduction. An even more striking indication of Cerularius's ambition is the following passage from the contemporary historian John Skylitzes, in which he reports that Cerularius even dared to wear the scarlet boots, reserved only for the emperor.

B. Cerularius Wears the Imperial Boots

(From John Skylitzes, *Synopsis historion*, MPG, vol. 122, cols. 368f., esp. 372a.)

But [Patriarch Michael], often failing in his constant and insolent demands [on the emperor], even resorted to threats and unseemly rebukes, and when he still could not persuade him, he even threatened him with expulsion from the throne, quoting the common and well-worn phrase: "I raised you up, oven [sic], and I shall pull you down." And he even presumed to put on the scarlet sandals, saying that such was the custom of the ancient priesthood, and that the patriarch in the new [order] ought to wear these. For he said that there was no or little difference between the priesthood and imperial authority, and indeed in the more precious matters [i.e., the spiritual], the priesthood was probably even greater and more estimable.

104.

Introduction. One of the extremely scarce documents remaining that lists the emperor's powers over his prelates (all of which pertain to administration of the church) is an accord drawn up between the patriarch and the emperors John V and his son Manuel II, who in 1380–82 secured this document from the church.

Imperial Privileges over the Church

(From V. Laurent, "Les droits de l'empereur en matière ecclésiastique: L'accord de 1380–82," *Revue des études byzantines* 13 [1955]: 5–20.)

Articles established by the [standing] synod assembled at the divine and imperial order at the convent of Studius in the reign of our deceased master and emperor John Palaeologus the Great and in the patriarchate of our very saintly and regretted patriarch Nilos; articles which have been approved as conforming to the canons and laws by the very saintly bishops, then given to the Holy Emperor as his privileges.

Article 1. Conforming to custom, the bishops will elect three candidates for a metropolitan see. When they have communicated the names to the patriarch with the aim of the ordination of one of them, the patriarch will make this known to the emperor and if the emperor has something to say against one of the three for reasons that he should specify, he will indicate it to the patriarch, who, after having discarded the name, will ordain the one he desires of the two remaining.

Article 2. Transfers, promotions, ranks, and sees as well as the assignment, for the sake of benefit, of another church to a bishop, belong to the emperor, without whose assent nothing can be done in the matter, since it is an ancient privilege of the crown.

Article 3. The same will obtain for the highest and the other great charges of the church. Nothing will be provided for apart from the advice of the emperor since that too is a privilege of the crown.

Article 4. Each bishop will preserve intact the limits of his diocese, and he will have every extension of this, in whatever manner may be ratified by the emperor. If any part of it has been taken away, the latter will have it returned to him and it will be restored to him. And let this point be observed during the life and after the death of the bishop, in manner that during the vacancy of the see, no one may have the right to subtract the least part from his rights, but these shall be preserved for the metropolitan who will come after him to receive and maintain.

Article 5. The patriarch will levy no excommunication which affects the function and the administration of the emperor as well as his revenues. That is, he shall cast no censure against an archon of the Senate, against those who are close to the emperor, or against those who are directly in his service. If it happens that one among them acts contrary to the canons, the patriarch will reprimand him. If he corrects it, that is fine. If not, he will disclose it to the emperor who will extract reparation. The emperor is in fact the defender of the church and the canons. If any one of the bishops finds himself in Constantinople by agreement of the emperor for important business, he shall not be constrained by the patriarch to return without the order of the emperor. If the emperor will decide to recall anyone of those to the seat of his metropolis by reason of affairs of an urgent nature, he shall not in any way be prevented by the patriarch.

Article 7. Every prelate just before being ordained will express in writing, at the moment of his profession of faith, the promise of being in everything the true and sincere friend of the *basileus*. He shall have always in everything the care and interest [at heart] of the empire and of Romania.

Article 8. All the synodal acts will be decreed by the bishops and also signed by them.

Article 9. All bishops concerned shall take care to observe all that is prescribed in these articles; they shall be applicable to all and they shall not admit for voting anyone who is not friendly to the emperor.

105.

Introduction. By the end of the fourteenth century, after the severe weakening of the empire, the relationship between the power of the emperor and that of the patriarch was almost completely reversed. Where once the imperial authority had been the chief support of the church, the patriarch now at times in fact had to exercise his authority in order to uphold the greatly reduced authority and prestige of the emperor, in particular before foreign rulers.

The following selection is taken from a letter written in 1395 by Patriarch Anthony of Constantinople to the grand prince of Moscow, Vasily I, who had earlier written disparagingly about the Byzantine emperor. Here is clearly exposed the disparity between the ideal, that is, the image of Byzantine imperial authority, and the now unfortunate reality.

A PATRIARCH DEFENDS THE AUTHORITY OF THE EMPEROR (1395)

(Letter of Patriarch Anthony, from F. Miklosich and I. Müller, eds., *Acta et Diplomata Graeca Medii Aevi* [Vienna, 1862], vol. 2, pp. 190–91.)

The holy emperor has a great place in the church, for he is not like other rulers or governors of other regions. This is so because from the beginning the emperors established and confirmed the [true] faith in all the inhabited world. They convoked the ecumenical councils and confirmed and decreed the acceptance of the pronouncements of the divine and holy canons regarding the correct doctrines and the government of Christians. They struggled boldly against heresies, and imperial decrees together with councils established the metropolitan sees of the archpriests and the divisions of their provinces and the delineation of their districts. For this reason the emperors enjoy great honor and position in the Church, for even if, by God's permission, the nations [primarily the Ottoman Turks] have constricted the authority and domain of the emperor, still to this day the emperor possesses the same charge from the church and the same rank and the same prayers [from the church]. The *basileus* is anointed with the great myrrh and is appointed *basileus* and *autokrator* of the Romans, and indeed of all Christians. Everywhere the name of the emperor is commemorated by all patriarchs and metropolitans and bishops wherever men are called Christians, [a thing] which no other ruler or governor ever received. Indeed he enjoys such great authority over all that even the Latins themselves, who are not in communion with our church, render him the same honor and submission which they did in the old days when they were united with us. So much more do Orthodox Christians owe such recognition to him. . . .

Therefore, my son, you are wrong to affirm that we have the church without an emperor, for it is impossible for Christians to have a church and no empire. The *Basileia* [empire] and the church have a great unity and community—indeed they cannot be separated. Christians can repudiate only emperors who are heretics who attack the church, or who introduce doctrines irreconcilable with the teachings of the Apostles and the Fathers. But our very great and holy *autokrator*, by the grace of God, is most orthodox and faithful, a champion of the church, its defender and avenger, so that it is impossible for bishops not to mention his name in the liturgy. Of whom, then, do the Fathers, councils, and canons speak? Always and everywhere they speak loudly of the one rightful *basileus*, whose laws, decrees, and charters are in force throughout the world and who alone, only he, is mentioned in all places by Christians in the liturgy.

C.
THE ECUMENICAL COUNCILS AND DOGMA

106.

Introduction. While the emperor could and did keep a firm hold on ecclesiastical administration, the formulation of dogma and canons, in Byzantine eyes, was the sole responsibility of a council, above all of an ecumenical ("universal") council. The church's predilection for councils, especially in the East (even during the early centuries of persecution) influenced the ecclesiastical policies of Constantine and his successors. Constantine himself, after experiencing difficulty in settling ecclesiastical disputes by imperial decree, resorted to the expedient of calling an ecclesiastical council of bishops from all parts of the empire to deal with the teachings of Arius, who affirmed that the Son was not of exactly the same nature as the Father and was therefore inferior and not truly God.

The Byzantines viewed the function of the ecumenical council to be the definition of dogma—not, strictly speaking, the "creation" of dogma, since the truth was believed already to exist, needing but to be "uncovered" (under the inspiration of the Holy Spirit). It was a question of stating formally what had always been "received" and believed. It should be noted that in every single instance, the councils were convened to meet a specific challenge to the faith posed by certain heretical groups. Thus an ecumenical council always defined dogma *against* heretical views (Arianism, Monophysitism, and the like).

The first ecumenical council, meeting at Nicaea in 325, set the precedent for the ecumenical councils of subsequent centuries. Thus while the emperor could call such a council, preside (through his legates) over its sessions, and often influence its decisions (by packing it or by subtle maneuvering), he had no vote; it remained, above all, an ecclesiastical assemblage. After the council the emperor would at once ratify, by civil legislation, the decrees of the council. (This kind of joint corpus of legislation was known as *nomocanones*.) But the ultimate approval of the council's decisions lay in their universal acceptance not only by the clergy but also by the people of the empire.

The following selections illustrate both the role of the emperor and the emphasis on universal consensus as the test of conciliar enactments. The first, from the fifth-century church historian Socrates, illustrates the role of the emperor in guiding, at least indirectly, the activities of the council in a dominant but not truly dictatorial manner. Socrates, after giving the Nicene Creed as originally formulated by the Fathers, then gives it as it was finally expressed, following modifications introduced by the emperor.

SOCRATES ON THE COUNCIL OF NICAEA (325)

(Translated by A. Zenos, from Socrates, *Ecclesiastical History*, in P. Schaff and H. Wace, eds., *A Select Library of Nicene and Post-Nicene Fathers of the Christian Church*, 2d ser. [reprint, Grand Rapids, Mich.: Wm. Eerdmans, 1976], vol. 2, pp. 10–12.)

[*Original Formulation of Creed*] When these articles of faith were proposed, there seemed to be no ground of opposition: nay, our most pious emperor himself was the first to admit that they were perfectly correct, and that he himself had entertained the sentiments contained in them; exhorting all present to give them their assent, and subscribe to these very articles, thus agreeing in a unanimous profession of them, with the insertion, however, of that single word *homoousios* [consubstantial], an expression which the emperor himself explained, as not indicating corporeal affections or properties; and consequently that the Son did not subsist from the Father either by division or abscision: for, said he, a nature which is immaterial and incorporeal cannot possibly be subject to any corporeal affection; hence our conception of such things can only be in divine and mysterious terms. Such was the philosophical view of the subject taken by our most wise and pious sovereign; and the bishops on account of the word *homoousios*, drew up this formula of faith:

[*The Nicene Creed*] "We believe in one God, the Father Almighty, Maker of all things visible and invisible:—and in one Lord Jesus Christ, the Son of God, the only-begotten of the Father, that is of the substance of the Father; God of God, Light of light, true God of true God; begotten not made, consubstantial with the Father; by whom all things were made both which are in heaven and on earth; who for the sake of us men, and on account of our salvation, descended, became incarnate, was made man, suffered and rose again on the third day; he ascended into the heavens, and will come to judge the living and the dead. [We believe] also in the Holy Spirit. But those who say 'There was a time when he was not,' or 'He did not exist before he was begotten,' or 'He was made of nothing,' or assert that 'He is of other substance or essence than the Father,' or that the Son of God is created, or mutable, or susceptible of change, the Catholic and apostolic Church of God anathematizes."

Now this declaration of faith being propounded by them, we did not neglect to investigate the distinct sense of the expressions "of the substance of the Father, and consubstantial with the Father." Whereupon questions were put forth and answers, and the meaning of these terms was clearly defined; when it was generally admitted that *ousias* [of the essence or substance] simply implied that the Son is of the Father indeed, but does not subsist as a part of the Father. To this interpretation of the sacred doctrine which declares that the Son is of the Father, but is not a part of his substance, it seemed right to us to assent. We ourselves therefore concurred in this exposition; nor do we cavil at the word "*homoousios*" having regard to peace, and fearing to lose a right understanding of the matter. On the same grounds we admitted also the expression "begotten, not made": "for *made*," said they, "is a term applicable in common to all the creatures which were made by the Son, to whom the Son has no resemblance. Consequently he is no creature like those which were made by him, but is of a substance far excelling any creature; which substance the Divine Oracles teach was begotten of the Father by such a mode of generation as cannot be explained nor even conceived by any creature." Thus also the declaration that "the Son is consubstantial with the Father" having been discussed, it was agreed that this must not be understood in a corporeal sense, or in any way analogous to mortal creatures; inasmuch as it is neither by division of substance, nor by abscission, nor by any change of the Father's substance and power, since the underived nature of the Father is inconsistent with all these things. That he is consubstantial with the Father then simply implies, that the Son of God has no resemblance to created things, but is in every respect like the Father only who begat him; and that he is of no other substance or essence but of the Father.

107.

Introduction. Although at the Council of Nicaea the Arian belief in the difference in substance between the Father and the Son was rejected in favor of the view that both Father and Son were of exactly the same substance (*homoousios*), some ecclesiastics believed that the Holy Spirit, the third person of the Trinity, differed in substance from the other two persons, being a kind of "creature" of the second person. This heresy was called Macedonianism. It was the task of the so-called Second Ecumenical Council, which met in Constantinople in 381, to define the nature of the Holy Spirit and to affirm its consubstantiality with the Father and the Son, and thus to assert the full divinity of the Holy Spirit. The words added to define the divine nature of the Holy Spirit are today read in the creed, which is called the Niceno-Constantinopolitan creed. This council of 381, though not at the time considered ecumenical, was recognized as such by the later Fourth Ecumenical Council at Chalcedon in 451. In the following selection the same fifth-century ecclesiastical historian Socrates describes the actions taken at the Second Ecumenical Council at Constantinople.

SOCRATES'S ACCOUNT OF THE SECOND ECUMENICAL COUNCIL

(Translated by A. Zenos, from Socrates, *Ecclesiastical History*, in P. Schaff and H. Wace, eds., *A Select Library of Nicene and Post-Nicene Fathers of the Christian Church*, 2d ser. [reprint, Grand Rapids, Mich.: Wm. Eerdmans, 1976], vol. 2, p. 121.)

The emperor making no delay summoned a Synod of the prelates of his own faith, in order that he might establish the Nicene Creed, and appoint a bishop of Constantinople: and inasmuch as he was not without hope that he might win the Macedonians over to his own views, he invited those who presided over that sect to be present also. There met therefore on this occasion of the Homoousian party, Timothy from Alexandria, Cyril from Jerusalem, who at that time recognized the doctrine of *homoousion*, having retracted his former opinion; Meletius from Antioch, he having arrived there previously to assist at the installation of Gregory; Ascholius also from Thessalonica, and many others, amounting in all to one hundred fifty. Of the Macedonians, the leaders were Eleusius of Cyzicus, and Marcian of Lampsacus; these with the rest, most of whom came from the cities of the Hellespont, were thirty-six in number. Accordingly they were assembled in the month of May, under the consulate of Eucharius and Evagrius, and the emperor used his utmost exertions, in conjunction with the bishops who entertained similar sentiments to his own, to bring over Eleusius and his adherents to his side. But they, paying little heed alike to admonitions and reproofs, chose rather to maintain the Arian dogma, than to assent to the "homoousian" doctrine. Having made this declaration, they departed from Constantinople; moreover they wrote to their partisans in every city, and charged them by no means to harmonize with the creed of the Nicene Synod, the bishops of the other party remaining at Constantinople. . . . The latter prelates moreover published a decree, prescribing "that the bishop of Constantinople should have the next prerogative of honor after the bishop of Rome, because that city was New Rome."* They also again confirmed the Nicene Creed.

*This was the famous canon 3, which raised the bishop of Constantinople second to Rome in honor and above the other bishops of the Greek East, especially Alexandria and Antioch (and Jerusalem).

108.

Introduction. Possibly the most important council of all was the fourth, held in Chalcedon in 451. While Nicaea (325) and Constantinople (381) had earlier dealt with the trinitarian question (defining the Godhead as one substance in three persons), the Third Ecumenical Council, at Ephesus (431), and the Fourth, at Chalcedon (451), had to solve the even more complex doctrinal question of Christology: the relationship of the two natures of Christ, the divine and the human, in one person. As had happened with Arianism, civil disturbances over the outcome of the council, especially in the eastern provinces of Egypt, Syria, and Palestine, illuminated the importance of and great interest in questions of ecclesiastical dogma to the empire at large.

At Chalcedon, after long and bitter sessions, Christ's two natures were defined as combined in one person, at once perfect God and perfect man, though each nature retained its own characteristic in Christ—to use the four famous phrases, "without confusion, without change, without division, and without separation." Paradoxical as these four terms may seem, they were worded so as to avoid the two poles of heresy: Nestorianism, which seemed to overstress the human element; and Monophysitism, which overemphasized the divine at the expense of the human nature of Christ. (At the Third Ecumenical Council in 431, Patriarch Nestorius had played a prominent role but was condemned, among other things, for calling the Virgin Mary *Chrestotokos* [Christbearing], not *Theotokos* [Godbearing.]).

A. The Decree of the Council of Chalcedon (451)

(In J. Ayer, Jr., ed., *A Source Book for Ancient Church History* [New York, 1941], p. 520.)

Following the holy Fathers, we all with one voice teach men to confess that the Son and Our Lord Jesus Christ is one and the same, that He is perfect in godhead and perfect in manhood, truly God and truly man, of a reasonable soul and body, consubstantial with His Father as touching His godhead, and consubstantial with us as to His manhood, in all things like unto us, without sin; begotten of His Father before all worlds according to His godhead; but in these last days for us and for our salvation of the Virgin Mary, the Theotokos, according to His manhood, one and the same Christ, Son, Lord, only begotten Son, in two natures, unconfusedly, immutably, indivisibly, inseparably; the distinction of natures being preserved and concurring in one person and hypostasis, not separated or divided into two persons, but one and the same Son and Only begotten, God the Word, the Lord Jesus Christ, as the prophets from the beginning have spoken concerning Him, and as the Lord Jesus Christ himself has taught us, and as the creed of the Fathers has delivered us.

B. Other Decisions or Statements of the Council of Chalcedon

(In *Source Book for Ancient Church History*, p. 520.)

This then we have done, having by a common sentence driven away the doctrines of error, and having renewed the unerring faith of the Fathers, proclaiming to all the Symbol of the Three Hundred and Eighteen [Fathers of the Council of Nicaea] and acknowledging, as of the same household, the Fathers who received this godly document, the One Hundred and Fifty, namely who afterwards met together in the great Constantinople and set their seal to the same faith . . . on account of those who would fain corrupt the mystery of the Incarnation, shamelessly and senselessly pretending that he who was born of the Holy Mary was a mere man; it hath accepted the Synodical Epistles of the blessed Cyril, Pastor of the Church of Alexandria, to Nestorius and to the Orientals as in keeping [with these Creeds] for the confutation of the Nestorian folly, and for the interpretation of the salutary Symbol to those who in their godly zeal desire the true understanding thereof. [We accept this] . . . for the overthrow of the impiety of Eutyches [i.e., extreme Monophysitism], inasmuch as it agrees with the confession of the great Peter [of Rome] and is a common monument erected against the heretics.

C. From the Concluding Statements

(Translated by R. Sellers, in *The Council of Chalcedon* [London, Society for Promoting Christian Knowledge, 1961], p. 224.)

If, then, anyone teaches what is thus contrary to the divine Scriptures, saying that one [nature] is the Son of God, and another [nature] the man of Mary made Son according to grace as we are, so that *there are two Sons*, one according to nature, Son of God and of God, and one according to grace, the man of Mary; or if anyone says that *the flesh of our Lord was from above* [heaven] and not of Mary the Virgin, or that the Godhead was changed into flesh, or *confused*, or made other than it was, or that *the Godhead of the Son is impassible*, or that the flesh of our Lord is not to be worshipped as human flesh [and not (rather) that it is to be worshipped as the flesh of (our) Lord and God]— such, the Catholic church anathematizes in obedience to the [divine] Apostle, who said, "If any man preacheth unto you any gospel other than that which ye received, let him be anathema" (Galatians 1:9).

109.

Introduction. Evidence for the fundamental importance of orthodox dogma in Byzantium is the fact that from the end of the fifth century onward, as a result of the Monophysite controversy, Byzantine emperors were all obliged, immediately before their coronation, to take an oath promising to defend the orthodox faith as defined by the first four (and later, seven) ecumenical councils. The conciliar definitions of faith had thus become inviolable. The following text, reconstructed from the fourteenth-century *Historia* of John Cantacuzene and the *De officiis* of Pseudo-Codinus of the same century, is part of the oath that emperors were required to take. There is no reason to believe that this oath, delivered to the patriarch orally and in writing, had changed substantially since the earlier centuries.

THE IMPERIAL OATH TO PRESERVE THE ORTHODOX CREED

(Translated and reconstructed by F. Brightman, in *Journal of Theological Studies* 2 [1901]: 387–88.)

I, _____, in Christ [our] God, faithful Emperor and Autocrator of the Romans, with my own hand set forth: I believe in one God . . . [the rest of the Creed follows]. Further I embrace and confess and confirm as well as the apostolic and divine traditions the constitutions and decrees of the seven ecumenical councils and of local synods from time to time convened and, moreover, the privileges and customs of the most holy Great Church of God. And furthermore I confirm and embrace all things that our most holy fathers here or elsewhere decreed and declared canonically and irreproachably. And all things which the holy fathers rejected and anathematized, I also reject and anathematize. And I believe with my whole mind and soul and heart the aforesaid Holy Creed. All these things I promise to keep before the Holy Catholic and Apostolic Church of God.

110.

Introduction. The Fifth and Sixth Ecumenical Councils met in response to attempts of the subsequent emperors to placate the powerful heresy of Monophysitism (the belief in one nature in Christ after the Incarnation), which had spread widely among the Christians of Egypt, Syria, and Palestine, areas not only rich but strategically situated in the empire. The Fifth Ecumenical Council, after violent conflict among the clergy, approved the condemnation suggested by Emperor Justinian of several writers whose works were most objectionable to the Monophysites. This effort to placate the Monophysites failed, however, owing to the unwillingness of the Monophysites to compromise their beliefs. Later Emperor Heraclius sought to conciliate the heretics by skirting the question of natures in Christ and emphasizing, instead, the problem of wills (*one* will in *two* natures). But this view was rejected and condemned as heresy by the Sixth Ecumenical Council.

A. DECREE OF THE FIFTH ECUMENICAL COUNCIL (553)

(Translated by H. Bettenson, in *Documents of the Christian Church* [Oxford, 1947], pp. 128–29.)

1. If anyone does not acknowledge the one nature or substance [*ousia*] of the Father, Son and Holy Spirit, their one virtue and power, a consubstantial Trinity, one Godhead worshiped in three persons [*hypostaseis*] or characters [*prosopa*], let him be anathema. For there is one God and Father, from whom are all things, and one Lord Jesus Christ, through whom are all things, and one Holy Spirit, in whom are all things.

2. If anyone does not confess that there are two begettings of God the Word, one before ages, from the Father, timelessly and incorporeally, the other in the last days, the begetting of the same person, who came down from heaven and was made flesh of the Holy and Glorious God-bearer and ever-virgin Mary, and was born of her, let him be anathema.

3. If anyone says that there was one God the Word who did miracles, and another Christ who suffered, or that God the Word was with Christ when he was born of a woman, or was in him, as one person in another, and not that there was one and the same Lord Jesus Christ, incarnate and made man, and that the miracles and the sufferings which he endured voluntarily in the flesh pertained to the same person, let him be anathema.

4. If anyone says that the union of God, the Word, to a man was effected in respect of grace, or working, or equality of honor, or authority, or was relative, or temporary, or "dynamic"; or that it was according to the good pleasure [of the Word], God the Word being pleased with the man . . . let him be anathema.

5. If anyone takes the one personality [*hypostasis*] of our Lord Jesus Christ in a sense which allows it to stand for several personalities, and by this means attempts to introduce two personalities or two characters in the mystery of Christ, and says that of those two characters introduced by him there is one personality in respect of worth and honor and adoration, as Theodore [of Mopsuestia, one of the condemned writers] and Nestorius have written in their madness; and slanders the holy Council of Chalcedon by alleging that the phrase "one personality" was there used with this impious intention; and does not confess that the Word of God was united to flesh in respect of personality [*kathhypostasin*] . . . let him be anathema.

6. If anyone applies the title "God-bearer" [*Theotokos*] to the glorious and ever-virgin Mary in an unreal and not in a true sense, as if a mere man was born, and not God the Word made flesh and born of her, while the birth is to be "referred to God the Word," as they say inasmuch as he was with the man that was born . . . let him be anathema.

10. If anyone does not confess that he who was crucified in the flesh, our Lord

Jesus Christ, is the true God and Lord of glory, and one of the Holy Trinity, let him be anathema.

B. DECISIONS OF THE SIXTH ECUMENICAL COUNCIL AGAINST MONOTHELETISM (680–81)

(From *Documents of the Christian Church*, pp. 130–31.)

We also preach two natural wills in him and two natural operations, without division, without change, without separation, without partition, without confusion. This we preach in accordance with the teaching of the holy Fathers. And two natural wills, not contrary (God forbid), as the impious heretics assert, but his human will following his divine and omnipotent will, not resisting it nor striving against it, but rather subject to it. For the will of the flesh had to be moved, but to be subjected to the divine will, according to the all-wise Athanasius. For as his flesh is said to be, and is, the flesh of God the Word so the natural will of the flesh is said to belong to God the Word, and does so belong; as he himself says, "I came down from Heaven not to do mine own will, but the will of the Father that sent me" (John 6:38), calling his own will of the flesh, since the flesh also was made his own.

For as his all-holy and immaculate ensouled flesh was not destroyed by being deified, but persisted in its own state and sphere; so also his human will was not destroyed by being deified, but was rather preserved, as Gregory the theologian says: "For the willing that we understand to be an act of the Saviour's will is not contrary to God but is wholly deified."

111.

Introduction. From 726 until 843 a great ecclesiastical, and particularly dogmatic, controversy wracked the empire: the conflict over the icons, beginning with the anti-icon decree of Emperor Leo III (probably in 726). Why Leo, in the midst of a dangerous and lengthy struggle with the Arabs, chose to attack the prevailing religious sentiment on the sanctity of icons ("likenesses," or "holy images") is not clear, though it is quite possible that, since Asia Minor (whence the army was primarily recruited) was largely iconoclastic in belief, he was thereby seeking to insure the support of the military.* (The vast tableland of Asia Minor, aside from the extreme east and the province of Cappadocia, possessed few if any monasteries, which always provided the focal points of support for the icons.) Leo's edict banning the icons caused a storm of protest and opposition, precipitating a grave conflict in both spheres of church and state.

The following documents reveal something of the intensity of both factions, the pro- and anti-icon groups (iconodules and iconoclasts). The first selection, written during the opening phase of the struggle, is by the eighth-century monk John of Damascus, and is titled *On Holy Images* (c. 730). John was also the author of a treatise which later came to be considered as a kind of semi-official statement of the dogma and beliefs of the Orthodox Church, the *Fountain of Knowledge.*

JOHN OF DAMASCUS DEFENDS VENERATION OF ICONS

(Translated by M. H. Allies, *St. John Damascene on Holy Images*
[London: Burns and Oates Ltd., 1898], pp. 10–17.)

For the invisible things of God since the creation of
the world are made visible through images. We see images in creation which re-
mind us faintly of God, as when, for instance, we speak of the holy and adorable
Trinity, imaged by the sun, or light, or burning rays, or by a running fountain, or
a full river, or by the mind, speech, or the spirit within us, or by a rose tree, or a
sprouting flower, or a sweet fragrance.

Again, an image is expressive of something in the future, mystically shadow-
ing forth what is to happen. For instance, the ark represents the image of Our
Lady, Mother of God; so does the staff and the earthen jar. The serpent brings
before us Him who vanquished on the cross the bite of the original serpent; the
sea, water, and the cloud the grace of baptism.

Again, things which have taken place are expressed by images for the remembrance either of a wonder, or an honour, or dishonour, or good or evil, to
help those who look upon it in after times that we may avoid evils and imitate
goodness. It is of two kinds, the written image in books, as when God had the law
inscribed on tablets, and when He enjoined that the lives of holy men should be
recorded and sensible memorials be preserved in remembrance; as, for instance,
the earthen jar and the staff in the ark. So now we preserve in writing the images
and the good deeds of the past. Either, therefore, take away images altogether
and be out of harmony with God who made these regulations, or receive them
with the language and in the manner which befits them. In speaking of the manner let us go into the question of worship.

Worship is the symbol of veneration and of honour. Let us understand that
there are different degrees of worship. First of all the worship of *latreia*, which
we show to God, who alone by nature is worthy of worship. Then, for the sake of
God who is worshipful by nature, we honour His saints and servants, as Joshua
and Daniel worshipped an angel, and David His holy places, when he says, "Let
us go to the place where His feet have stood." Again, in His tabernacles, as when
all the people of Israel adored in the tent, and standing round the temple in
Jerusalem, fixing their gaze upon it from all sides, and worshipping from that
day to this, or in the rulers established by Him, as Jacob rendered homage to
Esau, his elder brother, and to Pharoah, the divinely established ruler. Joseph
was worshipped by his brothers. I am aware that worship was based on honour,
as in the case of Abraham and the sons of Emmor. Either, then, do away with
worship, or receive it altogether according to its proper measure. . . .

Of old, God the incorporeal and uncircumscribed was never depicted. Now,
however, when God is seen clothed in flesh, and conversing with men, I make an
image of the God whom I see. I do not worship matter, I worship the God of
matter, who became matter for my sake, and deigned to inhabit matter, who
worked out my salvation through matter. I will not cease from honouring that
matter which works my salvation. I venerate it, though not as God. How could
God be born out of lifeless things? And if God's body is God by union, it is immutable. The nature of God remains the same as before, the flesh created in time is

quickened by a logical and reasoning soul. I honour all matter besides, and venerate it. Through it, filled, as it were, with a divine power and grace, my salvation has come to me. Was not the thrice happy and thrice blessed wood of the Cross matter? Was not the sacred and holy mountain of Calvary matter? What of the life-giving rock, the Holy Sepulchre, the source of our resurrection: was it not matter? Is not the most holy book of the Gospels matter? Is not the blessed table matter which gives us the Bread of Life? Are not the gold and silver matter out of which crosses and altar-plate and chalices are made? And before all these things, is not the body and blood of our Lord matter? Either do away with the veneration and worship due to all these things, or submit to the tradition of the Church in the worship of images, honouring God and His friends, and following in this the grace of the Holy Spirit.

* It is also likely that, in the context of the tremendous Byzantine losses to the Arabs, Leo III felt that God was punishing the Byzantines for what appeared to be their *worship* of the images (see also selection 114).

112.

Introduction. The next selection, on the other hand, reveals clearly the sentiments of the anti-icon party. It is the statement (as preserved in later anti-iconoclast writings) made by the iconoclast ecclesiastics at the first great iconoclast council, held at Hieria in 754 near Constantinople. It is a prime example of an expression of dogma pronounced by a council later to be deemed heretical, since its terms were not, in the long run, accepted. It demonstrates also the traditional requirement that pronouncements of a council of this kind could not be considered valid unless so agreed by a subsequent ecumenical council. Note that the only acceptable "icon," according to the iconoclast decisions of 754, was the bread and wine used in the Eucharist.

THE COUNCIL OF 754 CONDEMNS ICONS

(Translated by H. R. Percival, *The Seven Ecumenical Councils of the Undivided Church,* in P. Schaff and H. Wace, eds., *A Select Library of Nicene and Post-Nicene Fathers of the Christian Church,* 2d ser. [reprint, Grand Rapids, Mich.: Wm. Eerdmans, 1955], vol. 14, pp. 543–44.)

Satan misguided men, so that they worshipped the creature instead of the Creator. The Mosaic law and the prophets cooperated to undo this ruin; but in order to save mankind thoroughly, God sent his own Son, who turned us away from error and the worshipping of idols, and taught us the worshipping of God in spirit and in truth. As messengers of his saving doctrine, he left us his Apostles and disciples, and these adorned the Church, his Bride, with his glorious doctrines. This ornament of the Church the holy Fathers and the six Ecumenical Councils have preserved inviolate. But the before-mentioned demiurgos of wickedness could not endure the sight of this adornment, and gradually brought back idolatry under the appearance of Christianity. As then Christ armed his Apostles against the ancient idolatry with the power of the Holy Spirit, and sent them out into all the world, so has he awakened against the new idolatry his servants our faithful Emperors, and endowed them with the same wisdom of the Holy Spirit. Impelled by the Holy Spirit they could no longer be witnesses of the Church being laid waste by the deception of demons, and summoned the sanctified assembly of the God-beloved bishops, that they might institute at a synod a scriptural examination into the deceitful colouring of the pictures which draws down the spirit of man from the lofty adoration [*latreia*] of God to the low and material adoration of the creature, and that they, under divine guidance, might express their view of the subject.

After we had carefully examined their decrees under the guidance of the Holy Spirit, we found that the unlawful art of painting living creatures blasphemed the fundamental doctrine of our salvation—namely, the Incarnation of Christ, and contradicted the six holy synods. These condemned Nestorius because he divided the one Son and Word of God into two sons, and on the other side, Arius, Dioscorus, Eutyches, and Severus [were also condemned by preceding ecumenical councils] because they maintained a mingling of the two natures of the one Christ.

Wherefore we thought it right, to show forth with all accuracy in our present definition the error of such as make and venerate these, for it is the unanimous doctrine of all the holy Fathers and of the six Ecumenical Synods, that no one may imagine any kind of separation or mingling in opposition to the unsearchable, unspeakable, and incomprehensible union of the two natures in the one hypostatis or person. What avails, then, the folly of the painter, who from sinful love of gain depicts that which should not be depicted—that is, with his polluted hands he tries to fashion that which should only be believed in the heart and confessed with the mouth? He makes an image and calls it Christ. The name *Christ* signifies *God and Man*. Consequently it is an image of God and man, and consequently he has in his foolish mind, in his representation of the created flesh, depicted the Godhead which cannot be represented, and thus mingled what should not be mingled. Thus he is guilty of a double blasphemy—the one in making an image of the Godhead, and the other by mingling the Godhead and manhood. Those fall into the same blasphemy who venerate the image, and the same woe rests upon both, because they err with Arius, Dioscorus, and Eutyches, and with the heresy of the Acephali. When, however, they are blamed for undertaking to depict the divine nature of Christ, which should not be depicted, they take refuge in the excuse: We represent only the flesh of Christ which we have seen and handled. But that is a Nestorian error. For it should be considered that the flesh was also the flesh of God the Word, without any separation, perfectly assumed by the divine nature and made wholly divine. How could it now be separated and represented apart?

. . . The only admissible figure of the humanity of Christ . . . is bread and wine in the holy Supper. This and no other form, this and no other type, has he chosen to represent his incarnation. Bread he ordered to be brought, but not a representation of the human form, so that idolatry might not arise. And as the body of Christ is made divine, so also this figure of the body of Christ, the bread, is made divine by the descent of the Holy Spirit; it becomes the divine body of Christ by the mediation of the priest who, separating the oblation from that which is common, sanctifies it.

The evil custom of assigning names to the images does not come down from Christ and the Apostles and the holy Fathers; nor have these left behind them any prayer by which an image should be hallowed or made anything else than ordinary matter.

If, however, some say, we might be right in regard to the images of Christ, on account of the mysterious union of the two natures, but it is not right for us to forbid also the images of the altogether spotless and everglorious Mother of God, of the prophets, apostles, and martyrs, who were men and did not consist of two natures; we may reply first of all: If those fall away, there is no longer need of these. But we will also consider what may be said against these in particular. Christianity has rejected the *whole* of heathenism, and so not merely heathen sacrifices, but also the heathen worship of images. The Saints live on eternally with God, although they have died. If anyone thinks to call them back again to life by a dead art, discovered by the heathen, he makes himself guilty of blasphemy. Who dares attempt with heathenish art to paint the Mother of God, who is exalted above all heavens and the Saints? It is not permitted to Christians, who have the hope of the resurrection, to imitate the customs of demon-worshippers, and to insult the Saints, who shine in so great glory, by common dead matter.

113.

Introduction. The Iconoclast struggle went through several phases. By 787 the Iconodule (pro-image) party became dominant, and Empress Irene (who styled herself *basileus* and *autokrator*) called a council which became the Seventh Ecumenical Council. It met in Constantinople to pronounce on the restoration of the icons. A clear distinction was drawn between "reverence" (*proskynesis*) appropriate to a holy image (and its prototype) and actual worship (*latreia*) due to God alone. The icon was officially declared a channel of divine grace, extending from the prototype through the icon to the worshipper.

THE SEVENTH ECUMENICAL COUNCIL CONDEMNS ICONOCLASM (787)

(Translated by H. R. Percival, *The Seven Ecumenical Councils of the Undivided Church* in P. Schaff and H. Wace, eds., *A Select Library of Nicene and Post-Nicene Fathers of the Christian Church*, 2d ser. [reprint, Grand Rapids, Mich.: Wm. Eerdmans, 1955], vol. 14, · p. 550.)

We, therefore, following the royal pathway and the divinely inspired authority of our Holy Fathers and the traditions of the Catholic Church (for, as we all know, the Holy Spirit indwells her), divine with all certitude and accuracy that just as the figure of the precious and life-giving Cross, so also the venerable and holy images, as well in painting and mosaic as of other fit materials, should be set forth in the holy churches of God, and on the sacred vessels and on the vestments and on hangings and in pictures both in houses and by the wayside, to wit, the figure of our Lord God and Saviour Jesus Christ, of our spotless Lady, the Mother of God, of the honourable Angels, of all Saints and of all pious people: For by so much more frequently as they are seen in artistic representation, by so much more readily are men lifted up to the memory of their prototypes, and to a longing after them; and to these should be given due salutation and honourable reverence [*proskynesis*], not indeed that true worship of faith (*latreia*) which pertains alone to the divine nature; but to these, as to the figure of the precious and life-giving Cross and to the Book of the Gospels and to other holy objects, incense and lights may be offered according to ancient pious custom. For the honour which is paid to the image passes on to that which the image represents, and he who reveres the image reveres in it the subject represented. . . .

Those, therefore, who dare to think or teach otherwise, or as wicked heretics to spurn the traditions of the Church and to invent some novelty, or else to reject some of those things which the Church hath received, [the Gospels, the image of the cross, pictorial icons, or relics of martyrs], or evilly and sharply to devise anything subversive of the lawful traditions of the Catholic Church or to turn to common uses the sacred vessels or the venerable monasteries, if they be Bishops or Clerics, we command that they be deposed; if religious or laics, that they be cut off from communion.

114.

Introduction. A new struggle over the icons broke out in 815. Emperor Leo V, returning to the policy of early Iconoclast emperors, now attacked particularly the monks and their possessions. The following statement of Leo V, if not revealing all of the probably complex motivations for his restoration of Iconoclasm, does nevertheless very clearly show his personal distaste for the worship of "false idols" and the dangers he perceived icon worship could entail for the welfare of the Byzantine Empire itself. This latter consideration, some scholars believe, was in fact the principal motive behind Leo III's original edict.

The Iconoclast Views of Leo V

(From I. Bekker, ed., *Scriptor incertus de Leone Bardae filio* [Bonn, 1842], p. 349.)

Why are the Christians suffering defeat at the hands of the pagans (*ethnoi*)? It seems to me it is because the icons are worshiped and nothing else. And (for this reason) I intend to destroy them. For you see that those emperors who accepted and worshiped them [the icons] died either as a result of exile or in battle. But those alone who have not worshiped them died each one in his own bed and after death were buried with honor in the imperial tombs at the Church of the Holy Apostles. Thus I too wish to imitate these latter emperors and destroy the icons in order that I and my son may live for a long time, and that our line may reign until the fourth and fifth generation.

115.

Introduction. Finally, a second (and permanent) restoration of the icons was again effected by a woman, this time Empress Theodora, widow of the Iconoclast Emperor Theophilus. Theodora convoked an ecclesiastical council (not, however, considered an ecumenical council) in 843 at Hagia Sophia. The lengthy conciliar statement (*Synodikon* of Orthodoxy) pronounced there has ever since been referred to as the "Triumph of Orthodoxy." It is still read in all Orthodox churches on the first Sunday of Lent during a service officially known as "The Feast of Orthodoxy," at which time icons are borne in procession throughout the church.

ACCLAMATION OF ORTHODOXY

(From the *Synodikon* of Orthodoxy, in the *Triodion*, Greek Orthodox Church of America.)

. . . As the Prophets prophesized, as the Apostles taught, as the Church has received, as the teachers have dogmatized, as the Universe has agreed, as Grace has shown forth, as truth has revealed, as error was repudiated, as wisdom has pronounced, as Christ awarded:

Let us declare, let us assert, let us preach in like manner Christ our true God, and honor His Saints in words, in writing, in thoughts, in deeds, in Churches, in Holy Icons, worshipping Him as God and Lord and honoring them as His true servants.

This is the faith of the Apostles, this is the faith of the Fathers, this is the faith of the Orthodox, this is the faith which sustains the Christian *Oikoumene*. . . .

[There follow ringing statements declaring "eternal be the memory" of the truly Orthodox Fathers of the Church, including especially the Iconodule bishops Germanos, Tarasius, Nicephorus, Methodius, Ignatius, Photius, and so on. Then follows a much more extended list of anathematizations ("may they be eternally damned") against the anti-Orthodox adherents of the Iconoclast heresy, opponents of the orthodoxy of Gregory the Theologian (Gregory of Nazianzus), Athanasius, Cyril, Ambrose, Amphilocius, and Leo (pope of Rome). Finally anathemas are pronounced against the Messalians, and especially against Arius "the heresiarch," Nestorius, Paul of Samosata, Sabellius, Dioscorus, Severus, Eutyches, the Monotheletes, and the Jacobites. The *Synodikon* closes with the expression of eternal praise for the memory of the emperors and the patriarchs, and for all those living.]

116.

Introduction. The Seventh Ecumenical Council (787)—actually the Second Council of Nicaea—was the last of the councils to be considered ecumenical by the East. Increasingly, and with the passage of centuries, the decrees of the "seven ecumenical councils" came to be regarded in the Byzantine East as inviolable—something sacred to be preserved absolutely and without the slightest change.

A great and enduring crisis arose in the Orthodox Church during the last two or three centuries over the question of religious union of the Eastern church with the Western. The emperor and certain high-ranking Byzantine officials believed that the only power that could effectively aid Byzantium against Charles, king of Sicily, and later the increasingly grave Turkish danger to Constantinople, was the papacy. But the pope always insisted that military aid would be forthcoming only if the Byzantines accepted religious union with Rome—that is, accepted papal jurisdiction over the Eastern church. The Greek prelates insisted that a lasting religious union of East and West could be achieved only through the traditional means of a convocation of an ecumenical council. The pope always demanded that reunion precede any papal military aid, while the Greeks always insisted that no union would take place until military aid for Constantinople was first forthcoming.

The Byzantine attitudes were usually misunderstood in the West (see below, selections 156–63). But in the fourteenth century, the south Italian Byzantine, Barlaam, envoy of the Greek emperor to the papal court, in a speech delivered before the pope in Avignon (1339), offered a penetrating analysis of Byzantine attitudes, psychological as well as ecclesiastical, toward religious union. He especially indicated the reasons why the Greeks had refused to accept the validity of the Council of Lyons (1274): all five patriarchs had not attended, there was no official discussion, and therefore in Greek eyes it was not ecumenical (see selection 159).

Even after 787, however, local councils were still convoked and, even if not ecumenical, continued to be recognized as an effective means of making disciplinary decisions. A permanent council of bishops resident nearby (*synodos endemousa*, or holy synod) sat in the capital city, which served to assist (or occasionally even to act as a check on) the patriarch. For major decisions this permanent (or "standing synod") would be augmented by additional clergy and high imperial officials. The following selection describing the trial and condemnation of the heretic Bogomil, Basil, during the reign of Alexius I Comnenus (1081–1118) shows the cooperation of the emperor and the members of the standing synod on this particular occasion. (This is the single known example of the actual burning of a Byzantine heretic.)

A. The Trial of Basil the Bogomil (1110)

(From Anna Comnena, *Alexiade*, ed. B. Leib [Paris, 1945], vol. 3, pp. 218–19 and 226–27.)

After this, in the course of the [lacuna] year of Alexius's reign, a huge cloud of heretics arose, the nature of this type of heresy being new and not previously known to the church. Two very evil and worthless doctrines, already known in older times, now became amalgamated: the impiety (as one might say) of the Manichaeans (which we also call the heresy of the Paulicians) and the abomination of the Messalians. . . .

The notoriety of the Bogomils had already been diffused everywhere. (For a certain monk Basil shrewdly manipulated the impiety of the Bogomils; with twelve disciples whom he even called apostles and also with some women disciples whom he dragged around with him—women of evil habits and utterly corrupt—he propagated his evil everywhere.) The evil seized upon many souls like fire. But the soul of the emperor could not endure this and so he began to investigate the heresy. . . .

All the chief dignitaries of the holy synod and of the Nazireans [i.e., monks] and the patriarch of the time decreed that it was fitting that Basil be burned as a true heresiarch and utterly unrepentant. In agreement with them the emperor, after speaking with Basil several times and recognizing him as an evildoer who would not deny his heresy, thereupon ordered an immense pyre to be built in the Hippodrome. A huge pit was dug; and a large amount of wood (all consisting of tall trees) piled together made the structure look like a mountain. Then after the pyre was lit, a great crowd gradually gathered on the ground floor of the Hippodrome, all eagerly anticipating what would happen. On the opposite side, a cross was erected and the blasphemous man was granted a choice: if, dreading the fire and therefore changing his mind, he should move toward the cross, then he would be liberated from the fire. A group of heretics meantime were also watching their leader Basil. And he showed himself to be disdainful of any kind of punishment or menace. Indeed, while still standing away from the fire he laughed aloud and talked of marvelous happenings, affirming that angels would pluck him from the midst of the fire as he chanted these words of David: "It shall not come nigh thee; only with thine eyes shalt thou behold" [Psalm 90].

Then the crowd moved aside, thus permitting him an unobstructed view of the frightful sight of the burning pyre. (Indeed, even from a great distance away he could feel the fire and see the flames shooting skyward and thundering, so to say, and sending forth sparks of fire which flew to the top of the obelisk of stone placed in the middle of the Hippodrome.) At that point that audacious man seemed to cringe from the fire and to be distressed as if he were completely at a loss. He frequently averted his eyes, clapped his hands together, and struck his thigh. Though he was thus affected by the very sight of the fire, he remained adamant. The fire did not soften the steel in his soul, nor did the admonitions sent by the emperor win him over. For either the ultimate degree of madness had seized him, making him lose his mind because of the pressing exigency of circumstances and his misfortune and thus completely depriving him of his judgment concerning what was best for him, or, as is more likely, the devil had taken control of his soul and plunged him into the deepest darkness. Thus that abominable Basil stood insensible to every threat and all fear, staring now at the burning pyre, now at the spectators. He appeared to everybody to be truly mad, since he did not run to the pyre, nor did he draw back, but remained frozen and immobile in the place he had first occupied.

Commentary. Besides the pronouncements of the official ecumenical and local councils, summaries or interpretations of dogma were, at times, unofficially drawn up by certain individual ecclesiastics. John of Damascus (died ca. 750) is generally considered to have composed the best and most systematic summary of Orthodox teaching, a summary which achieved virtually official status. While living in the monastery of St. Savas in Palestine he wrote his *Exposition of the Orthodox Faith,* using Aristotelian concepts and terminology to explain and clarify Christian doctrine. In many important respects, however, his thought remained that of the Christian Neoplatonism of the early Fathers of the church. (On John see selection 111.)

Sometimes occasions arose when it became necessary for patriarchs to make pronouncements which, though not officially sanctioned by a council, served to clarify aspects of dogma, especially in connection with specific heresies. An example of this is the condemnation of the Bogomil heresy whose Manichaean beliefs (on the extreme dualism in the world of good and evil) spread rapidly from the Paulicians of Asia Minor to the area of Thrace in the Balkans after Paulicians had been forcibly settled there near the Bulgars (see selection no. 198).

We quote here from the letter of Patriarch Theophylact of Constantinople (933–56) to the Bulgar tsar, Peter, in which the patriarch in detail condemns followers of the Bogomil heresy. The letter is also a good example of the form of a Byzantine "anathema," which was pronounced against adversaries of the Orthodox church.

B. Patriarch Theophylact Anathematizes the Bogomils

(Translated by V. Sharenkoff, *A Study of Manichaeism in Bulgaria* [New York, 1927], pp. 63–65.)

In the name of the Holy Consubstantial and Worshipped Trinity, the Father, the Son, and the Holy Ghost, cursed be everyone who does not think and believe as does the Holy Divine Catholic Church, the Churches of Rome, of Constantinople, of Alexandria, of Antioch, and of the Holy City—in a word those from one end of the world to the other who do not accept the rules, decrees, and dogmas of the seven holy ecumenical councils.

Cursed be everyone who believes and admits that there exist Two Principles, good and evil, one the creator of light, the other of darkness; one the creator of man and the other of the angels and of the other creatures.

Cursed be those who talk idly that the guileful devil is the creator and ruler of matter of this whole visible world and of our bodies.

Cursed be those who slander the law of Moses and say that the prophets are not from the good.

Cursed be those who reject lawful marriage, slander it, and say that the increase and continuation of our generation is the institution of the devil.

Cursed be those who blaspheme and say that the Member of the Holy Trinity, the Son and Word of the same substance with God the Father, was man without sin in imagination and appearance but not in fact.

Cursed be those who fancy that the crucifixion, death and resurrection of Christ were only apparent.

Cursed be those who do not believe in the reality of the body and the blood of Christ, as it was said to the Apostles and handed down to them by Him in the "Take, eat," but who tell fables about the Gospel and Epistles.

Cursed be those who say idly that the Mother of God was not the Virgin Mary, the daughter of Joakim and Anna, but was the high Jerusalem into which, they say, Christ entered and from which he had emerged.

Cursed be those who invent the story that the eternal Virgin Mary, the Mother of God, after the indescribable birth of the Son and the Word of God had given birth to other children by sexual intercourse with a man.

Cursed be the authors and teachers of this ancient and newly appeared heresy. [There follow the names of specific heretics.]

D.
ADMINISTRATION OF THE CHURCH: THE SECULAR CLERGY

117.

Introduction. The ecclesiastical head of the church, the patriarch of Constantinople, was invested by the emperor in a magnificent ceremony befitting his high office. Under the patriarch there were metropolitans, archbishops, and bishops. (Metropolitan was the title of a bishop exercising provincial and not merely diocesan authority.) The following selection describes the patriarch's investiture in the fourteenth century—a ceremony virtually identical with that of earlier centuries.

INVESTITURE OF A PATRIARCH

(From Pseudo-Codinus, *De officiis*, ed. I. Bekker [Bonn, 1839], pp. 101–3.)

The prelates assemble who live in Constantinople, whether on the one hand they be many, or, if not, twelve (at least). . . . They sit in the place of voting, of course as many as are there, and three persons are chosen to be patriarch, whom God has inspired to be chosen. The most eminent archons of the church bring their names in writing to the emperor and the emperor selects from these the [one] name which God has inspired in him. Then the archons whom the emperor may select and the ecclesiastical archons who have been selected are sent by him to announce the vote to the one elected and chosen by the church and by the emperor. If the chosen one accepts, all is fine, but if he does not, they go to another, and if this one declines, they go to the last one. If perhaps also the third does not accept, a vote is again taken from the beginning, and after the one who is elected accepts, the emperor invests him in the following manner.

After the patriarchal throne is constructed of wood at the front of the *triklinium* [a large room in the imperial palace], carpeted by red porphyry cloth on which stands the imperial throne which is mentioned in the coronation of the emperor, the *triklinium* is divided by porphyry drapes, of the kind customarily used in the investiture of the despot. Then the emperor, wearing his crown and other ornaments of his rank, enters from his chambers, and sits on his throne, with all the archons standing nearby behind the partition wearing their decorations and official garb. And when the [patriarchal] throne, extending high up and located in the third part of the *triklinium* extending from the wall toward the emperor, has been covered by gold porphyry [cloth], there comes the candidate for patriarch (for he is called candidate until now) and sits upon it. Then when the porphyry [curtain] has been drawn apart, both emperor and patriarch stand up and at once all exclaim, "Many happy years." After this someone not from among the highest officials—despot or *sebastokrator*, or caesar—supports the candidate . . . (for when the patriarch sits they should not stand. Again when the emperor and empress are acclaimed it is not proper for them to stand. . .).

The most worthy and eminent of the archons, lifting him up by the hand, leads him before the raised throne. Then after the patriarchal staff is found there in the said enclosure, the emperor takes it from one of the nobles not wearing *skiadia* [a type of hat], and standing with his son (if the latter is present) in a loud voice proclaims the following: "May the Holy Trinity, through the empire given to us by it, constitute you archbishop of Constantinople, the New Rome, and ecumenical patriarch." And thus at once all shout acclamations. Then the patriarch approaches his throne and receives his [shepherd's] staff from the hand of the emperor. And after blessing the emperor the patriarch moves away. Then both sit on their thrones and emperor and patriarch are acclaimed. Then following the acclamation, when the drapes have been closed, the emperor returns to his chambers while the patriarch on horseback betakes himself to Hagia Sophia. His horse is covered with white cloth up to his neck, the nobles attending him being adorned with their special insignia.

118.

Introduction. Each bishop, situated in an important city of the empire, supervised the administration of his own diocese and his court, which included such officials as an *oikonomos* (in charge of administration of church property), a *chartophylax* (in charge of the chancery), a *skevophylax* (in charge of vestments, relics, etc.), and many others. This organization of ecclesiastics paralleled that of the patriarchal court in Constantinople in many respects.

One of the best records we have describing the election of a Byzantine bishop is provided by the *Epanagoge* (c. 880), written as noted by or under the influence of the patriarch Photius. Note the presence of laymen (*archontes* or "principal men" of the city) as well as clerical electors. The presence of such laymen underlines the central importance of religious officials to the life of the community at large.

ON THE ELECTION OF A BISHOP

(From the *Epanagoge Aucta*, in J. and P. Zepos, eds., *Jus graecoromanum* [Athens, 1930–31], vol. 6, pp. 66–67.)

We command that, if a bishop is to be elected, the clergy should be assembled together with the chief men of the city, and votes should be cast for three persons. Each of these [electors] should in his own handwriting declare that he has not rendered his vote because of any gift or promise or friendship or favor or any attempt whatever [to influence him] but through knowing that the persons involved are of the orthodox and catholic faith and of modest life, and in age above the thirtieth year; also that the candidate is not married . . . and has no concubines or illegitimate children. Of the three persons voted upon, let the best man be chosen by the will and judgment of the electors. Let him provide a *libellus* [letter] signed by himself attesting to the orthodoxy of his faith. . . . Let him also attest in his own handwriting that he has not made any gift or promise, or thereafter will make no gift either to anyone who elected him or to those who cast their votes for him, or to anyone at all in connection with his election.

We command those participating in the voting, that if they should consider any layman worthy of such an election [to bishop], that they should consider him together with the other three [who are] clerics or monks. However, in this case let the layman thus considered for the episcopal office not [immediately] be elected bishop but let him be inscribed among the clergy only after at least three months have passed, and thus [he will] be ordained bishop after he has been instructed in the holy canons and the sacred liturgy.

119.

Introduction. A view of the day-to-day activities of a high prelate in the period before the Arab conquest is afforded by the following passages from the life of St. John the Almsgiver, patriarch of Alexandria in the early seventh century Under John the patriarchate possessed its own fleet of ships, which in time of need he would dispatch to areas such as Sicily to procure grain for his people.

THE BISHOP TAKES CARE OF HIS PEOPLE

(Translated by E. Dawes and N. Baynes, *Three Byzantine Saints* [Crestwood, N.Y.: St. Vladimir's Seminary Press, and Oxford: A. R. Mowbray, 1977; originally published by Blackwell, Oxford, 1948], pp. 202, 221, 223.)

An indescribable number of fugitives from the Persians invaded Alexandria . . . and great scarcity of food prevailed. Therefore after he had spent all the money he had, the holy Patriarch [John] sent and borrowed about ten hundred pounds from divers good Christians . . . News was then brought that two of the Church's fast-sailing ships, which he had sent to Sicily for corn, had cast anchor in the harbor. . . .

In the greatness of his mind and the generosity of his purpose he supported them all liberally (the refugees as well as his flock), supplying most abundantly each one's necessities. . . . In addition to this he built a great many poor-houses and hostels for strangers and he decreed that all the corn and all the necessary expenditure for the feeding of their inmates should be paid for from the revenues of the church.

E.
MONASTICISM AS AN INSTITUTION

120.

Introduction. Admired for their asceticism, their disregard of worldly rank and station, and their search for spiritual perfection, the monks (and nuns) of Byzantium were, at their best, exemplars of the highest and most respected form of Christian life. As such they held a special place in the society of the Christian Byzantine Empire. These "holy men" exercised great moral authority over the common people, and emperors and high state officials paid them honor. (Some monasteries were not only centers of the contemplative life but also fulfilled certain social needs, serving, at various times and places, as asylums, hospitals, old-age homes, and places of exile. But this was not their major function.)

Early Byzantine Christianity knew various types of monasticism. There were anchorite (or eremitic) monks who lived absolutely alone, often in the deserts of Syria, Palestine, and Egypt, in order to remove themselves from worldly corruption. The cenobites lived together in common in a monastery. Besides these two basic types, there existed variations including the monks of the *laura* (hermits living in separate cells but in one area, under the direction of an abbot), and the idiorhythmic (self-regulated, hence rather undisciplined), groups of monks who in the later period were often found on Mount Athos.

The following celebrated passage by the fourth-century bishop Athanasius of Alexandria (d. 373) illustrates the traits of the earliest anchorite (eremite) monk, St. Anthony of Egypt, and reflects the motivation for monastic life which was to endure throughout the entire Byzantine period.

FROM ATHANASIUS, *LIFE OF SAINT ANTHONY*

(Translated by H. Ellershaw and A. Robertson, from Athanasius, *Life of St. Anthony*, in P. Schaff and H. Wace, eds., *A Select Library of Nicene and Post-Nicene Fathers of the Christian Church*, 2d ser. [reprint, Grand Rapids, Mich.: Wm. Eerdmans, 1976], vol. 4, pp. 196, 200, 210.)

After the death of his father and mother he was left alone with one little sister: his age was about eighteen or twenty, and on him the care both of home and sister rested. Now it was not six months after the death of his parents, and going according to custom into the Lord's House, he communed with himself and reflected as he walked how the Apostles left all and followed the Saviour; and how they in the Acts sold their possessions and brought and laid them at the Apostles' feet for distribution to the needy, and what and how great a hope was laid up for them in heaven. Pondering over these things he entered the church, and it happened the Gospel was being read, and he heard the Lord saying to the rich man, "If thou wouldest be perfect, go and sell what thou hast and give to the poor; and come follow Me and thou shalt have treasure in heaven." Anthony, as though God had put him in mind of the Saints, and the passage had been read on his account, went out immediately from the church, and gave the possessions of his forefathers to the villagers—they were three hundred acres, productive and very fair—that they should be no more a clog upon himself and his sister. And all the rest that was movable he sold, and having got together much money he gave it to the poor, reserving a little however for his sister's sake.

And again as he went into the church, hearing the Lord say in the Gospel, "be not anxious for the morrow," he could stay no longer, but went out and gave those things also to the poor. Having committed his sister to known and faithful virgins, and put her into a convent to be brought up, he henceforth devoted himself outside his house to discipline, taking heed to himself and training himself with patience. For there were not yet so many monasteries in Egypt, and no monk at all knew of the distant desert; but all who wished to give heed to themselves practised the discipline in solitude near their own village. . . .

And so for nearly twenty years he continued training himself in solitude, never going forth, and but seldom seen by any. After this, when many were eager and wishful to imitate his discipline, and his acquaintances came and began to cast down and wrench off the door by force, Anthony, as from a shrine, came forth initiated in the mysteries and filled with the Spirit of God. Then for the first time he was seen outside the fort by those who came to see him. And they, when they saw him, wondered at the sight, for he had the same habit of body as before, and was neither fat, like a man without exercise, nor lean from fasting and striving with the demons, but he was just the same as they had known him before his retirement. And again his soul was free from blemish, for it was neither contracted as if by grief, nor relaxed by pleasure, nor possessed by laughter or dejection, for he was not troubled when he beheld the crowd, nor overjoyed at being saluted by so many. But he was altogether even as being guided by reason, and abiding in a natural state. Through him the Lord healed the bodily ailments of many present, and cleansed others from evil spirits. And He gave grace to Anthony in speaking, so that he consoled many that were sorrowful, and set those at variance at one, exhorting all to prefer the love of Christ before all that is in the world. And while he exhorted and advised them to remember the good things to come, and the loving-kindness of God towards us, "Who spared not His own Son, but delivered Him up for us all," he persuaded many to embrace the solitary life. And thus it happened in the end that cells arose even in the mountains, and the desert was colonised by monks, who came forth from their own people, and enrolled themselves for the citizenship in the heavens. . . .

So he was alone in the inner mountain, spending his time in prayer and discipline. And the brethren who served him asked that they might come every month and bring him olives, pulse and oil, for by now he was an old man. There then he passed his life, and endured such great wrestlings, "Not against flesh and blood," as it is written, but against opposing demons, as we learned from those who visited him. For there they heard tumults, many voices, and, as it were, the clash of arms. At night they saw the mountain become full of wild beasts, and him also fighting as though against visible beings, and praying against them. And those who came to him he encouraged, while kneeling he contended and prayed to the Lord. Surely it was a marvellous thing that a man, alone in such a desert, feared neither the demons who rose up against him nor the fierceness of the four-footed beasts and creeping things, for all they were so many. But in truth, as it is written, "He trusted in the Lord as Mount Sion," with a mind unshaken and undisturbed; so that the demons rather fled from him, and the wild beasts, as it is written, "kept peace with him."

121.

Introduction. The next selection is taken from the so-called "longer rules" of the fourth-century Church Father, St. Basil the Great (d. 379), who is considered the most important founder and organizer of the main type of Byzantine monasticism, cenobitism. These rules illustrate the cenobitic monastic ideal.

AN EXAMPLE OF ST. BASIL'S "LONGER RULES"

(Translated by M. M. Wagner, *Saint Basil: Ascetical Works*, in series *Fathers of the Church* [Washington, D.C.: Catholic University of America Press, 1950], vol. 9, pp. 247–50, 289–91.)

I consider that [monastic] life passed in company with a number of persons in the same habitation is more advantageous in many respects. My reasons are, first, that no one of us is self-sufficient as regards corporeal necessities, but we require one another's aid in supplying our needs. The foot, to cite an analogy, possesses one kind of power and lacks another, and without the co-operation of the other members of the body it finds itself incapable of carrying on its activity independently for any length of time, nor does it have wherewithal to supply what is lacking. Similarly, in the solitary life, what is at hand becomes useless to us and what is wanting cannot be provided, since God, the Creator, decreed that we should require the help of one another, as it is written, so that we might associate with one another. Again, apart from this consideration, the doctrine of the charity of Christ does not permit the individual to be concerned solely with his own private interests. "Charity," says the Apostle, "seeketh not her own." But a life passed in solitude is concerned only with the private service of individual needs. This is openly opposed to the law of love which the Apostle fulfilled, who sought not what was profitable to himself but to many that they might be saved. Furthermore, a person living in solitary retirement will not readily discern his own defects, since he has no one to admonish and correct him with mildness and compassion. In fact, admonition even from an enemy often produces in a prudent man the desire for amendment. But the cure of sin is wrought with understanding by him who loves sincerely; for Holy Scripture says: "for he that loveth correcteth betimes." Such a one it is very difficult to find in a solitude, if in one's prior state of life one had not been associated with such a person. The solitary, consequently, experiences the truth of the saying, "Woe to him that is alone, for when he falleth he hath none to lift him up."

Moreover, the majority of the commandments are easily observed by several persons living together, but not so in the case of one living alone; for, while he is obeying one commandment, the practice of another is being interfered with. For example, when he is visiting the sick, he cannot show hospitality to the stranger and, in the imparting and sharing of necessities (especially when the ministrations are prolonged), he is prevented from giving zealous attention to [other] tasks. As a result, the greatest commandment and the one especially conducive to salvation is not observed, since the hungry are not fed nor the naked clothed. Who, then, would choose this ineffectual and unprofitable life in preference to that which is both fruitful and in accordance with the Lord's command?

Besides, if all we who are united in the one hope of our calling are one body with Christ as our Head, we are also members, one of another. If we are not joined together by union in the Holy Spirit in the harmony of one body, but each of us should choose to live in solitude, we would not serve the common good in the ministry according to God's good pleasure, but would be satisfying our own passion for self-gratification. How could we, divided and separated, preserve the status and the mutual service of members or our subordinate relationship to our Head which is Christ? It is impossible, indeed, to rejoice with him who receives an honor or to sympathize with him who suffers when, by reason of their being separated from one another, each person cannot, in all likelihood, be kept informed about the affairs of his neighbor. In addition, since no one has the capacity to receive all spiritual gifts, but the grace of the Spirit is given proportionately to the faith of each, when one is living in association with others, the grace privately bestowed on each individual becomes the common possession of his fellows. "To one, indeed, is given the word of wisdom; and to another, the word of knowledge; to another, faith, to another, prophecy, to another, the grace of healing," and so on. He who receives any of these gifts does not possess it for his own sake but rather for the sake of others, so that, in the life passed in community, the operation of the Holy Spirit in the individual is at the same time necessarily transmitted to all. He who lives alone, consequently, and has, perhaps, one gift renders it ineffectual by leaving it in disuse, since it lies buried within him. How much danger there is in this all of you know who have read the Gospel. On the other hand, in the case of several persons living together, each enjoys his own gift and enhances it by giving others a share, besides reaping benefit from the gifts of others as if they were his own.

122.

Introduction. Basil's ideas were amplified by the important ninth-century reformer of the cenobitic type of monasticism, Theodore of Studius (d. 826). Like Basil and his predecessor Pachomius, Theodore stressed absolute obedience; but at the same time he urged moderation in ascetic practice so that the cenobitic ideal could be carried out by all. In the so-called "Constitutions" of the Studite house (the largest monastic establishment in Constantinople), Theodore's rulings on monastic discipline were summarized: "There are many different rules which prevail in the holy monasteries . . . but our tradition is that which we have received from our great father and confessor, Theodore. . . . We are not alone in this, for a large section of the approved monastic world also accepts this as the best and the most royal rite which indeed avoids both extravagance and inadequacy."* In the selection that follows Theodore himself in a letter to a pupil explains something more of his ideal for the cenobitic monastic community. Note among other things his warnings against female company, even that of female animals.

REFORM RULES OF THEODORE OF STUDIUS

(Translated by A. Gardner, *Theodore of Studium[s]: His Life and Times* [London: Edward Arnold, 1905], pp. 71–74.)

Since, by the good pleasure of God, you have been promoted, my spiritual child Nicolas, to the dignity of abbot, it is needful for you to keep all the injunctions in this letter. Do not alter without necessity the type and rule that you have received from your spiritual home, the monastery. Do not acquire any of this world's goods, nor hoard up privately for yourself to the value of one piece of silver. Be without distraction in heart and soul in your care and your thought for those who have been entrusted to you by God, and have become your spiritual sons and brothers;—and do not look aside to those formerly belonging to you according to the flesh, whether kinsfolk, or friends, or companions. Do not spend the property of your monastery, in life or death, by way of gift or of legacy, to any such kinsfolk or friends. For you are not of the world, neither have you part in the world. Except that if any of your people come out of ordinary life to join our rule, you must care for them according to the example of the Holy Fathers. Do not obtain any slave nor use in your private service or in that of the monastery over which you preside, or in the fields, man who was made in the image of God. For such an indulgence is only for those who live in the world. For you should yourself be as a servant to the brethren like-minded with you, at least in intention, even if in outward appearance you are reckoned to be master and teacher. Have no animal of the female sex in domestic use, seeing that you have renounced the female sex altogether, whether in house or fields, since none of the Holy Fathers had such, nor does nature require them. Do not be driven by horses and mules without necessity, but go on foot in imitation of Christ. But if there is need, let your beast be the foal of an ass.

Use all care that all things in the brotherhood be common and not distributed, and let nothing, not even a needle, belong to any one in particular. Let your body and your spirit, to say nothing of your goods, be ever divided in equality of love among all your spiritual children and brethren. Use no authority over the two brothers of yours who are my sons. Do nothing, by way of command or of ordination, beyond the injunctions of the Fathers. Do not join in brotherhood or close relation with secular persons, seeing that you have fled from the world and from marriage. Such relations are not found in the Fathers, or but here and there, and not according to rule. Do not sit at a feast with women, except with your mother according to the flesh, and your sister, or possibly with others in case of necessity, as the Holy Fathers enjoin. Do not go out often, nor range around, leaving your fold without necessity. For even if you remain always there, it is hard to keep safe your human sheep, so apt are they to stray and wander.

By all means keep to the instruction three times a week in the evening, since that is traditional and salutary. Do not give what they call the little habit [of novice or postulant?] and then, some time later, another as the larger. For there is one habit, as there is one baptism, and this is the practice of the Holy Fathers. Depart not from the rules and canons of the Fathers, especially of the Holy Father Basil; but whatever you do or say, be as one who has his witness in the Holy Scriptures, or in the custom of the Fathers, so as not to transgress the commandments of God. Do not leave your fold or remove to another, or ascend to any higher dignity, except by the paternal decision. Do not make friends with any canoness, nor enter any women's monastery, nor have any private conversation with a nun, or with a secular woman, except in case of necessity; and then let it be so that two are present on either side. For one, as they say, is cause of offence. Do not open the door of the sheepfold to any manner of woman, without great necessity; if it is possible to receive such in silence, it is all the better. Do not procure a lodging for yourself, or a secular house for your spiritual children, in which there are women, for that were to run great risks; but provide yourself with what is necessary for journeys and other occasions from men of piety. Do not take as pupil into your cell a youth for whom you have a fancy; but use the services of some one above suspicion, and of various brothers.

Do not have any choice or costly garment, except for priestly functions. But follow the Fathers in being shod and clad in humility. Be not delicate in food, in private expenditure, or in hospitality; for this belongs to the portion of those who take their joy in the present life. Do not lay up money in your monastery; but things of all kinds, beyond what is needed, give to the poor at the entrance of your court; for so did the Holy Fathers. Do not keep a safe place, nor have a care for wealth. But let all your care be the guardianship of souls. As to the money, and various necessaries, entrust them to the steward, the cellarer, or to whosesoever charge it falls; but so that you keep for yourself the whole authority, and change offices among persons from time to time as you see fit, receiving account as you may demand, of the tasks entrusted to each. Do nothing, carry out nothing, according to your own judgment, in any matter whatever, in journeying, buying or selling, receiving or rejecting a brother, or in any change of office or in anything material, or in regard to spiritual failings, without the counsel of those who stand first in knowledge and in piety, one, two, three or more, according to circumstances, as the Fathers have directed. These commands, and all others that you have received, keep and maintain, that it may be well with you, and that you may have prosperity in the Lord all the days of your life. But let anything to the contrary be far from you in speech and in thought.

*J. Hussey, "Byzantine Monasticism," in *Cambridge Medieval History*, vol. 4, pt. 2, *Byzantium: Government, Church, and Civilization* [Cambridge, 1967], p. 166.

123.

Introduction. A later example of the cenobitic type of monasticism is that of the late tenth-century St. Nilus of Rossano in southern Italy, who founded the great monastery of Grottaferrata south of Rome (1004). The following selection gives some idea of the influence the Byzantine monasticism of southern Italy (which included a large number of small monasteries and anchorites) seems to have exerted on the Latin variety, and also provides a unique example, in this relatively late period, of monastic symbiosis, a harmonious dwelling-together of Greeks nd Latins in the same monastery.

FROM THE *LIFE* OF SAINT NILUS OF ROSSANO

(From the *Vita* of St. Nilus, in MPG, vol. 120, col. 127.)

Now our saintly father Nilus, while he wanted to obey God's will, did not intend to return to the areas of the East [Byzantium] to which he was invited by the *cubicularius* [a state official], for he suspected that there he would not be able to escape great esteem and favorable attention, since the fame of his virtue had come to the ears of the most pious emperors. Therefore he chose to go among the Latins, who, not knowing him, would not grant him honors. But the more he was seeking to flee glory, that much more did an aureole of celestial radiance surround him, and all came to look upon him as an apostle, and thus venerated him. When he arrived in Capua, he was received with great honor by [the Lombard] Prince Pandulf and the nobles of the city; indeed, they thought of enthroning him as bishop. And this would have happened had the prince not died. Then the nobles called on the abbot of Monte Casino (Aligernus, a most holy man) to grant to Nilus a monastery, whichever the latter preferred among the property of our saintly father, Benedict.

[Nilus then goes to this monastery and is received with pomp.]

. . . Nor did it seem to these monks that they were seeing or hearing anyone less than the great Anthony come from Alexandria, or the great Benedict, their divine [Latin] legislator and master, returned from the dead. So they thought and they were not far from the truth.

Then after he had comforted them with his personal presence and calmed them by spiritual joy (like a man sent by God), and in turn, after he had admired their regularity of habits and discipline (approving their customs in preference to ours [the Greek]), he went to a place called Vallelucio, dedicated to the Archangel Michael, accompanied by the abbot and the principal brothers of the monastery. There he was supposed to live with his [spiritual] sons. But the [Latin] abbot [of Monte Cassino] with his monks wanted him to return once more to the great monastery with his entire community, and there to celebrate the office in the Greek language. As the abbot said, "God is in all places and things, which the prophet had already prefigured in saying 'the lion and the lamb shall lie down together.'" This request the admirable Nilus tried to resist, saying "How can we chant of God in another land, we who for our sins are subject to humiliation in all the earth?" Nonetheless, in order to celebrate in a common faith, and in order that the great name of Christ be glorified, he complied with the request.

As the fruit of his lips he composed a hymn in honor of St. Benedict, including all the marvelous things written about his life. And then, accompanied by all his monks, more than sixty in number, he went to Monte Cassino and chanted the evening office with beautiful harmonies. He had with him intelligent monks expert in reading and chanting the psalms and hymns, whom he himself had trained.

When the office was over, all the [Latin] monks gathered around him with the permission of the lord abbot, as they continued to observe their own rule. Astounded by the splendor of the divine spirit hovering around his face, they wanted to hear words from his mouth. So they asked of him many questions: "Tell us, holy father, what is the proper work of a monk, and how can we attain mercy?" And the saintly one, responding in the Roman language [Latin], said, "The monk is an angel, and his work is compassion [*misericordia*], peace, the sacrifice of praise . . . ; thus equally it behooves that the true monk show compassion to his inferiors and to guests, his brothers and friends, and also brothers in his own community, with a spirit of peace, and not bear envy to those that have more than he. And he should have a sincere faith and hope in God and in him who is his father in the spirit [the abbot]. Whoever possesses these three qualities leads on earth the life of an angel; but he, on the contrary, who is without faith and nourishes hate and has not a compassionate heart, becomes a habitation of every evil, and is visibly revealed as a demon. From whatever moment he is made a monk, it is no longer in his power to be a man, but he becomes one of two, either an angel or devil. As for you, brother, I believe the best and wish you health." These and various other matters were treated by the saint.

124.

Introduction. Unlike anchorite monasticism, cenobitic monasticism was closely regulated. Early canons prescribed strict subordination of local monasteries to the local bishop. Later, however, some new monasteries came to be placed under the direct control and protection of the emperor or the patriarch, who sometimes even founded their own monasteries.

Here, in the introduction to his own *typikon* (monastic charter), Emperor Michael VIII Palaeologus presents his reasons for rebuilding the Monastery of St. Demetrius in Constantinople (c. 1261).

TYPIKON FOR THE MONASTERY OF ST. DEMETRIUS

(From C. Chapman, *Michel Paléologue: Restaurateur de l'empire Byzantin, 1261–82* [Paris, 1926], pp. 176–77.)

In former times the blessed George Palaeologus, distinguished for his burning piety and love of God . . . wanted to build—from foundations to roof—a temple in the center of the capital, a sanctuary dedicated to the name of the sainted Christian martyr. [This] venerable saint [Demetrius] is in fact the patron saint of the Palaeologi. But the Latin tyranny, opposed to the lofty idea which had inspired this construction, razed it and reduced it to dust. Indeed, one could hardly discern the traces of its former existence. When I came to power, by the grace of God and the assistance of the sainted martyr Demetrius, I rebuilt the devastated structure and with an open and generous hand I restored it to its former splendor. There I founded a monastery and there I established monks in the service of God. I assigned to them properties and sources of revenue sufficient for their expenses and corporal needs. Thus I realized an aim which is doubly praiseworthy: I payed my debt of gratitude to the sainted martyr for the greatest glory of God (and this had been the fundamental principle of my government), and I restored the memory of its blessed founder, our ancestor, among men. And finally, the third happy consequence of my action is that a monastery was founded where many monks now can live a holy life, pleasing to God: thus, those who pray for my reign will become more numerous, and more numerous in turn will be the gifts and heavenly favors which I will receive.

If it is true that "he who offers even a glass of cold water will surely be rewarded," according to the true words of Our Savior and Lord, then—as I have given means of fulfillment to those whose ascetic inclinations compel them to God's service, making it possible for them to follow their choice—how could these acts go unrewarded by him who said that "the whole world is not worth the sacrifice of one soul"? If, by this act and for these reasons, my reign has restored the sanctuary to the honor of God and his sainted martyr, Demetrius, may this monastery become, by the intercession of our glorious saint, a paradise. May it nurture monks who will be like ever-healthy and precious plants, producing each day that fruit which is virtue—for the glory of God, for the glory of the great martyr whose name our monastery is honored to bear, and also for the expiation of many sins which, of course, I have committed, being a man and having man's changing and corruptible nature.

125.

Introduction. As a rule the emperors respected the monks and the monastic life. In certain eras, however, when the state was endangered, several emperors became alarmed that vast tracts of lands were passing into monastic hands and that great estates, secular as well as ecclesiastic, were being created at the expense of peasant holdings (see selection 170). These emperors were also concerned that ecclesiastical lands, although theoretically liable to taxation like other landed property, sometimes paid little or no taxes.* Accordingly, they issued edicts restricting the increase of monastic property. The one below was issued in 965 by Emperor Nicephorus Phocas. Note that Phocas, nevertheless, supported his friend the monk Athanasius, in the founding of the famous monastery of the Laura on Mount Athos.

RESTRICTION AND CARE OF MONASTIC PROPERTY (965)

(From J. and P. Zepos, eds., *Jus graecoromanum* [Athens, 1931], vol. 1, pp. 251–52.)

Wherefore, desiring to lead you to observance of the commandments of Christ and to uproot utterly the sin of vanity which is hateful to God, and considering that all the good works we do, we do for the sake of God and not for human approbation . . . we order that those who wish to act piously and to perform acts of service and *philanthropeia* follow the injunction of Christ, that they, after selling their possessions, give the money to the poor. For he desires that we be munificent and extravagant beyond measure in our compassion, so that we not only share the money we possess with those who are in need, but even that we—after spending this money—proceed to the sale of our property. But if some are fond of elegance and magnificence (we call this their love of honor [*philotimon*]) and accordingly wish to found new monasteries, travelers' hostels [*xenones*], or homes for the aged, no one will forbid it. But since many of the already existing monasteries have become dilapidated and have fallen almost to the point of utter ruin, let them take care of these, let them stretch out their hand to such prostrate monasteries, let them display their love of God through them. As long as they ignore these already existing monasteries, averting their eyes from them and—as the Gospel says—turning away from them, and instead seek to found other new ones, we will not approve such actions, nor allow them at all. For we consider such activity to be nothing but love of vanity and obvious madness. Rather we decree that they ameliorate conditions in those already existing monasteries needing assistance; but let them not provide them with fields or lands or any buildings (for the monasteries' present land holdings, which they have possessed from the beginning, are sufficient). Indeed these [original] lands lie neglected and uncultivated owing to a lack of money. Therefore let those who possess lands and estates, and who consider it worthy to care for these monasteries, sell such lands to whomever among the lay population they desire, and [let them] provide to the monasteries slaves, oxen, sheep, and other animals. For if we allow those who possess land [to give it to monasteries]—since the law forbids that property of religious foundations be alienated—we will still confront the same problem as before, that is, we will have monasteries which are in unsound condition still uncared for, since they have neither enough manpower nor sufficient [financial] resources to work those lands which they already possess.

Therefore, from now on it is forbidden that anyone transfer lands or estates through any means to monasteries, *xenones*, or old-age homes, nor to bishops or metropolitans, for such actions offer no benefit to them. But if there are existing monasteries and religious foundations which—on account of poor management—have no lands remaining, they will not be prevented from acquiring any necessary land. This, however, may take place only after imperial investigation and with imperial approval. We do not prohibit the foundation of monastic cells or of the so-called *laurai* [see selection 120]. Rather we consider this a laudable action so long as the property belonging to such cells and *laurai* does not extend outside their enclosures.

*Certain scholars have recently stressed rather the view that these emperors were primarily interested in preventing monasteries from acquiring lands for whose cultivation they lacked sufficient labor.

126.

Introduction. The institution of the *charistikion* (the handing over of the administration of a monastery or monastic property to laymen) became rather widespread in the mid-eleventh century, at the time of increasing disturbances within the empire caused by nomadic Turkish invaders, pirates, or simply lawless inhabitants. Over the centuries (perhaps as far back as Emperor Justinian) the practice of granting *charistikion* to laymen had gone on because many monasteries in bad financial straits needed a lay protector, powerful and probably wealthy, to restore them to a condition of well-being. However, the institution led, in many cases, to abuse on the part of the lay protector, who often "milked" the monastery and its estates for his own purposes. By the late eleventh century, a continuing outcry by churchmen arose against the granting by the emperor of *charistikia* to laymen. A striking example of this ecclesiastical protest may be seen in the following (rhetorical and highly biased) selection from the treatise "On Monastic Discipline and Why Monasteries Should Not Be Handed over to Laymen," addressed to the emperor at the end of the eleventh century by John, patriarch of Antioch.*

A Patriarchal Indictment of the Practice of Granting Charistikia

(From P. Gautier, "Réquisitoire du Patriarche Jean d'Antioche contre le charisticiat," *Revue des études byzantines* 33 [1975]: 115–19.)

If it were to be affirmed that monasteries are given [to laymen] for their own welfare and maintenance, the monasteries which have been converted into private estates at once cry out and loudly remonstrate. We do not know if a monastery can be found which has been reestablished and restored by a *charistikarios.* But even if one should be found, God does not accept this illegal gift. At the present time monasteries which are free flourish and prosper, while those in servile condition fall into ruin. But you—you maintain precisely the same position as one who contends that perpetual servitude is better than liberty. And it is clear from the following that these monasteries are not granted for their own preservation and maintenance: for it is not ruined monasteries that are granted, but rather monasteries in good condition and whose revenues are flourishing; and the benefits which go along with certain donations [*charistikia*] reveal it more clearly. Among these it is said that the incomes which exceed the usual expense of the monastery return to the *charistikarios* as a profit without his accounting for them. And again, if it might be said that they [the *charistikarioi*] act in this manner because they are exempt from additional levies, let them take heed: to impose additional charges or not to do so depends on your [imperial] authority. Suppress those who impose them [i.e., excess levies] and there will no longer be need for exemptions. For he who says these things resembles an archon who, through the mediation of his subordinate, indirectly crushes a poor freeman with levies. Then, as if he were moved by pious sentiment for the poor man, he orders that his liberty at the same time as his goods be stripped from him and that he become a slave instead of a free man in order that he not be overwhelmed with burdens!

All that is a pretext, an excuse, a disguise for avarice. How is it that a holy church and monastery be granted to anyone—what evangelical and divine words have prescribed this, what apostolic exhortation has foreseen it, what patristic and canonical tradition has ordained it, what civil legislation from time immemorial has prescribed it? Even the [ancient] Greeks themselves never gave a pagan temple to anyone. Consequently, what logical person could term this a good thing, or useful, or appropriate, or considerate, or beneficial, or helpful? It is rather a violation and transgression, the ultimate disastrous transgression of law. . . .

It is necessary to speak of those who receive these donations and whom evil custom has called *charistikarioi*. As soon as one takes charge of the monastery, alas, he reveals incontinently the great whirlpool of his cupidity, and he sucks in all the goods of the monastery, not only houses, lands, livestock, and all kinds of revenues but even the churches themselves. He treats the abbot and monks as slaves and considers people and things without exception as his own and makes use of them without fear as if under the guise of his personal patrimony, without his ever conceiving that these things belong to God and his saints. . . . The immediate result is not only the end and extinction of all the pious solicitude fostered by the holy founders, which is bound up with the divine, the brilliant ceremonies of the Holy Feasts, the incense, and the doxologies. . . . In brief it is the disappearance of any form of piety as envisioned by the founders of the holy churches both for the monks and the laity. The revenues hitherto used for this purpose have been diverted to the sinful world and to the [sinful] prince of the world. Even worse, all canon, all rule, all monastic discipline have at once ended. For here there is no authority of the abbot, nor fear, nor humility, nor any other virtue.

* Like other patriarchs of Antioch, John resided in Constantinople rather than Muslim-controlled Antioch.

127.

Introduction. But the condemnation of the practice of *charistikion* was not universal, even among the clergy. Despite condemnation of the practice by Patriarch Sisinnius in 998, Patriarch Sergius in 1016 defended and reestablished it. In the following passage from the work of the greatest Byzantine canon lawyer (later patriarch of Antioch), Theodore Balsamon (d. c. 1195), he comments on the *charistikion* and quotes from the decree of Sergius's synod.

THEODORE BALSAMON DEFENDS THE PRACTICE OF CHARISTIKION

(From "Canones sanctae et universalis VII synodi," in MPG, vol. 137, cols. 956–57.)

Another *tomos* [decree], that of the lord Patriarch Sergius, was promulgated in the month of May, in the fourteenth indiction of the year 1016 and ratified by imperial signature, which interpreted the forty-ninth canon of the synod in Trullo (691–92) [which forbade alienation of church lands] and which prescribes that the divestiture of those gifts [given to the *charistikion* holder] which preserved the condition of the monasteries is not required, but rather the expulsion of those men who have seized the monasteries with the purpose of keeping them as secular hostelries. . . [Here follows the decree of 1016.] Therefore, we, assembled in this [standing] synod, through the authority given to us by the Holy Spirit, overturn that act [of Patriarch Sisinnius] which has taken away the gifts and the contributions [i.e. the *charistikion*], since his [Sergius's] act was not done with episcopal consent but rather at his own volition. Nor has his act been accepted by the Christ-loving emperor since it seems that the emperor himself grants monasteries beyond the authority of this act [of Sisinnius] which, moreover, is not for the benefit of the monasteries but for their complete destruction and disintegration. However, confirming and corroborating this ancient, novel, and useful custom [the *charistikion*] of our blessed and God-bearing fathers, we decree that these gifts and contributions be made unhindered for the preservation and betterment of the monasteries which have been endowed and enriched.

Commentary. During the grave internal dissension of the twelfth century and, even more, during the final two centuries of the declining empire, the imperial practice of granting *charistikion* to laymen increased so greatly as to constitute a grave threat to the well-being of the monasteries and monastic life. Though monastic properties were still canonically inalienable, by this time the appetite of landowners for acquiring more lands, especially in the remaining areas of Asia Minor and in the Peloponnesus, became so great that neither emperors nor patriarchs were effectively able to restrain them.

128.

Introduction. Little is known about church life in the Byzantine countryside. In the rural areas the country priest was in charge, as he is today. He usually came from the same village as the other inhabitants, and, like them, was probably little educated. But popular imagination in these rural areas especially seems to have been aroused more by the presence of monks, who, though usually not in ecclesiastical orders (not priests, that is), were looked upon as possessing a special sanctity or charisma. Indeed, since they followed the path of spiritual perfection, they were considered worthy of even higher respect than the secular prelates and ecclesiastics (those who had taken priestly vows).

The following selection illustrates something of the enthusiasm which a "wonder-working" monk or his relics could arouse among the faithful of a rural parish in the later fifth century.

THE CHARISMA OF MONKS

(Translated by E. Dawes and N. Baynes, from *The Life of St. Theodore of Sykeon* in *Three Byzantine Saints* [Crestwood, N.Y.: St. Vladimir's Seminary Press, and Oxford: A. R. Mowbray, 1977; originally published by Blackwell, Oxford, 1948], pp. 106–7.)

There lived in this village [presumably Mossyna] a very excellent smith—him the holy man ordered to make a very narrow iron cage that he might enter therein and standing in it pass his days of fasting. So the men of the village impelled by faith one and all brought their agricultural tools in order that his bidding might be executed, and in this way the cage was fittingly finished for his holiness.

He wanted to take it away at once and return to his own monastery, but the men of the village begged him to leave it there until they made a second one of wood on the same pattern, and to do them the favour of passing his accustomed period of seclusion in it the following winter, so that they might have it as a protection in memory of his holiness and afterwards they would give him the iron one.

He gave the promise on these conditions; then they assembled and accompanied him with a religious procession and reestablished him in his sanctified place during the Great Week of our Saviour's Passion and afterwards returned to their own homes.

Then they made the wooden cage and in the following winter they returned with a religious procession and fetched him and escorted him to their village. And he entered into the wooden cage, which was standing in the church of St. John the Baptist, and in it he observed his fast from Christmas to Palm Sunday. On that day he came out and the inhabitants of the village formed a religious procession and carrying the iron cage accompanied him and restored him before the feast to his own place. After receiving his blessing they returned to their homes. He had the cage suspended above the cave on the face of the rock in mid-air, and ordered iron rings to be made for his feet, fifteen pounds in weight, and similar ones for his hands, and a cross with a collar of eighteen pounds weight and a belt for his loins of thirty-three pounds and an iron staff with a cross on it.

F.
MONASTIC SPIRITUALITY

129.

Introduction. Unlike the West, there was in Byzantium no proliferation of monastic "orders," each with its own set of rules and objectives. While individual monastic *typika* might specify certain charitable obligations of the monastery, the chief purpose of Byzantine monasticism was not "social service" but the cultivation of the spiritual life. Emphasis was placed on achieving a mystical union with God already in this life (*theosis*) by means of prayer and contemplation.

Seeking union with God through retirement from the world and absorption in the techniques of attaining mystical oneness reached its climax in the great movement of Hesychasm (roughly, quietude) which flourished primarily in the fourteenth century among the monks of Mt. Athos in Greece. The Hesychasts had worked out a method of controlling their breathing while seated and gazing at their navels (which they considered to be the center of the body and site of the soul); in the course of this, so they believed, a divine light (the same as that seen by the Apostles on Mt. Tabor at the time of the Transfiguration) would be made manifest to them.

This Hesychastic method of seeking mystical union with God was believed by most Byzantines to be the final step in an evolution whose beginnings reached back to the early centuries of the church. One of the earliest exponents of mysticism among the early Greek Fathers was the late fourth-century St. Gregory of Nyssa. His writings, in particular the *Life of Moses*, from which we quote below, reveal his conviction that man could obtain spiritual union with God by proceeding through various stages: from knowledge obtained by the mind and the senses, to an ultimate contemplation which transcended apprehension. Thus the spiritual life is represented as moving from a luminous darkness to a clear light before attaining a vision of the divine.

FROM EARTHLY LIGHT TO LUMINOUS HEAVENLY DARKNESS

(Translated by H. Musurillo, *From Glory to Glory*, in *Texts from Gregory of Nyssa's Mystical Writings* [New York: Scribner, 1961], p. 29.)

What now is the meaning of Moses' entry into the darkness and of the vision of God that he enjoyed in it? . . . The sacred text is here teaching us that . . . as the soul makes progress, and by a greater and more perfect concentration comes to appreciate what the knowledge of truth is, the more it approaches this vision, and so much the more does it see that the divine nature is invisible. It thus leaves all surface appearances, not only those that can be grasped by the senses but also those which the mind itself seems to see, and it keeps on going deeper until by the operation of the spirit it penetrates the invisible and incomprehensible, and it is there that it sees God. The true vision and the true knowledge of what we seek consists precisely in not seeing, in an awareness that our goal transcends all knowledge and is everywhere cut off from us by the darkness of incomprehensibility. Thus that profound evangelist, John, who penetrated into this luminous darkness, tells us that "no man hath seen God at any time," teaching us by this negation that no man—indeed, no created intellect—can attain a *knowledge* of God.

130.

Introduction. The mystic whose body of works constitutes in a sense a fountainhead for Byzantine (as well as Western) mysticism is Pseudo-Dionysius the Areopagite. Though he lived probably in Antioch around 500 A.D. and was Neoplatonic and perhaps even a Monophysite, he was believed (especially in the West) to have been the Dionysius, the supreme court judge converted by St. Paul himself. Hence his great authority for the Christian church. A basic characteristic of Dionysius's mysticism is his emphasis on the so-called apophatic theology, that is, a theology defining not what God is but rather what he is not. For, of course, if God is definable, he would then be circumscribable, something impossible in Christian theology.

In the following translation of his celebrated *Mystical Theology*, Dionysius expresses the idea that since God is infinite, the best approach to "understanding" him is to state what he is not. Thus he stresses here that in seeking to attain union with God the initiate must first pass through a state of divine darkness before reaching the luminous light which is God.

FROM THE *MYSTICAL THEOLOGY* OF PSEUDO-DIONYSIUS THE AREOPAGITE

(From Pseudo-Dionysius the Areopagite, *The Mystical Theology and the Celestial Hierarchies* [Godalming, 1965], pp. 9–16.)

Supernal Triad, Deity above all essence, knowledge and goodness; Guide of Christians to Divine Wisdom; direct our path to the ultimate summit of Thy mystical Lore, most incomprehensible, most luminous and most exalted, where the pure, absolute and immutable mysteries of theology are veiled in the dazzling obscurity of the secret Silence, outshining all brilliance with the intensity of their Darkness, and surcharging our blinded intellects with the utterly impalpable and invisible fairness of glories surpassing all beauty.

Let this be my prayer; but do thou, in the diligent exercise of mystical contemplation, leave behind the senses and the operations of the intellect, and all things sensible and intellectual, and all things in the world of being and non-being, that thou mayest arise by unknowing towards the union, as far as is attainable, with Him who transcends all being and all knowledge. For by the unceasing and absolute renunciation of thyself and of all things thou mayest be borne on high, through pure and entire self-abnegation, into the superessential Radiance of the Divine Darkness.

But these things are not to be disclosed to the uninitiated, by whom I mean those attached to the objects of human thought, and who believe there is no superessential Reality beyond, and who imagine that by their own understanding they know Him who has made Darkness His secret place. And if the principles of the divine Mysteries are beyond the understanding of these, what is to be said of others still more incapable thereof, who describe the transcendental First Cause of all by characteristics drawn from the lowest order of beings, while they deny that He is in any way above the images which they fashion after various designs; whereas they should affirm that, while He possesses all the positive attributes of the universe (being the Universal Cause) yet, in a more strict sense, He does not possess them, since He transcends them all; wherefore there is no contradiction between the affirmations and the negations, inasmuch as He infinitely precedes all conceptions of deprivation, being beyond all positive and negative distinctions.

Thus the blessed Bartholomew asserts that the divine science is both vast and minute, and that the Gospel is great and broad, yet concise and short; signifying by this, that the beneficent Cause of all is most eloquent, yet utters few words, or rather is altogether silent, as having neither (human) speech nor (human) understanding, because He is super-essentially exalted above created things, and reveals Himself in His naked Truth to those alone who pass beyond all that is pure or impure, and ascend above the topmost altitudes of holy things, and who, leaving behind them all divine light and sound and heavenly utterances, plunge into the Darkness where truly dwells, as the Oracles declare that ONE who is beyond all. . . .

We pray that we may come unto this Darkness which is beyond light, and, without seeing and without knowing, to see and to know that which is above vision and knowledge through the realization that by non-seeing and by unknowing we attain to true vision and knowledge; and thus praise, superessentially, Him who is superessential, by the abstraction of the essence of all things; even as those who, carving a statue out of marble, abstract or remove all the surrounding material that hinders the vision which the marble conceals and, by that abstraction, bring to light the hidden beauty.

It is necessary to distinguish this negative method of abstraction [apophatic approach] from the positive method of affirmation [cataphatic] in which we deal with the Divine Attributes. For with these latter we begin with the universal and primary, and pass through the intermediate and secondary to the particular and ultimate attributes; but now we ascend from the particular to the universal conceptions, abstracting all attributes in order that, without veil, we may know that Unknowing which is enshrouded under all that is known and all that can be known, and that we may begin to contemplate the superessential Darkness which is hidden by all the light that is in existing things.

131.

Introduction. A later but important exponent of the "Dionysian" variety of mysticism in Byzantine religious thought was the early eleventh-century monk, Symeon the "New Theologian" (so called to distinguish him from John the Evangelist and especially Gregory of Nazianzus, who alone of Byzantine Fathers bore the epithet "theologian"). The selection following, on Symeon's life (949–1022), was composed by his disciple Nicetas Stethatus, and provides us with perhaps the most vivid picture that survives of a personal experience of the initial phase of "contemplation," which ultimately was supposed to lead to *theosis*.

THE VISION OF ST. SYMEON

(From "Vie de Symeon le nouveau theologien," ed. I. Hausherr, in *Orientalia Christiana* 12 [1918]: 8–11.)

One night, as he was praying (his purified understanding thereby being united with the First Intelligence), he saw a light coming from above, radiating its beams from heaven upon him: a pure and immense light illuminating everything, creating a brilliance equal to the light of day. He, too, was illumined by it, and it seemed to him that the entire building, including the cell which he inhabited, had disappeared, passing into nothingness in the twinkling of an eye. He found himself carried up into the air, completely forgetful of his body. In this state—as he told and wrote his intimates—he was both filled with a great happiness and overcome with hot tears. Amazed by the strangeness of this marvelous happening (for he had as yet not had any similar revelations), he cried out again and again, "Lord, have mercy on me." (This he knew only when he had returned to his ordinary state, for at the time he was not aware that he spoke out loud or that his words were heard beyond his room.)

In this state of great illumination he received the grace of seeing: a great, luminous cloud, formless, but full of the nameless glory of God, was made manifest to him. To the right of this cloud he saw his [spiritual] father, Symeon the Studite, standing upright and dressed in the clothes he habitually wore. He was staring fixedly at the divine light and praying without any distraction. Because he had been in this ecstatic mood for some time, Symeon did not know whether he had left his own body or whether he was still within it, as he later related. Finally, the great light began to recede little by little, and Symeon found himself conscious of his body and his cell. . . . Such is the effect of purity and so great the actions of divine love in virtuous souls.

132.

Introduction. An important characteristic of Byzantine monastic spirituality, especially Hesychasm, came to be an emphasis on ceaseless prayer, the constant repetition of the words "Lord Jesus Christ, Son of God, have mercy on me." The origins of this "Jesus Prayer" may be found in the monastery of St. Catherine of Sinai, established by Justinian in the sixth century. From there, in later centuries, the practice was carried to Crete. From the early fourteenth century onward, the greatest center of Byzantine monastic spirituality was Mt. Athos (a mountainous peninsula near Thessalonika), and it was there that such practices flourished with the growth of the Hesychast movement.

As already noted, the Athonite Hesychastic monks stressed, as an aid to contemplation (*theoria*), a physical regimen designed to control the body, especially the breathing function, so as to produce, the Hesychast monks affirmed, a vision of the same divine light which was believed to have surrounded Christ at his Transfiguration on Mt. Tabor. But this practice brought the opposition of a number of outspoken critics, most noteworthy among them the south Italian Byzantine monk, Barlaam, writing probably before 1341. Barlaam, emphasizing the utter incomprehensibility of God, severely criticized the Athonite monks' claims to see God (and thus to unite with God's manifestations or energies). Barlaam thought these claims ridiculous or—more serious—verging on the polytheistic.

BARLAAM ATTACKS THE HESYCHASTS

(From *Barlaam Calabro: Epistole Greche*, ed. G. Schirò [Palermo, 1954], pp. 323–24.)

I have been instructed by them [certain Athonite monks] in monstrosities and in ridiculous doctrines not even worthy of mention by one of sound mind or understanding—products of mistaken doctrines and reckless fantasy. Among such, they transmitted to me knowledge of certain wondrous disjunctions and reunions of the mind with the soul, the relations of demons with the soul, distinctions between red and white lights, and also intelligible entrances and exits which occur through the nostrils while breathing, vibrations present in the area of the navel [*omphalon*], and, lastly, the union of our Lord with the soul which occurs perceptibly within the navel and with full conviction of heart.

133.

Introduction. The Hesychast movement soon found a great champion in the monk Gregory Palamas, later archbishop of Thessalonika, one of the leading theologians and mystics of the Byzantine church. Palamas defended and clarified the Hesychast attempts to come close to God by preparing the senses for the reception of divine grace. He never denied that God was, in essence, transcendent and unknowable, and, drawing on the Greek patristic tradition, he made a clear distinction between God's essence and his energies (comparing them respectively to the sun and its rays), thus emphasizing both God's transcendence and his immanence. The Hesychast, then, by contemplation and prayer, could claim to know (or see) God through the experience of his energies, without impinging on—and thereby limiting—God's essence.

In 1351 high church officials met in council at the Blachernae Palace in Constantinople. Emperor John Cantacuzene, a devoted supporter of Hesychasm (for both political and personal religious reasons), presided over this synod, which had assembled to accept or reject the doctrines of Palamas and the goals of Hesychasm. Palamas, who had been goaded by such opponents as Barlaam and Nicephorus Gregoras into formalizing his beliefs, presented them at Blachernae in the form of a "Confession"—a formal declaration of belief from which we quote below. His views on the theology of Hesychasm were thereupon confirmed as official dogma of the Eastern church.

FROM THE "CONFESSION" OF GREGORY PALAMAS (1351)

(Translated by A. Papadakis, Palamas, "Confession of Faith," in "Palamas at the Council of Blachernae," *Greek, Roman and Byzantine Studies* 10 [1969]: 341–42.)

Moreover, we receive with joy the holy councils that have assembled through God's grace at different times and places for the firm establishment of piety and evangelical life; among which are those held in this great city in the celebrated Church of the Holy Wisdom of God, against Barlaam the Calabrian, and the man following him, Akindynus, who held the same views and with cunning hastened to vindicate him. These two teach that the grace common to the Father, Son and Spirit—the light of the age to come, in which the righteous will shine as the sun, just as Christ intimated when he shone on the mountain—and simply every power and operation of the Three Persons of the Godhead, and everything that differs from the divine nature in any way whatever, is created; and they too impiously separate the one Godhead into created and uncreated. And they label as atheists and polytheists (just as Jews, Sabellians and Arians believe of us) those who piously believe that the most sacred light is uncreated and every power and operation is divine—since nothing which issues naturally from God is created. But we properly cast out both the latter and the former as atheists and polytheists and totally excommunicate them from the company of the faithful, as the Holy Catholic and Apostolic Church of Christ did through the Synodal Tome and the Hagioretic Tome [pertaining to Mt. Athos.] We believe in one omnipotent Godhead in three hypostases, whose unity and simplicity are in no way lost on account of either the powers or the hypostases. Moreover, we look for the resurrection of the dead, and the life everlasting of the world to come. Amen.

134.

Introduction. Palamas wrote a number of works defending his position, perhaps the most important of which was his *Triads*. Here besides theology he stressed the spiritual methods of Hesychasm, which were in many ways based on the thought and practice of the eleventh-century mystic Symeon the New Theologian. We quote below from Symeon's influential tract, "Method [for Hesychasts] of Holy Prayer and Attention."

METHODS OF HOLY PRAYER AND ATTENTION

(From "Vie de Symeon le nouveau theologien," ed. I. Hausherr, in *Orientalia Christiana* 9 [1927]: 150–59.)

There are three ways of prayer and attention by which the soul raises itself or falls; it raises itself if these means are employed at the right time; it is cast down, if it undertakes them at the wrong time and in the wrong spirit. Sobriety [attention] and prayer are united like soul and body; one could not subsist without the other. The combination of the two is accomplished in two ways—first, sobriety opposes itself to sin like a cleanser and a guard that goes in front. As a result, prayer at once exterminates and reduces to nothing evil thoughts that one has tried to will away, since will power alone is not able to succeed. This then is the door of life and death—that is, attention and prayer. If we purify ourselves by sobriety, we improve ourselves. If, on the contrary, by letting ourselves go we neglect sobriety and soil it, we become evil.

Since we have indicated three kinds of attention and prayer, it is necessary to set forth all the features of each, so that he who wishes to acquire life and put it to work may do so without hesitation. Of these three states enumerated, choose the best and do not run the risk of accepting through ignorance the worst, that is, of being excluded from the best part.

The First Method of Prayer and Attention. The peculiarities of the first method are as follows: a man sets himself to pray and lifts his hands and eyes as well as spirit to heaven. The spirit, then forming one divine concept and imagining celestial beauties, hierarchies of the angels and dwellings of the mind, assembles briefly in his mind all that he has learned from the Holy Scriptures and excites his soul to divine love while gazing fixedly at the sky. It happens also that his eyes fill with tears, and his heart expands and he arises. He takes for divine consolation what he experiences and constantly wishes to devote himself to such an activity. There are signs of his errors, for the good exists only when he accomplishes it rightly. If then such a man devotes himself to utter silence, a solitary life without exterior relations, he can hardly escape from going out of his mind. But if, by chance, he does not fall into evil, it will at least be impossible for him to arrive at the possession of virtues and disinterest (apathy). It is this kind of attention that has strayed. Those are the sensitive ones who see light, perceive certain perfumes, hear voices, and [observe] many other similar phenomena. Some have been possessed entirely of a demon . . . and in their madness, wander from place to place; some others have been led astray, taking the devil for an angel of light, in which form he appeared to them without their recognizing him. . . . Some, instigated by the devil, have committed suicide . . . or hanged themselves. . . . From this, a man of sense can see what harm comes from this first method of attention and prayer—if it is considered as the final perfection in prayer. . . .

The Second Method of Prayer and Attention. The second method is this. When the spirit, retiring from external things and guarding against sensations from outside, and collecting all its thoughts, advances, forgetful of all vanities, the more it makes an examination of its thoughts, the more it applies its attention to the demands that the lips address to God, the more it attracts to itself captive thoughts, so that, overcome itself by passion, it uses violence to return to itself. To combat this, peace is impossible to arrive at and virtue too. . . . In his pride [the one who practices this] despises and criticizes others and praises himself, . . . and he is like a blind man who undertakes to lead the blind. Such is the second method. It does harm to the soul, and one should watch oneself carefully. Yet this method is better than the first, as moonlight is better than a dark night without a moon.

The Third Method of Prayer and Attention. Now we begin to speak of the third prayer. It is strange and hard to explain; for the ignorant . . . it is almost unbelievable. Few are those in whom one meets this. My view is that this great good has deserted us along with obedience. For obedience, disengaging its adherents from evil . . . frees them from cares and attachment to possessions, renders them constant and decisive in pursuit of their aim, if they find a sure guide at the same time . . . The beginning of this third method is not gazing upward to heaven, raising the hands or keeping the mind on heavenly things. . . . Nor is it guarding the senses with the mind and directing all attention on this, not watching for the devil's onslaughts on the soul from within. This is the second method and those [who follow it] become enslaved by demons. . . .

The third method of attention and prayer is the following: the mind should be in the heart. . . . It should guard the heart while it prays, revolve, remaining always within, and from the depths of the heart, offer prayers to God. . . . In a word, he who does not have attention in himself and does not guard his mind, cannot become pure in heart and so cannot see God. . . . You should observe three things above all: *Freedom from all cares*, not only bad and vain but even about good things; in other words, you should become dead to everything; your conscience should be entirely clear, and denounce you in nothing. You should have *complete absence of passionate attachment*, so that your thought inclines to nothing worldly. Keep your attention within yourself (not in your head but heart). Wrestling thus the mind will find the place of the heart. This happens when grace produces sweetness and warmth in prayer. From that moment, whenever a thought appears, the mind at once dispels it, before it has time to enter and become a thought or image, destroying it by [*repeating*] *Jesus' name* [prayer], "Lord Jesus Christ, have mercy upon me."

135.

Introduction. Because the state of *hesychia* fostered by the Athonite monks in the fourteenth century came to be looked upon by many monks as the most effective way to achieve mystical union with God (*theosis*), the Holy Eucharist among some monks began to lose its central importance. By contrast, in the following selection Nicholas Cavasilas (d. 1371), the last great Byzantine mystic, although very sympathetic to the Hesychast movement, reemphasizes with remarkable imagery the significance of the Holy Communion and its fundamental place in Christian life. This work of Cavasilas, who was probably a monk though not in clerical orders, became very popular in the devotional life of many Byzantine monks (and laymen), and may be compared in its influence to the near-contemporary Western work, *Imitation of Christ* attributed to Thomas à Kempis.

Nicholas Cavasilas on the Importance of the Eucharist

(From Greek text "The Life in Christ," in *Die Mystik des Nikolaus Cabasilas vom Leben in Christo*, ed. W. Gass [Greifswald, 1849], pp. 83–85 and 91.)

What can subsist, what that is absent can be introduced [into us] when Christ is completely with us, when he penetrates through all parts of us, possesses everything within us, and is all around us? He prevents the arrows launched from outside from hitting us, sheltering us from all sides, for he is our place of refuge. If by chance there is some imperfection within, he expels it. For he is the dweller who fills the entire abode with his presence. For we do not partake of some of his [attributes] but of him himself. Nor do we receive in our souls rays or light but [the solar] disk itself,* to the point of dwelling within and becoming one spirit with us. At once therefore our spirit and body and all our faculties become spiritual, since spirit is mixed with spirit, body with body, and blood with blood.

O the sublimity of the *mysteria* [sacraments]: For it is in such manner that the spirit of Christ is comingled with our spirit, his will with our will, his body with our body. What spirit is ours under the power of his spirit, what will is ours with his blessed will, and what is our dust with his unquenchable fire. . . . Thus perfect is the *mysterion* [sacrament], surpassing all other perfection, and leads through itself to the acme of what is good, since it is the final end of all human aspiration. We receive God himself in that sacrament and God unites with us in the most perfect union: for what union could be more intimate than to become one spirit with God. . . .

Wherefore, he has not only assumed flesh, but also taken soul and mind and will and all else belonging to man, so that he might be able to unite himself completely with our being and penetrate our entire being, and dissolve us in himself while uniting all his attributes with ours. For this reason he is unharmonious with sinners and cannot be united with them, since between him and men all is common except for sin. For he has assumed all our other attributes in the manner of man [*philanthropos*] and is united with us even more humanly. God has come to earth and lifted us up from below. He has made himself man and he has deified man.

*Cf. this with Palamas's analogy of the "super-essential" divinity as the sun, and the sun's rays as God's energies (see above, selection 133, introduction).

136.

Introduction. In the early Byzantine period of the fifth and sixth centuries, before the Arab conquest, the eastern areas of Palestine and Syria were especially famous for their monastic centers. Monkish writers of these areas were unsurpassed for their vigor and liveliness. Besides the well-known *Ladder to Paradise* of John Climacus (abbot of the house on Mt. Sinai), we may cite the varied stories from the *Spiritual Meadow* of John Moschus (d. 619). Written in a simple, popular style, this collection of stories, while not always reflecting the quality of spirituality, has great value from a devotional viewpoint and sometimes even provides edification to the reader. The stories constitute a special popular religious and literary genre.

THE SPIRITUAL MEADOW

(From John Moschus, *Le pré spirituel*, in *Sources chrétiennes* [Paris, 1946], vol. 12, ch. 31.)

Two monks went from the Aegean to Tarsus in Cilicia, and by God's will, entering into a hostelry to take their rest (for it was unbearably hot), they found there three young men who were going to the Aegean and who had with them a courtesan. The monks seated themselves apart from them. One of the monks drew from his bag the Holy Bible and began to read. When the courtesan with the young men observed the monk reading, she left the young people and went over to seat herself by the monk. But he rejecting her said to her: "Unfortunate one, you are very impudent; are you not ashamed of coming over here and sitting next to us?" She replied: "No, Father, do not condemn me. If I have committed all kinds of sins, yet the Master of the universe, the Lord Our God, did not repulse the courtesan who came to him." The monk answered: "But that courtesan did not remain a courtesan." She responded to him: "I have hope in the Son of the living God that after today I shall not remain in sin." And leaving the young men and abandoning all her possessions she followed the monks. She can be seen in a monastery near the Aegean which is called that of Nakkiba. I myself have seen her, now very old, living full of much wisdom. And it is from her that I heard of all this.

G.
CHURCHES, WORSHIP, AND HYMNODY

137.

Introduction. Byzantine spirituality was expressed not only in the monastic emphasis on the Jesus prayer and special exercises, but even more importantly, especially for laymen, in the liturgical life of the church. The liturgy was an attempt to provide a foretaste of heavenly bliss.

The impressiveness of the rich Byzantine ritual is indicated in the following selection from the *Russian Primary Chronicle*. Sent by Prince Vladimir of Kiev (987) to observe the manner of worship of various religions (among the Muslim Volga Bulgars and the Roman Catholic Germans), Russian envoys, after attending services in Hagia Sophia, are reported to have declared their preference for the Byzantine liturgy.

THE *RUSSIAN PRIMARY CHRONICLE* ON BYZANTINE LITURGY

(From Serge A. Zenkovsky, ed., *Medieval Russia's Epics, Chronicles, and Tales* [New York, 1963], pp. 67–68. Copyright © 1963 by Serge A. Zenkovsky. Reprinted by permission of the publisher, E. P. Dutton, Inc.)

On the morrow, the emperor sent a message to the patriarch to inform him that a Russian delegation had arrived to examine the Greek faith, and directed him to prepare the church and the clergy, and to array himself in his sacerdotal robes, so that the Russians might behold the glory of the God of the Greeks. When the patriarch received these commands, he bade the clergy assemble, and they performed the customary rites. They burned incense, and the choirs sang hymns. The emperor accompanied the Russians to the church, and placed them in a wide space, calling their attention to the beauty of the edifice, the chanting, and the offices of the archpriest and the ministry of the deacons, while he explained to them the worship of his God. The Russians were astonished, and in their wonder praised the Greek ceremonial. Then the Emperors Basil and Constantine invited the envoys to their presence, and said, "Go hence to your native country," and thus dismissed them with valuable presents and great honor.

Thus they returned to their own country, and the prince called together his vassals and the elders. Vladimir then announced the return of the envoys who had been sent out, and suggested that their report be heard. He thus commanded them to speak out before his vassals. The envoys reported: "When we journeyed among the Bulgarians, we beheld how they worship in their temple, called a mosque, while they stand ungirt. The Bulgarian bows, sits down, looks hither and thither like one possessed, and there is no happiness among them, but instead only sorrow and a dreadful stench. Their religion is not good. Then we went among the Germans, and saw them performing many ceremonies in their temples; but we beheld no glory there. Then we went on to Greece, and the Greeks led us to the edifices where they worship their God, and we knew not whether we were in heaven or on earth. For on earth there is no such splendor or such beauty, and we are at a loss how to describe it. We know only that God dwells there among men, and their service is fairer than the ceremonies of other nations. For we cannot forget that beauty. Every man, after tasting something sweet, is afterward unwilling to accept that which is bitter, and therefore we cannot dwell longer here." Then the vassals spoke and said, "If the Greek faith were evil, it would not have been adopted by your grandmother Olga, who was wiser than all other men." Vladimir then inquired where they should all accept baptism, and they replied that the decision rested with him.

138.

Introduction. The principal liturgy used by the Byzantines (and still in use today) in ordinary services is traditionally ascribed to St. John Chrysostom (though probably falsely). The other most used liturgy is ascribed to St. Basil. Actually, the latter differs from the former only in the substitution of a number of prayers spoken by the priest. While Chrysostom's liturgy was commonly used, that of Basil was used only on special feast days. There follow several of the more interesting sections of Chrysostom's liturgy with commentary.

THE BYZANTINE LITURGY

(Translated by G. Downey, *Constantinople in the Age of Justinian* [Norman, Okla.: University of Oklahoma Press, 1960], pp. 124–35. Copyright 1960 by the University of Oklahoma Press, Publishing Division of the University.)

[The liturgy opened with a blessing pronounced by the celebrant, "Blessed be the Kingdom of the Father and of the Son and of the Holy Ghost, now and for ever and from all ages to all ages." There followed a set of prayers for peace and salvation, said by the deacon, with responses sung by the choir. After these came a series of antiphonal anthems and prayers.

The celebrant and the deacon then entered the sanctuary, took the richly bound Gospel book from the altar, and carried it through the church and again into the sanctuary. There followed hymns for the day and then the appointed lessons for the day, first from the Acts or Epistles, then from the Gospels.

Between the reading of the Epistle and the Gospel the priest said a prayer for knowledge which shows very typically the stress which the Greeks of all periods—from Plato to Justinian—placed on wisdom and learning as the means by which man may seek "a heavenly citizenship":]

"O Merciful Master, cause the pure light of the knowledge of thee to shine in our hearts, and open the eyes of our mind to perceive thy message of Good Tidings; fill us with the fear of thy blessed commandments, that we, trampling down our fleshly desires, may seek a heavenly citizenship, and may do and consider all those things that are well pleasing to thee. For thou, Christ our God, art the source of light to our souls and bodies, and to thee we ascribe glory, with thine eternal Father and thine all-holy, righteous and life-giving Spirit, now and forever and from all ages to all ages."

[The reading was followed by another series of prayers, for bishops, priests, monks, and for the imperial family; and there was a litany for the departed. After another litany for peace, the celebrant and the deacon sang the Cherubic Hymn. . . . (See selection 318a.)

Ministers and people then joined in reciting the Creed and the Offertory began. The deacon went into the sanctuary and reverently began to fan the elements, using a metal fan of silver or gold, mounted on a long wooden staff, engraved to represent the six wings of the Seraphim. The celebrant next recited the prayer of thanksgiving and praise which was an eloquent confession of the goodness of God and his benefactions to men. The affirmation that his benefits are both "known and unknown, seen and unseen," shows the working of the Greek mind which acknowledges its limitations, in the presence of the unsearchable nature of God, and realizes that there are things which cannot, in this life, be known or seen. . . .

The service began to draw near its climax. The celebrant proceeded to describe the Last Supper, and at the breaking of the bread, he recited the words of Christ, "Take, eat; this is my body which is broken for you, for the remission of sins." When he described how Christ took the cup, the priest again repeated the words, "Drink ye all of this; this is my blood of the new covenant, which is shed for you and for many for the remission of sins." . . .

As these words (of the priest) were spoken, the deacon elevated the paten and the chalice, crossing his arms as he did so. At this point the celebrant began the long and beautiful prayer in which he called upon God to send down his Holy Spirit upon the people and their gifts, making the bread the precious Body of Christ, and making the cup his precious Blood, changing them, through the Holy Spirit, so that they might bring to those who receive them the means for the purification of the soul, the remission of sins, the fellowship of the Holy Spirit, and the fulfilment of the Kingdom of Heaven. One of the prayers said at this point gave typical expression to the constant awareness of the unity of all the faithful. The priest prayed that the bread and wine might] "unite us all, as many as are partakers in the one bread and cup, one with another, in the participation of the one Holy Spirit: to suffer no one of us to partake of the holy body and blood of thy Christ unto judgment or unto condemnation but that thereby we may find mercy and grace together with all the saints which have been well pleasing unto thee since the world began, our forefathers and fathers, patriarchs, prophets, apostles, preachers, evangelists, martyrs, confessors, teachers, and with all the spirits of the just in faith made perfect."

[The long prayer continued, commemorating the Virgin Mary; John the Baptist, the Forerunner; the apostles and saints; the faithful departed (mentioning any whose names had been given by the worshipers to the celebrant); all ecclesiastical rulers and Christian ministers; the Emperor and Empress and their court; the army; the city and those who dwelt in it; travellers; the sick; the suffering and captives (in the hands of the barbarians).

After prayers of thanksgiving and another litany, the celebrant again invoked the mystical presence of Christ:]

"Come and sanctify us, thou who sittest above with the Father and art here invisibly present with us, and do thou deign by thy mighty power to give to us of thy sacred Body and of thy precious Blood."

[The celebrant then partook of the elements himself, and administered the communion to the deacon. This was done with the doors of the sanctuary closed. After the ministers had said a prayer of thanksgiving, the doors of the sanctuary were opened and the congregation came forward to receive the communion. Before administering the elements, the priest said a further prayer as a final declaration and petition just before the bread and wine were distributed:]

"I believe, Lord, and I acknowledge that thou art of a truth the Christ, the Son of the Living God, which came into the world to save sinners, of whom I am chief. I believe also that this is indeed thy precious blood. Therefore, I pray thee, have mercy upon me, forgive me mine offences, voluntary and involuntary, whether in word or deed, whether witting or unwitting: and count me worthy to partake without condemnation of thy most pure mysteries, unto remission of sins and unto everlasting life. . . ."

[Each communicant, as he came forward, bowed and crossed his hands on his chest, while the priest, taking up the bread and wine together in a spoon, placed them in the mouth of the communicant.

When all the congregation had received the communion, the deacon, holding the paten over the chalice, recited the hymns of the Resurrection. These declared the power of Christ, who, slain after the institution of the Last Supper, rose again so that all men might partake of him:]

"We have seen Christ's resurrection, let us worship the Lord Jesus, for that he is holy, he only is without sin. . . . For, behold, from the cross is come joy unto all the world. . . . O Christ! O thou the Wisdom [*sophia*] and the Word and Power of God! Grant that we may partake of thee more truly, in that day of thy kingdom which shall have no night."

[The priest then blessed the people and went into the sanctuary, closed the doors, and said a final personal prayer of thanksgiving. After the singing of the Song of Symeon ("Lord, now lettest thou thy servant depart in peace . . .") and other hymns and prayers, the priest put off his vestments, and the service was at an end.]

139.

Introduction. Byzantine hymnography, another means for evoking feeling for the celestial, has been termed one of the supreme, most original creations of Byzantine culture. Unlike the meter of classical Greek poetry, that of Byzantine hymns was accentual rather than quantitative (a development paralleled in the medieval Western hymn). But unlike the texts of Western hymns, which often came to stress the human emotions (pain, suffering, joy), the Byzantine texts usually emphasized the sublimity of the heavenly realm.

Orthodox hymnody remained relatively constant in form throughout the Byzantine period, though there was more experimentation and variation than has usually been recognized. Several important changes were instituted, it is believed, in the fourteenth century by the Byzantine monk of Mt. Athos, John Koukouzeles, who was himself a Hesychast or had close connections with the Hesychast monks. He intensified musical expression by extending the intervals of pitch in the melody so as to produce a deeper emotional reaction in the listener (see selection 318d below).

The following are some selections from the most famous of all Byzantine hymns, the *Akathistos*, sometimes ascribed to the sixth-century Romanos the Melodist, by others to Patriarch Sergius or the poet George Pisides, but most probably written by an anonymous hymnographer of the sixth century. (For more on Byzantine hymns see selection 318.)

The Akathistos Hymn

(Translated by G. Meersseman, *The Acathistos Hymn* [Fribourg, 1958], pp. 25–37.)

To thee, protectress, leader of my army, victory.
I, thy city, from danger freed
   this song of thanks
inscribe to thee,
   mother of God.
Since thou hast an unconquerable power,
free me from all danger,
that I may sing to thee:
Hail mother undefiled.

A prince of angels
was sent from heaven
to greet the Mother of God,
and upon his unbodied word,
seeing thee, O Lord,
   take body,
he stood in ecstasy and
cried to thee this greeting:

Hail by whom gladness will be enkindled;
hail by whom the curse
   will be quenched.
Hail righting
   of the fallen Adam;
hail ransom
   of Eve's tears.

Hail height unscaled
　　by human reasonings;
hail depth inscrutable
　　even to angel's eyes.
Hail for thou art
　　the king's seat;
hail for thou bearest him,
　　who beareth all.
Hail thou star
　　that makest the sun to shine;
hail thou womb
　　of God's incarnation.
Hail thou by whom
　　all creation is renewed;
hail thou through whom
　　the Creator became a babe.
Hail mother undefiled.

The blessed virgin,
seeing herself chaste,
said unto Gabriel resolutely:
"The contradiction in thy assertion
seems very hard
　　to my soul.
Thou foretellest me a childbirth
by seedless conception, and criest:
　　Alleluia!"

The virgin, yearning to know,
the unknowable knowledge,
exclaimed to the servant:
"From my maiden womb
how may a child be born?
　　Tell me."
to her he answered
timorously, crying out:

Hail! initiated
　　into the unspeakable counsel;
hail! faith
　　in what has to remain secret.
Hail! of Christ's wonders
　　the beginning;
hail! of all tenets about him
　　the summary.
Hail! heavenly ladder
　　by which God came down;
hail! bridge that carries
　　the earth-born into heaven.

Hail! marvel much spoken of
by the angels;
hail! wounding most lamentable
for the demons.
Hail! who mysteriously
gavest birth to the light
hail! who the manner
to none hast taught.
Hail! who outsoarest
the learning of the wise;
hail! who enlightenest
the mind of the faithful.
Hail! mother undefiled.

The power from on high
overshadowed then
unto conception the undefiled maid,
and converted her fruitless womb
into a meadow sweet
to all men,
who sought to reap
salvation by singing thus:
Alleluia!

140.

Introduction. Byzantine churches were designed and decorated to evoke a sense of otherworldliness and provide an image of the heavenly kingdom to the throngs that gathered for worship. A passage from the sixth-century history of Procopius provides a glowing description of the features of the preeminent church of the empire, Hagia Sophia, dedicated by Justinian in 537.

PROCOPIUS DESCRIBES THE "GREAT CHURCH"

(Translated by W. Lethaby and H. Swainson, from Procopius, *De Aedificiis*, in *The Church of St. Sophia Constantinople* [New York: 1894], pp. 24–28.)

The emperor, thinking not of cost of any kind, pressed on the work, and collected together workmen from every land. Anthemius of Tralles, the most skilled in the builder's art, not only of his own but of all former times, carried forward the king's zealous intentions, organized the labours of the workmen, and prepared models of the future construction. Associated with him was another architect [*mechanopoios*] named Isidorus, a Milesian by birth, a man of intelligence, and worthy to carry out the plans of the Emperor Justinian. It is indeed a proof of the esteem with which God regarded the emperor, that he furnished him with men who would be so useful in effecting his designs, and we are compelled to admire the wisdom of the emperor, in being able to choose the most suitable of mankind to execute the noblest of his works. . . .

[The Church] is distinguished by indescribable beauty, excelling both in its size, and in the harmony of its measures, having no part excessive and none deficient; being more magnificent than ordinary buildings, and much more elegant than those which are not of so just a proportion. The church is singularly full of light and sunshine; you would declare that the place is not lighted by the sun from without, but that the rays are produced within itself, such an abundance of light is poured into this church. . . .

Now above the arches is raised a circular building of a curved form through which the light of day first shines; for the building, which I imagine overtops the whole country, has small openings left on purpose, so that the places where these intervals occur may serve for the light to come through. Thus far I imagine the building is not incapable of being described, even by a weak and feeble tongue. As the arches are arranged in a quadrangular figure, the stone-work between them takes the shape of a triangle, the lower angle of each triangle, being compressed where the arches unite, is slender, while the upper part becomes wider as it rises in the space between them, and ends against the circle which rests upon them, forming there its remaining angles. A spherical-shaped dome standing upon this circle makes it exceedingly beautiful; from the lightness of the building, it does not appear to rest upon a solid foundation, but to cover the place beneath as though it were suspended from heaven by the fabled golden chain. All these parts surprisingly joined to one another in the air, suspended one from another, and resting only on that which is next to them, form the work into one admirably harmonious whole, which spectators do not dwell upon for long in the mass, as each individual part attracts the eye to itself.

No one ever became weary of this spectacle, but those who are in the church delight in what they see, and, when they leave, magnify it in their talk. Moreover it is impossible accurately to describe the gold, and silver, and gems, presented by the Emperor Justinian, but by the description of one part, I leave the rest to be inferred. That part of the church which is especially sacred, and where the priests alone are allowed to enter, which is called the Sanctuary, contains forty thousand pounds' weight of silver.

141.

Introduction. Byzantine writers were unanimous in their praise of the magnificence of St. Sophia, a magnificence which encouraged worshipers to imagine themselves already on the threshold of the afterlife. Scholars believe that the imagery of St. Sophia's tremendous dome was intended to represent heaven, to be a kind of celestial canopy over the earth, with heaven and earth constituting the two halves of one great cosmic "egg". Justinian's contemporary, Paul the Silentiary, in his famous encomium on St. Sophia, draws on this kind of imagery when he describes the dome as "the great celestial helmet which, rounded in all respects like a sphere, embraces the top of the building like the radiant heavens."* He continues to describe the church vividly and in rich detail, as follows:

THE WONDERS OF ST. SOPHIA

(Translated by W. Lethaby and H. Swainson, from Paul the Silentiary, *Descriptio S. Sophiae*, in *The Church of St. Sophia Constantinople* [New York, 1894], pp. 42–52.)

Above all rises into the immeasurable air the great helmet [of the dome], which, bending over, like the radiant heavens, embraces the church. And at the highest part, at the crown, was depicted the cross, the protector of the city. And wondrous it is to see how the dome gradually rises, wide below, and growing less as it reaches higher. It does not however spring upwards to a sharp point, but is like the firmament which rests on air, though the dome is fixed on the strong backs of the arches. . . . Everywhere the walls glitter with wondrous designs, the stone for which came from the quarries of seagirt Proconnesus. The marbles are cut and joined like painted patterns, and in stones formed into squares or eight-sided figures the veins meet to form devices; and the stones show also the forms of living creatures. . . .

A thousand others [lamps] within the temple show their gleaming light, hanging aloft by chains of many windings. Some are placed in the aisles, others in the centre or to east and west, or on the crowning walls, shedding the brightness of flame. Thus the night seems to flout the light of day, and be itself as rosy as the dawn. . . .

Thus through the spaces of the great church come rays of light, expelling clouds of care, and filling the mind with joy. The sacred light cheers all: even the sailor guiding his bark on the waves, leaving behind him the unfriendly billows of the raging Pontus, and winding a sinuous course amidst creeks and rocks, with heart fearful at the dangers of his nightly wanderings—perchance he has left the Aegean and guides his ship against adverse currents in the Hellespont, awaiting with taut forestay the onslaught of a storm from Africa—does not guide his laden vessel by the light of Cynosure, or the circling Bear, but by the divine light of the church itself. Yet not only does it guide the merchant at night, like the rays from the Pharos on the coast of Africa, but it also shows the way to the living God.

*See D. Geanakoplos, "Church Construction and Caesaropapism," *Greek, Roman, and Byzantine Studies* 7 (1966): 184, quoting from Paul the Silentiary's *Descriptio S. Sophiae*.

H.
RELICS IN BYZANTIUM

142.

Introduction. The relics of Christianity most vener-
ated by the Byzantines dated from the earliest period of the Christian faith.
The true cross, the crown of thorns, the Virgin's robe, girdle, and shroud, and
the sponge used on Calvary—these were most revered. Of all relics, however,
the robe of the *Panagia* (Virgin Mary)—and to a lesser extent her girdle—were
looked upon by the inhabitants of Constantinople as their own special palla-
dium. The Virgin herself (especially the icon of the *Hodegetria*, depicting the
"Virgin who leads") was considered the city's special protector.

Since the ancient relics were highly prized by other Christian peoples in the
West and in the East as well, it is not surprising that a traffic in relics soon developed or that some relics were removed, forcibly or by stealth, from their
original resting places. Many sources, Greek, Latin, and Slavic, tell us about the
fate of such relics. The following passage from the *History of the War against the
Persians*, written by the sixth-century Greek historian Procopius, relates how a
piece of the true cross served to inspire the Christian populace of Apamea (in
Syria) against the invading Persians.

The Power of the True Cross

(From Procopius, *History of the Wars*, Loeb Classical Library [Lon-
don, 1914], vol. 1, pp. 354–56.)

In Apamea there exists a piece of wood the length of
an arm, a portion of the cross upon which, it is agreed, Christ not unwillingly
endured punishment in Jerusalem and which in ancient times had been brought
there secretly by a Syrian. The ancient inhabitants [of Apamea], believing that
this would be a great source of protection for themselves and their city, made a
kind of wooden box in which they placed the cross. They decorated the box with
much gold and precious stones and entrusted it to three priests, who were to
guard it with the utmost care. On a certain day of every year they remove the
cross from its box and the entire population worships it. Now the people of Apamea, upon learning of the approach of the Persian army against them, became
very fearful. And when they heard that [the Persian ruler] Chosroës was not at
all to be trusted, they came to Thomas, the bishop of their city, and beseeched

him to show the cross to them, so that they might die, having worshiped it for the last time. And he did as they wished.

Then indeed a wondrous sight appeared which surpassed both description and belief. For as the priest who was bearing the cross displayed it to the people, a flame of fire followed and it illuminated a portion of the roof above him with a great and unaccustomed light. While the priest walked around in all parts of the church, the blaze followed upon him, constantly retaining its position above his head in the roof. The people of Apamea, joyously marveling over the miracle, rejoiced and wept, and at once everyone gained confidence concerning their safety. And [Bishop] Thomas, after traversing the entire church, replaced the wood of the cross in the box and covered it. And suddenly the flame had ceased.

143.

Introduction. So prized were the relics of saints among all Byzantine classes, especially the lower, that it was not uncommon for the bones of famous holy men to be stolen from one village by citizens of another. We even hear of cases of collusion between a monk and villagers, even before the monk's death, to preserve his bones for the village and thwart their being stolen by relic-mongers from rival towns. The following brief selection from an office of the liturgy of the Russian Orthodox church commemorates the stealing ("translation") in 1087 by merchants from Bari of the bones of the fourth-century Greek St. Nicholas from the town of Myra in Byzantine Asia Minor and their transfer to Bari in southern Italy.*

THEFT OF THE BONES OF ST. NICHOLAS OF MYRA

(Translated by F. Dvornik, in *The Slavs: Their Early History and Civilization* [Boston, 1956], p. 24.)

The city of Bari rejoices, and with it the whole universe exults in hymns and spiritual canticles. . . . Like a star the relics [of St. Nicholas] have passed from the East to the West. . . . And the city of Bari has received divine grace by their presence. If now the country of Myra is silent, the whole world, enlightened by [Nicholas] the holy worker of miracles, invokes him with songs and praise.

*Curiously, whereas December 6 is and was from early centuries celebrated in both Latin and Orthodox (Greek *and* Russian) church calendars as the feast day of St. Nicholas of Myra, the ancient Rus of Kiev evidently celebrated a second day also in his honor—the day on which, in 1087, Italian merchants stole his relics and brought them to Bari. This latter celebration was undoubtedly taken to Kiev by the Rus members of the imperial Byzantine Varangian guard, then in service in southern Italy. The distant descendant of the Greek St. Nicholas of Myra is the modern Santa Claus.

144.

Introduction. At the end of the eleventh century, Emperor Alexius I Comnenus, in a (possibly spurious) letter seeking aid for Constantinople written to the count of Flanders, enumerates the many and remarkable relics to be found in Constantinople. Since Alexius's aim was to secure Western aid for Constantinople against the Turks, he hoped to arouse Western interest by his enumeration of all the precious relics, holy to all Christians, located in his capital. (This enumeration of relics should be compared with the far fuller list of holy relics in the Byzantine capital described over a century later [1204] by the French knight, Robert of Clari. See below no. 279.)

THE RELICS OF CONSTANTINOPLE

(Translated by E. Joranson, "The Problem of the Spurious Letter of Emperor Alexius to the Count of Flanders," *American Historical Review* 55 [1950]: 815.)

In that [city] are the most precious relics of the Lord, to wit: the pillar to which he was bound; the lash with which he was scourged; the scarlet robe in which he was arrayed; the crown of thorns with which he was crowned; the reed he held in his hands, in place of a scepter; the garments of which he was despoiled before the cross; the larger part of the wood of the cross on which he was crucified; the nails with which he was affixed; the linen cloths found in the sepulcher after his resurrection; the twelve baskets of remnants from the five loaves and the two fishes; the entire head of St. John the Baptist with the hair and the beard; the relics or bodies of many of the Innocents, of certain prophets and apostles, of martyrs and, especially, of the protomartyr St. Stephen, and of confessors and virgins, these latter being of such great number that we have omitted writing about each of them individually. Yet, all the aforesaid the Christians rather than the pagans ought to possess; and it will be a great muniment for all Christians if they retain possession of all these, but it will be to their detriment and doom if they should lose them. However, if they should be unwilling to fight for the sake of these relics, and if their love of gold is greater, they will find more of it there than in all the world; for the treasure-vaults of the churches of Constantinople abound in silver, gold, gems and precious stones, and silken garments, i.e., vestments, which could suffice for all the churches in the world; but the inestimable treasure of the mother church, namely St. Sophia, i.e., the Wisdom of God, surpasses the treasures of all other churches and, without doubt, equals the treasures of the temple of Solomon.

Again, what shall I say of the infinite treasures of the nobles, when no one can estimate the treasure of the common merchants? What is contained in the treasures of the former emperors? I say for certain that no tongue can tell it; because not only the treasure of the Constantinopolitan emperors is there contained, but the treasure of all the ancient Roman emperors has been brought thither and hidden in the palaces. What more shall I say? Certainly, what is exposed to men's eyes is as nothing compared with that which lies hidden. Hasten, therefore, with your entire people and fight with all your strength, lest such treasure fall into the hands of the Turks and the Patzinaks; because, while they are infinite, just now sixty thousand are daily expected, and I fear that by means of this treasure they gradually will seduce our covetous soldiers, as did formerly Julius Caesar who by reason of avarice invaded the kingdom of the Franks, and as Antichrist will do at the end of the world after he has captured the whole earth. Therefore, lest you should lose the kingdom of the Christians and, what is greater, the Lord's Sepulcher, act while you still have time; and then you will have not doom, but a reward in heaven. Amen.

145.

Introduction. Nor were supernatural powers in Constantinople believed to be limited to relics. Robert of Clari, the Latin knight present at the Latin sack of the capital in 1204, mentions the curative powers attributed to various parts of the building of Hagia Sophia.

HEALING POWERS OF COLUMNS IN HAGIA SOPHIA

(Translated by E. McNeal, *Robert of Clari: The Conquest of Constantinople* [New York, 1936], pp. 106–7.)

[In Hagia Sophia] there was no column not of jasper or porphyry or some other precious stone, nor was there one of these columns that did not work cures. There was one that cured sickness of the reins [kidneys] when it was rubbed against, and another that cured sickness of the side, and others that cured other ills. . . .

On the ring of the great door of the church, which was all of silver, there hung a tube, of what material no one knew; it was the size of a pipe such as shepherds play on. This tube had such virtue as I shall tell you. When an infirm man who had some sickness in his body like the bloat, so that he was bloated in his belly, put it in his mouth, however little he put it in, when this tube took hold it sucked out all the sickness and it made the poison run out of his mouth and it held him so fast that it made his eyes roll and turn in his head, and he could not get away until the tube had sucked all the sickness out of him. And the sicker a man was the longer it held him, and if a man who was not sick put it in his mouth, it would not hold him at all, much or little.

I.
TENSION BETWEEN EAST AND WEST: THE ECCLESIASTICAL SCHISM BETWEEN ROME AND CONSTANTINOPLE

146.

Introduction. Under Constantine and his successors the Christian church and the Roman Empire became virtually coterminous. There was one Christian church, one Christian society, whose many local churches, though occasionally separated by schisms and language differences, nevertheless were bound together by common religious and cultural ideals. But due to wars and invasions, as the Roman Empire lost much of its western territory to Germanic tribes and some of its eastern provinces to the Arabs, the fabric of the religious as well as the political unity of East and West began to unravel.

The Byzantine Empire, centered in Constantinople, in time became increasingly identified with the "Greek" cultural tradition and in religion with the interests of the patriarchate of Constantinople. The Western church, on the other hand, headed by the papacy, early on became entirely Latin in language and "Western" in culture. By the seventh century, in fact, the Western church came to look less to the Roman Emperor in Constantinople and more to the German "barbarian" kings for protection and leadership.

This reorientation of papal interest and policy culminated on Christmas Day in the year 800, when Pope Leo III crowned Charlemagne, king of the "Germanic" Franks, as "Roman" Emperor. In Western eyes the empire had now been transferred ("translated") to the Franks by authority of the pope. To the Byzantines such claims appeared ridiculous, directly conflicting with the fundamental Byzantine belief in the inalienable unity of the Roman Empire. Indeed, the actions of the pope and Charlemagne appeared as the insubordination of "barbarians" toward the legitimate Roman sovereign, the Byzantine emperor in Constantinople.

Despite the development of a virtual political schism between East and West, the coronation of Charlemagne was, curiously, almost ignored by the monastic chronicler Theophanes, the principal Byzantine source for the period. Writing about the events of 800 he seems to be more interested in the anointing of Charlemagne ("from head to foot") in contrast to Eastern practice, where the emperors were apparently not anointed until after the Latin occupation of 1204.

A Byzantine View of Charlemagne's Coronation

(From Theophanes, *Chronographia*, ed. C. de Boor [Leipzig, 1883], vol. 1, pp. 472–73.)

In this same year there was an uprising of the relatives of the blessed Pope Hadrian in Rome, who incited the people to rise against Leo the Pope. And after seizing him they blinded him. . . . Leo fled to Charles, king of the Franks, who took sharp revenge on his enemies and reestablished him again on his own throne. And from this time onward Rome was under the authority of the Franks. The pope recompensed him [Charlemagne] by crowning him emperor of the Romans in the church of the Holy Apostle Peter, anointing him with oil from head to foot and clothing him in the imperial garb and crown, in the month of December, the 25th, the ninth indiction.

[In another passage, p. 475, Theophanes describes events surrounding the coronation:]

In this year on December 25, in the ninth indiction, Charles, king [*rex*] of the Franks, was crowned by Leo the Pope. And although he wanted to attack Sicily he delayed preparing a fleet, instead preferring to marry Irene [the dowager Byzantine Empress], and he sent for this purpose envoys the following year [801], in the tenth indiction. . . And these envoys from Charles and from Pope Leo arrived at [the court of] the most pious Irene, seeking to secure a marriage between Charles and her, and to unite East and West. This would have happened had it not been prevented by the frequent objections [speeches] of Aetius [one of her eunuch advisers.]

147.

Introduction. The first major ecclesiastical confrontation between Rome and Constantinople came in the mid-ninth century, over the naming of Photius as patriarch of Constantinople. Photius, at that time a layman, was appointed in the year 858 to the patriarchal throne, succeeding the monk Ignatius, who had resigned under great political pressure. Ignatius's supporters then appealed to Rome against the "usurper" Photius, a fact which served to raise basic questions on church unity and the authority of the pope in the "universal" church. What right, for example, did the pope have to supervise the administration of churches outside his own Western patriarchate?

Another conflict between the churches of East and West concerned jurisdiction over Illyricum (roughly the Balkan peninsula), south Italy, and Sicily. During the Iconoclast struggle of the eighth and early ninth centuries, the Byzantine Emperors had removed both areas from the jurisdiction of the pope and transferred them to the patriarchate of Constantinople. With the restoration of the icons, however, Rome insisted on return of the two provinces to papal control. This dispute was especially important because of the question of whether the Bulgars would be converted to Christianity under Roman or Byzantine auspices.

The following selection is taken from the letter sent by Pope Nicholas I to the Byzantine Emperor Michael III (865 or 866). Written in reponse to an earlier letter of the emperor, the epistle stresses the most fundamental difference dividing the two churches: papal primacy and jurisdiction over the entire church, which was offered as the fundamental reason the pope should adjudicate the difference between Photius and Ignatius.

AFFIRMATION OF PAPAL SUPREMACY OVER THE EASTERN CHURCH

(From MGH, *Epistolae*, vol. 3, pp. 454–80.)

But if you seek to learn from us, as from ministers of Christ and dispensers of his mysteries, we shall show you quite clearly. But if you truly consider it unimportant to learn and you lift up your steps against the privileges of the Roman church, beware lest they be turned against you. Indeed, it is hard for you to struggle against the flow of a river and hard to kick against the pricks. Then if you do not hear us, let it be so . . . especially since the privileges of the Roman church of Christ, made firm in the mouth of the Blessed Peter, deposited in the church itself, observed from antiquity, and celebrated by the holy ecumenical synods perpetually venerated by all churches, in no way may be diminished, in no way infringed upon, in no way altered, since the basis which God established no human should dare to move, and that which God has established remains firm and valid. . . .

These privileges of this holy church—given by Christ, not by synods, privileges both celebrated and venerated, which have brought us not so much honor as burden, although we have obtained this honor not through our merits but by command of the grace of God through the blessed Peter and in the blessed Peter—oblige and compel us to have solicitude for all the churches of God. For the company of the blessed Apostle Paul was added to that of the Blessed Peter. . . . These, like two great lights of heaven, having been divinely placed in the Roman church, have illuminated magnificently the whole world by the splendor of their brightness. Like the reddening sun, they give luster from themselves as well as through their disciples, as if they were shining rays of light. Through their presence, the West has been made [the equal] of the East. . . . These things, then, I say compel [me] to aid Ignatius, the patriarch, as a brother who has been deposed by no rule or ecclesiastical order. For among other things, he [Peter] through whom all these privileges are given to us, heard from God: "Whenever you are able . . . help your brother."

These divinely inspired privileges have mandated that—because Photius, with Ignatius still alive, not through the [proper] entry but from another place ascended to the Lord's flocks, overthrew the shepherd, and dispersed our sheep —he must move away from the position which he has usurped and from the communion of Christians. And since we consider nothing about the person of Ignatius or of Photius more discreet, mild, or useful than that each should come to an investigation to be renewed in Rome, we desire this greatly and we admonish for your own good that you assent.

148.

Introduction. Though the dispute over the appointment of Photius was initially over ecclesiastical discipline, the graver charge against Rome of doctrinal error was made by Photius, namely, that the Latins had added to the Nicene-Constantinopolitan creed the term *filioque* to express the belief that the Holy Spirit proceeds not (just) from the Father but from the Father *and from the Son* (*filioque*). In response to Rome's refusal to recognize Photius as legitimate patriarch, Photius summoned a council in Constantinople (867) consisting of the Eastern bishops, where he "deposed" Pope Nicholas on the grounds of heresy.

The charges against the pope were enumerated in a circular letter sent by Photius to the three other Eastern patriarchs. These charges were to remain the basis for the standard Eastern complaints against Rome on dogmatic, ecclesiastical, and disciplinary grounds* until the end of the Byzantine Empire (and in fact up to the present day). We quote here what Patriarch Photius wrote about the Latin doctrine of *filioque*. (On Photius see also selections 258, 299.)

PHOTIUS CHARGES ROME WITH DOCTRINAL DEVIATION

(From Photius's encyclical letter, in MPG, vol. 102, cols. 728–29.)

Where have you learned this [i.e., that the Holy Spirit proceeds from the Son]? From what Gospel is this term taken? From which council does this blasphemy come? Our Lord and God says "the Spirit which proceeds from the Father." But the fathers of this new impiety state, "the Spirit which proceeds from the Son."

Who will not close his ears against the enormity of this blasphemy? It goes against the Gospel, it is arrayed against the Holy Synods, and it contradicts the blessed and holy Fathers: Athanasius the great, Gregory renowned in theology, the [royal] robe of the Church [who is] the great Basil, and the golden-mouth of the *ecumene*, that sea of wisdom truly named Chrysostom. But why should I mention this Father or that one? This blasphemous term, which militates against God, is at the same time armed against everyone: the holy prophets, the Apostles, bishops, martyrs, and the voices of God himself.

*For Byzantine objections to other Latin liturgical and disciplinary practices see selections 150–51 below.

149.

Introduction. At the center of the dispute between Constantinople and Rome over jurisdiction was the conflict between the Greek theory of the "pentarchy," that is the "collegial" authority over the Christian church exercised by the bishops of the five great sees: Rome, Constantinople, Alexandria, Antioch, and Jerusalem, and the papal view of Roman primacy of jurisdiction, de jure as well as de facto, over *all* the sees of Christendom. Theodore of Studius (d. 826) expresses Byzantine views on the pentarchy in a letter to a Byzantine ecclesiastical colleague.

THEODORE OF STUDIUS ON THE ECCLESIASTICAL PENTARCHY

(From F. Dvornik, *Byzantium and the Roman Primacy*, trans. Edwin A. Quain, S.J. [New York: Fordham University Press, 1966/1979], p. 101.)

We are not discussing worldly affairs. The right to judge them rests with the Emperor and the secular tribunal. But here it is question of divine and heavenly decisions and those are reserved only to him to whom the Word of God has said: "Whatsoever you shall bind upon earth, will be bound in Heaven and whatsoever you shall loose on earth, shall be loosed in Heaven" (Matt. 16:19). And who are the men to whom this order was given?— the Apostles and their successors. And who are their successors?—he who occupies the throne of Rome and is the first; the one who sits upon the throne of Constantinople and is the second; after them, those of Alexandria, Antioch and Jerusalem. That is the Pentarchic authority in the Church. It is to them that all decision belongs in divine dogmas. The Emperor and the secular authority have the duty to aid them and to confirm what they have decided.

150.

Introduction. After some complex maneuvering on both sides, the "Photian schism" was eventually healed and the unity of the church restored. However, the resurgence of the Western empire under the German Ottonian emperors (later tenth century) and their successors led to new ecclesiastical difficulties between the Eastern and Western churches.

These German emperors were concerned with ecclesiastical reform in the German empire and Italy and grew impatient with the corruption of the papacy, which had at the time become virtually a plaything of the Roman nobility. At length, the German rulers succeeded in placing their own reform candidate on the chair of St. Peter.

The introduction of a "German papacy," beginning with Pope Leo IX (d. 1054), brought with it a group of eager ecclesiastical reformers such as Stephen of Lorraine and Humbert of Silva Candida. Both of these held exalted views of papal authority and were largely unfamiliar with the ecclesiastical and political traditions of the Byzantine world. Byzantium, for its part, accustomed to the low prestige and corruption of the tenth-century papacy, now seems to have underestimated the growing strength of the papal reforming party. Even more important, Byzantium at this time was divided between proponents of Patriarch Cerularius and those of Emperor Constantine IX Monomachus. The emperor favored a political alliance with the papacy in order to counter the growing strength of the new Norman invaders in southern Italy, while the ambitious patriarch opposed such an alliance and used charges of Latin religious error to support his position. In the selection which follows Cerularius's spokesman, Archbishop Leo of Ochrida (in Byzantine Bulgaria), notes for the Greek bishop of Trani, in Byzantine southern Italy, certain Byzantine religious practices derived from the early church and asks that those bishops who have been following other practices (Latin, that is) change them to conform to the Byzantine. The most important of these divergences of practice concerned the *azyma*, the Latin use of unleavened bread in the Eucharist, instead of leavened, which was the Greek practice. The Greeks believed the Latin *azyma* followed too closely the Jewish use of unleavened bread for the Passover holiday.

PATRIARCH MICHAEL CERULARIUS'S SPOKESMAN CRITICIZES LATIN RELIGIOUS PRACTICES

(From MPG, vol. 120, cols. 836–44.)

God's great love and the depth of his compassion have persuaded me to write to your sanctity, and through you to all the archbishops of the Franks and to the most venerable pope himself, in order to mention the question of the *azyma* and of the Sabbath, in which [practices] you improperly commune with the Jews in the manner of the Mosaic law. For those [the Jews] were instructed by Moses to observe the Sabbath and [the practice of] the *azyma*. But Christ is our Paschal [Lamb], who, so as not to be considered pagan, was circumcised and at first celebrated the lawful Passover, and after ceasing [to observe] that, inaugurated a new practice for us. The holy evangelist, in the Gospel according to Matthew concerning the Last Supper, speaks thus: "On the first [day] of the Passover festival, Jesus' disciples came to him saying, "Lord, where do you wish that we prepare for you the Passover festival?' . . ." [Passage follows on Jesus' and the Apostles' Passover.]

But since this [Jewish] law has ceased, the *azyma*, of necessity, according to the same Apostle, also ceased. And the same thing [occurred] in connection with the paralytic, whom he [Jesus] made whole on the Sabbath, and because of this [i.e., Jesus' non-observance of the Jewish Sabbath], the ones who keep the Sabbath and also the *azyma*, saying that they are Christians, are neither good Jews nor good Christians. Rather, they are similar to the skin of a leopard, as Basil the Great tells us, of which the hair was neither black nor wholly white. . . .

These things, O man of God, you, knowing many times over and having taught them thus to your own people, and having written them, now order these things to be changed among those who follow the same practice, so you may gain the salvation of your own soul. Also send to the archbishops and bishops of the [episcopal] thrones of Italy, and have them take an oath that they will change these things in order that you may have the greatest reward both in these matters as in other good things of yours. And if you do this I will write to you, in a second letter, of greater and more extensive matters as further evidence of the true and divine faith and glory of God and the salvation of those choosing to believe correctly in the orthodox manner, for whom Christ gave his own soul.

151.

Introduction. The complicated mid-eleventh-century political situation of internal rivalry within Byzantium, Norman threats against the empire's Italian possessions, and the new muscle of the reformed papacy supported by the German rulers form the background for the well-known schism of 1054 between the Latin and Byzantine churches. The papal legation to Constantinople, headed by the haughty Cardinal Humbert, arrived in the Byzantine capital ready, it appears, to humble Patriarch Michael and expecting to conclude a formal alliance with Emperor Constantine IX against the Normans. After an unsatisfactory meeting with the patriarch, the legation was well received by the emperor. But the clash between Humbert and Michael resulted in the famous scene in the cathedral of Hagia Sophia, where the papal legates deposited a bull of excommunication on the holy altar and left the church, "shaking the dust from their feet as if they had been in the house of heretics." It should be noted that the text of the bull actually praised the "orthodoxy" of "the emperor and his people" and excommunicated *only* Patriarch Michael Cerularius "and his followers." (To be sure, the passage of time would soon make the entire population of the Eastern empire in effect followers of Cerularius.)

The translation of the papal legation's bull of excommunication, below, is followed by a translation of the Greek counter-excommunication against the legates, the result of the hastily convoked "Standing Synod" under the tutelage of Patriarch Cerularius. Since this Greek document has evidently not hitherto been translated, we quote substantial portions from it here.

Reciprocal Excommunications (1054)

A. HUMBERT'S ANATHEMA OF CERULARIUS

(From C. Will, ed., *Acta et scripta* [Leipzig-Marburg, 1861], pp. 153–54.)

Humbert, by the grace of God cardinal-bishop of the Holy Roman Church; Peter, archbishop of Amalfi; Frederick, deacon and chancellor, to all sons of the Catholic church:

The holy Roman, first, and Apostolic See, toward which, as toward the head, belongs the special solicitude of all churches, for the sake of the peace and benefit of the church, has deigned to appoint us *apocrisiarii* [legates] to this city, in order that, according to our instructions, we might come over and see whether in fact the clamor still continues which, without ceasing, comes to its [Rome's] ears or, if that is not so, in order that the Holy See might find out about it. Therefore, above all else, let the glorious emperors, the clergy, the Senate, and the people of this city of Constantinople, and the entire Catholic church, know that we have noted here a great good, on account of which we deeply rejoice in the Lord, but also we have perceived a very great evil because of which we are extremely saddened.

For, with respect to the pillars of the empire and its wise and honored citizens, the City is most Christian and orthodox. However, with regard to Michael, falsely called patriarch, and his followers in folly, too many tares [*zizania*] of heresies are daily sown in its midst. For as the Simoniacs sell God's gift; as the Valesians castrate their guests and promote them not only to the priesthood but even to the episcopate; as the Arians rebaptize people already baptized (especially Latins) in the name of the Holy Trinity; as the Donatists affirm that, excepting for the Greek church, Christ's church and the true sacrifice [of the Mass] and baptism have perished from the whole world; as the Nicolaites permit and defend [carnal] marriage for ministers of the holy altar; as the Severians maintain that the law of Moses is accursed; as the Pneumatomachians [enemies of the Holy Spirit] or Theoumachians have deleted from the creed the procession of the Holy Spirit from the Son;* as the Manichaeans declare, among other things, that anything fermented is alive; as the Nazarenes maintain the bodily cleanliness of the Jews to such a point that they deny baptism to infants who die before the eighth day after birth and [deny] communion to menstruating women or those about to give birth or if they [the women] were pagan they forbid them to be baptized; also, they [the Nazarenes], preserving their hair and beards, do not receive into communion those who, according to the custom of the Roman church, cut their hair and shave their beards. Although admonished by our Lord Pope Leo regarding these errors and many other of his deeds, Michael [Cerularius] himself has with contempt disregarded these warnings. Moreover, to us his [Leo's] ambassadors who are seeking faithfully to stamp out the cause of such great evils, he denied his presence and any oral communication, and he forbade [us the use of] churches to celebrate Mass in, just as earlier he had closed the Latin churches [in Constantinople], and, calling the Latins *azymites* [users of unleavened bread in communion], he hounded them everywhere in word and deed. Indeed, in the persons of its sons, he cursed the Apostolic See, in opposition to which he signed himself "ecumenical patriarch." Wherefore, not putting up with this unheard-of slander and insult to the first, holy Apostolic See, and seeing the Catholic faith assaulted in many ways, we, by the authority of the undivided and Holy Trinity and that of the Apostolic See, whose embassy we constitute, and by the authority of all the orthodox fathers of the seven [ecumenical] councils and that of the entire Catholic church, whatever our most reverend lord the pope has denounced in Michael and his followers, unless they repent, we declare to be anathematized:

"May Michael, false neophyte patriarch, who only out of human fear assumed the monastic habit, now known notoriously to many because of his extremely wicked crimes, and with him Leo the archdeacon called bishop of Ochrida, and his treasurer [*sacellarius*] Michael, and Constantine who with profane feet trampled upon the Latins' sacrifice [the Eucharist], and all their followers in the aforesaid errors and presumptions, be anathematized, Maranatha,' with the Simoniacs, Valesians, Arians, Donatists, Nicolaites, Severians, Pneumatomachians, Manichaeans, and Nazarenes, and with all heretics, indeed with the devil and his angels, unless by some chance they repent. Amen. Amen. Amen."

B. MICHAEL CERULARIUS AND THE STANDING SYNOD ANATHEMATIZE THE PAPAL LEGATION

(From Will, *Acta et scripta*, pp. 155–68.)

Decree in response to the bull of excommunication cast before the holy altar by the legates of Rome against the most Holy Patriarch Michael in the month of July of the 7th indiction [1054]:

When Michael, our most holy despot and ecumenical patriarch was presiding [over the Orthodox church] certain impious and disrespectful men (what else, in fact, could a pious man call them?)—men coming out of the darkness (they were begotten of the West)—came to this pious and God-protected city from which the springs of orthodoxy flow as if from on high, disseminating the teachings of piety to the ends of the *ecumene*. To this city [Constantinople] they came like a thunderbolt, or an earthquake, or a hailstorm, or to put it more directly, like wild wolves trying to defile the Orthodox belief by the difference of dogma. Setting aside the Scriptures, they deposited [an excommunication] on the holy altar according to which we, and especially the Orthodox church of God, and all those who are not in accord with their impiety (because we Orthodox want to preserve what is Orthodox and pious) are charged with, among other things, the fact that unlike them we do not accept the shaving of our beards. Nor did we want to transform what is natural for men into the unnatural [i.e., we favor marriage for the lower clergy, rather than celibacy]. In addition, we do not prohibit anyone from receiving communion from a married presbyter. In addition to all this, we do not wish to tamper with the sacred and holy creed, which holds its authority inviolate from synodal and ecumenical decrees, by the use of wrongful arguments and illegal reasoning and extreme boldness. And unlike them we do not wish to say that the Holy Spirit proceeds from the Father and the Son—O what artifice of the devil!—but rather we say that the Holy Spirit proceeds from the Father. But we declare that they do not follow the Scripture which says "Do not shave your beards." Nor do they want to fully understand that God the Creator in an appropriate way created woman, and he decreed that it was improper for men to be alone. But they dishonor the fourth [canon] of the Synod of Gangra, which says to those who despise marriage: "If one would hesitate to receive communion from a married presbyter, let him be anathematized." In addition, they respect and honor the sixth synod which says . . . that those who are about to become deacons or to be worthy of being ordained presbyters should not have relations with their wives. And we, who continue to observe inviolate the ancient canons of the apostolic perfection and order, wish to affirm that the marriage of ordained men [priests] should not be dissolved and they should not be deprived of having sexual relations with their wives which from time to time is appropriate. So if anyone is found to be worthy of the office of deacon or subdeacon, he should not be kept from this office and he should be restored to his lawful wife, in order that what God has himself ordained and blessed should not be dishonored by us, especially since the Gospel declares "Those whom God has joined together, let not man put asunder. . . ." If someone then dares against the apostolic canons to remove anyone of the clergy, that is presbyter, deacon, or subdeacon, depriving him of his lawful bond with his wife, let him be excommunicated. And likewise if some presbyter or deacon wants to cast aside his wife on the pretext of piety, let him be excommunicated, and if he persists, let him be excommunicated.

Moreover, they [Latins] do not wish to comprehend, and insist that the Holy Spirit proceeds not only from the Father but also from the Son, although they have no evidence from the Evangelists [the Gospels] nor from the ecumenical councils for this blasphemy against the holy doctrine. For the Lord Our God speaks of "the spirit of the Truth, [which] proceeds from the Father." But the fathers of this new impiety speak of "the Spirit which proceeds from the Father and the Son." But if the Holy Spirit proceeds from the Father, then this property of his is affirmed. And if the Son is generated from the Father, then this property of the Son is likewise affirmed. But if, as they foolishly maintain, the Holy Spirit proceeds from the Son, then the Spirit which proceeds from the Father has more properties than even the Son. For the origin from the Father himself is common to both the Spirit and the Son. As to the procession of the Spirit from the Father, this is a property belonging alone to the Spirit, but the Holy Spirit does not also proceed from the Son. But if the Spirit has more properties than the Son, then the Son would be closer to the essence of the Father than the Spirit. And thus there would appear again on the scene the drama of the heresy of Macedonius against the Holy Spirit. And apart from what has been said, they do not wish at all to accept that what is not common to the omnipotent and consubstantial triad, belongs to only one of the three.[‡] But the procession of the Holy Spirit is not common to the three. Thus it is only the property of one of the three.

But they come against us and against the Orthodox church of God, not as from the elder Rome but as from some other place, arriving before the most pious emperor. But they intrigued against the faithful and even "counterfeited" their arrival with the pretext that they came from Rome, and pretending that they were sent by the pope. But the truth is that they were sent by the fraudulent Argyrus [the Byzantine commander in Italy] and his numerous admonitions and counsels, and they arrived by their own accord and not at all as messengers of the pope. And they even produced fraudulent letters which allegedly had been given them by him. This fraud was detected, among other things, also from the seals which were clearly tampered with. This document written against us in Italian [Latin] letters was deposited by this impious man [Humbert?] in the presence of the subdeacons who were officiating in the second week on the holy altar of the Great Church of God. Later it was removed from the holy altar by the subdeacons, and the subdeacons suggested that it be taken back, but as the legates did not accept it, it was thrown on the ground and fell into many hands. And so that the blasphemies contained in it not be publicized, Our Mediocrity [Cerularius] took it. Then, after this, Our Mediocrity asked certain men, the *protospatharios* Kosmas, Romanus, Pyrrhus, and the monk John the Spaniard to translate it from Latin into Greek. After the document had been translated by them, the content of their words was as follows:

"Whoever contradicts the faith and the sacrifice of the Roman and Apostolic See, let him be anathema and not accepted as orthodox, but let him be called proazymite and the new Antichrist. Humbert, by the grace of God, bishop of the Holy Roman Church, Peter, archbishop of Amalfi, Frederick, deacon and chancellor of all the children of the Catholic church."

. . . This was in essence the contents of the impious, distasteful document. Our Mediocrity, unable to tolerate such audacity and impudence against our piety by remaining silent or to permit it to remain unpunished, communicated this to our powerful and sacred emperor. And he, after it was reported to him (when the legates had been away from the city for only one day), sent messengers to bring them back to the great city, and they returned quickly. But they refused to come before Our Mediocrity or to face the holy and great synod and to give any answer about the impious acts they had committed. But besides delivering the document, they even insisted further that they had even more to say than what had been written [in the document] against our faith and would prefer to die rather than to come to face us and the synod. These things were reported to us and to the synod by the powerful and sacred emperor through the response of the noble *magister*, the master of petitions, and the *chartophylax*, the most beloved of God. When the legates did not want to appear before us and the synod, our powerful and sacred emperor would not allow them to be brought by force because they held the office of legates. But because it would be improper and completely unworthy for such impiety against our faith to go unpunished, the emperor found a perfect solution for the matter by sending an honorable and respectful letter to Our Mediocrity through Stephan, the most holy monk and *oikonomos* [steward] of the Great Church, John the *magister* and master of petitions, and Constans the vestiarius and consul of the philosophers (*Hypatos ton philosophon*)[*] which read as follows:

"Most holy lord, Our Majesty, after examining what has happened, has found that the root of the evil was committed by the interpreters and by the party of Argyrus [the Latin commander of the Byzantine army in Italy, a political enemy of Cerularius]. And concerning those who are alien and foreign and have been influenced by others we can do nothing. But those responsible we have sent to Your Holiness in order that they might be instructed properly and through their example others may not do such foolishness. Let the document with the anathema be burned in the presence of all including those who have counseled, published, and written it, and even those who have some idea about it. For Our Imperial Majesty has commanded that the *vestarches*, the son-in-law of Argyrus, and the *vestes* his son, be incarcerated in prison, in order that they might be punished there, since they are responsible for the matter. In the month of July, the seventh indiction."

So read the imperial and sacred decree. And in accordance with the foresight of our most pious emperor, that impious document and those who deposited it or gave an opinion on its composition were placed under anathema in the great *secretum* in the presence of the legates sent to the emperor. This was decreed on the fourth day, which is the first of the present week, on the twentieth of the present month of July, and the report of the fifth synod will be read, according to custom, before the people, and this impious document once more will be anathematized along with those who edited it, wrote it, or had something to do with it either in will or act. And the original of the impious document deposited by these irreligious and accursed men was not burned, but was placed in the depository of the *chartophylax* in order that it be to the perpetual dishonor of those who have committed such blasphemies against us and as permanent evidence of this condemnation. It should also be known that on the twentieth day of the present month, during which the blasphemies against the Orthodox faith were anathematized, there were also present those who convened today with us, the hierarchy and all the metropolitans of the standing synod and the archbishops, namely Archbishop Leo of Athens, the *synkellos* Michael Sylaios, the *synkellos* Nicholas Euchaneias, the *synkellos* Demetrius of Caria, and also Archbishop Paul of Lemnos, Leo Cotradia, and Antonius Ziccia.

[*] Here the Roman delegation has completely twisted the matter of the *filioque* (see above, selection 148).
[†] Perdition at the coming of Christ the Lord.
[‡] Here is clearly implied the Greek emphasis on the "threeness" of the Trinity and the Latin stress rather on the "unity."
[§] See selection 302a.

152.

Introduction. Although in the historic exchanges between Humbert and Cerularius in 1054 the question of the *filioque* (see selection 148) was, surprisingly, not of the greatest significance, that of the *azyma* was (see selection 150). In the following selection, Nicetas Stethatus, a strong-willed monk from the monastery of Studius in Constantinople, issued a reply to Cardinal Humbert's accusation on the question of the *azyma*, presenting the Byzantine position (1054).

A. THE QUESTION OF THE *AZYMA*

(Translated by J. Erickson, "Leavened or Unleavened: Some Theological Implications of the Schism of 1054," *St. Vladimir's Theological Quarterly* 14 [1970]: 9–10.)

Those who still partake of the azymes are under the shadow of the Law and eat of the table of the Jews, not of the reasonable and living table of God nor of the bread which is both supersubstantial and consubstantial to us men who have believed. For we have been taught to ask for supersubstantial bread from on high. For what is supersubstantial if not that which is consubstantial to us? But the bread which is consubstantial to us is nothing other than the Body of Christ, who was born consubstantial to us according to his humanity. But if our lump's [lumpish] nature (which the Word assumed) is living [or possesses a soul], you, by partaking of the azymes, do not eat bread which is supersubstantial and consubstantial to us. For indeed the azymes plainly are lifeless [or without a soul], as the very nature of things even more plainly teaches.

Introduction. Humbert's response, which flatly rejected Stethatus's argument as futile sophistry, included the following:

B. HUMBERT'S RESPONSE ON THE *AZYMA*

(From Erickson, "Leavened or Unleavened," p. 11.)

As for what you also said—that the consubstantial and the supersubstantial are the same—it is altogether worthless. For although the Lord Jesus is consubstantial to us in humanity, in divinity—in which he is consubstantial to the Father—he is supersubstantial to us. Thus, although the breads of a human table are consubstantial to themselves, the bread of the divine table is supersubstantial to them.

Commentary. Important as this encounter between Humbert and Cerularius later became in the development of the rupture between the churches, the "schism" of 1054 was, at the time, hardly noted by contemporary Byzantine historians. Indeed, it was primarily the hindsight of subsequent historians that invested it with the importance it now has.*

Although attempts were made almost immediately to heal the religious schism, on a popular level little notice seems then to have been paid it. Pilgrims continued to travel between East and West, and embassies were exchanged between pope and patriarch. But while the schism was not yet definitive, the altercation of 1054 clearly indicates the growing estrangement of Eastern and Western Christendom. That this estrangement would eventually become a complete rupture was, ironically enough, one result of a great movement, the Crusades, probably initially launched by a pope (Urban II) as an attempt, at least in part, to heal the ecclesiastical differences between East and West (see selections 268–70).

*The most recent scholarship has stressed that Pope Leo IX died before Humbert and the other two legates reached Constantinople, a fact which, technically, stripped the papal legates of their authority. It has also been shown that the name of the pope had not been commemorated in the diptychs of St. Sophia since as early as 1009—a fact which also tends to decrease the significance of 1054 as marking the *definitive* point of schism between the two churches. On the diptychs, see selection 98c.

153.

Introduction. The most basic, underlying ecclesiastical issue between East and West was the papal claim to primacy of *jurisdiction* over the Greek and other churches. While the Byzantines almost invariably accepted papal primacy of *honor* over all churches, including the Greek, they would not accept papal interference in the internal affairs of the Eastern church. This issue continued to be argued until the very end of the Byzantine Empire. In a debate held in Constantinople in 1136, the Latin bishop, Anselm of Havelburg, used (as the Latins usually did) Christ's words to St. Peter ("Thou art Peter, and upon this rock [*petra*] I will build my church, and the gates of hell shall not prevail against it") as a basis to argue in behalf of Rome's primacy. Nicetas, Greek bishop of Nicomedia, countered Anselm's arguments with the following rather moderate views:

A BYZANTINE MODERATE'S VIEW OF PAPAL PRIMACY

(From F. Dvornik, *Byzantium and the Roman Primacy*, trans. Edwin A. Quain, S.J. [New York: Fordham University Press, 1966/1979], pp. 145–46.)

I neither deny nor do I reject the Primacy of the Roman Church whose dignity you have extolled. As a matter of fact, we read in our ancient histories that there were three patriarchal sees closely linked in brotherhood, Rome, Alexandria, and Antioch, among which Rome, the highest see in the empire, received the primacy. For this reason Rome has been called the first see and it is to her that appeal must be made in doubtful ecclesiastical cases, and it is to her judgment that all matters that cannot be settled according to the normal rules must be submitted.

But the Bishop of Rome himself ought not to be called the Prince of the Priesthood, nor the Supreme Priest, nor anything of that kind, but only the Bishop of the first see. Thus it was that Boniface III [607], who was Roman by nationality, and the son of John, the Bishop of Rome, obtained from the Emperor Phocas confirmation of the fact that the apostolic see of Blessed Peter was the head of all the other Churches, since at that time, the Church of Constantinople was saying that it was the first see because of the transfer of the Empire.

In order to make sure that all the sees profess the same faith, Rome sent delegates to each of them telling them that they should be diligent in the preservation of the true Faith.* When Constantinople was granted the second place in the hierarchy because of the transfer of the capital, this custom of the delegations was likewise extended to that see.

We find that, my dear brother, written in the ancient historical documents. But the Roman Church to which we do not deny the Primacy among her sisters, and whom we recognize as holding the highest place in any general council, the first place of honor, that Church has separated herself from the rest by her pretensions. She has appropriated to herself the monarchy which is not contained in her office and which has divided the bishops and the churches of the East and the West since the partition of the Empire. When, as a result of these circumstances, she gathers a council of the Western bishops without making us (in the East) a part of it, it is fitting that her bishops should accept its decrees and observe them with the veneration that is due to them . . . but although we are not in disagreement with the Roman Church in the matter of the Catholic faith, how can we be expected to accept these decisions which were taken without our advice and of which we know nothing, since we were not at that same time gathered in council? If the Roman Pontiff, seated upon his sublime throne of glory, wishes to fulminate against us and to launch his orders from the height of his sublime dignity, if he wishes to sit in judgment on our Churches with a total disregard of our advice and solely according to his own will, as he seems to wish, what brotherhood and what fatherhood can we see in such a course of action? Who could ever accept such a situation? In such circumstances we could not be called nor would we really be any longer sons of the Church but truly its slaves.

*Perhaps Nicetas was thinking of the delegations which carried letters announcing the enthronement of patriarchs, with their professions of faith.

154.

Introduction. Greek suspicions of Latin Crusader intentions were emphatically confirmed by the Fourth Crusade (1204), which, diverted primarily by Venetian pressure from its original mission to the Holy Land, ended up capturing and sacking Constantinople and establishing a new, Latin empire on the ruins of the old Byzantine state. The following excerpt from the Acts of Pope Innocent III's Fourth Lateran Council (1215) reveals, as Innocent himself indicates, the Greek reaction to the Latin occupation and to the foreign liturgical acts being performed in the Greek churches.

GREEK OPPOSITION TO LATIN LITURGICAL
PRACTICES (1215)

(From C. Hefele, *Histoire des conciles* [Paris, 1872], vol. 8, ch. 4, p. 124).

It is proper that we should favor and honor the Greeks in our day who return to the obedience of the Apostolic See, sustaining their customs and rites as much as we are able, God willing. Nevertheless, we do not wish nor ought we to hesitate in these matters which bring danger to the soul and detract from ecclesiastical honor. For after the church of the Greeks, with help from certain parties, had withdrawn from obedience to the Apostolic See, so much did the Greeks begin to abominate the Latins, that among other things which they committed in derogation of them [the Latins], whenever Latin priests might conduct services on their [Greek] altars, they did not desire [again] to celebrate the liturgy [*sacrificare*] until they had washed from it this "iniquity." And the Greeks with rash impudence even presumed to rebaptize those already baptized by the Latins; and, further, just as we know, they had no fear whatever in doing this. Therefore, desirous of removing so great a scandal from the church of God, in accord with the sacred [Lateran] council, I forcefully decree that they [the Greeks] no longer presume to do such things, and conform with filial obedience to the sacred Roman church, their mother, in order that there may be one flock and one shepherd. If, however, anyone presumes to act contrary to this bull, let him be excommunicated and be deposed from any ecclesiastical office and benefice.

155.

Introduction. During the early years of the Latin occupation of Constantinople, some Greek citizens sought to resolve the difficult ecclesiastical situation in Constantinople, or at least to make the best of it, by writing to Pope Innocent III seeking the appointment of a Greek as well as a Latin patriarch in the capital city, as had been for a long time the case in Jerusalem and Antioch. The Latin would presumably preside over clergy of the Latin community and the Greek over the Orthodox.

GREEK CITIZENS OF LATIN CONSTANTINOPLE
PROPOSE A DUAL PATRIARCHATE

(From "Graecorum ad Innocentium III Pontificem Romanum Epistola," in MPG, vol. 140, col. 292.)

Many patriarchs and emperors have desired to see that day [of the union of the two churches], but this they were denied. You, Lord, after the passing of many generations, shall be granted this grace, to unite East and West, and you shall become and be called the thirteenth Apostle. . . . Since, then, small is the gap between Latins and Greeks which loosens the unity of the one church, seek to assemble an ecumenical council and send out representatives of your Magnificence, and let it be proclaimed, and let all that is in doubt be resolved. If you yourself be the coworker of God, according to Paul the great Apostle, we are ready, Lord, even to leave the jurisdictional authority of Constantinople and to attend a council to be held in East or West. . . . For this [reason] we write daily to our Western brothers of this area, both cocelebrants and cobishops, to be ready to assemble in Constantinople.

But it is necessary before the council that we have a patriarch of our own views and of our language who may teach and hand down our customs and receive our confession. For that reason both in Jerusalem and in Antioch where there is one king, there are two prelates, one for the Greek and one for the Latin of the same teachings and language and thus similar to each [people]. For it is not proper to confess your secrets through an interpreter to a patriarch of another language, even if perhaps agreement of opinion exists. Thus these considerations should be observed until union is accomplished.

156.

Introduction. The bitter Latin occupation of Constantinople lasted fifty-seven years, until the city was recovered by Emperor Michael Palaeologus in 1261. The occupation had exacerbated Greco-Latin relations in the extreme, making any successful reunion of the churches very difficult if not impossible thereafter. Nevertheless, because of the threat to Byzantium posed by Charles of Anjou, and then for a far longer time by the Ottoman Turks, many attempts were made by Byzantine Emperors of the last two centuries to unite the churches with the aim of securing papal military aid. Of thirty such attempts, two succeeded—though only very briefly—in bringing about ecclesiastical union.

The first was concluded at the Council of Lyons in 1274. In a letter brought by imperial envoys to Lyons, Emperor Michael VIII repeated the profession of faith earlier demanded of him by Pope Clement IV (containing the *filioque*) and declared his acceptance of the Roman faith and papal primacy. He strongly urged, however, that the Greek church be permitted to retain its creed as recited before the religious schism and also its own rites and liturgy, provided they did not conflict with the ecumenical councils and patristic writings recognized by the councils.

MICHAEL VIII RECOGNIZES ROMAN DOCTRINE AND PAPAL SUPREMACY

(From J. Mansi, *Sacrorum conciliorum nova et amplissima collectio* [Venice, 1770], vol. 24, cols. 67ff. Cf. also D. Geanakoplos, "Bonaventura, the Two Mendicant Orders, and the Greeks at the Council of Lyons (1274)," in D. Baker, ed., *The Orthodox Churches and the West* [Oxford, 1976], esp. p. 191.)

[After repeating the Roman profession of faith sent him by the pope, Michael writes:]

The Holy Roman Church also possesses the highest and fullest primacy and authority over the universal catholic church, which primacy she sincerely and humbly recognizes that she has received with the fullness of power from the Lord Himself in the person of the Blessed Peter, chief or head of the Apostles, whose successor the Roman pontiff is. And as he ought to defend above all the truth of the Faith, so if questions arise concerning the Faith, they shall be defined by his judgment. Anyone who is accused can appeal to his authority in matters pertaining to the tribunals of the church. And in all matters pertaining to ecclesiastical jurisdiction, one may have recourse to his judgment. All the churches are subject to his jurisdiction and the prelates shall give obedience and reverence to him. His plenitude of power is so established that it admits the other churches to partake of his solicitude. This same Roman Church has honored many of the churches with various privileges, and especially the patriarchal churches. But its prerogative is always reserved except in general councils as in various other occasions. . . .

I request of Your Greatness, however, that our [Greek] church be permitted to recite the sacred creed as it had been before the schism and up to our time, and that we may remain in observance of the rites we had before the schism—these rites not being contrary to the faith declared above nor to the divine command-ments, nor to the Old or New Testament, nor to the doctrine of the sacred ec-umenical councils and of the Holy Fathers approved by the holy Councils cele-brated under the spiritual leadership of the Church of Rome.

157.

Introduction. At Lyons on 6 July 1274 religious union was signed between the churches of East and West. The ceremonies ac-companying the signing are described in the following selection from the *Or-dinatio* (a Latin book of ceremonies) of the council.

CEREMONIES OF UNION AT LYONS (1274)

(From the *Ordinatio*, in A. Franchi, *Il Secondo Concilio di Lione* [Rome, 1965], pp. 82–83.)

In the same year and month, the 28th, on the feast-day of the Apostles Peter and Paul, the lord pope celebrated mass in the cathe-dral of St. John at Lyons, all the cardinals being there who had been summoned to the council. The Epistle was read in Latin and Greek, and the Evangelium was chanted by Cardinal Octobonus in Latin, and after him in Greek, by a Greek deacon [dressed] in the vestments in which the Greeks are accustomed to chant. After this, Brother Bonaventura preached a sermon until the end.

Afterwards the creed was chanted, namely, "I believe in one God" in Latin with Lord Erard Antisiodorensis and . . . bishops, who, like cantors or *primicerii* [chiefs], led the chorus in chant, following the canons of this church. Imme-diately afterward the patriarch with all the Greeks, archbishops of Calabria, and Brother William of Moerbeke of the order of the Dominicans, and Brother John [Parastron] of Constantinople of the Franciscan order, a penitentiary of the lord pope, who [both] knew the Greek language, also solemnly chanted, in a loud voice, the creed; and when they came to the article "Which proceeds from the Father and the Son," chanted [it] solemnly and devotedly three times.

When the creed was finished, the same patriarch, the archbishop, and the logothete [George Acropolites], with all the others [Greeks], chanted solemn praises, in the Greek language, to the lord pope. And after this the Mass was continued and completed by the lord pope, with the said Greeks standing next to the altar.

158.

Introduction. After the signing of ecclesiastical union at Lyons by the pope and the representatives of the Byzantine Emperor (a leading civil official and the ex-patriarch of Constantinople), the Byzantine population as a whole violently refused to accept the union. This was primarily on the grounds that no public discussion had taken place at Lyons and, more important, that the four Eastern patriarchs had not been present. A furor thereupon arose in Constantinople and Emperor Michael Palaeologus was forced to take repressive measures. The following short selection reveals the sentiments of the Byzantine populace as they hooted at the Byzantine envoys returning from Lyons. As one of the Byzantine envoys, George Metochites, wrote in his *On the Procession of the Holy Spirit*:

A. Metochites on the Byzantine Reaction to the Council of Lyons

(Translated in D. Geanakoplos, *Interaction of the Sibling Byzantine and Western Cultures in the Middle Ages and Italian Renaissance* [New Haven, 1976], p. 46.)

Instead of a conflict of words, instead of refutative proof, instead of arguments drawn from the Scriptures, what we envoys constantly hear [from the Byzantine people] is, "*Frangos kathestekas*" ([" By accepting union with Rome] You have become a Frank . . ."). Should we who are pro-unionists, simply because we favor union with Rome, be subjected to being called supporters of a foreign nation [*alloethneis*] and not Byzantine patriots?

Introduction. The following selection—a dialogue that supposedly took place between a Greek priest and a Latin bishop—constitutes part of a *libellus* (pamphlet) circulated illegally by anti-unionists, probably monks, and is significant because it reveals the views and prejudices, often wrong, of the lower (as well as upper) level of the Byzantine populace with regard to Latin religious beliefs and customs. Such prejudices held by the vast bulk of the Byzantine population helped make union so difficult to achieve.

B. The Libelous *Libellus* of c. 1274

(From A. Vassilife, *Anecdota Graeco-byzantina* [Moscow, 1893], pp. 179–88.)

I ask you [said the Greek priest to the Latin bishop] about the heresy you Franks have. Why do you not call the super-holy *Theotokos* the Mother of God but [only] Santa Maria, that is, you make her simply a saint?"* But we call her more than holy, *Theotokos*, because she bore the king of heaven and earth. Why do you not use three fingers to cross yourself from your face down to your breast and your navel . . . but cross yourselves from the other side with your two fingers? . . . Why do you not worship and kiss the holy icons with love and faith but you fall on your knees and whisper and with your two fingers you make the sign of the cross on the ground and then kiss it and trample upon it and go away appearing as if you have trampled upon the cross? Why do you eat strangled meat? Why do you open your veins in your glass and then wash it and drink from it? Why do you feed dogs from your plates, then you wash the dishes and eat from the same platter? . . . Why do you eat meat and cheese on Monday, the first day of Lent, when demons shudder and angels exult and we Christians abstain even from water, whereas you do not fast in the whole of Lent? . . .

Another thing—you do not chant the Alleluia until Holy Friday, but you walk barefooted and you carry the cross from one corner [of the church] to another†. . . . Why do your priests not marry? As Basil the Great says: "No one attached to bodily pleasures is worthy to serve the king of Glory." Christ, however, as a concession to the weakness of the body, ordered a virgin boy to take [to marry] a virgin girl, and they are called virgins because the first wedding is called a virginal wedding. The church considers a virginal wedding something precious. For this reason the church says: "Those whom God has joined together let no man put asunder," for the church is heaven on earth. For that reason [the weakness of the flesh] the church does not forbid the priest to take a wife, but you [Latin priests] do not marry.

Instead you have concubines and your priest sends his servant to bring him his concubine and he puts out the candle and he keeps her for the whole night. Then he comes out of his cell and asks forgiveness before the other priests who have done the same, saying: "Forgive me, my brethren, that I have had bad thoughts" and he receives pardon and he enters the church to celebrate the liturgy.‡

*The Greeks refer to the Virgin as *Panagia* (all-holy).
†Perhaps referring to the Western stations of the cross.
‡For a detailed explanation of the entire dialogue, see D. Geanakoplos, *Interaction of the Sibling Byzantine and Western Cultures in the Middle Ages and Italian Renaissance* (New Haven, 1976), ch. 8.

159.

Introduction. The union at the Council of Lyons, it should be noted, was signed primarily as a result of Michael Palaeologus's attempts to thwart the threat to Constantinople of the newly enthroned king of Sicily, the formidable Charles of Anjou. But the success of Lyons was ephemeral. The reasons for its ultimate failure, from the Byzantine point of view, are succinctly stated by the Byzantine ambassador Barlaam, in his address to the pope in 1339.

BARLAAM EXPLAINS THE BYZANTINE INSISTENCE ON AN ECUMENICAL COUNCIL (1339)

(From MPG, vol. 151, cols. 1332ff.; translated by D. Geanakoplos, "Byzantium and the Crusades," in K. Setton, *A History of the Crusades* [Madison, Wis., 1975], vol. 3, ch. 3, pp. 55–56.)

The emperor does not dare to manifest publicly that he desires union with you. If he did declare this, a great number of princes and men of the people, in the fear that he would renew the experience of Michael Palaeologus [see above, selection 157, on Council of Lyons], would seek an occasion to put him to death. . . . You have two means peacefully to realize the union. You can either convince the scholars, who in their turn will convince the people, or persuade both people and learned men at the same time. To convince the learned men is easy, since both they and you seek only the truth. But when the scholars return home they will be able to do absolutely nothing with the people. Some men will arise who, either from jealousy or from vainglory, and perhaps believing they act rightly, will teach all exactly the opposite of what you will have defined. They will say to the Greeks, "Do not let yourselves be seduced by these men who have sold themselves for gold and are swelled up with pride; let them say what they wish, do not change anything of your faith." And they will listen to them. . . .

To persuade therefore both the people and the learned men together there is only one way: a general council to be held in the East. For the Greeks admit that all that has been determined in a general council conforms to the faith. You will object, saying that already at Lyons a council to treat of union was held. But no one of the Greeks will accept that the Council of Lyons was ecumenical unless another council declares it so. The Greeks present at Lyons had been delegated neither by the four patriarchs who govern the Eastern church nor by the people, but by the emperor alone, who, without seeking to gain their consent, wanted to achieve union by force. Therefore send legates to the four patriarchs; under their presidency a general council will be held which will make union. And all of us who will have been present at this council will say to the people, "Here is what the Holy General Council has decreed. It is your duty to observe its decisions." And all will submit.

160.

Introduction. The last and greatest attempt to reconcile the churches of East and West was made at the Council of Florence in 1438–39. This celebrated confrontation of East and West—the most important in the entire Middle Ages—was primarily the result of two considerations: first, papal desires to use a successful union with the Greeks against challenges to papal authority from the rival conciliar party within the Western church; second, the now desperate Greek attempt to stave off Turkish capture of the capital city of the empire, Constantinople.

Interminable squabbles broke out almost at once over the problem of the *filioque* and the *azyma*, over protocol regarding the order of precedence in the seating of pope, patriarch, and emperor, and over still other problems, liturgical and even psychological. These considerations, so bitterly and lengthily discussed, are well illustrated in the following documents. The first, taken from the *Memoirs* of Sylvester Syropoulos, a rabidly anti-unionist cleric of St. Sophia, shows the reaction of the Greek patriarch and his prelates to the demand that they kneel and kiss the foot of the pope upon meeting.

PATRIARCHAL OBJECTIONS TO KISSING THE FOOT OF
THE POPE (1438)

(From Les "Mémoires" de Sylvestre Syropoulos, ed. V. Laurent [Paris, 1971], pp. 230–31.)

[The patriarch exclaimed:]
Whence has the pope this right? Which synod gave it to him? Show me from what source he derives this privilege and where it is written. The pope claims he is the successor of St. Peter. But if he is successor to Peter, then we too are the successors of the rest of the Apostles. Did they kiss the foot of St. Peter?

[The Latin reply, as quoted in the same source, was that the practice of kissing the pope's foot] is an ancient custom observed by bishops, kings, and even the emperor of the Germans, as well as the cardinals who are holy and superior to the emperor. [In fact the practice reverted back to the directive, *Dictatus papae*, of Pope Gregory VII of the eleventh century.]

Commentary. The two statements quoted above clearly reflect differences in the Greek and Latin attitudes toward the church: the Greek, conservative and ever maintaining ancient tradition "handed down from the Fathers" (*patroparadoton*), and the Latin, more innovative (one might say) and flexible, often in order to aggrandize papal authority, which had developed especially in the late eleventh and twelfth centuries.

161.

Introduction. At Florence the complex, acrimonious arguments over the *filioque* and other disputed questions lasted over one and one-half years. The following selection, taken from the so-called *Acta graeca*, the record of the council written (in Greek) by a Byzantine pro-unionist prelate who attended, reveals a good deal of the mental turmoil that most of the Greek clergy were undergoing in Florence during the council's sessions. Various Byzantine bishops are recorded as saying the following in private session:

BEHIND THE SCENES AT THE COUNCIL OF FLORENCE

(From Quae supersunt actorum Graecorum concilii Florentini, ed. J. Gill [Rome, 1953], vol. 2, pp. 399–401).

[Isidore, Byzantine metropolitan of Russia:] It behooves us to unite spiritually and bodily with Rome or leave with nothing done. To leave is easy, then; how to go later, or where, or when, I do not see. . . .

[Dositheos of Monembasia:] And how do you propose that we return home? With expenses paid by the pope? Do you wish us to betray our dogma? I would rather die than ever to Latinize [*latinizein*]!

[Isidore of Russia:] Nor do *we* want to Latinize, but we say that the procession of the Holy Spirit is attributed also to the Son not only by the Western Fathers but also the Eastern. Therefore it is right to agree with our own Fathers and unite with the Roman church.

[Bishop Antony of Heraclea:] And who are greater—the Eastern Fathers and synods, all our saints—or the Western? Thus we should follow the majority, [that is,] those who say the Holy Spirit proceeds from the Father and not from the Son.

[Mark Eugenicus, bishop of Ephesus:] The Latins are not only schismatics, but heretics, and about this our church is silent, because they [Latins] are many in number. But we have not left them except insofar as they are heretics. So we should not unite with them unless they delete the addition [*filioque*] from the creed as we do.

[Archbishop Bessarion:] So those who say the Holy Spirit proceeds from the Son are heretics?

[Mark:] Yes.

[Bessarion:] Spare me, God; and the saints who say this are heretics? "May their lips be mute who speak against the saints." Now listen carefully: The Eastern and Western Fathers do not differ, but the Holy Spirit is spoken of by all, and if you wish to, compare the writings of both and [you will] see that the saints agree.

[Mark:] And who knows which of their books have been corrupted?

[Bessarion:] And who dares to say this?

162.

Introduction. Sylvester Syropoulos, grand *ecclesiarch* of Hagia Sophia, in his *Memoirs* provides insight into the wrangling behind the scenes at the Council of Florence. He depicts, on the one hand, those Greeks who were in favor of religious union (often but not always for political reasons) and, on the other, those intransigent Greeks who refused union under any circumstances. The scene here described by Syropoulos took place shortly after union was agreed upon but not yet signed. He, like many Greeks, considered the Greek unionists "Latinizers."

A Greek Prelate Describes Greek Disputes over Union

(From *Les "Mémoires" de Sylvestre Syropoulos*, ed. V. Laurent [Paris, 1971], p. 445.)

Another day we met again according to custom at the patriarch's lodgings. We debated there the question of [religious] union, and the supporters of "Latinism" contented themselves with praising the harmony and the "peace." The bishop of Heraclea observed: "It would be good if you would furnish us with the declaration which you have sent to the Latins. We have heard it only once, though we should have seen and examined it several times." At once the bishop of Nicaea [Bessarion] replied: "It would be shameful for you to say you have forgotten it after having heard it once. You should not have forgotten what was said and heard here." Thus he replied to and avoided the request of the bishop of Heraclea. These are the kinds of examination and studies that [the Greek] bishops thought they should devote to this declaration and agreement concerning the faith.

But some others said: "The difference is small which separates us from the Latins, and, if our side should wish it, this difference could be easily bridged." When the bishop of Ephesus [Mark] responded that the difference, on the contrary, was great, they replied to him: "It is *not* heresy and you should not call it that, for none of the scholars and holy men [i.e., the Fathers of the church] who lived before you have called it heresy." Then the bishop of Ephesus replied: "It *is* a heresy and those who have preceded us have considered it to be that. Only they did not want to condemn the Latins as heretics because they had hopes of converting them and were seeking their friendship. If you wish it, I shall myself show you why they [in the past] were considered heretics." At once the bishops of Mytilene and of Lacedaemon angrily exclaimed: "Who are you to treat the Latins as heretics?" They rose near the patriarch and, together approaching closer to the bishop of Ephesus, they chastised him shamelessly with reproaches and sarcasm. "How long," they cried, "shall we bear in silence what you say?" And they could hardly restrain themselves from rushing upon him to tear him to pieces with their teeth and hands. Finally they said: "We are going to tell the pope that you called him a heretic and either you will prove it or suffer as you deserve." And they left very troubled. Then the grand *protosynkellos*, about to leave but still near the patriarch, said: "I know very well that if we achieve union they [the Latins] will anathematize us before we have even reached Venice. If we do not achieve it, on the other hand, they will still anathematize us. It would be better, then, to make union and as a result have them anathematize us." Questioned by the *protekdikos*, he expressed this idea still more clearly, leaving his hearers perplexed.

163.

Introduction. In the end, the Council of Florence failed, despite the support of the emperor and certain nobles and high church officials, because of the opposition of the bulk of the Byzantine populace, the monks and nuns, and most of the clergy. A certain proportion of the population apparently even preferred what seemed an inevitable Turkish conquest to what they believed would be a second Latin occupation of their capital in the wake of religious union. The horrors of the Latin seizure of Constantinople from 1204 to 1261 could not be forgotten. These Byzantine feelings of opposition to Rome and the West, religious, political, and even "ethnic" in nature, continued all the way to 1453, and in certain respects have left their mark even until today.

The fifteenth-century Byzantine rather pro-unionist historian, Ducas, describes the Byzantine populace's hostile reception of the Greek delegates as they returned from the Council of Florence.

THE BYZANTINE RECEPTION OF THE GREEK LEGATES
FROM FLORENCE (1439)

(From Ducas, *Historia Turcobyzantina, 1341–1462*, ed. [Bucharest, 1958], pp. 315, 317.)

After the emperor had received them graciously and accorded them the honor befitting their station, they began to discuss the question of union. The emperor and some members of the clergy declared themselves in favor of it. But the greatest number of those in the priestly and monastic orders—abbots, archimandrites, and nuns—but why do I say the greatest number? (for it was the nuns who prevailed upon me to speak and to write)—not a single one of these agreed to the union. Even the emperor himself feigned his acceptance of it. Then those who appeared to be in favor of the union—priests and deacons of the clergy, the emperor, and the Senate—came to the Great Church, seeking to celebrate the divine liturgy in harmony and to recite the prayers with untroubled minds.

At this time the schismatic party went to the Monastery of the Pantocrator, to the cell of Gennadios, the former George Scholarios, and asked him "What are we to do?" He was in seclusion in his cell, and taking a piece of paper he expressed his thoughts and counsel in writing. His words were: "Wretched Romans, how you have gone astray! You have rejected the hope of God and trusted in the strength of the Franks; you have lost your piety along with your city which is about to be destroyed. Lord have mercy on me. I testify before you that I am innocent of such transgression. Know, wretched citizens, what you are doing. Along with your impending captivity, you have forsaken the faith handed down from your fathers [*patroparadoton*] and assented to impiety. Woe unto you, when you are judged!" This and many other things he had written, he placed on the door of his cell; he secluded himself inside and what he wrote was read.

Then all the nuns, who believed themselves to be pure and dedicated servants of God in Orthodoxy, in accordance with their own sentiment and that of their teacher Gennadios, cried out the anathema, and along with them the abbots and confessors and the remaining priests and laymen. They condemned the doctrinal definition of the council [of Florence] and all those who had acquiesced to it, all those who were now acquiescing, and all who would do so in the future. The common and low-born people, leaving the courtyard of the monastery, entered into the taverns and, holding bottles of unwatered wine in their hands, anathematized the unionists and drank to the intercession of the icon of the Mother of God [the *Hodegetria*]. And they beseeched her to guard and aid the city now against Mehmed, as she had formerly done against Chosroës, Kaghan, and the Arabs. "We need neither the aid of the Latins nor Union. Keep the worship of the azymites far from us."

PART IV
Social and Economic Life

♦ ♦ ♦ ♦ ♦ ♦ ♦ ♦ ♦ ♦ ♦ ♦ ♦ ♦ ♦ ♦ ♦

A.
RURAL LIFE: PEASANTS AND MAGNATES

164.

Introduction. While the life of the imperial court in Constantinople, the church, and the aristocracy is comparatively well documented, the life of the peasant, the backbone of the Byzantine Empire, remains largely obscure. Typical of the agricultural organization of early fourth-century Byzantium, was the great landed estate, which had hundreds of sharecroppers working its lands. In order to prevent the sharecroppers, termed *coloni*, from fleeing their onerous duties and heavy taxes, Constantine and succeeding emperors bound these workers to the soil. Fugitive *coloni*, on discovery, were by law required to be returned to their land. The following selection, taken from the Theodosian Code, illustrates something of the legal status of the *coloni* in the late fourth century.

The Legal Status of the Coloni

(Translated by C. Pharr, *The Theodosian Code and Novels and the Sirmondian Constitution* [Princeton: Princeton University Press, 1952], 5-17-1, 2 and 5-18-1, 3, pp. 115–16.)

[Emperor Constantine to the provincials, 332:]

Any person in whose possession a colonus that belongs to another is found not only shall restore the aforesaid colonus to his birth status but also shall assume the capitation tax for this man for the time that he was with him.

Coloni also who meditate flight must be bound with chains and reduced to a servile condition, so that by virtue of their condemnation to slavery, they shall be compelled to fulfill the duties that befit freemen.

[Emperors Gratian, Valentinian, and Theodosius to the praetorian prefect, 386:]

If any person through solicitation should receive a colonus belonging to another or by concealment should harbor him, he shall be compelled to pay six ounces of gold for him if he is a colonus belonging to a private person, and a pound of gold if he is a colonus belonging to an imperial patrimonial estate.

On Inquilini and Coloni. [Emperors Honorius and Theodosius Augustuses to Palladius, praetorian prefect, 419:]

If a person who is a colonus or inquilinus by birth status has departed from a landholding thirty years before and if, through a continuous period of silence, he has not been brought back to his native soil, every unfounded action against him or the person who perchance now possesses him shall be completely excluded. It is Our will that this same number of years shall be observed likewise for future times.

But if within this period of thirty years any colonus by birth status has departed from a landholding, whether he escaped through flight or was abducted by his own wish or through solicitation, and if there should be no doubt concerning his status, We order that all controversy shall be removed and that he, together with his family, shall be restored without delay to the status to which he was born.

But if perchance the man whose ownership is contested should be destroyed by the lot of fate, We command that, with swift execution of the order, his offspring shall be recalled to the legal claims of the fields, along with all their peculia [private property] and wages, just as though the man who had died were surviving.

In the case of women, to be sure, it is Our will that there shall be a different regulation. Thus if women who are proved to be colonae by birth status have departed twenty years before from the land to which they were obligated, all right of recovery shall cease. But We do not permit the owners to lose their right to recover those women who are proved to have departed within the aforementioned period of time and concerning whose status there is no doubt. However, this condition shall be observed, namely, that a substitute woman shall not be refused, together with a third part of the offspring of the fugitive colona, that have been begotten by a colonus belonging to another, provided that substitutes for the children may also be furnished.

165.

Introduction. The following is a deed of surety for a serf (*colonus*) dated 579, and drawn up in Egypt in the reign of one of Justinians's successors.

DEED OF SURETY FOR A COLONUS (579)

(Translated by A. S. Hunt and C. C. Edgar, in *Select Papyri: Non-literary Papyri*, Loeb Classical Library [Cambridge, Mass.: Harvard University Press, 1932], vol. 1, pp. 77–81.)

To the most magnificent heirs of Apion of glorious memory, patrician, landowners in this illustrious city of Oxyrhynchus, through their servant Menas who is acting on their behalf and assuming for his masters, the said all-honoured persons, the rights and obligations of the agreement, from Aurelius Pamouthius, lead-worker, son of George and Anniana, of the city of Oxyrhynchus. I acknowledge of my free will, swearing the divine and imperial oath, that I accept from your magnificence, through your representatives, the charge of and responsibility for Aurelius Abraham son of Herminus and Herais, who comes from the estate of Great Tarouthinas belonging to your magnificence in the Oxyrhynchite nome and is enrolled as your farmer, engaging that he shall uninterruptedly remain and abide on his proper estate along with his family and wife and animals and all his household gear, I being answerable for all that regards his person or his status as your bondsman, and that he shall in no wise leave the said estate or remove to another place; and if he is required of me by your magnificence through your representatives at any date and for any reason whatsoever, I will bring and deliver him in a public place debarred from every sanctuary and subterfuge, even where I received him, in the guard-room of your said honourable house. If I fail to do this, I agree to pay down for his desertion and my failure to deliver him 8 gold solidi, to be really and truly exacted. This deed of surety, made in a single copy, is valid, and in answer to the formal question I have given my assent. (Subscribed) Executed by me, Anastasius. (Endorsed).

166.

Introduction. Under the strain of the Persian, Slavic, and Arab invasions of the sixth and seventh centuries, rural organization underwent significant changes. Though great landed estates by no means disappeared, sources indicate that a second form of rural organization was emerging in the empire, especially in Asia Minor and the Peloponnesus: the free peasant village. There thus arose in the empire what did not exist in most of Western Europe of the time, a free peasantry, working its own land, but paying rather stringent taxes to the state in addition to providing a source for military recruitment. It was these free peasants, with the services and revenues they rendered to the state, who were the backbone of the empire. Details of the everyday life of the peasants of this period may be found in legal codes and, on occasion, in the lives of saints (hagiography), which themselves are often expressions of provincial life (see selection 317). The following are provisions drawn from the so-called *Farmer's Law* of the late seventh or early eighth centuries, which governed the conduct of these free peasants.

From *The Farmer's Law*

(Translated and edited by W. Ashburner, "The Farmer's Law," *Journal of Hellenic Studies* 32 [London, 1912]: 87–95.)

The farmer who is working his own field must be just and must not encroach on his neighbour's furrows. If a farmer persists in encroaching and docks a neighbouring lot—if he did this in ploughing-time, he loses his ploughing; if it was in sowing-time that he made this encroachment, he loses his seed and his husbandry and his crop—the farmer who encroached.

If a farmer without the landowner's cognizance enters and ploughs or sows, let him not receive either wages for his ploughing or the crop for his sowing—no, not even the seed that has been cast.

If two farmers agree one with the other before two or three witnesses to exchange lands and they agreed for all time, let their determination and their exchange remain firm and secure and unassailable.

If two farmers, A and B, agree to exchange their lands for the season of sowing and A draws back, then, if the seed was cast, they may not draw back; but if the seed was not cast they may draw back; but if A did not plough while B did, A also shall plough.

' If two farmers exchange lands either for a season or for all time and one plot is found deficient as compared with the other, and this was not their agreement, let him who has more give an equivalent in land to him who has less; but if this was their agreement, let them give nothing in addition.

If a farmer who has a claim on a field enters against the sower's will and reaps, then, if he had a just claim, let him take nothing from it; but if his claim was baseless, let him provide twice over the crops that were reaped.

If two territories contend about a boundary or a field, let the judges consider it and they shall decide in favour of the territory which had the longer possession; but if there is an ancient landmark, let the ancient determination remain unassailed.

If a division wronged people in their lots or lands, let them have licence to undo the division.

If a farmer on shares reaps without the grantor's consent and robs him of his sheaves, as a thief shall he be deprived of all his crop.

A share holder's portion is nine bundles, the grantor's one: he who divides outside these limits is accursed.

If a man takes land from an indigent farmer and agrees to plough only and to divide, let their agreement prevail; if they also agreed on sowing, let it prevail according to their agreement.

If a farmer takes from some indigent farmer his vineyard to work on a half-share and does not prune it as is fitting and dig it and fence it and dig it over, let him receive nothing from the produce. . . .

If a farmer takes over the farming of a vineyard or piece of land and agrees with the owner and takes earnest-money and starts and then draws back and gives it up, let him give the just value of the field and let the owner have the field.

If a farmer enters and works another farmer's woodland, for three years he shall take its profits for himself and then give the land back again to its owner.

If a farmer who is too poor to work his own vineyard takes flight and goes abroad, let those from whom claims are made by the public treasury gather in the grapes, and the farmer if he returns shall not be entitled to mulct them in the wine.

If a farmer who runs away from his own field pays every year the extraordinary taxes of the public treasury, let those who gather in the grapes and occupy the field be mulcted twofold.

Concerning Herdsmen. If a neatherd in the morning receives an ox from a farmer and mixes it with the herd, and it happens that the ox is destroyed by a wolf, let him explain the accident to its master and he himself shall go harmless.

If a herdsman who has received an ox loses it and on the same day on which the ox was lost does not give notice to the master of the ox that "I kept sight of the ox up to this or that point, but what is become of it I do not know," let him not go harmless, but, if he gave notice, let him go harmless.

If a herdsman receives an ox from a farmer in the morning and goes off and

the ox gets separated from the mass of oxen and goes off and goes into cultivated plots or vineyards and does harm, let him not lose his wages, but let him
make good the harm done.

If a herdsman in the morning receives an ox from a farmer and the ox disap-
pears, let him swear in the Lord's name that he has not himself played foul and
that he had no part in the loss of the ox and let him go harmless.

If a guardian of fruit is found stealing in the place which he guards, let him
lose his wages and be well beaten.

If a hired shepherd is found milking his flock without the owner's knowledge
and selling them, let him be beaten and lose his wages.

If a man is found stealing another's straw, he shall restore it twice over.

If a man takes an ox or an ass or any beast without its owner's knowledge and
goes off on business, let him give its hire twice over; and if it dies on the road, he
shall give two for one, whatever it may be. . . .

If a man steals an ox or an ass and is convicted, he shall be whipped and give it
twice over and all its gain.

If while a man is trying to steal one ox from a herd, the herd is put to flight
and eaten by wild beasts, let him be blinded.

If a man finds an ox in a wood and kills it, and takes the carcass let his hand be
cut off.

If a slave kills one ox or ass or ram in a wood, his master shall make it good.

If a slave, while trying to steal by night, drives the sheep away from the flock
in chasing them out of the fold, and they are lost or eaten by wild beasts, let him
be hanged as a murderer.

If a man's slave often steals beasts at night, or often drives away flocks, his
master shall make good what is lost on the ground that he knew his slave's guilt,
but let the slave himself be hanged. . . .

If a man is found in a granary stealing corn, let him receive in the first place a
hundred lashes, and make good the damage to the owner; if he is convicted a
second time, let him pay twofold damages for his theft; if a third time, let him be
blinded.

If a man at night steals wine from a jar or from a vat or out of a butt, let him
suffer the same penalty as is written in the chapter above.

If people have a deficient measure of corn and wine and do not follow the
ancient tradition of their fathers but out of covetousness have unjust measures,
contrary to those that are appointed, let them be beaten for their impiety.

If a man delivers cattle to a slave for pasture without his master's knowledge
and the slave sells them or otherwise damages them, let the slave and his master
go harmless.

If, with his master's knowledge, the slave receives beasts of any sort and eats
them up or otherwise does away with them, let the slave's master indemnify the
owner of the beasts. . . .

Where a man destroys another's beast on any pretence, when he is recognized,
let him indemnify its owner.

If a man harvests his lot before his neighbour's lots have been harvested and
he brings in his beasts and does harm to his neighbours, let him receive thirty
lashes and make good the damage to the party injured.

If a man gathers in the fruits of his vineyard and while the fruits of some lots are still ungathered brings in his beasts, let him receive thirty lashes and make good the damage to the party injured.

If a man lawlessly, when he has a suit with another, cuts his vines or any other tree, let his hand be cut off.

If a man who is dwelling in a district ascertains that a piece of common ground is suitable for the erection of a mill and appropriates it and then, after the completion of the building, if the commonalty of the district complain of the owner of the building as having appropriated common ground, let them give him all the expenditure that is due to him for the completion of the building and let them share it in common with its builder.

If after the land of the district has been divided, a man finds in his own lot a place which is suitable for the erection of a mill and sets about it, the farmers of the other lots are not entitled to say anything about the mill.

If the water which comes to the mill leaves dry cultivated plots or vineyards, let him make the damage good; if not, let the mill be idle.

If the owners of the cultivated plots are not willing that the water go through their plots, let them be entitled to prevent it.

167.

Introduction. The devastation wrought by the invaders, especially during and after the reign of Heraclius (610–41), also brought about a reduction in the population. This factor in turn produced a great demographic transformation in the empire, particularly in the countryside of Asia Minor. In place of many of the great estates there now appeared, as noted above, villages populated by free peasants. Some of these were soldiers who, in return for service to the state, were paid by gifts of land in the countryside taken from the imperial fisc. Each village was responsible for the payment of taxes to the state. Indeed, if any villager defaulted in payment, his neighbors were obliged *collectively* (*allelengyos*) to make up the deficit. According to the eighth-century chronicler Theophanes: "The independent villager is to be enrolled in the army, and other members of his commune are collectively to pay 185 *nomismata* for his [military] equipment while assuming the tax payments that are due from him to the government."* The following is a selection from the *Anonymous Fiscal Treatise* of the early tenth century (probably c. 913) which not only gives a good idea of the legal status of the free peasant villages (*choria*), but also shows some modifications in the tax system made since the time of *The Farmer's Law*, especially the mitigation of some of the harsher features of the collective responsibility for payment of taxes (*allelengyon*).

THE ANONYMOUS FISCAL TREATISE ON VILLAGES

(Translated by C. Brand, "Two Byzantine Treatises on Taxation," *Traditio* 25 [1969]: 49–50. Reprinted by permission of Fordham University Press.)

A field is one thing and a hamlet [*agridion*, little field] another. For the field is the entire improved [cultivated] area, while a hamlet is an individual division of the large village land, which also has individual cultivation. Therefore it is named "little field" for the sake of ease, like "city" and "little city." Hamlets arose either when some of the villagers did not remain at the site of the village, or when they did not possess the so-called enclosed gardens equally with the others and therefore transferred their dwellings and cultivated and lived in a [separate] part of the entire village land. Similarly the fathers of some, dying with many children, left to some of them the nearer fields which they held in the village land, to others the outer fields; then those who received their hereditary property in the outer fields, not being able to dwell and live far from it, moved their dwellings thither and improving the place made it into a hamlet. Others again, either enriched in cattle and slaves or crowded by poor neighbors and unable to live in the seat of the village, removed into some part of the whole taxable area of the village land and likewise improving it made the same thing. And inquiring, you would find many origins whence hamlets arose. . . .

The so-called separately established [idiostatic] hamlets and proasteia came into being this way. When the country has been devastated by some incursion of foreigners or by some other act of divine wrath and since the surviving neighbors are likely to remove on account of being compelled [to pay taxes] even for what has been devastated, there came an inspector sent by the emperor, and, having investigated, he remitted their tax either of the whole place or in part for the devastated parcels. Then if these owners returned within thirty years, the sympatheia [remission] is restored [to full taxability]; but if they did not return and the thirty-year period has passed, another inspector is again sent and removes the former sympatheia to the register of klasma [desolated land]. So when these things have happened, either the inspector who created the klasma or another one after him separates into a special part the land pertaining to those parcels which have been made klasma and surveys it and inscribes it on the bureau's register, and he will make separate and enroll the survey of the remaining devastated taxable area of the village land and thereafter this division which has been made klasma might be sold or given or hired out by contractual or leaseholding right or entrusted to some [government] bureau and thus be inhabited and improved; then because it falls in another property register and is not included within the register of the whole village land, it is called a separately established [idiostatic] hamlet or proasteion. For what has been made into klasma by the inspector and has been divided by the inspector from the taxable area of the village land and surveyed and marked off into a special part is separately established, so that neither is it among the parcels nor does it have any fiscal community [i.e., joint tax obligation] with the remaining taxable area of the village.

Commentary. From the later eighth century onward, as some measure of peace returned to the countryside, great landed estates under such magnate families as the Phocas, Scleroi, and Comnenoi again gradually became prominent. The great estates began to envelop many tracts of uncultivated lands left in the empire and, most significantly, to encroach on the free peasant holdings, even on those of the farmer-soldier. By the tenth century the soldier's holding (apparently) differed from other, free peasant holdings in that the holders of soldier's land were specifically required to provide money and supplies to equip soldiers in the field although not under all circumstances to serve in the army.

*Translated by D. Geanakoplos from Theophanes, *Chronographia*, ed. C. De Boor (Leipzig, 1883), p. 486.

168.

Introduction. One of the most famous records that remain of the life and especially the mentality of the rural aristocracy is the *Strategikon* of Kekaumenos, dating from the last half of the eleventh century. It is a manual of advice from a provincial, or rural, noble of high class to his young sons, filled with counsels for proper conduct in a variety of situations. It is a remarkable testimony showing the life and habits of the provincial aristocracy in both the capital and the country, and also the close family ties of this aristocratic class.

Advice from a Provincial Noble

A. Do Not Put Up Your Friends at Home

(From *Cecaumeni strategicon et incerti scriptoris de officiis regiis Libellus*, ed. B. Wassiliewsky and V. Jernstedt [St. Petersburg, 1896], pp. 42–44 and 73–74.)

If you have a friend living in another place and he passes through the town in which you live, do not install him in your house, but let him go elsewhere. Send him what he needs and he will receive you more favorably. For in your house, hear how many problems you will have: One is that your wife, your daughters, and your daughters-in-law will not be able to come forth from their chambers and therefore will not properly take care of your house. If it is necessary, however, that they appear, your friend will crane his neck to inspect them. In your presence he will pretend merely to acknowledge them; but if he is alone with them, he will note with curiosity how they walk and turn, and their girdle and glance and, in a word, he will study them from head to foot, in order later to imitate them to the great amusement of the members of his own household. Then he will have contempt for your servants, your table, the disposition of your household, and he will question you about your revenues, whether you own this or that. But why do I say so much? When he finds a chance, he will pursue your wife with amorous attentions and gaze at her with intemperate eyes, and, if he is able to, he will even seduce her. And when he departs, he will brag unworthily about what he did. But even if he does not speak of it, your enemy, in conflict with you, will proclaim it. . . .

A certain nobleman notable for his wealth, high station, and very high-birth, who had his residence in the City, had a beautiful wife whose brother was a general. Even more than beauty she was endowed with a fine spirit, intelligence, and virtue, and was knowledgeable in the Scriptures. The emperor, having often heard much praise of her, sent messengers asking to meet with her, promising both to her and her husband honors and many other good things. But her husband did not know of this. So then the emperor sent her husband out to serve as judge in a theme. Since the ruler could not persuade her [to acquiesce], he quieted down. But after three years [of service] the husband returned from his theme and was happy in his own home. Then a certain handsome youth, also of high station but unrelated, presented himself as a relative. And he said to her husband within their palace, "I," he said, "am related to the lady there." And many other things he said to him in order to ingratiate himself with the husband. And so the judge received him in his house. But he [the youth] was deceitful to him and succeeded in getting on friendly terms with him. What is the point of all this? Briefly, he had sexual relations with her who was once happy but now pitiable. When this drama became known, shame and sorrow, and especially pain, possessed her husband and relatives, but the youth prided himself for his act as if he had accomplished one of the labors of Hercules. And that which an emperor and promise of ranks and riches were unable to accomplish, habit and a friend did.

B. Keep Your Lands and Stay Away from the Imperial Court

(From *Cecaumeni strategicon*, pp. 76–78.)

No one has ever dared to revolt against the emperor and the Roman Empire, breaking the peace, without destroying himself. That is why I counsel you, dear children whom God has given me, always to align yourself on the side of the emperor and in his service. For the emperor who sits in the city of Constantine always triumphs. . . .

If you have in your own land fortified places or estates of which you are the owner and governor, do not let yourself be seduced by gold, by honorific titles, or by great promises of the emperors to cede your land to the emperor in exchange for riches and possessions. Not even if you will receive the quadruple part of its value; but preserve your own land, small as it might be or little in value. For it is better to be an independent friend than a servant without liberty. For in the eyes of the emperor and of all, you will remain a considerable personage, honored, esteemed, and noble, so long as you and your children and the children of your children remain in possession of your land and of your power. At the hour you lose your land and are despoiled of your power, you will still be loved by the emperor. But very soon you will be disdained by him and will count for nothing before him. You will understand then that you are no longer a friend but a servant. And from this moment, your inferior will also become formidable before you; if you displease him he will go to find the emperor and will accuse you of fomenting intrigues against him or of wishing to return to your former land. Perhaps you may not [later] even be able to remember what you were accused of. It is better for you to be in your land. And honor the emperor and also love all of your fellows. . . .

There was a certain chief of the Arabs by name of Apelzarach who, coming before the . . . Emperor Lord Romanus, was loaded with expensive gifts and honors and then released to return to his land by the emperor. And again he came to Constantinople, but the second time he was ignored. Slighted, he wanted to leave but was not allowed to do so by the emperor. He was then retained for two years in the Queen City, each year expecting exile and destruction. However, after two years the emperor released him to return to his own land. When he had arrived at and crossed the iron bridge beyond Antioch, he assembled all his servants and all those living at his house. Then holding his head in both hands, he asked of them: "What is this?" "Your head, our master," they responded, laughing. "I give thanks to God," he replied, "that I passed Chrysopolis with my head on my body, and now I have reached the mountains of Arabia. For those who trip up their heels fall into their own traps."

Thus, now, it is necessary to tell you to speak truly and act honorably and be content with your lot. If you ever wish to go to render homage to the imperial power, in some way to make your devotions in the holy churches and to see the beauty and order of the palace and the city [Constantinople], do it once. But thereafter you will become a servant and not a friend.

169.

Introduction. The famous Byzantine epic poem, *Digenes Akritas* (see selections nos. 9, 253, and 315) of the tenth-eleventh century, provides an idealized portrait of one member of the provincial nobility in the role of military leader, in this case on the border between the empire and Muslim territory in the East around the area of Mesopotamia.

OPENING VERSES OF *DIGENES AKRITAS*, BORDER WARLORD

(Translated by J. Mavrogordato, *Digenes Akritas* [Oxford, 1956], pp. 3–4.)

Honours triumphs and the praise
Of the thrice-blessed Borderer Basil,
The very noble, most brave
Who had his strength as gift from God,
And overthrew all Syria,
Babylon, all Harziane,
Armenia, Kappadokia,
Amorion and Ikonion,
And that famous and great fortress,
The mighty and the fortified,
Ankyra I mean, and all Smyrna
And the seaside subduing.
I will declare his works to you
Which in this present life he did.
How warriors mighty and brave
He overawed, and all wild beasts,
Having to help the grace of God,
And of God's mother unconquerable,
Of the angels and archangels,
Of the prize-bearing great martyrs,
Of both the glorious Theodores,

The host's leader and the recruit,
Of noble George of many trials,
And wonder-working martyr of martyrs
Glorious Demetrios, defender
Of Basil, boast and pride of him
Who had victory on his adversaries
The Agarenes and Ishmaelites,
And barbarous Skyths who rage like dogs.

170.

Introduction. Repercussions from the resurgence of
the landed aristocracy were soon to become serious for the state. The decline
of the soldier-holdings obviously weakened the military strength of the empire,
inasmuch as the aristocrats were reluctant to fulfill the obligations incumbent
upon possession of their lands. Moreover, the decline of the free peasant villages reduced the tax base of the empire, thus endangering the state's financial
stability. The new rural aristocrats, especially of Asia Minor, were to prove po-
litically dangerous for the central government: following their own personal
ambition, they would frequently lead revolts against the emperor.

The central government, which had sporadically recognized the dangers inherent in the decline of the free peasant holdings, finally began in the reign of
Romanus I Lecapenus (tenth century) to issue laws to secure continued peasant
control of rural lands. The basic purpose of all these laws was to allow to the
peasants alone the right to purchase the land of their peers (called *penetes*, the
poor), and thus to block any further acquisition of lands by the great landed
magnates (termed the *dynatoi*, powerful). The document below and the one
following it (selection 171) are the edicts of Emperor Romanus Lecapenus (922
and 934) on the subject of alienation of peasant lands.

EDICT OF ROMANUS I (922) ON REFORM OF LAND
TENURE REGULATIONS

(From J. and P. Zepos, eds., *Jus graecoromanum* [Athens, 1931],
vol. 1, pp. 201–2.)

It is an old law that no one be impeded by relatives
or business partners from selling to whomever he may wish. But another law
plainly forbids that someone be able to sell [his land] to another except to the
inhabitants of his own *metrocomia.** But we, making great provision for our taxpayers and at the same time for the public revenues, and also bearing in mind
additional military and local fiscal responsibilities [*leitourgias*] and the collective
liability for taxation, correct this ambiguity and the contradiction of these [two
laws], concisely and unambiguously, through this sacred edict:

1. From now on in every city, country[side], and province, if perchance there
are people who possess in common a dwelling or field or vineyard or some other
such [common] immovable property from a divided or undivided inheritance, or
from a common purchase or from some similar sort of acquisition (either inheri-

tance or new purchase), or, on the other hand, if there are people whose lands are intermingled not on account of joint ownership but by [possessing] property that is adjacent to each other's in a certain place, or [if they are] neighbors who share a collective liability for taxation or simply live in proximity [to each other], if any of these should wish to alienate their own property either through purchase, *emphyteusis* [a kind of perpetual usufruct], or lease, we decree that they not alienate such property to anyone else, unless they first inform those whom we now list according to the order of preference [*protimesis*]: first, that close relatives, on both sides, be notified, then those who are bound together by an arrangement of joint ownership. After these are those whose lands are simply interspersed [among those of the seller], even if they happen to be total strangers to the one who is divesting himself of his land. Then come the neighbors who share a joint liability for taxation [*homoteleis*], and finally those who are linked because of contact [of their lands] in some area. (By *homoteleis* we mean all those listed together under the same assessment [of taxes in a specific place], even if they in fact remit their individual payments in differing areas.)

In the case in which there are many neighbors on every side of the property, let this order of preference be utilized by formal notification [of the sale] to each person in the same sequence as listed above, so that, when those who receive preference, petition equally [to buy the property], those who are named in succession, if they wish, may come to terms [with the owner]. If, however, everyone who comes enjoys the same grade of privilege—in order that no one be given preference before the others in making an offer—let a similar announcement be made beforehand to all in order that they in the proper manner and without delay, within thirty days, pay from their own resources or from some other source the authorized price or whatever a purchaser in good faith might offer. As for those, however, who do not make an offer at the specified price for these lands within this stated period of time, they will no longer have the legal right of *protimesis*. . . .

2. We forbid the powerful [*dynatoi*] to obtain anything belonging to the more humble [*eutelesteroi*], either by means of adoption or simple gift, or on account of death or testament, or through usufruct or patronage [*prostasia*], or by informal concession, unless they are relatives. But [let the *dynatoi*] not make any new purchases or leases or exchanges from owners in any villages or hamlets in which they do not already personally possess property. And if *proasteia*⁺ are offered for sale which do not belong to these *dynatoi* but to other persons, or if lands which are called *klasmatika*⁺ or any other lands belonging to the treasury are to be alienated, let these [small landowners] again be given preference in purchasing. When such men, acting of their own free will, refuse to do so, only then is it permissible to enter into an agreement with the *dynatoi*. . . . If any powerful person attempts to effect [an illegal transaction] he will be deprived of the property and will forfeit to the treasury the amount of the price. However, after ten years without a complaint against those making such [illegal] arrangements (either by receiving a gift or acquiring something through testament from any one of those who are awarded preferential rights by this decree), there will be no inquiry by the treasury.

3. Together with these things, we decree that all soldiers' properties [*stratiotika ktemata*]—as many as have been alienated by whatever means in the last thirty years, or will henceforth be alienated—be restored free of charge to cover the responsibility and the benefits enjoyed owing to obligation for military service, unless after the alienation there remains to the soldier a sufficient amount for the fulfillment of the next campaign. Insofar as it lacks [this], the alienation is voided.[§]

* A local semi-independent unit of government and taxation roughly corresponding to a village.
† "Estates," a term generally referring to any lands near a village that were not included in that village's collective tax liability, but were assessed separately.
‡ Abandoned lands which, after a certain indeterminate period of time, had been removed from a village's fiscal responsibility and whose ownership had reverted to the government.
§ The authenticity of this last, third article has been questioned.

171.

SECOND LAW OF ROMANUS ON RESTORATION OF PEASANT LANDS (934)

(From J. and P. Zepos, eds., *Jus graecoromanum* [Athens, 1931], vol. 1, pp. 207–13.)

We decree therefore that in every area and district which our authority, after God, controls, the ones who reside there possess their appointed dwellings, freely and unhindered. If time allows that a man retain possession of this land, let it be the inherited acquisition of his children or relatives, or [let] the testament of the owner be fulfilled according to his intentions. But if in the course of human life and the misfortunes of time induced by need or deprivation or even perhaps by simple desire, [the owner] should either fully or partially seek to alienate the property of his household lands, let this sale be first offered to men of the same or nearby lands or villages. We do not issue these laws out of hatred or jealousy for the stronger, but we decree them for the benefit and patronage of the poor and for the common salvation. . . . Therefore let no one of the illustrious *magistri* [important court officials] or patricians, nor those honored with positions of [civil] authority, generalships, or [other] military or civil titles, nor anyone counted as part of the senate [*synkletos*], nor the commanders of themes and their lieutenants, nor the most holy metropolitans, archbishops, bishops, abbots, and church *archontes* [high lay patrons of the church], nor those who enjoy the patronage of and control over imperial or religious foundations—either for their own advantage or for that of the crown or church—ever dare clandestinely to enter into any land or village, in part or entirely, either by means of sale or gift or inheritance or on whatever pretext. Rather, when such acquisition has been found to be invalid, let these officials be ordered to withdraw from and to return free of charge these acquisitions and any improvements made upon them to their [original] owner or his relatives. If there are no heirs [let the property go] to inhabitants of the same lands or villages. For the authority of such [powerful] persons has exacerbated the great suffering of the poor because of the multitude of their retainers and hirelings and those who are linked with and attend their prominent positions—[a fact] which includes prosecutions, forced services, other consequent distresses and straitened circumstances, and has brought about no little common ruin for [i.e., apparent to] those who observe carefully, unless the present law, anticipating [such a situation], acts to prevent it.*

The habitation of the common people displays the great benefit derived from the people's employment, the joint payment of the taxes, the collective obligation to support the army, which will be completely lost if the common people die out. And it is necessary to rid ourselves of those who abet the disruption of civil stability, to cast off any harmful [element] and to uphold the common welfare. Let these things henceforth be observed for the common benefit and the condition of our subjects. It is necessary to offer the applicable remedy not only for the benefit of those in the future but also for those already present. For many, taking as a given the poverty of the poor (which time, the bearer of all things, has brought, or rather [which] the multitude of our sins, by forcing out divine mercy, has introduced in place of benevolence, compassion, and goodness, when they see the poor suffering from hunger, they buy up cheaply—some with silver, some with gold, some with grain or other offerings—the possessions of the wretched poor. They are more ferocious than the impending dearth [itself], and in the times coming afterwards, they are, for the wretched people of the villages, like the pestilential appearance of some disease or a kind of gangrene, as they fasten themselves upon the body of the villagers and [inflict] complete destruction.

Therefore, from the past first indiction, that is from the time the famine came and went, whoever of the illustrious people whom the present edict [above] has forbidden [to buy up lands] has gained control of fields or village lands, either in full or in part, or has seized properties in them, [we decree] that they be ejected from them but that they receive the price which they paid either from the original owners or from their heirs or relatives, or if these are poor, from others who are joint taxpayers or from a group coming forward to pay the price. But regarding improvements on such lands, let those who give back the lands, whether they are well-off and willing or poor and unwilling, return the [building] materials to those who are regaining possession even if they have added such improvements at personal expense, although these [improvements] do not in themselves reflect the labor and profit of the poor. And so much regarding the apparently just method of purchase. Moreover, we decree that gifts or inheritances or other such cunning types of acquisitions or seizures be void now and for the past [retroactively], and that nothing shall be inquired on behalf of these powerful evildoers, but that these lands be restored without payment to their proper owners, or if these men have disappeared through some chance, that they be granted to their children or relatives.

If divine providence or something else incomprehensible transforms the situation of some persons for the better, snatching away lower fortune and changing it to a better one, we think it just that they remain in the same inheritance and position they held from the beginning and that they not, in the course of increasing the measure of their personal fortune, act to plunder their less fortunate neighbors. . . .

The return of payments [made by the rich to purchase land] which has been mentioned above requires harmonious detailed investigation, not careless or arbitrary judgment. For when a free and noncompulsory sale has been completed and the appropriate payment of the price has been observed, the calculation for the amount of repayment (which may ameliorate the hardship of poverty) will be fairly preserved in a certain small appendix to the law. Let at once the return of the lands and their restitution be made to the ones who had sold them or to their heirs or relatives, or if these are not present, to their fellow, joint taxpayers. If these people are wealthy, then let the price originally paid be returned, but if they are poor let them not be forced to repay quickly so that the payment now imposed may not seem heavier and more oppressive than the benefit and security awaited in the future. . . . But in order to circumvent any new chicanery and to carry out what has been ordained, let a period of three years of postponement [for repayment] be designated so as to bring prosperity to the poor and enable them without hardship to offer the [appropriate] restitution. . . .

When someone becomes, or wishes to become, a monk for the sake of appearance, and hands over his property to the holy monastery, let those things which at that time seemed good not receive any disturbance. Reaping sufficient benefit from the present decree, let [the monastery] receive the proper price of the property, if this [act of the new monk] was carried out in good faith for the sake of salvation and not for the sake of deceit, circumvention, and cunning. This will not be reckoned as more to the advantage of the holy foundations than of the poor, inasmuch as the first are relieved of discord and disputes and unfree property, while [the latter] avoid and turn away from the causes of calamities: discoveries [of older deeds to the land?] and limitations; [then] let the property remain for men who are living and still bound to the flesh, and not for those uncorrupted persons [monks] who are responsible for the failings of mankind.

*The translation follows the original Greek sequence of tenses which is confused here.

172.

Introduction. Despite the moderate success of Romanus's efforts to arrest the decline of the small peasantry (and of the soldiers' holdings), the accession of Emperor Nicephorus Phocas to the throne in 963 marked a significant change in imperial land policy. As a representative of the landed military aristocracy of Asia Minor, Phocas removed certain restrictions imposed by his predecessors on the purchase of peasant properties by large landowners and magnates.*

LAW OF NICEPHORUS II PHOCAS ON PROPERTY AND SOCIAL STATUS (966–67)

(From J. and P. Zepos, eds., *Jus graecoromanum* [Athens, 1931], vol. 1, pp. 253–54.)

When those who ruled before us promulgated legislation—on account of the poverty existing at that time—banning the *dynatoi* from purchasing the [lands] of the poor [*penetes*] and *stratiotai* [soldiers], and thereby gaining advantage for themselves, they added to this [legislation] that the poor receive the right of preference [*protimesis*] even in [purchasing] property of the *dynatoi*, not only on the basis of joint ownership but even on the basis of collective liability for taxation. And they completely shut out the ones who are daily increasing [in wealth] by not providing them with the opportunity for making new gains. Rather they forced even those formerly well-off to live in want and straitened circumstances, since the poor receive preferential treatment in purchasing. And since they [earlier emperors] had no thought for the security of those [*dynatoi*], they appeared biased and, through these edicts, they weakened and ruined Roman power in its entirety. . . .

We decree that the legislation promulgated by those who have formerly ruled remain in force, except only in one respect: We order that certain legislation be rescinded, so that the poor might not have the right of *protimesis* for property being publicly sold by a lender [*daneistes*, a misreading probably for *dynastes*, powerful man], neither on the basis of joint ownership nor of collective tax liability, if *stratiotai* or civilians [*politikoi*] may be found. We order that some prominent person, that is, one who may appear for the benefit and tranquility of the neighboring poor, regain ownership of this property; but any person who, after obtaining ownership of the property, is so evilly inclined as to cause harm to his neighbors, [we decree] that he be expelled as a wicked and violent man not only from his new acquisition, but from his patrimonial possessions. We also desire that the *dynatoi* contract purchases only from the *dynatoi*, and that the *stratiotai* and poor transact purchases only with those who have similar social status. And just as we forbid the *stratiotai* and *penetes* from purchasing possessions of the *dynatoi*, thus also we forbid the latter to purchase lands of the poor and also of impecunious *stratiotai*, and we desire that the *dynatoi* not cite joint ownership or collective tax liability in the aim of opposing justice, for the sake of which we make law for everyone and do not show more concern for some than for others.

* Not all scholars agree that Phocas's edicts mark a genuine reversal of Romanus's policy.

173.

Introduction. The next selection, also taken from an edict of Emperor Nicephorus Phocas, specifically concerns the disposition of soldiers' lands or properties which had been alienated.

LAW OF NICEPHORUS II PHOCAS ON LANDS
BELONGING TO MILITARY MEN (C. 967)

(From J. and P. Zepos, eds., *Jus graecoromanum* [Athens, 1931], vol. 1, pp. 255–56.)

The *protospatharios* Basil, who is in charge of petitions, had stated that he returns to the *stratiotai*, free of charge, lands which are recovered since they [the *stratiotai*] are found performing the obligations of military service incumbent upon these same lands. And he has pointed out that it seems vexatious for someone not to have legal authority to sell anywhere a portion of the lands which are under his control, however much and of whatever sort may be the additional property which he owns.

Wherefore, we desire that such a law be in effect for those *stratiotai* who, until now, have sold their lands, so that immovable income-producing property worth four pounds [of gold] be set aside for each soldier by reason of his liability for military service. And if he has this amount and is found to have sold another piece of his land and he then seeks to regain it, he may do so through his right of *protimesis*, not without compensation but rather through payment [to the new owner] of the lawful price. But if the *stratiotes* has sold a portion of this holding— of the immovable income-producing property worth four pounds—such is to be restored [to him] without payment.

Hereafter, however, when land of the mail-clad and armor-bearing men undergoes transfer, we decree that no common *stratiotes* anywhere be able to sell with assurance immovable holdings from this [land], unless in addition he has income-producing, immovable property worth twelve pounds [of gold]. But if he has sold off anything from a holding which amounts to such a sum, [we decree] that he recover it without payment, while if he possesses anything in addition to this [that is, twelve pounds], sells it, and then seeks to regain it, that he not recover it without charge, but by paying a fitting price.

174.

Introduction. Emperor Basil II, who had endured several revolts led by the landed aristocracy, in his turn wisely sought to restore to the peasantry lands lost by them to the great magnates. We quote here from Basil's law of 996 (the most drastic of all) concerning peasant properties which had been seized by, or sold (under pressure, often at a low price) to powerful nobles.

BASIL II PROTECTS PEASANT PROPERTIES (996)

(From J. and P. Zepos, eds., *Jus graecoromanum* [Athens, 1931] vol. 1, pp. 263–67.)

1. Whereas our imperial majesty, by the grace of God from whom we have received the imperial authority, has undertaken to scrutinize the legal cases initiated by both rich and poor, we have found that

those powerful [*dynatoi*] who desire to aggrandize [their lands] have a legitimate excuse for their personal covetousness, that is, the prescription of up to forty years,* and that they anxiously await to pass through this period either by means of bribes and gifts or through the power they possess and then to enjoy in full ownership whatever they have wrongly appropriated at the expense of the poor. Therefore we have promulgated the present legislation, which on the one hand rectifies what has previously occurred but, on other hand, also curbs the present-day *dynatoi* and forbids those in the future from undertaking such things [to attack the poor], since they now have the knowledge that they [the *dynatoi*] will get no assistance from this quarter. Not only will they themselves be stripped of the property belonging to others, but so also will their children and whomever else they leave it to as heirs. From this we wish it to be clear that our imperial majesty does not without purpose or investigation overturn ownership [based upon] prescription of long-standing, but takes pity on the poor and watches out for the common welfare and conditions and embraces justice and provides a remedy against this fearful passion of desire for aggrandizement. Because of this circumstance we have been very disturbed on behalf of the poor, and we have observed with our own eyes (when we traversed the themes of our empire and set out on campaigns) the avarice and injustices every day perpetrated against the poor. Indeed how can time be of any assistance at all since, as has happened, the *dynatos*, who is powerful and prosperous and aggrandizes himself at the expense of the poor man, will profit from the passage of time and will bequeath to his heirs his power and wealth? . . .

For when one who happens to be powerful acquires property in communities of peasant villages or enlarges [his property] with more [land], and when his successors take over his authority as well as his wealth and provide no opportunity for the poor man to take legal action against them for the things they have evilly expropriated and taken from him, it is clear that whatever amount of time may elapse in these matters, the poor man will [ought] in no case to be prevented from seeking and gaining the return of his own property. For unless we do this, we will provide an excuse for the one who is avaricious to declare: "Since I am today prosperous and the poor man is unable to take action against me, if my son also prospers, and on account of our prosperity the time prescribed by law elapses, or if I myself live through this period [of time] prosperously, we [will] hold the property irrevocably, and it is in my interest to be acquisitive [at others' expense]." . . .

Therefore, we decree by our present enactment, that those properties which have been acquired by the *dynatoi* in communities of peasant villages up to the initial law of our great-grandfather Emperor Romanus the Elder and which derive their validity from written documents or supporting witnesses, be preserved and kept in their owner's hands, as has been declared in earlier laws. For this reason we seek written privileges and supporting witnesses to be adduced, so that the *dynatoi* might not by means of subterfuge allege that the lands recently acquired by them carry over to them by written documents from a long time ago. But from that time when the written prescription was issued through the law published by our great-grandfather Emperor Romanus the Elder, until the present (which is the first of January of the ninth indiction of the year 996 and also into the future), [we declare] that in no way at all can time [elapsed] have [legal] validity or be made use of against the poor, when they have dealings with the *dynatoi*, but their possessions should be given back to the poor, nor [should anything be brought up] concerning the return of any costs [paid] or necessary improvements made by the *dynatoi*, because they have been discovered to transgress the aforementioned law and are indeed liable to be called to account. For when the aforesaid emperor, our great-grandfather Emperor Romanus the Elder, wrote and said: "From now I forbid the *dynatoi* to acquire property among lands in peasant villages," he meant that he forbade them forever and for eternity, and he did not give them [a prescription of] time as a method of assistance.

We do not decree the aforementioned [regulations] only for the future, but we also make this enactment retroactive to the previous period about which we have spoken [i.e. since 922, the date of Romanus's first law]. For if we do not rectify those past actions which are now being brought into legal question, how would those in the future be protected and those [evildoers] who may come later be cowed?

2. Since we have found many [of our] subjects listed in [imperial] surveys recorded in chrysobulls, and many such cases have been brought before our tribunal, we decree that those surveys which are adduced [as evidence] have no validity, nor shall those utilizing them derive any legal benefit from the ambiguity which may exist in these documents. For the surveys are not issued with imperial knowledge or assent but for the benefit of those receiving them. Moreover, the chief secretaries who draw up the chrysobulls are neither present nor do they observe when the [actual] measuring [of the property] or the notification [of the results] occurs. For this reason, as has been made clear, we wish that those surveys in which ambiguity exists be considered invalid and have no effect. But if such surveys happen to be among the archives of the imperial treasury or in some other [legally] substantiating documents, we command that they be heeded and obeyed.

Commentary. By the mid-eleventh century it was clear that this imperial policy of providing a vigorous check on the acquisition of peasant lands by the landed magnates could not be sustained after the death of such a strong leader as Emperor Basil II. After his death the throne was occupied by members of the landed aristocracy from Asia Minor (for example, Isaac Comnenus) or members of the rival civil bureaucracy in Constantinople (the Ducas family, for instance), the latter of whom naturally tended to neglect the countryside and the army in favor of the capital city and their own bureaucratic interests.

In the twelfth century the conditions of the relatively few remaining free peasants in Asia Minor deteriorated even further. The instability of the rural scene drastically worsened as a result of the sudden Seljuk conquests of most of Anatolia, a fact which brought about a great reduction in the population of what had been the very heartland of the empire.

* Referring to a kind of statute of limitations, according to which an irregular transaction not discovered until forty years later could not be prosecuted at law.

175.

Introduction. The Latin occupation of Constantinople (1204–61) did little to improve the lot of the Byzantine peasant. Indeed, peasant conditions in the areas of the old empire came more and more to parallel those experienced by the Western European serf. However, the Latin conquest did serve to stimulate Greek interest in effective means for restoring the Byzantine Empire, especially in remedying the social and economic ills plaguing Byzantium. Thus in the Greek "Empire" of Nicaea (a Byzantine successor state) in western Asia Minor, the far-sighted Greek Emperor John III Vatatzes (1222–54), realizing the significance of the free peasantry (as well as of a native industry and native Greek army), enacted legislation in behalf of agrarian reform. The Byzantine historian Nicephorus Gregoras describes the encouragement of agriculture around Nicaea in Asia Minor under John Vatatzes.

AGRARIAN CONDITIONS IN NICAEA UNDER JOHN VATATZES

(From Nicephorus Gregoras, *Byzantine historia*, ed. I. Bekker and L. Schopen [Bonn, 1829], vol. 1, pp. 42–43.)

The emperor himself marked out a piece of land, arable and suitable for wine-growing, which he adjudged sufficiently able to supply the needs of the imperial table as well as the many things the beneficent and socially aware emperor was concerned with. He had the land administered by those who knew something about agriculture and vineyard cultivation, and he had a great abundance of fruit grown. But that was not all. In addition he acquired herds of cattle, sheep, and pigs, and domesticated birds of every kind. The young of these beasts brought to him each year a rich income. He also summoned others to do the same, not only his relations but also the other nobles. He desired that each be able to supply his wants from his own resources so that he would not lay an avaricious hand on the common, socially inferior man. At the same time he desired that Byzantine society be henceforth completely cleansed of injustice. In a short time the barns were full of fruit and the roads and streets, the pens and stalls, were hardly able to contain all the livestock and poultry.

An advantage befell the Byzantines in that the Turks were afflicted by a severe famine. All roads which led to the Byzantine realm were filled with the comings and goings of this race of people: men, women, and children. And the wealth of the Turks emptied itself in great abundance into the hands of the Byzantines: gold, silver, clothing, and other things, whatever precious and luxury items in every form they had to offer.

One could then see how valuable things were put down in order to purchase a bit of food. Every fowl, cow, and goat was dearly paid for. In this manner the houses of the Byzantines became in the shortest time full of the riches of the barbarians and the imperial treasury chambers were overflowing with money. To explain the entire situation by one little example: the men who tended the imperial fowl annually collected and sold the eggs which had been laid. In a short time this brought in so much money that a crown, set with many colored gems and pearls, could be made for the empress. To this crown the emperor gave the name "egg-crown," as it had been made out of sale of the eggs. This is an example of the emperor's wise internal policy.

Commentary. In the last phase of the empire, the Palaeologan period of the late thirteenth, fourteenth, and fifteenth centuries, the lot of the peasant declined even further. In those areas not already conquered by the Ottoman Turks, great landowners, imperial scions or ecclesiastical officials, held *pronoia* of the emperor—and therefore could be virtually independent rulers. A *pronoia*, as noted above in selection 45, was a grant of land from the emperor which now virtually always entailed exemption of the land from imperial taxation and performance of other state duties. In return the holder of the *pronoia* was to provide troops for the imperial army, along with his own military service. (In some ways the *pronoia* resembled the Western feudal fief, except primarily for the absence of subinfeudation and the hierarchy of lords.) On these lands of the pronoiar the peasants were subject to the demands and whims of their lord. Their lot, in effect, was much the same as that of a Western serf.

By the end of Byzantium, the peasant's original function, that of supplying grain (especially for the capital), had almost disappeared. Indeed, the population of Constantinople had shrunk so much that practically all food could be grown within the walls, or immediately outside them. The sad lot of the peasant, who had been so important for the well-being of Byzantine society, pointed to the end of the empire. And, indeed, the peasant's fate may be considered a kind of barometer of the ups and downs of the history of the empire itself.

B.
THE TOWN DWELLER

176.

Introduction. Though the Byzantine Empire, like other ancient and medieval kingdoms, depended on the countryside for sustenance, town life was always a significant and characteristic feature of its society. As in the ancient world, government, administration, and cultural life centered in general on the *poleis* (cities) of the Byzantine Empire. From the earliest period the Byzantine government took great interest in maintaining and improving the quality of life in the towns. The imperial government thus often took measures to oversee the organization of cities, to provide education for the youth, (sometimes) to make available medical care, and not least to carry out public works. This was especially true of the capital cities, but also of other great cities of the empire, such as Antioch and Alexandria. The following selections give two examples of the imperial aim to foster a harmonious, congenial urban life. The first selection documents the efforts of emperors Honorius and Theodosius II to provide a stable and moderately priced grain supply for Constantinople (409). The second selection deals with governmental regulation by Theodosius II of the activities of professors in the cities of Constantinople and Rome (425).

A. The Capital's Grain Supply

(Translated by C. Pharr, *The Theodosian Code* [Princeton, 1952], 14-16-1, p. 417.)

Emperors Honorius and Theodosius Augustuses to Monaxius, Prefect of the City:

For the prevention of famine, five hundred pounds of gold have been collected, partly by the inquiries of Your Excellency and partly by the gratifying contribution of the Most August Senate, and We so consecrate this amount to this account that if any sum should be found under the title of purchase for the buying of grain, it shall be disclosed in the tribunal of the City prefect, under attestation in the public records, so that the sum collected and its increment, which accrues from the sale of wheat, shall be subjected to the scrutiny of the Fathers. Therefore, all usurpation attempted contrary to this title shall cease, so that neither by the authority of your office nor under the plea of any occasion, even an honorable one, shall any person be allowed in any manner to violate these carefully considered regulations. Otherwise he shall not only appear to violate the protection of so many decrees, but he shall also be punished by a property loss, and whatever he takes from this quantity of gold, he shall pay two-fold that sum to the grain treasury. Moreover, if any person should wish to purchase grain privately for his own use within Our Most August City, he shall have the license to make such purchases.

B. REGULATIONS FOR PROFESSORS

(From *Theodosian Code.* 14-8-3, p. 414.)

We order to be removed from the practice of vulgar ostentation all persons who usurp for themselves the name of teachers and who in their public professorships and in their private rooms are accustomed to conduct with them their students whom they have collected from all quarters. Thus if any of these teachers, after the issuance of the words of this divine imperial sanction, should perhaps again attempt to do that which We prohibit and condemn, he shall not only undergo the brand of infamy that he deserves, but he shall know that he will also be expelled from the very city where he conducts himself thus illicitly. But by no threat of this kind do We prohibit those teachers who are accustomed to give such instruction privately within very many homes, if they prefer to keep themselves free for such students only whom they teach within the walls of private homes. If, moreover, there should be any teacher from the number of those who appear to be established within the auditorium of the Capitol, he shall know that in every way he is interdicted from teaching such studies in private homes. He shall also know that if he should be apprehended doing anything contrary to the imperial celestial statutes, he shall obtain no benefit from those privileges which are deservedly conferred upon those persons who have been commanded to teach only in the Capitol.

Therefore, Our auditorium shall specifically have three orators and ten grammarians, first of all among those teachers who are commended by their learning in Roman oratory. Among those professors also who are recognized as being proficient in facility of expression in Greek, there shall be five sophists in number, and likewise ten grammarians. Since it is Our desire that Our glorious youth should be instructed not only in such arts, We associate authorities of more profound knowledge and learning with the aforesaid professors. Therefore, it is Our will that to the other professors, one teacher shall be associated who shall investigate the hidden secrets of philosophy, two teachers also who shall expound the formulas of the law and statutes. Thus Your Sublimity shall provide that to each of these teachers a designated place shall be specifically assigned, in order that the students and teachers may not drown out each other, and the mingled confusion of tongues and words may not divert the ears or the minds of any from the study of letters.

177.

Introduction. While the emperors took an active interest in the quality of life in the capital cities, much of the responsibility for administering provincial cities in the early period fell upon local senators (*curiales* or decurions). In addition to their responsibility for imperial tax payments, the decurions as the local magistrates (they were coerced to perform municipal duties, duties which could not by law be evaded) carried out many public works such as maintenance of law and order, some forms of justice, and construction and upkeep of public buildings. The following two imperial edicts show (a) the financial liability of the *curiales* who were in charge of public works (385) and (b) the customary role of *curiales* (and others) in the repair and maintenance of the walls (396).

On Duties of Municipal Senators (Curiales)

A. FINANCIAL LIABILITY

(Translated by C. Pharr, *The Theodosian Code,* 15-1-24, pp. 425–26.)

If the charge of public works has been enjoined upon any man or if money has been decreed for construction in the customary manner, he, together with his heirs, shall be held liable for fifteen years after the completion of the work. Thus, if any defect in construction should appear within the statutory time, it shall be repaired from the patrimony of such persons, except in cases of fortuitous circumstances.

B. RESPONSIBILITY FOR WALLS

(From *Theodosian Code,* 15-1-34, p. 427.)

All governors of provinces shall be admonished by letter that they must know that the municipal senates and inhabitants of each city shall build new walls or make the old walls stronger, and the expense thereof shall, of course, be arranged in such a way that the tax assessment shall be apportioned according to the ability of each man. An estimate shall be made of the cost of the future work, and in accordance therewith the land of the citizens shall be assessed, so that no more or less than necessity requires shall be demanded, lest the urgent completion of such work should be hindered. A definite sum must be assessed against each taxable unit of land so that the burden of defraying the expense may be imposed equally on all.

178.

Introduction. Even by the time of Theodosius II, however, this system of municipal senates' running the cities was virtually moribund. And the best efforts of later rulers to revive it met with no success. Thus the cities fell more and more under the administrative control of imperial officials. This process was virtually completed by the beginning of the seventh century, although the laws on the *curiales* were only officially abrogated by the edict promulgated by Leo VI (late ninth or early tenth century). In this law Leo notes specifically that the older regulation on the *curiales* had been for some time a dead letter.

Abrogation of Laws on Duties of Curiales

(From *Les novelles de Léon VI le Sage*, ed. P. Noailles and A. Dain [Paris, 1944], pp. 183–85.)

In general in all circumstances of life it is necessity that each time points to the manner of action, and those things which present some usefulness we favor. On the other hand, those which offer no advantage we discard. According to this principle it is necessary to establish harmony in the composition of this chapter of laws. . . . We say this because among the ancient laws certain ones concerned with the decurions and the *curiales* impose on the decurions duties which are onerous and difficult to carry out, and at the same time give to the *curiales* the privilege of promoting certain magistrates and administering the cities in an independent fashion. Now, in view of the change in civil affairs, that is, since everything depends entirely on the imperial solicitude and administration, these laws shall by our decree be expunged from the legal codes, for it is in vain that they would find a place there.

179.

Introduction. One of the most striking features of life in many Byzantine cities in the early period, especially at the time of Emperors Anastasius and Justinian, was the activity of certain groups of the population, normally associated with the racing factions of the Hippodrome in Constantinople. These racing factions had their roots in two different groups in ancient Roman society: (1) the "fans" of the horse-racing groups which competed at the public games, the Blues and the Greens, and (2) the often rowdy partisans of theatrical performances. In the fifth century the amalgamation by the emperors of public entertainment united both groups under the rubric of "circus factions," forming a new, rather volatile social force. Recent scholarship, in contrast to older views, holds that the Blues and Greens had no genuine religious or political policies and that these two factions should not be construed as champions of the popular (democratic) will against that of the emperors. Rather their organizations seem to have played three roles: (1) in imperial ceremonies, when they greeted the emperor at the Hippodrome; (2) in rivalries which could and did explode in bloody riots; and (3) in time of sudden danger, when they provided a kind of urban militia to defend the city walls.

The first selection gives the historian Procopius's description of the Blue and Green factions in the time of Justinian (527–65). (For their subsequent role in the violent "Nika" riot against that ruler see selection 183.)

BYZANTINE RACING FACTIONS

(From Procopius, *History of the Wars*, Loeb Classical Library [London, 1914], vol. 1, pp. 218 and 220.)

The population in every city has for a long time been divided into two groups, the Greens and the Blues; but only recently, for the sake of these names and the places which they occupy while watching the games, have they come to spend their money, to abandon their bodies to the cruelest tortures, and to consider it a not unworthy thing to die a most disgraceful death. The members [of each faction] fight with their opponents not knowing for what reason they risk their lives, but realizing full well that even when they vanquish their opponents in brawls, they will be carted off to prison and that, after they have suffered the most extreme tortures, they will be killed. Therefore, there arises in them an endless and unreasoning hatred against their fellow men, respecting neither marriage nor kinship nor bonds of friendship, even if those who support different colors might be brothers or some other kind of relatives. Neither human nor divine affairs matter to them compared to winning these [street] fights. When some impious act is committed by one of them against God, or when the laws and the state are injured by their comrades or opponents, or perhaps when they lack the necessities of life, or their country is suffering dire need, they ignore all this as long as events turn out well for their own "faction." For this is what they call the bands of rioters. Even women participate in this abomination, not only accompanying the men but, if the occasion arises, even opposing them, although they do not go to the public spectacles nor are they motivated by any other reason. Thus I, for my part, consider [their actions] nothing else than a sickness of the soul. And this is how things are among the people of every city.

180.

Introduction. The next selection records a famous conversation between a representative of the Green faction and the herald (*mandator*) of Emperor Justinian near or in the Hippodrome (though one modern scholar believes it took place at a later period). The Greens complain that Justinian is unfair to them and partisan to the Blues, but their allegations are contemptuously ignored by the imperial herald.

THE GREENS AND THE BLUES

(Translated by D. Munro and G. Sellery, from the *Chronicle* of Theophanes, in *Medieval Civilization* [New York: Century Co., 1910], pp. 104–7.)

Greens: Long live Emperor Justinian! May he be ever victorious! But, O best of Princes, we are suffering all kinds of injustice. God knows we cannot stand it any longer. Yet we are afraid to name our persecutor, from fear that he may become more angry and that we shall incur still greater dangers.

Herald: I do not know of whom you are speaking.

Greens: Our oppressor, O thrice August! lives in the shoemakers' quarter.

Herald: No one is doing you any injury.

Greens: A single man persecutes us. O Mother of God, protect us!

Herald: I do not know this man.

Greens: Oh, yes, you do! You know very well, thrice August, who is our executioner at present.

Herald: If any one is persecuting you, I do not know who it is.

Greens: Well, Master of the World, it is Calopodios.

Herald: Calopodios has nothing to do with you.

Greens: Whoever it is will suffer the fate of Judas, and God will very soon punish him for his injustice.

Herald: You didn't come here to see the show, but only to insult the officials.

Greens: Yes, if any one annoys us he will suffer the fate of Judas.

Herald: Shut up, you Jews, Manicheans, Samaritans!

Greens: You call us Jews and Samaritans; may the Mother of God protect us all equally!

Herald: I want you to get baptized.

Greens: All right, we'll get baptized.

Herald: I tell you, if you don't shut up, I'll have your heads cut off.

Greens: Each one seeks to have power, in order to be safe. If our remarks hurt you, we hope that you will not be at all irritated. He who is divine ought to bear everything patiently. But, while we are talking, we shall call a spade a spade. We no longer know, thrice August, where the palace is or the government; the only way we know the city now is when we pass through it on an ass's back. And that is unjust, thrice August.

Herald: Every freeman can appear publicly wherever he likes, without danger.

Greens: We know very well we are free, but we are not allowed to use our liberty. And if any freeman is suspected of being a Green, he is always punished by public authority.

Herald: Jail-birds, don't you fear for your souls?

Greens: Let the color which we wear be suppressed, and the courts will be out of a job. You allow us to be assassinated, and, in addition, you order us to be punished. You are the source of life, and you kill whomsoever you choose. Truly, human nature cannot endure these two opposites. Ah! Would to heaven that your father Sabbatios had never been born. He would not have begotten an assassin. Just now a sixth murder took place in the Zeugma; yesterday, the man was alive, and in the evening, Master of all things, he was dead.

Blues: All the murderers in the Stadium belong to your party.

Greens: You do the killing, and you escape punishment.

Blues: You do the killing, and you keep on talking; all the assassins in the Stadium belong to your faction.

Greens: O Emperor Justinian! They complain, and yet no one is killing them. Come, let's discuss it; who killed the dealer in wood in the Zeugma?

Herald: You did.

Greens: And the son of Epagathos, who killed him, O Emperor?

Herald: You did that, too, and you accuse the Blues of it.

Greens: That will do. May the Lord have mercy on us! Truth is getting the worst of it. If it is true that God governs the world, where do so many calamities come from?

Herald: God is a stranger to evil.

Greens: God is a stranger to evil! Then why are we persecuted? Let a philosopher or a hermit come to solve the dilemma.

Herald: Blasphemers, enemies of God, will you not keep still?

Greens: If your Majesty orders us we shall keep still, thrice August, but it will be against our will. We know all about it, but we are silent. Adieu. Justice, thou dost not exist any longer. We are going away; we'll become Jews. God knows, it is better to be a pagan than a Blue.

Blues: Oh, horrors! We don't want to see them any longer; such hatred frightens us.

Greens: We hope the bones of the spectators will be thrown into the sewer some day.

181.

Introduction. Rivalry between Blues and Greens was not limited of course to exchanging verbal abuse in the Hippodrome of Constantinople; conflict between the factions often erupted into open warfare elsewhere as well. In this selection, John, bishop of Nikiu, describes party strife in Egypt shortly before the Persian conquest (c. 608–10).

A. BLUES AND GREENS IN EGYPT

(Translated by R. H. Charles, *Chronicle of John Bishop of Nikiu* [London, 1916], p. 175.)

And taking advantage of the war between Bonosus and Nicetas [rival Byzantine generals], artisan guilds [the Greens] arose and perpetrated outrages on "the Blues" and gave themselves shamelessly to pillage and murder. And when Nicetas was apprised of these facts he had them arrested, and reproved them, and said unto them: "Do no outrage henceforth to any one." And he established peace amongst them. And he named prefects in all the cities and repressed plundering and violence, and he lightened their taxes for three years. And the Egyptians were very much attached to him.

Introduction. Perhaps due to this sort of suppression by the Byzantine authorities, both Greens and Blues in Egypt joined to aid the Arabs against their own government. As John of Nikiu reports:

B. TREASON OF BLUES AND GREENS

(From *Chronicle of John of Nikiu*, pp. 187–88.)

And Menas who was the leader of the Green faction, and Cosmas the son of Samuel, the leader of the Blues, besieged the city of Misr [Egypt] and harassed the Romans [Byzantines] during the days of the Moslem.

Commentary. In time the capital's Blues and Greens, primarily through their role in court ceremonial, achieved a measure of respectability and their members a certain degree of affluence. Thus, by the late seventh century they gradually ceased to exercise their explosive, divisive force in Byzantine society and had become merged into the court and its ceremonial. Indeed, the leaders of the two groups, called demarchs, became relatively high-ranking dignitaries in the court hierarchy. (See selection 28.)

182.

Introduction. The density of population in Constantinople during Justinian's reign and afterward* brought to the fore the problem of insufficient living and working space in the capital. The class most affected by the crowded conditions (lack of sufficient sanitation, poor condition of the streets, the heat and cold) was of course the lowest class, the small tradesmen and the poor. Already in Justinian's time there are indications of a growing influx of people into the capital city, who would all too often lack adequate housing and enter the ranks of the poor, while engaging perhaps in violent or illegal acts. Following is the preface to Justinian's *Novella* 80 (539), which deals essentially with the problem of *coloni* fleeing their lands but also acknowledges the great influx of people into Constantinople.

CONSTANTINOPLE'S URBAN PROBLEMS

(From Justinian, *Novella* 80, from R. Schoell, ed., *Corpus Iuris Civilis*, vol. 3, *Novellae* [Berlin, 1912], p. 391.)

With the aid of God, we continually possess complete foresight so that the object which has been given to us for our philanthropy [i.e., the people] is preserved unharmed. Then, so as to take care of the people, we have established laws of complete justice, and that which little by little declines we strive to repair. Especially do we design administrative acts which correct the lesser evils of the ones who commit offenses. Therefore we have established praetors of the people in this great city—a most useful provision for all types of matters—provisions approved by all the inhabitants of this our imperial city. As a result of this practice, we have thought to regulate something else which requires attention and to establish justice by law and authority.

We have found that little by little the provinces are becoming denuded of their inhabitants, and this great city of ours becomes disturbed by a great multitude of all kinds of people, especially those from the rural areas, who have left their own towns and their agricultural pursuits in order to take refuge here.

*Under Justinian the population of Constantinople was perhaps 400,000 and in the Comnenan period, possibly 300,000 to 400,000 people. Scholarly tendency today, based on demographic and topographic factors (assessing space required for monuments and squares, and the like) is to scale down the population figures for Constantinople at its height (later tenth and early eleventh centuries) from the formerly high estimate of one million inhabitants to perhaps 600,000. These are all estimates, however.

183.

Introduction. Since the lower and middle classes ordinarily had no voice in government, on rare occasions they would vent their frustration and disapproval in violent protest against imperial authority, at times even rebelling and bringing about a change of policy, of ministers of state, or even of ruler. In the following selection the sixth-century historian Procopius describes the famous Nika riot of 532 in which the two Hippodrome parties (Blues and Greens) united to spark a popular uprising against the oppressive taxation policies of the minister of state, John the Cappadocian, and nearly toppled Emperor Justinian himself.

The Nika Riot

(From Procopius, *History of the Persian Wars*, Loeb Classical Library [London, 1914], vol. 1, pp. 223–29 and 233–37.)

At that time the civil officials who were in charge of the population in Byzantium [Constantinople] led away for execution some of the rioters. But rioters of the two factions, coming together and making peace with each other, seized the prisoners and went directly to the public jail where they freed all who were imprisoned for rioting or any other illegal act. The prison attendants who worked for the city government were indiscriminately killed. But those citizens who kept their wits about them fled to the opposite shore, and the city was put to the torch as if occupied by enemy troops. . . . At this time the praetorian prefect was John the Cappadocian and the imperial legal adviser was Tribonian, a native Pamphilian. (The Romans term this official the quaestor.) Of these two men, John was totally ignorant of the liberal arts and even lacked a primary education. He had learned nothing while attending elementary school except how to write the letters, and this very badly. But, on the strength of his innate ability, he became the most powerful man we have ever known. He was exceedingly competent in determining a necessary course of action and in finding a way out of difficulties. . . . Neither the word of God nor the opinion of men influenced him; rather, for the sake of personal profit he concerned himself with destroying the lives of many men and ruining entire cities. . . .

On the fifth day of the revolt in the late afternoon, the Emperor Justinian issued an order to Pompeius and Hypatius, the nephews of the former Emperor Anastasius, that they return to their homes as quickly as possible, either because he suspected them of fomenting some new plot against his person, or, it may be, fate simply intervened. But these two men, fearing that the populace would force them onto the imperial throne (as in fact turned out to be the case), said that it would be improper for them to abandon their emperor while he was in such a dangerous position. When he heard this the emperor became even more suspicious and ordered that they immediately be ejected from the palace. Thus the two men went home and, as long as it was night, remained there in peace.

But on the next day at sunrise it was discovered by the populace that both men were no longer living in the palace. The entire people then went to them and declared Hypatius *basileus*; and they tried to carry him off to the marketplace in order that he might receive the symbols of supreme power. But his wife Maria, who was the same age as her husband and who possessed a great reputation for prudence, held on and would not let go of him. Crying out loudly and summoning all their relatives, she shouted that the people were leading her husband to his death. But the mob prevailed by means of force and she unwillingly let go of her husband. After he had been brought against his will to the Forum of Constantine, the people summoned him to the throne. Since they did not have a diadem or anything else custom decrees that an emperor should wear, they placed a gold necklace on his head and then proclaimed him *basileus* of the Romans. Since members of the Senate had already assembled in the forum—except for those who were left behind in the imperial palace—many people were of the opinion that they ought to go and storm the palace. . . .

When Hypatius arrived at the Hippodrome, he went straight up to the place where the emperor customarily sits and seated himself on the imperial throne from which the emperor was accustomed to watch the equestrian and athletic games. Mundus [a general] entered from the palace through the gate which is named "the snail" on account of the fact that the descent from it is circular. Belisarius [another general of Justinian] ascended at first directly toward Hypatius himself and the imperial box, and when he came to the adjoining [small] structure where in the past a guard of soldiers used to be stationed, he called out to his troops, instructing them to open the door as quickly as possible so that they might move against the tyrant [Hypatius]. But since it seemed judicious to the soldiers that they support neither emperor until one clearly became the victor, they evaded carrying out this order by pretending not to hear anything. Therefore Belisarius returned to Justinian and informed him that all was lost for them, inasmuch as the soldiers guarding the palace were in revolt against him. The emperor then ordered Belisarius to go to the gate called Chalke and the Propylaea there. But instead the latter, at great risk and with great exertion, traversing the ruins and half-burned areas, went to the Hippodrome. When he came to the Blue Colonnade, which is to the right of the imperial throne, he thought at first to proceed against Hypatius himself. But since there was a small door which had been closed and which was guarded on the inside by Hypatius's bodyguard, he feared that the populace would discover him while he was having difficulties in this constricted area, would kill both him and all the troops who were following him, and thus with little difficulty would move against the emperor.

Belisarius, then, considering that he had to attack the people who took their stand in the Hippodrome—a huge mob pushing against each other in complete disorder—took his sword from its sheath and ordered his men to do the same, and shouting and running, he attacked them. But the populace, massed together in no rational order, when they saw that armored soldiers (who had a great reputation for bravery and experience in combat) were striking mercilessly with their swords, broke into flight. Then, when a great cry of victory arose (as is customary on such occasions), Mundus, who was stationed nearby thought of entering the fray (for he was a bold and vigorous man). But he did not know precisely what to do under the present circumstances, until he saw Belisarius involved in the combat. Immediately he made an attack into the Hippodrome through the gate called the "Gate of Death." Now Hypatius's bodyguard, attacked from both sides, was destroyed. When it became clear who was victorious and that a great slaughter of the people had already occurred, two nephews of Emperor Justinian, Boraides and Justus, dragged Hypatius from the throne and no one dared to raise a hand against them. They led him off and presented him, along with Pompeius, to the emperor. And on that day there perished among the populace more than thirty thousand.

184.

Introduction. Perhaps the greatest problem of the poor in Constantinople was housing. Although no one was supposed to sleep in the streets of the capital, a funerary oration written by Leo VI on his father Basil I (late ninth century) suggests that the government kept arcades and other roofed public areas open during the winter so that the poor, who often slept on the sidewalks, would not freeze at night.

A POOR MAN AND FUTURE EMPEROR FINDS REFUGE IN CONSTANTINOPLE

(From A. Voigt and I. Hausherr, "Oraison funèbre de Basil I" par son fils Léon le Sage," *Orientalia Christiana* [1932], vol. 6, pt. 1, p. 51.)

From the time of his infancy and during his adolescence, the All-powerful, by means of several signs, predicted to him [Emperor Basil I] that he would secure the imperial throne. [So for the first time the impoverished Basil made the long journey to Constantinople to enter the service of Emperor Michael III.] Then, very fatigued, he did not think he could do better than to lie down just as he was, on the pavement, in a church which was dedicated to the defender of the truth, Diomides. And that martyr [Diomides] appeared on that very night, predicted to him his acquisition of the empire, [and] recommended to him to take care of his [Diomides'] church [building]. At the time it was not much more than a mass of ruins. But later when the oracle had come to pass, the church was magnificently restored through his [Basil's] active care . . . and placed in the hands of the monks.

185.

Introduction. The life of the poor in the larger cities must have been hard, especially after the fall of Egypt to the Persians in the seventh century, which led in 618 to the end of the distribution of free bread, hitherto doled out to the urban masses of Constantinople by the emperors. Invariably a large number of poor people, unable or unwilling to find work, became beggars in the streets of the capital city, relying on the Christian charity of passersby. In this selection describing the sometimes strange forms of charity assumed by a certain ninth-century ascetic named Andrew, we read of his encounter with a group of the poor in Constantinople.

THE POOR OF THE CAPITAL CITY

(From Nicephorus the Presbyter, *Vita S. Andreae Sali*, in MPG, vol. 111, col. 656.)

Some lovers of Christ gave to him [Andrew] money voluntarily, though he did not seek this. But Christ was looking out for him. As much as they gave, he accepted. During the whole day he received twenty to thirty [copper] pieces and more. He knew an out-of-the-way place where the poor gathered and he went there, holding in his hand the coins as if he were playing with them so they would not know what he was up to, and, sitting in the midst of these poor people, he played with the coins. When one of the poor tried to grab some of the coins, he struck him. Then the other beggars, running to the aid of their comrade, hit Andrew with their staves. He, taking this as a pretext for flight, then scattered all the coins and each grabbed some for himself and kept them.

186.

Introduction. The lifestyle of the urban aristocracy, in comparison to that of the middle class, much less the poor, was luxurious. Indeed at times their concerns seem to have been strikingly modern. In the following selection Emperor Leo VI issues an edict regulating the construction of balconies on the houses of the well-to-do, paying special attention to protecting their view of Constantinople and its surroundings (see selection 325).

SPACE REGULATIONS FOR CONSTANTINOPLE'S RESIDENTIAL BUILDINGS WITH BALCONIES

(From *Les novelles de Léon VI le Sage*, ed. P. Noailles and A. Dain [Paris, 1944], no. 113, p. 373.)

The regulations established elsewhere by the ancients on the subject of building houses as well as walls are excellent ones, and very justly the space between adjoining inheritances has been fixed to amount to a maximum length of ten feet. But the condition of these constructions [houses] with respect to those that are called balcony-belvederes (which take their name from the sun, being called *solaria*) has received at law neither mention nor regulation. This condition is now in need of decision, that is, [we need] to define and resolve the difficulties that, as might be expected, can arise.

Thus we decree that also for these constructions, the *solaria*, the space between neighboring properties should conform to the measure which has been fixed for the properties erected. And in effect the same [is true] for these last [*solaria*], that because of the view one has fixed on a space of ten feet: similarly, it is for the same reason here that one will justly fix the same space, although one might be able to demand, because of this view, a greater distance. If, then, it is to prevent the first from having a better view than the second, that the adjoining inheritance be separated by ten feet, here it would be necessary to separate them all the more since the kinds of construction are better suited in this regard. For it is certain that he who is seated in his house or who is engaged in some task, is not visible because of the numerous obstacles which interpose themselves. But in these tasks on the balcony (or, as many say, corbel) in question, no obstacle obstructs their view. . . .

That is why we have decreed that no one can construct a building of this kind unless at least ten feet separate him from his neighbor. Also, if one desirous of altering the roof of his house recovers it with plaques of marble, he cannot carry out this change unless he separates himself from his neighbor by at least the said ten feet. But if another kind of qualification is involved, namely, that a very long interval of time has elapsed since the building has been constructed, the legal rule of delay [applies], or indeed of a right based on a friendly accord in virtue of which the beneficiary has proceeded to construction; [thus] we decree that the work remain in the state in which it is without having to observe the interval of ten feet.

187.

Introduction. The urban aristocracy, the highest class in Constantinople, technically was, in part at least, lineally descended from the senators whom Constantine had brought from old Rome when he transferred his capital to Constantinople. Though the wealth of these aristocrats consisted largely of their country estates, their preferred residence was certainly the so-phisticated capital—the *megalopolis,* the Queen City, or simply "the City"—where they were frequently in attendance at court, participating in the lavish ceremonials and in the complex court intrigues.

These landed magnates constituted only one part of the urban aristocracy. Another perhaps even more important part consisted of families who tended to monopolize the high posts in the civil bureaucracy. Michael Psellus (1018–c. 1079), historian, personal secretary to the emperor, and egotist par excellence, has left us a self-portrait in his *Chronographia.* The man his writings reveal may be taken as not untypical of these self-confident, often arrogant, civil aristocrats of the capital bureaucracy.

MICHAEL PSELLUS: SELF-PORTRAIT

(From Michael Psellus, *Chronographie,* ed. E. Rénauld [Paris, 1926], vol. 1, pp. 138–40.)

As to my career, even before the fruit was mature, the blossom foreshadowed an (illustrious) future. The emperor himself did not yet know me, but his entire entourage did, some recounting to him one of my abilities, others praising another, while also adding that eloquence graced my lips. And I shall say something about this here. At the time of our birth, certain natural virtues or their opposites are bestowed upon us. By "virtue" I mean not ethical virtue or political, or whatever surpasses and attains to the ideal or perfection of the Creator. But rather, just as certain bodies at their very birth come into the world endowed with beauty while on others nature bestows from the very beginning blemishes and wrinkles, so certain souls may be immediately distinguished as most graceful and cheerful, while others are somber and drag along with them deep gloom. In time, the innate graces of the first type become increasingly apparent, but in the second case, everything miscarries, and not even rational thought is well organized [in them].

At any rate, I have been informed that my speech is elegant, even in simple phrases, and without my striving for it a natural mellifluousness flows forth. I would not of course be aware of this, if many had not told me so in the course of conversation, and if they had not listened to me attentively. This [quality] first brought me into contact with the emperor, the eloquence of my language thus constituting my entrée to him and providing a foretaste of my innermost spirit. When I first entered his presence I expressed myself without fluency or elegance; yet I described my family and the kind of preparation I had received in literature. The emperor [Constantine IX], like those who are overcome with divine rapture without others observing it, was as a result seized by a boundless joy. And he almost embraced me, so affected was he at the sound of my voice. For others access to him was fixed and limited, but for me, on the other hand, the doors of his heart were opened and, as little by little I grew closer to him, all of his secrets were revealed to me. May no one blame me if I have digressed somewhat from the main theme of my work, nor see in this a display of personal vanity. For if I say something of this nature, it is actually entirely relevant to the aim of my history. For it was not possible otherwise to speak of my entry [into the imperial presence] without first indicating the cause, and since I wished to reveal this cause, it was necessary to relate some details about myself.

188.

Introduction. The eunuchs residing in the capital city constituted another element in the social fabric of the empire up to about the time of the Latin conquest. During the earlier centuries they were looked upon with scorn not only because of their sexual inadequacy but because most of them were foreign-born. By the ninth century, however, when they were generally native-born Byzantines, society tended to look upon them somewhat more favorably, especially since a surprising number were men of unusual ability who were able to achieve the elevated status of imperial minister or keeper of the imperial wardrobe or bedchamber (*protovestiarios* or *parakoimomenos*). Because of their inability to produce offspring to whom they could transmit their possessions and power, eunuchs were particularly useful to the emperors who could command their personal loyalty. Sometimes, as in the tenth century, a eunuch such as the *praepositus* Baanes, the *parakoimomenos* Basil, or the *parakoimomenos* Joseph Bringas conducted affairs of state in the absence of the emperor on military campaigns. And several even became patriarchs of Constantinople. Indeed in order to aid in the career of their sons, some parents, despite imperial prohibition of the practice, went so far as to have them castrated.

The changed image of the eunuch in the Byzantine mind of the ninth and tenth centuries is shown in the following selection from the *Novellae* of Emperor Leo VI, which views their deformity compassionately as a deformity of the work of God, and even allowed eunuchs to adopt children.

A. Edict of Leo VI regarding Eunuchs

(From *Les novelles de Léon VI le Sage*, ed. P. Noailles and A. Dain [Paris, 1944], no. 60, p. 223.)

Our Majesty, being of the view that it is good not to add onto the hardship that the eunuchs have undergone from men, a second liability on the part of the law, decrees that, if any eunuch wishes to adopt a child, this should not be hindered. For I believe that this benefit seems the more necessary especially where the greatest gain may be realized. For the eunuchs in particular, legal adoption is all the more advantageous because only in this way can they become fathers; and so they will be able to enjoy the cares which children give—cares of which it is not humane to deprive them simply because they have already been deprived of their sexual organs.

Introduction. Eunuchs constituted a special category in the bureaucracy. But their position was not an easy one: the general Byzantine population still tended to mock them, and one particular emperor who made use of their services even called them "of an effeminate soul, perverse by natural predilection, alert to invent many kinds of mischief and to carry such out . . . ; they are instruments of moral depravity, instructors in illicit arts, and harbingers of vice." In the following selection Michael Psellus of the eleventh century discusses the character—this time in some respects praiseworthy—of the eunuch John the Orphanotrophos, brother of Emperor Michael IV.

B. The Eunuch John the Orphanotrophos

(From Michael Psellus, *Chronographie*, ed. E. Rénauld [Paris, 1926], vol. 1, pp. 59–60.)

I wish to say something more concerning John, but I shall relate nothing which is vacuous or a lie. For I personally observed this man at an age when I was beginning to grow a beard, and I listened to him speak and witnessed him in action. I have thus made a careful assessment of his character. I realize that some of his actions were highly admirable while others were not. In that period his character consisted of various facets: he was quick-thinking and if any man ever was shrewd it was he; and his piercing eyes revealed these qualities. He carried out his duties with great care, indeed in an extremely industrious manner. He was highly experienced in all aspects of government, but he showed himself to be most intelligent and shrewd in matters of public finance. Not wishing to be a source of trouble but at the same time not desirous of being slighted by anyone, he did no harm to any person, though in his dealings with people his countenance would become fierce, thereby filling all with fear. His very appearance was a source of distress to many. Indeed many, shuddering at the very sight of him, abandoned their evil ways. He was truly a bulwark for the emperor, as well as a brother. During neither days nor nights did he relax from his concerns. Even when involved in his own pleasures or when attending festivities, ceremonies, or public festivals, he did not neglect those duties which were incumbent upon him. Nothing at all escaped his notice nor did anyone wish to do so, for everyone feared him and dreaded his vigilance. At untimely hours of the night he would suddenly ride off on his horse and examine every section of the capital, passing through all of the inhabited quarters at once like a flash of lightning. Since all were suspicious of these random inspections, they concealed themselves and shut themselves in; everyone remained in his own home and public gatherings [tended to] disappear.

Such were the qualities for which John may be commended, but he had others of an opposite sort. His nature was changeable, for he accommodated himself so as to agree with every opinion [expressed] in his presence. In the course of the same interview he would appear to be of several minds. From afar he would criticize those persons who approached him, but when they drew near he would receive them graciously, as if only then seeing them for the first time. And if anyone brought him some information such as was able to preserve the empire, John, in order not to be beholden to anyone, would pretend that he had known about the matter for some time and would reproach the informant for his slowness. The latter went away feeling ashamed, while John took appropriate measures, and, at an early stage, completely excised the trouble. He wished to spend his life in greater magnificence and to manage [public] affairs in a truly imperial manner, but his character constituted an impediment to this ambition, since he was unable to purge his nature of his innate greed. Wherefore, once he had begun to drink (and he was certainly dominated by this habit), he forthwith reveled in every kind of indecency. Yet not even then did he lose sight of concerns of state, nor did he ever relax the savage-beast look on his face or the solemnity of his expression.

189.

Introduction. Another segment of the population in many cities, especially Constantinople, was the Jewish community. Unlike pagans and heretics, the Jews were in general not persecuted in Byzantium. They were tolerated and usually not to be subjected to forcible conversion. Nonetheless, they were set apart from the Orthodox Christians by certain more or less severe civil disabilities. In the following passage from the Theodosian Code it is specified that Jews were to be excluded from the imperial service. The rather mild provision of this code was with certain exceptions to mark Byzantine policy toward the Jews in later centuries.

The Theodosian Code and Jews

A. A Grudging Religious Toleration (412)

(Translated by C. Pharr, *The Theodosian Code* [Princeton, 1952], 16-8-21), pp. 469–70.)

No person shall be trampled upon when he is innocent, on the ground that he is a Jew, nor shall any religion cause any person to be exposed to contumely. Their synagogues and habitations shall not be burned indiscriminately, nor shall they be injured wrongfully without any reason; moreover, even if any person should be implicated in crimes, nevertheless, the vigor of our courts and the protection of public law appear to have been established in Our midst for the purpose that no person should have the power to seek his own revenge.

But just as it is Our will that the foregoing provision shall be made for the persons of the Jews, so We decree that the Jews also shall be admonished that they shall not by any chance become insolent and, elated by their own security, commit any rash act in disrespect of the Christian religion.

B. Prohibited from Imperial Service (418)

(From Pharr, *The Theodosian Code*, 16-18-24, p. 470.)

Those persons who live in the Jewish superstition shall hereafter be barred from seeking entrance to the imperial service. To these persons who have undertaken the oaths of enlistment in the imperial service as members of the secret service or as palatines We grant the right to complete such service and to end it within the statutory periods. . . . We decree, however, that those persons who are bound to the perversity of this race and who are proved to have sought armed imperial service shall unquestionably be released from the cincture of office, and they shall not be protected by the patronage of their earlier merits. However, We do not prohibit Jews instructed in liberal studies from acting as advocates, and We permit them to enjoy the honor of the compulsory public service of decurions, which they obtain through the prerogative of birth and splendor of family.

190.

Introduction. The following selection is from the Byzantine monk Antiochus Strategos on the fall of Jerusalem to the Persians in 614. It shows not only the prevailing Byzantine prejudice against the Jews but also reflects the fact that the Jews had, at times, sought to escape the Byzantine restrictions placed upon them by aiding the Persian and later the Arab enemies of the empire, whom they often viewed as "liberators."

The Jews, "Betrayers" of Jerusalem to the Persians

(Translated by F. Conybeare, "Antiochus Strategos' Account of the Sack of Jerusalem (614)," *English Historical Review* 25 [1910]: 508.)

Thereupon the vile Jews, enemies of the truth and haters of Christ, when they perceived that the Christians were given over into the hands of the enemy, rejoiced exceedingly, because they detested the Christians; and they conceived an evil plan in keeping with their vileness about the people. For in the eyes of the Persians their importance was great, because they were the betrayers of the Christians. And in this season then the Jews approached the edge of the reservoir and called out to the children of God, while they were shut up therein, and said to them: "If ye would escape from death, become Jews and deny Christ; and then ye shall step up from your place and join us. We will ransom you with our money, and ye shall be benefited by us." But their plot and desire were not fulfilled, their labours proved to be in vain; because the children of Holy Church chose death for Christ's sake rather than to live in godlessness: and they reckoned it better for their flesh to be punished, rather than their souls ruined, so that their portion were not with the Jews. And when the unclean Jews saw the steadfast uprightness of the Christians and their immovable faith, then they were agitated with lively ire, like evil beasts, and thereupon imagined another plot. As of old they bought the Lord from the Jews with silver, so they purchased Christians out of the reservoir; for they gave the Persians silver, and they bought a Christian and slew him like a sheep. The Christians however rejoiced because they were being slain for Christ's sake and shed their blood for His blood, and took on themselves death in return for His death. . . .

When the people were carried into Persia, and the Jews were left in Jerusalem, they began with their own hands to demolish and burn such of the holy churches as were left standing. . . .

How many souls were slain in the reservoir of Mamel! How many perished of hunger and thirst! How many priests and monks were massacred by the sword! How many infants were crushed under foot, or perished by hunger and thirst, or languished through fear and horror of the foe! How many maidens, refusing their abominable outrages, were given over to death by the enemy! How many parents perished on top of their own children! How many of the people were bought up by the Jews and butchered, and became confessors of Christ! How many persons, fathers, mothers, and tender infants, having concealed themselves in fosses and cisterns, perished of darkness and hunger! How many fled into the Church of the Anastasis, into that of Sion and other churches, and were therein massacred and consumed with fire! Who can count the multitude of the corpses of those who were massacred in Jerusalem?

191.

Introduction. The official policy of grudging toleration toward the Jews was followed until the reign of Justinian, who, because of his insistence on unity of faith within the empire, began to persecute not only the Jews but—together with the long-persecuted Manichaeans—the Nestorians, the Monophysites, and others who deviated from the Orthodox faith. The clearest and most damaging laws against the Jews were issued, however, by Leo III, the Isaurian, in the early eighth century, who attempted to force baptism upon them. Leo's reasons were unclear, but he may well have been influenced by a desire to gain divine favor in view of the renewed Muslim Arab threat to Constantinople. In addition, he was reacting to the influence Jews had gained, for from the seventh century on Byzantine theological polemic became very concerned, among other things, with Jewish attacks upon Christianity. Later emperors too at times resorted to forcible conversion or imposed restrictions on Jews. The following is the edict of Leo VI (886–912) prescribing that Jews must live in accordance with the rites of Christianity or suffer the consequences of apostasy.

JEWS SHALL LIVE IN ACCORDANCE WITH THE RITES OF CHRISTIANITY

(Translated by H. Agylaeus, from the *New Constitutions of Leo VI*, in S. Scott, ed., *The Civil Law* [Cincinnati: Central Trust Company, 1932], vol. 17, p. 255.)

Those who formerly were invested with Imperial authority promulgated various laws with reference to the Hebrew people, who, once nourished by Divine protection, became renowned, but are now remarkable for the calamities inflicted upon them because of their contumacy towards Christ and God; and these laws, while regulating their mode of life, compelled them to read the Holy Scriptures, and ordered them not to depart from the ceremonies of their worship. They also provided that their children should adhere to their religion, being obliged to do so as well by the ties of blood, as on account of the institution of circumcision. These are the laws which I have already stated were formerly enforced throughout the Empire. But the Most Holy Sovereign from whom We are descended, more concerned than his predecessors for the salvation of the Jews, instead of allowing them (as they did) to obey only their ancient laws, attempted, by the interpretation of prophesies and the conclusions which he drew from them, to convert them to the Christian religion, by means of the vivifying water of baptism. He fully succeeded in his attempts to transform them into new men, according to the doctrine of Christ, and induced them to denounce their ancient doctrines and abandon their religious ceremonies, such as circumcision, the observance of the Sabbath, and all their other rites. But although he, to a certain extent, overcame the obstinacy of the Jews, he was unable to force them to abolish the laws which permitted them to live in accordance with their ancient customs.

Therefore We desiring to accomplish what Our Father failed to effect, do hereby annul all the old laws enacted with reference to the Hebrews, and We order that they shall not dare to live in any other manner than in accordance with the rules established by the pure and salutary Christian Faith. And if anyone of them should be proved to have neglected to observe the ceremonies of the Christian religion, and to have returned to his former practices, he shall pay the penalty prescribed by the law for apostates.

Commentary. This severe-sounding edict of Leo VI was however only sporadically enforced and in time the Jews were again free to practice their religious rites. A number of Jews in the later period (especially after 1261) became dressers of furs and tanners of hides and lived in a quarter (called Vlanka) situated just outside the city wall. In summary, it may be said that, in contrast to the often violent persecution in the medieval West, the history of the Jews in Byzantium was in general one of relative toleration marked by sporadic persecution and permanent civil disabilities. The Jews lived in rather close association with the Byzantine Christians but they were usually denigrated by the latter.

192.

Introduction. In some respects the zenith of Byzantine urban life came in the twelfth century after the recovery of the empire from its semicollapse in the mid-eleventh century (see introduction). The following is an account by the (late) twelfth-century traveler, Benjamin, a Jew of Tudela, Spain, who describes Constantinople and other urban centers of the empire during the Comnenan period. Although Benjamin was primarily interested in Jewish communities in the East, he provides interesting insights about the Byzantine population as well.

A Spanish Jew's View of Byzantine Cities

(Translated by A. Sharf, *Byzantine Jewry* [New York, 1971], pp. 134–36.)

Thebes is a large city with about two thousand Jews. They are the best in the land of Greece at making garments of silk and of purple cloth. . . . There are none like them in all the land of Greece, except for the city of Constantinople. Salonica . . . is a very large city with about five hundred Jews. . . . The Jews suffer oppression there. They work in the silk industry. Constantinople is the capital of all the lands of Yavan which is called Greece. And there is the throne of King Manuel, the emperor. He has twelve kings under him, each with his own palace in Constantinople. They possess castles and cities and they rule over the whole land. . . .

. . . The city of Constantinople is eighteen miles in circumference, half towards the sea and half towards the land.* It lies between two arms of the sea: one which flows from the Sea of Russia, one from Spain. . . . The Greeks who live there have a wealth of gold and jewels. They walk about dressed in silk, with patterns of gold sewn or embroidered on their garments. They ride their horses like princes. . . . It has men learned in all the books of the Greeks. . . . But to fight their wars against Mas'ud, King of the Turks, they hire men from all the nations they call "strangers," for they have no stomach for fighting and are weak as women in war. . . . The Greeks hate the Jews, whether good or bad, and hold them under a heavy yoke. . . . Yet the Jews are rich, kind and charitable. They observe the commandments of Scripture and cheerfully bear the yoke of their oppression. The name of the place where the Jews live is Pera [across the Golden Horn from Constantinople].

*According to Eustathius of Thessalonika, Constantinople at this time had a population of 60,000 Venetians (he probably meant Latins in general).

193.

Introduction. In 1261 the reconqueror of Constantinople from the Latins, Michael VIII, sought to restore the capital and its population to their former condition, as we see from the following several passages taken from the historians Gregoras and Pachymeres.

A. Michael VIII Restores His Capital City (1261)

(From Nicephorus Gregoras, *Byzantina historia*, ed. I. Bekker and L. Schopen [Bonn, 1829], vol. 1, pp. 87–88.)

Constantinople was then an enormous desolate city, full of ruins and stones, of houses razed to the ground, and of the few remains of the great fire. . . . Enslaved, it had received no care from the Latins except destruction of every kind day and night. The first and most important immediate task facing the emperor was as much as possible to cleanse the city and transform its great disorder into good order, to strengthen the churches which had completely collapsed, and to fill the emptied houses with people.

B. Repopulation of Constantinople

(From Pachymeres, *De Michaele et Andronico Palaeologis* [Bonn, 1835], vol. 1, pp. 163–64 and 168.)

His first task within the city was to bring in and settle those people who had fled earlier to settle along the sea, and second to distribute (by lot) to those outside and inside the city, lands for cultivation. . . . Also to award rich lands to the monasteries. And third, for those who were [living] crowded together, to provide a place on which they could build. . . . He had in mind from necessity the repopulation of the city with light-armed soldiers. After distributing land in the city to a great many Laconians who had just come from the Morea, he gave them places to live—lands which were distributed—and he rewarded them with annual payments and many other acts of magnanimity both within and outside the city, since these Laconians have great usefulness in war.

194.

Introduction. During the fourteenth century there occurred in Thessalonika what seems to have been a "popular" urban revolt. This revolt is interesting not only because it was directed against unpopular measures of the government, but because it may even have taken on aspects of a class struggle between the lower and the upper strata of society. Actually the population of Thessalonika seems to have consisted of several classes: a small group of provincial nobility, a fairly large middle class including great merchants, tradesmen, and craftsmen, and, finally, the poor or the common people. (One may add to these a considerable number of monks and priests, in particular visiting monks from neighboring Mt. Athos.) The tension between these various classes—especially the dissatisfaction of the lower classes with the rich, whether civil administrators or churchmen—became particularly serious in the mid-fourteenth century. In 1342 a group (probably) consisting mainly of the malcontent poor fomented the so-called "Zealot Revolution" which expelled the nobles and confiscated their property. The causes of this famous revolution are not entirely clear, though it is known that such urban unrest was common in Byzantium in this period (and in the West as well).*

With the support of the "guild" of the sailors, the Zealot party shared control of the city government with government administrators sent from Constantinople. But following a massacre in 1345 of a hundred or more members of the upper class, the Zealots succeeded in establishing a virtual republic. Only in 1350 was Emperor John Cantacuzene able to reimpose imperial control over the city.

The following selection, though from the pen of John Cantacuzene, an opponent of the Zealots, reveals something of the movement's aims and mood.

THE ZEALOT REVOLT

(From John Cantacuzene, *Historia* [Bonn, 1831], vol. 2, pp. 234–35.)

In Thessalonika, since the *protostrator*, as we said, was doubtful over which emperor to associate himself with and openly pondered the matter, something even more reprehensible occurred—he tolerated the so-called Zealots, who chose to fight on behalf of the Palaeologan emperor against the Emperor Cantacuzene and who were gradually increasing in numbers. He did this on the one hand lest he should seem openly favorable to the side of Emperor Cantacuzene. For his wife and daughter, who were in Byzantium, . . . caused him great indecision, lest on account of him they be subjected to many misfortunes. This also made him indifferent [toward the Zealots], the fact that not only the garrison of Thessalonika, which was not small, but also the powerful members of the citizenry had chosen the side of the Emperor Cantacuzene (citizens whom he believed confidently would, whenever they might wish, suppress the Zealots).

And then, when the Zealots, on account of his [the *protostrator*'s] neglect, became somewhat greater in number, and when they incited the people [*demos*] against the rich [*dynatoi*], and when the *protostrator* was recognized as doing the bidding of the Emperor Cantacuzene, the Zealots attacked in a mob and drove out from the city about a thousand people. A small crowd formed as a result of the skirmishing, in which a few even of the household of the *protostrator* were wounded, and they also captured some of the rich [*dynatoi*] who were unable to escape along with the others at the time of the first attack. After the Zealots had taken possession of the city, they rushed to the houses of the fugitives and razed them and seized their goods and did other things, things that men would do who were driven by poverty and urged on to reckless violence on account of the immense wealth [of the rich]. They came to such a point of murder and audacity that some dared even the most terrible things. Seizing the cross from the holy sanctuary, they used it as a banner and said they were fighting under it (although they were actually led by the enemy of the cross). And if someone was involved in legal dispute with another, he, seizing the cross, displayed it alongside his opponent's house as if the cross itself had given a signal. And at once, it was [deemed] necessary to raze the house to its foundation, since the people [*demos*] were driven by irrational force and hope of profit.

For two or three days Thessalonika was devoured as if by enemy soldiers, and nothing was done there which was not customary for captured cities. The victors, at night and during the day, roved around in groups, expressed themselves with cries and shouting, and plundered and carried away the property of the vanquished. The victims, lamenting, hid in intolerable places, accepting the situation as inescapable, [fearing] lest suddenly they might be killed. Since the revolt would cease when corrupt citizens were lacking, the Zealots, who from the poorest and most ignoble status had suddenly become rich and arrogant, seized everything for themselves, and either drew the middle class toward them or forced them (reluctantly) to accept them. Or the Zealots condemned wisdom and reasonableness as being "Cantacuzenism." In Thessalonika, then, such things were happening.

*The civil war between adherents of Cantacuzene and of John V Palaeologus also played a role.

195.

Introduction. In the last decades of the Palaeologan period, as a result especially of over half a century of intermittent Turkish sieges and pressures on the capital—which caused hundreds, rather thousands, of Greeks to flee to other areas (primarily Italy, and Venice in particular)—the city of Constantinople had largely fallen into disrepair, with the population declining at the end to only some fifty to seventy thousand persons. The historian George Sphrantzes relates that, at the beginning of the final siege of Constantinople in 1453 by the Ottoman Turks, the Emperor Constantine XI had a count made of all men able to bear arms and it totaled only 4,973 men.

A DEPOPULATED CAPITAL

(From George Sphrantzes, *Chronikon*, ed. I. Bekker [Bonn, 1838], p. 240.)

The number of men who were in the city to oppose such a great [Turkish] army were four thousand, nine-hundred and seventy-three, without the foreigners who numbered barely two thousand men. I knew this was true for the following reason: the emperor had ordered the demarchs and generals to register exactly everyone in his area, both the laymen able to stand guard as well as the monks, and [to find out] what weapons each of them had for defense. Thus each of the demarchs gave a listing of his area to the emperor. Then he, calling me, said, "This service concerns you and should be done but in secret. Take the lists of the census and go to your home. Calculate exactly how many men there are and what weapons and shields and arrows and war machines there are." When I finished what the emperor had asked of me I returned to my lord emperor, pale and in sorrow. And the numbers remained secret, known only to him and to me.

C.
RESETTLEMENTS AND FORCED MIGRATIONS

196.

Introduction. The governmental policy of Byzantium was above all directed by and for the overriding interests of the state. Though Byzantine Christian principles of course emphasized the worth of the individual, the individual's role in areas other than religion was usually subordinated to the political exigencies of the state. This may be seen especially in the imperial attempts to reorganize the empire as early as the later seventh and eighth centuries. At that time and also later, entire peoples, especially dangerous minority groups, might be transported from one section of the empire to another. Heretical Paulicians, for example, were in the tenth century transported by Emperor John Tzimisces from their home in eastern Asia Minor to severely depopulated Thrace, where they were given lands in the aim of having them serve as a buffer against enemy incursions. Similarly, Slavs of the Balkans were at various times transplanted to Asia Minor and even to the Syrian frontier to repopulate areas devastated by the Arabs or to serve in the army.

Ethnic and cultural changes also resulted from voluntary emigration to escape religious persecution. Noteworthy was the re-Hellenization of Calabria in southern Italy and especially Sicily by Byzantine monks (and sometimes laymen) who fled there seeking to escape the Persian and Arab invasions and, later, the fury of the Iconoclastic emperors. These monks transformed areas originally Greek, then subsequently largely Latin in language and culture, into outposts of Byzantine civilization.

The following excerpts from the lives of three popes included in the famous *Liber pontificalis*, allow us to infer that by the middle of the seventh century there was a very sizable Greek population in Sicily, part of which had emigrated from the Byzantine East.

BYZANTINE REFUGEES IN SOUTHERN ITALY AND SICILY

(From *Liber pontificalis*, ed. L. Duchesne [Paris, 1955], vol. 1, pp. 359, 368, 371.)

Leo the younger, Sicilian by nation, whose father was Paul, sat ten months and seventeen days, a very eloquent man, sufficiently instructed in divine Scripture, erudite in Greek and Latin languages and especially in chanting and psalmody. . . .

Conon, born of a Thracian father, educated in Sicily, after coming to Rome assumed the honor of presbyter of this church. . . .

Sergius, Syrian by nation of the region of Antioch, was born of a father named Tiberius in Palermo, Sicily, sat twelve years, eight months, twenty-three days. Coming to Rome in the pontificate of Adeodatus of holy memory [pope from 672 to 676], he was included among the clergy of the Roman church.

197.

Introduction. The selection which follows, in contrast, illustrates a resettlement dictated by state policy. It is a celebrated passage from the *Chronicle of Monemvasia*, recording the reestablishment in Patras in the early ninth century, by the emperor, of the Byzantine population which had fled to southern Italy before the invading Avars and their tributary Slavic troops.

THE RESETTLEMENT OF PATRAS

(From "The Chronicle of Monemvasia," ed. N. Bees, in *Byzantis* [1909], vol. 1, pp. 37ff.)

In another incursion they [the Avars] placed under their control all of Thessaly and Greece, Old Epirus, Attica, and Euboia. They attacked and forcibly subjugated the Peloponnesus, expelling and destroying the noble and Hellenic peoples, and they themselves settled there. Those Greeks who were able to flee from the blood-stained hands of the Avars scattered themselves in various places: the inhabitants of the city of Patras resettled in the area of Rhegium in Calabria, the Argives on that island called Orobe, and the Corinthians came to dwell on the island named Aegina. At this same time some of the Lakones, abandoning their ancestral homeland, sailed off to the island of Sicily, and even today they are still in an area of Sicily called Demena, calling themselves Demenitai instead of Lacedaemonians but preserving their own Laconian dialect. Others discovered an inaccessible region [in the Peloponnesus] on the coast, and founded a strong city there—naming it Monemvasia because there was only one entrance to it—and they settled there with their own bishop. Their herdsmen and farmers settled in rugged areas in the vicinity and have recently been called Tzaconians. Thus the Avars, after they had conquered the Peloponnesus and settled there, held it for 218 years, that is from the year [587 A.D.], after creation of the world 6096 the sixth year of the reign of Maurice, until 6313 [805 A.D.] which was the fourth year of the reign of the elder Nicephorus, whose son was Stauracius.

They were under the control of neither the Roman emperor nor anyone else. Only the eastern portion of the Peloponnesus, from Corinth to Malea, remained free from the Slavic nation on account of the rugged and inaccessible terrain in these areas. The Roman emperor used to appoint a "*strategos* of the Peloponnesus" over this region. One of these *strategoi*, a member of the Scleros family from Lesser Armenia, attacked the Slavic tribes, defeated and utterly destroyed them, and enabled the ancient inhabitants to recover their possessions. When he heard about this, the above-mentioned Emperor Nicephorus became filled with joy and desired to restore the cities there, to rebuild the churches which the barbarians had destroyed, and to convert these barbarians to Christianity. Wherefore, having made inquiry concerning the colony in which the [former] inhabitants of Patras dwelled, he ordered that they be resettled, along with their own bishop (who at that time was named Athanasius) on their former lands. He also granted to Patras the privileges of a metropolitanate; previously it had enjoyed the status of an archbishopric. And he rebuilt their city and the holy churches of God from the ground up, while Tarasius was still patriarch.

198.

Introduction. One of the most striking examples of state policy of population transfer is the action of Emperor John Tzimisces (969–76) in moving to Thrace (especially to the town of Philippopolis) an entire people, the heretical Paulicians. They, however, were put there not only to separate them from their kinsmen in eastern Asia Minor—and thus weaken resistance there to the Byzantine state (as already noted)—but so that they could act as a buffer against the Bulgars who repeatedly threatened Constantinople.

FORCED RESETTLEMENT OF THE PAULICIANS

(From Anna Comnena, *Alexiade*, ed. B. Leib [Paris, 1945], vol. 3, pp. 178–81.)

At one time, it seems, Philippopolis had been a great and beautiful city. But since the ancient period when the Tauroi and Scythians had enslaved the city, it was reduced to the state in which we found it during the reign of my father—a state which leads us to conjecture that it had once been a great city. It had suffered among other things from the fact that many heretics resided there. For the Armenians took possession of this city, and also the so-called Bogomils, about whom and whose heresy we shall later speak at an opportune time.

Moreover, there lived there the completely ungodly Paulicians, a separate branch of the Manichaeans, who as their name indicates, were followers of Paul and John,* and who became imbued with the impiety of Mani which they transmitted undiluted to their followers. I would have liked to outline summarily the doctrine of the Manichaeans and to hasten to refute their atheistic doctrines. But since I realize that the heresy of the Manichaeans is regarded by all as ridiculous and since I am at the same time eager to continue my account, I shall omit this refutation. . . .

These disciples of Mani and of Paul and John, the sons of Callinike, who were very savage and crude in their beliefs and did not hesitate to shed blood for them—these, that remarkable ruler among emperors, John Tzimisces, conquered in battle. Leading them out of Asia as slaves, he transported them from the lands of the Chalybes and Armenians to Thrace. He forced them to reside in the area around Philippopolis, first because he wanted to expel them from their fortified cities and castles which they tyrannically ruled, and also because he knew that they would be the most secure guardians against the incursions of the Scythians, from which the territory around Thrace had often suffered. For the Scythians used to cross the mountain passes of the Haemus and to overrun the plains below.. . . .

But John Tzimisces, having transformed our enemies of the Manichaean heresy into allies, established them as a worthy force of arms against these Scythian nomads. Henceforth the urban areas, delivered from most of these raids, breathed freely again. However, the Manichaeans, who were free and unsubmissive by nature, comported themselves in their customary manner and reverted to their usual conduct. Since all the people of Philippopolis except for a few were Manichaeans, they tyrannized over the Christians there and seized their belongings, caring little or nothing for the messengers from the emperor. Their number then increased and all those in the vicinity of Philippopolis were heretics. And there joined them now also another distasteful stream, that of the Armenians, and still another from the filthiest springs of Jacob. And the city was, so to say, the confluence of all impurities, for even if the others [the immigrants] differed [from them] with respect to beliefs, they agreed with the Manichaeans in their seditious spirit.

* Paul and John, it seems, were brothers who lived in Samosata, a center of Manichaeism. These are not the New Testament Paul and John.

199.

Introduction. The following selection mentions the defeat and capture of a large group of Serbs and their subsequent settlement (1129–30) in Asia Minor in the area of Nicomedia by Emperor John II Comnenus.

RESETTLEMENT OF SLAVS IN ASIA MINOR

(From Nicetas Choniates, *Historia*, ed. I. Van Dieten [Berlin, 1975], vol. 1, p. 16.)

But a little later he [Emperor John II] proclaimed a military campaign against the nation of the Triballians—others would call them Serbs—which was ravaging the area and breaking the truce. From them he took an immense booty and he gave many of the benefits of it to his army. And he moved to the East the greater part of those taken in battle and he assigned to them as a place to live the territory around Nicomedia. After dividing up a very ample amount of land [among them] he recruited some of them into his army and others he made tributary.

D.
COMMERCE AND INDUSTRY IN BYZANTIUM

200.

Introduction. Although agriculture was the lifeblood of the Byzantine economy, commerce and to a lesser extent industry from the beginning also played a very important role in the economic life of the empire. Constantinople was the major trade entrepôt between East and West, uniting the Latin West with the Persians and (later) the Muslim world, and even bringing contacts with the Indies far in the East. In the early centuries, Byzantine merchants (along with Jewish and Syrian inhabitants of the empire) were active all along the vast trade routes stretching from Spain to the Far East. The range of the Byzantine merchant can be seen in the following brief selections. The first is by the early sixth-century Byzantine merchant-sailor (and later monk) Cosmas Indicopleustes (the "sailor-around-the Indies").

BYZANTINE TRADE WITH THE FAR EAST

(Translated by J. McKindle, *The Christian Topography of Cosmas Indicopleustes* [London: Hakluyt Society, 1897], pp. 47, 53, 356.)

Now this country of silk is situated in the remotest of all the Indies, and lies to the left of those who enter the Indian sea, far beyond the Persian Gulf, and the island called by the Indians Selediba [Ceylon]. . . . The island being, as it is, in a central position, is much frequented by ships from all parts of India and from Persia and Ethiopia, and it likewise sends out many of its own. And from the remotest countries, I mean Tzinitza [China] and other trading places, it receives silk, aloes, cloves, sandalwood, and other products and these again are passed on to marts on this side.

201.

Introduction. Byzantine traders were also to be found in the Latin West in appreciable numbers in the early medieval centuries. The following passage from the *History of the Franks* by the seventh-century bishop of Tours, Gregory, briefly refers to the so-called "Syrian" and also Jewish merchants in Gaul. These, coming originally from Byzantine areas, settled in the West but preserved their commercial contacts with the East.

GREGORY OF TOURS ON THE "SYRIAN" (BYZANTINE) MERCHANTS

(Translated by L. Thorpe, from Gregory of Tours, *History of the Franks* [London, 1974], p. 433.)

[When the (Merovingian) king entered Orleans] a vast crowd of citizens came out to meet him carrying flags and banners and singing songs in his praise. The speech of the Syrians contrasted sharply with that of the Jews, as they each sang his praises in their own tongue.

202.

Introduction. The Jewish traveler from Spain, Benjamin of Tudela, of the late twelfth century describes Constantinople and its multiethnic traders in the following manner:

CONSTANTINOPLE, EMPORIUM FOR THE WORLD

(Translated by A. Sharf, *Byzantine Jewry* [New York, 1971], p. 135.)

All kinds of merchants come [to Constantinople] from Babylon and Shin'ar, from Persia and Medea, from all the kingdoms of Egypt, from the land of Canaan, from the kingdom of Russia, from Hungary, from the land of the Petchenegs, from Khazaria, from Lombardy and from Spain. It is a tumultuous city; men come to trade there from all countries by land and by sea. There is none like it in all the world except for Baghdad, the great city which is Ishmael's. . . .Constantinople has countless buildings. Year by year tribute is brought to it from all the land of Greece, whereby castles are filled with garments of silk, purple and gold. Such buildings, such riches can be seen nowhere else in Greece. They say that the city's daily income, what with the rent from shops and markets and what with the customs levied on merchants coming by sea and by land, reaches twenty thousand gold pieces.

203.

Introduction. Merchants from the towns also, it seems, played a prominent role in Byzantine commerce, especially in the smaller fairs of the Byzantine countryside. For reference to such rural fairs (probably little more than weekly country markets) in the late tenth century, during the important reign of Emperor Basil II, we have the testimony of one of his legal enactments (996).

ON THE REGULATION OF RURAL FAIRS

(From J. and P. Zepos, ed., *Jus graecoromanum*, [Athens, 1931], vol. 1, pp. 271–72.)

We desire that that which has been called into question concerning the right of [holding] fairs receive an appropriate order. For some have been rendered impoverished, and they make accusation that, while formerly they held a fair established on their own property, the organizers of the fair went away and abandoned those former owners of the fair who found themselves deserted, while on the lands of those receiving them they established a new fair. We order, if ever at any time such a thing happens, if all the fair operators and merchants—both those native to the area and those from outside the area—depart as a group and of their own accord from the old owner of the fair and go to other lands, setting up a new fair, that they possess a free and unimpeded right to do so, if they wish to transfer the site of the fair, and they should not at all be compelled by force but voluntarily betake themselves there.

If, however, there occurs a dispute among the fair operators and some elect to remain in those places where previously they held the fair while others depart and establish themselves in other areas, then the distinction [priority] of time should prevail and the ones who have departed, whatever their number, should be joined in union with those who choose to stay; and the ancient right of the area should be in force. Since changes or transfers of fairs may be divided into four types (for transfers usually occur from the *dynatoi* [powerful] to the *dynatoi* or from the weak to the weak, or from the powerful to the weak, or the weak to the powerful), the things which have just been decreed shall apply only to the first three cases, that is to transfers from the powerful to powerful, or from the weak to weak, or from the strong to the weak. The fourth type, however, shall be the object of our more personal and more beneficent interpretation. For since the *dynatoi* have a strong tendency to withdraw fairs from the lawful possession of the weak, we decree that in this situation such removal shall not take place, that is, the transfer of a fair from the weak to the *dynatoi*, unless the entire fair is transferred without compulsion and altogether to another area in which a fair has already long been established, since there are two good reasons present in this case, the right of temporal priority and the assent and congregation of all members. For in the three other cases even one reason alone seemed to be enough, either simple agreement (when the entire fair is transferred) or merely priority of time (when the fair divides and splits into two parts); but in this fourth case we decree that there should be a conjunction of the two reasons in order that the transfer of fairs be legitimized from the weak to the *dynatoi*: the joint agreement of everyone and the right of priority of time.

I extend my hand completely therefore as a succor to the poor and I curb the excess of power of the *dynatoi*, a thing which was earlier the care also of my blessed [great] grandfather, Lord Romanus the Elder, concerning the alienations of lawfully owned immovable property from the weak to the *dynatoi*.

204.

Introduction. The site of the most famous fair in the Byzantine world came to be the city of Thessalonika, which in the last century or two ranked next to the capital itself in importance. There merchants came from all over the East as well as the West. This fair was probably larger in size than the famous contemporary fair at Champagne in France. The following selection, taken from the *Timarion*, a satirical work in imitation of the ancient writer Lucian, describes the fair of Thessalonika as it was in the mid-twelfth century, a period in which that city not only was of economic importance, but was becoming significant culturally as well.

The Great Fair at Thessalonika

(Translated by H. Tozer, "Byzantine Satire," *Journal of Hellenic Studies* 2 [1881]: 244–45.)

The Demetria is a festival, like the Panathenaea at Athens and the Panionia among the Milesians, and it is at the same time the most important fair held in Macedonia. Not only do the natives of the country flock together to it in great numbers, but multitudes also come from all lands and of every race—Greeks, wherever they are found, the various tribes of Mysians [i.e. people of Moesia] who dwell on our borders as far as the Ister and Scythia, Campanians and other Italians, Iberians, Lusitanians, and Transalpine Celts [this is the Byzantine way of describing the Bulgarians, &c., Neapolitans, Spaniards, Portuguese, and French]; and, to make a long story short, the shores of the ocean send pilgrims and suppliants to visit the martyr, so widely extended is his fame throughout Europe. For myself, being a Cappadocian from beyond the boundaries of the empire, [this country was now under the Seljouk sultans of Iconium] and having never before been present on the occasion, but having only heard it described, I was anxious to get a bird's eye view of the whole scene, that I might pass over nothing unnoticed. With this object I made my way up to a height close by the scene of the fair, where I sat down and surveyed everything at my leisure. What I saw there was a number of merchants' booths, set up in parallel rows opposite one another; and these rows extended to a great length, and were sufficiently wide apart to leave a broad space in the middle, so as to give free passage for the stream of the people. Looking at the closeness of the booths to one another and the regularity of their position, one might take them for lines drawn lengthwise from two opposite points. At right angles to these, other booths were set up, also forming rows, though of no great length, so that they resembled the tiny feet that grow outside the bodies of certain reptiles. Curious indeed it was, that while in reality there were two rows, they presented the appearance of a single animal, owing to the booths being so near and so straight; for the lines suggested a long body, while the crossrows at the sides looked like the feet that supported it. I declare, when I looked down from the heights above on the ground plan of the fair, I could not help comparing it to a centipede, a very long insect with innumerable small feet under its belly.

And if you are anxious to know what it contained, my inquisitive friend, as I saw it afterwards when I came down from the hills—well, there was every kind of material woven or spun by men or women, all those that come from Boeotia and the Peloponnese, and all that are brought in trading ships from Italy to Greece. Besides this, Phoenicia furnishes numerous articles, and Egypt, and Spain, and the pillars of Hercules, where the finest coverlets are manufactured. These things the merchants bring direct from their respective countries to old Macedonia and Thessalonica; but the Euxine also contributes to the splendour of the fair, by sending across its products to Constantinople, whence the cargoes are brought by numerous horses and mules. All this I went through and carefully examined afterwards when I came down; but even while I was still seated on the height above I was struck with wonder at the number and variety of the animals, and the extraordinary confusion of their noises which assailed my ears—horses neighing, oxen lowing, sheep bleating, pigs grunting, and dogs barking, for these also accompany their masters as a defence against wolves and thieves.

205.

Introduction. While the fairs in both city and countryside of the empire were generally administered by native Greek merchants, the carrying trade between Byzantium and the outside world, especially the West, from at least the tenth century onward passed increasingly into the hands of foreign merchants—and above all, to the Latins.

In the manual, *On the Administration of the Empire*, written c. 950 by the Byzantine Emperor Constantine Porphyrogenitus, we have an invaluable description, unique of its kind, of the famous Rus "Varangian" trade route in the tenth century, from Kiev north to the Baltic and from Kiev south to the Black Sea—and ultimately to Constantinople. This segment describes the portage techniques used by the Rus merchants to cross between the Dnieper and other rivers on the way to Byzantium.

THE VARANGIAN ROUTE TO CONSTANTINOPLE

(Translated by R. Jenkins, from Constantine Porphyrogenitus, *De administrando imperio*, ed. G. Moravcsik [Washington, D.C., 1967], pp. 57–63.)

The "monoxyla" [small boats] which come down from outer Russia to Constantinople are from Novgorod, where Sviatoslav, son of Igor, prince of Russia, had his seat, and others from the city of Smolensk and from Teliutza and Chernigov and from Vyshegrad. All these come down the river Dnieper, and are collected together at the city of Kiev, also called Sambatas. Their Slav tributaries, the so-called Krivichians and the Lenzanenes and the rest of the Slavonic regions, cut the "monoxyla" on their mountains in time of winter, and when they have prepared them, as spring approaches, and the ice melts, they bring them on to the neighbouring lakes. And since these [*lakes*] debouch into the river Dnieper, they enter thence on to this same river, and come down to Kiev, and draw [*the ships*] along to be finished and sell them to the Russians. The Russians buy these bottoms only, furnishing them with oars and rowlocks and other tackle from their old "monoxyla," which they dismantle; [*and so*] they fit them out. And in the month of June they move off down the river Dnieper and come to Vitichev, which is a tributary city of the Russians, and there they gather during two or three days; and when all the "monoxyla" are collected together, then they set out, and come down the said Dnieper river. And first they come to the first barrage, called Essoupi, which means in Russian and Slavonic "Do not sleep!"; the barrage itself is as narrow as the width of the Polo-ground; in the middle of it are rooted high rocks, which stand out like islands. Against these, then, comes the water and wells up and dashes down over the other side, with a mighty and terrific din. Therefore the Russians do not venture to pass between them, but put in to the bank hard by, disembarking the men on to dry land leaving the rest of the goods on board the "monoxyla"; they then strip and, feeling with their feet to avoid striking on a rock [lacuna]. This they do, some at the prow, some amidships, while others again, in the stern, punt with poles; and with all this careful procedure they pass this first barrage, edging round under the river-bank. When they have passed this barrage, they re-embark the others from the dry land and sail away, and come down to the second barrage, called in Russian Oulvorsi, and in Slavonic Ostrovouniprach, which means "the Island of the Barrage." This one is like the first, awkward and not to be passed through. Once again they disembark the men and convey the "monoxyla" past, as on the first occasion. Similarly they pass the third barrage also, called Gelandri, which means in Slavonic "Noise of the Barrage," and then the fourth barrage, the big one, called in Russian Aeifor, and in Slavonic Neasit, because the pelicans nest in the stones of the barrage. At this barrage all put into land prow foremost, and those who are deputed to keep the watch with them get out, and off they go, these men, and keep vigilant watch for the Pechenegs. The remainder, taking up the goods which they have on board the "monoxyla," conduct the slaves in their chains past by land, six miles, until they are through the barrage. Then, partly dragging their "monoxyla," partly portaging them on their shoulders, they convey them to the far side of the barrage; and then, putting them on the river and loading up their baggage, they embark themselves, and again sail off in them. When they come to the fifth barrage, called in Russian Varouforos, and in Slavonic Voulniprach, because it forms a large lake, they again convey their "monoxyla" through at the edges of the river, as at the first and second barrages, and arrive at the sixth barrage, called in Russian Leanti, and in Slavonic Veroutzi, that is "the Boiling of the Water," and this too they pass similarly. And thence they sail away to the seventh barrage, called in Russian Stroukoun, and in Slavonic Naprezi, which means "Little Barrage." This they pass at the so-called ford of [*Vrar*], where the Chersonites cross over from Russia and the Pechenegs to Cherson; which ford is as wide as the Hippodrome, and, measured upstream from the bottom as far as the rocks break surface, a bow-shot in length. It is at this point, therefore, that the Pechenegs come down and attack the Russians. After traversing this place, they reach the island called St. Gregory, on which island they perform their sacrifices because a gigantic oak-tree stands there; and they sacrifice live cocks. Arrows, too, they peg in round about, and others bread and meat, or something of whatever each may have, as is their custom. They also throw lots regarding the cocks, whether to slaughter them, or to eat them as well, or to leave them alive.

From this island onwards the Russians do not fear the Pecheneg until they reach the river Selinas. So then they start off thence and sail for four days, until they reach the lake which forms the mouth of the river, on which is the island of St. Aitherios. Arrived at this island, they rest themselves there for two or three days. And they re-equip their "monoxyla" with such tackle as is needed, sails and masts and rudders, which they bring with them. Since this lake is the mouth of this river, as has been said, and carries on down to the sea, and the island of St. Aitherios lies on the sea, they come thence to the Dniester river, and having got safely there they rest again. But when the weather is propitious, they put to sea and come to the river called Aspros, and after resting there too in like manner, they again set out and come to the Selinas, to the so-called branch of the Danube river. And until they are past the river Selinas, the Pechenegs keep pace with them. And if it happens that the sea casts a "monoxylon" on shore, they all put in to land, in order to present a united opposition to the Pechenegs. But after the Selinas they fear nobody, but, entering the territory of Bulgaria, they come to the mouth of the Danube. From the Danube they proceed to the Konopas, and from the Konopas to Constantia, [*and from Constantia*] to the river of Varna, and from Varna they come to the river Ditzina, all of which are Bulgarian territory. From the Ditzina they reach the district of Mesembria, and there at last their voyage, fraught with such travail and terror, such difficulty and danger, is at an end. The severe manner of life of these same Russians in winter-time is as follows. When the month of November begins, their chiefs together with all the Russians at once leave Kiev and go off on the "poliudia," which means "rounds," that is, to the Slavonic regions of the Vervians and Drugovichians and Krivichians and Severians and the rest of the Slavs who are tributaries of the Russians. There they are maintained throughout the winter, but then once more, starting from the month of April, when the ice of the Dnieper river melts, they come back to Kiev. They then pick up their "monoxyla," as has been said above, and fit them out, and come down to Romania [Byzantium].

206.

Introduction. Trade along the Varangian route to Constantinople was secured by the Rus as the result of wars which opened up the great market of Constantinople to their traders. In the treaties ending these conflicts the Greeks had to accept the stipulation that economic privileges be provided to Rus merchants in the capital city. The following selection from the *Russian Primary Chronicle* concerns the treaty of 911 by which Byzantium conferred such economic privileges on Kievan Prince Oleg's merchant subjects.

BYZANTINE-RUSSIAN TREATIES

(Translated by S. Cross and O. Sherbowitz, *Russian Primary Chronicle* [Cambridge, Mass.: Medieval Academy of America, 1930], pp. 65–68.)

[The Rus proposed the following terms:] The Rus who come hither shall receive as much grain as they require. Whosoever come as merchants shall receive supplies for six months, including bread, wine, meat, fish, and fruit. Baths shall be prepared for them in any volume they require. When the Rus return homeward, they shall receive from your Emperor food, anchors, cordage, and sails and whatever else is needed for the journey.

[The Greeks declared:] If Rus come hither without merchandise, they shall receive no provisions. Your prince shall personally lay injunction upon such Rus as journey hither that they shall do no violence in the towns and throughout our territory. Such Rus as arrive here shall dwell in the St. Mamas quarter. Our government will send officers to record their names, and they shall then receive their monthly allowance, first the natives of Kiev, then those from Chernigov, Pereyaslavl', and the other cities. They shall not enter the city save through one gate, unarmed and fifty at a time, escorted by an agent of the Emperor. They may conduct business according to their requirements without payment of taxes.

Thus the Emperors Leo and Alexander made peace with Oleg, and after agreeing upon the tribute and mutually binding themselves by oath, they kissed the cross, and invited Oleg and his men to swear an oath likewise. According to the religion of the Rus, the latter swore by their weapons and by their god Perun, as well as by Volos, the god of cattle, and thus confirmed the treaty.

Oleg gave orders that sails of brocade should be made for the Rus and silken ones for the Slavs, and his demand was satisfied. The Rus hung their shields upon the gates as a sign of victory, and Oleg then departed from Tsar'grad. The Rus unfurled their sails of brocade and the Slavs their sails of silk, but the wind tore them. Then the Slavs said, "Let us keep our canvas ones; silken sails are not made for the Slavs." So Oleg came to Kiev, bearing palls, gold, fruit, and wine, along with every sort of adornment. The people called Oleg "the Sage," for they were but pagans, and therefore ignorant.

207.

Introduction. The carrying trade between Byzantium and the West from the late tenth century on passed increasingly into the hands of merchants from Italy: Venetians, Genoese, Pisans, and in certain respects earliest of all, Amalfians. In the beginning these Italian merchants had to pay the standard duty of ten percent at Constantinople and at the custom house at Abydos on the Hellespont. Increasingly, however, because of the empire's growing military needs, far-reaching trading concessions were granted to several of these cities in exchange for naval aid against Byzantium's enemies.

The first of the chrysobulls granting commercial privileges to Venetian merchants in Constantinople (and probably in other important Byzantine cities) was issued in 992 by Emperor Basil II in return for the use of Venetian ships to transport Byzantine soldiers to southern Italy, where they were needed to defend against Arab attacks.

Imperial Concessions to Venetian Merchants (992)

(From G. Tafel and G. Thomas, eds., *Urkunden zur Älteren Handels- und Staatsgeschichte der Republik Venedig* [Vienna, 1856], vol. 1, pp. 36–39.)

It is most compassionate and laudable for us to give heed not only to petitions which are in our hands, but also, with foresight and piety, to those foreign entreaties which pertain to the state. For thereby sufficiently gracious piety may be shown toward misfortune, and over a long distance an expression of imperial piety may be given.

Wherefore, when the doge of the Venetians and he who is subject to him, on behalf of the entire [Venetian] people, made entreaty to Our Majesty, they requested that everyone coming for the purpose of trade with his own ship, whether from his own province or from another province or city, pay nothing other than two *solidi* [gold coins] and that from this time forth they pay only such a sum. Accordingly, we interrogated many merchants and found that it was more, that is, they are accustomed to paying more than thirty *solidi* per ship to Our Divinely Crowned Majesty. For, on the one hand, in view of the obligation of Christian peoples and having faith that God is with us, and, on the other, on account of the promise which they [the Venetians] made long ago—as can be ascertained not only at this divinely founded and protected city*—[they pledge] that according to ancient custom they [the Venetians] with ready willingness [should render] indefatigable services, and that perhaps when Our Majesty moves into Longobardia they should labor to provide land transportation, to give service with their ships, and not to make an [occasion of] profit or [undue] mention of it.

Therefore the emperors give heed to their petition and order through this chrysobull that every [Venetian] pay nothing to the public [fisc] for the transport from Abydos except two *solidi* per ship, when coming [to Constantinople] with merchandise from Venice or some other province. When however these merchants depart [from the empire, let them pay] fifteen *solidi*, so that the total payment from each ship comes to seventeen *solidi*.

These same Venetians are accustomed to bring to [lacuna] of the palace, whoever that may be, and let [permission] be granted to them by the *kommerkiarios* [a Byzantine customs official] himself, that they may move about and whenever they wish, that they may return to their own province.

Let no one for the sake of greed have the authority to detain them more than three days, and let this be done only when it is a matter of necessity to the state that [their departure] be opposed by force.

In addition, the same Venetians should not, for their protection, carry in their own ships Amalfians, Jews, Lombards, citizens of Bari, or anyone else who may have business in Constantinople, but should bring in only Venetian businessmen. If they do so [i.e. carry in foreigners], not only will they be unable to protect them, but they will lose their own privileges. Furthermore, we order this, that Venetian ships and the Venetians themselves, only by the man who is then logothete of the palace [*logothetes ton oikeiakon*], may be searched, weighed, and judged, in accordance with ancient custom. If perchance a legal dispute arises between the Venetians and others, [again] only this same logothete may investigate and make a decision [and] never any other magistrate. Therefore, we order and command [this] to everyone, the logothetes themselves, the *chartularii* who are under his control, the *notarii parathalassarii* [notarial officials of the shore], the *limenarchai* [harbor officials], the *hypologos* of the treasury, and those who are termed *xylokalami*, the *kommerkiarii* of Abydos, and to [all] other men who are members, in even the smallest capacity, of the imperial service. Indeed, it will not be permitted that anyone of the public [fisc] ever have the authority to disturb, seize, or search the Venetians or their ships for any reason, nor that they dispute with the Venetians about these matters nor for any reason investigate them. Wherefore Our Imperial Majesty entrusts them [the Venetian merchants] to the care of the logothete of the palace alone, and solely by him may they be judged. [They should] observe all the requirements which have been mentioned above and provide, along with their other services [to the empire], their ships as transportation for our army whenever Our Majesty may wish to send it to Longobardia [Byzantine southern Italy].

* The Latin is garbled here. No Greek original exists for this treaty or for that of 1082, this Latin version being perhaps that of an interpreter.

208.

Introduction. The chrysobull of 1082, issued by Emperor Alexius I Comnenus in favor of the Venetians, was the most famous and far-reaching of all edicts concerning Byzantine-Western trade relations. According to this chrysobull, the Venetians, in return for naval aid to Alexius against the Normans of southern Italy, were released from the payment of any customs duties whatsoever in the course of their trade with Byzantium. Moreover, they were given a special quarter of their own (located on the Golden Horn) in Constantinople, and the right to trade in all the main maritime cities of the empire. It is noteworthy that Byzantine merchants themselves were required to pay the normal customs duties.

EXTRAORDINARY PRIVILEGES FOR THE VENETIANS (1082)

(From G. Tafel and G. Thomas, eds., *Urkunden zur Älteren Handels- und Staatsgeschichte der Republik Venedig* [Vienna, 1856], vol. 1, pp. 51–53.)

No one is ignorant of those things which have been done by the faithful Venetians, how after they had gathered together different types of ships, they came to Epidamnus (which we call Dyrrachium) and how they provided for our assistance numerous seaborne fighting men, how their fleet conquered by force the wicked expedition [of the Normans], and how they lost some of their own men. We also know how even now they continue to be our allies, and about those things which have been done by their rowers [*thalattokopi*], men who work on the sea. Even if we should not mention this, everyone knows it perfectly well.

Wherefore, in recompense for their services of this kind, Our Majesty decrees through this present chrysobull, that the Venetians annually receive a gift of twenty pounds [of gold], so that they might distribute this among their own churches in whatever manner they see fit. We honor their noble doge with the most venerable dignity of *protosebastos* and the full stipend which pertains to it, and we designate this honor not only for the person of [the present] doge, but decree that it be continuous and perpetual for all his successors who will come afterwards and to whom the ducal office is transmitted. We also assign to their patriarch the title of *hypertimos*, that is, "most honorable," with a stipend of twenty pounds. And we give this honor [likewise] not to this one man alone, but to all those who will succeed him, so that the honor might also be continuous and perpetual. We decree also that the most holy church of the Apostle and Evangelist St. Mark in Venice receive every year three *nomismata* from every one of all the Amalfians who own workshops in the great city [Constantinople] and in all of Romania [the empire], since they are under the authority of the same patriarch. In addition, those workshops situated in the quarter of Perama [on the Golden Horn across from Pera], together with their upper chambers, which have an entrance and exit throughout, which extend from the Ebraica [gate] up to the Vigla [gate], both inhabited or uninhabited, and in which Venetians and Greeks stay—[all of] these we grant to them as factories, as well as three docks [*scalae*] which end in this aforementioned area. We also grant to St. Akyndinos the property, that is, a mill, lying alongside this church, which belongs to the house of Peter and which has an income of twenty bezants [Byzantine gold coins]. Similarly, we give the church of the Holy Apostle Andrew in Dyrrachium, together with all the imperial payments except the one which is set aside there to be given to the [harbor] barges.

It is also granted to the Venetians that they may conduct business in every type of merchandise in all parts of the empire, that is around great Laodicea, Antioch, Mamistra, Adana, Tarsus, Attalia, Strobilos, Chios, Ephesus, Phocea, Dyrrachium, Valona, Corfu, Bonditza, Methone, Coron, Nauplia, Corinth, Thebes, Athens, Negropont, Demetrias, Thessalonika, Chrysopolis, Perithorion, Abydos, Redestos, Adrianople, Apros, Heraclea, Selymbria, and the megalopolis itself [Constantinople], and indeed in all other places which are under the authority of our pious clemency, without their paying anything at all for any favor of commerce or for any other condition on behalf of their business—[payments] which are made to the fisc [*demosion*] such as the *xylokalamos, limenatikos, poriatikos, kaniskios, hexafolleos, archontikios* [i.e. charges for mooring ships, disembarking, and unloading cargo, and taxes on imports, exports, purchases, and sales], and exemption from all other taxes which have to be paid to engage in commerce. For in all places of business Our Majesty has given them the permission that they be free of such exactions. And the Venetians are removed [from the authority of] the *eparchos parathalassitos* [sic] himself, the *heleoparochos*, the *genikos*, the *chartularii*, the *hypologoi*, and of all officials of this sort. Let no one who carries out imperial or other duties presume to be contemptuous of the provisions which have been specified here. For permission has been granted to the Venetians to deal in whatever types of goods and merchandise anyone may mention, and they have the ability to make any purchase and remain free from all exactions [*dationes*].

. . . Nor may anyone hold opinions contrary to those [expressed here], nor take any [legal] action against all [of the Venetians] on account of the transfer [of ownership] of his workshops and of the *scalae*. Let absolutely no one infringe upon the rights which are here made explicit, whether ecclesiastical, private, public, or of the holy [imperial] house. For such rights now belong to the Venetians, faithful servants of Our Majesty, and [will remain so] henceforth in the future, since they display great benevolence and a correct attitude toward Romania [the empire] and toward Our Imperial Majesty, and they promise to serve the empire wholeheartedly in perpetuity, and they desire and declare that they will fight for the Roman state and in behalf of the Christians.

Commentary. The Venetian desire to secure complete control of the lucrative Byzantine trade was undoubtedly one of the most basic causes of the Latin conquest of Constantinople in 1204.

209.

Introduction. In 1261, just before his recapture of Constantinople from the Latins, Emperor Michael VIII Palaeologus, in order to counter the pervasive Venetian influence in Constantinople, granted large trading concessions to the Genoese, bitter rivals of the Venetians.

Besides the exemption from all custom duties for all Genoese merchants, Michael granted them as their preserve, with virtual right of extraterritoriality, the quarter of Constantinople called Galata, which was situated directly across the Golden Horn from the main part of the capital. We quote below a modern summary of the specific provisions of the celebrated Treaty of Nymphaeum (1261) in which these extraordinary concessions were granted to the Genoese.

PROVISIONS OF THE TREATY OF NYMPHAEUM (1261)

(Adapted from D. Geanakoplos, *Emperor Michael Palaeologus and the West* [Cambridge, Mass.: Harvard University Press, 1959], pp. 87–89.)

(1) A permanent alliance was signed by the Emperor and Genoa for the purpose of making war on Venice. (2) A Genoese squadron of up to fifty ships was to be put at the disposition of Palaeologus, to be dispatched at the Emperor's request and provisioned at his expense. (3) Genoese merchants were granted the right to trade, free of duty, in all parts of the Byzantine Empire, such territories to include those already in Michael's possession as well as those to be conquered in the future. In return, Greek merchants in Genoa would be exempt from duties. (4) A *loggia, pallazzo*, church, bath, and houses were to be assigned to Genoese merchants in Constantinople, Aenos, Cassandria near Thessalonika, Smyrna, Adramyttion, and the isles of Crete, Negropont, Chios, and Lesbos. In each locality the Genoese would be governed by their own consuls with administrative and judicial authority, civil as well as criminal. These officials would guarantee that traitors to Palaeologus would undergo the same punishment as those unfaithful to Genoa. (5) Michael was to exclude from Greek waters

and markets (including the Black Sea) the warships and merchants of Genoese enemies, except for the Pisans, "the faithful subjects of our imperial majesty." (6) Once Constantinople was taken, the Genoese were to receive back all their former possessions in the city, in addition to such Venetian property as the church of Santa Maria, loggias, cemetery, and the Venetian fortified palace. But this provision regarding Venetian possessions was to be implemented only on condition that Genoa provide immediate aid in taking the capital. (7) The Greek city of Smyrna would be handed over to the Genoese in absolute possession with the proviso that the rights of its ecclesiastics and nobles be respected. (8) Genoa pledged to permit the export to the Greeks of arms and horses; to prevent the arming of warships against Michael in Genoese waters; to allow Genoese to enter Greek military service (for which the Commune would supply arms and horses and the Emperor the pay); to instruct Genoese subjects resident in Greek territories to aid in defending such areas in case of attack; and, finally, to require the captains of Genoese vessels in Greek waters during wartime to place themselves under imperial orders. (9) Michael would present an annual donative of 500 *hyperpyra* and a pallium to the Archbishop of Genoa: (10) It was forbidden for a Genoese to become a Greek subject.

210.

Introduction. But the Genoese merchants in Constantinople in their turn soon became even more successful—and overbearing—than the Venetians. The Greek historian Gregoras estimates that in the mid-fourteenth century Constantinople received annually far less in port duties than the Genoese colony of Galata, situated just across the Golden Horn from Constantinople.

GENOESE COMMERCIAL SUCCESSES AT BYZANTINE EXPENSE

(From Nicephorus Gregoras, *Byzantina historia*, ed. L. Schopen and I. Bekker [Bonn, 1830–45], vol. 2, pp. 841–42.)

While the emperor [John Cantacuzene] was occupied with these matters, the Latins of Galata happened to attack Byzantium, not because they had any genuine or obvious reason to conquer it but in fact lest the Byzantine navy increase in size and the customs duties which they collected on their own from the merchants would be diminished. For from the beginning it had been permitted to them to construct certain small and insignificant buildings. However, with the passing of much time, the Genoese had gradually achieved great wealth and power. It so happened that the [Byzantine] princes were fighting among themselves over the empire, and since Byzantine affairs were deeply disturbed by these wars, they [the Genoese] secretly and treacherously supported now one side and now the other, promising to enter an alliance and give assistance in men and weapons on land and sea. Hence they took over not only the facility of movement of the Byzantines and almost all the duties from the sea [trade], but also many public functions of various sorts that brought money to the treasury.

Thus there [in Galata] the sum of approximately 200,000 *hyperpyra* in duties is collected every year, while in Byzantium barely 30,000 a year. Consequently they [the Genoese] become ever more overbearing.

211.

Introduction. Emperor Michael VIII, realizing the danger to the imperial economy from Genoese commercial successes, was finally forced to adopt restrictive measures against Genoese traders. The following passage from the pen of the Greek historian Pachymeres describes the anti-Greek activities of the Genoese merchants (probably after 1274) and Michael's attempts to take punitive measures against them, using his newly reconstituted imperial fleet.

MICHAEL PALAEOLOGUS BRINGS THE GENOESE TO ACCOUNT

(From Pachymeres, *De Michaele et Andronico Palaeologis*, ed. I. Bekker [Bonn, 1835], vol. 1, pp. 421–25.)

Then the emperor . . . resolved to suppress the insolence of the Genoese. Formerly the Venetians had surpassed them in power and in riches, because having a greater number of vessels they engaged in a larger volume of commerce and secured greater gain. But since, through the liberality of the emperor, they [the Genoese] became masters of the Black Sea, they made themselves so very assiduous in seeking to control this sea at all times, and even during the severe weather of winter, that they became more powerful than the Venetians, and even the Romans [Byzantines] themselves. Thus they conducted themselves insolently to the hurt of other peoples.

The emperor had rewarded a noble Genoese, named Manuel, son of Zaccaria, with [the gift of] the mountain area which is situated in Phocea on the western side, where there are alum mines, from which he [Manuel] drew a great profit. But as he wanted to secure still greater profits, he requested the emperor to prohibit the Genoese from bringing from the East the alum they needed for the dyeing of their cloths. After this wish was granted to him, the Genoese who resided in Constantinople accepted this, but the others, [from the home city], far from deferring to that order, constructed a huge vessel, sailed from their port, traversed the Bosporus from Thrace and entered into the Black Sea without rendering to the emperor the accustomed honor. Having approached from the north, they for a long time committed acts of piracy on this sea. Thus coming upon a vessel filled with cargoes of various merchandise, primarily of alum, they pillaged it and set sail for their own land [Genoa].

The emperor, greatly angered by this outrageous defiance, pondered how he might take revenge on those who had humiliated him. But they were not at all unaware of this and therefore proceeded with more than usual care and diligence, altering course to avoid ambushes of Greek ships, whose pilots were under imperial orders to watch for them and to make every effort to seize them. Then, on the return trip, as the Genoese began to leave the mountains of the east, they easily took advantage of every kind of wind in order to avoid coming upon any of our vessels. But when they reached Pharos they found that there was insufficient wind, and that they lacked the north wind, the one that the sailors call *Tanaites*. . . . After they waited several days for this wind, it began to blow and so at that very moment they raised their sails and sailed forth happily. They had covered the sides of their vessels with skins of cows in order to withstand the Greek fire [used as a naval weapon by the Byzantines].

When Michael Palaeologus heard of this, he sent an order to the Genoese who lived in Pera, to stop their compatriots. And these did what they could, but the latter remained defiant, as was reported to him [the emperor]. Then, realizing this was an insupportable affront to his authority and that the pirates would return with impunity to Genoa, he sent against them all the vessels he could spare under the command of Alexios Alyates, the *vestiarios*, who at once crossed the Bosporus, imbuing his men with an extraordinary ardor, stressing to them that he would prefer to lose his command than to fail to achieve victory.

When all his forces were then drawn up in battle array, some on the ships and others on the banks, they attacked the Genoese vessel. Yet though they did everything they could possibly do, they were unable to achieve anything. The strength of the wind that the Genoese had at the stern and the height of their vessel prevailed over the efforts of the Byzantines. When the Byzantines pursued it, they were not able to catch it, and when they attacked it from the sides, they were repulsed without trouble. The emperor from time to time sent out fresh troops on new ships, spurring them on with promises and threats. But, unfortunately, one saw that everything he did only served to render him ridiculous before his enemies.

Things being what they were, he was advised to place his troops on a large Catalan vessel which was alongside, in order to reduce the wind of the Genoese ship, while others [Greeks] would attack it from all sides. When this advice was followed, the Catalan vessel deprived the Genoese ship of the wind, and thus, having rendered it almost immobile, provided the means for the others to attack it. They battled it each in turn and fought so valiantly that after a long and stubborn resistance, they seized the ship and led it into one of our ports. The Genoese were treated as they merited. Some had their eyes put out as punishment for their defiance of Our Majesty.

Another similar incident still further excited [Greek] public hatred against the Genoese. A Genoese said to a [Greek] sailor: "We will soon become masters of Constantinople," and the [Greek] sailor, having given him a slap in the face by which he hoped to take out his eye, killed him on the spot with a stroke of his sword. When the emperor heard of this, he demanded his sailor of the Genoese, but since they would not hand him over (as they had killed him), [the emperor] ordered Manuel Muzalon to exterminate them. At this moment the troops which were in Constantinople and its environs were assembled. They surrounded the homes of the Genoese and awaited the orders of the emperor in order to put them to death. Then the Genoese, terrified by so formidable a spectacle, lost much of their arrogance and, prostrating themselves on the ground as if with a cord around their necks, asked for clemency from the emperor. Thus they appeased his anger by their submission and purchased their lives with gold.

Commentary. Evidence has been accumulating that in the later fourteenth and early fifteenth centuries, far from disappearing, the Byzantine merchant began to thrive. But Greek merchant enterprise remained limited to local shipping and was almost entirely subordinate to the far stronger and more extensive Italian merchant activity with its greater capital, complex trade network, and domination of the money markets. As a result of their earlier treaties with Byzantium (see selections 207–9 above), the Genoese and Venetian merchants continued to enjoy virtually complete exemption from the payment of imposts to the imperial government. Indeed, some Greek merchants, in order to enjoy these same privileges and secure the protection of Italian commercial law, even sought to obtain Venetian or Genoese citizenship.

More numerous in Constantinople (and Genoese-controlled Pera) than the Greek merchants, however, were Greek tradesmen and artisans who controlled almost all the retail business of the capital. The Byzantine guild system, though much changed, seems still to have been in existence but now, owing to socioeconomic conditions and possibly the example of the Italian guilds, served less to benefit the Byzantine government than the guildsmen themselves.

Thus, in these last years of the Byzantine empire, a kind of Greco-Italian symbiosis in the economic sphere was often in evidence. The Greeks (despite the strong Orthodox "patriotism" of most) apparently often adopted certain Italian business practices and at times became partners in Italian commercial ventures in order to benefit from the Italian merchants' larger capital funds, more effective mercantile methods, and elaborate banking procedures—in a word, the Italians' developing capitalist practices.

The end result of this considerable Greco-Italian interaction in business affairs, however, was a Byzantine economy heavily dominated by the powerful Italian merchants, who were thus in a position to manipulate the Byzantine economy for their own ends. This situation, which contributed immensely to the weakness of the Byzantine state, was a vital factor leading to the final fall of Constantinople in 1453. But before this tentative, fragmentary picture of Byzantine urban society and commerce in the last century or so can be fully clarified, much research remains to be done in the Italian and Greek archival materials such as notarial documents, manuals of commerce, and merchants' account books.

212.

Introduction. In contrast to the West in the earlier medieval period, industry was an important part of the Byzantine economy. The largest industries of the empire were centered in Constantinople, where the large urban population and the immense needs of the government provided a large market for manufactured goods. Strict governmental control extended over all the activities of the merchants and artisans as well as such professionals as notaries, bankers, lawyers, even pharmacists—that is, over the activities of the "middle class" in general.

This organization is best understood through study of the famous *Book of the Eparch* (the eparch, or prefect, was the chief official, the governor so to speak, of Constantinople). This document, compiled probably in the tenth century from older materials, is the best description left to us of the Byzantine guild system, controlled economically and socially by the government. Its regulations in many ways resemble those of the Western guild organization, which itself may well have been somewhat influenced by the Byzantine system, since Venice, Genoa, and Pisa from the twelfth century on were in close touch with Byzantium, and their merchants held entire quarters in the capital. But the Byzantine guilds differed from the Western primarily in that their main goal was to assure the Byzantine government and its people a stable supply at all times of basic commodities at controlled prices. The Western guilds, on the other hand, were primarily formed to secure a monopoly for the artisans themselves. The result in Byzantium, up to about the end of the twelfth century, was a reasonably stable economy, though by no means an aggressive one.

A prime example of a large and profitable industry was the silk industry. Its products were used for political and ecclesiastical "diplomacy"—that is, as gifts to foreign princes—as well as in Byzantine upper-class homes and churches. Unlike smaller, less-developed industries, the silk industry was broken down into several steps of production, with the workers in each phase being rigidly organized into separate guilds. The *Book of the Eparch* provides fascinating insight into the organization of the Byzantine silk industry. Note especially the way in which members of one type of silk guild were forbidden to engage in certain activities outside their own guild. This was to prevent monopolization of the silk industry by a few wealthy men.

A. Government Regulation of the Silk Industry

(Translated by E. Freshfield, *Roman Law in the Later Roman Empire: Byzantine Guilds, Professional and Commercial Ordinances of Leo VI c. 895*, from the *"Book of the Eparch"* [Cambridge: Cambridge University Press, 1938], pp. 16–17 and 20–23.)

Merchants of Silk Stuffs. The silk merchants will be concerned in the purchase of silk garments. They will not engage in other purchases except those articles they require for their personal use, and they are forbidden to sell the latter. They are moreover forbidden to resell to persons who are "strangers" to the city the articles which are on the prohibited list, that is to say purple of the distinctive dyes [red or violet], so as to prevent exportation of these out of the Empire. Offenders will be flogged and liable to confiscation.

Silk merchants whether freemen or slaves who purchase from the nobility or silk buyers, or from anyone else, garments exceeding ten *nomismata* in value shall declare the same to the eparch so that he may know where these articles are to be sold. Offenders will suffer the above-named punishments.

Anyone else who has not declared to the eparch the peach-coloured or red garments or mantles of two-thirds dye will be punished.

Any person who fails to inform the eparch of a sale of an article destined for aliens of the Empire, so that the eparch may certify the transaction, shall be held responsible.

To obtain admittance to the guild of silk merchants five members of the craft must testify to the eparch that the candidate is a person worthy to exercise the craft. He shall then be admitted to it, he shall open a shop, and carry on business. His entrance fee to the guild is six *nomismata*.

To obtain a license to acquire the workshop of a silk merchant the tax is ten *nomismata*. The recommendation of the eparch is necessary.

Every person exercising at one and the same time the craft of silk merchant and silk dyer shall be put to his election to choose one or other of these crafts to the exclusion of the other. Anyone attempting to carry on both crafts shall be liable to the aforesaid punishments.

Care must be taken to ensure that strangers who lodge in caravanserais do not purchase prohibited or unsewn garments, unless for their personal use; and in the latter case the articles must have been manufactured in Constantinople.

When strangers leave the city their departure must be notified to the eparch so that he may take cognizance of the articles they have purchased.

Anyone helping them to evade this obligation shall be flogged, shaved and have his property confiscated.

Every silk merchant who secretly or openly causes the rent of any other silk merchant to be raised, shall be flogged, shaved and shall be liable to confiscation.

Raw Silk Merchants. Merchants in this class are limited to exercising their own trade, and must do so publicly in the public places which are assigned to them. Anyone contravening this shall be flogged, shaved and banished.

Every raw silk merchant who employs a workman for wages must only engage him for one month. He shall not advance him more than a month's salary, that is to say the amount he can earn in thirty days, and whoever pays in excess of that sum shall forfeit the excess.

A raw silk merchant is forbidden to engage an employee of another member of his craft until such employee has worked for the latter for the full period for which he was engaged. Any contravention is to be punished by the forfeit of that part of the salary which he the employee has received without having worked for it.

For each cantar of raw silk the raw silk merchant shall pay to the exarchs [of the guild] one *keration*. All those craftsmen whose scales or weights do not bear the sealed impress of the eparch shall be flogged and shaved.

Individuals who have come to lodge with raw silk in the caravanserais have no fee to pay for selling it. They shall only pay their rent and for the right of sojourn. Nor shall those who buy raw silk be required to pay any fee.

At the opening of the market all the members of the guild shall contribute according to their means to a fund to purchase the raw silk which shall then be rationed among them in proportion to their respective contributions.

If a rich raw silk merchant wishes to sell to one of his poorer brethren raw silk acquired from some importer, the profit he may secure shall not exceed one *ouggia* per *nomisma*.

Every raw silk merchant who does not have a fixed salary but imports raw silk in his own name for some rich or influential person or for a silk dyer, shall be flogged and shaved, and cease to be a member of the guild.

Anyone who by means of a trick tries to raise the price of raw silk after having received from the purchaser earnest money for the same, shall be condemned to forfeit it.

Every raw silk merchant convicted of having travelled outside the city to buy raw silk shall cease to be a member of the guild.

Raw silk merchants shall sell their wares in the public streets and not in their private premises, lest such sales be made to persons who are not authorized to buy. Anyone contravening shall be flogged and shaved.

The raw silk merchants shall not be permitted to dress silk but only to trade in it. Persons contravening shall be liable to the aforesaid punishments.

The folk called *melatharioi* shall not trade in pure silk either secretly or openly, and those who disobey shall be liable to the aforesaid punishments.

Raw silk merchants are forbidden to sell raw silk to Jews or to tradesfolk who would resell it outside the city. Persons contravening will be flogged and shaved.

Silk Dyers. Dyers are forbidden to make up the purple of the so-called prohibited grades, that is to say in the series of great mantles, including those of self colour or those where the purple alternates with dark green or yellow in half-tint. They may dye peach tint where that colour is combined with others, or common turbans of slavonian style slashed with scarlet bands. Peach-coloured purple and fine dresses of [?] "two palms" length must be declared to the eparch and also the cloaks worth more than ten *nomismata*, even if of divers colours.

Anyone who has purchased garments made outside the city and delivers them to the imperial store shall be flogged and shaved.

Anyone wishing to open a workshop must, if he is a freeman, be guaranteed by five persons. If he is a slave his master must be surety for him; providing him also with adequate means. In both cases the guarantors will be subject to the same liabilities as the person for whom they stand surety. And he shall pay an entrance fee of three *nomismata*.

Introduction. We also quote from the regulations prescribed for another guild in the *Book of the Eparch*, that of the bankers and money lenders.

B. BANKERS AND MONEY LENDERS

(From *Roman Law in the Later Roman Empire*, pp. 25–27.)

Any person seeking admission to the corporation of bankers must produce the evidence of honorable and honest men who will answer for him that he will not contravene the regulations, that is to say that he will not sweat [file] or clip either *nomismata* or *miliaresia*, that he will not "coin", and, in case a public duty demands his services, he will not entrust to any of his slaves the duties of his craft since that might lead to grave abuses. Anyone contravening this will have his hand cut off.

Money-changers are expected to denounce to the eparch the itinerant vendors of cash who stand on the market squares or public streets. They must be prevented from infringing obligations and service; and if such changers wittingly fail to notify the eparch they shall be liable to the above-named punishments.

Money-changers shall not discount the *miliaresia* if the same are of good alloy and bear for authenticity the Emperor's effigy. They will take them at the rate of twenty-four *oboloi*. If the *miliaresion* is not of good alloy they will value it and pay on its value. Persons contravening this rule will be flogged, shaved and have their property confiscated.

Every banker must employ two men to tally his money. He shall caution them, and if one of them happens to infringe the rules, the banker who was responsible for him and the man himself shall suffer the above-named penalties.

Every money-changer who does not declare to the eparch that he has received counterfeit *nomisma* or *miliaresion* and indicate the presenter thereof shall be flogged, shaved and banished.

Bankers are forbidden to give credit or cash to their employees and then instruct them to stand in the squares or streets to obtain any profit that they may be able to secure. They are also forbidden to quit their banks or to entrust them to other persons even on the days of [the sovran's distribution of] largesse, or of his service. Any person contravening this shall be flogged, shaved and have his property confiscated.

213.

Introduction. Besides the large industries in Constantinople, small craftsmen and other artisans existed throughout the entire Byzantine period, especially in the provincial towns. Sources on the conditions of life for such workers are very scarce. One important source of information, still largely untapped, is the *Lives* of local saints which contain sporadic references to their working conditions. The following variegated selection is composed of small pieces of information on tradesmen and craftsmen from many levels of society in Asia Minor during the sixth and seventh centuries, that is, before the Arabic invasions.

TRADESMEN AND CRAFTSMEN IN EARLY BYZANTINE ASIA MINOR

(Material within brackets is my own; that within quotations is taken directly from the sources as translated by H. Magoulias, "Trades and Crafts in the Sixth and Seventh Centuries as Viewed in the Lives of the Saints," *Byzantinoslavica* 37 [1976]: 11–35. Magoulias, as do I, also draws upon passages translated in E. Dawes and N. Baynes, *Three Byzantine Saints* [Crestwood, N.Y.: St. Vladimir's Seminary Press, and Oxford: A. R. Mowbray, 1977; originally published by Blackwell, Oxford, 1948], pp. 185–86.)

[The building worker most frequently mentioned in hagiographic sources is the mason or stonecutter. In the *Life* of St. Nicholas Sionites it is related that, when stonecutters were unable to remove a huge rock to be used for construction purposes, St. Nicholas, who had mastered the technique of leverage, succeeded so that] "not only men but even slaves obeyed him." [In the *Life* of another saint, John of Ephesus mentions the quarries of a town and the techniques of transporting the dressed stone to the monastery. He also notes the importance of builders in the conduct of war, recording that the Persian ruler Chosroës in 566 seized Byzantine stonecutters and builders,] "all kinds of artificers [whom he commanded] to make a cutting through a hill which lay on the East of the city [of Nisibis] outside the aqueduct, in order to divert the water supply. . . ."

[The *Life* of St. Nicholas of Sion (near Myra in Asia Minor) mentions carpenters whom the saint ordered] "to make a wooden chest for storing corn and pulse for the monastery's use. . . ."

[Artists are mentioned especially if they were monks, as in this statement from the *Life* of St. Symeon the Stylite the Younger,] "who blessed the monk John, praying 'May God instruct you, child, in the art of sculpture.'"

[In the *Life* of St. Theodore of Sykeon it is related that] "the monks, together with the abbot Christophorus, wished to have a picture of Theodore as a permanent memorial and to secure his blessing. They summoned a painter without Theodore's knowledge: he could only see the Saint through a small aperture but managed to paint a good likeness. . . ."

[One of the most remarkable of all stories attesting to the extreme lengths some monks would go to in their ascetic practices is found in the same *Life* of St. Theodore of Sykeon, who commissioned in a village] "a very excellent smith . . . to make a very narrow iron cage that he might enter therein and standing in it pass his days of fasting. . . ." [The saint had the cage suspended above the cave of the rock in mid-air and ordered iron rings to be made for his feet] "of fifteen pounds in weight and similar ones for his hands, and a cross with a collar of eighteen pounds weight and a belt for his loins of thirty-three pounds and an iron staff with a cross on it."

[Candlemakers were, for obvious reasons, always important in Byzantine life. Stephanus, a deacon of St. Sophia in Constantinople, in his *Miracula of St. Artemius*, relates that he bought some candles] "which had no protective covering; the candlemaker had no other candles with the exception of one other pair for which, he apologized, he had already received payment." [But the deacon, because of the rain and muddy streets, dropped the candles, so he returned to the candlemaker who let him have the other customer's candles. This took place, interestingly enough, in the quarter of Constantinople called Oxeia near the church of St. John the Baptist, where candlemakers sold their wares in a building called Jordan.]

214.

Introduction. An important support for the far-flung Byzantine trade up to the mid-eleventh century was the virtually universal acceptability of the Byzantine gold coin, the *nomisma*. For over six hundred years, from the reign of Anastasius to the reign of Constantine IX in the mid-eleventh century, the *nomisma* remained completely undepreciated, a record unique in history. Indeed, the coin was so widely utilized in trade that large caches of *nomismata* have been found as far east as Ceylon as well as in the island of Wisby in the North Sea. Cosmas Indicopleustes (early sixth century) in his famous work remarks on the wide circulation of the Byzantine *nomisma*. There is reason to believe that the story he tells is apocryphal since variations on it appear in other literatures. Yet it gives a good idea of the universal regard for the *nomisma*.

A. The Byzantine Nomisma in the Far East

(Translated by J. McKindle, *The Christian Topography of Cosmas Indicopleustes* [London: Hakluyt Society, 1897], pp. 73 and 368–70.)

[The Roman Empire] has many bulwarks of its safety in that it is the foremost power in the world, in that it was the first to believe in Christ, and in that it renders services to every department of the Christian economy. There is yet another sign of the power which God has accorded to the Romans. I refer to the fact that it is with their coinage all the nations carry on trade from one extremity of the earth to the other. This money is regarded with admiration by all men to whatever kingdom they belong, since there is no other country in which the like of it exists. . . .

Now I must here relate what happened to one of our countrymen, a merchant called Sopatrus, who used to go thither on business, but who to our knowledge has now been dead these five and thirty years past. Once on a time he came to this island of Taprobane on business, and as it chanced a vessel from Persia put into port at the same time with himself. So the men from Adulê with whom Sopatrus was, went ashore, as did likewise the people of Persia, with whom came a person of venerable age and appearance. Then, as the way there was, the chief men of the place and the custom-house officers received them and brought them to the king. The king having admitted them to an audience and received their salutations, requested them to be seated. Then he asked them: In what state are your countries, and how go things with them? To this they replied, they go well. Afterwards, as the conversation proceeded, the king inquired Which of your kings is the greater and the more powerful? The elderly Persian snatching the word answered: Our king is both the more powerful and the greater and richer, and indeed is King of Kings, and whatsoever he desires, that he is able to do. Sopatrus on the other hand sat mute. So the king asked: Have you, Roman, nothing to say? What have I to say, he rejoined, when he there has said such things? but if you wish to learn the truth you have the two kings here present. Examine each and you will see which of them is the grander and the more powerful. The king on hearing this was amazed at his words and asked, How say you that I have both the kings here? You have, replied Sopatrus, the money of both—the *nomisma* of the one, and the drachma, that is, the miliaresion of the other [the Persian].* Examine the image of each, and you will see the truth. The king thought well of the suggestion, and, nodding his consent, ordered both the coins to be produced. Now the Roman coin had a right good ring, was of bright metal and finely shaped, for pieces of this kind are picked for export to the island. But the miliaresion, to say it in one word, was of silver, and not to be compared with the gold coin. So the king after he had turned them this way and that, and had attentively examined both, highly commended the *nomisma*, saying that the Romans were certainly a splendid, powerful, and sagacious people. So he ordered great honour to be paid to Sopatrus, causing him to be mounted on an elephant, and conducted round the city with drums beating and high state.

These circumstances were told us by Sopatrus himself and his companions, who had accompanied him to that island from Adulê; and as they told the story, the Persian was deeply chagrined at what had occurred.

* He uses Byzantine terms to describe the Persian coinage.

B. TABLE OF RELATIVE BYZANTINE COINAGE VALUES
(C. FIFTH TO MID-ELEVENTH CENTURIES)

(From K. Setton, "On the Importance of Land Tenure and Agrarian Taxation in the Byzantine Empire from the Fourth Century to the Fourth Crusade," *American Journal of Philology* 74 [1953]: 257.)

1 gold pound = 72 *nomismata*
1 *nomisma* = 12 *miliaresia* [silver] = 24 *keratia* = 288 *folleis* [copper]
1 *miliaresion* = 2 *keratia* = 24 *folleis*
1 *keration* = 12 *folleis*

215.

Introduction. With the rising governmental need for money to stave off foreign invasions as well as the declining resources of the empire after it passed the height of its power in 1025, the Byzantine coinage began to be depreciated and decline in value. The very first evidence, however, is perhaps from the reign of Nicephorus II Phocas (963–69) and, certainly, from the reign of Constantine IX (1042–55). There is also definite evidence of debasement of the coinage under Alexius Comnenus (1081–1118), in whose reign new coins of lesser gold content were put into circulation. Alexius's practice of debasing the coinage and following an inflationary policy in turn produced high prices and shortages in goods. Under Alexius the debased gold *nomisma*, previously worth twelve silver *miliaresia*, fell to one-third of its value (four *miliaresia*).*

By the beginning of the thirteenth century, the Byzantine gold *nomisma*, which formerly held undisputed primacy in international trade, came to contain far less precious metal than its original face value. Thus from the mid-thirteenth century it was increasingly displaced by the newly minted gold coins of Florence, Venice, and Genoa. By the time of Michael VIII Palaeologus (1259–82) the gold coin contained a little less than ⅔ of its weight in gold. During the reign of his successor Andronicus II and later in the fourteenth century, a period of particularly severe Byzantine distress, the *hyperpyron*, as the *nomisma* came to be called, had sunk to only half its original gold content. The selection which follows is taken from the contemporary history of Pachymeres and succinctly describes the rapid debasement of the Byzantine gold coin.

DEBASEMENT OF THE BYZANTINE GOLD COINAGE

(From Pachymeres, *De Michaele et Andronico Palaeologis* [Bonn: 1835], vol. 2, pp. 493–94.)

But the *nomisma* was debased to conform to the necessities of the time. For earlier, in the reign of John Ducas [Vatatzes], the weight of the gold coin consisted of two-thirds solid gold,[†] a value which his son and successor [Theodore II Lascaris] maintained. But later, under Michael Palaeologus, after the recapture of Constantinople and with the payments of gold which necessarily followed this, especially to the Italians, the old legends [on the coin] were replaced by the image of the city, stamped on the reverse, and the value of the *nomisma* was diminished by a carat so that the gold coin contained only fifteen carats of gold out of twenty-four. After the death of this emperor, at the beginning [of Andronicus's reign], the *nomisma* contained fourteen carats of solid gold as opposed to ten [of alloy], but now in our time the relative amounts of solid gold and alloy are equal.

Commentary. By the later fourteenth century the *hyperpyron* seemed to have no fixed value. Contemporaries affirmed that its purchasing power grew smaller by the day: to quote Nicephorus Gregoras about the monetary chaos of his time: "Each day the *nomisma* declines in value: in one day, in fact, ten *nomismata* descended to the value only of eight nomismata."[‡]

---

[*] See G. Ostrogorsky, *History of the Byzantine State* (New Brunswick, 1969) p. 369, whose opinion is based primarily on coin hoards and archaeology.

[†] See D. Zakythinos, *Crise monétaire et crise économique* (Athens, 1948), p. 8, and G. Ostrogorsky, *History of the Byzantine State* (New Brunswick, 1969), p. 484, who say "two thirds." Cf. Pachymeres, *De Michaele et Andronico Palaeologis*, vol. 2, p. 493, for Greek text: *to dimoiron tou talantou ton nomismaton chrysos en apefthos.*

[‡] From Nicephorus Gregoras, *Byzantina historia*, ed. L. Schopen and I. Bekker (Bonn, 1855), vol. 3, p. 52.

E.
HOME AND FAMILY

216.

Introduction. In Byzantium the basic unit of society was the extended family, consisting not only of parents and their immediate offspring, but of grandparents, grandchildren, uncles and aunts, all often living in close association. Well-planned marriage alliances were of considerable importance to strengthen the position and material well-being of a family. The following selection, quoting from the laws of the eighth century *Ecloga* (726) concerning marriage contracts, indicates some of the considerations involved, especially those of property, and implies that romantic love as a factor in choice of spouse was very low on the list of priorities. Recall that the average Byzantine lifespan was far less than ours.

THE CONTRACT OF MARRIAGE

(Reprinted with permission of Bowes & Bowes at The Bodley Head, from by E. Freshfield, trans., *A Manual of Roman Law: The "Ecloga"* [Cambridge, 1926], pp. 72–74.)

The marriage of Christians, man and woman, who have reached years of discretion, that is for a man at fifteen and for a woman at thirteen years of age, both being desirous and having obtained the consent of their parents, shall be contracted either by deed or by parol.

A written marriage contract shall be based upon a written agreement providing the wife's marriage portion; and it shall be made before three credible witnesses according to the new decrees auspiciously prescribed by us. The man on his part agreeing by it continually to protect and preserve undiminished the wife's marriage portion, and also such additions as he may naturally make thereto in augmentation thereof; and it shall be recorded in the agreement made on that behalf by him, that in case there are no children, one-fourth part thereof shall be secured in settlement.

If the wife happens to predecease the husband and there are no children of the marriage, the husband shall receive only one-fourth part of the wife's portion for himself, and the remainder thereof shall be given to the beneficiaries named in the wife's will or, if she be intestate, to the next of kin. If the husband predeceases the wife, and there are no children of the marriage, then all the wife's portion shall revert to her, and so much of all her husband's estate as shall be equal to a fourth part of his portion shall also inure to her as her own, and the remainder of his estate shall revert either to his beneficiaries or, if he be intestate, to his next of kin.

If the husband predecease the wife and there are children of the marriage, the wife being their mother, she shall control her marriage portion and all her husband's property as becomes the head of the family and household.

217.

Introduction. Much documentary information has remained illustrating Byzantine inheritances. The *Novellae* of Leo VI the Wise, for example, fully specify what percent of the deceased's estates was to be left to the widow, what was to be reserved for the children, and so on. Wills, as noted, together with marriage contracts, sales, and the like had, by law, to be drawn up by the notaries of the city.

The following selection (*novella* 28) from the law code of Leo VI (886–912) prescribes regulations for the inheritance and administration of property willed to the young, reflecting a very advanced approach to the question of the age of "discretion."

INHERITANCES AND GUARDIANS FOR THE YOUNG

(From *Les novelles de Léon VI le Sage*, ed. P. Noailles and A. Dain [Paris, 1944], no. 28, pp. 111–13.)

Since . . . the legislators have taken steps to foresee the assignment of guardians for minors who shall look after them with a father's solicitude, bring help to the feebleness of their age, and conserve their goods intact through appropriate measures, we have considered how best to complete this legislation. In what way is it incomplete? In that [it is decreed that] it may be only by decision of the emperor that guardians should abandon the administration of their properties, that the young might assume this administration on reaching the required age, (for boys twenty years of age, for girls eighteen years), and that they acquire the full disposition through having arrived at the age of wisdom when one may properly and usefully manage one's fortune. But since wisdom does not befall all in the same manner, it should not be necessary to decide in so simple a manner, since not all the young come to wisdom at the same point by the sole circumstance of age; rather, they should be called when they are in a position to take over their own property.

218.

Introduction. Though in the Byzantine world the oldest male was generally the head of the household, the unifying and some-times dominant figure within the home itself, from the lowest to the highest echelons of society, was the mother. The following selection, taken from the history of Anna Comnena, vividly (if a little exaggeratedly) portrays the character and personality of her grandmother, a vibrant and influential woman, Anna Dalassena, mother of Emperor Alexius I Comnenus.

A MATRIARCH OF THE EARLY TWELFTH CENTURY

(From Anna Comnena, *Alexiade*, ed. B. Leib [Paris, 1967], vol. 1, pp. 123–25.)

One might be amazed that my father accorded his mother such high honor in these matters and that he deferred to her in all respects, as if he were turning over the reins of the empire to her and running alongside her while she drove the imperial chariot, contenting himself simply with the title of emperor. Indeed, he had already passed beyond the period of boyhood, an age especially when lust for power grows in men of such nature [as Alexius]. He took upon himself the wars against the barbarians and whatever battles and combats pertained to them, while he entrusted to his mother the complete management of [civil] affairs: the selection of civil magistrates, the collection of incoming revenues and the expenses of the government. A person who has reached this point in my text may blame my father for entrusting management of the empire to the *gynaiconites* [women's section of the palace]. But if he had known this woman's spirit, how great she was in virtue and intellect and how extremely vigorous, he would cease his reproach and his criticism would be changed into admiration. For my grandmother was so dextrous in handling affairs of state and so highly skilled in controlling and running the government, that she was not only able to manage the Roman empire but could have handled every empire under the sun. She had a vast amount of experience and understood the internal workings of many things: she knew how each affair began and to what result it might lead, which actions were destructive and which rather were beneficial. She was exceedingly acute in discerning whatever course of action was necessary and in carrying it out safely. She was not only acute in her thought, but was no less proficient in her manner of speech. Indeed, she was a persuasive orator, neither verbose nor stretching her phrases out at great length; nor did she quickly lose the sense of her argument. What she began felicitously she would finish even more so. . . .

But, as I was saying, my father, after he had assumed power, managed by himself the strains and labors of war, while making his mother a spectator to these actions, but in other affairs he set her up as ruler, and as if he were her servant he used to say and do whatever she ordered. The emperor loved her deeply and was dependent upon her advice (so much affection had he for his mother), and he made his right hand the executor of her orders, his ears paid heed to her words, and everything which she accepted or rejected the emperor likewise accepted or rejected. In a word, the situation was thus: Alexius possessed the external formalities of imperial power, but she held the power itself. She used to promulgate laws, to manage and administer everything while he confirmed her arrangements, both written and unwritten, either through his signature or by oral commands, so that he seemed the instrument of her imperial authority and not himself the emperor. Everything which she decided or ordered he found satisfactory. Not only was he very obedient to her as is fitting for a son to his mother, but even more he submitted his spirit to her as to a master in the science [*episteme*] of ruling. For he felt that she had attained perfection in everything and far surpassed all men of that time in prudence and in comprehension of affairs.

219.

Introduction. Nevertheless, Byzantine women remained under certain legal constraints: they could not, for example, act as witnesses in the signing of a contract except under special circumstances.

WOMEN SHALL NOT ACT AS WITNESSES IN THE EXECUTION OF CONTRACTS

(Translated by H. Agylaeus, in S. P. Scott, ed., *The Civil Law, The Novels of Emperor Leo VI* [Cincinnati: Central Trust Company, 1932], vol. 17, p. 249.)

I do not know why the ancient authorities, without having thoroughly considered the subject, conferred upon women the right of acting as witnesses. It was, indeed, well known, and they themselves could not fail to be aware that it was dishonorable for them to appear frequently before the eyes of men, and that those who were modest and virtuous should avoid doing so. For this reason, as I have previously stated, I do not understand why they permitted them to be called as witnesses, a privilege which resulted in their frequently being associated with great crowds of men, and holding conversation with them of a character very unbecoming to the sex. . . .

And, indeed, the power to act as witnesses in the numerous assemblies of men with which they mingle, as well as taking part in public affairs, gives them the habit of speaking more freely than they ought, and, depriving them of the morality and reserve of their sex, encourages them in the exercise of boldness and wickedness which, to some extent, is even insulting to men. For is it not an insult, and a very serious one, for women to be authorized to do something which is especially within the province of the male sex?

Wherefore, with a view to reforming not only the errors of custom, but also of law, We hereby deprive them of the power of acting as witnesses, and by this constitution forbid them to be called to witness contracts under any circumstances. But, so far as matters in which they are exclusively interested are concerned, and when men cannot act as witnesses, as, for instance, in confinements, and other things where only women are allowed to be present, they can give testimony as to what is exclusively their own, and which should be concealed from the eyes of men.

220.

Introduction. Though strictly forbidden under canon law, mixed marriages between Byzantines and infidel Arabs (and later

Turks) were by no means unknown, nor were marriages between Byzantine merchants and heathen Slavs (before their conversion). A different type of mixed marriage was that between Latins and Greeks. Although considered normal in the Constantinian period, it had virtually ceased to occur after the sixth century, with the exception of an occasional dynastic marriage, as in southern Italy. Such marriages, however, increased in number with the growing Latin influx into the East after the tenth century. Some Greeks, especially ecclesiastics, were never able to believe that any good could come of Greco-Latin unions. Thus the learned Demetrios Chomatianos, archbishop of Ochrida in the thirteenth century, wrote: The Orthodox partner in a mixed marriage celebrated by a Catholic priest should be excommunicated, and any Greek priest who imparts his blessing to such a union should be suspended.* (Chomatianos's view, it should be noted, was rather extreme and apparently unenforced.) The fruit of such unions, called Gasmules (half-breed, probably from the words *bât* (stupid person) and *moulos* (bastard), were often looked upon with disdain by Latins and Greeks alike. Yet they were at the same time often grudgingly admired. (On Gasmules see also selection 85.)

BETWEEN EAST AND WEST: THE GASMULES

(From Pachymeres, *De Michaele et Andronico Palaeologis*, ed. I. Bekker [Bonn, 1835], vol. 1, p. 309.)

The Gasmules of the City (whom the Byzantines call two-raced) are born of Byzantine women to Italian men, . . . And they derive zealousness in battle and prudence from the Byzantines and impetuosity and audacity from the Latins.

Commentary. Many Gasmules became merchants, others were hired to replenish the Byzantine fleet by Michael VIII (1259–82) or, in the later period, they acted as interpreters and go-betweens between the emperor and Western rulers, and they even gave their services to the Turks. Gregoras, too, in his *History* describes them as "raised in both Greek and Latin customs so as to derive from the Greeks the ability to go into battle prudently and from the Latins audacity."[†] In the last two centuries, because of the increasingly strong position of the Latins in the East vis à vis the Greeks, the Gasmules often preferred to "pass" as Latins.

*Trans. D. Geanakoplos from J. Pitra ed., *Analecta sacra et classica spicilegio Solesmensi parata* (Paris-Rome, 1891), p. 713.

[†]Gregoras, *Byzantina historia*, ed. L. Schopen and I. Bekker (Bonn, 1829), vol. 1, p. 98.

221.

Introduction. Many records on slaves exist in Byzantine archives up to the twelfth or thirteenth century, after which records of sales and manumissions of slaves are scarce. Legally slaves were considered property and there were penalties, for example, if a free woman had relations with a slave. An example of the severe Byzantine legal and moral view toward slavery can be seen in the following edict of Emperor Constantine I as recorded and interpreted in the *Theodosian Code*.

A. Constantine I on Responsibility of Owners for Disciplining Slaves (329)

(Translated by C. Pharr, *The Theodosian Code* [Princeton, 1952], 10-9-2, p. 235.)

Whenever such chance attends the beating of slaves by their masters that the slaves die, the masters shall be free from blame if by the correction of very evil deeds they wished to obtain better conduct on the part of their household slaves. In the case of such actions, in which it is to the interest of the master to keep a slave that is his own property unharmed, it is Our will that no investigation shall be made as to whether the punishment appears to have been inflicted with the intention of killing the man or simply as correction. For it is Our pleasure that a master shall not be pronounced guilty of homicide for the death of a slave when he exercises his domestic power in simple punishments. If at any time, therefore, slaves depart from the human scene when fatal necessity is imminent as a result of correction by beating, the masters shall fear no criminal investigation.

Interpretation: If a slave should die while his master is punishing a fault, the master shall not be held on the charge of homicide, because he is guilty of homicide only if he is convicted of having intended to kill the slave. For disciplinary correction is not reckoned as a crime.

Introduction. Early emperors had decreed that slaves' property belonged to, or at the slaves' death reverted to, their masters. In the next selection, drawn from the *Novellae* of Leo VI (early tenth century), more generous provision is made for the disposition of the property of imperial slaves. This suggests that, perhaps under the church's influence, there had been some amelioration by the time of Leo VI's reign in the treatment of slaves compared to the harsh treatment accorded them in the earlier period.

B. Disposition of Property of Imperial Slaves

(Translated by S. P. Scott, *The Civil Law* [Cincinnati: Central Trust Company, 1932], vol. 17, p. 241.)

Although the following provision is apparently plausible, and has been legally enacted, still, it seems to me to exceed the bounds of equity; for it declares that slaves shall not be permitted to dispose of their property, and, even though it may have been obtained by their arduous labors, and with many privations, their masters shall be entitled to it. And, indeed, it is surprising that the law originally enacted on this subject was not drawn up with more moderation and justice, and that those responsible for the same adopted it, just as if it had been framed by others.

Moreover, I do not approve of this law and I shall not permit it to apply to my slaves; but, on the contrary, I grant them full authority to manage their own estates, and, hereafter, the slaves of the Emperor shall be the actual owners of their property; so that, when they are in health, or ill, if they think that they are in danger of death, they shall not be deprived of the power of disposing of their property in any way that they may desire, and the ownership of whatever they possess shall not be taken from them under the pretext of servitude. Therefore, this law shall be applicable to Imperial slaves. Magistrates, and the remainder of the people, however, shall have the power to observe the ancient statutes having reference to the property of slaves, when they are not willing to acquiesce in this Our decree.

222.

Introduction. The style of Byzantine clothing changed with the passing of centuries. In the early years of the Roman Empire, as during the earlier Republican period, the standard clothing for men was the toga. By the fourth and fifth centuries, however, this garb seems to have fallen out of fashion, and it even became necessary for the emperors to legislate the compulsory wearing of togas by all members of the senatorial class. In place of the toga a variety of clothing became popular, including pants, boots, and garments made out of animal pelts, adopted from barbarian Germanic usage. Imitation of barbarian fashions in the fourth and fifth centuries is attested to in the following selections in which the emperors prohibit the wearing of boots, skins, or pants within the cities of the empire. The unusual severity of punishment established for violation of these edicts (dated 382 and 397) clearly reveals how much the emperors feared the growing influence of barbarian Germanic customs on Roman society.

A. CLOTHING TO BE WORN WITHIN THE CITY

(Translated by C. Pharr, *The Theodosian Code* [Princeton, 1952], p. 415.)

No Senator shall vindicate for himself a military garb, even without the exception of the early morning hours, provided that he resides within the walls, but he shall lay aside the awe-inspiring military cloak and clothe himself with the sober robes of everyday costume and a civilian cloak. When, moreover, a meeting of the whiterobed Order [the Senate] is being held or a case of a Senator is being tried at a public hearing of a judge, We command the aforesaid Senator to be present clad in his toga.

. . . Within the venerable City [Rome or Constantinople] no person shall be allowed to appropriate to himself the use of boots or trousers. But if any man should attempt to contravene this sanction, We command that in accordance with the sentence of the Illustrious Prefect, the offender shall be stripped of all his resources and delivered into perpetual exile.

We command that no person shall be allowed to wear very long hair, no one, not even a slave, shall be allowed to wear garments made of skins within our most sacred City, and hereafter no person shall be able to appropriate to himself the right to wear such clothing with impunity. Moreover, if any freeman should disregard the severity of this Our sanction, he shall not escape the toils of the law; if a slave, he shall be vindicated to the public works. We sanction that it shall forthwith be made known that such usage is forbidden, not only within the City but also in the neighboring districts.

Introduction. An example of the unique dress fancied in the period of Emperor Justinian (in the sixth century) by the circus factions, the Greens and Blues of the capital, is provided for us by the historian Procopius.

B. The Outlandish Dress of the Circus Factions

(Translated by H. B. Dewing, from Procopius, *The Anecdota or Secret History*, Loeb Classical Library [Cambridge, 1935], p. 81.)

As to fashions in dress, they all insisted on being well clad in fine garments, clothing themselves in raiment too pretentious for their individual rank. . . . And the part of the tunic which covered the arms was gathered by them very closely about the wrist, while from there to each shoulder it billowed out to an incredible breadth. And as often as their arms were waved about, either as they shouted in the theatres and hippodromes, or urged men on to victory in the customary manner, this part of their garments would actually soar aloft, causing the foolish to suppose that their bodies must be so fine and sturdy that they must needs be covered by such garments, not taking into consideration the fact that by the loosely woven and empty garment the meagreness much rather than the sturdiness of their bodies was demonstrated. Also their cloaks and their drawers and especially their shoes, as regards both name and fashion, were classed as "Hunnic."

223.

Introduction. The basileus alone, as vicar of the one God, was permitted to wear the insignia and clothing of the imperial office: the imperial diadem, the purple buskins (lesser dignitaries wore black ones), vestments laden with heavy silk brocade, purple (virtually red) garments. Anna Comnena describes the dress of the emperors at the turn of the twelfth century.

Imperial Vestments

(From Anna Comnena, *Alexiade*, ed. B. Leib [Paris, 1945], vol. 1, pp. 115–16.)

Constantine Porphyrogenitus, the son of the Empress Maria, after the dethronement of his father Michael Ducas, voluntarily put away the purple buskins and put on common black ones. But Nicephorus Botaneiates, the one who ruled after Ducas the father of Constantine, having seized the scepter, directed him to put away these black shoes and ordered him to wear buskins of many-colored silk, since he felt compassion for the young man and admired him for his handsomeness as well as his aristocratic extraction. He forbade him to wear shoes completely of red [i.e. imperial purple] but permitted certain portions of the cloth to be red in color.

After the accession of Alexius Comnenus the Empress Maria, the mother of

Constantine, persuaded by the counsels of the caesar, requested from the emperor a written assurance confirmed in letters of red-and a gold seal, not only that she be maintained in security together with her son, but that he rule jointly with him [Alexius]; also that he wear buskins and be crowned and acclaimed with him [Alexius] as emperor. She succeeded in her request, receiving a chrysobull confirming all her demands. The shoes woven of silken fabric that Constantine was in the habit of wearing were then taken away and footwear was substituted wholly of red. With respect to donations and chrysobulls, he signed in red ink immediately after the Emperor Alexius and in processions he followed him wearing an imperial tiara.

224.

Introduction. In the twelfth century, the scholar-bishop Eustathius of Thessalonika describes for us the dress of David, the Byzantine commander who lost Thessalonika to the Normans (1185)—an event which led to the almost unmentionable atrocities perpetrated in that city (at least as he records them—see below selection 275).

A. THE DRESS AND MANNER OF A BYZANTINE MILITARY OFFICIAL

(From Eustathius, *La espugnazione di Tessalonica*, ed. S. Kyriakedes [Palermo, 1961], p. 83.)

In the days that preceded the greatest intensity of battle, and then during the course of the battle, he [David] was never seen either clothed in powerful armor or riding a noble steed. He mounted a mule and had on a brocaded [garment] and sandals of the latest style. He covered his head in the Iberian [south of the Black Sea] manner, with a strange red covering. This was a barbarian custom (the barbarians have a special name to designate it), and it was made in this manner: it is formed of many folds which on the flounce fall with little regularity, while in the front it is sufficiently large to protect the face from the sun. Moreover, he did not assume the martial attitude, but he appeared in an effeminate manner in order to escape the rays of the sun.

Introduction. In the early thirteenth century in Anatolian Nicaea (while Constantinople itself was in the hands of the Latins) Italian-style clothing was evidently in vogue, as is indicated by the following passage describing an edict of the Emperor John Vatatzes.

B. EMPEROR JOHN VATATZES FORBIDS THE WEARING OF ITALIAN AND ORIENTAL CLOTHING

(From Nicephorus Gregoras, *Byzantina historia*, ed. I. Bekker and L. Schopen [Bonn, 1829] vol. 1, p. 43.)

The emperor saw that the Byzantines were squandering their riches unnecessarily in order to buy clothing from foreign peoples—variegated garb which the Babylonian and Assyrian weavers [probably Persian and Syrian] had made, and elegant things which were woven by the hands of the Italian weavers. For this reason he promulgated a law that if any one of his subjects wore such [foreign] clothing both he and his family would be dishonored. One was to wear only clothing produced on Byzantine land and by the hands of Byzantine ["Roman"] weavers.

225.

Introduction. During the last period of the empire Byzantine dress was especially influenced by styles from the East. Particularly popular was the habit of flaunting heavy brocades and stiff turbans. In 1438–39 when the Byzantine Emperor John VIII Palaeologus and his retinue of seven hundred came to the Council of Florence to negotiate religious union, Westerners were surprised at the difference between Byzantine clothing and their own. The Byzantines were mostly bearded and wore oriental-looking garments with conical-shaped hats—most of which reflected the influence of the Muslim East. A view of Byzantine dress at this council is provided by the Italian humanist Vespasiano da Bisticci in his *Lives of Illustrious Men*. (For the Council of Florence see also selections 160–63.)

An Italian Renaissance View of Byzantine Dress

(Translated by W. George and E. Water, from Vespasiano da Bisticci, *Renaissance Princes, Popes and Prelates* [New York, 1963], pp. 25–26.)

During this ceremony the Emperor occupied the place where the Epistle is read by the high altar, in which same place, as I have already said, were all the Greek prelates. All Florence was there to witness this noble function. Opposite to the Pope's seat, on the other side, was a chair covered with a silken cloth on which sat the Emperor, clad in a rich robe of damask brocade and a cap in the Greek fashion, on the top of which was a magnificent jewel. He was a very handsome man with a beard of the Greek cut.* Round about his chair were posted the many gentlemen of his retinue, clad in the richest silken robes made in Greek fashion; their attire being most stately, as was that of the prelates and of the laymen also. It was a very wonderful thing to behold this goodly ceremony: the reading of the Gospel in both the Greek and Latin tongues as is done on Easter eve in Rome. I will not pass on without a word of special praise of the Greeks. For the last fifteen hundred years and more they have not altered the style of their dress; their clothes are of the same fashion now as they were in the time indicated. This may be seen in Greece in a place called the fields of Philippi, where were found many records in marble in which may be seen men clothed in the manner still used by the Greeks.

* For an English view in 1400 of Emperor Manuel II's dress and appearance see selection 18.

F.
PHILANTHROPY AND PUBLIC WELFARE

226.

Introduction. As the "imitator of Christ" (*mimetes Chrestou*) and the successor to Hellenistic notions of kingship, the Byzantine Emperor was expected to be *philanthropos* (loving mankind) and benefactor of the people. This expectation is clearly revealed in the following passage from the sixth-century *Exposition on Kingship* by Agapetus.

ETHICAL VALUES FOR A RULER

(From Agapetus, *Expositio Capitum Amonitoriorum . . . imperatori Justiniano,* MPG, vol. 86, col. 1164.)

You should know this, O divinely created icon of piety, that the more God considers you to be worthy of his great bounty, the larger is the obligation which you owe to him. Thus you should render your debt of gratitude to your Benefactor, who accepts this payment as grace and renders his own grace in exchange for grace. God is forever himself the original giver of grace and repays grace rendered [him] as if it were a debt. Thus from us he seeks gratitude, but not in our offering of good words, rather in our acts of piety.

There is nothing which can bring a man such good reputation as not only to be able to do what he desires but to desire and to carry out acts of kindness [*philanthropeia*]. Accordingly, inasmuch as God in his own grace has granted you the authority which your benevolence toward us needed for our sake, may you, equally, will and accomplish all things as is pleasing to him who first accorded you such authority.

227.

Introduction. The duty of philanthropy was not restricted to the emperor, however. An example of private charity on the part of the church or private individuals may be found in the following passage from a biography of the early seventh-century monk (later patriarch of Alexandria) John, called "the Almsgiver."

The Philanthropy of John "the Almsgiver"

(Translated by E. Dawes and N. Baynes, *Three Byzantine Saints* [Crestwood, N.Y.: St. Vladimir's Seminary Press, and Oxford: A. R. Mowbray, 1977; originally published by Blackwell, Oxford, 1948], pp. 229–31.)

Another good habit this Saint also adopted, namely sleeping on the cheapest of beds and using only very poor coverings in his own cell. One of the city's landowners once went into the Patriarch's room and saw that he was only covered with a torn and worn quilt, so he sent him a quilt costing 36 nomismata and besought him earnestly to cover himself with that in memory, he said, of the giver.

John took and used it for one night because of the giver's insistence, but throughout the night he kept saying to himself (for so his chamber-attendants related), "Who shall say that humble John"—for he ever called himself that—"was lying under a coverlet costing 36 nomismata whilst Christ's brethren are pinched with cold? How many are there at this minute grinding their teeth because of the cold? and how many have only a rough blanket half below and half above them so that they cannot stretch out their legs but lie shivering, rolled up like a ball of thread? How many are sleeping on the mountain without food or light, suffering twofold pangs from cold and hunger? How many would like to be filled with the outer leaves of the vegetables which are thrown away from my kitchen? Verily, if you live like that and pass your life in such ease, do not expect to enjoy the good things prepared for us on high; but you will certainly be told, as was that other rich man: Thou in thy lifetime receivedst thy good things, but the poor evil things; and now they are comforted, but thou art in anguish? Blessed be God! You shall not cover humble John a second night. For it is right and acceptable to God that 144 of your brothers and masters should be covered rather than you, one miserable creature." For four rough blankets could be bought for one nomisma. Early on the following morning, therefore, he sent it to be sold, but the man who had given it saw it and bought it for 36 nomismata and again brought it to the Patriarch. But when he saw it put up for sale again the next day he bought it once more and carried it to the Patriarch and implored him to use it. When he had done this for the third time the Saint said to him jokingly, "Let us see whether you or I will give up first!" For the man was exceedingly well-to-do, and the Saint took pleasure in getting money out of him, and he used to say that if with the object of giving to the poor anybody were able, without ill-will, to strip the rich right down to their shirts, he would not do wrong, more especially if they were heartless skinflints. For thereby he gets a twofold profit, firstly he saves their souls, and secondly he himself will gain no small reward therefrom. And to confirm this saying he would adduce as trustworthy evidence the tale about St. Epiphanius and John the Patriarch of Jerusalem—to wit that the former would skilfully steal away the Patriarch John's silver and give it to the poor.

228.

Introduction. Nevertheless, in practice as well as in theory, it was the emperor who exercised the principal role in establishing hospitals, orphanages, homes for the aged, lodgings for travelers, and so on. The *orphanotrophos* (literally, guardian of the orphans) was an official of the court, sometimes of great importance and often included in the highest political councils.

The care that Byzantines took to relieve human suffering and to prolong life was notable. Not only had they inherited and put to good practical use the knowledge of ancient Greek and Roman medicine, but in a few cases they even were able to improve upon their heritage. As one modern scholar puts it, "Many operations of present-day surgery, orthopedics, obstetrics-gynecology, otolaryngology, and hygiene methods, epidemiology, anesthesiology and physiology, considered as scientific advances in recent years, were known to medieval Greek physicians."* Of specific public hospitals in Constantinople, we know only very few by name. Yet hospitals and philanthropic institutions certainly existed from early times not only in Constantinople, Antioch, and Alexandria, but later in Thessalonika, Nicaea, Ephesus, and other provincial towns.

John Koukouzeles, the fourteenth-century reformer of Byzantine chant (see selection no. 318d), was an orphan of Slavic-Greek parentage, and was raised and educated in a monastic establishment originally founded for orphans by Emperor Alexius Comnenus (d. 1118). In the following selection Anna Comnena describes her father's solicitude for the orphans and the poor.

A PHILANTHROPIC EMPEROR

(From Anna Comnena, *Alexiade*, ed. B. Leib [Paris, 1945], vol. 3, p. 217.)

The name of this place is "the orphanage." It is called the orphanage on account of the philanthropy of the emperor toward orphans and war veterans. But the name especially applies to his solicitude for the orphans. There are [government] departments which handle all these matters and accounts are required from the administrators of the goods of these poor people. Chrysobulls also provide assurance as to the inalienable rights of those who are maintained there. A large and important group of clerics was assigned to the church of the great herald, Paul, along with a great amount of lighting. If you should enter this church you would see choirs chanting on either side: he appointed to this church of the apostles male and female singers in the manner of Solomon. He made the work of the deaconesses the object of his care and devoted much attention to the nuns who had come as emigres from Iberia. In the past they were in the habit of begging from door to door whenever they came to Constantinople, but the solicitude of my father led him to construct a very large convent for them and provide food and clothing appropriate to them. Let that famous Alexander of Macedon brag about Alexandria in Egypt, Bucephalus in Media, and Lysimachia in Ethiopia. But Emperor Alexius could not take pride in cities thus erected by him (which we know he built everywhere) as much as he prided himself on this "city."

Now, when you enter the area, these churches and holy monasteries would be on your left, while on the right of the great church [of St. Paul] stands the grammar school for all the orphans who have been gathered from all races. Over this presides a master and boys stand around him, some concerned with grammatical questions, while others compose what are called *schedoi*.[*] It is possible even to see a Latin being instructed there; a Scyth Hellenizing [his tongue] [i.e., learning Greek]; a Roman [Byzantine] studying Greek texts; and an illiterate Hellene [Greek] learning to speak Greek correctly. Such was the great interest taken by Alexius in literary studies. . . .

[Alexius also occupied himself with the care of captives taken in battle and other foreigners, as well as with the orphaned and handicapped of his own realm.]

[*] J. Theodorides, "Byzantine Science," in R. Taton, ed., *History of Science Ancient and Medieval* (New York, 1957), p. 440.

[†] Commentaries on specific passages in the text. On *schedographia*, see below, selection 305.

229.

Introduction. Probably the most important philanthropic institution established in Byzantium was the *xenon* of the monastery of the Pantokrator founded in Constantinople by Emperor John Comnenus (1136). *Xenones* were houses for travelers and, along with homes for the aged, sometimes offered medical services. Indeed, the *xenon* of the Pantokrator was a medical center almost in the modern sense of the term, and provided preventive as well as therapeutic care. The charter (*typikon*) establishing that institution provides information on the services available there: a general hospital, a home for the aged, a "psychiatric" clinic, and what we would term outpatient service. The following is a selection from the *typikon* of the *xenon* of the Pantokrator.

THE XENON OF THE PANTOKRATOR

(From A. Dmitrievskii, *Opisanie Liturgitseskich Rukopisej Typika* [Kiev, 1895], vol. 1, p. 682.)

Since a *xenon* has been established by Our Majesty, which ought to have beds for fifty patients, I desire and ordain that there be such a number for the repose of sick people. From among these fifty, ten [beds should be] for those with disturbances from wounds or crippled limbs and eight for those suffering from illnesses of the eyes and of the intestines and other severe ailments. For the women who are ill, there will be set aside twelve beds, and the remainder shall be given over to those sick who are simply recovering. But if there is often a lack of injured or of those with eye diseases or of those afflicted with very serious diseases, then the number [of beds] shall be filled with other such persons, those having *any* kind of illness. Let each bed have one blanket with pillow and coverlet but in the winter also with two heavy ones.

When these fifty beds are divided into five clinics, there shall be in each clinic an extra bed in which there shall be placed one of the sick who cannot be moved at all, either because of the acuteness of the illness, or because of great weakness, or sometimes even because of the severity of the wounds he has suffered. They [the patients] should be attended to constantly because of the unpredictability of their illnesses or because of the more serious complications that may follow. [There should be] shirts and outer clothing in the number of fifteen or twenty, so that when they arise they might have a change of clothing. And their clothing should be washed and guarded for them so that they can wear it when they have been cured and depart. Every year [let there be taken] from these beds and from the rest of the clothing whatever is totally worthless in order that it might be exchanged. And also the pillows, so that they may be repaired and the wool replaced and the torn clothes exchanged and again sewn for the repose of those bedridden.

230.

Introduction. That *philanthropeia* was an efficacious means to secure forgiveness of sins and to benefit the souls of the deceased is clearly implied by Symeon, metropolitan of Thessalonika (d. 1429), who in a theological treatise wrote the following:

PHILANTHROPEIA AND THE SOUL

(From Symeon of Thessalonika, *De fine et exitu nostra et vita*, MPG, vol. 155, col. 693.)

Through memorial [services] for the dead, prayers, Holy Communion, and good works [i.e., *philanthropeia*] for the poor, remission and forgiveness [of sins] and release from punishment are granted not only to those who have sinned and then died in repentance, but also to those who have lived righteously. . . . Let every one of the faithful know that, if he loves a deceased relative, he does him a great deal of good by offering [charity] on his behalf, and that he is the source of great joy for [the soul of] his relative whenever he gives to the poor or ransoms captives [of war].

231.

Introduction. As a result of this belief in the helpfulness of philanthropy for attaining salvation, patriarchs and bishops, monasteries and wealthy private individuals made provision for charitable purposes such as the foundation of churches and hospitals. An example of the philanthropic inclination of private citizens is the following statement of the fourteenth-century scholar-statesman Theodore Metochites (d. 1332), who commends the citizens of the city of Nicaea for their acts of philanthropy, especially their care of the sick and the poor.

PHILANTHROPEIA IN THE CITY OF NICAEA

(From Theodore Metochites, "Nikaefs," in K. Sathas, *Mesaioneke Bibliotheke* [Venice, 1872], vol. 1, p. 145.)

And regarding those things, I say, those communal homes and hospitals for the poor [living] in sickness and penury it is not so much the external appearance of the buildings that is to be commended as the display of compassion, the *philanthropeia* of both kinds: toward the treatment of sickness through medical help and toward the alleviation of hunger.

Commentary. Despite all the activity by emperors, churchmen, and others, Byzantine philanthropy in the last analysis displayed a striking weakness. Following perhaps too literally the evangelical precept, "Let not thy right hand know what thy left hand is doing," bread and money were often distributed as an act of charity but without effort at systematic eradication of poverty or rehabilitation of the indigent. In other words, it was aimed fundamentally at saving the soul of the person giving and seemed to lack any real awareness of larger responsibilities for public welfare or design for social amelioration of the lower classes.

G.
BYZANTINE AMUSEMENTS

232.

Introduction. Byzantine amusements ranged from participation in the magnificent ceremonies of the imperial and patriarchal courts to the morbid Byzantine fascination with death and deformity. Above all, the interests of the citizen of Constantinople centered on the Hippodrome. If Hagia Sophia was for God and the palace was for the emperor, the Hippodrome was intended for the amusement of the people. At the Hippodrome the emperor had his own great private box (the *kathisma*) facing on the side of the palace. Regarding the emperor's entrance into the Hippodrome the Arab historian of the late eleventh century, Marvazi, in his *Taba'i al-hayawan* relates:

THE EMPEROR APPEARS IN THE HIPPODROME

(Translated by V. Minorsky, "Marvazi on the Byzantines," in *Mélanges H. Grégoire, Annuaire de l'Institut de philologie et d'histoire orientales et slaves* 10 [1950]: 462.)

On the day before the day of assembly, a proclamation is made in the town that the Basileus intends to visit the Hippodrome. The people hasten thither for the spectacle and jostle in throngs and in the morning the king comes with his intimates and servants, all of them dressed in red. He sits on an eminence overlooking the place and there appears his wife called *dizbuna* [*despoina*] with her servants and intimates, all of them dressed in green, and she sits in a place opposite the king. Then arrive the entertainers and players of string instruments and begin their performance.

Commentary. There were special seats in the Hippodrome reserved for Byzantine ministers and also for foreign ambassadors. The Pisans, for example, in a twelfth-century treaty with the Byzantine Emperor specifically prescribed that they should have choice seats at all Hippodrome spectacles! Other leaders of the court, less privileged foreign guests and, of course, the population in general sat in the less distinguished sections of the large arena.

In the Hippodrome the entertainment varied from the symbolic pageantry in honor of the emperor (for instance, at the opening of the New Year) to combats between wild animals, athletic matches, and exhibitions of clowns, jugglers, acrobats, musicians, dwarfs, and mimes.

At regular intervals the Byzantine state and church provided, for the edification of the populace, "official" ceremonies—processions in the Hippodrome or Hagia Sophia, or, much more rarely, the celebration of great military triumphs through the capital. These elaborate processions, modeled after, or rather continuing, the tradition of the ancient Roman triumph, slowly wended their way from the Golden Gate along the Mese (the principal thoroughfare cutting through the city) and ended at the Cathedral of Hagia Sophia. What all of these ceremonies emphasized was imperial ideology—the emperor as Vicar of God—while at the same time of course providing diversion for the people. (See selection no. 283 for description of a triumphal procession as late as the thirteenth century.)

233.

Introduction. The most exciting of Byzantine amusements was probably the chariot races held in the Hippodrome of Constantinople. In the following passage we derive an impression of these races from the same foreign visitor quoted above, the Islamic writer Marvazi.

CHARIOT RACES IN THE HIPPODROME

(Translated by V. Minorsky, "Marvazi on the Byzantines," in *Mélanges H. Grégoire, Annuaire de l'Institut de philologie et d'histoire orientales et slaves* 10 [1950]: 462.)

Beforehand they prepare agile and trained horses and eight horses are brought [foward]. They also have in readiness two big vehicles [chariots] embellished with gold. To each of them four horses are harnessed, and in them two men take their places dressed in clothes woven of gold. Then they let the horses go, urging them on until they reach the two gates, and outside this gate there is a place with idols and statues and the drivers have to wheel around them three times in competition with one another. Whoever wins is laden with gifts. If the victory is with the king's party, it is a cause of rejoicing and good augury, and it is said: "Victory will be ours over the Muslims." If, however, the lady's [empress's] party wins, the king takes it as a bad omen and says, "The Muslims will be victorious over us." They call this day "the Day of the Hippodrome."

234.

Introduction. The leisure time of the ordinary Byzantine city dweller tended to be spent in the bath, the tavern, and at the various sporting events. The baths, scattered throughout the capital and in other important cities as well, were a place of relaxation and gossip for all classes of citizens. As in Turkey to this day (a legacy from the Byzantines), going to the baths constituted almost a full day's activity for both men and women who, according to law, bathed separately. The recreational (and frivolous) value of baths in Byzantine life is reflected, if in an oblique manner, in the following paraphrase of a condemnation of them attributed to the early seventh-century ascetic monk of Asia Minor, St. Theodore of Sykeon.

FUN AT THE BATHS

(Translated by E. Dawes and N. Baynes, *Three Byzantine Saints* [Crestwood, N.Y.: St. Vladimir's Seminary Press, and Oxford: A. R. Mowbray, 1977; originally published by Blackwell, Oxford, 1948], p. 178.)

Many in Constantinople, especially those in high places, were accustomed to go to the baths after communicating [taking the Eucharist]. Theodore condemned the practice. A number of the cathedral clergy came to Theodore and asked him whether his condemnation had support in scripture or was based on a special revelation. Theodore replied that God had revealed to him that those who take a bath after receiving the Eucharist through wantonness and for bodily enjoyment commit a sin. "For no one who has anointed himself with myrrh and perfumes washes off the pleasant scent thereof and no one who has lunched with the emperor straightway runs to the baths."

Commentary. Villagers too frequented bathhouses, as is revealed from the *Vita* of Symeon the Stylite the Younger, which tells of a village woodworker who sought out the saint in order to be cured of a demon who had cast him down in the bathhouse.*

*In H. Delehaye, *Vita S. Symeonis Stylitae Iunioris*, in *Les saints stylites* (Brussels, 1923), p. 256; summary by the editors.

235.

Introduction. The tavern, suspect to both the imperial government and the church, was a place where the ordinary citizen could meet, if he was so inclined, with the more nefarious elements of society. Besides excessive drinking, assaults and other transgressions of law might take place there—including the chief Byzantine vice, gambling. Especially popular were games of chance involving the use of dice. Checkers, a form of backgammon, and chess were also popular.

In the dark back streets of the larger cities were also to be found houses of prostitution and other dens of iniquity (although material on these of course is not very profuse in the sources).

Among common amusements was that of observing the antics of dancing bears. Well known is the case of Theodora, celebrated wife of the sixth-century Emperor Justinian, who in the days before her marriage to Justinian, as daughter of a bearkeeper, performed on the stage for the amusement of the public. The following passage from Procopius's famous *Secret History* gives a very hostile account of Theodora's checkered past.

THEODORA'S CHECKERED PAST

(From Procopius, *Secret History* [*Anecdota*], Loeb Classical Library [Cambridge, 1960], pp. 102 and 104.)

In Byzantium [Constantinople] there was a man called Acacius, who was in charge of the animals used in the hunt [i.e. in the

Hippodrome], a member of the Green Faction; they called him Master of the Bears. During the reign of Emperor Anastasius this man had died of illness, leaving behind three daughters, Comito, Theodora, and Anastasia, the eldest of whom was not yet seven years old. And his widow, reduced thus to destitution, married another man. . . . When these children became old enough, their mother had them at once go on the stage there—since they were comely to the eye—not all at the same time, however, but rather when each girl seemed to her ripe for this kind of work. The first of these, Comito, had already become well-known among the whores of her age. Theodora, the one next in line, dressed in a little tunic with sleeves as befitting a slave girl, was in the habit of following her [mother] around. She performed various services, especially carrying on her shoulders the stool her mother used to sit on in gatherings.

236.

Introduction. In the same section of his extremely biased *Secret History*, Procopius gives a more than intimate glimpse of Theodora's amours and her sexual exploits prior to her being raised to the imperial throne.

FUN AND GAMES WITH THEODORA

(From Procopius, *Secret History* [*Anecdota*], Loeb Classical Library [Cambridge, 1960], pp. 106, 108, 110.)

Later she consorted with the actors in all activities of the theater, sharing performances with them on stage and taking part in the buffoonish ribaldry intended to make the audience laugh. For she was extraordinarily clever and possessed of a biting wit, and soon became admired for this kind of performance. She had no sense of shame, and no one ever saw her embarrassed; rather without any hesitation she would perform the most shameful acts. Her character was such that while being beaten or struck over the head, she would make jokes and raucously burst out laughing. She would expose naked those things, front and back, which it is customary to keep unseen and hidden from men.

She would make jokes even when idling with her lovers, and by fooling around with new techniques of intercourse she always successfully won over the hearts of licentious men. Since she did not expect that propositions would be made by the men whom she encountered, she herself instead made jokes and moved her hips as she laughed so as to tempt every man who came along, especially beardless youths. Never was anyone more addicted to all forms of hedonistic gratification. Often when she went to a bring-your-own-food dinner party with ten or more vigorous young men for whom intercourse was a constant occupation, she lay with all of them for the entire night. When all of them were too exhausted to continue, she would sleep with each of their servants, some thirty in number. Even then she did not sate her lust.

Once, having gone to a certain official's house during the drinking, in the sight of all the revelers (so they say), she got up on the edge of the couch near their feet and brazenly took off her clothes, not hesitating to exhibit her lewdness. Although she made use of her three orifices, she used to complain of Nature, angry that it had not made her nipples larger than normal, so that she might be able to enjoy intercourse in yet another manner. She was frequently pregnant but managed almost always immediately to bring about an abortion.

Even in the theater, in sight of the entire audience, she would often undress and parade naked among the people, with only a girdle around her groin and genitals. She was not even ashamed to exhibit these to the public. Regulations did not permit that anyone there be entirely nude; one had to wear at least a girdle around the groin. In such attire she would lie down on her back on the floor and certain slaves, whose duty it was, would sprinkle grains of barley over her genitals. Geese, specially trained for this purpose, would pick them up one by one with their beaks and eat them. When she arose she did not blush but rather seemed proud of her performance. For she was not only without shame herself but encouraged shamelessness even more in others.

237.

Introduction. The marketplace could provide a lively place of entertainment for the masses. The following piece (sixth-century) describes one of the presumably numerous outdoor entertainers who plied their trade in the streets and marketplaces of many cities in the empire.

A Trained Dog Does Tricks in the Marketplace

(From John Malalas, *Chronographia,* ed. L. Dindorf [Bonn, 1831], pp. 453–54.)

In this same period an itinerant man appeared from Italy, having with him a blond dog which, when called by his master, performed remarkable tricks. When his master was in the marketplace and while a crowd observed, the dog surreptitiously gathered up the rings from the observers and put them in the ground, covering them with earth. Then the man told his dog to give back each ring to each owner and the dog, checking matters out, returned to each person the ring that belonged to him.

The same dog was also given various *nomismata* engraved with images of several emperors and he sorted them all out according to their names. Before a large crowd of men and women, when asked, the dog pointed out the women who had fornicated, the men who were pimps, adulterers, and misers, and the lofty-minded. And all he indicated accurately. Whereupon many said that the dog was possessed of the spirit of the Pythia [the priestess-prophetess at the ancient oracle of Delphi].

238.

Introduction. The upper classes, besides attending the spectacles available to all at the Hippodrome, had their own special kinds of amusements. Chief among these was hunting, especially in Asia Minor where the estates of the nobility were generally located. The following selection describes the hunting expedition for pleasure of Emperor John II Comnenus, which unfortunately brought about his death (1143).

THE PASTIME OF THE HUNT

(From John Kinnamos, *Epitome rerum ab Ioanne et Alexio Comnenis gestarum,* ed. A. Meineke [Bonn, 1836], p. 24.)

It is useful to relate the way in which the emperor [John Comnenus] died. A huge boar, such as the lands of Cilicia and the Taurus Mountains produce in abundance, appeared before him while he was hunting. He met the charging animal (it is said) with the spear that he held in his hand. After the spearpoint had been buried in its chest, the boar became infuriated at the blow and pressed more strongly against the emperor so that John's arm, which had been turned aside from a straight position by the boar's violent resistance, was deflected against the quiver full of arrows which he customarily held suspended from his shoulder. His wrist was cut by the tips of the arrows and a wound immediately resulted. A bloody foam flowed out of the wound, but a thin membrane—which the common people vulgarly term *ekdera*—was applied in order to bind the cut and to heal the wound so that it might not become inflamed and painful. But this [*ekdera*] later became the cause of inflammation. For the poison from the tip of the arrow entered into its material and thus spread to the rest of the emperor's body. But this happened later.

239.

Introduction. In the mid-twelfth century, with the increased contact with Western chivalric practices, the Byzantine Emperor Manuel I Comnenus introduced a vogue for jousts after the Western fashion, even jumping, on occasion, into the Hippodrome himself to participate in mock battle. Such Western-style tournaments were promoted by Manuel I for the edification of his people. Many Byzantines, however, looked down on these Latin practices as "barbarian," degrading, and not befitting the imperial pageantry of the Hippodrome. The following passage from the history of the fourteenth-century Nicephorus Gregoras discusses the celebration with tournament and joust (*zostra*) which took place at Didymoteichon in Thrace on the occasion of the birth of an heir to the throne.

LATIN-STYLE JOUSTS AND TOURNAMENTS IN BYZANTIUM

(From Nicephorus Gregoras, *Byzantina historia*, ed. I. Bekker and L. Schopen [Bonn, 1829], vol. 1, pp. 482ff.)

The following summer the wife of the emperor [Andronicus III], Empress Anna, who was pregnant, gave birth at Didymoteichon on June 18 to a son, John the emperor. And hearing this the emperor returned back very speedily to Didymoteichon. Exulting with joy he put away the mourning garments he was wearing because of the death of his grandfather and put on more splendid ones. Then he celebrated two games (resurrecting somehow the likeness of the Olympic games), which earlier he had often sponsored but now in a more sumptuous manner. These games had been earlier devised by the Latins for the purpose of exercising the body when there was no war. One of these was a type of single combat which is called by the Latins "joust." And the participants are divided according to tribes and peoples and fraternal groups. Then each side arms itself, and individuals who so wish fight against each other, making themselves in every way cataphracts. Then with each one taking his spear, the end of which has three [sharp] points, they attack each other and collide forcefully, pushing against each other violently with their lances. The one knocking his opponent from his horse is proclaimed victor. Then by lot even the emperor participated in such single combat so that sometimes he was almost mortally wounded. For this reason he was counseled by the older men not to participate in such activities. For it was not proper for the emperor to be struck by his inferiors; this was a contest in which danger existed.

The second of the games is called "tournament." It goes this way. The contestants are divided according to tribes and peoples and fraternal groups and all are armed similarly. And after selections are made by lot, they elevate as leaders two of them, one from each group. This [tournament], which earlier had been gradually dying out, now occurs constantly. The emperor himself was among those who, like a common soldier, obeyed the leader selected. When both sides, in equal number, had assailed each other wielding sturdy clubs, the emperor himself struck others and was struck back freely. This was the rule of the contest: whoever wounded or perchance killed another was not culpable. After the end of this contest, both sides received back their own leader, and among them even the emperor did not leave his subordinate position, each side parading in good order in two separate files until they disbanded.

240.

Introduction. While the works of ancient Greek playwrights remained known and were studied either in schools or privately, it seems clear that these plays were not actually performed on stage, probably owing to ecclesiastical censure of their too overtly pagan content. However, theatrical performances of a more contemporary type—of a kind of musical comedy or of a ribald genre—were presented. This and other facets of Byzan-

tine life and amusements helped to satisfy the Byzantine people's passionate
love for the theatrical. (Cf. selection 314.)

There seem to have been some plays of a religious nature composed in Byzantium. The only surviving example of this genre is the eleventh- or twelfth-
century *Chrestos Paschon*, formerly wrongly attributed to the fourth-century
Church Father, Gregory of Nazianzus. The following is the (anonymous) author's introduction to this rather inferior work.

A Drama on Christ's Passion in Imitation of Euripides

(From *Grégoire de Nazianze [?], La Passion du Christ tragédie*, ed.
A. Tuilier [Paris, 1969], pp. 124–26.)

Preface

"Dramatic presentation of our Holy Father Gregory
the Theologian [sic] containing, in the manner of Euripides, the incarnation in
our behalf of our Savior Jesus Christ and his world-redeeming Passion."

Since, after piously hearing some verses, you wish now to hear some religious
poems, listen attentively. I shall now present to you in the manner of Euripides a
recital of the world-redeeming Passion. You will learn all the mysteries from the
mouth of the Virgin Mother and from that of the disciple who was dear to the
Master's heart. First the Virgin Mother will begin her recital; she will be seen
lamenting as a mother at the moment of his Passion. Her lamentations will recall
from the beginning the fate which has earned her the name Mother of the Word
in order to reveal today the suffering that her Son had unjustly to undergo. If we
had not been misled by our own weakness we would not have been condemned
to death from the beginning of the world, the ruses of the serpent would not
have abased us, the duplicity of the monster would not have engendered death
and we would not have suffered the sad fate which we justly merited. To triumph
over evil, it would not have been necessary that the Master of life, the divine
Logos, become man and desire to die in atoning through goodness for what was
lost and in returning life to humankind. If the Word had remained in its [origi-
nal] glory, this woman would not have become Mother of the Lord; she would
not have suffered; she would not have cried out in pain as she saw him suffering
today in so unjust a manner. Here then are the actors of my drama: the All-Holy
Mother [*Panagia*], the chaste and pure virgin [John the Theologian], and the
women who appear with the Mother of the Lord.

PART V
Byzantium and the World

A.
THE GERMANS AND THE HUNS

In the eyes of its inhabitants the Byzantine Empire, theoretically, included all the territories of the ancient Roman Empire. Although its borders in actuality were considerably smaller, nevertheless, except for the Nicene and last Palaeologan period (1204–1453), the empire, like its Roman predecessor, may be called a multi-ethnic (or multi-national) state. Just as for most of its existence the empire included within it many diverse ethnic groups, so at the same time it had a rich and varied relationship with many peoples living outside its borders.

While racial or national prejudice seems to have been of little consequence in Byzantine life (except in the last two centuries with respect to the Latins and Turks), there was what we may term "cultural" prejudice. Regardless of one's ethnic ancestry, the principal qualification for social acceptance among the upper classes at least, besides of course Orthodox Christianity, was a "Hellenic" education (*paideia*). This meant a knowledge of the Greek language and at least some acquaintance with the Greek classical authors—a necessary attribute if one was not to be viewed as a "barbarian."

241.

Introduction. In the second century A.D., the barbarian Germanic Goths migrated southward into southern Russia, where they came into contact with the more advanced civilization of the Greek cities of that area. By the fourth century some Goths had accepted Christianity. This was especially the result of the work of the Arian bishop Ulfila, born on Gothic territory but educated as an Arian in Constantinople. He invented a Gothic alphabet (based in part on Greek letters) and translated the Bible into Gothic (341). As a result of his missionary work the Goths became Arian Christians. We quote from Sozomen, the early fifth century Byzantine historian.

ULFILA CONVERTS THE GOTHS (341)

(Translated by C. Hartranft, from Sozomen, *Church History*, in P. Schaff and H. Wace, eds., *A Select Library of Nicene and Post-Nicene Fathers of the Christian Church*, 2d ser. [reprint, Grand Rapids, Mich.: Wm. Eerdmans, 1976], vol. 2, p. 373.)

The vanquished [Gothic] nation, being pursued by their enemies, crossed over into the Roman territories. They passed over the river, and dispatched an embassy to the emperor, assuring him of their co-operation in any warfare in which he might engage, provided that he would assign a portion of land for them to inhabit. Ulphilas, the bishop of the nation, was the chief of the embassy. The object of his embassy was fully accomplished, and the Goths were permitted to take up their abode in Thrace.

Ulphilas, their bishop, originally held no opinions at variance with those of the Catholic Church; for during the reign of Constantius, though he took part, as I am convinced, from thoughtlessness, at the council of Constantinople, in conjunction with Eudoxius and Acacius, yet he did not swerve from the doctrines of the Nicaean council. He afterwards, it appears, returned to Constantinople, and, it is said, entered into disputations on doctrinal topics with the chiefs of the Arian faction; and they promised to lay his requests before the emperor, and forward the object of his embassy, if he would conform to their opinions. Compelled by the urgency of the occasion, or, possibly, thinking that it was better to hold such views concerning the Divine nature, Ulphilas entered into communion with the Arians, and separated himself and his whole nation from all connection with the Catholic Church. For as he had instructed the Goths in the elements of religion, and through him they shared in a gentler mode of life, they placed the most implicit confidence in his directions, and were firmly convinced that he could neither do nor say anything that was evil. He had, in fact, given many signal proofs of the greatness of his virtue. He had exposed himself to innumerable perils in defense of the faith, during the period that the aforesaid barbarians were given to pagan worship. He taught them the use of letters, and translated the Sacred Scriptures into their own language. It was on this account, that the barbarians on the banks of the Ister followed the tenets of Arius.

242.

Introduction. In the fourth century divisions of Goths participated as mercenary troops in the Roman (Byzantine) armies. They served faithfully until the Goths, pressed by the fierce Huns from the Asiatic East, had to cross the Danube into Byzantine territory. Mistreated by the Byzantines, they attacked and defeated the Byzantine army under Emperor Valens at the famous battle of Adrianople in 378. We quote from Jordanes, the historian of the Goths, on this battle.

The Goths Defeat and Kill Valens at Adrianople (378)

(Translated by C. Mierow from *The Gothic History of Jordanes* [New York: Barnes & Noble, 1960], p. 90.)

When the Emperor Valens heard of this [the Gothic uprising] at Antioch, he made ready an army at once and set out for the country of Thrace. Here a grievous battle took place and the Goths prevailed. The Emperor himself was wounded and fled to a farm near Hadrianople. The Goths, not knowing that an emperor lay hidden in so poor a hut, set fire to it (as is customary in dealing with a cruel foe), and thus he was cremated in royal splendor. Plainly it was a direct judgment of God that he should be burned with fire by the very men whom he had perfidiously led astray when they sought the true faith, turning them aside from the flame of love into the fire of hell. From this time the Visigoths, in consequence of their glorious victory, possessed Thrace and Dacia Ripensis as if it were their native land.

243.

Introduction. But the Gothic problem was one of internal danger to Byzantium as well as external. Not only did Gothic armies continue to give trouble until pacified by the measures of Emperor Theodosius I, but they rapidly infiltrated into the government, even taking over important official posts in Constantinople as well as assuming the supreme army office of *magister militum* (master of the soldiers). A protest penned by the philosopher Synesius in Cyrene (North Africa) addressed (after 399) to the Emperor Arcadius reflects the reaction of certain social groups to the German danger; Synesius saw the Goths as a pernicious threat to the existence of the Roman state. He suggests their expulsion from Constantinople and the army, the formation instead of a native Roman army, and the relegation of the Goths to tilling the soil outside Constantinople.

Synesius Cautions against the Gothic Threat

(Translated by A. Fitzgerald, *The Letters of Synesius of Cyrene* [London, 1926], pp. 13–24.)

The least pretext will be used by the armed [Goths] to assume power and become the rulers of the [Roman] citizens. And then the unarmed will have to fight with men well exercised in military combats. First of all they [the Goths] should be removed from commanding positions and deprived of senatorial rank; for what the Romans in ancient times considered of highest esteem has become dishonorable because of the influence of the foreigners. As in many other matters, so in this one, I am astonished at our folly. In every more or less prosperous home we find a Scythian [Goth] slave; they serve as cooks and cupbearers; also those who walk along the street with little chairs on their backs and offer them to people who wish to rest in the open, are Scythians.

But is it not exceedingly surprising that the very same light-haired barbarians with Euboic headdress, who in private life perform the function of servants, are our rulers in political life? The Emperor should purify the troops just as we purify a measure of wheat by separating the chaff and all other matter, which, if allowed to germinate, harms the good seed. Your father, because of his excessive compassion, received them [the barbarians] kindly and condescendingly, gave them the rank of allies, conferred upon them political rights and honors, and endowed them with generous grants of land. But not as an act of kindness did these barbarians understand these noble deeds; they interpreted them as a sign of our weakness, which caused them to feel more haughty and conceited. By increasing the number of our native recruits and thus strengthening our own army and our courage, you must accomplish in the Empire the things which still need to be done. Persistence must be shown in dealing with these people. Either let these barbarians till the soil following the example of the ancient Messenians, who put down their arms and toiled as slaves for the Lacedaemonians, or let them go by the road they came, announcing to those who live on the other side of the river [Danube] that the Romans have no more kindness in them and that they are ruled by a noble youth!

244.

Introduction. In 476 the German (Herul) leader Odovacar deposed the Western emperor, the young Romulus Augustulus, and sent the imperial insignia of office to Emperor Zeno in Constantinople and was himself recognized by Zeno as *magister militum* for Italy, governing (in theory at least) as the emperor's viceroy. Jordanes, historian of the Goths, thus succinctly describes the deposition of the last emperor in the West.

ODOVACAR DEPOSES ROMULUS AUGUSTULUS (476)

(Translated by C. Mierow from *The Gothic History of Jordanes* [New York: Barnes & Noble, 1960], p. 119.)

Now when Augustulus had been appointed Emperor by his father Orestes in Ravenna, it was not long before Odovacar, king of the Torcilingi, invaded Italy, as leader of the Sciri, the Heruli and allies of various races. He put Orestes to death, drove his son Augustulus from the throne and condemned him to the punishment of exile in the Castle of Lucullus in Campania. Thus the Western Empire of the Roman race, which Octavianus Augustus, the first of the Augusti, began to govern in the seven hundred and ninth year from the founding of the city, perished with this Augustulus in the five hundred and twenty-second year from the beginning of the rule of his predecessors and those before them, and from this time onward kings of the Goths held Rome and Italy. Meanwhile Odovacar, king of nations, subdued all Italy and then at the very outset of his reign slew Count Bracila at Ravenna that he might inspire a fear of himself among the Romans. He strengthened his kingdom and held it for almost thirteen years, even until the appearance of Theodoric, of whom we shall speak hereafter.

245.

Introduction. Meanwhile, Emperor Zeno was concerned over the threat of another Gothic people, the Ostrogoths (East Goths). In order to rid himself of this new menace and at the same time to punish the now recalcitrant Odovacar, he sent the Ostrogoths under their able king, Theodoric, to Italy. There Theodoric was able to seize from Odovacar the principal Byzantine fortress city of Ravenna, thus founding the Ostrogothic kingdom of Italy (493). Italy was to remain under Ostrogothic rule until its reconquest by the Byzantine Emperor Justinian in the mid-sixth century.

THEODORIC THE OSTROGOTH, KING OF ITALY

(From *Anonymus Valesianus*, ed. V. Gardthausen [Leipzig, 1875], par. 57, pp. 294–95, 297.)

In the consulate of Olybrius, Odovacar the king left Ravenna at night, after going into Pineta with the Heruls against the camp of the patrician Theodoric, and they [Theodoric and his men] cut off the army on both sides. Levila, Odovacar's *magister militum* was killed while fleeing in the river Bedente. And Odovacar, now defeated, fled to Ravenna on the Ides of July. There Odovacar under compulsion gave his own son Thelon as a hostage to Theodoric, in good faith that he would be safe. Thus Theodoric entered Ravenna. In a few days, Odovacar, plotting against him [Theodoric], was discovered shortly before entering the palace, and Theodoric with his own hand anticipated him and killed him with a sword in Lauritum. On the same day the men of Odovacar's army were all killed on Theodoric's order wherever they could be found, along with all their children. And Zeno the emperor died in Constantinople and Anastasius was made emperor.

Theodoric had sent Faustus Nigrus to Zeno on a legation. But when Zeno's death was found out, before the legation could return, as Theodoric had entered Ravenna and killed Odovacar, the Goths made Theodoric their king, without waiting for the decree of the new *princeps* [Anastasius]. . . . Later Theodoric received a wife from the Franks by name of Augoflada . . . and after peace was made with Emperor Anastasius through the mediation of Festus regarding his assumption of the throne [i.e., without imperial consent], the emperor sent back all the insignia of the palace [throne] which Odovacar had [previously] sent to Constantinople.

246.

Introduction. The most important Germanic tribe to settle in the West was the Franks. Like most of their predecessors the Franks were eager to obtain official confirmation of their authority over the areas (Gaul) in which they settled. The following selection from Bishop Gregory of Tours relates how King Clovis of the Franks obtained from Emperor Anastasius (491–518) the coveted Roman title of consul.

KING CLOVIS OF THE FRANKS, ROMAN CONSUL

(Translated by E. Bréhaut from Gregory of Tours, *History of the Franks* [New York: W. W. Norton, 1969], p. 47.)

Clovis received an appointment to the consulship from the emperor Anastasius, and in the church of the blessed Martin he clad himself in the purple tunic and chlamys and placed a diadem on his head. Then he mounted his horse, and in the most generous manner he gave gold and silver as he passed along the way which is between the gate of the entrance [of the church of St. Martin] and the church of the city, scattering it among the people who were there with his own hand, and from that day he was called *consul* or *Augustus*. Leaving Tours he went to Paris and there he established the seat of his kingdom.

247.

Introduction. Constantinople, because of its strategic location astride two continents and at the confluence of three seas—not to mention its great wealth—was constantly endangered by invading forces. A chief route into Europe from Asia was across the Russian steppes and down to the Black Sea. Constantinople was threatened by a long series of invasions by central Asiatic peoples, but (except for the Latin conquest of 1204) the walls of the city were never breached until the final siege by the Turks in 1453. One of the first and most ferocious of such Asiatic (Turkic) peoples were the Huns. In the earlier part of the fifth century the Byzantine historian Priscus (the bulk of whose work is now lost) wrote a vivid description of his visit to the Huns as envoy of the Byzantine Emperor to the court of the much-feared Hunnic leader, Attila.

A BYZANTINE EMBASSY TO THE HUNS

(Translated by J. B. Bury, *History of the Later Roman Empire* [New York, 1958], vol. 1, pp. 279–88.)

We set out with the barbarians, and arrived at Sardica, which is thirteen days for a fast-traveller from Constantinople. . . .

Having waited for some time until Attila advanced in front of us, we proceeded, and having crossed some rivers we arrived at a large village, where Attila's house was said to be more splendid than his residences in other places. . . .

Attila sat in the middle on a couch; a second couch was set behind him, and from it steps led up to his bed, which was covered with linen sheets and wrought coverlets for ornament, such as Greeks and Romans use to deck bridal beds. The places on the right of Attila were held chief in honour, those on the left, where we sat, were only second. Berichus, a noble among the Scythians, sat on our side, but had the precedence of us. Onegesius sat on a chair on the right of Attila's couch, and over against Onegesius on a chair sat two of Attila's sons; his eldest son sat on his couch, not near him, but at the extreme end, with his eyes fixed on the ground, in shy respect for his father. When all were arranged, a cup-bearer came and handed Attila a wooden cup of wine. He took it, and saluted the first in precedence, who, honoured by the salutation, stood up, and might not sit down until the king, having tasted or drained the wine, returned the cup to the attendant. All the guests then honoured Attila in the same way, saluting him, and then tasting the cups; but he did not stand up. Each of us had a special cup-bearer, who would come forward in order to present the wine, when the cup-bearer of Attila retired. When the second in precedence and those next to him had been honoured in like manner, Attila toasted us in the same way according to the order of the seats. When this ceremony was over the cup-bearers retired, and tables, large enough for three or four, or even more, to sit at, were placed next the table of Attila, so that each could take of the food on the dishes without leaving his seat. The attendant of Attila first entered with a dish full of meat, and behind him came the other attendants with bread and viands, which they laid on the tables. A luxurious meal, served on silver plate, had been made ready for us and the barbarian guests, but Attila ate nothing but meat on a wooden trencher. In everything else, too, he showed himself temperate; his cup was of wood, while to the guests were given goblets of gold and silver. His dress, too, was quite simple, affecting only to be clean. The sword he carried at his side, the latchets of his Scythian shoes, the bridle of his horse were not adorned, like those of the other Scythians, with gold or gems or anything costly.

After the songs a Scythian, whose mind was deranged, appeared, and by uttering outlandish and senseless words forced the company to laugh. After him Zerkon, the Moorish dwarf, entered. He had been sent by Attila as a gift to Aetius, and Edecon had persuaded him to come to Attila in order to recover his wife, whom he had left behind him in Scythia; the lady was a Scythian whom he had obtained in marriage through the influence of his patron Bleda. He did not succeed in recovering her, for Attila was angry with him for returning. On the occasion of the banquet he made his appearance, and threw all except Attila into fits of unquenchable laughter by his appearance, his dress, his voice, and his words, which were a confused jumble of Latin, Hunnic, and Gothic. Attila, however, remained immovable and of unchanging countenance, nor by word or act did he betray anything approaching to a smile of merriment except at the entry of Ernas, his youngest son, whom he pulled by the cheek, and gazed on with a calm look of satisfaction. I was surprised that he made so much of this son, and neglected his other children; but a barbarian who sat beside me and knew Latin, bidding me not reveal what he told, gave me to understand that prophets had forewarned Attila that his race would fall, but would be restored by this boy. When the night had advanced we retired from the banquet, not wishing to assist further at the potations.

B.
BYZANTIUM AND THE PERSIANS, ARABS, AND ARMENIANS

248.

Introduction. From time immemorial, eastern areas in central Aṣia had exercised a strong influence on the Mediterranean world. Thus it is not surprising that certain eastern customs found their way into the Byzantine imperial court and were readily adopted into its ceremonies. From the Persians the Roman emperors Aurelian and later Diocletian borrowed the use of the diadem and the act of *proskynesis* (obeisance to the emperor by prostration on the floor). After smashing the power of the Persians, the one great rival of Byzantium up until the early seventh century, the Byzantine Emperors Heraclius and his successors officially adopted the title *Basileus* (ruler of all the *ecumene*) to add to the earlier title of *autokrator*. The term *basileus* is analogous to the Persian title Shah (king of kings).

The opening phrase from an edict of Heraclius (629) illustrates this new use of the term *basileus*: "Heraclius and [his son] Heraclius, the New Constantine, Faithful Emperors [*basileis*] in Christ".*

Nevertheless, Byzantine relations with the Persians were most notable for the constant rivalry and violent acrimony between them, which led to several periods of almost uninterrupted warfare. In the following account of the Persian capture of Jerusalem (614) written by the Byzantine monk, Antiochus Strategos, who lived in the *laura* of St. Saba (in Jerusalem), we observe the negative Byzantine attitude toward the conquering Persians, the legacy of centuries-long hostility.

THE PERSIAN CAPTURE OF JERUSALEM AS SEEN BY A BYZANTINE MONK

(Translated by F. Conybeare, "Antiochus Strategos' Account of the Sack of Jerusalem (614)," *English Historical Review* 25 [1910]: 506–7.)

The beginning of the struggle of the Persians with the Christians of Jerusalem was on the 15th April, in the second indiction, in the fourth year of the Emperor Heraclius. They spent twenty days in the struggle. And they shot from their ballistas with such violence, that on the twenty-first day they broke down the city wall. Thereupon the evil foemen entered the city in great fury, like infuriated wild beasts and irritated serpents. The men however who defended the city wall fled, and hid themselves in caverns, fosses, and cisterns in order to save themselves; and the people in crowds fled into churches and altars; and there they destroyed them. For the enemy entered in mighty wrath, gnashing their teeth in violent fury; like evil beasts they roared, bellowed like lions, hissed like ferocious serpents, and slew all whom they found. Like mad dogs they tore with their teeth the flesh of the faithful, and respected none at all, neither male nor female, neither young nor old, neither child nor baby, neither priest nor monk, neither virgin nor widow. . . .

Meanwhile the evil Persians, who had no pity in their hearts, raced to every place in the city and with one accord extirpated all the people. Anyone who ran away in terror they caught hold of; and if any cried out from fear, they roared at them with gnashing of teeth, and by breaking their teeth forced them to close their mouths. They slaughtered tender infants on the ground, and then with loud yelps called their parents. Their parents bewailed the children with vociferations and sobbings, but were promptly despatched along with them. Any that were caught armed were massacred with their own weapons. Those who ran swiftly were pierced with arrows, the unresisting and quiet they slew without mercy. They listened not to appeals of supplicants, nor pitied youthful beauty, nor had compassion on old men's age, nor blushed before the humility of the clergy. On the contrary they destroyed persons of every age, massacred them like animals, cut them in pieces, mowed sundry of them down like cabbages, so that all alike had severally to drain the cup full of bitterness. Lamentation and terror might be seen in Jerusalem. Holy churches were burned with fire, others were demolished, majestic altars fell prone, sacred crosses were trampled underfoot, life-giving icons were spat upon by the unclean. Then their wrath fell upon priests and deacons: they slew them in their churches like dumb animals.

*From J. and P. Zepos, eds., *Jus graecoromanum* (Athens, 1931), p. 36.

249.

Introduction. The collapse of the Persian Empire in the early seventh century facilitated the extraordinarily rapid rise and expansion of the newly Islamized Arabs. In many ways the Arabs took the former place of the Persians in Byzantine eyes, inheriting both the hostility and also the cultural interaction accompanied by Byzantine respect for highly refined eastern culture. The Arabs, like the Persians, were never considered by the Byzantines as "barbarians." All of these factors led to closer Byzantine ties with the Arabs than with other peoples, extending from the seventh century to at least the twelfth.

Ironically, at the time of the first Arab penetration across the extreme eastern borders of the empire (mid-seventh century), the Arabs, to judge by the Byzantine chroniclers, were viewed as either a heretical Jewish sect or an insignificant dissident Christian group. But the Byzantines soon learned how unique and vital the new Islamic civilization was, and by the end of the seventh century Syria, Palestine, Egypt, and North Africa were all permanently lost to the Arabs. Some measure of this Islamic success, however, was certainly due to the widespread disaffection felt by the largely Monophysite population of the eastern Byzantine areas, who often looked upon the invading Arabs as liberators, not as conquerors. We quote, from the *History of the Patriarchs of Alexandria*, a section from the life of the Monophysitic-Coptic Patriarch Benjamin I (622–61). The text reveals the preference of the Christian Monophysites for Arab rather than Orthodox Christian hegemony.

Toward the Arab Conquest of Egypt

(Translated and edited by B. Evetts, *History of the Patriarchs of Alexandria*, pt. 1, ch. 1, from *Patrologia Orientalis*, vol. 1, pp. 489–97.)

And in those days [Emperor] Heraclius saw a dream in which it was said to him: "Verily there shall come against thee a circumcised nation, and they shall vanquish thee and take possession of the land." So Heraclius thought that they would be the Jews, and accordingly gave orders that all the Jews and Samaritans should be baptized in all the provinces which were under his dominion. But after a few days there appeared a man of the Arabs, from the southern districts, that is to say, from Mecca or its neighbourhood, whose name was Muhammad; and he brought back the worshippers of idols to the knowledge of the One God, and bade them declare that Muhammad was his apostle; and his nation were circumcised in the flesh, not by the law, and prayed towards the South, turning towards a place which they called the Kaabah. And he took possession of Damascus and Syria, and crossed the Jordan, and dammed it up. And the Lord abandoned the army of the Romans before him, as a punishment for their corrupt faith, and because of the anathemas uttered against them, on account of the council of Chalcedon, by the ancient fathers.

When Heraclius saw this, he assembled all his troops from Egypt as far as the frontiers of Aswân. And he continued for three years to pay to the Muslims the taxes which he had demanded for the purpose of applying them to himself and all his troops; and they used to call the tax the *bakt*, that is to say that it was a sum levied at so much a head. And this went on until Heraclius had paid to the Muslims the greater part of his money; and many people died through the troubles which they had endured.

So when ten years were over of the rule of Heraclius together with the Colchian, who sought for the patriarch Benjamin, while he was fleeing from him from place to place, hiding himself in the fortified churches, the prince of the Muslims sent an army to Egypt, under one of his trusty companions, named Amr son of Al-Asi, in the year 357 of Diocletian, the slayer of the martyrs. And this army of Islam came down into Egypt in great force, on the twelfth day of Baunah, which is the sixth of June, according to the months of the Romans.

Now the commander Amr had destroyed the fort, and burnt the boats with fire, and defeated the Romans, and taken possession of part of the country. For he had first arrived by the desert; and the horsemen took the road through the mountains, until they arrived at a fortress built of stone, between Upper Egypt and the Delta, called Babylon. So they pitched their tents there, until they were prepared to fight the Romans, and make war against them; and afterwards they named that place, I mean the fortress, in their language, Bâblûn Al-Fustât; and that is its name to the present day.

After fighting three battles with the Romans, the Muslims conquered them. So when the chief men of the city saw these things, they went to Amr, and received a certificate of security for the city, that it might not be plundered. This kind of treaty which Muhammad, the chief of the Arabs, taught them, they called the Law; and he says with regard to it: "As for the province of Egypt and any city that agrees with its inhabitants to pay the land-tax to you, and to submit to your authority, make a treaty with them, and do them no injury. But plunder and take as prisoners those that will not consent to this and resist you." For this reason the Muslims kept their hands off the province and its inhabitants, but destroyed the nation of the Romans, and their general who was named Marianus. And those of the Romans who escaped fled to Alexandria, and shut its gates upon the Arabs, and fortified themselves within the city.

And in the year 360 of Diocletian, in the month of December, three years after Amr had taken possession of Memphis, the Muslims captured the city of Alexandria, and destroyed its walls, and burnt many churches with fire. And they burnt the church of Saint Mark, which was built by the sea, where his body was laid; and this was the place to which the father and patriarch, Peter the Martyr, went before his martyrdom, and blessed Saint Mark, and committed to him his reasonable flock, as he had received it. So they burnt this place and the monasteries around it. . . .

When Amr took full possession of the city of Alexandria, and settled its affairs, that infidel, the governor of Alexandria, feared, he being both prefect and patriarch of the city under the Romans, that Amr would kill him; therefore he sucked a poisoned ring, and died on the spot. But Sanutius, the believing duke, made known to Amr the circumstances of that militant father, the patriarch Benjamin, and how he was a fugitive from the Romans, through fear of them. Then Amr, son of Al-Asi, wrote to the provinces of Egypt a letter, in which he said: "There is protection and security for the place where Benjamin, the patriarch of the Coptic Christians is, and peace from God; therefore let him come forth secure and tranquil, and administer the affairs of his Church, and the government of his nation." Therefore when the holy Benjamin heard this, he returned to Alexandria with great joy, clothed with the crown of patience and sore conflict which had befallen the orthodox people through their persecution by the heretics, after having been absent during thirteen years, ten of which were years of Heraclius, the misbelieving Roman, with the three years before the Muslims conquered Alexandria. When Benjamin appeared, the people and the whole city rejoiced, and made his arrival known to Sanutius, the duke who believed in Christ, who had settled with the commander Amr that the patriarch should return, and had received a safe-conduct from Amr for him. Thereupon Sanutius went to the commander and announced that the patriarch had arrived, and Amr gave orders that Benjamin should be brought before him with honour and veneration and love. And Amr, when he saw the patriarch, received him with respect, and said to his companions and private friends: "Verily in all the lands of which we have taken possession hitherto I have never seen a man of

God like this man." For the Father Benjamin was beautiful of countenance, excellent in speech, discoursing with calmness and dignity.

Then Amr turned to him, and said to him: "Resume the government of all thy churches and of thy people, and administer their affairs. And if thou wilt pray for me, that I may go to the West and to Pentapolis, and take possession of them, as I have of Egypt, and return to thee in safety and speedily, I will do for thee all that thou shalt ask of me." Then the holy Benjamin prayed for Amr, and pronounced an eloquent discourse, which made Amr and those present with him marvel, and which contained words of exhortation and much profit for those that heard him; and he revealed certain matters to Amr, and departed from his presence honoured and revered. And all that the blessed father said to the commander Amr, son of Al-Asi, he found true, and not a letter of it was unfulfilled.

250.

Introduction. The next selection, by the Arab historian Al-Baladhuri, gives an Arab view of an event discussed in the previous selection, the conquest of the great Byzantine port of Alexandria (642) and the disposition of its property by the conquerors.

ALEXANDRIA CAPTURED BY THE ARABS

(Translated by P. Hitti, in *The Origins of the Islamic State* [New York: Columbia University Press, 1916], vol. 1, pp. 346–49.)

'Amr [the Arab commander] kept his way until he arrived in Alexandria whose inhabitants he found ready to resist him, but the Copts [the Monophysites] in it preferred peace. Al-Mukaukis [Alexandria's commander] communicated with 'Amr and asked him for peace and a truce for a time; but 'Amr refused. Al-Mukaukis then ordered that the women stand on the wall with their faces turned towards the city, and that the men stand armed, with their faces towards the Moslems, thus hoping to scare them [Moslems]. 'Amr sent word, saying, "We see what thou hast done. It was not by mere numbers that we conquered those we have conquered. We have met your king Heraclius, [the Byzantine Emperor], and there befell him what has befallen him." Hearing this, al-Mukaukis said to his followers, "These people are telling the truth. They have chased our king from his kingdom as far as Constantinople. It is much more preferable, therefore, that we submit." His followers, however, spoke harshly to him and insisted on fighting. The Moslems fought fiercely against them and invested them for three months. At last, 'Amr reduced the city by the sword and plundered all that was in it, sparing its inhabitants of whom none was killed or taken captive. He reduced them to the position of *dhimmis* [Christian protected minority] like the people of Alyunah. He communicated the news of the victory to 'Umar through Mu'awiyah ibn-Hudaij al-Kindi (later as-Sakuni) and sent with him the [usual] fifth [of booty].

The Greeks wrote to Constantine, son of Heraclius, who was their king at that time, telling him how few the Moslems in Alexandria were, and how humiliating the Greeks' condition was, and how they had to pay poll-tax. Constantine sent one of his men, called Manuwil [Manuel], with three hundred ships full of fighters. Manuwil entered Alexandria and killed all the guard that was in it, with the exception of a few who by the use of subtle means took to flight and escaped. This took place in the year 25. Hearing the news, 'Amr set out at the head of 15,000 men and found the Greek fighters doing mischief in the Egyptian villages next to Alexandria. The Moslems met them and for one hour were subjected to a shower of arrows, during which they were covered by their shields. They then advanced boldly and the battle raged with great ferocity until the "polytheists" [Christians] were routed; and nothing could divert or stop them before they reached Alexandria. Here they fortified themselves and set mangonels [a type of catapult]. 'Amr made a heavy assault, set the ballistae [machine like a crossbow for hurling large missiles] and destroyed the walls of the city. He pressed the fight so hard until he entered the city by assault, killed the fathers and carried away the children as captives. Some of its Greek inhabitants left to join the Greeks somewhere else; and Allah's enemy, Manuwil, was killed. 'Amr and the Moslems destroyed the wall of Alexandria in pursuance of a vow that 'Amr had made to that effect, in case he reduced the city. . . . (From 'Amr an-Nakid from Yazid ibn-abi-Habib):* 'Amr ibn-al-Asi conquered Alexandria, and some Moslems took up their abode in it as a cavalry guard.

* This indicates the oral source of transmission for the text.

251.

Introduction. Somewhat later, because of the role played by the Muslim Caliphate of Baghdad, the Byzantines began to look upon Islam as a rival "world religion"—a false religion, to be sure, but a powerful one and a major force to be reckoned with. In accordance with this view and also the undeniable fact of Islamic political and cultural eminence, some Byzantines came to regard the Arab caliph of Baghdad as virtually the equal of the emperor. Illustrative of this attitude are two letters from the early tenth-century patriarch Nicholas I Mysticus, regent of the empire, one to the Caliph of Baghdad and the other to the emir of Crete. In the first he writes that "two lordships" rule the world, the Roman-Christian and the Islamic. In the second he stresses the friendship between Patriarch Photius and the Muslim emir's father despite religious differences.

A. Two Lordships Rule the World

(Translated by R. Jenkins and L. Westerink, *Nicholas I Patriarch of Constantinople: Letters* [Washington, D.C.: Dumbarton Oaks, 1973], p. 3.)

All earthly authority and rule depend from the rule and authority that are above: and there is no authority among men, nor any potentate who succeeds to his power on earth by his native ability, unless the Author and Ruler and only Potentate in the Highest shall approve his succession.

Therefore it is right, if possible, that all of us who have obtained power among men, even though there should be nothing else to promote our mutual contact and converse through words, yet for this very reason—that we have obtained the gift of our authorities from a common Head—it is right that we should not omit day by day to make contact with one another, both by letters and by the emissaries who serve us in our affairs. This is even more incumbent on those who hold mighty rules and authorities, inasmuch as these have been more signally honored, and are (as it were) brothers superior to and preferred above their brethren, and entrusted with the administration of the greatest rules and authorities. What do I mean by this? I mean there are two lordships, that of the Saracens and that of the Romans, which stand above all lordship on earth and shine out like the two mighty beacons in the firmament. They ought, for this very reason alone, to be in contact and brotherhood and not, because we differ in our lives and habits and religion, remain alien in all ways to each other, and deprive themselves of correspondence carried on in writing.*

B. "FRIENDSHIP" BETWEEN PATRIARCH PHOTIUS AND THE EMIR OF CRETE

(From MPG, vol. 111, cols. 36–37.)

Your Sagacity must have noted that the highest of the high priests of God, the illustrious Photius (who is my father in the Holy Spirit) was joined to the father of Your Majesty in bonds of friendship. Indeed there was no other person of his religion and country so friendly to you. Since he was a man of God and learned with regard to human and divine matters, he realized that, though a dividing wall of worship separated us, yet the attributes of human wisdom, intelligence, dependability of conduct, love for mankind, and every other attribute that adorns and elevates human nature with its presence, ignites, in those persons who care for that which is good, friendship toward those imbued with the qualities they have.

*M. Canard has convincingly shown that this letter was addressed to the Caliph of Baghdad, not to the Emir of Crete as earlier believed.

252.

Introduction. Embassies were constantly being exchanged on the highest level between Constantinople and Baghdad, and even, to a lesser extent, between Constantinople and distant Muslim Cordoba. Complex negotiations over a multitude of interests were the rule. We quote from the detailed account of a late tenth-century Arab envoy, sent from the court of Baghdad to the court of Emperor Basil II in Constantinople to negotiate regarding Bardas Skleros, a Byzantine claimant to the throne who had gone to Baghdad hoping for Arab support against Basil. Note the almost modern fondness for complexity of negotiations, including mention of copies in triplicate.

AN ARAB AMBASSADOR IN CONSTANTINOPLE

(Translated by H. Amedroz, "An Embassy from Bagdad to the Emperor Basil II," *Journal of the Royal Asiatic Society* [1914], pp. 921–25.)

So I proceeded to Constantinople and made my entry after I had been met and most courteously escorted by court officials. I was honourably lodged in the palace of the Kanikleios Nicephorus (the envoy come with me) who stood in favour with the Sovereign. Next I was summoned to the presence of the Chamberlain [i.e., the eunuch Basil], who said: "We are acquainted with the correspondence which bears on your message, but state your views." Thereupon I produced the actual agreement, which he inspected and then said: "Was not the question of relinquishing the land-tax on Abu Taghlib's territory [at Mosul], both past and future, settled with al-Bākilāni in accordance with your wishes, and did he not assent to our terms as to restoring the fortresses we had taken, and as to the arrest of Bardas? Your master accepted this agreement and complied with our wishes, for you have his ratification of the truce under his own hand." I said that al-Bākilāni had not come to any arrangement at all; he replied that he had not left until he had settled the terms of agreement, of which the ratification under the hand of his sovereign was to be forwarded, and that he had previously produced his letter approving the whole of the stipulations. Accordingly I was driven to find some device in order to meet this position.

I said this: "Ibn al-Bākilāni came to no agreement with you; it was Ibn Kūnis who made this compact and took a copy of it in the Greek language." At this the Chamberlain broke out, and asked Ibn Kūnis "Who has authorized this?" to which he answered that neither he nor Ibn al-Bākilāni had settled anything, and I withdrew.

A few days later the Chamberlain summoned me and resumed reading the agreement. He paused at a point where it spoke of "what might be settled with Ibn Shahrām on the basis of what was contained in the third copy," and said that this was the one copy, but where were the other two? On referring to this passage I saw the blunder that had been committed in letting this stand, and said: "The meaning of the passage is that the agreement was to be in triplicate, one part to remain with the Byzantine ruler, one to be in Aleppo, and the third in the capital [Baghdad]." This Ibn Kūnis traversed, saying that his instructions had been to note down the exact sense of the agreement, and the Chamberlain said that this copy was the ruling one; that the second copy referred to giving up the fortresses, whilst the third omitted all mention of Aleppo; that the agreement had been signed on the terms agreed upon with Ibn al-Bākilāni, and the sole object in sending this copy was to procure the sovereign's hand and seal thereto. To which I said: "This cannot be so; my instructions are merely what I have stated as regards Aleppo and the fortresses, in accordance with the agreement which you have seen." He replied: "Were Bardas [i.e., Scleros] here in force and you had made us all prisoners you could not ask for more than you are asking; and Bardas is, in fact, a prisoner." . . .

I replied: "Your supposed case of Bardas being here in force is of no weight, for you are well aware that when Abu Taghlib, who is not on a par with the lowest of ʿAdud al-Daula's followers, assisted Bardas he foiled the Byzantine sovereigns for seven years; how would it be, then, were ʿAdud al-Daula to assist him with his army? Bardas, although a prisoner in our hands, is not exposed, as your captives are, to mutilation; his presence in the capital is the best thing for us, for we have not made a captive of him. It may be that he will fret at our putting him off, will despair of us, become estranged, and go away; but at present he is acting with us and is reassured by the pomp and security he witnesses at the capital. We hold in truth, all the strings."

My words impressed and nonplussed him greatly, for he knew them to be true, and he said: "What you ask cannot be granted; we will ratify, if you will, what was agreed on with al-Bākilāni—else, depart." I replied: "If you wish me to depart without having had a hearing from the Sovereign I will do so." To this he said that he spoke for the Sovereign, but that he would ask an audience for me.

And in a few days time I was summoned and attended. The Byzantine Sovereign [Basil] caused what had passed to be repeated to him in my presence, and said: "You have come on a reprehensible errand; your envoy came and procured our consent to certain terms, which included the restoring of the fortresses taken during the revolt; you are now asking to have ceded other fortresses which were taken by my predecessors. Either consent to what was originally stipulated or go in peace." I replied: "But al-Bākilāni agreed on nothing, for, as for the document he brought, you deprived us under its terms of half our territory; how can we admit such a thing against ourselves? Of these fortresses in Diyār Bakr none are held by you; now Diyār Bakr belongs to us: all you can do is to dispute it, and you do not know what will be the issue of the struggle." Here the Chamberlain interposed, saying: "This envoy is skilled in controversy and can make up a fine story: death is better for us than submission to these terms: let him return to his master." The Sovereign then rose, and I withdrew.

253.

Introduction. The literary work which comes closest to being a "national" Byzantine epic, the famous *Digenes Akritas*, probably composed in the tenth or eleventh century, not only reveals the military aspects of the Byzantine-Arab relationship, but in many ways depicts a symbiosis of life on the eastern frontier. This is evident in the very name of the hero, Digenes (literally, "two-raced"), the son of a converted Muslim father and a Christian mother. For extracts from *Digenes Akritas* see selections 9, 169, and 315.

254.

Introduction. Somewhat in the same manner that a modern corporation will guard its trade secrets from a rival, so the Byzantines, jealously guarded their technological advances. In the following selection from Theophanes Continuatus, we find the Emperor Theophilus (829–42) refusing a specific request from the Arab caliph of Baghdad for the services of the Byzantine mathematician Leo, even though the caliph was willing to pay a substantial amount in gold pieces for Leo's expertise.

LEO THE MATHEMATICIAN

(From Theophanes Continuatus, ed. I. Bekker [Bonn, 1838], pp. 188–90.)

And so Mamoun [Abbasid caliph—after hearing of Leo the mathematician from one of his students who had been captured and brought to Baghdad] immediately wrote letters to Leo, which contained the following sentiments: "Just as we recognize the tree by its fruit, so we know the teacher by his student. Although you have a command of the science of those things relating to virtue and profound knowledge, you are nevertheless unknown to your fellow countrymen; nor have you received the fruits of your wisdom and knowledge (for certainly you have garnered no honors from them). Thus do not consider it unworthy to come to us and share your teaching with us. If you do so, the entire Saracen people will hearken unto you, and you will be honored with money and gifts in a way that no one has ever been honored before." After Mamoun had given these letters to the youth [Leo's student] and indulged him with gifts, he instructed him to find Leo. Mamoun promised the youth honors and gifts and even, if he so desired, [the privilege] of returning again to his home, but only if he should persuade Leo to depart from the land of the Romans.

When the youth arrived in the imperial city and stood face to face with his teacher, the sight of his teacher warmed and, so to speak, inflamed him, moving him to tears which wet not only his cheeks but also his neck and chest. At first Leo was struck speechless at what happened, knowing neither who the young man was nor why he acted in such a manner. For [his pupil's] appearance, altered by time and the hardship of captivity, indicated that this was some other young man and not the one whom he had known. But when the youth slowly revealed his identity by stating his name and the areas of his study, and when he related the events of his captivity and the cause for his release and arrival [in Constantinople] while placing the letters [from Mamoun] into Leo's hands, both together then ended their sorrow and lamentation. But since Leo thought that it would hardly be safe for him to be caught having secretly received letters from the enemy, he went to the logothete (this was Theoctistus . . .) and explained to him all the things [related by] the captive, his student, and at the same time he gave him the letters of the *ameramnoune* (al-Mamoun).* It was for this reason that Leo came to the emperor's attention and that his services were acquired by the emperor. For both his student and the letters of Mamoun brought Leo's wisdom, heretofore hidden away in a corner, into the open. The logothete showed the letters to [Emperor] Theophilus, who summoned Leo, gave him a large sum of money, and publicly appointed him to teach in the Church of the Forty Holy Martyrs.

Not long afterwards, when Mamoun realized that the philosopher did not desire to abandon his home for another land, he sent [to Leo] in writing difficult problems in geometry, astrology, and other subjects, solutions for which he desired to receive. After Leo had considered each problem, he solved it, setting forth solutions for [all] of them. . . . When he received these letters, the *ameramnoune* (al-Mamoun) was overwhelmed with desire for this man and called out loudly, since he admired Leo's wisdom and knowledge. Whereupon, he immediately dispatched a letter not to Leo but to the emperor, which was of this tenor: "I had desired, as the act of a friend and student, to come to you. But since the authority which has been entrusted to me by God and the multitude of people who are under my hand and power do not permit this, I ask that you send [to me] for a brief time the man you have who is famous for his knowledge of philosophy and other disciplines and that you persuade him to stay with me, so that he may impart to me his knowledge and virtue for which I have such high regard. Do not decline to do this on account of the differences between our religions and peoples, but rather, since a man of such authority asks you, fulfill my request as between good and proper friends. In return for this I will present you twenty *centenarii* of gold [2,000 pounds] as a gift, along with peace and perpetual and endless treaties." With such means did Mamoun [seek to] buy Leo's departure [from the empire] and presence [in Baghdad]. Theophilus, however, answered that it was senseless to give away to others his own precious possession and to make known to other peoples things for which the Roman nation is marveled at and honored by everyone. And he did not accede to Mamoun's request.

* Probably a Greek transliteration of the Arabic term Amir al-Mu'minin ("commander of the faithful").

255.

Introduction. The Armenians, caught first between Byzantines and Persians, then between Byzantines and Arabs, and still later between Byzantines and Turks, were never well-liked in the empire, partly because, religiously, they were dissident Monophysites. Nevertheless, they were numerous in Byzantium and from the sixth century on they were of capital importance in Byzantine affairs. (Some of the greatest Byzantine emperors—Nicephorus Phocas, John Tzimisces and probably Heraclius—were of Armenian descent.)

The precarious position of the Armenians, within and outside the empire, may be observed in the next two selections. The first, from the seventh-century Armenian historian Sebeos, reveals the plans of the Byzantine Emperor Maurice (d. 602) and the Persian ruler to split Armenia between their two empires and to resettle the Armenian people elsewhere.

LETTER OF EMPEROR MAURICE ON THE ARMENIANS

(From F. Macler, *Histoire d'Héraclius par l'évêque Sebèos* [Paris, 1904], pp. 30–31.)

[Sebeos has Maurice address the Persian ruler as follows:]

The Armenians are scoundrels and an unsubmissive nation. They dwell between us and constitute a source of disturbance. I shall round up my [Armenians] and send them off to Thrace; let you send yours to the east. If they die there, it will be that many enemies who will perish. But if, on the other hand, they kill others, it will be that many enemies whom they kill. As for us, we shall live peacefully. If however they remain in their own country, we will never have any rest.

256.

Introduction. This scurrilous poem by the famous ninth-century Byzantine poetess-nun Kasia reflects something of the prejudices, however exaggerated here, of a large part of Byzantine society toward the Armenian people. The poem also may perhaps be taken as evidence of the oft-expressed view that religious issues covered deeper social and cultural antagonisms, not only between Greeks and Monophysite Armenians but even between Greeks and Chalcedonian (Orthodox) Armenians.

KASIA ON THE ARMENIANS

(From C. Trypanis, *Medieval and Modern Greek Poetry* [Oxford, 1951], p. 43.)

The most terrible race of the Armenians
Is deceitful and evil to extremes,
Mad and capricious and slanderous
And full of deceit, being greatly so by nature,
Once a wise man said of them appropriately:
Armenians are evil even when they are obscure.
On being honored they become more evil;
On acquiring wealth they (become] even more evil
    on the whole;
But when they become extremely wealthy and
    honored,
They appear to all as evil doubly compounded.

Commentary. The traditional antagonism of Greek for Armenian and vice versa reached its culmination at the time of the battle of Manzikert (1071), when the treachery of the Armenians was in some part responsible for the annihilation of the Byzantine army by the Seljuk Turks.

C.
BYZANTIUM AND THE SLAVS

257.

Introduction. A special relationship existed between the Byzantines and the Slavs. True, the Slavs were often a menace to the external security of the empire, but they adopted, as a people, Orthodox Christianity. Although it cannot be said that most of the Slav states were de jure parts of the empire, their acceptance of a common religion and common political theory (one modern historian calls them part of the Byzantine "Commonwealth," meaning the Orthodox world)* gave them a special relationship to the provinces of the empire. They did not, however, receive one vital element of Byzantine civilization: the Greek classical heritage. The Slavs, even those in the higher levels of society, rarely learned the Greek language, since all the religious service books and other ecclesiastical texts were translated into Slavonic. Thus, because of Byzantine emphasis on Hellenic culture, though the Byzantines recognized the Slavic powers (Moravians, Bulgars, Rus, and Serbs) as fellow Orthodox from a religious point of view, they at the same time viewed the Slavs as culturally inferior and potentially dangerous—neighbors who had to be handled with care.

The degree of Slavic settlement and influence in what is today Greece is a much debated question. We simply note here the famous *Chronicle of Monemvasia* concerning the Avars and the Slavs in the Peloponnesus, an area which was constantly raided by the Slavs between 587 and 805 (see above, selection 197).

The Bulgars were originally a Turanian (Turkic) people who ultimately were assimilated by the more numerous Slavs living in the Balkans, around the area of modern-day Bulgaria. Following many bloody encounters between the Byzantine and Bulgar armies, the Bulgars became, in the eyes of the Byzantines of the tenth and eleventh centuries, the most dangerous of all of Byzantium's enemies. The threat of the so-called "First Bulgarian Empire" was ended in 1016 only by the crushing victory of Emperor Basil II the Bulgaroktonos ("Bulgar-slayer").

An earlier emperor, Nicephorus I, who had seen the defeat of the Slavs in Greece, was killed in 811 in battle against the Bulgars, who at that time were led by Khan Krum. The following selection describes the campaign.

ON EMPEROR NICEPHORUS, WHO LEFT HIS BONES IN BULGARIA

(From I. Dujcev, "La chronique byzantine de l'an 811," *Travaux et mémoires* [Paris, 1965], vol. 1, pp. 210–12.)

In the ninth year of the reign of the Emperor Nicephorus, he penetrated into Bulgaria, desiring to crush it. He took with him his son Staurakios and his son-in-law Michael, also named Rhangabe, as well as all the patricians, *archontes*, and dignitaries, and all the military forces, and the sons of the *archontes*, from fifteen years on up, of which he formed his son's company, bestowing upon it the name of Ikanatri. As they entered the defiles, the Bulgars, learning of the great size of the advancing army and feeling unable to withstand it, abandoned all their goods and fled into the mountains. Thus Nicephorus penetrated and installed himself in the residence of the prince of Bulgaria, called Krum. But finding there an army of Bulgars left to defend it, he engaged in combat with them and killed them all. Meantime fifty thousand others had come to meet him, and he gave battle and crushed them.

Entering into the residence of Krum, he inspected his treasures and, finding there a rich booty, he had it distributed to his soldiers: money of copper, vestments, and various other objects of value, according to a list. He also opened storehouses and distributed wine to all his men so they could assuage their thirst. Then, promenading through the residence and walking on the terraces, he exulted and said, "See, God has delivered all this into my hands. I want to build here a city in my name, so that I may be famous among all future generations." After a few days, he left the residence of the impious Krum and, as he departed, burned all the houses as well as the enclosure constructed of pieces of wood. Then, without devoting any care to his withdrawal, he began rapidly to march across all of Bulgaria, intending to push to Sardica, thinking that he had gotten rid of the Bulgars. At the end of fifteen days, he had come to the point of completely neglecting his affairs. His spirit was no longer the same, and like a man beside himself, he lost his head. He fell into complete mental confusion and became paralyzed by the attitude of presumption. He no longer left his tent, addressed a word, or gave an order to anyone. Although some clamored against him and sent his son to counsel him to leave that place, he paid no attention. [The rest of the passage describes Nicephorus's defeat and capture by the Bulgar khan.]

*They were actually an integral part of the Byzantine church. The patriarch, for example, named a Byzantine prelate as Metropolitan of Kiev (later Moscow) until about the mid-fifteenth century. See selection 265.

258.

Introduction. The most significant development in early Slavic history was their conversion to Christianity, a process set in motion by the two so-called "Slavic apostles," Cyril and Methodius. Born in Byzantine Thessalonika, the two brothers Constantine (later renamed Cyril), formerly professor of philosophy in Constantinople, and Methodius, an *hegoumenos* (abbot), were in 863 sent by Patriarch Photius to convert the Slavic Moravians in what is today part of Czechoslovakia. Through their efforts not only the Moravian people but ultimately many other Slavic peoples, including the Bulgars and the Russians, accepted Christianity. Hardly less important, they received an alphabet, which constituted in effect the beginnings of Slavonic literature. The two brothers translated into Slavonic the Bible, the Psalter, and other Byzantine liturgical writings.

The following account, drawn from the famous *Life* of Methodius (which was written by one of his Slavic disciples, as the parallel *Life* of his brother Constantine was written by Methodius), emphasizes not only their proselytizing mission but also the achievement of creating a new Slavonic literature based on the Byzantine heritage.

THE *VITA* OF METHODIUS

(From F. Dvornik, *Les légendes de Constantin et de Methode vues de Byzance* [Prague, 1933], pp. 385–88.)

It happened at this time that Rastislav, the Slavic ruler, and Sviatopluk [prince of Moravia] dispatched [an envoy] from Moravia to the Emperor Michael to tell him: "By the grace of God we are well. There have come among us to teach a number of Christians, some Italians, Greeks, Germans who have taught us in different fashions. But we Slavs are simple people and we have no one to teach us the truth and to explain to us the meaning [of Scripture]. Send us then, Lord, a man capable of teaching us the whole truth."

Emperor Michael said to Constantine the philosopher: "Do you hear, O philosopher, this word? No one else except you can do it. Here are some gifts for you, go there and take with you your brother Methodius, the *hegoumenos*. For both of you are from Thessalonika and all the Thessalonians speak Slavic well." They were of course unable to refuse God and the emperor, according to the word of St. Peter, who said: "Fear God and respect the emperor." But when they had heard the great word [call], they began to pray with the others who were molded with the same spirit as they. And then afterward God revealed to the philosopher the Slavonic writing. After having at once combined the letters and composed a sermon, he took the road for Moravia, leading Methodius with him. Again the latter began humbly to obey the philosopher, to serve him, and to teach with him. And at the end of three years they returned from Moravia, after having taught some disciples.

259.

Introduction. With the conversion of the Moravians by Cyril and Methodius, the Bulgars found themselves surrounded by Christian powers and at the same time subject to increasing Christianizing influences, especially from followers of the two apostles who came to Bulgaria. For these reasons as well as very possibly out of sincere religious conviction, the khan of the Bulgars, Boris, decided to adopt Christianity for his people and personally became Christian in 864. As already noted, conversion under the auspices of Constantinople marked a tremendous increase in Byzantine political and cultural influence, but also aroused the resentment of the powerful group of conservative boyars (nobles), whose political and social position was threatened. The contemporary Western source, the *Annals of St. Bertin*, relates the violent initial reaction of the boyars to conversion from Byzantium.

INITIAL BULGAR OPPOSITION TO CONVERSION

(From *Annales Bertiniani*, ed. Waitz, MGH SS, p. 85 [a. 866].)

The king of the Bulgars, who in the preceding year (with God inspiring him and warning the people of his kingdom with signs and afflictions) had considered becoming a Christian, received holy baptism. But because his nobles believed this [conversion] to be to their detriment, they incited the people against him so they would slay him. Indeed, a multitude from the ten [provinces] gathered around his palace. But he, after invoking the name of Christ and accompanied by forty-eight men all fervent Christians who had remained with him, ventured forth against that entire multitude. Then when he went out from the gates of the city, there appeared to them and to those who were with him seven priests. And each one of them held a burning candle in his hand and thus they went forth preceding the king and those accompanying him.

To those who had revolted against him, it seemed that a great building burning above them would fall upon them, and the horses of those who were with the king, as it seemed to those on the other side, stood erect and struck them [the rebels] with their front legs. Such a great fear seized them that they sought neither to flee nor to defend themselves, but only prostrated themselves and were unable to move. The king, however, killed fifty-two of the nobles who had especially incited the people against him. The rest of the people he permitted to depart unharmed.

Commentary. Despite these early difficulties and the temporary flirtation of Boris with the papacy, in the end the conversion of the Bulgars was successfully accomplished by the Byzantines.

260.

Introduction. Perhaps the oldest piece of evidence regarding the earliest Byzantine knowledge of the Rus comes from the same Western source, the *Annals of St. Bertin*, which, under the year 839, refers to Greek envoys and Rus representatives together at the Western imperial court.

BYZANTINES AND RUS AT A WESTERN COURT

(Translated by G. Vernadsky, *A Source Book for Russian History* [New Haven, Conn., and London: Yale University Press, 1972], vol. 1, p. 11.)

There came the Greek envoys sent by Emperor Theophilus. . . . He also sent with them certain men who said that they [their tribe] were called Rhos, and that their king, known as chacanus [khagan], had dispatched them to him [the Byzantine Emperor Theophilus], for the sake of friendship, as they had asserted. He [Theophilus] asked . . . that the emperor [the Western emperor, Louis the Pious] allow them to return home across his possessions since the roads by which they had come to Constantinople were cut by wild and ferocious tribes and he [Theophilus] did not want them to face danger in case of returning by the same route. The emperor [Louis] investigated diligently the cause of their coming and discovered that they were Swedes by origin.

261.

Introduction. Since the Rus were a people initially hardly known to the Byzantines, the suddenness of the first Rus attack on Constantinople must have been terrifying to the Byzantines. Patriarch Photius himself, in one of the most expressive of his homilies, describes the shock and sheer terror provoked in Constantinople by the earliest attacks of the yet unconverted Rus in 860–61.

HOMILY OF PHOTIUS ON THE FIRST ATTACKS OF THE RUS

(Translated by C. Mango, *The Homilies of Photius* [Cambridge, Mass.: Harvard University Press, 1958], pp. 95–110.)

I know that you are all aware—both those who are skilled in comprehending God's rejection of men, and those who are somewhat more ignorant of the Lord's decrees—indeed, I believe that all of you alike perceive and understand that the danger let loose on us, and the sudden incursion of the tribe came upon us from no other source than the wrath and anger of the Lord Almighty. For, to be sure, the Godhead is good and above anger and every passion, inasmuch as its nature surpasses every material affection (which has been allotted a position of subordination beyond all comparison), yet He could be said with propriety to be wrath and angered, whenever an action, deemed worthy of anger and wrath, draws from Him fitting condemnation for its perpetrators; in which manner the calamity which has just overtaken us has also burst out, revealing to our faces the censure of our sins. Nay, nor did it resemble other raids of barbarians, but the unexpectedness of the attack, its strange swiftness, the inhumanity of the barbarous tribe, the harshness of its manners and the savagery of its character proclaim the blow to have been discharged like a thunderbolt from God.

An obscure nation, a nation of no account, a nation ranked among slaves, unknown, but which has won a name from the expedition against us, insignificant, but now become famous, humble and destitute, but now risen to a splendid height and immense wealth, a nation dwelling somewhere far from our country, barbarous, nomadic, armed with arrogance, unwatched, unchallenged, leaderless, has so suddenly, in the twinkling of an eye, like a wave of the sea, poured over our frontiers, and as a wild boar has devoured the inhabitants of the land like grass, or straw, or a crop (O, the God-sent punishment that befell us!), sparing nothing from man to beast, not respecting female weakness, not pitying tender infants, not reverencing the hoary hairs of old men, softened by nothing that is wont to move human nature to pity, even when it has sunk to that of wild beasts, but boldly thrusting their sword through *persons* of every age and sex. . . .

Nobody would be able to describe in words the Iliad of ills which overtook us then. And who, on seeing these things, would not admit that the cup mixed by the Lord's anger, which had boiled over at our transgressions, was not poured out on us to its very dregs? . . .

Do you recollect that unbearable and bitter hour when the barbarians' boats came sailing down at you, wafting a breath of cruelty, savagery and murder? When the sea spread out its serene and unruffled surface, granting them gentle and agreeable sailing, while, waxing wild, it stirred up against us the waves of war? When the boats went past the city showing their crews with swords raised, as if threatening the city with death by the sword? When all human hope ebbed away from men, and the city was moored only with recourse to the divine? When quaking and darkness held our minds, and our ears would hear nothing but, "The barbarians have penetrated within the walls, and the city has been taken by the enemy"? For the unexpectedness of the event and the unlooked-for attack induced, so to speak, everybody to imagine and hear such things—a symptom that is indeed common among men in such cases: for what they fear excessively they will believe without verification to have happened even when it has not; whereas that of which they have had no previous apprehension they will reject by the arbitrary power of their judgment even when it has come upon them. Verily, there was mourning then, and lamentation and woe.

262.

Introduction. The important *Russian Primary Chronicle* offers a portrait of the Russian Princess Olga of Kiev, who was probably the first Rus of noble status to be converted to Orthodoxy (954 or 955). Her example, however, was not followed by her pagan son, Sviatoslav.

PRINCESS OLGA BECOMES A CHRISTIAN

(Translated by Serge A. Zenkovsky, *Medieval Russia's Epics, Chronicles and Tales* [New York, 1963], pp. 61–62. Copyright © 1963 by Serge A. Zenkovsky. Reprinted by permission of the publisher, E. P. Dutton, Inc.)

Olga was the precursor of the Christian land, even as the dayspring precedes the sun and as the dawn precedes the day. For she shone like the moon by night, and she was radiant among the infidels like a pearl in the mire, since the people were soiled, and not yet purified of their sin by holy baptism. But she herself was cleansed by this sacred purification. She put off the sinful garments of the old Adam, and was clad in the new Adam, which is Christ. Thus we say to her, "Rejoice in the Russians' knowledge of God," for we were the first fruits of their reconciliation with him.

She was the first from Russia to enter the kingdom of God, and the sons of

Russia thus praise her as their leader, for since her death she has interceded with God in their behalf. The souls of the righteous do not perish. As Solomon has said, "The nations rejoice in the praise of the righteous, for his memory is eternal, since it is acknowledged by God and men". . . . For God protected the sainted Olga from the devil, our adversary and our foe.

263.

Introduction. The most decisive event in early Russian history occurred in 988–89, when Prince Vladimir, grandson of Olga, was converted to Christianity; he, in turn, had all the people of his Kievan state baptized in the Dnieper River. The following selection from the *Russian Primary Chronicle* relates why he selected Orthodoxy over the religion of the German Catholics, and over Islam, the religion of the (Volga) Bulgars.

VLADIMIR'S ROAD TO CONVERSION

(Translated by Serge A. Zenkovsky, ed., *Medieval Russia's Epics, Chronicles, and Tales* [New York, 1963], pp. 66–67, 70. Copyright © 1963 by Serge A. Zenkovsky. Reprinted by permission of the publisher, E. P. Dutton, Inc.)

Vladimir summoned together his vassals and the city elders, and said to them: "Behold, the Bulgarians came before me urging me to accept their religion. Then came the Germans and praised their own faith; and after them came the Jews. Finally the Greeks appeared, criticizing all other faiths but commending their own, and they spoke at length, telling the history of the whole world from its beginning. Their words were artful, and it was wondrous to listen and pleasant to hear them. They preach the existence of another world. 'Whoever adopts our religion and then dies shall arise and live forever. But whosoever embraces another faith, shall be consumed with fire in the next world.' What is your opinion on this subject, and what do you answer?" The vassals and the elders replied: "You know, O Prince, that no man condemns his own possessions, but praises them instead. If you desire to make certain, you have servants at your disposal. Send them to inquire about the ritual of each and how he worships God."

Their counsel pleased the prince and all the people, so that they chose good and wise men to the number of ten, and directed them to go first among the Bulgarians and inspect their faith. The emissaries went their way, and when they arrived at their destination they beheld the disgraceful actions of the Bulgarians and their worship in the mosque; then they returned to their own country. Vladimir then instructed them to go likewise among the Germans, and examine their faith, and finally to visit the Greeks. They thus went into Germany, and after viewing the German ceremonial, they proceeded to Constantinople where they appeared before the emperor. He inquired on what mission they had come, and they reported to him all that had occurred. When the emperor heard their words, he rejoiced, and did them great honor on that very day.

On the morrow, the emperor sent a message to the patriarch to inform him that a Russian delegation had arrived to examine the Greek faith, and directed him to prepare the church and the clergy, and to array himself in his sacerdotal robes, so that the Russians might behold the glory of the God of the Greeks. When the patriarch received these commands, he bade the clergy assemble, and they performed the customary rites. They burned incense, and the choirs sang hymns. The emperor accompanied the Russians to the church, and placed them in a wide space, calling their attention to the beauty of the edifice, the chanting, and the offices of the archpriest and the ministry of the deacons, while he explained to them the worship of his God. The Russians were astonished, and in their wonder praised the Greek ceremonial. Then the Emperors Basil and Constantine invited the envoys to their presence, and said, "Go hence to your native country," and thus dismissed them with valuable presents and great honor.

Thus they returned to their own country, and the prince called together his vassals and the elders. Vladimir then announced the return of the envoys who had been sent out, and suggested that their report be heard. He thus commanded them to speak out before his vassals. The envoys reported: "When we journeyed among the Bulgarians, we beheld how they worship in their temple, called a mosque, while they stand ungirt. The Bulgarian bows, sits down, looks hither and thither like one possessed, and there is no happiness among them, but instead only sorrow and a dreadful stench. Their religion is not good. Then we went among the Germans, and saw them performing many ceremonies in their temples; but we beheld no glory there. Then we went on to Greece, and the Greeks led us to the edifices where they worship their God, and we knew not whether we were in heaven or on earth. For on earth there is no such splendor or such beauty, and we are at a loss how to describe it. We know only that God dwells there among men, and their service is fairer than the ceremonies of other nations. For we cannot forget that beauty. Every man, after tasting something sweet, is afterward unwilling to accept that which is bitter, and therefore we cannot dwell longer here." Then the vassals spoke and said, "If the Greek faith were evil, it would not have been adopted by your grandmother Olga, who was wiser than all other men." Vladimir then inquired where they should all accept baptism, and they replied that the decision rested with him. . . .

264.

Introduction. During the final decades of the empire, the Russians, chafing under the tight rein imposed by the Byzantine emperor and patriarch on the Russian church, began increasingly to show signs of insubordination and a desire for independence. The catalyst which moved the Russians to an open break from Byzantine ecclesiastical control was the Council of Florence (1438–39), where the Byzantines, for political reasons, concluded religious union of the Eastern and Western churches. The Rus took that occasion to name a metropolitan of Kiev, without securing patriarchal approval, thus in effect proclaiming the ecclesiastical independence of their church from Byzantium. Indeed, they began to proclaim that now their church alone remained the bastion of pure Orthodoxy, the Greek church having become apostate through religious union with heretical Rome.

The following text, taken from the Russian *Voskresensk Chronicle*, recounts what happened in Moscow at the news of the proclamation of ecclesiastical union in Florence. It indicates, too, the official Muscovite reaction to the conduct of the Greek-born metropolitan, Isidore of Kiev, who had been a chief proponent of union.

RUSSIAN REACTION TO THE COUNCIL OF FLORENCE AND METROPOLITAN ISIDORE

(Translated by G. Vernadsky, *Source Book for Russian History* [New Haven, Conn., and London: Yale University Press, 1972], vol. 1, pp. 126–27.)

[A.D. 1440:] Isidore came to the Russian land, into the God-protected city of Moscow [in March 1441], to the pious and Orthodox grand prince Vasilii [II] Vasilievich, concealing within himself the deceit of the Latin heresy. . . . And he ordered that the Latin cross be carried before him. . . . Then during the commemorative prayers of the holy service he mentioned first and lauded, instead of the holy ecumenical patriarchs, the Roman pope Eugene, to whom he had delivered the holy faith of Greek Orthodoxy for gold. Upon the conclusion of the holy service Isidore ascended the pulpit and ordered that the edict of the false-minded and apostate council be read in a loud voice. In it were written the Latin deceits, hateful and foreign to God: separating the Holy Trinity, saying that the Holy Ghost proceeds from the Son as well as from the Father, and joining to this their sophistry concerning unleavened bread, saying that it is proper for the body of Christ to be transformed both as fermented and unfermented bread; and concerning the dead it was written thus: those who have met death with humility, in the true faith and in penitence to God, but have not succeeded in performing the penance for their sins which their confessors have pronounced, such men will be purified after death by the purification of sins. But they did all this among themselves through sophistry, in order to deceive the true Orthodox faith and, having deceived it, to sever Christianity from the law of God.

[The Grand Prince] heard from [Isidore's] lips the name of the pope mentioned first, recognized the heresy of that rapacious wolf Isidore, did not accept the blessing from his hand, and called him a heretical Latin deceiver; and, quickly accusing him, he covered him with shame and called him a wolf rather than a shepherd and teacher; and he soon ordered that he be removed from his throne as metropolitan, as a mad deceiver and apostate from the faith, and ordered him to go into a monastery. . . . Isidore . . . left stealthily at night, the doors being open, took to flight with his pupil the monk Grigorii, and thus fled to Rome, whence he had come and brought the evil Latin heresies. The God-knowing worker of piety, the Orthodox grand prince Vasilii Vasilievich, did not send anyone after him to bring him back, not wishing to detain him, as someone bereft of reason and hateful to God.

265.

Introduction. Isidore's see in Moscow remained empty from the time of his deposition until 1448, when the Russian church finally took the drastic step of selecting its own metropolitan. (Virtually all previous Russian metropolitans had been appointed by Constantinople.) Nevertheless, the Rus ruler, Vasilii, felt constrained to report this event to the Byzantine Emperor in this manner (cf. selection 333):

THE RUSSIANS ELECT THEIR OWN METROPOLITAN

(Translated by G. Vernadsky, *A Source Book for Russian History* [New Haven, Conn., and London: Yale University Press, 1972], vol. 1, p. 127.)

And by the will of God, by the grace of the Holy Ghost, and by those divine sacred rules, having assembled the prelates of our land and acting by means of our fathers, these Russian prelates, we have appointed our aforementioned father, Iona, bishop of Riazan', to be metropolitan of Kiev and all Russia. But we have done this from great necessity, and not from haughtiness or insolence; and we ourselves observe piety in everything, in accordance with the ancient Orthodoxy bequeathed to us . . . in which we shall remain to the end of our earthly life, and to the end of the ages. And our Russian church of the most holy Russian metropolitanate asks and seeks the blessing of God's holy ecumenical Orthodox apostolic church of God's wisdom, Sancta Sophia in Tsar'grad [Constantinople], and shall obey it in everything in accordance with ancient piety.

D.
BYZANTIUM AND THE WEST

266.

Introduction. Byzantine attitudes toward the West are more complicated than those toward other peoples earlier discussed, for East and West were "sibling" civilizations in that they shared the heritage of the Christian Roman Empire. The awareness of this common political and cultural heritage was, however, not only a source of unity; it became in time also a source of misunderstanding. West and East agreed that, ideally, there was but one world empire headed by one Christian emperor. Thus when Charles the Great and the pope established, in 800, what they claimed was a "restoration" of the Roman Empire, the Byzantines, themselves already in possession of the imperial title, were doubtless incensed. Nevertheless, the Byzantine court, at the time preoccupied with the more pressing danger of the Arabs and the Bulgars in the east and north, seemed at first to pay little attention to the new development in the West. For Theophanes' report of the initial Byzantine reaction, see selection 146.

The growing tension between feelings of unity and antipathy in the relations between East and West is well expressed in the following letter of the Byzantine Emperor Michael II (and his son) to Charlemagne's son, Louis the Pious, describing the method of his accession to the throne. Note especially the contrast between the appeal to Christian unity made at the end with the insulting salutation to the man who considered himself Roman Emperor in the West.

A BYZANTINE EMPEROR WRITES TO THE KING OF
THE FRANKS (824)

(From P. Lemerle, "Thomas le Slav," *Travaux et mémoires* [Paris, 1965], vol. 1, pp. 256–58.)

Michael and Theophilus [son of Michael], faithful in God, *imperatores Romanorum* [emperors of the Romans] to his dear and honorable brother Ludovico, the glorious King of the Franks and Lombards, who is called their emperor[!]:

At the time of our predecessor Leo [V, the Armenian], there appeared a certain Thomas, pupil of the devil. While he was in the service of one of the greatest nobles at the time when Irene [the empress] directed the empire, he lay with the wife of his master. When the fact was known, he fled to the Persians [i.e., the Arabs]. He remained there from the time of the said Irene to that of Leo, and abjured Christianity, in order the better to gain from the numerous infidels, Saracens, and others. He made them believe he was Constantine, son of the Empress Irene, that another in his place had had his eyes removed [Irene had blinded her son], and that he had fled in good health and safely. With those whom he attached to himself, he set out to rob and pillage. He gained over others by force, by gold, by the promise of honor and of titles. . . .

As the Emperor Leo was incapable of containing the assault of the tyrant, certain malcontents formed a conspiracy against him, and he was assassinated. Then they brought together, according to ancient custom, the patriarch, the nobles, the senators, and the *archontes* from various provinces, and by unanimous assent, we were raised to the throne—for they knew us and loved us, especially because of the pressing danger coming from the traitor-murderer.

We found the Christians divided. A great number followed the tyrant, and because of that we have not been able to combat him effectively. He has therefore profited to attract many men to his side; by means of our [traitorous] fleets and *dromones* [ships] he came by way of Thrace and Macedonia, besieged Constantinople and blockaded it by sea in December in the fifteenth indiction [of 821]. . . . The battle was joined and God gave us victory. It was a miracle. . . . Finally we took Thomas alive, and all those with him, Greeks and foreigners. His hands and feet were cut off, and he died on the gallows. Of his two pretended adopted sons, one was killed by our faithful [men] in Asia, the other condemned to the same punishment as Thomas. We took alive all the Saracens, Armenians, and others who had escaped from the combat, and we wreaked our vengeance on them according to God's will. . . . From this time all the Christians of our empire have returned to unity and concord.

We have adjudged it necessary to inform you of this—you our peaceful friend and spiritual brother, and to associate you in our joy, in order that together, *as befits those of the same faith and religion,** we may thank God. In truth, we should have done this from the beginning of our reign. But the revolt of Thomas kept us from this. Now that he is dead and all our people are gathered together again, God gives us the possibility of doing this.

*My italics.

267.

Introduction. By the tenth century, political, religious, and economic circumstances had driven East and West further and further apart. The growing Byzantine contempt for what they called the "barbarian" West's cultural and political pretensions and arrogance, on the one hand, and Western revulsion for Byzantine "perfidy," superciliousness, and "effeminacy," on the other, comes through in the passage quoted here. It is taken from the reminiscences of Liudprand of Cremona, emissary of the Western Emperor Otto I to the Byzantine Emperor Nicephorus Phocas. Liudprand was sent to Constantinople to arrange a marriage between Otto's son and a

Byzantine princess, Theophano. In conversation with Emperor Nicephorus Phocas (c. 969) Liudprand said the following:

LIUDPRAND IN CONSTANTINOPLE

(From Liudprand, *Relatio de legatione Constantinopolitana*, MPL, vol. 136, col. 913.)

That land, which you claim belongs to your empire, the inhabitants and language thereof reveal belongs to the kingdom of Italy. The Lombards have held it in their power, and Louis, emperor of the Lombards or Franks, liberated it with much bloodshed from the hands of the Saracens. For seven years Landulf, prince of Benevento and Capua, placed it under his own power; nor would it, even up to the present day, have escaped the yoke of slavery to him and his descendants, had not the [Byzantine] Emperor Romanus at great expense purchased the friendship of our King Hugh. This was the reason that he joined in marriage his own nephew and namesake with the illegitimate daughter of our King Hugh. But, as I understand, you ascribe to my lord not a feeling of appreciation but one of impotence in that, after acquiring Rome and Italy, he left them for so many years to you.

The bond of friendship which you say you have wished to make by marriage [*parentela*] we consider a fraud and an insult. You demand a truce, which you have no right to request and we have no reason to grant. In order that we might be rid of all deceit, let the truth not be kept silent: my lord has sent me to you so that, if you agree to give in marriage the daughter of Emperor Romanus and Empress Theophano to his son, my master the August Emperor Otto, may you affirm it before me with an oath, and I will confirm with an oath those things which my lord in grateful recompense will do and observe on your behalf. My lord has now handed over to you, his brother [ruler], the best pledge of friendship, by giving [to you] all of Apulia, which was under his control.

268.

Introduction. The ecclesiastical schism of East and West did perhaps more than anything else to exacerbate tensions. Yet in the last analysis, even more immediately responsible for the deterioration of Byzantine-Western relations were the Western expeditions called the Crusades. Initially, Emperor Alexius I Comnenus in 1082 had requested the aid of Western mercenary troops to stem the invasion of the Seljuk Turks in Asia Minor. In the West, however, under the vigorous leadership of the reformed papacy, Alexius's call(s) for aid may have become the basis for a veritable movement of entire armies. These Western Crusades were intended not only to restore the Holy Sepulcher in Palestine to Christianity but probably, at least implicitly, to bring East and West back into ecclesiastical union but under papal leadership.

We quote from a letter, possibly written by Emperor Alexius to his friend, the count of Flanders, requesting Western aid for Byzantium (c. 1090?). Whether or not the letter is genuine, it is more or less contemporary with the First Crusade (1096) and certainly reflects the desire of Alexius for some form

of Western military assistance, though probably not in the form of entire organized Latin armies that might prove a threat to Byzantium itself.

ALEXIUS'S (SUPPOSED) LETTER OF APPEAL TO THE WEST

(Translated by E. Joranson, "The Problem of the Spurious Letter
of Emperor Alexius to the Count of Flanders," *American Historical
Review* 55 [1950]: 812–15.)*

O most illustrious count and especial comforter of
the Christian faith! I wish to make known to your prudence how the most sacred
empire of the Greek Christians is being sorely distressed by the Patzinaks and the
Turks, who daily ravage it and unintermittently seize [its territory]; and there is
promiscuous slaughter and indescribable killing and derision of the Christians.
But since the evil things they do are many and, as we have said, indescribable, we
will mention but a few of the many, which nevertheless are horrible to hear and
disturb even the air itself. For they circumcise the boys and youths of the Christians over the Christian baptismal fonts, and in contempt of Christ they pour the
blood from the circumcision into the said baptismal fonts and contrive still further desecrations; and thereafter they violently drag them around in the church,
compelling them to blaspheme the name of the Holy Trinity and the belief
therein. But those who refuse to do these things they punish in diverse ways and
ultimately they kill them. Noble matrons and their daughters whom they have
robbed [of their possessions] they, one after another like animals, defile in adultery. Some, indeed, in their corrupting, shamelessly place virgins before the
faces of their mothers and compel them to sing wicked and obscene songs, until
they have finished their own wicked acts . . . likewise, at the dishonoring of their
daughters, the mothers are in turn compelled to sing wicked songs, [though]
their voices sound forth not a song but rather, we believe, a plaint, as it is written
concerning the death of the Innocents. . . . The holy places they desecrate and
destroy in numberless ways, and they threaten them with worse treatment. . . .
For almost the entire land from Jerusalem to Greece, and the whole of Greece
with its upper regions, which are Cappadocia Minor, Cappadocia Major, Phrygia, Bithynia, Lesser Phrygia (i.e., the Troad), Pontus, Galatia, Lydia, and the
principal islands Chios and Mytilene, and many other regions and islands which
we cannot even enumerate, as far as Thrace, have already been invaded by them,
and now almost nothing remains except Constantinople, which they are threatening to snatch away from us very soon, unless the aid of God and the faithful
Latin Christians should reach us speedily. For even the Propontis, which is also
called the Avidus and which flows out of the Pontus near Constantinople into the
Great Sea, they have invaded with two hundred ships, which Greeks robbed by
them had built; and they are launching them with their rowers, willy-nilly, and
they are threatening, as we have said, speedily to capture Constantinople by land
as well as by way of the Propontis. These few among the innumerable evil things
which this most impious people is doing we have mentioned and written to you,
count of the Flemings, lover of the Christian faith! The rest, indeed, let us omit,
in order not to disgust the readers. Accordingly, for love of God and out of sym-

pathy for all Christian Greeks, we beg that you lead hither to my aid and that of the Christian Greeks whatever faithful warriors of Christ you may be able to enlist in your land—those of major as well as those of minor and middle condition and as they in the past year liberated Galicia and other kingdoms of the Westerners somewhat from the yoke of the pagans, so also may they now, for the salvation of their souls, endeavor to liberate the kingdom of the Greeks.

*Joranson thinks this version was composed in 1105–6 (based in part perhaps on an earlier letter of Alexius) as propaganda to aid the Norman Bohemund's proposed crusade of 1105–6 *against* Byzantium.

269.

Introduction. An often overlooked source for the origins of the First Crusade (useful despite inaccuracies because of certain additional material it provides) is a later thirteenth-century Byzantine historian, now identified as Theodore Scutariotes. He discusses the shrewd appeal of Emperor Alexius to the West for the dispatching of troops to recapture the Holy Sepulcher—troops which he then proceeded to use for his own ends: to recapture for Byzantium parts of Asia Minor from the Seljuk Turks.

ALEXIUS AND THE FIRST CRUSADE

(From *Anonymous Summary Chronicle*, ed. K. Sathas, in *Bibliotheca Graeca medii aevi* [Paris, 1894], vol. 7, pp. 184–85.)

Reflecting that by himself he was unable to sustain this all-important combat [against the Turks], Alexius understood that it was necessary to make an alliance with the Italians; he did this by dissembling, shrewd manipulation, and cunning. Indeed he found what he considered to be a heaven-sent pretext in that this people [the Latins] considered it intolerable that the Persians [i.e. Seljuk Turks] controlled Jerusalem and the life-giving Sepulcher of Our Savior Jesus Christ. He sent embassies to the bishop of the elder Rome and to those that are called kings and nobles in those regions [of the West] and, through the use of appropriate arguments, he induced not a few of them to leave their homelands, and he succeeded in directing them by every means to this task. For this reason many of them, numbering in the thousands and tens of thousands, did not come slowly on foot but (more quickly) crossed the Ionian Sea to Constantinople. After he had exchanged oaths of loyalty and made treaties with them, he went off to the East and, through divine assistance, the aid of his allies, and his own efforts, he quickly forced the Persians [Turks] to abandon the lands of the Romans; he freed the cities and restored Roman power in the East to its former glory. Such a man was this emperor: great in making plans and great in performing deeds.

270.

Introduction. If Pope Urban had any hopes that his crusade would promote better religious relations, perhaps even ecclesiastical union between the Byzantine and Western churches, they were not to be realized. For from the first the Byzantines were suspicious of these armed "barbarians" who claimed to be on a religious mission to Jerusalem. The following account by Anna Comnena, daughter of the Byzantine Emperor Alexius Comnenus, reflects the typical Byzantine reaction to the Western Crusaders (1096).

ANNA COMNENA ON THE CRUSADERS

(From Anna Comnena, *Alexiade*, ed. B. Leib [Paris, 1967], vol. 2, pp. 206–9.)

Alexius had no time to relax when he heard a report of the approach of innumerable Frankish armies. He feared their arrival since he knew the Latins' uncontrollable spirit, their unstable and changeable character, as well as all the rest that pertains to the Celtic temperament with its inevitable consequences: how greedy for money they were and how they always seemed without scruple and ready to break their own agreements for any reason whatever. He had always heard this mentioned and it was quite true. Yet, not at all discouraged, Alexius prepared himself completely so that he would be prepared for war if such a contingency arose. But the actual events were more frightful than the rumors, for the entire West, as many of the barbarian peoples as lived in the lands between the Adriatic [Sea] and the Straits of Gibraltar, all were moving en masse with their families through Europe toward Asia.

Now here in outline is the cause of this mass movement. A certain Celt named Peter, with the surname Koukoupetros, went off to worship at the Holy Sepulcher, and after suffering many frightful things at the hands of the Turks and Saracens who were plundering all of Asia, barely and only with great difficulty succeeded in reaching home. But he could not bear to have failed in his plan [to go to Jerusalem]. And so he wished to make a second journey, but realizing that it was not wise for him by himself to make the trip to the Holy Sepulcher (for something worse might happen to him), he worked out a clever scheme. It was to preach in all the lands of the Latins: "A divine voice has called me to proclaim before all the counts of France, that all [of you] should leave your homes and go off to worship at the Holy Sepulcher and with all your might and soul should strive to free Jerusalem from the hands of the Agarenes [Muslims]." And he actually succeeded [in his aims]. As if he had imbued the hearts of all with a divine voice, he made preparations in order that all Celts should assemble, one after another from all areas, with arms and horses and all other implements of war. They were full of ardor and passion and they filled every highway. A number of people, more numerous than the sands of the shore and the stars, accompanied these Celtic soldiers, bearing palms and with crosses on their shoulders. Women and children left their own countries. Like certain rivers which flow together from all directions, they moved toward us, for the most part through Dacia [modern Rumania].

The incidents surrounding the coming of the barbarians occurred in the following manner, and there was in it something strange, although recognizable to intelligent people. For the arrival of these many people did not occur at the same time, nor did they come by the same route (for how could such a great multitude, coming from many different areas, cross the Adriatic in such great numbers?) Some of them first, some second, others behind, and so on, all making the voyage, then marched overland. As I said, a plague of locusts preceded each army. All [the Greeks] then, after seeing this phenomenon once or twice, believed that locusts were the forerunners of the Frankish battalions. And when certain groups had begun to cross the Straits of Lombardy [i.e. Otranto in the old Byzantine theme of Longobardia], the emperor summoned certain of the commanders of the Byzantine forces and sent them off to the regions of Dyrrachium and Avlona, charging them to receive the voyagers benevolently and to provide them, from all lands [of the empire], abundant supplies along their route. And [he also ordered them] to observe the armies discreetly, following them so that, should they notice them making raids or turning off to plunder any adjoining areas, they should restrain them by means of light skirmishing. There accompanied these [Byzantine] officers certain specialists in the Latin dialect[s] whose duty it was to suppress any conflicts arising between Byzantines and Latins.

271.

Introduction. During the Second Crusade (1147) which, like most such Western expeditions, passed through Constantinople, Odo of Deuil accompanied the French army as chaplain to the French King Louis VII. A section of the account Odo wrote on his experiences in the East reveals the Western conviction that the religious customs of the Byzantines were "blasphemous, even heretical." From this conviction it was but one step for some Westerners to deny even the Christianity of the Byzantines.

A. A Latin Cleric's Opinion of Greek Religious Practices

(Translated by V. Berry, from Odo of Deuil: *De profectione Ludovici VII in orientem* [New York: Columbia University Press, 1948], p. 57.)

If our priests celebrated mass on Greek altars, the Greeks afterwards purified them with propitiatory offerings and ablutions, as if they had been defiled. All the wealthy people have their own chapels, so adorned with paintings, marble, and lamps that each magnate might justly say, "O lord, I have cherished the beauty of Thy house." . . . But, O dreadful thing! We heard of an ill usage of theirs which could be expiated by death; namely, that every time they celebrate the marriage of one of our men, if he has been baptized in the Roman way, they rebaptize him before they make the pact. We know other heresies of theirs, both concerning their treatment of the Eucharist and concerning the procession of the Holy Ghost. . . . Actually, it was for these reasons that the Greeks had incurred the hatred of our men, for their error had become known even among the lay people. Because of this they were judged not to be Christians, and the Franks considered killing them a matter of no importance and hence could with the more difficulty be restrained from pillage and plundering.

Introduction. And yet when the French Crusader leaders, including Odo, heard the Greek service for St. Dionysius, whom they

identified with France's own Saint Denis, they were moved. Denis was erroneously identified by the French with Dionysius, the Athenian pupil of St. Paul
(wrongly believed to have written the Dionysian corpus of mystical works and
to have gone to Gaul and there converted the Germanic Parisii). Probably
the author of these famous mystical writings (today referred to as Pseudo-
Dionysius) lived about 500 around Antioch (see selection 130).

B. Greeks and Franks on the Feast Day of Saint Dionysius

(From Odo of Deuil, *De profectione*, p. 69.)

Since the Greeks celebrate this feast, the emperor
knew of it, and he sent over to the king a carefully selected group of his clergy,
each of whom he had equipped with a large taper decorated elaborately with
gold and a great variety of colors; and thus he increased the glory of the ceremony. These clergy certainly differed from ours as to words and order of service,
but they made a favorable impression because of their sweet chanting; for the
mingling of the voices, the heavier with the light, the eunuch's, namely, with the
manly voice (for many of them were eunuchs), softened the hearts of the Franks.
Also, they gave the onlookers pleasure by their graceful bearing and gentle clap-
ping of hands and genuflections.

272.

Introduction. Even as late as the twelfth century,
when the empire's territory had been considerably diminished, the Emperor
Manuel I Comnenus (1143–80), following the ancient Byzantine dream of
unity, tried to reconquer long-lost parts of formerly Byzantine Italy. In his attempts to recover these lands (as well as others in the East), Manuel made use
of Latins in Byzantine administrative posts, to the objection and anger of many
Greeks. The Latin historian and courtier of the Crusader-founded Latin Kingdom of Jerusalem, William of Tyre, who was partial to Manuel, describes Manuel's policy and at the same time reveals the prejudices and misperceptions of
Greeks and Latins in the period after the first two Crusades (1096 and 1147).

Mutual Hostility

(Translated by E. A. Babcock and A. C. Krey, from William of
Tyre, *A History of Deeds Done beyond the Sea* [New York: Columbia
University Press, 1943], vol. 2, pp. 461–62.)

During the reign of Manuel, beloved of God, the
Latins had found great favor with him—a reward well deserved because of their
loyalty and valor. The emperor, a great-souled man of incomparable energy, re-
lied so implicitly on their fidelity and ability that he passed over the Greeks as
soft and effeminate and entrusted important affairs to the Latins alone. Since he
held them in such high esteem and showed toward them such lavish generosity,
men of the Latin race from all over the world—nobles and men of lesser degree—regarded him as their great benefactor and eagerly flocked to his court.

As a result of this eager deference, his affection toward the Latins increased more and more, and he was constantly improving their status.

The Greek nobles, especially the kindred of the emperor, and the mass of the people as well, naturally conceived an insatiable hatred toward us and this was increased by the difference between our sacraments and those of the Greek church, which furnished an additional incentive to their jealousy. For once having separated insolently from the church of Rome, in their boundless arrogance they looked upon everyone who did not follow their foolish tradition as a heretic. It was they themselves, on the contrary, who deserved the name of heretic, because they had either created or followed new and pernicious beliefs contrary to the Roman church and the faith of the apostles Peter and Paul against which "the gates of hell shall not prevail."

For these and other reasons they had for a long time cherished this hatred in their hearts and were ever seeking an opportunity, at least after the death of the emperor, to destroy utterly the hated race of the Latins, both in the city and throughout the entire empire, that in this way they might satisfy their inexorable animosity.

273.

Introduction. Nicetas Choniates, who lived during the same era as William of Tyre, describes from the Byzantine point of view the feelings of hostility toward the Latins during Manuel's reign—in particular Byzantine resentment of what appeared to be the "Latinophron" (Latin-minded) policies of that emperor.

A BYZANTINE VIEW OF MANUEL'S FAVORS TO THE LATINS

(From Nicetas Choniates, *Historia*, ed. I. Van Dieten [Berlin, 1975] vol. 1, pp. 203–5.)

Nevertheless it must be admitted that he [Manuel I] did not act so from a grand desire to undertake new enterprises, but from the knowledge he had of the power of the Latin peoples, and from his apprehension that, as he said, they might all join together in order completely to destroy the empire, just as a torrent formed of various rivulets can ravage the entire country. He desired to foresee this evil, or at least to scotch it at birth. . . . But the prudence of his conduct was clearly revealed only after his death, when the vessel of the empire, deprived of so sage a pilot, was almost ready to be shipwrecked.

I would not know how to dissimulate the fact that he had an excessive passion for increasing taxes, for selling charges. But from these he gave generously to the monasteries, to the churches, and to the Greek poor, but especially to the foreign peoples, above all to the Latins. . . . He was prodigal and benign also to the chamberlains and eunuchs of the bedchamber and indeed also to the servants who are of foreign races . . . who are semibarbarous and who more easily sputter rather than speak [Greek]. And he gave them many riches so that they overflowed with piles of money and every kind of ornament. . . . To these lacking any education and knowing only vestiges of the Greek language . . . to these [the Latins], as if they were the most obedient and faithful of officials, he not only assigned the highest magistracies, but he appointed them as judges in the most difficult matters, when circumstances required a most expert knowledge of jurisprudence and of the laws. When it was a question of naming an appointee to a province (and this he did often), he would send with them a Byzantine by birth and speech and wisdom, but only the better to be able to collect the tax. But the foreigner, as the supervisor, was in charge and had to approve with seals the taxes collected which had to be sent to the emperor. . . . In thus distrusting the Byzantines, as if there were among them only thieves and as if their birth and education had given them less probity than that of the foreigners, he lost their affection and drew upon himself rather the hatred of the Byzantines.

274.

Introduction. After Manuel I's reign, Greek hatred of the Latins, so long smoldering, burst forth in 1182 in the revolt of Andronicus Comnenus (a relative of Manuel) against the government. Killing many nobles, he seized the palace and the capital with the help of the anti-Latin populace. William of Tyre describes the Greek revenge on the Latins in Constantinople.

THE BYZANTINES TAKE THEIR REVENGE

(Translated by E. Babcock and A. C. Krey, from William of Tyre: *A History of Deeds Done beyond the Sea* [New York, 1943], pp. 464–65.)

This change of affairs spread consternation among the Latins, for they feared that the citizens would make a sudden attack upon them; in fact they had already received warning of such intention from certain people who had private knowledge of the conspiracy. Those who were able to do so, therefore, fled from the wiles of the Greeks and the death which threatened them. Some embarked on forty-four galleys which chanced to be in the harbor, and others placed all their effects on some of the many other ships there.

The aged and infirm, however, with those who were unable to flee, were left in their homes, and on them fell the wicked rage which the others had escaped. For Andronicus, who had secretly caused ships to be prepared, led his entire force into the city. As soon as they entered the gates these troops, aided by the citizens, rushed to that quarter of the city occupied by the Latins and put to the sword the little remnant who had been either unwilling or unable to flee with the others. Although but few of these were able to fight, yet they resisted for a long time and made the enemy's victory a bloody one.

Regardless of treaties and the many services which our people had rendered to the empire, the Greeks seized all those who appeared capable of resistance, set fire to their houses, and speedily reduced the entire quarter to ashes. Women and children, the aged and the sick, all alike perished in the flames. To vent their rage upon secular buildings alone, however, was far from satisfying their unholy wickedness; they also set fire to churches and venerated places of every description and burned, together with the sacred edifices, those who had fled thither for refuge. No distinction was made between clergy and laymen, except that greater fury was displayed toward those who wore the honorable habits of high office or religion. Monks and priests were the especial victims of their madness and were put to death under excruciating torture.

Among these latter was a venerable man named John, a subdeacon of the holy Roman church, whom the pope had sent to Constantinople on business relating to the church. They seized him and, cutting off his head, fastened it to the tail of a filthy dog as an insult to the church. In the midst of such frightful sacrilege, worse than parricide, not even the dead, whom impiety itself generally spares, were suffered to rest undisturbed. Corpses were torn from the tombs and dragged through the streets and squares as if the insensate bodies were capable of feeling the indignities offered them.

The vandals then repaired to the hospital of St. John, as it is called, where they put to the sword all the sick they found. Those whose pious duty it should have been to relieve the oppressed, namely the monks and priests, called in footpads and brigands to carry on the slaughter under promise of reward. Accompanied by these miscreants, they sought out the most secluded retreats and the inmost apartments of homes, that none who were hiding there might escape death. When such were discovered, they were dragged out with violence and handed over to the executioners, who, that they might not work without pay, were given the price of blood for the murder of these wretched victims.

Even those who seemed to show more consideration sold into perpetual slavery among the Turks and other infidels the fugitives who had resorted to them and to whom they had given hope of safety. It is said that more than four thousand Latins of various age, sex, and condition were delivered thus to barbarous nations for a price.

In such fashion did the perfidious Greek nation, a brood of vipers, like a serpent in the bosom or a mouse in the wardrobe evilly requite their guests—those who had not deserved such treatment and were far from anticipating anything of the kind; those to whom they had given their daughters, nieces, and sisters as wives and who, by long living together, had become their friends.

275.

Introduction. The literature of both West and East gives vivid descriptions of the havoc wreaked by the Greeks against the Latins in Constantinople during the riots of 1182 and 1185. Less well-known, however, is the description of the even more horrible acts of violence perpetrated by the Norman conquerors in their sack, in 1185, of Thessalonika, the second city of the empire. The Byzantine scholar-bishop Eustathius wrote the account.

Norman Atrocities and Devastation in Thessalonika

(From Eustathius of Thessalonika, *L'espugnazione di Tessalonica*, ed. S. Kyriakedes [Palermo, 1961], pp. 112–14.)

The [Latin] barbarians, having entered every part of the city, beginning from the eastern gates, cut down our men and piled them on the ground, those thick maniples [a Roman army unit] of human crops that Hades loves to feed on. Those who fled through the streets fell in them and were stripped and robbed. Thus the streets took on the sorrowful look of cemeteries and the sun witnessed what it should not. Nor could those who remained in their houses leave them. It was not possible to find a house in which any person might have been spared, except in the houses where many people lived. Some died in their domestic surroundings, their houses becoming their tombs, to speak in the words of the psalmist. Others who fled outside were at the mercy of the violence. At first, the fallen ones lay each in his place, but then the enemy, after slackening in their relentless drive and taking vengeance on the mute earth, so to say, behold, there were added to them cadavers of animals. And so the cadaver of a human was coupled with the carcass of an ass; another had lying next to him a dog. And the greater part of the bodies of men and animals were placed in the position of embracing or kissing. One man was placed together with a domestic cat. The barbarians spared no animals of any kind, not even small dogs, which were running around and yelping. So that our city now almost lacked any animal life. And if any dog was spared, when a Greek passed, it barked at him and ran behind him, but if it were a Latin, it withdrew whimpering. Even these understood in what evil circumstances they found themselves. And someone was able to compare them with the silent frogs in Serifos [Greek island] and to some Italian grasshoppers of the same character. Thus even the dogs among us are silent.

The incursion through the streets of the city and the devastation of the houses cannot, of course, be considered anything new in wartime. But the profanation of the holy churches—that may be viewed as waging war on God. Indeed the barbarians, breaking into each church, committed such impieties as to provoke divine reaction. And how many priests, who held up their sacred stoles as cuirasses, did they not strike, some on the divine altar itself, still others outside, where it happened that the assassins found them attending to the divine service. How many laymen, who invoked in a loud voice the *Kyrie eleison* ["Lord have mercy"] were decapitated, while the barbarians demanded of them what was this *Kyrie eleison*, and derided them. Chaste women were contaminated in the sanctuaries by the lust of the enemy, and offenses against their purity were carried out against married women, and against virgins not required to lead a chaste life and against the spouses [nuns] of God who are witnesses against the guilty. If this had happened to only one of them, the evil would of course have been less, but it became so common among these women, one might say like a urinal used by all, that one cannot lament them enough.

Yet I can say one good thing of the barbarians—that some of them who rushed to kill the faithful as they stood in the churches, first carried them outside and killed them there, thus rendering the evil less wicked. But in truth the majority profaned the objects of the divine cult, destroying the sacred images that had no material value.

276.

Introduction. Mounting Byzantine fears of the designs of Western Crusaders on Byzantium were dramatically realized with the Fourth Crusade of 1204. Financed by Byzantium's ungrateful mercantile stepchild, Venice, the Crusaders sacked Constantinople itself and established on its ruins a Latin empire which was to last for fifty-seven years. Latins justified this act by claiming that they warred against schismatic Christians, even heretics. The Western Crusader-knight Robert of Clari gives the following account of the Latin army's deliberations before the conquest.

LATIN CLERGY URGE CONQUEST OF CONSTANTINOPLE

(Translated by E. H. McNeal, from Robert of Clari, *The Conquest of Constantinople* [New York: Columbia University Press, reprint 1964], 1936, p. 94.)

Finally the [Latin] bishops and the clergy of the host consulted together and gave judgment that the battle was a righteous one and that they were right to attack them. For anciently they of the city had been obedient to the law of Rome, but now they were disobedient to it, saying that the law of Rome was worth nothing and that all who believed in it were dogs. And the bishops said that on this account they were right to attack then, and that it was not at all a sin, but rather a righteous deed. . . . And the bishops said that they would assail all those who should attack them, in the name of God and by the authority of the apostolic. Then the bishops commanded the pilgrims all to confess themselves well and to take communion, and not to be afraid of attacking the Greeks, for they were the enemies of God and worse than the Jews.

277.

Introduction. The French nobleman Geoffrey of Villehardouin, an eyewitness, supports Robert of Clari's account of the treasures of Constantinople with his report of the amount of booty divided among the conquering Crusaders (cf. selection 279).

THE LATINS DIVIDE THE SPOILS

(Translated by F. Marzials, from Geoffrey of Villehardouin, *La conquête de Constantinople*, in *Villehardouin and De Joinville: Memoirs of the Crusades* [London, 1908, reprint 1955], pp. 65–66.)

The booty gained was so great that none could tell you the end of it: gold and silver, and vessels and precious stones, and samite and cloth of silk, and robes vair and grey, and ermine, and every choicest thing found upon the earth. And well does Geoffrey of Villehardouin, the Marshal of Champagne, bear witness, that never, since the world was created, had so much booty been won in any city. . . . That which was brought to the churches was collected together and divided, in equal parts, between the Franks and the Venetians. . . . After the division had been made [the Crusaders] paid out of their share fifty thousand marks of silver to the Venetians, and then divided at least one hundred thousand marks among themselves. . . . If it had not been for what was stolen, and for the part given to the Venetians, there would have been at least four hundred thousand marks of silver, and at least ten thousand horses—one with another.

278.

Introduction. Greek accounts of the Latin sack of Constantinople in 1204 are (as might be expected) even less reticent in their relation of the atrocities and looting perpetrated by the Latins. But they join to this an indescribable feeling of sorrow and anguish for the desecration of their beloved capital and lament the disappearance of so many monuments and relics dear to their history. In the following, a virtual funeral oration for the "City," the Greek metropolitan of Ephesus, Nicholas Mesarites, mourns the events of 1204.

CRUSADERS RUN WILD IN CONSTANTINOPLE

(From A. Heisenberg, "Neue Quellen zur Geschichte des lateinischen Kaisertums und der Kirchunion, Der Epitaphios des Nikolaos Mesarites auf seinen Bericht Bruder Johannes," *Sitzungsberichte der bayerischen Akademie der Wissenschaft. Philosophisch- philologische und historische Klasse* [1922], 5 Abhandlung, 46 [1922–23]: 46.)

And so the streets, squares, houses of two and three stories, sacred places, nunneries, houses for nuns and monks, sacred churches, even the Great Church of God and the imperial palace, were filled with men of the enemy, all of them maddened by war and murderous in spirit, all clad in armor and bearing spears, swords and lances, archers and horsemen boasting terribly, barking like Cerberus and exhaling like Charon, as they sacked the sacred places and trampled on the divine things [and] ran riot over the holy vessels. . . . Moreover, they tore children from their mothers and mothers from their children, and they defiled the virgins in the holy chapels, fearing neither God's anger nor man's vengeance. They searched breasts of women to find out whether some womanly ornament or gold was attached or hidden in the body; hair was loosened and head-coverings removed, and those without homes or money were struck down.

279.

Introduction. It is to the simple French knight Robert of Clari that we owe the most detailed account, from the Western point of view, of the astounding number and variety of early Christian relics seized in

Constantinople by the Western forces of the Fourth Crusade (on relics, see also selections 142–45).

THE SACRED RELICS OF CONSTANTINOPLE

(Translated by E. McNeal, from Robert of Clari, *The Conquest of Constantinople* [New York, 1964], pp. 102–5.)

When the city was captured and the pilgrims were quartered, as I have told you, and the palaces were taken over, then they found in the palaces riches more than a great deal. And the palace of Boukoleon was very rich and was made in such a way as I shall tell you. Within this palace, which was held by the marquis, there were fully five hundred halls, all connected with one another and all made with gold mosaic. And in it there were fully thirty chapels, great and small, and there was one of them which was called the Holy Chapel, which was so rich and noble that there was not a hinge nor a band nor any other part such as is usually made of iron that was not all of silver, and there was no column that was not of jasper or porphyry or some other rich precious stone. And the pavement of this chapel was of a white marble so smooth and clear that it seemed to be of crystal, and this chapel was so rich and so noble that no one could ever tell you its great beauty and nobility. Within this chapel were found many rich relics. One found there two pieces of the True Cross as large as the leg of a man and as long as half a *toise*, and one found there also the iron of the lance with which Our Lord had His side pierced and two of the nails which were driven through His hands and feet, and one found there in a crystal phial quite a little of His blood, and one found there the tunic which He wore and which was taken from Him when they led Him to the Mount of Calvary, and one found there the blessed crown with which He was crowned, which was made of reeds with thorns as sharp as the points of daggers. And one found there a part of the robe of Our Lady and the head of my lord St. John the Baptist and so many other rich relics that I could not recount them to you or tell you all the truth.

Now there was still another relic in this chapel which we had forgotten to tell you about. For there were two rich vessels of gold hanging in the midst of the chapel by two heavy silver chains. In one of these vessels there was a tile and in the other a cloth. And we shall tell you where these relics came from. There was once a holy man in Constantinople. It happened that this holy man was covering the house of a widow with tile for the love of God. And as he was covering it, Our Lord appeared to him and said to him (now this good man had a cloth wrapped about him): "Give me that cloth," said Our Lord. And the good man gave it to Him, and Our Lord enveloped His face with it so that His features were imprinted on it. And then He handed it back to him, and He told him to carry it with him and touch the sick with it, and whoever had faith in it would be healed of his sickness. And the good man took it and carried it away; but before he carried it away, after God had given him back his cloth, the good man took it and hid it under a tile until vespers. At vespers, when he went away, he took the cloth, and as he lifted up the tile, he saw the image imprinted on the tile just as it was on the cloth, and he carried the tile and the cloth away, and afterwards he cured many sick with them. And these relics were hanging in the midst of the chapel, as

I have told you. Now there was in this chapel still another relic, for there was an image of St. Demetrius which was painted on a panel. This image gave off so much oil that it could not be removed as fast as it flowed from the picture. [And there was another palace in the city, called the palace of Blachernae.] And there were fully twenty chapels there and at least two hundred chambers, or three hundred, all connected with one another and all made of gold mosaic. And this palace was so rich and so noble that no one could describe it to you or recount its great nobility and richness. In this palace of Blachernae there was found a very great treasure, for one found there the rich crowns which had belonged to former emperors and the rich ornaments of gold and the rich cloth of silk and gold and the rich imperial robes and the rich precious stones and so many other riches that no one could number the great treasure of gold and silver that was found in the palaces and in many other places in the city.

280.

Introduction. Constantinople contained some of the great masterpieces of statuary which had survived from Greek antiquity, many of which had been collected by Emperor Constantine from throughout the empire and placed in his new capital city. While the Byzantines understandably viewed these pagan art works equivocally—especially after the Iconoclastic struggle—they nevertheless appreciated the cultural continuity which the statues represented. In a section of his *Historia* commonly referred to as *On the Statues*, Nicetas Choniates describes the lamentable fate of many of these works of classical art and other treasures during the Latin sack of Constantinople in 1204.

DESTRUCTION OF ANCIENT ART IN THE LATIN SACK OF CONSTANTINOPLE

(From Nicetas Choniates, *Historia*, ed. I. Van Dieten [Berlin, 1975], pp. 647–51.)

From the very beginning they [the Latins] revealed their race to be lovers of gold; they conceived of a new method of plundering, which had completely escaped the notice of all who had [just] sacked the imperial city. Having opened the graves of those emperors which were in the burial ground situated in the area of the church of Christ's Holy Apostles, they stripped all of them during the night and, if any golden ornament, pearl, or precious stone still lay inviolate in these [tombs], they sacrilegiously seized it. When they found the corpse of the Emperor Justinian, which had remained undisturbed for so many years, they marveled at it, but they did not refrain from [looting] the funerary adornments. We may say that these Westerners spared neither the living nor the dead. They manifested [toward all], beginning with God and his servants [i.e. the clergy], complete indifference and impiety: quickly enough they tore down the curtain in the Great Church [Hagia Sophia], the value of which was reckoned in millions of purest silver pieces, since it was entirely interwoven with gold.

Even now they were still desirous of money (for nothing can satiate the avarice of the barbarians). They eyed the bronze statues and threw them into the fire. And so the bronze statue of Hera, standing in the agora of Constantine, was broken into pieces and consigned to the flames. The head of this statue, which could hardly be drawn by four oxen yoked together, was brought to the great palace. The [statue of] Paris [also called] Alexander opposite it, was cast off its base. This statue was connected with that of the goddess Aphrodite to whom the apple of Eris [Discord] was depicted as being awarded by Paris. . . .

These barbarians—who do not appreciate beauty—did not neglect to over-turn the statues standing in the Hippodrome or any other marvelous works. Rather, these too they turned into coinage [*nomisa*], exchanging great things [i.e. art] for small [i.e. money], thus acquiring petty coins at the expense of those things created at enormous cost. They then threw down the great Hercules Tri-hesperus, magnificently constructed on a base* and girded with the skin of a lion, a terrifying thing to see even in bronze. . . . He was represented as stand-ing, carrying in his hands neither quiver nor arrows nor club, but having his right foot and right hand extended and his left foot bent at the knee with the left hand raised at the elbow. . . . He [the statue of Hercules] was very broad in the chest and shoulders and had thick hair, plump buttocks, and strong arms, and was of such huge size, I think, as Lysimachus [Lysippus?] considered the real Hercules to have been—Lysimachus who sculpted from bronze this first and last great masterpiece of his hands. The statue was so large that the rope around his thumb had the size of a man's belt and the lower portion of the leg, the height of a man. But those [i.e. the Latins] who separate manly vigor from other virtues and claim it for themselves (considering it the most important quality) did not leave this Hercules (although it was the epitome of this attribute) untouched.

* The base was perhaps shaped like a basket.

281.

Introduction. Along with the misery caused by the Latins after 1204, local acts of usurpation caused by Byzantine nobles evoked hardly less reaction on the part of the population. There survive records of Greeks, even prelates, who castigated some of their own people for their trans-gressions or acts of usurpation. Here is a selection from a letter (dated 1208) of the metropolitan of Athens, Michael Choniates, written to console his nephew for the death of the latter's young son, killed by Leo Sgouros, a Greek usurper of power in the Peloponnesus during this period.

MICHAEL CHONIATES LAMENTS SGOUROS'S SEIZURE OF THE PELOPONNESUS

(From *Michael Akominatou Ta Sozomena* [Athens, 1880], vol. 2, pp. 169–70.)

Alas, but we have been enriched by more evils. It was not enough for us to be tyrannized by foreigners and consigned to the lot of slaves, but this man [Sgouros], allegedly of the same [Greek] people, has added to the great distress we suffer from our injuries. His fire, even before the approach of the Italians, had engulfed many parts of Greece and the Peloponnesus, and its coals still burn after their arrival. Compared to him even the Italians seem blameless. For the evils which they have caused seem more benevolent than those caused by this man, our countryman, and to the Romans [Byzantines] the foreigners appear more civilized and on the whole fairer. For example, no one has fled to such a fellow Greek from the cities enslaved by the Italians, since that would be nothing else than fleeing the smoke to fall into the fire. Indeed, as many as are able to escape from this man's garrisons desert to the Latins with a glad heart, as if they were departing from hell itself. And the evidence of events attests to this. For where are so many of the inhabitants of Argos, Hermione, and Aegina? Where are the prosperous citizens of Corinth? Has not everyone departed, unseen and unheard of? But indeed the Athenians and Thebans [under Latin domination] and Chalcidians and those who live along the coast remain at home and have not yet fled their dwellings.

282.

Introduction. In the year following the Latin occupation of Constantinople in 1204, Pope Innocent III wrote a letter to scholars at the University of Paris calling for the establishment, in effect, of a branch of the university in Constantinople. He invited professors and students to go from the West to Byzantium. The plan was probably not implemented, but it is significant as perhaps the most striking of the increasingly numerous Western attempts to infiltrate Byzantine society, in this case by striking at its most vulnerable point, the education of the youth. In 1248 another pope asked the chancellor of the University of Paris to provide for the study of scholars from the East (probably Greeks and perhaps Syrians and Armenians).

A Branch of the University of Paris in Constantinople

(From *Chartularium Universitatis Parisiensis,* ed. H. Denifle and A. Chatelain [Paris, 1889], vol. 1, pp. 62–63.)

[Pope Innocent III to the Masters and Scholars of the University of Paris:]

We have heard with very great joy that our most Christian and dearest son in Christ, B[aldwin I], the illustrious emperor of Constantinople, acts and exerts himself with all the means at his disposal in behalf of those things by which the Christian religion can and should be propagated. And, so that the edifice [the Latin church and empire in the East] which has recently in great measure been constructed may not collapse, he labors with ardent zeal and diligent solicitude. Thus, recently expanding into branches of good deeds the [seeds of] devotion which have been planted in his heart, he has humbly requested that we admonish and induce you [professors and students] by apostolic letters to go to Greece and to restore the study of letters there in that very place where it is known that this study had its inception. We are all the more inclined to grant the emperor's requests since we have frequently observed the extreme sincerity of his faith.

Therefore we anxiously beseech your university and admonish you, through the apostolic letters which we send, carefully to recall how many difficulties and aggravations your forefathers have endured so that they might learn the elements of liberal studies during their youth. Thus, let it not be displeasing that many of you go to this land [the East], full of silver and gold and jewels, abundant in grain, oil, and wine, and overflowing with all good things, so that—for the honor and glory of him from whom comes the gift of all knowledge [scientia]—they [you] might benefit themselves [yourselves] and others there, receiving the reward of eternal glory in addition to temporal riches and honors.

283.

Introduction. The jubilant words of the Byzantine historian George Acropolites record the long-awaited recovery of Constantinople from the Latins in 1261 by Emperor Michael VIII Palaeologus and provide a vivid description of the ceremonies attached to Byzantine repossession of the capital. The main theme of these ceremonies stressed "divine sanction" for the rule of Michael Palaeologus (he had previously gained the throne through usurpation: see selection 23).

THE BYZANTINE RECOVERY OF CONSTANTINOPLE: THANKSGIVING AND CELEBRATION

(From George Acropolites, *Historia*, ed. A. Heisenberg [Leipzig, 1903], vol. 1, pp. 186–88.)

The emperor reached Constantinople on the fourteenth day of August, but he did not wish to enter the city the same day, so he pitched his tents in the monastery of Cosmidion. . . . And after spending the night there and arising, he made his entrance as follows: since the Patriarch Arsenios was not present . . . it was at once necessary that one of the prelates pronounce the prayers. George, metropolitan of Cyzicus . . . whom they call Kleidas, fulfilled this task. Getting up on one of the towers of the Golden Gate and having with him also the icon of the *Theotokos*, the image named after the monastery of the *Hodegetria*, he recited prayers for all to hear. Then the emperor, putting aside his mantle, fell to his knees on the ground, and with him all those behind fell to their knees. And after the first prayer was over, the deacon motioned them to rise, and all standing chanted *Kyrie eleison* [Lord have mercy] one hundred times.

When this was over, another prayer was recited by the prelate. And then the same thing happened as after the first. And this was done until the completion of all the prayers. When the religious part of the ceremony had been performed, the emperor entered the Golden Gate in a way which honored God more than the emperor, for he marched on foot with the icon of the Mother of God [Hodegetria] preceding him. And he went up to the monastery of Studius, and after leaving there the icon of the most immaculate Mother of God, he mounted his horse and went to the Church of the Wisdom of God [St. Sophia]. There he worshiped Our Lord Christ and rendered proper thanks to him. Then he arrived at the Great Palace and the Byzantine population was filled with great and immense joy and exultation. For there was no one who could not dance or exult with joy, being scarcely able to believe this event because of its unexpectedness and the enormous outpouring of jubilation. Since it was necessary that the patriarch also be in Constantinople, . . . after a few days the emperor entered the holy building, the temple of Great Wisdom, in order that he might hand over the *cathedra* [the patriarch's throne] to the prelate. And finally there assembled with the emperor all the notables of the archons and the entire multitude. Then the emperor, taking the arm of the patriarch, said, "Take your throne now, O lord, and enjoy it, that of which you were so long deprived."

284.

Introduction. Despite the Greek recovery of Constantinople in 1261, the empire was much weaker than ever before; in fact, many of the problems existing before 1204 were exacerbated by the Latin occupation. One aspect of Byzantine-Western relations that became ever more dangerous was the increasing encroachment of the Italian maritime states (and, in the fourteenth century, the Catalans) on the trade of Constantinople. In the following selection, a chrysobull of Andronicus II (issued in 1320), the emperor grants special privileges to Catalan merchants.

EMPEROR ANDRONICUS II GRANTS COMMERCIAL PRIVILEGES TO THE CATALANS

(Translated by M. Varouxakis and D. Geanakoplos, from F. Miklosich and J. Müller, eds., *Acta et diplomata Graeca medii aevi* [Vienna, 1869], vol. 3, pp. 98–100.)

As His Majesty the King of Aragon, Valencia, Sardinia, Corsica, Count of Barcelona and dearest uncle of Our Majesty, Lord James, has sent to me, the emperor, a letter carried by the Catalan merchants Berengarius, Bonatus Remigi, Guillaume Bertolini, and Tommasio de Podio, asking me not to permit any disturbances in connection with their commerce, thanks to my love and genuine affection for him, and also asking that I order that not only they, but also all others who will come in the [near] future and even later into the territories of my empire, might be granted the same freedom from molestation—not only did I accept that [provision] immediately, with eagerness, but in addition, on account of the love and genuine affection that I bear for His Majesty the King and dearest uncle of Our Majesty, I gave the order that they might have more privileges regarding the tax [*kommerkion*] that they should pay for their commerce, and that they might be completely exempt from the tax that they formerly paid. Thus, I issue this chrysobull by which it is decreed that the above-named merchants and others might travel to our empire without any impediment [including] all those from the country of His Majesty the King, my dearest uncle, who would wish to come here, to the holy, glorious, God-grown and God-saved Constantinople and to other territories of my empire, as often as they wish; and they might engage in their commerce freely and without any impediment, paying a tax (*kommerkion*) of two *hyperpyra* per hundred [i.e. 2%] on imports and another two *hyperpyra* for exports,* and they shall not have to pay more and their persons shall remain inviolate and their merchandise free of molestation from any of my subjects and no harm should come to them or oppression or robbery on the part of my subjects. Besides this, after this request of these merchants, if it happens that any of their ships be in danger after a storm on sea and [if] they should come to shore in any of my empire's areas, the inhabitants of this land or others shall not have the right to rob or take advantage of the merchandise that will be saved, but the merchandise must be kept intact, because whoever does any harm to the shipwrecked merchants and steals from the cargo, they [the Byzantines] will be obliged to return the goods and to indemnify them [the Catalans] for the entire cargo, whatever they have stolen, and they are to be punished as infringers of this chrysobull. As soon as this chrysobull is issued, the Catalan merchants, after having paid the tax mentioned, will remain undisturbed and will not suffer injustice or harm or attack from anyone. For this reason the present chrysobull of our reign is issued for their benefit and is given to the merchants that are here and to other Catalans who will wish to come from the land of my aforementioned dearest uncle, His Majesty the King, here or in the other territories of my empire, for assurance and power and security.

*Cf. the Venetians (and the Genoese) who after 1261 generally paid no duties. See selections 209 and esp. 211.

285.

Introduction. The effects of the Western conquest remained in one way or another firmly ingrained in the Byzantine psyche all the way to the fall of the empire in 1453. After 1204, in fact, the West, much more even than before, was regarded by the Byzantines as openly aggressive. And after the Greek recovery of Constantinople in 1261, all efforts toward rapprochment of the two peoples, especially on the ecclesiastical level, were generally regarded in Byzantium simply as Western ploys for the recovery of political and military as well as ecclesiastical control over the Byzantine East. (For the perceptive statement by Barlaam on Byzantine suspicions of Western, especially papal, proposals for religious union, see above, selection 159.)

One of the most basic but not always clearly articulated fears of the Greeks was what they termed "Latinization" (*latinizein*) of their society and even culture. The Westerner who most explicitly advocated such a policy was the fourteenth-century Dominican Crusader-propagandist, William of Adam. In particular he advocated sending one child from each Greek family to the West to be brought up in the Latin fashion and faith.*

Some years earlier the French publicist Pierre Dubois (who flourished in 1308) had even suggested the sending of educated Latin girls to the East to marry important Greeks (especially clerics!) so as, ultimately, to "convert the entire Greek people to the Latin faith."

PIERRE DUBOIS'S METHOD OF LATINIZING THE BYZANTINES

(From Pierre Dubois, *De recuperatione terre sancte*, ed. V. Langlois, in *Collection de textes pour servir à l'étude . . . de l'histoire* [Paris, 1891], ch. 61, pp. 51–52.)

Let Latin girls be instructed in medicine and surgery and in the subjects antecedent to these. When these girls have been thus instructed and have a knowledge of writing, those noble-born and of especial skill and attractive in face and figure shall be adopted as daughters and granddaughters by the greater princes of their own [Latin] regions of the Holy Land and of other nearby areas. They will be so adorned [in skills] provided by the said foundation† that they will be considered children of princes and may appropriately be given as wives to the greater princes, clerics, and other rich men of the East. . . .

It would be very expeditious [for the West] that the Eastern [mainly Byzantine] prelates and priests secure such wives, for it is their [Byzantine] custom to marry [but, necessarily, *before* ordination] and they have been extremely unwilling to follow the Roman and other Western clergy in renouncing their right to be married.‡ Thus, these wives, possessing this kind of education and believing in the articles of faith and sacraments of the Roman church, would then teach their own children and their husbands to accept the Roman faith, to believe and sacrifice in the Latin manner.

---

*William Adam, *Directorium ad passagium faciendum* in *Recueil des historiens des croisades. Documents Arméniens*, vol. 2 (1906), pp. 367f.
† Elsewhere Dubois describes this foundation, to be established to convert the Orthodox East in the final aim of recovering the Holy Land.
‡ Dubois was against clerical celibacy.

286.

Introduction. An almost inevitable result of the Latin occupation of Constantinople was the development of an even stronger sense of identification on the part of many among the Byzantine people with their ancient Greek, or Hellenic, heritage. This feeling had emerged in the Byzantine successor state of Nicaea (Asia Minor) already during the period of the Latin Empire. The result was that less emphasis was now placed by some on the continuity of a multi-national "Roman" past (of course most of the non-Greek-speaking areas of the empire had been lost centuries before). Rather the tendency emerged to identify with a sense of Greek "ethnicity," not only with Orthodoxy but with ancient Greek culture. New and more systematic efforts, especially in the cultural realm, were thus made to return to classical Greek rather than Roman ideals, although the notion of Byzantium constituting the continuation of the "Roman" Empire never died out.

With this increased sense of their "Greekness," there also emerged among the Byzantines an increasing feeling that the Latins were in many ways alien to them, even a lower form of existence in the Christian *ecumene*. Nevertheless, the achievements of medieval Latin civilization, especially from the thirteenth century onward, began to be investigated and even admired by a very small, well-educated minority of *Latinophrones* ("Latin-minded" Greeks). Some of them even felt that reforms in the Byzantine economy and culture on the model of the Latin West were a precondition for survival of the Byzantine state!

Appreciation even for Western Scholasticism became notable among a few fourteenth-century Byzantine theologians and scholars. But in most cases Byzantine theologians learned Western theological arguments only in order to the better to oppose them. In contrast is the example of the emperor's private councillor, the influential *Mesazon* Demetrius Cydones (c. 1324–97/8), who translated into Greek Thomas Aquinas's *Summa contra Gentiles*. As Cydones explained, he began his study of Latin in order to be able, without the aid of translators, to read Western chancery documents, and in the process became fascinated by Aquinas's use of Aristotle, "who," in effect he affirmed, "is one of our own."

Cydones's Apologia for His Interest in the Teachings of Aquinas

(Translated by M. Varouxakis and D. Geanakoplos, from G. Mercati, *Studi e testi*, no. 56, *Notizie di Procoro e Demetrio Cidone . . .* [Vatican, 1931], pp. 362–63.)

When that very fine teacher [Cydones' Dominican instructor] saw this, he was overjoyed, his reward being the benefit of his student. And wishing to increase both knowledge and glory together, he gave me a book in order that I might exercise my mind on it as much as possible. It was a work on theology of a man who surpassed everyone in this respect. But now no one is ignorant of Thomas [Aquinas], [everyone knows] the great number of his writings, the moderation of their meaning, and his use of syllogisms out of which all proceeds, and he is known to those even outside Stelon [the Pillars of Hercules].

Of his books this one is the most perfect because it brings to flower the man's wisdom. Yet he [my teacher], on his part, merely wanted to acquaint me with the terms used in the book, just as grammarians often urge children to read the best parts of Homer and Hesiod. He did not expect me even to approach the depth of the thought or the elegance of the language. But I, as if I had received something that belonged to me, did not neglect any part of what I was reading, none of the terminology which was not very common, nor also the deepest part of the meaning. No matter how difficult and peculiar it was, I easily understood it. And then it became increasingly remarkable that, as if by divine aid, I could understand this, and I began to have so much courage that it seemed that by my own personal volition I would show it to my friends who scoffed at me and did not believe that I had succeeded in this task. In addition, in my customary mode of thinking, I, for my part, wanted to tell my friends what I believed was good, and I brought to Greece many of those chapters, [and] when we had some leisure time I gave them to the emperor to read. He listened with pleasure to what I told him and he praised me for my efforts in this regard, and he encouraged me not to hesitate but to try to interpret the book with all my attention, affirming that there would accrue great profit from this book for the cause of the Greeks in the future.

Thus I obeyed him and with great pleasure I undertook the work [of translation] of this book and whatever he urged me to do, and,—as they say, from his nails you will recognize the lion—beginning with a little bit at the beginning, I worked out the entire book. It was considered such a worthwhile study that as soon as the emperor received it he copied it out, and many of the highest ranking persons [of the imperial court] did the same and were able to learn something useful from it. And now the work of Thomas against the Greeks is to be found in the hands of many people, bringing honor to the writer and much benefit to those who read it.

287.

Introduction. Western advances in technology, which by the fourteenth century had clearly surpassed the Byzantine, were feared but also admired, at least by certain Greek intellectuals. To be sure, for centuries Byzantium had adopted isolated elements of Western culture, for example, nautical terms such as *scala* (landing wharf), *cassela* (chest), *marangon* (ship's carpenter). And we have cited the example of Emperor Manuel I's adoption of the custom of the Western joust (see selection 239). But for the first time some Byzantines could conceive of Western technology as surpassing the Byzantine, and even think of adopting aspects of it in order to counteract the growing Turkish menace. Very revealing in this respect is a letter (c. 1444) of the Byzantine cardinal of the Roman Church, Bessarion, who states that young Greeks, in order to benefit their country, should go to Italy to study the mechanical arts, arms manufacturing, shipbuilding and iron-working.

Bessarion Urges the Greeks to Adopt Western Technology

(From "Letter of Bessarion to the Despot of the Morea Constantine Palaeologus" (c. 1444), in S. Lambros, ed., *Neos Hellenomnemon* [Athens, 1906], vol. 3, pp. 43–44.)

It would also be good to do this, to send some selected young men to Italy in order that they might learn the skills that are needed, for the reason that these techniques are very rare and unique and easy, both in theory and in practice, and do not take long to master and to be taught. . . . I heard that the Peloponnesus, especially the area around Sparta itself, is full of iron metal and all that is lacking is men who know how to extract it and to construct weapons and other things. . . . These four skills, my excellent lord, engineering, iron-working, weapons manufacture, and naval architecture . . . are needed and useful to those who [wish to] prosper. Send four or eight young men here to the West, together with appropriate means [money]—and let not many know about this—so that when they return to Greece [Hellas] they can pass on the knowledge to other Greeks. There are, in addition, however, four other [arts] worthy of mention, the skill of glass-making, that of silk manufacture, the manufacture of wool [clothing], and still more, the science of dyes.

288.

Introduction. After the recapture of Constantinople by Michael VIII Palaeologus in 1261, as a result primarily of the great outpouring of patriotic sentiment from Greeks in the Byzantine world (including Nicaea, "Greece," Trebizond, and probably even Epirus), there occurred the so-called "Palaeologan Renaissance" or rather revival and intensification of classical Greek culture. (Manifestations of this had been seen even earlier in the state of Nicaea.)* The "renaissance" took many forms, but one important field was certainly art, where a new emphasis on the expression of emotion, a stronger sense of dynamism, almost of "realism" or "naturalism," was observable in some of the great works produced. This was true of some of the painting, especially of the "Macedonian" or "Constantinopolitan" school. Other paintings were in a less dramatic, somewhat softer style called "Cretan." (See selection 332.)

Nevertheless, most Byzantines could not (or apparently would not) understand the expression of realism when they saw it in contemporary Western painting. The traditional Byzantine attitude toward Latin religious art is well reflected by the following two passages, the first from the work *Against Heresies* by Symeon, metropolitan of Thessalonika, in the mid-fifteenth century, and the second from the *History of the Council of Florence* by the Greek cleric of St. Sophia, Sylvester Syropoulos.

Typical Byzantine Attitudes toward Later Latin Religious Art

A. Byzantine Views of Western Icons

(Translated by C. Mango, *The Art of the Byzantine Empire, 312– 1453* [Englewood Cliffs, N.J.: Prentice-Hall, 1972], pp. 253–54.)

What other innovation have they [the Latins] introduced contrary to the tradition of the Church? Whereas the holy icons have been piously established in honor of their divine prototypes and for their relative worship by the faithful . . . and they instruct us pictorially by means of colors and other materials† (which serve as a kind of alphabet)—these men, who subvert everything, as has been said, often confect holy images in a different manner and one that is contrary to custom. For instead of painted garments and hair, they adorn them with human hair and clothes, which is not the image of hair and of a garment, but the [actual] hair and garment of a man, and hence is not an image and a symbol of the prototype. These they confect and adorn in an irreverent spirit, which is indeed opposed to the holy icons.

B. Latin Religious Art Unappreciated by Byzantines

(From *Art of the Byzantine Empire*, p. 254.)

When I‡ enter a Latin church, I do not revere any of the [images of] saints that are there because I do not recognize any of them. At the most, I may recognize Christ, but I do not revere him either, since I do not know in what terms he is inscribed. So I make the sign of the cross and I revere this sign that I have made myself, and not anything that I see there.

*On the emergence, after 1204, of a Byzantine sense of identification with the ancient Greek heritage or of a sense of Greek "ethnicity," see selections 158, 161, and 163.

†On the Byzantine theory of icons following John of Damascus, see selection 111, also 112–13.

‡Syropoulos is here quoting the words of another Greek prelate.

E.
THE TURKS

289.

Introduction. The last invaders, ultimately fatal for Byzantium, were the Turks. The first wave of Turks, the Seljuks, began to penetrate into eastern Asia Minor after the fatal battle of Manzikert (1071). Here the fourteenth-century Byzantine historian, Nicephorus Gregoras, describes the effects of early Seljuk Turkish advances into Anatolia.

MOURNFUL EVENTS AS THE TURKS ADVANCE

(From Nicephorus Gregoras, *Byzantina historia*, ed. I. Bekker and L. Schopen [Bonn, 1829], vol. 1, pp. 141–42.)

When the barbarians fearlessly seized our borders on the edges of Asia, making them their dwellings and dividing the lands they had enslaved into satrapies, they encircled all the land from the sea around Pontus and Galatia up to the sea around Lycia and Caria and the River of Egoumedon. Who would be more able to describe at greater length those terrible events which are worthy of description in the *Iliad* itself? They continually, day and night, beset the Romans and contribute to the disintegration of the Roman [Empire], for the barbarians advanced as much as possible. If we would try to narrate these events in a chapter, it would be impossible to do justice to them in emotion and language. And an insufficient impression would be made of these happenings which are worthy of tears. It is impossible to describe, one by one, all the things that occurred. Moreover, it would bring forth a river of tears from the eyes of those tender in heart and sensitive, and we shall think that we are writing a lament rather than narrating a history. Therefore, not everything can be said or described. . . .

On the first attack those barbarians took as spoil a very great and innumerable host of men and women. Whatever could be carried away they divided as booty among themselves.

290.

Introduction. At the end of the thirteenth century the Ottoman Turks, a small tribe related to the Seljuks, began their own amazingly rapid advance across Asia Minor. Quickly they reached Amorium in central Anatolia, then Brusa (which became their capital), and still later Adrianople in European Thrace. In the following selection Demetrius Cydones, the Byzantine *Mesazon* (private councillor to the emperor) during part of the critical fourteenth century, laments the harsh fate of the Greek Christians at the hands of the Ottomans in Asia Minor.

CYDONES LAMENTS TURKISH CONQUESTS IN ASIA MINOR

(From Demetrius Cydones, *Oratio pro subsidio latinorum*, in MPG, vol. 154, col. 965.)

Indeed the entire region which used to sustain us, extending to the east from the Hellespont to the mountains of Armenia, they [the Turks] have stripped away. They have completely destroyed cities, despoiled churches, looted graves and filled everything with blood and corpses. They have even polluted the souls of the inhabitants, forcing them to reject the true God and to take part in their own filthy rites, and, alas! they have insolently abused the bodies [of Christians]. Having been stripped of all their possessions and even of their freedom, they [the inhabitants] are now reduced to sick likenesses of slaves. And these unfortunate ones are forced, with the slight energy that remains to them, to serve the personal comforts of their masters.

291.

Introduction. One may speculate as to what would have happened had the medieval Greek East and the Latin West been able, not only in theory but in practice, to combine their erudition and technical and military skills in order to achieve a united front against the Turks. There were, however, certain Byzantines who, perhaps still mindful of the potential of the old multi-ethnic type of empire, preferred to throw in their lot with the Turks. It was, it seems, their hope that with the Greek Christian faith and culture joined to the Turkish military ability and energy, a new and greater "Roman" (or perhaps "Greco-Turkish") empire could emerge. This may well have been an underlying hope of the author of the letter quoted below, George of Trebizond, a Byzantine emigré-intellectual born in Crete who went to Italy and who, some years before the fall of Constantinople to the Turkish Sultan Mehmed II in 1453, wrote to the latter in the following manner:

A GRECO-TURKISH EMPIRE?

(From G. Zoras, *George of Trebizond and His Efforts for Greco-Turkish Cooperation* (in Greek) [Athens, 1954], quoting from George's treatise, pp. 95–98 and 164.)

You see, dear Emir and true Sultan, that the entire race of man is divided into three parts, Jews, Christians, and Muslims, of which the Jewish people is small and very diffused, while the Christian is large and great and has great power, wisdom, and knowledge. If one unites these two races of men, Christians, I say, and Muslims, in one faith and dogma, I swear that God himself in heaven and on earth shall be praised by all men both on earth and in heaven, and he [the accomplisher of union] shall be elevated to the rank of the angels. This, wonderful Emir, no one except you can accomplish. . . .

The Christians condemn the Muslims as imprudent and unlearned, the Muslims [condemn] the Christians as idolatrous, and both condemn each other as impious. . . . The worst is that both Christians and Muslims all say it is impossible for such a holy union to come about. . . . Then they point to how great the differences are between us, Christians and Muslims, so great that they cannot be overcome. But ignorance has increased the differences. For Christians and Muslims cannot even converse together because of ignorance of each other's language. And the schism and hatred between us and you has increased, especially because even before learning anything—how the other speaks, believes, and what his creed is—each condemns the other in a way that is unjust and not pleasing to God. But I, having heard from some of the teachings of the *Koran*, do not believe the differences are so many that they cannot be removed; rather they are small and easily reconcilable if one diligently studies the writings of each side. . . .

But first, in order that the argument be clear to us, let us enumerate the chief differences between you and us. They are three. First, that the Muslim says that the Christians believe in three gods, father, mother, and son; second, that we believe that Christ is the Son of God and is God; third, that we believe Christ was crucified and died and was buried, and being resurrected, lives into eternity as true God. These are the differences separating Muslims from Christians; others of custom and manner of life are not important. . . . But O *Basileus* of *Basileis* and Lord of Lords, dearest Emir and Sultan most magnificent, listen benevolently regarding God and examine this argument through your wise men there [and see] if it agrees with the *Koran*, especially with the truth. And if it agrees with the *Koran* and the truth, you may find those things written here, most noble Sultan; seek to unite the *ecumene* [universe] and you shall become, as is appropriate for you, *basileus* not only of all the earth but of the heavens. Do we Christians believe in many gods? Let it not be, let it not be, O Emir and Sultan. . . . Accursed be he who believes in many gods. . . . In one God we believe, simple, without beginning, without end, whose substance and nature none can apprehend, not even the angels of heaven. . . .

Whence then came this lie . . . that we believe in three gods? From Satan and the Jews who, being an evil people and enemies of the truth, slandered us Christians to you Muslims and made both of us war against each other, so that they could take joy from our slaughter, those who do not understand their own Scriptures, those violating the Mosaic law, who understand it not spiritually but bodily, who have nothing good, nothing manly, neither science nor empire nor strength anywhere. . . . [And if you accomplish this union of Muslims and Christians] compared to your greatness, Alexander the Great, and Caesar Augustus, and Constantine [the Great] himself shall appear small.

292.

Introduction. The Byzantines, though long aware of the powerful Turkish menace to the life of the empire, never systematically studied the Turks from a political or cultural point of view. They usually failed, for example, in this later period to adapt to the Turkish methods of hit-and-run warfare. Their information on Turkish religious practices and beliefs was meager and colored by hostility and superstition. Useful, then, is the following account written by a highly educated Greek prelate, Gregory Palamas (later to become the famous Hesychast leader on Mt. Athos), who in 1354 was captured at Gallipoli by the Ottoman Turks. Taken to the court of the Turkish Sultan Orkhan, he engaged in debate over the religious beliefs of Christianity and Islam.

After his escape to Constantinople he wrote down his firsthand impressions of the Turks and included an eyewitness transcription of his debate with the Muslims, which took place in the presence of the Turkish sultan and was presided over by "Palapanos" [Balabanos], a close associate of the sultan. Palamas first defended the Christian doctrine of the Trinity (a concept which struck many Turks as polytheistic), stating, "God has both word and spirit, which are with him and in him without beginning and without separation. God was never, nor will he ever be, without spirit or word. Therefore, all three persons of the trinity are one, and one the three." Later the discussion turned to other differences between Christian and Muslim beliefs and practices. Passages from the transcript of the debate follow.

GREGORY PALAMAS AMONG THE OTTOMAN TURKS

(Translated by D. Sahas, "Captivity and Dialogue: Gregory Palamas and the Muslims," *Greek Orthodox Theological Review* 25 [1980]: 422–23.)

The presiding Palapanos, after he called for silence, said to the bishop [Palamas], "The master [Orkhan] demands from you to answer the question how we accept Christ, love him, respect him, confess him to be God's word and breath, and we also place his mother near to God, and yet you do not accept our prophet nor do you love him?" Then the bishop said: "He who does not believe in the words of a teacher cannot love the teacher himself; that is why we do not love Muhammad. Our Lord God Jesus Christ has said to us that he will come again to judge the entire world. He also commanded us not to receive anyone else until He will come back to us again. He also said to those who disbelieved in him: "I have come in my Father's name, and you do not receive me, nor did you accept me; if another comes in his own name, him you will receive." That is why the disciple [St. Paul] of Christ writes to us: "But even if an angel preaches to you contrary to that which you have received from us let him be accursed."

Then . . . [they] said to the bishop: "Circumcision was handed down by God from the very beginning. Even Christ Himself was circumcised. How then, you do not circumcise yourselves?" Then the bishop: "Since you are referring to the old law and to what was handed down by God to the Hebrews at that time—for traditions of God also were the keeping of the Sabbath, the Jewish passover, sacrifices which were to be offered exclusively by the priests, the altar in the interior of the temple, and the dividing curtain—since all these and other such things have also been handed down by God, why do you not cherish any of them and you do not practice them?" . . .

They interrupted him again saying: "Why do you place many representations [images] in your churches and you venerate them, even though God wrote and said to Moses: 'Thou shalt not make a likeness of anything, whatever things are in heaven above, and whatever are in the earth beneath, and whatever are in the sea'?" And the bishop said again: "Friends are venerated by each other, but they are not made gods. It is evident to everyone that this is, indeed, what Moses learned from God and this is what he taught the people then. However, this same Moses again and at that time, left almost nothing of which he did not make a representation. He made the area beyond the curtain to be like and represent the celestial [reality]. Also, since the Cherubim are in heaven, he made representations of them and placed them into the innermost sanctuary of the temple. As to the exterior of the temple, he made it to represent the earthly [reality]. If anyone, then, had questioned Moses 'Why have you anyway made such things, since God forbids the icons and the likeness of things in heaven and of things on earth?', he would have, certainly, answered that 'icons and representations are forbidden so that one may not worship them as gods. However, if one is to be elevated through them toward God, this is good!' The Greeks, too, praised created things but they did so as if they were gods. We praise them too, but we elevate ourselves through them to the glory of God."

293.

Introduction. In 1369 the Ottoman Turks began the first of a series of intermittent sieges of Constantinople itself. The first of any real consequence was that of 1422 under Sultan Murad. John Cananus, a Byzantine chronicler of the early fifteenth century, has left a vivid account of this siege.

JOHN CANANUS DESCRIBES MURAD'S SIEGE OF
CONSTANTINOPLE (1422)

(From John Cananus, *Relation of the Siege of Constantinople*, [in Greek], MPG, vol. 156, cols 61–65.)

In the year 1422, on Tuesday 10 June at eight o'clock in the morning, there came upon us an army of about ten thousand Muslims, led by their general, an evil, bloodthirsty man called Michalpas. In one sweep they took every city and country under the imperial authority. They also took all the area around our city, while they ravaged, pillaged, and captured everyone. They slaughtered many men, while they carried others beyond Iconium and Araza-petas Kefas. They licentiously disgraced the women, circumcised the infants, and destroyed and exterminated all animals either yoked or free. . . . As I already mentioned, the first army of Muslims came on the tenth of June and shut us up in the city, and on the twentieth of June there appeared another army of Muslims, like a cloud of hail, spreading destruction and darkening all the land that belonged to the Romans; like a streak of burning lightning they set fire to and burned everything, and uprooted all fruit-bearing trees and even the trunks of the vineyards; and every other form of evil and destruction they committed against us. Finally came their great general, the emir, their lord.

Such a great mass of soldiers, generations on generations, crowds upon crowds, both infantry and cavalry, had gathered that the whole region was covered by them. At the command of the Turkish despot, Murad-Bey, they began to make a palisade. This palisade, greater than any other, stretched from one end of the city, the Golden Gate, to the other, the Xyloporta. The palisade came as close to the walls as an arrow could. It was solid and fortified with large beams of timber and thick planks. They placed a web of entwined branches in front of the palisade to deflect the arrows and spears and the stones hurled by the Romans. Behind the palisade they made room for soldiers of the army (who were from all nations) to stand. They were also to fight from behind the palisade with spears and bows, and with the large and small weapons of the nonprofessional troops whom they brought for this purpose. With their large war machines they hoped to destroy the walls of the city and thus capture it. . . . The Turks were expecting that the stones of the greater bombardments would destroy the fallen tower, and because the place does not have a guard to hinder the Turks, they would enter the outer wall and push back the Romans from the opening and enslave the city.

But this expectation of the infidels came to naught, for the stones of their large [siege engine] hit the collapsed tower seventy times, and they did not harm the Romans, nor did this benefit the Turks. For the place and the ditch and the tower were near the [gate] of St. Kyriake, between the [gates] of St. Romanus and Charses [Charisius], near the river called Lycus. So much concerning the uselessness of the bombardment.

Who can tell of all the other machines of the enemy, which they brought for the siege of the city and the extermination of the Romans? Of the many, I shall now mention a few. They constructed many large wooden towers on iron wheels, as high as the city walls, or even higher. They had bull and buffalo teams (belonging to the nonprofessional troops) ready to pull the towers with ropes near the trench and to fight from them, and to destroy the wall. . . . Opposite the doors of the city they made gigantic wooden towers with wheels tied with iron, so that whoever saw them and hadn't known of the attack on the walls and the uselessness of the towers [against the walls] was made to wonder and to fear greatly.

Others were looking for the aqueducts which brought water to the fountains of the city, in order to secretly enter the city by night and thus to surprise, seize, and capture it.

The despot of the Turks also dispatched heralds to proclaim to all the ends of the earth that the emir promised to deliver all the riches and people of the city to the Muslims. This he did to gather all the Muslims, and this ruse worked. For as the proclamation was made known to all the nations of Muslims—that the city was promised to be delivered up to booty and slavery—from almost every corner of the earth and every tribe the Muslims came to profit, not only the profiteers in looting and war, but the adventurers and the *sailides* [i.e. the merchants], perfumers, shoemakers, and even some Turkish monks. For this reason, everyone assembled: the soldiers for booty, the merchants to buy the loot; some came to buy prisoners, some women; others came to take the men and still others, the infants; others came to seize the animals and others, goods; and the Turkish monks came to get our nuns and free booty from the despot of the Turks. In expectation, then, there gathered from all the corners of the earth innumerable masses of Muslims, and all marveled as they beheld the fierceness of the host.

294.

Introduction. The final, climactic event in Byzantine history was, of course, the siege and capture of the City early in the morning on Tuesday, 29 May 1453, by the Ottoman Sultan Mehmed II. Chaos and disorder seemed to rule in the capital during the three-month-long siege, in particular because of conflict between the proponents of ecclesiastical union with Rome and their opponents. George Scholarios (who later as Gennadios became the first patriarch appointed by the Turkish sultan) had succeeded Mark of Ephesus as champion of the anti-unionists. Just before the fall, many anti-unionists, angered and provoked by a unionist ceremony recently performed in Hagia Sophia, flocked to Scholarios's monastic cell. There they found, nailed to the door, a placard on which Scholarios had written the following powerful words:

SCHOLARIOS WARNS THE BYZANTINES

(From Ducas, *Ducae historia Turcobyzantina, 1341–1462*, ed. V. Grecu [Bucharest, 1958], p. 317.)

Wretched Romans, how you have gone astray! You have rejected the hope of God and trusted in the strength of the Franks; you have lost your piety along with your city which is about to be destroyed. Lord have mercy on me. I testify before you that I am innocent of such transgression. Know, wretched citizens, what you are doing. Along with your impending captivity, you have forsaken the faith handed down from your fathers [*patroparadoton*] and assented to impiety. Woe unto you when you are judged!

295.

Introduction. The fall of Constantinople, for centuries the true capital of Christendom, the city "guarded by God," had an extremely traumatic effect on the Greek psyche. For decades thereafter laments were composed by the educated literatus and common citizen alike, mourning the loss and destruction of the capital. One Greek historian of the capture, Ducas, a witness to the capture and sack of the city in 1453, lamented the fallen city and its people in these moving words:

O MY CITY!

(From Ducas, *Ducae historia Turcobyzantina, 1341–1462*, ed. V. Grecu [Bucharest, 1958], pp. 385–87.)

And the entire City [its inhabitants and wealth] was to be seen in the tents of the [Turkish] camp, the city deserted, lying lifeless, naked, soundless, without either form or beauty. O City, City, head of all cities! O City, City, center of the four corners of the world! O City, City, pride of the Romans, civilizer of the barbarians! O City, second paradise planted toward the west, possessing all kinds of vegetation, laden with spiritual fruits! Where is your beauty, O paradise, where the beneficent strength of the charms of your spirit, soul, and body? Where are the bodies of the Apostles of my Lord, which were implanted long ago in the always-green paradise, having in their midst the purple cloak, the lance, the sponge, the reed, which, when we kissed them, made us believe that we were seeing him who was raised on the Cross? Where are the relics of the saints, those of the martyrs? Where the remains of Constantine the Great and the other emperors? Roads, courtyards, crossroads, fields, and vineyard enclosures, all teem with the relics of saints, with the bodies of nobles, of the chaste, and of male and female ascetics. Oh what a loss! "The dead bodies of thy servants, O Lord, have they given to be meat unto the fowls of the heaven, the flesh of thy saints unto the beasts of the earth round about New Sion and there was none to bury them [Psalm 78:2–3]."

O temple [Hagia Sophia]! O earthly heaven! O heavenly altar! O sacred and divine places! O magnificence of the churches! O holy books and words of God! O ancient and modern laws! O tablets inscribed by the finger of God! O Scriptures spoken by his mouth! O divine discourses of angels who bore flesh! O doctrines of men filled with the Holy Spirit! O teachings of semi-divine heroes! O commonwealth! O citizens! O army, formerly beyond number, now removed from sight like a ship sunk into the sea! O houses and palaces of every type! O sacred walls! Today I invoke you all, and as if incarnate beings I mourn with you, having Jeremiah as [choral] leader of this lamentable tragedy!

PART VI
Byzantine Culture
◆ ◆ ◆ ◆ ◆ ◆ ◆ ◆ ◆ ◆ ◆ ◆ ◆ ◆ ◆ ◆ ◆ ◆

A.
INFLUENCE OF THE CLASSICS

296.

Introduction. Unlike the medieval West, where until quite late learning was almost exclusively confined to the clerical caste, Byzantium, throughout its history, possessed a considerable number of educated laymen. The core of the education typical of this group was training in the ancient Greek classics, particularly in rhetoric, that is, the art of speaking and writing well. The elegant form of classical works was especially admired and imitated, though of course the Christian works were not neglected. Indeed, from at least the time of the late fourth-century Cappadocian Church Fathers (Basil, Gregory Nazianzus, and Gregory of Nyssa), much of the content of the pagan Greek classics, especially dealing with philosophy and rhetoric, had been assimilated into—or grafted onto—a Christian framework, rendering it for all practical purposes acceptable to the church. As a result, the potential for conflict between the pagan classics and Christianity was probably more subtly regulated in Byzantium than in the West.

The following selection from the fourth-century St. Basil the Great's "Advice to Young Men on Studying Greek Literature" (advocating qualified acceptance of the poetry, prose, and philosophic works of the classics) is illustrative of what became the typical Byzantine attitude to the writings of pagan Greece. The more extreme of the Greek monks, however, were unable to accept this compromise, rejecting the reading of classical works as unchristian and immoral.

A. ST. BASIL ON THE STUDY OF CLASSICAL GREEK LITERATURE

(Translated by R. J. Deferrari and M. R. McGuire, *St. Basil: The Letters*, Loeb Classical Library [Cambridge, Mass., 1934], vol. 4, pp. 387–93 and 431. Reprinted by permission of Harvard University Press.)

But that this pagan learning is not without usefulness for the soul has been sufficiently affirmed; yet just how you should participate in it would be the next topic to be discussed.

First, then, as to the learning to be derived from the poets, that I may begin with them, inasmuch as the subjects they deal with are of every kind, you ought not to give your attention to all they write without exception; but whenever they recount for you the deeds or words of good men, you ought to cherish and emulate these and try to be as far as possible like them; but when they treat of wicked men, you ought to avoid such imitation, stopping your ears no less than Odysseus did, according to what those same poets say, when he avoided the songs of the Sirens. For familiarity with evil words is, as it were, a road leading to evil deeds. On this account, then, the soul must be watched over with all vigilance, lest through the pleasure the poets' words give we may unwittingly accept something of the more evil sort, like those who take poisons along with honey. We shall not, therefore, praise the poets when they revile or mock, or when they depict men engaged in amours or drunken, or when they define happiness in terms of an over-abundant table or dissolute songs. But least of all shall we give attention to them when they narrate anything about the gods, and especially when they speak of them as being many, and these too not even in accord with one another. For in their poems brother is at feud with brother, and father with children, and the latter in turn are engaged in truceless war with their parents. But the adulteries of gods and their amours and their sexual acts in public, and especially those of Zeus, the chief and highest of all, as they themselves describe him, actions which one would blush to mention of even brute beasts—all these we shall leave to the stage-folk.

These same observations I must make concerning the writers of prose also, and especially when they fabricate tales for the entertainment of their hearers. And we shall certainly not imitate the orators in their art of lying. For neither in courts of law nor in other affairs is lying befitting to us, who have chosen the right and true way of life, and to whom refraining from litigation has been ordained in commandment. But we shall take rather those passages of theirs in which they have praised virtue or condemned vice. For just as in the case of other beings enjoyment of flowers is limited to their fragrance and colour, but the bees, as we see, possess the power to get honey from them as well, so it is possible here also for those who are pursuing not merely what is sweet and pleasant in such writings to store away from them some benefit also for their souls. It is, therefore, in accordance with the whole similitude of the bees, that we should participate in the pagan literature.

And since it is through virtue that we must enter upon this life of ours, and since much has been uttered in praise of virtue by poets, much by historians, and much more still by philosophers, we ought especially to apply ourselves to such literature. For it is no small advantage that a certain intimacy and familiarity with virtue should be engendered in the souls of the young, seeing that the lessons learned by such are likely, in the nature of the case, to be indelible, having been deeply impressed in them by reason of the tenderness of their souls. Or what else are we to suppose Hesiod had in mind when he composed these verses which are on everybody's lips, if he were not exhorting young men to virtue?—that "rough at first and hard to travel, and full of abundant sweat and toil, is the road which leads to virtue, and steep withal."

Introduction. Another expression of the qualified
tolerance of the Byzantines for pagan literature is expressed in the following
touching verses by the eleventh century writer and later Metropolitan John
Mauropous. Mauropous was so impressed by the similarity of Plato and Plutarch's lofty moral sentiments to the teachings of the gospel that he pleaded to
Christ Himself to save both the philosopher and the historian-moralist from
the fires of eternal damnation. One cannot but compare Mauropous' sentiments to those of the fourteenth century Italian Dante, who in his *Divine Comedy*, for rather similar reasons, "spared" the pagan philosophers Aristotle and
Plato from the punishment of Hell by relegating them to Limbo. Mauropous
addresses the following poignantly worded epigram to Christ:

B. MAY CHRIST SAVE PLATO AND PLUTARCH FROM
ETERNAL DAMNATION

(From *Iohannis Euchaitorum metropolitae quae in codice vaticano
graeco 676 supersunt*, ed. P. de Lagarde [Göttingen, 1881], no. 43.)

If perchance you wish to exempt certain pagans
    from punishment, my Christ,
May you spare for my sake Plato and Plutarch,
For both were very close to your laws in both
    teaching and way of life.
Even if they were unaware that you as God reign
    over all,
In this matter only your charity is needed,
Through which you are willing to save all men
    while asking nothing in return.

297.

Introduction. The first "golden age" of Byzantine literature was that of the sixth century, which produced a number of distinguished literary figures, most of them connected with Emperor Justinian's
government and court. Characteristic of this period is John the Lydian, lawyer,
scholar, and civil servant, who has recorded something about the scholarly aspect of governmental service. Besides studying Aristotle and Plato, he had to
learn Latin (then still very important for government administration). After
gaining a post in the civil bureaucracy, John became an intimate of Emperor
Justinian. The selection which follows, an order of Justinian to John's superior
(c. 554), reveals the high esteem shown to government officials of literary talent. (On John the Lydian, see also selection 26; on the influence of the classics
in the later period see below, selections 308–18).

APPRECIATION FOR LITERARY EXCELLENCE

(Translated by G. Downey, *Constantinople in the Age of Justinian*
[Norman, Okla.: University of Oklahoma Press, 1960], p. 155.
Copyright 1960 by the University of Oklahoma Press, Publishing
Division of the University.)

In the most learned John, We have perceived knowl-
edge of literature, skill in language and grace in poetry, in addition to his wide
learning; and We have seen that he has made himself, by his own labors, most
accomplished in the Latin tongue, and that while he has borne himself nobly in
the service of Your Excellency's legal staff, he has also chosen, in addition to that
service, to devote his life to study, and to dedicate himself wholly to literature.
Believing that it would be unworthy of Our times to leave without reward a man
who has attained such a degree of merit, We command Your Excellency to reward him from the public treasury with such and such payment. Also let this
most learned man know that We do not stop with this, but that We shall honor
him with greater appointments and Imperial generosities, thinking it unseemly
that such eloquence should receive small reward, and praising him if he will
share with many others the talent he possesses.

298.

Introduction. Theophylact Simocattes, adviser to
Emperor Heraclius (610–41), in the *proemium* to his history, provides a very
revealing statement concerning the educated Byzantine attitude toward the use
of reason and the high place accorded to the study of history. He draws a
relevant example from the fountainhead of Greek literature, Homer.

ON THE IMPORTANCE OF REASON AND THE STUDY OF HISTORY

(From Theophylact Simocattes, *Ekumenike Historia*, ed. C. de Boor
[Leipzig, 1887], pp. 36–38.)

Man is adorned not only by the endowments of na-
ture but also by the fruits of his own efforts. For reason, which he possesses, is an
admirable and divine trait by which he renders to God his adoration and homage.
Through reason he enters into knowledge of himself and does not remain ignorant of the ordering of his creation. Accordingly, through reason men come together with each other and, turning away from external considerations, they direct their thoughts toward the mystery of their own nature.

Reason has given many good things to men and is an excellent helpmate of
nature. The things which nature has withheld from man, reason provides in the
most effective manner, embellishing those things which are seen, adding spice to
those that are tasted, roughening or softening things to the touch, composing
poetry and music for the ear, soothing the soul by lessening discord, and bringing sounds into concord. Is not reason also the most persuasive master of the

crafts?—reason which has made a well-woven tunic from wool, which from wood has constructed carts for farmers, oars for sailors, and small wicker shields for soldiers as protection against the dangers of the battlefield.

Most important of all, reason provides the hearer with that pleasure which reflects the greatest amount of experience, the study of history, which is the instructor of the spirit. Nothing can be more seductive than history for the minds of those who desire to learn. It is sufficient to cite an example from Homer to demonstrate this: Soon after he had been thrown on the beach by violent waves of the sea, the son of Laertes, Odysseus, almost naked and with his body emaciated from the mishap of the shipwreck, was graciously received at the court of Alcinous. There he was clothed in a bright robe and given a place at the table of the king. Although only just arrived, he was granted permission to speak and an opportunity to relate his adventures. His recital pleased the Phocaeans so much that the banquet seemed to have changed into a theater. Indeed, they lent him an attention altogether remarkable, nor did they feel during his long narration any tedium, although he described the many misfortunes he had suffered. For listening brings an overwhelming desire [to hear more] and thus easily accepts a strange tale.

It is for this reason that in learning the poets are considered most estimable, for they realize that the spirits of men are fond of stories, always yearning to acquire knowledge and thirsty for strange narrations. Thus the poets create myths for men and clothe their phrases with adornments, fleshing out the fables with method, and embellishing their nonsense with meter as if with enchanted spells. This artifice has succeeded so well that poets are considered to be theologians, intimately associated with the gods. It is believed that through the poets' mouths the gods reveal their own personal affairs and also whether a felicitous or a calamitous event will happen to men in their lifetime.

This being so, one may term history the common teacher of all men: it shows which course to follow and which to avoid as profitless. The most competent generals are those who have been instructed by history, for history reveals how to draw up troops and by what means to outmaneuver the enemy through ambush. History renders these generals more prudent because they know about the misfortunes of others, and it directs them through observation of the mistakes of others. Similarly, it has shown that men become happier through good conduct, pushing men to higher peaks of virtue through gradual advances. For the old man history is his support and staff, while for the young, it is the fairest and wisest instructor, applying [the fruit of] great experience to new situations and thus anticipating somewhat the lessons of time. I now dedicate my own zeal and efforts to history, although I know that I am undertaking a greater task than I am able to fulfill effectively, since I lack elegance of expression, profundity of thought, purity of syntax, and skill in composition. If any parts of my work should prove pleasing in any way, let this be ascribed rather to the result of chance than to my own skill.

299.

Typical of the Byzantine attitude to classical learning, especially literature and philosophy, are the works of the learned Patriarch Photius (late ninth century). Under his influence a "renaissance" or renewal of interest in classical Greek learning occurred after the so-called Dark Age of the seventh to mid-ninth centuries, itself a result of the destructive Arabic invasions and chaos which saw Byzantine culture sink to its lowest level. Through Photius's writing of his famous *Bibliotheca* (or *Myriobiblon*), a three volume collection of summaries (or "book reviews") of ancient Greek literature and some Christian writings, he helped to preserve the corpus, or at least a knowledge, of the names and content of classical Greek writings, a number of which would otherwise have been lost to us.

The following selection, typical of those in Photius's *Bibliotheca*, is concerned with the Greek historian Dionysius of Halicarnassus, who lived in the time of Augustus and whose work on early Roman history is important as are his writings on literary criticism. Note Photius's acute observations on Dionysius's style.

FROM PHOTIUS'S *BIBLIOTHECA* ON DIONYSIUS OF HALICARNASSUS

(From *Photius Bibliothèque*, ed. R. Henry [Paris, 1959], vol. 1, chap. 83, pp. 190–91.)

There were then read [in our circle] the twenty books of the history of Rome of Dionysius of Halicarnassus, son of Alexander. He begins with the arrival of Aeneas in Italy after the fall of Troy. He reviews in extreme detail the founding of Rome and the birth of Remus and Romulus, in a word, all the succession of events until there broke out the war of the Romans against Pyrrhus of Epirus. He narrates in detail the history of the latter and ends in the third year of the 128th Olympiad, after which he says that Polybius of Megalopolis began his history. He flourished in the time of Augustus. He sailed to Italy [from the Greek East] at the time when the civil war ended between Augustus and Antony. He lived there, as he says, twenty-two years, learned thoroughly the language of the Romans, made a profound study of their antiquities, and, after learning everything about their history, began [to write] his treatise.

With respect to his style and vocabulary, he tends toward innovative expressions and he forces his language into uncommon usages. The great detail of his narration keeps his thought simple and does not let him get carried away toward a disagreeable dryness. He also employs a good deal of digression, which relaxes and relieves the reader of the fatigue brought on by the recital. To put it briefly, the elegance of his language, [although] obscured by the abundance of detail and digressions, alleviates a style which possesses a tendency to coarseness.

300.

Introduction. Another glimpse of Byzantine attitudes toward the classics can be found in the persistent preoccupation, throughout the entire Byzantine period, with the question of who was the greater philosopher, Plato or Aristotle. While much of Byzantine religious thought, like that in the tradition of the earliest Greek Christian Fathers, would seem to be more compatible, at least in spirit, with Platonism or Neoplatonism, learned Byzantine laymen in general preferred Aristotle; for Aristotle, like Galen in medicine, Ptolemy in astronomy, or Isocrates in rhetoric, dealt primarily with things of this world (the "outer" learning noted below, selection 303) and was therefore deemed by the church safer to study. In addition, he provided more useful, practical knowledge and, above all, taught techniques of logic and reason that could be easily applied. Plato, on the other hand, though fascinating in philosophic content, was for many too dangerous, for he dealt with many matters considered by the Byzantine church in particular to be more appropriate to theology. (The church above all feared a recrudescence of certain of Origen's heretical Neoplatonic views.)

Perhaps the most famous comparison between Aristotle and Plato was written after 1453 (c. 1466) in Renaissance Italy by the Byzantine (unionist) scholar and patron of learning, Cardinal Bessarion, formerly archbishop of Nicaea. He compared the two classical philosophers from the point of view of their closeness to Christian dogma and beliefs, and reached the conclusion that Plato was more assimilable to Christianity.

Aristotle and Plato Compared

(From Bessarion, *In calumniatorem Platonis*, in E. Garin, *Filosofi Italiani del Quattrocento* [Florence, 1942], pp. 276–82.)

We always speak of Aristotle with maximum respect, and any wish to denigrate him, in order to defend Plato, is base and insolent; let it be far from us. Let us recall indeed that both are supremely wise and let us believe that we should be grateful to both for the benefits they have brought to humankind. . . . In this comparison of philosophy [between Aristotle and Plato] let us not exalt one with praise, covering the other with insults and contumely, as does our adversary [George of Trebizond]. We should respect and venerate both. . . .

The basic feature of our demonstration will consist of our showing in the words of Plato himself the opposite of what our adversary [George] opposes. . . . But before confronting this question I proclaim openly that I do not follow the views of Plato in the sense that I approve all [of him] and regard him as equivalent to our faith. I do not in fact accept either the preexistence of souls or the multiplicity of gods, or souls of the sky and the stars, or many other things for which the pagans are condemned by the church. . . . Although they [Plato and Aristotle] are both in fact pagans, both strangers to our faith, yet it will not be useless to clarify which of the two may have been nearer the truth and closer to our [Christian] faith. Indeed I do not intend in any way to offend Aristotle, even if it shall appear that I prefer Plato. . . .

It is not necessary to seek reasons for the divine, because it is grasped only through faith and the divine teachings in which we believe, since, otherwise, there would be no regard for our faith as the doctors of the church precisely hold. Thus no one would think that Aristotle or Plato ought to be honored for having venerated or affirmed in their writings the divine Trinity. Both were in reality deprived of such doctrine and ignorant of our faith. But while, without doubt, Aristotle in some place does not speak or think much on the Trinity, Plato certainly has spoken much about the Trinity, but in a manner quite different from the teachings of our religion. We do not deny that in Plato there has been, in the mediation of his natural light, a certain prefiguration of our own religion, which the Creator and Lord later revealed more clearly in the divine doctrine of his Son and in his goodness. But from that similarity we believe that we can draw not a little usefulness, in that we may be transported by the doctrine of Plato to the more perfect state of our faith. In such a manner there should arise, indeed almost burst forth, from the philosophy of Plato, certain principles of a true theology. If one wrongly distances himself from scriptural perfection and adheres to the doctrine of Plato, the fault should be his and not that of Plato. Plato in fact is worthy of the highest praise because even those who profess themselves Christians, in very few matters seek to remove themselves from his opinions—which would certainly not be the case if Plato had not had a certain similarity and conformity to the Christian faith.

B.
BYZANTINE EDUCATION

301.

Introduction. The structure of Byzantine education resembled the classical Greco-Roman system and the course of study followed by humanists during the Italian Renaissance, a humanism itself influenced by the Byzantine tradition. Both Byzantine and Western Renaissance traditions contrast sharply with Western medieval practices, in which the emphasis, at least from the end of the twelfth century on, was on logic and dialectics (Scholasticism) rather than on the humanities.

In Byzantium, children, sometimes girls as well as boys, began their education at about the age of six by studying grammar. (As the Byzantines put it, they learned to "Hellenize" their tongue.) Along with reading and writing, their lessons in time also stressed study of the classical Greek authors, read together with standard (usually Byzantine) commentaries. Basic to this study was the reading of the supreme epic poet Homer, whose works were often memorized. Michael Psellus, the statesman-philosopher of the mid-eleventh century, for example, knew Homer entirely from memory.

Indeed, throughout the entire Byzantine period Homer was the primary staple of education. The following selection, drawn from the famous *Commentary on the Iliad* by the later twelfth century bishop and educator Eustathius of Thessalonika, probably constitutes part of an introductory lecture he gave to students beginning their study of the *Iliad.* Here Eustathius stresses not only Homer's literary beauty and psychological insight but his influence on all subsequent Greek literature as well as his importance as a foundation for the Byzantine student's later studies. (For Eustathius' vivid historical account of the Norman capture of Thessalonika in 1185 see selection 275.)

INTRODUCTION TO A COURSE ON HOMER

(Trans. R. Browning in "Homer in Byzantium," *Viator*, vol. 6 [1975], pp. 17–18.)

It would be perhaps best to shun the sirens of Homer by blocking one's ears with wax or turning away in another direction, so as to avoid their spell. If one does not shun them, but reads the poem, he will not pass by willingly even if many bonds restrain him, nor if he did pass by would he be grateful. . . . From Ocean flow all rivers, all springs and all wells, according to the old saying. And from Homer comes, if not all, at any rate much of the material of later writers. For there is no one, whether his concern be with higher things, or with nature or with human affairs or with any subject of profane literature, whatever it be, who has passed by Homer's hostelry without being entertained but all have stopped there. And some have stayed with him to the end of their days, enjoying his catering, while others have merely satisfied some need and taken something from his store to put in their own work.

Commentary. So widespread was knowledge of Homer among educated Byzantines that Michael Psellus refers to him simply as "the poet," while Anna Comnena (who quotes or paraphrases Homer no less than sixty-six times in her *Alexiad*) does not even bother to explain those references, expecting her readers to catch the allusions at once.

Having mastered grammar and studied Homer and other basic classical literary texts, the student advanced to what the Byzantines stressed above all, rhetoric and rhetorical theory. The study of rhetoric offered not only effective techniques for professional use in public affairs, courts of law, and the civil service. Even more important, it provided the indispensable means for entry into educated Byzantine society, whose manner of expression and even of thought was penetrated through and through by imitation of the classical Greek literary tradition.

The rhetorical authors particularly studied were Demosthenes, Plutarch, Isocrates (whom the Byzantines seem to have preferred to Demosthenes) and, above all, Hermogenes* of the second century A.D., whose detailed theoretical treatises on rhetoric were considered the most instructive. Along with rhetoric the four arts of the *quadrivium*—arithmetic, geometry, music and astronomy—were also studied, again almost entirely from ancient classical models. Primary and secondary Byzantine education were often entrusted to private masters, although it seems that some sort of government-sponsored schools (about which we have little information) may at times also have existed.

* Bessarion, in Renaissance Italy, referred to Hermogenes as "the glory of the Greeks in rhetoric." On Bessarion see D. Geanakoplos, *Greek Scholars in Venice* (Cambridge: Harvard University Press, 1962), passim.

302.

Introduction. For advanced education in the fields of law, medicine, or philosophy, the Byzantine student would attend the University (perhaps, more accurately, the "Higher School") of Constantinople. Founded in the fifth century by Emperor Theodosius II, it seems to have existed, despite several interruptions, virtually throughout the entire life of the Byzantine state.* We know that the "higher school" disappeared sometime in the eighth or early ninth century (but probably not, as is sometimes affirmed, owing to Leo III's Iconoclastic policy) and was apparently restored in the mid-ninth century by the Emperor Theophilus and the Caesar Bardas and, again later, by Constantine IX. In the last century or so, however, the higher school seems to have lost its government sponsorship and was displaced by a number of privately run "higher schools." (For the edict of Theodosius II concerning the foundation and organization of the first university or higher school, in 425 in Constantinople, see above, selection 176b.)

One of the more important episodes in the history of Byzantine higher education was the reopening by Constantine IX in 1045 of the university, or higher school, in particular of its law school, after the neglect of letters by the soldier-emperor Basil II. After considerable discussion, both a faculty of law (under John Xiphilinus, later patriarch) and one of philosophy (under Michael Psellus) were constituted. The event is described by the historian Michael Attaleiates in the following passage:

A. Constantine IX Reestablishes the "Higher School"

(From Michael Attaleiates, *Historia*, ed. I. Bekker [Bonn, 1853], pp. 21–22.)

And so, having brought the war successfully to a close, the emperor led a quiet life and gave himself freely to civil matters, establishing a faculty of law. And, reaching to heaven, he also made provision for the teaching of philosophy, establishing as Chief of the Philosophers a man superior to the rest of us in knowledge.[†] And he urged the young to study the sage writings and teachings of the professors with this able teacher.

Introduction. The preamble to the chrysobull of Constantine IX establishing the faculty of law reads as follows:

B. The Rule of Law in Byzantium

(From J. and P. Zepos, eds., *Jus graecoromanum* [Athens, 1931], vol. 1, pp. 618–19.)

And what other preoccupation, what other work or imperial undertaking is more appropriate than the making of provisions for laws? It is an honor for the emperor, according to the saying, to love judgment. And justice and [the providing for] judicial decree is an accomplishment of the throne itself. These things indeed do not usually accrue to the emperor except from law and through law, by which emperors rule [peoples] and dynasts and archons conquer territory, even if by these same laws the imperial and divine authority [of the emperor] may be deprived of legitimate lordship, since the authority [of law] rules over all, and [he] does not rule by the authority of anything else over everything on earth.[‡]

---

[*] Some recent researchers object to the term "university" on the grounds that its organization differed greatly from medieval Western universities.

[†] Certain scholars, however, believe that there was at this time no *formal* faculty of philosophy and consider the term "Chief of the Philosophers" (*Hypatos ton philosophon*) to be rather an honorary title. There were, of course, always individual professors teaching privately who were paid by their students or sometimes by the government. See selection 151.

[‡] The meaning of this passage seems to be that, though the emperor is law incarnate (*nomos empsychos*), he is, at the same time, subject to the law.

303.

Introduction. Byzantine education comprised two kinds of learning: what were called "outer" (profane) and "inner" (theological). Individuals could pursue profane learning more or less freely so long as they did not advocate views that would contradict the teachings of the Byzantine church. Thus individuals could study the Greek classics, but attempts to foster paganism or other religious beliefs in the empire were exceedingly rare. The following passage is taken from the writings of Michael Psellus (1018–79?), the eleventh-century professor of (Neoplatonic) philosophy at the "Higher School" of Constantinople as well as a leading statesman and historian. It reflects his attitude toward the study of rhetoric, philosophy, literature, and Christian mysticism, and suggests the limits to which intellectual speculation in secular philosophy could go.

MICHAEL PSELLUS ON THE TWO KINDS OF LEARNING

(From Michael Psellus, *Chronographie*, ed. E. Rénauld [Paris, 1926], vol. 1; pp. 137–38.)

It is clear that there are two branches of literature. Rhetoric constitutes the one and philosophy the other. The former, knowing nothing of more profound things, issues forth in a mighty current of words, concerns itself with the composition of parts of a discourse, and sets forth certain theories for the development and division of political orations. It embellishes the spoken word and is characteristic in general of political speeches.

Philosophy, on the other hand, cares less about the beauty with which words are put together and rather traces the nature of things and explains the secrets of contemplation. Nor does philosophy mount to heaven with lofty language; rather, that cosmos which exists there, it explicates in many fashions. But I have not considered it necessary, as certainly the majority of men have, to embrace only the art of rhetoric and to neglect philosophy, or to study only philosophy, that is, to enjoy the riches of such learned knowledge and to neglect the flower [art] of speaking, the science of syntax and composition. Wherefore, many already reproach me when I compose a rhetorical composition into which I introduce, not inelegantly, some scientific proof. And again they reproach me when, demonstrating a philosophic proposition, I embellish it with certain graceful arts [of rhetoric], lest the mind of the reader find difficulty because of the weightiness of the argument and thus not comprehend my philosophic reasoning.

There is, however, a certain other philosophy superior to this, which the mystery of our Christian faith helps to complete (this mystery is twofold, divided in its nature [into human and divine] and in time [into finite and infinite], not to speak of another duality between logical proof and the understanding and knowledge inspired in some persons by God). And it is this philosophy [the divine] rather than the other [the profane] which I have zealously pursued.

I have followed the definitions [i.e., doctrines] of the great Fathers of the Church, while I have myself also contributed to the body of divine teachings. If then someone—and I say this simply and without vanity—should wish to praise me for my writings, let him not praise me for these [the religious ones] and may he not extol me for having read many books. I do not in fact deceive myself out of *amour propre*, nor am I unaware of my limitations. I know that my ability is very small when compared to that of those orators ["sophists"] and philosophers who have surpassed me. But if anyone lauds my efforts, let it instead be because I have not drawn my small amount of wisdom from any existing fount but rather from those sources which I have found sealed [bottled up], which I myself was able to open and purify, and which have allowed me to extract the waters hidden in their depths only through long and exhausting effort.

304.

Introduction. Psellus's most famous pupil, John Italus, a Greek-Italian from Byzantine southern Italy, was not as fortunate as his mentor. His speculations, based on pagan Greek philosophical tenets and suggesting the mortality of the soul, led (during the reign of Alexius I, 1081–1118) to his trial and condemnation for heresy and his deposition from his chair of philosophy at the university. (Contrast this with Western society, where relapsed heretics were often burned at the stake.)* Anna Comnena, daughter of Alexius, describes (with much prejudice) the condemnation of Italus.

SUPPRESSING THE TEACHINGS OF ITALUS

(From Anna Comnena, *Alexiade*, ed. B. Leib [Paris, 1945], vol. 2, pp. 38–40.)

At the moment when Italus was at the height of his popularity with the students I have already mentioned, he treated everybody contemptuously. Most of the stupid ones he pushed toward revolt and he incited not a few of his students to insurrection. I would mention some of them if time had not dulled my memory. But these things occurred before the accession of my father to the imperial throne. When he [Alexius] found that there was a total lack of culture and literary art (letters being banished to some far off place) he hastened to stir up whatever sparks there were hiding under the ashes. And those who were favorably disposed toward study (for there were some, though only a few, and these were standing merely in the antechamber of Aristotelian philosophy), he unceasingly encouraged to study, but he recommended to them that the study of the Divine Books precede that of Hellenic culture.

Having found that Italus was creating disturbances everywhere and was misleading many, he entrusted an examination of Italus to the *sebastokrator* Isaac, a man who was very highly learned and possessed the noblest qualities. And when Isaac found that this man held such beliefs, he made him appear at a public tribunal and refuted him. Then, by order of his brother the emperor, he deferred the matter to an ecclesiastical tribunal. Since Italus was not able to hide his ignorance, he vomited doctrines alien to the doctrines of the church. And in the midst of officials of the church he did not cease ridiculing and doing certain other things of a rude and barbaric nature. The presiding dignitary over the church was then Eustratius Garidas, who in order perhaps to change him for the better, retained him in the area of Hagia Sophia. But Patriarch Garidas would almost more easily have succumbed to the evil of Italus than impart to the latter more correct beliefs. According to common opinion, Italus even won him over completely. What then happened?

The populace of Constantinople moved en masse to the church seeking Italus. And he would probably have been thrown down from a great height to the middle of the church, had he not escaped to the roof of this holy building and hidden himself in a hole. Since his evil beliefs were discussed by many in the palace, not a few nobles were corrupted by his seductive doctrines and on this account the emperor was profoundly grieved. The heretical dogmas Italus taught were summarized in eleven propositions, which were sent to Alexius. The emperor ordered Italus to anathematize these propositions from the ambo in Hagia Sophia, [standing] bareheaded, and with all the people listening and repeating the anathema after him.

Nevertheless, although this was done, Italus remained unyielding and again, among many people, he openly espoused his doctrines. Although warned by the emperor, in barbaric undisciplined fashion he rejected the remonstrance. Consequently, Italus was personally anathematized; though later, when he had abjured his beliefs for a second time, the anathematization was lightened. His teachings remained anathematized, but his name was involved [only] rather obliquely; for many in fact, so far as they knew, it was not included in the ecclesiastical anathema. At a later time he altered his ideas on dogma, and of those views on which he had been wrong he repented. He repudiated his belief in transmigration of souls⁺ and his insults to the holy icons of the saints, and strove to reinterpret his views on the theory of ideas⁺ in a somewhat more orthodox manner. It was clear that he now condemned himself regarding those points on which he had formerly gone astray.

---

*Though on one famous occasion a heretic suffered this punishment in Byzantium, when the leader of the Bogomil religious sect was burnt alive by Alexius Comnenus (cf. above, selection 116a).
⁺Plato's belief.

305.

Introduction. The Byzantine educational system, although remarkable for its time (especially when compared with that of the West for most of the medieval period) was nevertheless not without its critics. The princess Anna Comnena (who, like many daughters of wealthy families did not attend formal school but was privately tutored) in her history, the *Alexiad*, deplores the stilted, pedantic method of education in her era and sets forth her own ideals of education. Note especially her strong objection to the excessive use of the device of *schedographia*. *Schedographia* was a technique used in grammatical and literary instruction which consisted of short commentaries (*schedoi*) on specific textual passages explaining grammatical forms and vocabulary, drawing analogies, and analyzing style.

ALEXIUS COMNENUS AND THE STATE OF EDUCATION

(From Anna Comnena, *Alexiade*, ed. B. Leib [Paris, 1945], vol. 3, p. 218.)

The technic of the use of *schedoi* is an invention of the younger men of our generation. I omit mention of the followers of Stylianus, of Longibardus, and of those who compile collections of words of all kinds, of the followers of Atticus and of those [clergy] who belong to the holy roster of our Great Church [Hagia Sophia]. These I skip over. But now the studies of these sublime writers, of the poets and even of the historians, and of the experience derived from them are not even deemed of secondary importance. Gambling and all other illegal activities are now the preoccupation. I say this because I deplore the complete neglect of the *enkyklios paideia* [i.e. "general" education].* For this condition inflames my spirit, because I have spent so much time on these studies. Indeed, when I finished my instruction in childhood, I advanced to the study of rhetoric and came into contact with philosophy. Amidst these sciences I also plunged into the poets and historians, thereby polishing the rough edges of my speech. For this reason, with the help of rhetoric, I condemned the incredible complexity of *schedographia*. But let these reflections be part of my history, not as a digression but as support for my argument [i.e. for *enkyklios paideia*].

*More specifically, this consisted of the "cycle" of Byzantine education, including grammar, rhetoric, philosophy, science, and mathematics, capped by study of theology.

306.

Introduction. Not long after his recovery of Constantinople (1261) from the destructive Latin occupation (during which the Byzantine "Higher School" was doubtless closed)* Emperor Michael VIII took steps to reestablish higher educational programs in the capital (schools for higher education had already emerged at Nicaea and Epirus). The scholar-statesman George Acropolites was appointed to oversee the process. The emperor himself was personally involved in this effort, confirming faculty appointments, endowing schools, even granting holidays to schoolboys. The following excerpt from the history of Pachymeres concerns the appointment of the monk Manuel Holobolos to head what seems to have been the revived Patriarchal School for educating the clergy.†

EMPEROR MICHAEL VIII REVIVES EDUCATION, ESPECIALLY AT THE PATRIARCHAL SCHOOL

(From Pachymeres, *De Michaele et Andronico Palaeologis*, ed. I. Bekker [Bonn, 1835], vol. 1, p. 283.)

Since Michael Palaeologus with remarkable ardor hoped to advance the study of the sciences [i.e. letters], he [the Patriarch Germanos] took under his patronage Holobolos, a man of rare erudition, and he resolved to secure for him the chair of Professor of the Church, as much to honor science with the appointment of a person who was so learned an ecclesiastic as to console him by the exercise of an affection which he had preserved for him. So, going to find the emperor, he [Patriarch Germanos] said: "It is a long time since George Acropolites, the grand logothete, occupied himself at your order to instruct in letters. Now that he is old in years and should be left alone to rest from work, it is proper at this time to consider the advancement of young men, and especially of young ecclesiastics, who need to become well educated in order one day to be able to acquit themselves worthily in the duties of holy orders to which they will be promoted. Grant then, if it please you, the request that I seek in the name of the church, in favor of Holobolos, to assign to him the post of Acropolites."

The emperor willingly granted the request of the patriarch, for he had the magnificent intention of reestablishing Constantinople in its ancient splendor. For this purpose, he placed two communities of ecclesiastics in two churches, the one in that of All the Apostles [Church of the Holy Apostles] and the other in that of Blachernae.

He [the emperor] founded a school of grammar in the Church of St. Paul and assigned some revenues to its master and his students. He looked upon them with such favor that he would on occasion visit them, to be informed of the progress the students were making in their studies, to distribute small gifts, and even to grant them a holiday, according to the old custom. Having then looked with favor upon the request of the patriarch, he gave orders to them that Holobolus be freed from the monastery in which he had been confined. Germanos, very joyous over this, received Holobolus with extraordinary manifestations of esteem and affection, granted him the emoluments of professor, and put him in charge of teaching.

Commentary. In the last half century of the empire we know that there existed in Constantinople several "higher schools" private in nature. The most famous was that at the Katholikon Mouseion of the Xenon where, among others, the noted philosopher John Argyropoulos and the famous rhetorician Manuel Chrysoloras taught. Both these men later became famous for their teaching at the *studium* ("university") in Florence, Italy, Argyropoulos in the mid-fifteenth century as professor of Aristotelianism and Platonism, and Chrysoloras earlier in 1397 as the initiator of systematic Greek studies in the Italian Renaissance (cf. selections 330–31.)

*See selection 282 on the Latin emperor's attempt to found a Latin university.
†The sources sometimes confuse the Higher School with the Patriarchal School, in part because the two schools seem to have shared the same faculty.

307.

Introduction. Although we have been discussing education among the upper classes of the Byzantine Empire, it is important to remember that large segments of the population remained totally illiterate, especially the poor in rural areas and many towns. The question of literacy is of course a vast one with many ramifications. One should be specific about the century, geographical location, and social status of persons or schools under consideration. It seems clear, however, that those individuals who received a complete education in the Greek classics were probably only a small percentage of those educated. Indeed, throughout most of the middle and later Byzantine periods a full literary education was sometimes difficult to obtain outside of the capital city or perhaps Thessalonika.

Nevertheless, the basic ability to read and write—functional literacy, as one might say—was probably rather widespread after the ninth century. The vast number of the provincial officials and the clergy could certainly read and write, and signatures on documents reveal that most monks and many laymen were also literate. Even in the army, particularly among the officers and higher-ranking enlisted men, literacy must have been common, if only for the reason that orders were usually transmitted down through the ranks in written form. As one scholar has put it, unlike in medieval Western Europe in Byzantium "the ability to read and write did not mark out a man sharply from his fellows for life." * In the following two selections from the *Vitae* of Constantine-Cyril (ninth century), one of the Byzantine Apostles to the Slavs, and of the monk St. Stephen the Younger (eighth century), we may observe two different degrees of literacy and also Constantinople's importance for advanced literary study.

Literacy in the Byzantine World

A. Cyril, Apostle to the Slavs

(From *Vita* of Constantine-Cyril, in A. Vaillant, ed., *Textes vieux-slaves* [Paris, 1968], vol. 1, *Textes et glossaire*, p. 27.)

And Constantine [Cyril], giving himself over to study [in Thessalonika], stayed at home learning the writings of St. Gregory the Theologian. And, penetrating into a myriad of [unfamiliar] terms and into profound thought, he was unable to understand them and therefore he fell into a great depression. There was there, however, a stranger who knew grammar; he went to find him and begged him to teach him, falling to his knees, saying: "Please teach me the art of grammar." [But the stranger was no longer teaching.] . . . When, however, Constantine's grace, intelligence and application to study came to the ears of the imperial official called the logothete, the latter sent for him in order that he might study near the emperor. The boy, at this news, set out with joy for the capital city. When he arrived at Constantinople he was placed in the charge of masters to teach him. In three months he learned all the grammar and applied himself to other studies. He studied Homer and geometry and with Leo and Photius dialectic and all the teachings of philosophy, and in addition rhetoric, arithmetic, astronomy, music, and all the other "Hellenic" [i.e, pagan Greek] teachings.

B. St. Stephen the Younger

(From *Vita* of St. Stephen the Younger, MPG, vol. 100, col. 1081.)

And then when the parents [in Constantinople] of this very holy boy, St. Stephen the Younger, saw that he had passed beyond the age of infancy and had attained the age of six years and should be occupied with learning letters, they entrusted him to teachers [in the capital] who would teach him the elements of the "holy letters."

*R. Browning, "Literacy in the Byzantine World," *Byzantine and Modern Greek Studies* 4 [1978]: 39–54.

C.
BYZANTINE LITERARY TYPES

308.

Introduction. Byzantine literary production, in its imitation of the ancient classics, is often criticized for its lack of creative originality and dismissed as overly concerned with sheer rhetorical skill. There was in fact usually a wide disparity between the classically influenced written (that is, literary) language and the living vernacular language of everyday speech. Nevertheless, though all too often closely imitative, Byzantine literature did produce many finely written and informative historical writings, verse chronicles, much highly refined epistolography, and often subtly expressed satire and epigrams. It includes an epic as interesting as any in the medieval world, and, perhaps most important, many marvelously expressive works of religious poetry, in particular hymnography, whose music has disappeared but whose poetic texts remain to enthrall the modern reader who can understand their idiom. Below we provide examples of most of the various types of literature reflected in Byzantine writings.

In his sophisticated history Michael Psellus provides us with one of the clearest definitions in all of Byzantine literature of the fundamental importance and use of rhetoric in Byzantine culture. There is no doubt that rhetoric—elegant style and manner of presentation—was in fact what most Byzantine writers prized above all.

THE IMPORTANCE OF RHETORIC

(From *Michel Psellus Chronographie*, ed. E. Rénauld [Paris, 1928], vol. 2, p. 68.)

Rhetoric is characterized not only by persuasive deception and ambiguous arguments having to do with [certain] hypotheses, but it also draws upon an exact art [*Mousa*]; it philosophizes through ideas; it blooms through its artful arrangement of words. And thus it appeals to its audience from two points of view.

Rhetoric articulates [differing] meanings clearly without confounding them by confusion [*syngheousa tais epiplokais*], but by categorizing and separating them in a gentle manner, it brings them to the fore. The power of rhetoric lies neither in confusion nor in ignorance but in its appropriateness for the times and circumstances. [This is true] even if someone should speak simply and without recourse to ornate phrasing or long sentences.

309.

Introduction. One of the most important literary genres was the writing of history. Historians writing in the style of the ancient Greeks abounded from the foundation of Constantinople to the very last days of the empire. Their works constitute a remarkable quarry of information not only for Byzantine but for Latin, Slavic, Hungarian, Arabic, and Turkish history as well. We have earlier cited excerpts from the historians Procopius, Theophanes, Michael Psellus, Anna Comnena, and others. Here we quote again from Anna Comnena (d. after 1147), who expatiates on her own attitude to history.

Anna Comnena on Writing History

(From Anna Comnena, *Alexiade*, ed. B. Leib [Paris, 1945], vol. 3, pp. 173–75.)

But perhaps the reader, arriving at this point in my narrative and reading this passage, might say that my work is biased in nature. But I—by the dangers undergone by the emperor on behalf of the well-being of the Byzantine people, and by the trials and misfortunes of my father which he endured on behalf of the Christians—I do not speak or write such things in the aim of extolling my father. Indeed, wherever I see that my father made an error, I contravene the law of nature and maintain the truth. Although I consider my father dear, I hold truth dearer. When two things are equally cherished, as a philosopher somewhere said, it is best to prefer the truth. But I both speak and write according to the events themselves, neither deliberately suppressing them nor deleting what happened. And here is the proof.

I do not write the history of ten thousand years ago; rather there are those alive today who knew my father and relate his deeds to me. From these much of my history has been put together, each one recalling something else according to what he remembers and all being in agreement. Most of the time, moreover, we ourselves lived and talked with our father and mother. For our existence was not confined to the home and spent in seclusion and luxury. From my very cradle, I swear by my God and his mother, troubles and misfortunes and calamities in succession gripped me, some from outside, some from within. Regarding my personal characteristics, I could not say; let those in attendance in the *gynaikonites* [women's section] speak and describe them. As to those things that happened to me from without: [to describe] how many enemies the evil of men inflicted against me when I had not yet reached my eighth year, it would be necessary to have the Siren of Isocrates, the eloquence of Pindar, the impetuosity of Polemo, the Calliope of Homer, the lyre of Sappho, or some other ability beyond those. For there are none of these terrible things, small or large or near or far, which did not at once oppress us. And the flood clearly overwhelmed me at that time and up to now, and until the very moment I write these words the sea of calamities advances upon me and waves upon waves strike me. But I am getting away [from the point], drifting into my own misfortunes.

Now that I have collected my wits, I shall return, just as if I were going against the current, to my previous narrative. Some things, as I said, I know from my own experience; other things I have found out from those who served on expeditions in various capacities with the emperor and who, through intermediaries, sent us information on what happened in the wars. Above all, many times I heard with my own ears the emperor and George Palaeologus discussing these things. I myself put together the majority of these facts, especially during the reign of the third in succession after my father, when all flattery and lying had disappeared with his grandfather. For all flatter the one who occupies the throne, but they show no flattery to one who is no longer around and they relate the bare facts, describing them exactly as they happened.

310.

Introduction. Satire was a favorite genre of Byzantine authors and the public alike, and some Byzantine satirical works are acknowledged minor masterpieces. Using the writing of the ancient Greek world, Lucian especially, as model, Byzantine writers satirized not only political and social conditions but also religion and the church. Above all with mordant wit some Byzantine writers satirized the monks. For example, the twelfth-century poet-monk Ptochoprodromos* (who, it should be noted, wrote essentially in the vulgar, that is the spoken Greek of the period) lampooned not only the clergy but especially the "fat, slothful monks," in a way foreshadowing the attacks of a Boccaccio or Erasmus. The following selection by Ptochoprodromos cleverly lampoons, through the use of a kind of fable, the wealth of the abbot of his own monastery in contrast to the poverty of a poor scholar—himself.

Satire

A. POVERTY AND "WISDOM"

(From Ptochoprodomos, in *Poeti bizantini*, ed. R. Cantarella [Rome, 1948], vol. 2, pp. 224–25.)

Because of my misery I blaspheme often; and I am told: "Take care not to continue [to do so] in order that after death you may not be condemned to the everlasting worms, to inferno, and to darkness." But I, O my lord of the universe [emperor Manuel I], these three condemnations I encounter already here even before death in that poverty which is constantly devouring and consuming me; and the inferno is this benumbing which makes me shiver as from freezing cold. I have nothing to put on my back, and since I have nothing for my back I constantly shiver. Darkness, too, O my lord is this obscurity that I feel all over, O ruler, when I have no bread. When I have nothing to eat my sight fails and I collapse. Here [already on earth] are the obscure darkness, the inferno, and the worms. But, my omnipotent Lord, Christ the Savior of mankind, will now save me from these tortures through your liberality, and from these he will liberate me by his grace.

And you, O powerful one, ruler of the four regions of the earth, lend your ears a little to me, your servant, so that I may relate to you what happened to me a little while ago. In the cell of the abbot of my monastery, they were cooking very salted loin sausage with all the trimmings, the kind that you are acquainted with, and when the table was prepared and it was served up, they [the abbot and his companions] sat down to eat. Then your servant, seeing them seated around as they were accustomed, ran to sit among them. But they threw me out exclaiming all together, "Learn to make haste to come and sit down. You are a learned *papas* [a poor priest or monk]—eat your own stuff and don't gaze at our meal. It is not food for your gullet. If you are hungry, O learned one, go and buy something to eat."

While all, O ruler, spoke to me in this way, a disturbance from the cellar was heard and all arose and suddenly left, believing that the house was collapsing and they would be crushed because all was completely rotten. And I, when I saw the loin sausage served up with the ribs, began to reflect, "What they said does not apply to me: 'it is not food for your gullet'. Behold, the incomparable judgment of the God-man justly has brought me the sausage." Thus speaking, O ruler, I took my knife and began to fill my mouth until I was full. Then, O ruler, I too went down to see along with them whence came the disturbance, after having left my cat on the table so that they would believe it was responsible for the consuming of the meat. But later, when they all returned to the cell and saw the cat on the table, they cast stones and said, "May you be dead because you have eaten that wonderful sausage." But later, catching on to my shrewdness and smiling a little, they exclaimed in one voice, "It is the *papas* who has eaten the sausage and we blamed the poor cat!" And they found their plates completely cleaned and there was no need at all to wash them.

Commentary. In another poem addressed to Emperor Manuel Comnenus (twelfth century), Ptochoprodromos recounts (again in vulgar Greek verses) the fate of a scholar dying of hunger.

B. Ptochoprodromos's Lament on a Poor Scholar (Himself!)

(From *Poeti bizantini*, vol. 2, pp. 216–17.)

O illness why do you torment me? Why, O malignant one, after having shrunken me like a dishcloth, after having sucked all the marrow from my bones and having torn the fibers of my being, have you lacerated my flesh and poisoned all my innards with voracious lips, similar to ferocious bears, or to the bite of a poisonous animal, to a viper or a lion? Dying of my misfortunes, I am nevertheless among the living and the furies give me a second existence among mortal men. Since I belong neither to men (since I am not truly alive) nor to those truly dead, I hold on to half a life. I breathe the air and see the splendor of the sun and speak and feel all the evils that torment me. For this reason alone am I counted among the living, but for all the rest I resemble the dead. Neither does sleep, sleep the father of dreams, rest on my eyelids night or day to mitigate my unhappiness, nor do I have food that feeds life or anything else. . . .

Christ the Lord, the Messiah, you who determined all at the beginning and as God led all things hostile by nature into the bonds of love so that the world might remain stable . . . rid me of this horrible pain in my stomach and my liver, and instill peace that gives surcease to the pain in my shrunken limbs. I am able to bear no more of this terrible evil.

Commentary. Contrary to what would appear to be the popular appeal of these works, the Ptochoprodromic satires were evidently written in the aim of catering to elitist court patrons under Emperor Manuel I Comnenus.

*His name means "poor" Prodromos. It is uncertain if he should be identified with the well-known poet Theodore Prodromos, a professional writer who wrote a vast amount of poetry characterized by a classicizing style and elegant diction.

311.

Introduction. During the Byzantine era scholars produced many tools for literary scholarship: lexica, grammars, encyclopedias, epitomes of earlier works, commentaries, and rules for writing panegyrics, orations, and other compositions. These works, though seemingly arid, should not be too lightly dismissed, for they often constitute not only the basis for our knowledge of the ancient classical texts but also provide a key to the method of interpreting them.

We quote here a typical entry on the work of the late fourth-century patriarch of Constantinople and theologian, St. Gregory of Nazianzus, contained in perhaps the most comprehensive of Byzantine dictionaries, the tenth-century Suda *Lexicon*. Note the encyclopedic style of the entry in which various facts are strung together to provide information for the reader.

AN ENTRY FROM THE SUDA *LEXICON*

(Trans. D. Geanakoplos and M. Varouxakis, from the *Sudae Lexicon*, ed. I. Bekker [Berlin, 1854], p. 250.)

Gregory, Bishop of Nazianzus (which is a way-station in Cappadocia), was a highly educated man and a great friend of Basil of Caesarea, Bishop of Cappadocia. He was not only a scholar and skilled in writing poetry but was learned in philosophy and a very keen orator; he wrote a great many works contained in thirty thousand verses. His writings consist of the following works: "On the Death of [his] Brother Caesarius," a funerary sermon for his father, another for his sister Gorgonia, a work on compassion for the poor, one in praise of the Maccabees, works in praise of Cyprianus, Athanasius, and Hero the Philosopher, two sermons against the Emperor Julian, two discourses against Eunomius, one sermon on theology, one discourse on the Son, another discourse on the Holy Ghost, a panegyric, ten sermons, and many other works which are very well known to all. He followed the style of Polemon of Laodicea, who was a sophist at Smyrna, and became master of the orator Aristides. He also wrote another work in hexameters, in which virgins and marriage are discussed by these two men, along with other matters. He also wrote on other subjects: in all, thirty thousand verses in various meters. Gregory Philostorgius, the Arian, writes about him [Gregory of Nazianzus] in his *History*, saying [quotation from Philostorgius missing in original manuscript] and he [Philostorgius] wrote these things because he was an Arian. When Gregory [Nazianzus] arrived in his homeland, he placed a bishop over his own church, and he himself went to live as a monk. After six years had passed he died, in the thirteenth year of Theodosius's reign.

312.

Introduction. The most popular Byzantine literary forms were the letter and the oration. Almost all Byzantine literary and political figures of any importance collected and published their own letters. (Some even wrote commentaries on their letters!) At first glance most of these letters seem more concerned with fine turns of phrase and subtle literary devices than with the communication of ideas. But in Byzantium an epistle was much more than the medium of a message. Rather, it often expressed the deepest sentiments of the writer and provided an exquisite aesthetic pleasure to its recipient. Indeed, an expertly crafted letter was considered to provide a more intimate link between writer and recipient than even a personal encounter.

The letters of a highly educated scholar-statesman of Byzantium's unhappy fourteenth century, Demetrius Cydones, reflect these deeply prized Byzantine qualities. We quote from a moving epistle Cydones wrote around 1395–1400 to his master and friend, Emperor Manuel II Palaeologus, as the shadows of Turkish war and conquest lengthened over Byzantium.

EPISTLE: A THRENODY FOR CONSTANTINOPLE

(From Demétrius Cydonès: *Correspondance*, ed. G. Cammelli [Paris, 1930], pp. 129–31.)

Oh, what is this thick and dense cloud which stretches over the land of the Romans? What is this flood which covers everything? What is this plague which attacks us, not allowing us time to catch our breaths, pushing us toward death? These misfortunes have for some time wasted us, and little by little, like the sickness of consumption, have enfeebled the body of the community, for many evils have already preceded this present ruin. But now misfortune is at its height. Formidable events no longer threaten, but worse, we are surrounded by evils more terrible than those of the past. We are besieged on all sides. Nevertheless, we all would have hoped that God would have granted us, through you, freedom from these calamities.

. . . I pity this unhappy place [Constantinople], the only one left to us—should

I call her city or fatherland? Today she submits to the rule of others instead of ruling over all as she did formerly. I curse myself for not preferring exile and hearing from others about the misfortunes of my country rather than, upon my return,* seeing them for myself and learning about them firsthand. I will still find remedy in this, in a new exile, unless God is reconciled to us, through your intercession, and sends us aid. For the vessel of hope is never empty while man yet draws breath. As I wait, I beg God not to let the light of Israel be extinguished completely. I wait to hear from him, from God (may he keep you safe as his agent) that he will do us some great good.

*He had gone to Italy.

313.

Introduction. Panegyrics, sermons, invectives, exhortations, and other types of orations abound through virtually the entire Byzantine period. One modern specialist in Byzantine literature has with perhaps only slight exaggeration termed the Byzantine literati "almost hysterically panegyrist!" The following selection is a panegyric addressed by the court encomiast Manuel Holobolos to Emperor Michael VIII Palaeologus on the first Christmas after that Emperor had recovered Constantinople from the Latins in 1261—of course one of the most important events in Byzantium's later history. A comparison of this thirteenth-century encomium with the fourth-century Tridecennial Oration of Eusebius addressed to Emperor Constantine reveals the remarkable persistence of this literary genre (see selection 1).

ORATION: PANEGYRIC ON MICHAEL VIII's RECOVERY OF CONSTANTINOPLE

(From Ch. Siderides ed., "Manuel Holobolos, Encomium to Michael VIII Palaeologus," (in Greek), *Epeteris Hetaireias Byzantinon Spoudon*, vol. 3 [1926] p. 191.)

May you live then, O Emperor, for many long years, may your days if possible be numbered as great as the days of the sky, and may that vineyard, the governance of the Romans [Byzantines], flourish as does its Caretaker at the right hand of God, and extend its borders up to the sea and to the rivers. And may our lord and emperor [God] fight on your side at our time of battle and misfortune. You the great hope of the Romans, after God the beauty of the earth, the scion of the graces and of great men in your youth and brief career, may you initiate the cosmic four seasons, and may all the ends of the earth be under the rule of your government. Indeed, O emperor, extend and guide and rule in behalf of truth and benignity and justice, just as once sang David, the forefather [*theopator*] of the Lord [i.e. Christ], the prophet and king.

314.

Introduction. That the classical tragedies were read but not performed in Byzantium (probably because of ecclesiastical censure) seems generally accepted by historians today. However, there is some indication that some kind of stage performances such as mimes, were on occasion presented in Constantinople. One bit of evidence comes from the strongly anti-Byzantine, Latin envoy Liudprand (mid-tenth century), who writes:

DRAMA IN BYZANTIUM

(Translated by F. Wright from Liudprand, *Relatio de legatione Constantinopolitana,* in *Liudprand of Cremona: The Embassy to Constantinople* [New York, 1930], p. 253.)

On the nineteenth of July he [Emperor Nicephorus Phocas] sent off his motley fleet, I viewing the spectacle from my detestable abode. The next morning, that being the day on which these flippant Greeks celebrated the ascension of the Prophet Elijah with stage plays [*ludi scenici*], he ordered me again to attend him.

Commentary. Of course the liturgy of the Byzantine church itself was in a real sense a drama of the life of Christ. Another type of Christian religious drama that was probably read but not performed was the eleventh- or twelfth-century *Chrestos Paschon* ("Christ Suffering") which, closely related to the liturgy, is reminiscent of though unrelated to Western miracle plays. (See above, selection 240, for the prologue to this play.)

315.

Introduction. More original, but again revealing in some ways the influence of Homer's epic poems, is the work which some believe comes closest to being the "national" Byzantine epic, *Digenes Akritas.* The sole remaining poem of its type in Byzantine literature, it is actually two poems joined together into a lengthy song of praise for the imperial warrior who lived on the embattled Byzantine-Arab frontier in the ninth to eleventh centuries. (Compare this to the near-contemporary medieval French *Chanson de Roland,* which is set on the contested Franco-Moorish frontier.) It was this eastern frontier which protected the Byzantine world against the infidel and barbarian world, Orthodox Christendom against Islam. *Digenes Akritas* then reflects the heroic ideals of the military aristocracy who saved Byzantium from the Arab flood which threatened to engulf it.

Digenes ("two-raced") is a Byzantine "border fighter" (*akritas*), born of an Arab father, who had converted to Christianity, and his Greek spouse. At his best Digenes exhibits qualities that the Byzantines prized highly: undeviating loyalty to the emperor, love for Orthodoxy, and devotion to his friends. Notable also is the characterization of the figures portrayed, the care devoted to theological matters, the solicitude for proper protocol and etiquette, and, not least for a hero of Digenes's proportions, the occasional remorse suffered by him for his sexual exploits. (For other extracts see selections 9 and 169.)

EPIC: BORDER FIGHTS AND BEAUTIES, FROM *DIGENES AKRITAS*

(Translated by J. Mavrogordato, *Digenes Akritas* [Oxford, 1956], pp. 83, 89.)

His father the Emir from those times forth
That with the sun went circling round the sky
Lived meditating the ways of the Lord,
And every day in gladness with his wife,
Together with his son and all his friends,
Until he reached the gateways of old age,
Having left all feats of bravery to his son.
And when the well-born Digenes the fair
Himself came to the measure of his prime
And among men was counted a right man;
Then on a day he sprang to horse and rode,
Took up the spear and took the club he had,
Gathered his company and took them with him.
And as they went with toil along the way
He heard tell about reivers [raiders] passing brave
That hold the narrows and do braveries,
And envy came on him to know the men.
So going off alone he found a reed-bed;
In it there was a dreadful lion, flayed
By the hands of the wondrous Ioannikios.
Digenes the Borderer, when he saw the lion,
Sighed from the bottom of his soul, and said:
"O eyes of mine, when shall you see those braves?"

. . . .

So then this also will I tell you, dearest,
How that at that same time the handsome Doukas,
Wondrous general of part of Romania,
Had a most lovely girl called Evdokia,
Whose name the Borderer was always hearing,
Boundless her beauty, glorious her descent.
So on a day he leapt to horse and rode,
And took his boys and went off to the chase.
And when the chase was done, they made for home.

* * *

The great general's house was on the road;
When they came near to it he gave a call:
"When a boy loves a very lovely girl,

And there he passes by and sees her beauties,
His heart is tamed, he would not live on earth."
Those in the house when the sweet sound they
    heard
They were amazed as once was that Odysseus
When in his ship he heard the Sirens' song.
Nor of the youth unhearing stayed the Girl,
All-beautiful, renowned, herself far-heard,
Her beauty priceless, glorious her descent,
Whose substance, and possessions, all her wealth
Impossible to count or quite imagine.
Only her dwelling none can celebrate;
All gold and marble was it, all mosaicked.

316.

Introduction. The atmosphere created in both East
and West by the long-lasting Crusades encouraged the writing of "romances"
with their content of high romantic adventure, noble quests, and exotic back-
grounds. These accentual narrative poems, composed in both Byzantium and
the Latin West especially during the thirteenth and fourteenth centuries, seem
so similar that it would not be unreasonable to accept the theory of reciprocal
influences. The earliest example of the Greek romance, from which we quote
below, was the thirteenth century *Romance of Callimachos and Chrysorrhoë*, about
the tender love affair of a youth and his maiden, now believed to have been
written by Andronikos Comnenos Ducas, a relative of Emperor Andronikos II.
The work was composed in the so-called Byzantine fifteen-syllable "political"
verse. These romantic poems evidently originally came from the upper class
cultural elite but their popularity soon spread downwards to other classes.

ROMANCE: ROMANTIC INTERLUDE

(From *Le roman de Callimaque et de Chrysorrhoë*, ed. M. Pichard
[Paris, 1956] pp. 29–30.)

The Graces pressed themselves into the service [of
the maiden and the youth] and participated in the bath with the young maiden.
What mouth can speak of her grace! None would know how to enumerate such a
collection of attractions. But anyone who would have been present at the bath
would have contemplated a spectacle both ravishing and extraordinary.

So much charm did her body have in the bath. A noble body with skin clear as
crystal doubles its attractiveness and grace in a bath. Then they [the youth and
the maiden] left the bath; at the side of the bath a bed was spread on the ground.
One might say that the water of the bath was of gold, but what was it compared
to the beauty of an [entire] pavement of gold. There was a bed there, but what
an increase in grace it assumed from contact with the body of the young girl.
Who can relate, who can describe in detail, the pleasure of which he was the
witness.

The kings of the golden castle lived in the midst of great pleasure and grace in equal measure.

317.

Introduction. Unlike most of Byzantine literature, which was written for the upper classes in a highly stylized imitation of ancient Greek literature, hagiographical writings (lives of the saints) were originally written in vernacular Greek and appealed to all classes because of their delight in the miraculous and their often fascinating examples of conduct to inspire the pious. The writer to whom we owe most of our knowledge of these Byzantine lives of saints is Symeon Metaphrastes ("the translator"). In the early tenth century he compiled a huge collection of such lives but rewrote them in a form more in keeping with the dictates of the classical Greek style. The original vernacular texts have thus been lost. The following is an example of hagiography dating from the beginning of the seventh century.

HAGIOGRAPHY: St. Theodore of Sykeon Performs an Exorcism

(Translated by E. Dawes and N. Baynes, *Three Byzantine Saints* [Crestwood, N.Y.: St. Vladimir's Seminary Press, and Oxford: A. R. Mowbray, 1977; originally published by Blackwell, Oxford, 1948], pp. 146–47.)

The slave girl of a magnate had been possessed secretly by a demon for twenty-eight years so that she was always ill and did not know what caused the malady. Her master brought her to the Saint praying that either by death or a restoration to health she might be liberated from her sickness. Saint Theodore took hold of her head and prayed that the cause of her illness might be made known and driven away. Immediately the demon in her was disturbed and tore her, shouting: 'You are burning me, iron-eater, spare me, strangler of demons, I adjure you by the God who gives you power against me.' Theodore bade the demon be silent and told the girl to return in a week's time. On the following Wednesday she came and once more the demon in her became excited and abusive: 'Oh this violence that I suffer from this harlot's child! Twenty-eight years I have possessed this girl and none of the saints found me out, and now this harlot's son has come and has made me manifest and handed me over to dread punishment. Cursed be the day on which you were born and the day that brought you here!' Theodore rebuked the demon with the sign of the Cross: 'Even if I am the harlot's son, nevertheless to the glory of our Lord Jesus Christ the Son of God I bid you in His name leave the girl and never take possession of her again.' The demon shouted in reply: 'I do your bidding and go out of her, but after three days she will die.' The Saint answered: 'Come forth and the will of the Lord be done. For a God-fearing man may not trust you, since your words are vain and false.' The demon tore the girl, threw her down at the Saint's feet and went out of her. And she, coming to herself, said: 'It is through your holy prayers, father, that I have been healed, for I saw the demon coming out of my mouth like a foul crawling thing.' Theodore prayed over her and dismissed her, bidding her remain in the church for seven days. And the word of the demon proved to be false, for after some days the girl and her master returned to the Saint giving glory to God.

318.

Introduction. Byzantium's supreme and most truly original literary contribution lay probably in the sphere of liturgical poetry, that is religious hymns combining text and music. (The literary texts remain but the music, unfortunately, has not survived.) Unlike classical Greek poetry, which followed a quantitative metrical system (it employed long and short sounds measured by the "quantity" of time held), this liturgical poetry was based on an accentual system (that is, long and short syllables in terms of accent-emphasis). It thus became more understandable to the average Byzantine, since spoken Byzantine Greek, like modern Western languages, was an accentual language.

Orthodox hymnology remained more or less constant in form throughout the Byzantine period, though there was more experimentation and variation than has usually been recognized. In the beginning of the sixth century the first important step in its development was taken with the appearance of the *kontakion*, an elaborate poetical homily or sermon set to music and coming after the Gospel lesson. Prior to the *kontakion* there had appeared the *troparion*, a short laudatory hymn which regularly preceded the *kontakion* in the liturgy and, though melodically independent, was linked to the *kontakion* by the refrain ending each of the stanzas. The master hymn writer of *kontakia* was the poet-monk Romanos the Melodist (d. 518), whose greatness of vision and powerful dramatic diction, along with his skillful handling of meter, are probably unparalleled in Christian hymnology. At the end of the seventh century the *kontakion* was displaced by another musical-poetic form, the canon, usually longer and sometimes more stilted in style, and derived from the nine Old Testament odes of the Canticles.

The prime example of Byzantine liturgical poetry is certainly the celebrated (anonymous) *kontakion*, the *Akathistos Hymnos*, perhaps written by Romanus the Melodist or possibly Patriarch Sergius or the poet George Pisides. Most probably it dates from the sixth century. It early became known in the West, especially in Venice.

A. THE *TROPARION*: THE *CHERUBIC HYMN*

Introduction. A famous example of the *troparion* is the (short) Cherubic Hymn, wrongly attributed to the eminent theologian-poet-monk of the eighth century, John of Damascus. This is chanted each Sunday in the liturgy and evokes the angels of the Cherubim.

(From the liturgy of the Greek Orthodox Church of America.)

Let us who mystically represent the Cherubim
And sing the thrice-holy hymn to the life-creating
  Trinity
Now set aside all earthly cares,
That we may welcome the King of all

Invisibly escorted by angelic hosts.
Alleluia, Alleluia, Alleluia.

B. The KONTAKION: THE AKATHISTOS HYMNOS (SEE SELECTION 139)

C. THE CANON: ANDREW OF CRETE'S GREAT CANON

Introduction. To Andrew of Crete (eighth century) is traditionally (though wrongly) attributed the invention of the *canon*. His *Great Canon*, a penitential hymn chanted in Lent, is considered to be the "king of canons."

(From Greek text, in E. Wellesz, *A History of Byzantine Music and Hymnography* [Oxford, 1961], p. 205.)

The end approaches, O soul,
It is near, and you take no heed.
You do not prepare yourself.
Time is growing short. Arise.
Near at the door there stands the judge.
Like a dream, like a flower,
The span of life runs out.
Why are we shaken by vain thoughts?

Be sober, O my soul, meditate on
The works which you have done,
And set them before your eyes,
While allowing your tears to flow.
Confess freely your acts and thoughts
To Christ and be justified.

D. ON THE LIFE OF JOHN KOUKOUZELES

(Translated by D. Geanakoplos from E. Williams, "John Koukou-zeles' Reform of Byzantine Chanting for Great Vespers in the Fourteenth Century" [Ph.D. diss., Yale, 1968], pp. 351 and 312.)

He built a small cell outside the monastery and a church of the Archangels in which to practice quietude [*hesychia*] for a certain number of days, that is to say, Monday and Tuesday and the rest of the week-days. On Sundays and the feast-days of Lent he was not absent from the right hand choir of the great church [at the Athonite monastery of the Great Laura] singing and praising God day and night. . . .

And loving peace most of all, Philotheos [the patriarch?] abdicated his throne entirely of his own volition, having tended his flock only four years pleasing to God. And he left to seek quietude at the Great Laura. At that time he found there the divine swan, John the Melodist, the siren tongue to whom the Mother of God had given that gold "coin," and who at this particular time was chanting, from the *Akathistos Hymnos*, "*Angelos protostates*" [Prince of Angels] or the "*Epi soi hairei*" [Hail to you] for Philotheos who was then present.

Commentary. Compare also the remarkable prose treatise of Nicholas Cavasilas (also fourteenth century) on the mystical meaning of the Eucharist in the liturgy (see above, selection 135).

319.

Introduction. "Devotional" poetry, too, was an important literary genre, written largely though not always by monks. Since it was primarily the monks who carried Orthodoxy to the Slavic lands (see selection 258), including Moravia, Bulgaria and Russia, the religious poems of the monks served as a very significant means for the dissemination of Byzantine culture, especially the Orthodox faith. Symeon the "New Theologian" (949– 1022) was one of the monks who wrote such poems. A great mystic and theologian as well as a remarkable poet, he has left us several exquisite examples of poetry depicting the spiritual condition of man, especially the overflowing love and ineffable joy that spring forth from his soul when he mystically communicates with God (termed in Byzantium *theosis*). For Symeon prayer is association and dialogue with God. The first poem depicts the spiritual condition of one (a monk) who has reached this height. On *theosis*, see also selection 131.

"DEVOTIONAL" POETRY: MONASTIC LOVE FOR THE DIVINE

(Reprinted from H. Magoulias, trans., *Byzantine Christianity: Emperor, Church and the West* [Detroit, 1970], pp. 77–78, by permission of the Wayne State University Press. Copyright © 1970 by Rand McNally & Company. All rights reserved.)

"Who Is the Monk?"

The monk is he who is uninvolved with the world
And unceasingly speaks to God alone.
Seeking, he is seen, loving, he is loved
And ineffably becomes an illuminated light.
Glorified he appears to be impoverished
And becoming familiar he is a stranger.
O strange and ineffable marvel.
Possessing infinite wealth I am a pauper
And thinking I have nothing I possess much.
And I say "I thirst" while having an abundance of
     waters. . . .

"The Paradox of Love"

In love there is no fear whatever,
Nor again does love without fear in the soul bear
     fruit.
The tree blossoms and bears fruit through labor.
Again its fruit uproots the whole tree.
The fruit remains alone; how can there be fruit
     without the tree?

Commentary. Symeon's aim was to reach the common people by using a metrical form that could easily be understood and remembered. His devotional poetry, like the *kontakia*, accordingly was composed not in the classical quantitative meters but in simple accentual meters.

320.

Introduction. Byzantine literature had no real popular, secular, lyric poetry.* The epigram, a poetic form half-way between the lyric and the epic, was a short piece of usually a few lines expressing a barbed comment or witty antithesis in couplets. It was a true miniature work of art which gave immense pleasure to the Byzantines. Everyone wrote epigrams, even the monks. Some of the best of this genre were written by the court official (and later monk and bishop) John Geometres in the late tenth century. We translate below, insofar as the clever word-play may be reproduced, several of his epigrams addressed to pagan Greek and Christian writers and one to both pagan Athens and Christian Constantinople. (For another epigram to Christ, written by John Mauropous, see selection 296B.)

A. THE EPIGRAM: JOHN GEOMETRES

(From John Geometres, *Carmina Varia*, in MPG, vol. 106, cols. 947, 950.)

To Aristotle
The mind described the mind, nature described
     nature,
But I speak of Aristotle as the ultimate of both.

To Plato
Plato, proclaiming the soul immortal,
Bequeathed immortal glory in life.
Plato the glorious, who broadened[†] human
     thought,
As he broadened the profound doctrine of the soul
Broadened his glory throughout the world.

On St. Gregory the Theologian
The Syrian was inspired by God,
The Phoenician was erudite in many disciplines,
But the Cappadocian [Gregory] was superior to
     both.

To Athens and to Constantinople
Earth erected the city of Erechtheus
But heaven constructed the New Rome.
Beauty is stronger than earth,
How much more, the brilliant pole.[†]

Introduction. Another type of verse was the Verse Chronicle, often written by court officials in praise of an emperor's victories. An example is the rather weighty panegyric composed by Theodosius the Deacon in the tenth century on the occasion of Nicephorus Phocas's recapture of the island of Crete from its Arab conquerors. Note his admixture of classical and Christian strains of thought.

B. Verse Chronicle: Theodosius the Deacon

(From *De Expugnatione Cretae* [Bonn Corpus, 1838], vol. 29, pp. 301, 302, 305–6.)

The Capture of Crete

The entire land of Rome, and sea and city,
Mountains, valleys, stars, waters of constantly
    flowing rivers,
Let the multitude of the stars above, exult.
Let the order of angels dance,
Because the wild beast has been slain,
The fierce-looking monster, crushed,
And the intolerable wound to the earth, healed . . .
Let nations, and cities, and country areas learn of
    the new power of the greatest Roman.
Let them know of the sleepless cares
Which the emperor suffered on our account . . .

Rouse yourselves sword-bearers of the land of
    Africa
For the city of Tarsus is disturbed.
Receive the ancient malediction, O tribe of Arabs
From the lance of the powerful Roman . . .
O Christ, child of the Father before the centuries
Provide such glory to your emperor.
Who would sigh over the tomb of Polyxenes?
Who over the captivity of the Phrygians?
O chorus of young men to whom the care of the
    thoughts of Homer,
The old man, is in your hearts . . .
[Take care] lest you be deceived by the old man's
    words
Lest you be lured by his "confabulated" songs.
For he, though wise, uttered falsehoods
And provided blind charms of words.
Applaud the capture of Crete, which
Time took by the sword of the wise kings.
Crete, fatherland of Zeus,
Zeus the tyrant, the fictitious genius
Who found the fire eternal[9]
Since he sought to be called God on earth . . .

Thus the city of the Cretans suffered shock
As it became as before a city of Rome.
O much-yearned-for city, excellent city,
Renowned city, most wealthy city.
Tarsus heard and digs out trenches.
Erects a tower and fortifies the gates with iron
And does all to preclude, through other
    misfortunes,
The burden of captivity in the future.

Introduction. Still another type of verse that became especially common in the twelfth century among the upper class, was the so-called "didactic" verse, a rather odd scholarly genre of poetry composed in the aim of instructing students and uninitiated devotees of classical literature in the intricacies of the art. The proverbial exponent of such poetry was John Tzetzes, who wrote in the fifteen-syllable verse pattern for easy memorization by his pupils. We know that he composed an erudite didactic poem, *Homer*, at least partly at the request of the Latin spouse of Emperor Manuel I Comnenus, Bertha of Sulzbach, who wished to improve her knowledge of Greek. The following verses constitute scholia for the instruction of students reading the treatises on rhetoric of the ancient Greek writer Hermogenes, who was extremely popular in Byzantium.

C. DIDACTIC VERSE: JOHN TZETZES

(From "Tzetzis Scholia in Hermogenem," in *Anecdota Graeca*, ed. J. Cramer, vol. 4 [Oxford, 1836], p. 62.)

On Hermogenes

Book two: On narration
. . . Such then is the function, on the one hand, of
    the proemium,
On the other, of the narration. What function does
    each serve?
The first serves to attract the attention of the
    hearers
To what we shall discuss in the narration.
And it exhorts to a need for narration,
Either with a view to disapproval or approval of the
    matter dealt with,
Extolling and demonstrating the notable
    achievement.

Book three: On inventions
By the end of the discourse there are four parts,
Proemium, narration, argument, with final
    conclusions.
In the second book takes place discussion of the
    seven forms;

Now in the third we discuss the teaching of main
   arguments,
Those parts which are introductions and
   resolutions of the chief issues
About which I also wrote at greater length earlier,
And directed the discourse to Emperor Marcus
   [Aurelius].*
Which I often succeeded in demonstrating to you
   through my own efforts
And I taught you this *viva voce.*

* Possibly because the archaizing, often stilted quality of the literary Byzantine language did not lend itself to freer forms of expression.
† Greek, *platyno,* to broaden—pun on Plato's name.
‡ Greek for pole is polos—pun on "Constantinoupolis."
§ Homer, the pagan poet, wrote "lies" and Zeus, the chief god, burns eternally in Hell.
# Hermogenes lived during the reign of Marcus Aurelius, second century A.D.

D.
BYZANTINE SCIENCE

321.

Introduction. In science as in literature the Byzantines were followers of the ancient Greeks. Byzantine manuscript copies of the writings of the ancients on science abound. In order to give the reader an idea of the Byzantine scientific fields of study, we offer selections from each of several important areas: medicine, surgery, mechanics and mathematics, physics, astronomy, and astrology.

The first selection, from the twelfth-century Western historian, William of Tyre, who lived in the Latin Kingdom of Jerusalem, describes the care and talent for medicine shown by the Emperor Manuel I Comnenus.

EMPEROR MANUEL COMNENUS AS SURGEON

(Translated by E. Babcock and A. C. Krey from William of Tyre, *History of Deeds Done beyond the Sea* [New York: Columbia University Press, 1943], p. 280.)

They [Baldwin, King of Jerusalem, and Manuel I] were riding through the forest, as hunters do in pursuance of that sport, when, on the solemn day of the Ascension of our Lord, an accident befell them. The king, borne along on his fleet horse, was riding over rough ground covered with low-growing shrubs and brambles, when he was flung headlong to the ground from his horse and suffered a fractured arm.

As soon as the emperor learned of the accident, he took upon himself, with the most gracious sympathy, the office of surgeon; he knelt down by the king and attentively ministered to him, as if he himself were merely an ordinary person. Meanwhile, his nobles and kinsmen were dumb with wonder and dismay. That the emperor, regardless of his imperial majesty, should lay aside his august dignity and show himself so devoted and friendly to the king appeared to all unseemly. When, on account of this accident, they returned to Antioch, he visited the king daily, himself renewed the poultices and healing ointments, and then carefully replaced the bandages. Indeed, he could scarcely have shown more solicitude had Baldwin been his own son.

322.

Introduction. Byzantine medical treatises exerted their influence beyond the borders of the empire. The thirteenth-century work of the Byzantine Nicholas Myrepsos, court physician to John Vatatzes of Nicaea, was used as a textbook on pharmacology at the University of Paris until 1651. The tract, *Epitome*, of the seventh-century doctor, Paul of Aegina (based in great part on Hippocrates and Galen) remained the principal medical text of Byzantium until the end of the empire. It emphasized the practical aspects of medicine, and its surgical section became celebrated not only in Byzantium but among Western and Arab doctors as well. (See also selection 229.)

On Fracture and Contusion of the Thigh and the Nose

(Translated and edited by Francis Adams, from *The Seven Books of Paulus Aegineta* [London, 1843], vol. 2, pp. 443–44, 466–67.)

The case of a broken thigh is analogous to that of the arm, but in particular, a fractured thigh is mostly deranged forwards and outwards, for the bone is naturally flattened on those sides. It is to be set by the hands, with ligatures, and even cords applied, the one above and the other below the fracture. When the fracture takes place at one end, if at the head of the thigh, the middle part of a thong wrapped round with wool, so that it may not cut the parts there, is to be applied to the perinæum, and the ends of it brought up to the head and given to an assistant to hold, and applying a ligature below the fracture, we give the ends of it to another assistant to make extension. If it is fractured near the knee, we apply the ligature immediately above the fracture, and give the ends to an assistant, with which to make extension upwards; and while we put a ligature round the knee to secure it, and while the patient lies thus, with his leg extended, we arrange the fracture. Pieces of bone which irritate the parts, as has been often said, are to be taken out from above; and the rest of the treatment we have already described in the section on the arm. The thigh gets consolidated within fifty days. The manner of arranging it afterwards will be described after delivering the treatment of the whole leg.

The under part of the nose being cartilaginous does not admit of fracture, but it is liable to be crushed, flattened, and distorted; but the upper part being of a bony substance is sometimes fractured. . . . When, therefore, the nose is fractured in its under parts, having introduced the index or little finger into the nostril, push the parts outwards to their proper position. When the fracture is of the inner parts this is to be done with the head of a probe immediately, during the course of the first day, or not long afterwards, because the bones of the nose get consolidated about the tenth day. But they are to be put into the proper position with the index-finger and thumb externally. In order to prevent the bones from changing their position, two wedge-like tents, formed of a twisted linen rag, are to be applied, one to each nostril, even if but one part of the nose be deranged, and these are to be allowed to remain until the bone or cartilage gets consolidated. . . .

If the nose become inflamed we may use some anti-inflammatory application to it, such as that from juices [*diachylon*], the one from vinegar and oil, and such like; or a cataplasm of fine wheaten flour boiled with manna or gum may be applied, both for the sake of the inflammation and in order to keep the nose in position. When the nose is distorted to either side, Hippocrates directs us, after it has been restored to its proper position, to take a piece of leather of a finger's breadth, and having spread one of its ends with taurocolla or gum, to fasten one extremity of it on that side of the nose to which it inclines, and after it dries to bring the thong by the opposite ear to the occiput and forehead, and to fix the other end of the thong firmly there, so that the nose being drawn sideways may take the proper position in the middle. This practice, however, is not much approved of by the moderns. If the bones of the nose are broken into small pieces we must make an incision or enlarge the wound, and having removed the small bones with a hair forceps, unite the divided parts with sutures, and use the applications for recent wounds and those of an agglutinative nature.

323.

Introduction. Despite their almost complete servility to ancient science, the Byzantines did make a few original contributions. Paul the Silentiary, in a passage from his lengthy poem in praise of Hagia Sophia (after 562), describes, for example, the engineering and architectural feat of the architects Anthemius of Tralles and Isidore of Miletus in constructing the church's immense dome (see above, selection 141). Note that Isidore had revised the text of Archimedes, the greatest mathematician of antiquity, and that Anthemius had composed several important mathematical texts of his own.

The chief handbook on mathematics used by the Byzantines was the early fourth-century treatise, *Synagoge*, of Pappus of Alexandria. We quote from Pappus's definition of the science of "mechanics" (an overall Byzantine term referring primarily to stresses and balances), mastery of which was vital for engineers and architects.

PAPPUS ON MECHANICS AND MATHEMATICS

(Translated by G. Downey, *Gaza in the Early Sixth Century* [Norman, Oklahoma, 1963], p. 123.)

The science of mechanics has many important uses in practical life, and is held by philosophers to be worthy of the highest esteem, and is zealously studied by mathematicians, because it takes almost first place in dealing with the nature of the material elements of the universe. For it deals generally with the stability and movement of bodies, and their motions in space . . . using theorems appropriate to the subject matter. . . . Mechanics can be divided into a theoretical and a manual part. The theoretical part is composed of geometry, arithmetic, astronomy and physics, the manual of work in metals, construction work, carpentering and the art of painting, and the manual execution of these things. The man who has been trained from his youth in the aforesaid sciences as well as practised in the aforesaid arts, and in addition has a versatile mind, will be the best builder and inventor of mechanical devices.

324.

Introduction. Early in the sixth century the Byzantine philosopher and mathematician John Philoponus of Alexandria (a famous commentator on Aristotle) anticipated modern scientific theory by proving, in opposition to Aristotle, that a vacuum can exist. Moreover, he attacked Aristotle's position on the laws regulating falling bodies. We quote below from his commentary on Aristotle's *Physics.*

PHILOPONUS AGAINST ARISTOTLE

(Translated and edited by M. Cohen and I. Drabkin, in *Source Book in Greek Science* [New York, 1948], pp. 217–21.)

Weight, then, is the efficient cause of downward motion, as Aristotle himself asserts. This being so, given a distance to be traversed, I mean through a void where there is nothing to impede motion, and given that the efficient cause of the motion differs, the resultant motions will inevitably be at different speeds, even through a void. . . . Clearly, then, it is the natural weights of bodies, one having a greater and another a lesser downward tendency, that cause differences in motion. For that which has a greater downward tendency divides a medium better. Now air is more effectively divided by a heavier body. To what other cause shall we ascribe this fact than that that which has greater weight has, by its own nature, a greater downward tendency, even if the motion is not through a plenum? . . .

And so, if a body cuts through a medium better by reason of its greater downward tendency, then, even if there is nothing to be cut, the body will none the less retain its greater downward tendency. . . . And if bodies possess a greater or a lesser downward tendency in and of themselves, clearly they will possess this difference in themselves even if they move through a void. The same space will consequently be traversed by the heavier body in shorter time and by the lighter body in longer time, even though the space be void. The result will be due not to greater or lesser interference with the motion but to the greater or lesser downward tendency, in proportion to the natural weight of the bodies in question. . . .

Sufficient proof has been adduced to show that if motion took place through a void, it would not follow that all bodies would move therein with equal speed. We have also shown that Aristotle's attempt to prove that they would so move does not carry conviction. Now if our reasoning up to this point has been sound it follows that our earlier proposition is also true, namely, that it is possible for motion to take place through a void in finite time. . . .

Thus, if a certain time is required for each weight, in and of itself, to accomplish a given motion, it will never be possible for one and the same body to traverse a given distance, on one occasion through a plenum and on another through a void, in the same time.

For if a body moves the distance of a stade through air, and the body is not at the beginning and at the end of the stade at one and the same instant, a definite time will be required, dependent on the particular nature of the body in question, for it to travel from the beginning of the course to the end (for, as I have indicated, the body is not at both extremities at the same instant), and this would be true even if the space traversed were a void. But a certain *additional time* is required because of the interference of the medium. For the pressure of the medium and the necessity of cutting through it make motion through it more difficult.

Consequently, the thinner we conceive the air to be through which a motion takes place, the less will be the *additional time* consumed in dividing the air. And if we continue indefinitely to make this medium thinner, the additional time will also be reduced indefinitely, since time is indefinitely divisible. But even if the medium be thinned out indefinitely in this way, the total time consumed will never be reduced to the time which the body consumes in moving the distance of a stade through a void. . . .

If, then, by rarefying the medium you will never eliminate this additional time, and if in the case of motion through a plenum there is always some portion of the second hour to be added, in proportion to the density of the medium, clearly the stade will never be traversed by a body through a void in the same time as through a plenum. . . .

But it is completely false and contrary to the evidence of experience to argue as follows: "If a stade is traversed through a plenum in two hours, and through a void in one hour, then if I take a medium half as dense as the first, the same distance will be traversed through this rarer medium in half the time, that is, in one hour: hence the same distance will be traversed through a plenum in the same time as through a void." For Aristotle wrongly assumes that the ratio of the times required for motion through various media is equal to the ratio of the densities of the media. . . .

But this is completely erroneous, and our view may be corroborated by actual observation more effectively than by any sort of verbal argument. For if you let fall from the same height two weights of which one is many times as heavy as the other, you will see that the ratio of the times required for the motion does not depend on the ratio of the weights, but that the difference in time is a very small one. *And so, if the difference in the weights is not considerable, that is, if one is, let us say, double the other, there will be no difference, or else an imperceptible difference, in time, though the difference in weight is by no means negligible, with one body weighing twice as much as the other.*

Now if, in the case of different weights in motion through the same medium, the ratio of the times required for the motions is not equal to the inverse ratio of the weights, and, conversely, the ratio of the weights is not equal to the inverse ratio of the times, the following proposition would surely be reasonable: "If identical bodies move through different media, like air and water, the ratio of the times required for the motions through the air and water, respectively, is not equal to the ratio of the densities of air and water, and conversely."

Now if the ratio of the times is not determined by the ratio of the densities of the media, it follows that a medium half as dense will not be traversed in half the time, but in longer than half. Furthermore, as I have indicated above, in proportion as the medium is rarefied, the shorter is the *additional* time required for the division of the medium. But this additional time is never completely eliminated; it is merely decreased in proportion to the degree of rarefaction of the medium, as has been indicated. . . . And so, if the *total* time required is not reduced in proportion to the degree of rarefaction of the medium, and if the time added for the division of the medium is diminished in proportion to the rarefaction of the medium, but never entirely eliminated, it follows that a body will never traverse the same distance through a plenum in the same time as through a void.

325.

Introduction. We are told that the great architect (*mechanikos*) Anthemius of Tralles was able to produce an explosion ("a small earthquake") by harnessing steam pressure. The following passage from the sixth-century historian, Agathias, relates the story of a dispute between Anthemius and a member of the Senate, Zeno, a teacher of rhetoric. Anthemius, vanquished by the eloquence of Zeno, took his revenge by producing tremors through the use of steam—something that so discomfited Zeno that, stung by the laughter of the imperial courtiers, he hurried to the palace to complain to the emperor.

ANTHEMIUS'S LITTLE EARTHQUAKE

(From Agathias, *Historia*, ed. R. Keydell [Berlin, 1967], bk. 5, chs. 6–7.)

A certain man named Zeno, belonging to the guild of lawyers and very well known to the emperor, lived near Anthemius, and it seemed proper to each that their houses be united and divided by a single boundary. After a time a quarrel arose between them, either concerning some customary favor which had been overlooked or over the fact that the newer house [Zeno's] had constructed a balcony of above average height and spoiled the other's view, or about something else of the many causes of dispute which arise between neighbors.

Anthemius, seeing himself overcome in court, since he was not able to equal the rhetorical eloquence of his opponent, harassed him by means of mechanical artifice. Zeno had a room in the upper part of the building, very large, conspicuous, and elaborately decorated, in which he commonly spent much of his time and entertained his friends. Beneath this room happened to be a portion of Anthemius' house. . . . Then Anthemius, having filled many large kettles with water, dispersed them around his room and put on them leather tubes, wide at the bottom so as to completely cover the [kettle's] rims, with the tops getting proportionately smaller, like upside down trumpets. He affixed the tops on beams and platforms and pinned them precisely so that when the tube was squeezed, the air went in an upward motion through the empty tube, going up to the bare ceiling as much as possible, so that, encompassed by the hide [of the tube], it was carried out of the tube. Having set this up with no one noticing, he lit a fire under the bottoms of the kettles and made a great flame. When the water heated up and evaporated, the vapor rose and entered the tube and quickly thickened. Not having any exit, the vapor crept up the tubes, and since it was increasingly constricted, sped up. Striking continuously against the roof it shook the entire room above and overturned its furniture. And those staying with Zeno awakened and were afraid and went out into the street, screaming and amazed at the marvel. Zeno, wandering in the public places, inquired of his friends how the earthquake had seemed to them, and why they were not killed. And they replied, "Shut up," and "Go away," and "It never happened."

326.

Introduction. In the fifteenth century several Byzantine thinkers attempted to reform the existing calendar by developing one that corresponded more closely to the rotation of the earth and movements of the planets than the Julian calendar. Among these was the famous Neoplatonic philosopher (and rejector of Christianity) Gemistus Pletho, from whose *Nomoi* (*Laws*) we quote the following passage:

A. PLETHO'S CALENDAR

(From Pletho, *Traité des lois*, ed. C. Alexandre [Paris, 1858], pp. 389f.)

Concerning the services of worship for the gods . . . [it is advisable] to use the natural months and years, with the months being calculated according to the moon and the years by the solstices of the sun, beginning anew at each winter solstice when the sun has gone farthest away from us and begins again its progression toward us. The day of the old and new moon has been determined by those who are most experienced in astronomy as the day on which the moon is joined with the sun. The next day is new moon day which begins at midnight, immediately after the conjunction of the two gods [the sun and moon]. From this point are calculated all the remaining days of the month—the full months having thirty days, the hollow months having one day less. The evening of each night is reckoned as part of the preceding day, the dawn as part of the following day, and midnight marks the division between two days.

The days of the month are counted in this manner: after the new moon comes the second day of the beginning of the month. After the eighth day of the beginning of the month comes the seventh day of the middle of the month, then the sixth, and so forth going backwards to the second, after which comes the middle of the month. . . . The intercalary month is inserted whenever the twelfth month does not reach the winter solstice. To determine the solstices of the sun we employ the most accurate sundials available.

Introduction. The greatest of Byzantine philosophers, Pletho, held views remarkable for his time. Deeply disturbed (as were many other intellectuals) over the terrible condition of the empire, he sought to revitalize the Byzantine state. One means he proposed was the replacement of traditional Christianity by paganism, actually a form of Neoplatonism in which the gods were not to be personal deities but philosophical categories. For him the model for life should be ancient "Hellenism," not Rome and its Christianity. Such views he expressed in his works in which he set forth, in imitation of Plato, a constitution for his Hellenic state. There were to be two classes, the army which would fight and pay no taxes and the peasants, who would till the soil. Lands would be held in common.

B. Pletho's Suggestions for a New Order

(From Pletho, Letter to Manuel II, in S. Lambros, *Palaiologeia kai Peloponnesiaka* [Athens, 1926], vol. 3, pp. 254, 256, 260.)

The produce of the labor of all should in justice be assigned to three different recipients—first, to the laborer himself; secondly, to the person who provides the stock for the labor; and thirdly, to the person who ensures security for the whole community. The laborers are ploughmen, diggers, and shepherds; the stock for their labor is oxen, vines, flocks, and the like. Those who ensure security for the whole community are the soldiers, who face danger on its behalf, and the officers and other persons who are in control of the several branches of common affairs and manage each branch whether great or small—with the king at their head, in control of all branches, guiding and managing them all. . . .

The army being organized on this basis [as a regular, permanent body], each infantry soldier should have one helot assigned to him, and each mounted man should have two; and thus each soldier—while enjoying his own produce so far as his military service permits him to labor on the land—will be able to count on the share of produce paid to him by his helot [an ancient Spartan term] . . . and will be in a position to serve in the army with proper equipment and to remain permanently with the standards. . . .

I would . . . suggest that all the land should be the common property of all its inhabitants, as perhaps it is by nature, and that no man should claim any part as his private property. Every man who wishes to do so should be allowed to plant a crop, wherever he will, to erect a house, and to plough as much land as he wishes and is able to plough, on the assumption that he will have that amount at his disposal in so far as, and on condition that, he does not neglect to till it while he is its occupant. Meanwhile, he should pay no rent to any person, and should not be let or hindered by any person, other than one who has anticipated him in cultivating it, and this according to the rule regulating all common property that does not belong to any one man more than it does to another. . . .

Introduction. In order to begin revitalization of the moribund Byzantine state, Pletho singled out the province of the Peloponnesus, which he believed to be the best area for regeneration precisely because of its long-tradition of "Hellenism." In the following letter addressed to his friend Emperor Manuel II Palaeologus, he emphasizes the ideal of a revived Hellenic, no longer Roman, state.

C. The Peloponnesus: Quintessential Hellenic Land

(From Pletho, Letter to Manuel II, in S. Lambros, *Palaiologeia kai Peloponnesiaka* [Athens, 1926], vol. 3, p. 247–50.)

The Greeks [Hellenes] cannot find any other land more familiar and appropriate to them than the Peloponnesus because it is close to Europe and to the other islands. This land, it seems, the Greeks always inhabited from the time that man is mentioned. And it was not conquered or plundered by foreigners in the way that other peoples frequently have left one land and gone to inhabit another, expelling and being expelled. But the Greeks, on the contrary, seem always to have possessed this land and starting from this place have acquired no little property elsewhere, and this without abandoning the Peloponnesus. Of all this land [Greece], the Peloponnesus, it is agreed, is the one which brought the final and most well-known lineage to the race of the Greeks [*genos Hellenon*]. And because of this they proved to be the greatest and most glorious Greeks. . . . This should be taken into consideration by all those considered as Greeks, and particularly by the emperors.*

Commentary. Pletho attended the Council of Florence with the Byzantine delegation in 1438–39. There he created a great stir because of his lectures on Plato's *Dialogues*, whose original Greek texts were unknown to the Italian humanists. In Florence he also wrote a tract for the humanists on the philosophic differences between Plato and Aristotle. It was his influence which ultimately induced Cosimo de'Medici to found the famous Platonic Academy in Florence, with far-reaching results for the culture of the entire Italian Renaissance.

*Pletho's suggested reforms were never put into action. Pletho lived at Mistra near ancient Sparta in the Peloponnesus.

327.

Introduction. There was always in Constantinople an "enlightened" segment of the population who maintained interest in the sciences. Already in the late thirteenth century, the statesman-scholar George Acropolites was able to forecast an eclipse of the sun. The same is true of the polymaths of the fourteenth century, the Palaeologan scholars Theodore Metochites and Nicephorus Gregoras.

Gregoras Predicts an Eclipse of the Sun

(From letters to John Chrysoloras and Michael Kaloeidas, in *Nicephore Gregoras: Correspondance*, ed. R. Guilland [Paris, 1927], pp. 137 and 153.)

After the eclipse of the sun, which took place as I had predicted, these people [a group of pseudo-wise men whom Gregoras in ancient style terms "sophists"] proposed some new questions to me of the same kind, that is unimportant, uninteresting, and incapable of holding the attention of an audience of savants. . . . After the eclipse of the sun took place—which I had earlier clearly predicted*—there would then take place that about which I spoke in not very clear terms. It would occur very close to twelve o'clock on 14 May of the first indiction† and it would be more important than all others that we have seen. After the latter eclipse, there would be still another. But I must again observe silence, because of these uninitiated [the "sophists"] and in order to allow those to deal with this who are just being introduced into the mysteries of science.

*The eclipse of 30 November 1331.
†There was an eclipse of the sun on 14 March 1333.

328.

Introduction. Throughout the Byzantine period and especially in times of distress, the Byzantines often had recourse to the advice of astrologers who at various times exerted a not inconsiderable influence on the course of events. Indeed, many Byzantine emperors employed in their courts astrologers or soothsayers whom they consulted. (As Charles Diehl says, "There was not a usurper who did not claim that predictions had foretold his ascension to the imperial throne.") Not all members of society, however, accepted the statements of astrologers; the intelligent Emperor Alexius Comnenus (1081–1118) called astrology a "very pernicious science." We quote here from Anna Comnena's *Alexiad* on the significance of divination and astrology during the reign of her father, Alexius.

A. Anna Comnena on Astrology

(From Anna Comnena, *Alexiade*, ed. B. Leib [Paris, 1945], vol. 2, pp. 57–59.)

A certain mathematician named Seth,* who prided himself greatly on his astrological skill, had predicted in an oracular pronouncement the death of Robert [Guiscard, the Norman conqueror of Byzantine southern Italy], after his crossing over to Illyricum. He wrote down the prediction on paper, and sealing it, he entrusted it to certain confidantes of the emperor, directing that they hold the document for a time. Then when Robert died, at Seth's instruction they opened the document. The oracle ran as follows: "A great enemy from the West who has stirred up many things will suddenly die." All marveled at the skill of the man, for he had reached the acme of his science. Let us briefly leave our recital of events and digress for a moment concerning the nature of oracles.

The discovery of divination is rather new and I do not believe that antiquity had this knowledge. For neither in the time of Eudoxus, the very great astronomer, was there a method of divination, nor did Plato know the art; not even Manetho, who knew about the influence of the stars, fully understood it. They did not know how [to draw up] a horoscope with which they could predict the future, and to fix cardinal points, and to note carefully the entire order [of the heavens], and all other things which the one who invented this method passed on to posterity and which are readily intelligible to those who engage in such nonsense.

I once for a little time had a fancy for this "art," not in order that I might practice such a thing (God forbid) but that I, knowing its foolish talk well, might better refute those addicted to it. I write thus not for the sake of ostentation, but in order that I might point out that many of the sciences progressed under this emperor [Alexius], who patronized philosophers and philosophy itself. Toward this study of astrology, however, he appeared somewhat hostile because, I think, it persuaded many of the guileless to shift their hopes away from heaven and to gape at the stars. That is the real reason that the emperor made war on astrology. There was not, however, on account of this any lack of astrologers at this time, but even the aforesaid Seth flourished then. This Egyptian from Alexandria was deeply involved in the secret mysteries of astrology. When he was questioned by many he gave very accurate forecasts, at times even without using an astrolabe, but made his prophecies through a certain kind of pebble-casting [presumably lecanomancy]. This was not at all magic, but a certain numerological skill of the Alexandrian. When the emperor saw the youth flocking to him and considering him as a prophet, he twice questioned him, and both times the Alexandrian responded properly to the questions. Then, fearful lest harm come to many and that all might turn toward the foolishness of astrology, he drove him from the city, exiling him to Rhaidestos, though showing great consideration for him so that his needs were taken care of by the imperial treasury.

*The famous Symeon Seth.

Introduction. Astrology was taken seriously in earlier Byzantine times as well. We quote an astrological canon (horoscope), retold by the tenth-century Emperor Constantine VII in his treatise *De administrando imperio*, which predicted the rise of Byzantium's powerful rival, the Arabs, and their penetration of Byzantine territory.

B. AN ASTROLOGICAL PREDICTION ON THE ARABS

(Translated by R. Jenkins, from Constantine Porphyrogenitus, *De administrando imperio*, ed. G. Moravcsik [Washington, D.C.: Dumbarton Oaks, 1967], p. 81.)

[Chapter heading]
From the canon which Stephen the astrologer cast from the stars concerning the Exodus of the Saracens [Arabs], in what year of the foundation of the world

it took place, and who then held the sceptre of the empire of the Romans.

The Exodus of the Saracens took place on the third day of the month of September of the tenth indiction, in the twelfth year of Heraclius, in the year from the creation of the world 6130. And the horoscope of these same Saracens was cast in the month of September, on the third day of the month, the fifth day of the week. At this same time Mouameth was first chief of the Arabs, whom the Arabs call Mahomet, who was also their prophet, and he held rule over the Arabs nine years.

329.

Introduction. Despite the relatively high state of Byzantine science in many spheres, superstition existed on all levels of Byzantine society. The historian of the fall of Byzantium in 1453, Critoboulos, shared the superstitious beliefs of much of the Greek populace, as demonstrated in a passage from his *History of Mehmed the Conqueror*, quoted below. In him coexisted both a dedication to reason and historical investigation, and a belief in the supernatural and magic.

CRITOBOULOS ON OMENS BEFORE THE FINAL CONQUEST

(Translated by C. Riggs, Critoboulos, *History of Mehmed the Conqueror* [Princeton: Princeton University Press, 1954], pp. 58–59.)

During those same days there occurred the following divine signs and portents of the terrors that were very soon to come to the city. Three or four days before the battle, when all the people in the City were holding a religious procession, men and women together, and marching around with the Icon of the Mother of God, this latter slipped suddenly from the hands of its bearers without any cause or power being apparent, and fell flat on the ground. And when everybody shouted immediately, and rushed to raise up the icon, it sank down as if weighted with lead, and as if fastened to the ground, and became well-nigh impossible to raise. And so it continued for a considerable time, until, by a great effort and much shouting and prayers by all, the priests and its bearers barely managed to raise it up and place it on the shoulders of the men.

This strange occurrence filled everyone with much terror and very great agony and fear, for they thought this fall was no good omen—as was quite true. Later, when they had gone on but a short distance, immediately after that, at high noon, there was much thunder and lightning with clouds, and a violent rain with severe hail followed, so that they could neither stand against it nor make any progress. The priests and the bearers of the icon and the crowds that followed were depressed and hindered by the force of the waters that flowed down and by the might of the hail. Many of the children following were in danger of being carried away and drowned by the violent and powerful rush of water, had not some men quickly seized them and with some difficulty dragged them out of the flood. Such was the unheard-of and unprecedented violence of that storm and hail which certainly foreshadowed the imminent loss of all, and that, like a torrent of fiercest water, it would carry away and annihilate everything.

EPILOGUE

330.

Introduction. Constantinople's capture by the Turks in 1453 understandably alarmed the West, and certain Western leaders, especially the pope, became more than ever interested in launching a new "crusade" to recover Constantinople and then perhaps to use it as a springboard to recover Jerusalem. Byzantine scholar-emigres in the West, aware of this reasoning, played upon it to urge the recapture of Constantinople. In the following selection the humanist Bessarion, former Byzantine archbishop of Nicaea and then cardinal of the Roman church, on 13 July 1453—only one and a half months after Constantinople's fall and immediately after he himself had heard the terrible news—wrote to the doge of Venice, urging his aid against the Turks for reasons of Christian solidarity and for self-defense.

BESSARION PLEADS FOR WESTERN AID AGAINST THE TURKS

(Translated by J. B. Ross and M. M. McLaughlin, *The Portable Renaissance Reader* [New York, 1953], pp. 70–73. Copyright © 1953 by The Viking Press, Inc.; copyright renewed 1981 by Viking Penguin Inc. Reprinted by permission of Viking Penguin Inc.)

Wretched me! I cannot write this without the most profound sorrow. A City [Constantinople] which was so flourishing, with such a great empire, so many illustrious men, such very famous and ancient families, so prosperous, the head of all Greece, the splendour and glory of the East, the school of the best arts, the refuge of all good things, has been captured, despoiled, ravaged, and completely sacked by the most inhuman barbarians and the most savage enemies of the Christian faith, by the fiercest of wild beasts. . . .

To me, however, has been given the opportunity freely to implore aid, not for my fatherland, not for the good of my city, but for the safety of all, for the honor of Christians. On this occasion I could explain in great detail how much danger threatens Italy, not to mention other lands, if the violent assaults of the most ferocious barbarians are not checked. But I am not sure that these arguments are not better known to your Senate than to me. And this letter hastens to its close. I say but this one thing briefly. One of two things must happen; either your Highness, together with other Christian princes, must curb and crush the violence, not to say madness, of the barbarian, in these very beginnings, not only to safeguard yourselves and your own, but also in order to take the offensive against the enemy; or the barbarian, when he has shortly become master in what remains of Greece, which is now still subject to our rule, and in all our islands and also in Pannonia and Illyricum, may bring Italian affairs to a most dangerous crisis.

There is no one who may not hope, however, that Christian princes will take the offensive the more readily, seeing that there are such important reasons, so grave, so serious, so urgent. They would act for the common good, for the Christian religion, and for the glory of Christ, especially if they were summoned by your Highness and your Senate, whose authority is very great. . . .

Why do you think the barbarian has burst forth with such great insolence? Doubtless because he has learned that Christian princes, waging wars against each other, have stained their hands with the blood of their own people, have defiled their arms with the blood of Christians. These things make the enemy bold; relying on them, he has lately assaulted the chief city of Greece, and has conquered, ravaged, and destroyed it. But if he should learn that, with our own hostilities resolved, united and harmonious as Christian princes should be, we would rise up to defend the Christian religion, believe me, he would not only refrain from invading foreign lands, but would withdraw to that place within his own territories which is most favourable for defence.

Rise up then, renowned prince, and when the mutual animosities of Christians have been extinguished (and this will be easy for you, who are exceedingly influential in authority and wisdom), awaken, awaken at once, and arouse their peaceful and tranquil spirits. Exhort them, challenge them, induce them to join you, before the enemy takes the Peloponnesus, in dedicating themselves to avenging the violence of the barbarian, to destroying the enemy of the Christian faith, to recovering that city which formerly belonged to your republic, and which would be yours again once victory had been achieved. Nothing you could do would be more profitable for your empire, more advantageous for Italy, and for the whole commonwealth of Christians; nothing more acceptable to the immortal God; nothing more glorious for your own fame. If your highness knows anything that my smallness can contribute to this task, either by calming the spirits of our people or by exhorting them to wage war on the barbarians, I shall spare no labour, no care or solicitude.

331.

Introduction. Byzantine cultural influences did not end with the fall of Constantinople in 1453. Indeed, many learned Greek refugees to western and eastern Europe took with them Byzantine philosophic ideas and the literary and philological techniques of the Palaeologan Renaissance. These qualities enriched both the civilization of the Italian Renaissance (where ancient Greek learning, as preserved and taught by Byzantines, helped mold the character of Italian humanism), and that of the Slavs, especially in Muscovy (Russia). Of course some Byzantine scholars had appeared in Italy considerably before 1453, for example Manuel Chrysoloras, who in 1397 began the first systematic teaching of Greek in the Italian Renaissance: see selections no. 300 and 306. And later in the sixteenth century the post-Byzantine monk from Mt. Athos, Maxim "the Greek," brought to Muscovite Russia some elements of the learning as well as the Hesychast beliefs of the Byzantine Palaeologan period.

In his oration delivered at the University of Padua, Italy in 1463, one of these Byzantine humanist exiles, Demetrius Chalcondyles, on the occasion of his appointment to the newly instituted chair of Greek studies at Padua, set forth for his Venetian-Paduan audience (possibly a bit exaggeratedly) the benefits to be derived from the study of Greek learning. Chalcondyles' most telling point was that if the ancient Romans had sent their sons to study Greek literature in Athens, how much more should the Venetians, their "successors," seek to learn Greek.

CHALCONDYLES AT PADUA ON THE IMPORTANCE OF LEARNING GREEK

(From "Chaldondyles' Discourse" in D. Geanakoplos, *Interaction of the Sibling Byzantine and Western Cultures in the Middle Ages and Italian Renaissance* [New Haven: Yale University Press, 1976], pp. 261–63 and 256–57.)

. . . I think that the study of Greek literature has been of great use and rhetorical embellishment in the first place for the human race and that no one imbued with some study of letters is ignorant of it. For who could be so inexpert and so uncultivated in liberal arts as not to know that every branch of knowledge was cultivated and flourished especially among the Greeks who were the originators and cultivators of almost all the sciences. . . . Almost all of the Romans understood Greek as well as their own language, and they preferred to express the feelings of their minds and the meaning and nature of things more often in Greek than in Latin. . . . The Romans, in fact, who were masters on land and sea and learned in addition at home and in school in almost every branch of knowledge that exists, were accustomed to send to their children to Athens [to study]. . . .

Since Latin grammar is joined to Greek and seems to depend upon it, how can anyone have a complete grasp of it unless he knows Greek letters? Nor can he know the derivation of many words and their specific meanings, nor the declension of many nouns, nor the quantity of syllables, nor want to speak correctly and elegantly if he is ignorant of Greek letters. No one can say rightly, I believe, that some Latin authors wrote some works concerning these things and that therefore it is not necessary to know Greek literature. For they [the Latin authors] speak thus about these things [Greek letters] so that the learners may have knowledge of them, so that they may not be completely ignorant of them, so that they might speak about this not imperfectly regarding those who have touched a bit there as at the fountain itself (so to speak)—as if anyone desirous of quenching his thirst would seek the swamp rather than the fountain and, being hungry, would prefer to have dessert instead of solid food! In the same way I think this should be said about those things that seem to pertain to poets, oratory, and every branch of speaking, since no one would maintain that a poem or an oration can be written without nouns, correct diction, figures [of speech], brilliant style, and subject matter. And since both skills have been handed down abundantly and copiously by them and have been put to use in their [Latin] poems, orations, and histories most fully and perfectly, the old Latin authors, the poets as well as the orators and historians, confirm my opinion: none of them [Latin authors] was ignorant of Greek letters. Indeed, several of them venerated Greek literature so thoroughly that one wonders whether they knew Greek or Latin literature better.

332.

Introduction. As an example of the diffusion of Byzantine culture, especially of the influences of Palaeologan painting, we might cite the remarkable Byzantine painter Theophanes "the Greek" (Feofan Grek in Russian.) After executing paintings in forty churches of Constantinople and its environs in the second decade or so of the fourteenth century, he went after mid-century to Muscovy where he left his paintings in the church of the Assumption in the Kremlin and in that of the Transfiguration in Novgorod. His style had considerable influence on Russian iconography as attested especially by the fact that Andrei Rublev, the greatest of all medieval Russian painters, has now been shown to have been his pupil.

No work definitely attributable to Theophanes survives in Constantinople. The masterly (anonymous) depiction of Adam in the famous fresco of the Anastasis [*Christ Raising Adam and Eve from Hell*, detail reprinted below), in the church of the Chora (*Karije Djami*) in Constantinople, has sometimes incorrectly been ascribed to the "school" or "associates" of Theophanes. At any rate, the painting reflects the qualities of intensified emotion, including more intense coloration and greater dynamism, imbuing a good deal of the art of the Palaeologan Renaissance*—a movement which, as we have seen, owed much of its impetus to the general Byzantine euphoria over the recovery of Constantinople from the Latins in 1261 (see selection 288.) It is very striking that Giotto, who marks the transition in Italian art from medieval to Renaissance, painted his masterpieces in the Arena chapel of Padua almost simultaneously with Theophanes' execution of his own in Constantinople.

Somewhat parallel to the case of Theophanes in Muscovy, but coming after 1453 in the West, is that of the post-Byzantine painter Domenikos Theotokopoulos, better known as El Greco ("the Greek"), who was born several decades after Constantinople's fall to the Turks. As a young man he studied in his native island, Venetian-held Crete, where he evidently remained until the age of twenty-five and was exposed to certain artistic trends continuing from the Palaeologan Renaissance. After several years of study in Renaissance Venice, he went to Toledo, in Spain, where he produced most of his great works. These reflect a new synthesis of (Palaeologan) Byzantine and apparently some Western characteristics, molded together of course by his own unique genius.[†]

THE PAINTERS THEOPHANES "THE GREEK" AND EL GRECO

*This type of Palaeologan art is sometimes termed the "Metropolitan" style. As noted earlier, some Palaeologan painting (formerly referred to as the "Cretan" school) was more traditional and reflected rather softer qualities. But such distinctions in Palaeologan painting are not very clear.

[†]On El Greco see D. Geanakoplos, *Byzantine East and Latin West* (Oxford: Blackwell), pp. 150–52.

Detail of the head of Adam from *Christ Raising Adam and Eve from Hell*, anonymous. From a fresco in the Kariye Djami, Constantinople. Courtesy of Dumbarton Oaks, Center for Byzantine Studies, Washington, D.C.

333.

Introduction. The fall of Constantinople to the Turks evoked a strong reaction in Russia, despite Russian opposition to the religious union of the Eastern and Western churches pronounced at the Council of Florence. In the following selection the fall of Byzantium's capital is discussed by the Russian *Voskresensk Chronicle.* Note the stress on divine punishment for the sins of the Greeks in abandoning Orthodoxy; also the suggestion of the religio-political doctrine, the famous "Third Rome" theory, later more clearly formulated by the monk Philotheus.

A. A Muscovite Response to the Fall of Constantinople

(Translated by G. Vernadsky, *A Source Book for Russian History* [New Haven, Conn., and London: Yale University Press, 1972], vol. 1, p. 160.)

Since it was so, and since [the fall of Constantinople] had happened thus because of our sins, the lawless [Sultan] Mehmed seated himself on the tsar's throne, the noblest of all [thrones] on earth, and they ruled the rulers of the two halves of the earth, and conquered the conquerors of the proud Artaxerxes . . . and destroyed the destroyers of most marvelous Troy, defended by seventy and four kings. But understand, O accursed ones. If all the signs concerning this city that were foretold by Methodius of Patara and Leo the Wise* have come to pass, the last shall not be avoided but shall likewise come to pass; for it is written: "The Russian race with the former founders [i.e. Byzantines] shall conquer all the Mohammedans and shall receive the City of the Seven Hills with its former lawful masters and shall reign in it."

Introduction. We quote below the doctrine of the Russian monk Philotheus [Filofei] of Pskov, the "Third Rome" theory (early sixteenth century), which emphasized the passing of the "Roman" Empire from Rome to Constantinople and, finally, to Moscow.

* Authors of famous Byzantine books of prophecy.

B. Moscow, the Third Rome

(Translated by N. Zernov, *The Russians and Their Church* [London and New York, Macmillan Co., 1945], p. 51.)

The Church of old Rome fell for its heresy; the gates of the second Rome, Constantinople, were hewn down by the axes of the infidel Turks; but the Church of Moscow, the Church of the new Rome, shines brighter than the sun in the whole universe. Thou art the one universal sovereign of all Christian folk, thou shouldst hold the reins in awe of God; fear Him Who hath committed them to thee. Two Romes are fallen, but the third stands fast; a fourth there cannot be. Thy Christian kingdom shall not be given to another.

APPENDIX A

• • • • • • • • • • • • • • • •

TABLE OF BYZANTINE EMPERORS

324–37	Constantine I
337–61	Constantius
361–63	Julian
363–64	Jovian
364–78	Valens
379–95	Theodosius I
395–408	Arcadius
408–450	Theodosius II
450–57	Marcian
457–74	Leo I
474	Leo II
474–75	Zeno
475–76	Basiliscus
476–91	Zeno (again)
491–518	Anastasius I
518–27	Justin I
527–65	Justinian I
565–78	Justin II
578–82	Tiberius I Constantine
582–602	Maurice
602–10	Phocas
610–41	Heraclius

641	Constantine III and Heraclonas
641	Heraclonas
641–68	Constans II
668–85	Constantine IV
685–95	Justinian II
695–98	Leontius
698–705	Tiberius II
705–11	Justinian II (again)
711–13	Philippicus
713–15	Anastasius II
715–17	Theodosius III
717–41	Leo III
741–75	Constantine V
775–80	Leo IV
780–97	Constantine VI
797–802	Irene
802–11	Nicephorus I
811	Stauracius
811–13	Michael I Rangabe
813–20	Leo V
820–29	Michael II
829–42	Theophilus
842–67	Michael III
867–86	Basil I
886–912	Leo VI
912–13	Alexander
913–59	Constantine VII
920–44	Romanus I Lecapenus
959–63	Romanus II
963–69	Nicephorus II Phocas
969–76	John I Tzimisces
976–1025	Basil II
1025–28	Constantine VIII
1028–34	Romanus III Argyrus
1034–41	Michael IV

1041–42	Michael V
1042	Zoe and Theodora
1042–55	Constantine IX Monomachus
1055–56	Theodora (again)
1056–57	Michael VI
1057–59	Isaac I Comnenus
1059–67	Constantine X Ducas
1068–71	Romanus IV Diogenes
1071–78	Michael VII Ducas
1078–81	Nicephorus III Botaneiates
1081–1118	Alexius I Comnenus
1118–43	John II Comnenus
1143–80	Manuel I Comnenus
1180–83	Alexius II Comnenus
1183–85	Andronicus I Comnenus
1185–95	Isaac II Angelus
1195–1203	Alexius III Angelus
1203–4	Isaac II (again) and Alexius IV Angeli
1204	Alexius V Murtzuphlus
1204–22	Theodore I Lascaris
1222–54	John III Ducas Vatatzes
1254–58	Theodore II Lascaris
1258–61	John IV Lascaris
1259–82	Michael VIII Palaeologus
1282–1328	Andronicus II Palaeologus
1328–41	Andronicus III Palaeologus
1341–91	John V Palaeologus
1347–54	John VI Cantacuzenus
1376–79	Andronicus IV Palaeologus
1390	John VII Palaeologus
1391–1425	Manuel II Palaeologus
1425–48	John VIII Palaeologus
1449–53	Constantine XI Palaeologus

APPENDIX B

◆ ◆ ◆ ◆ ◆ ◆ ◆ ◆ ◆ ◆ ◆ ◆ ◆ ◆ ◆ ◆ ◆ ◆ ◆ ◆

CHRONOLOGICAL TABLE OF CONTENTS

APPENDIX C

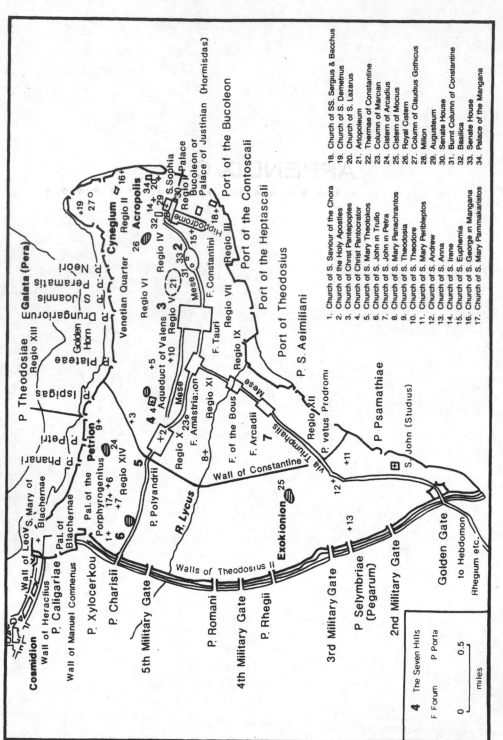

Constantinople. From *Cambridge Medieval History*, vol. 4, *The Eastern Roman Empire*, edited by J. B. Bury (Cambridge: Cambridge University Press, 1927).

The map contains the following labels and legend:

Cosmidion
Wall of Heraclius
P. Caligariae
Wall of Manuel Comnenus
P. Theodosiae
Regio XIII
Galata (Pera)
S. Joannis
Peramatis
Neori
Drungariorum
Golden Horn
Plateae
Ispigas
Phanari
P. Petri
P. of the Blachernae
Pal. of Blachernae
Wall of Leo
S. Mary of Blachernae
Petrion
Porphyrogenitus
Pal. of the Porphyrogenitus
P. Xylocerkou
P. Charisii
5th Military Gate
Regio XIV
Regio X
Aqueduct of Valens
Venetian Quarter
Cynegium
Acropolis
Regio II
Regio VI
Regio IV
Regio V
Mesè
F. Tauri
F. Amastrianon
Mesè
P. Polyandrii
R. Lycus
Regio XI
F. of the Bous
F. Arcadii
Regio IX
Mesè
Regio VII
Regio VIII
F. Constantini
Regio III
S. Sophia
Palace
Bucoleon or
Palace of Justinian (Hormisdas)
Port of the Bucoleon
Port of the Contoscali
Port of the Heptascali
Port of Theodosius
P. S. Aeimiliani
Port of P. S. Aeimiliani
Regio XII
P. vetus Prodromi
Exokionion
Wall of Constantine
Via Triumphalis
P. Psamathiae
P. Psamathiae
S. John (Studius)
P. Romani
4th Military Gate
P. Rhegii
P. Selymbriae (Pegarum)
3rd Military Gate
Golden Gate
to Hebdomon
Rhegum etc.
2nd Military Gate
Walls of Theodosius II
Hippodrome

The Seven Hills
F Forum   P Porta
0   0.5
miles

1. Church of S. Saviour of the Chora
2. Church of the Holy Apostles
3. Church of Christ Pantepoptes
4. Church of Christ Pantocrator
5. Church of S. Mary Theotokos
6. Church of S. John in Trullo
7. Church of S. John in Petra
8. Church of S. Mary Panachrantos
9. Church of S. Theodosia
10. Church of S. Theodore
11. Church of S. Mary Peribleptos
12. Church of S. Andrew
13. Church of S. Anna
14. Church of S. Irene
15. Church of S. Euphemia
16. Church of S. George in Mangana
17. Church of S. Mary Pammakaristos
18. Church of SS. Sergius & Bacchus
19. Church of S. Demetrius
20. Church of S. Lazarus
21. Artopoleum
22. Thermae of Constantine
23. Column of Marcian
24. Cistern of Arcadius
25. Cistern of Mocius
26. Royal Cistern
27. Column of Claudius Gothicus
28. Million
29. Augusteum
30. Senate House
31. Burnt Column of Constantine
32. Basilica
33. Senate House
34. Palace of the Mangana

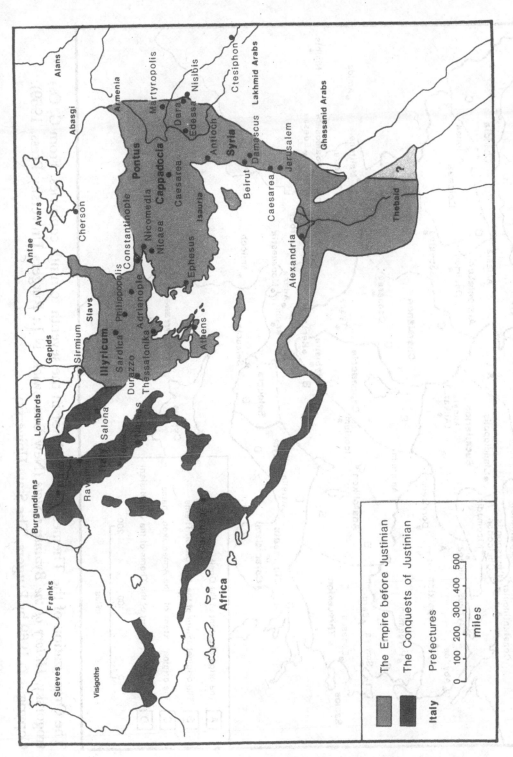

The Byzantine Empire in 565 A.D. under Emperor Justinian. From N. Baynes and H. Moss, eds., *Byzantium: An Introduction to East Roman Civilization* (Oxford: Clarendon Press, 1961).

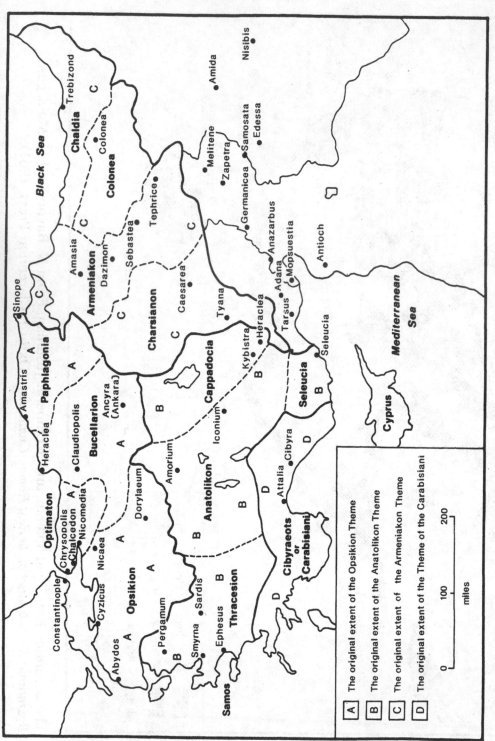

The Organization of the Themes in Asia Minor in the seventh to ninth centuries. From G. Ostrogorsky, *History of the Byzantine State* (New Brunswick, N.J.: Rutgers University Press, 1969). Copyright © 1969 by Rutgers, The State University.

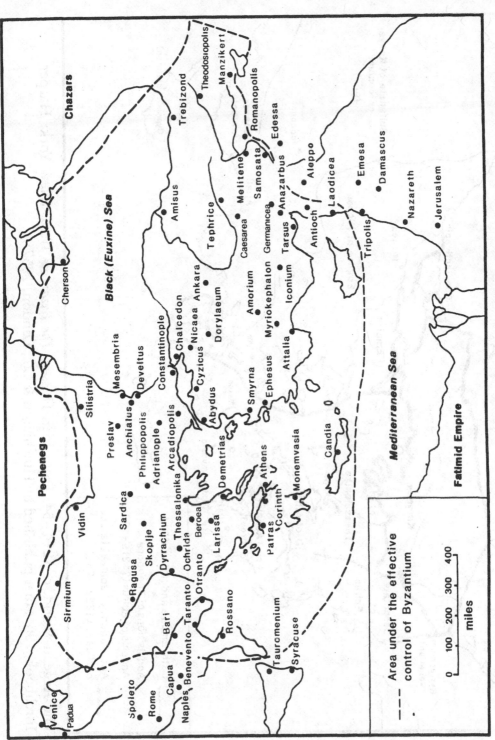

The Byzantine Empire in the middle of the eleventh century A.D. From R. Jenkins, *Byzantium: The Imperial Centuries, A.D. 610–1071* (London: Weidenfeld & Nicolson; originally published by Random House, New York, 1966).

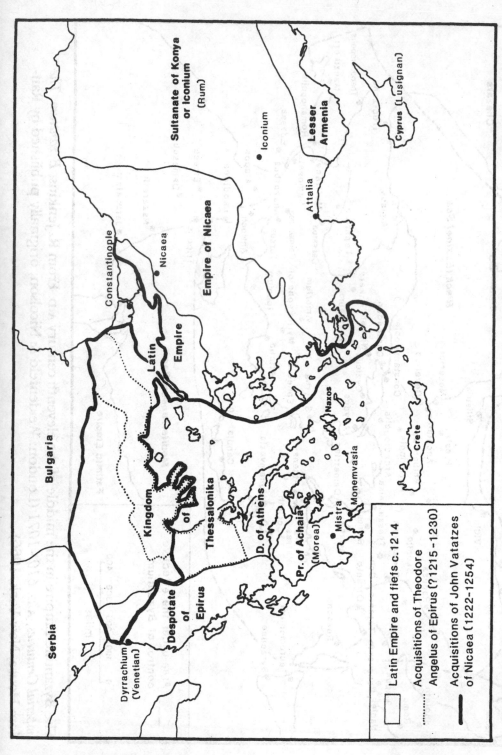

The Aegean World, c. 1214–54. From Joan Hussey, *The Byzantine World* (New York: Harper Torchbook, 1961; first published by Hutchinson & Co., London, 1957).

Map labels:

Serbia
Bulgaria
Dyrrachium (Venetian)
Despotate of Epirus
Latin Empire
Constantinople
Nicaea
Empire of Nicaea
Sultanate of Konya or Iconium (Rum)
Iconium
Attalia
Lesser Armenia
Cyprus (Lusignan)
Kingdom of Thessalonika
D. of Athens
Pr. of Achaia (Morea)
Mistra
Monemvasia
Naxos
Crete

Legend:
Latin Empire and fiefs c. 1214
Acquisitions of Theodore Angelus of Epirus (?1215–1230)
Acquisitions of John Vatatzes of Nicaea (1222–1254)

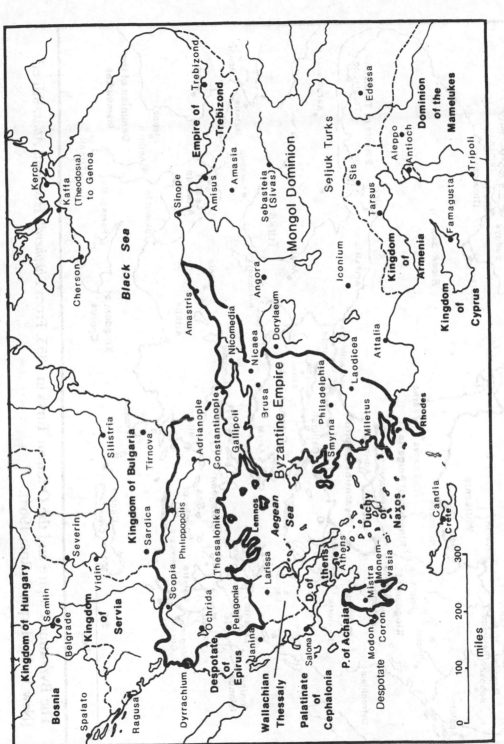

The Byzantine Empire in 1265 shortly after Michael VIII's recovery of Constantinople from the Latins. From *Shepherd's Historical Atlas*, 9th ed. (New York: Harper & Row, 1964).

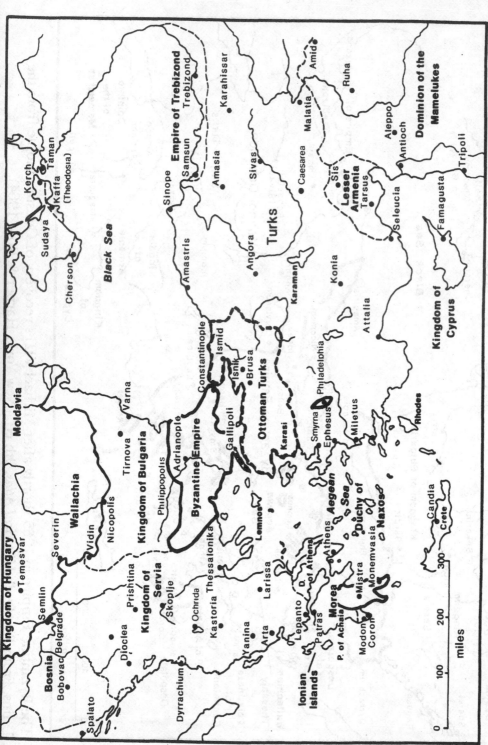

The Byzantine Empire and the Ottoman Turks in 1355. From *Shepherd's Historical Atlas*, 9th ed. (New York: Harper & Row, 1964).

INDEX

◆ ◆ ◆ ◆ ◆ ◆ ◆ ◆ ◆ ◆ ◆ ◆ ◆ ◆ ◆